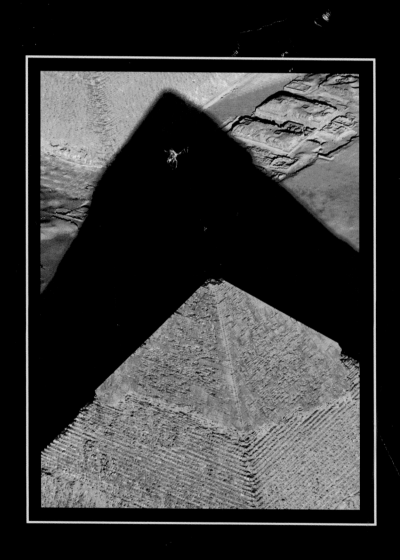

EDITED BY
ZAHI HAWASS

PROJECT EDITORS
Laura Accomazzo
Valeria Manferto De Fabianis

GRAPHIC DESIGN
Paola Piacco

WHITE STAR PUBLISHERS

PYRAMIDS

**TREASURES
MYSTERIES
AND NEW DISCOVERIES
IN EGYPT**

Preface

Four and a half millennia after they were built, the pyramids of Egypt continue to capture the imagination of people all over the world. I am extremely fortunate to have spent much of my career as an expert on these monumental tombs. I lived for many years in the shadow of the Great Pyramid of Khufu on the Giza Plateau, watching the sun come up in the morning and send its rays to cover the surface of the stones. In the evening, I would climb to the top of the pyramid to see the sunset. Since the 1980s, I have been excavating around the pyramids at Giza, where we have made many important discoveries. More recently, I have also excavated at Saqqara, near the pyramid of the first king of the Sixth Dynasty, Teti; in the area of the Gisr el-Mudir; and near the pyramid of Khendjer at South Saqqara.

In the years since *Treasures of the Pyramids* was published, a number of important discoveries have advanced our knowledge of the pyramids of the Old and Middle Kingdoms. In 2008, we discovered a queen's pyramid next to the pyramid complex of Teti, which lies near the eastern edge of the Saqqara plateau, in the northern part of the site. We found this while clearing a huge mound of sand left behind by a previous excavator. The small pyramid, which had been buried beneath this debris, consists of six steps. We found a polished casing stone 2.5 meters west of the lowest step. The angle of the outer surface was almost 51 degrees, allowing us to reconstruct a total height for the original pyramid of about 15 meters. Robbers had cut a shaft straight from the upper step of the pyramid directly into the burial chamber. We followed their route and found a sarcophagus with the remains of a mummy, most likely the queen herself, along with several objects. Although no inscriptions associated with this pyramid were found, I suggest that it might have been built for Teti's mother, Sesheshet.

At Saqqara, we are working to stabilize the Step Pyramid of Djoser. Over the last few years, we have been studying a master plan for the conservation of this pyramid, and have learned that the superstructure is in poor condition. There are a number of reasons for this, including earlier restoration done on the north side of the pyramid that changed the balance of the monument. The substructure is also in critical condition. The burial chambers, which lie 29 meters beneath the ground, are also falling apart, despite wooden supports placed there during the 26th Dynasty. We have begun to dress stones similar to the ones used in the original construction of the pyramid, and place them using mortar of lime and sand. We have finished the south, east, and north faces of the pyramid. We also found a new tunnel opening from the east face into the interior of the pyramid.

In the substructure, we recleared and cleaned the burial chamber, and also erected metal scaffolding so we can restore the wall of the chamber. The most interesting discovery we made here involved many relief fragments carved with stars, and also the known names of the daughter of Djoser, that were buried inside the pyramid. In addition, we found several new tunnels, increasing the total length of the corridors and chambers beneath the pyramid to more than 7 km.

I had always believed that Imhotep, the architect of the Step Pyramid, had been buried under the west side of the pyramid. We know that Senenmut, Hatshepsut's architect, could have been imitating him, and was buried in the complex of her memorial temple at Deir el-Bahari. During our new clearance work at Saqqara, we found a Second Dynasty tomb to the west of the Step Pyramid, with a burial shaft more than 10 m deep. We still believe that Imhotep should be buried somewhere in this area.

Also on the west of the pyramid, in the area of the Gisr el-Mudir, we have located a large cemetery. We were alerted to its presence a number of years ago by thieves who were illegally digging in the area at night. We have found a number of tombs here: the first was the tomb of the royal physician, Qar (discovered in the late 1990s); more recently, we have uncovered the Dynasty 5 tomb of Shepsesbu-Ptah, who had many titles, including Inspector of the Royal House and Priest of the Pyramid of Isesi. We also found the tomb of Shenwa, an expedition leader whose tomb contained many interesting scenes, such as the manufacture of beds.

Another important discovery was made in 2008 by Nicole Alexanian, director of the German expedition at Dahshur. Using magnetometric measurements and test drillings, she has located the causeway of the Bent Pyramid of Seneferu at Dahshur. In the next season, she began to uncover this important structure, and found that it was 150 m long, 6.35 m wide, and had a vaulted roof. The interior walls were plastered with yellow and white. Fragments of relief were found nearby, given us more information about the decoration of Old Kingdom causeways. Near the causeway is evidence for another structure; the excavator suggests that this is part of an ancient harbor.

Back at Giza, we found a new group of tombs located south of the cemetery of the pyramid builders. Based on the architectural style, these can be dated to the reign of Khufu, and include the tomb of an overseer surrounded by the tombs of the workmen who served under him.

We have been planning to reveal the secrets still hidden behind the doors inside the Second Chamber of the Great Pyramid. These lie deep within the pyramid, at the ends of the horizontal shafts leading from the south and north walls. A team from Leeds University has been planning the work. We do not know when we will carry out this project, but we hope it will be in the near future.

Finally, through satellite images, we were able to see underground structures near the pyramid complex of King Khendjer of Dynasty 13 at South Saqqara. There appears to be a pyramid here, still buried. We have uncovered one big limestone block from this pyramid. Nearby are four inscribed chapels dating from the Old Kingdom, and emplacements to the north of the pyramid of Khendjer that may be bases for trees.

As we can see, many secrets are still to be uncovered near the pyramids: the pyramids will continue to capture our hearts for thousands of years to come.

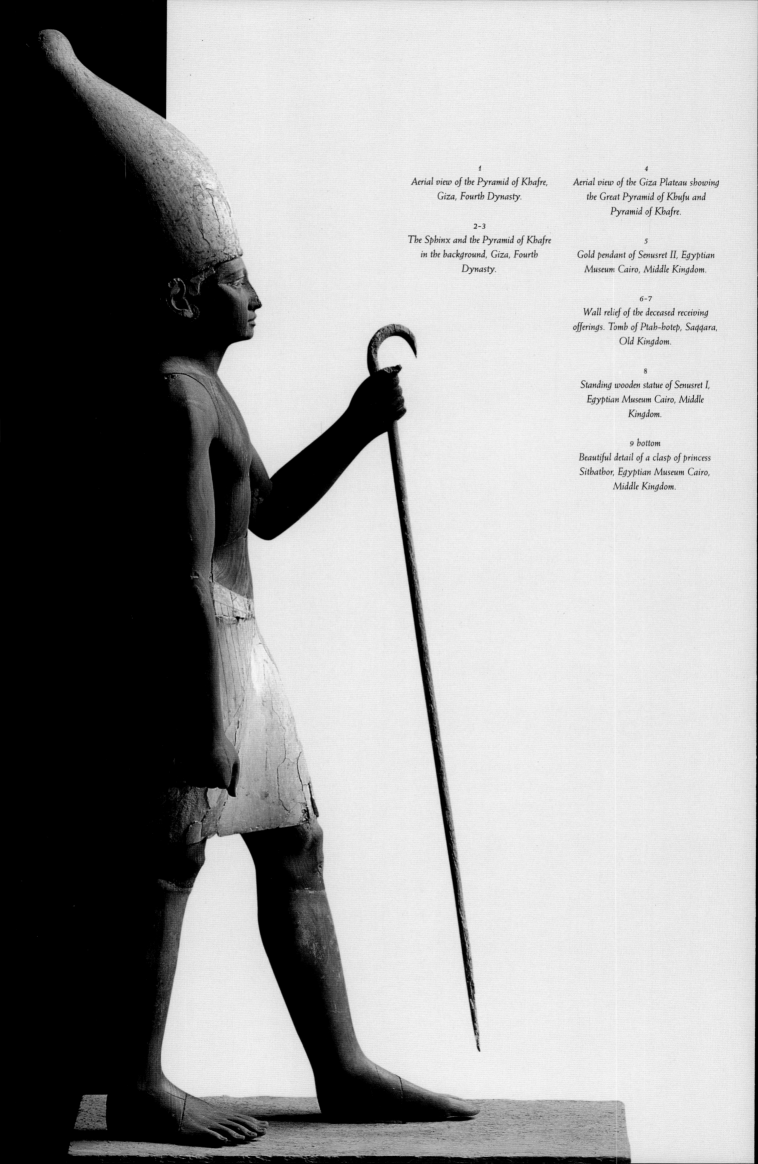

The Contributors

ZAHI HAWASS

World-renowned archaeologist Zahi Hawass has served in the field of Egyptian archaeology for over 40 years. He began as an inspector of antiquities and reached the top in 2011, when he was appointed Minister of Antiquities. Dr. Hawass received his doctorate from the University of Pennsylvania in 1987. He has written numerous books and made many major discoveries near the pyramids of Giza, such as the tombs of the pyramid builders. He plans to reveal the secrets behind the doors found inside the Great Pyramid soon. One of Dr. Hawass' most significant research efforts was the Egyptian Mummy Project (EMP), which used modern forensic techniques such as CT scanning and DNA analysis to answer questions about human remains from ancient Egypt. Through the EMP, Dr. Hawass was able to identify the mummy of Queen Hatshepsut, uncover the family of King Tutankhamun and solve the mystery of the murder of Ramesses III. He has received many prizes and awards, including five honorary doctorates from top universities around the world. Dr. Hawass has appeared in many documentary films shown all over the world, and has published articles in many international magazines. *Time Magazine* honored him as one of its Top 100 Most Influential People for 2005.

MATTHEW ADAMS

Matthew Douglas Adams is Research Scholar at the Institute of Fine Arts, New York University and holds a Ph.D. from the University of Pennsylvania. He has worked at Abydos since 1981, and is Associate Director of the Abydos Early Dynastic Project. He is the author of several articles and reviews.

JAMES P. ALLEN

He is Wilbour Professor of Egyptology at Brown University and Vice-President of the International Association of Egyptologists and has served as Cairo Director of the American Research Center in Egypt and as Curator at the Metropolitan Museum of Art. Dr. Allen is author of numerous books and studies on ancient Egyptian language, texts, and religion, as well as on the history of the Middle Kingdom and Amarna Period.

DIETER ARNOLD

He is Curator at the Metropolitan Museum of Art, New York, and has for forty years been conducting excavations in Egypt, at Thebes, El-Lisht and Dahshur, among other sites. He is the author of numerous books on Egyptian architecture, including *Building in Egypt: Pharaonic Stone Masonry*, *Temples of the Last Pharaohs*, and *The Pyramid Complex of Senwosret III at Dahshur*.

VASSIL DOBREV

Author of several scientific studies, since 1987, Dobrev has worked on the excavations of the pyramids and temples of King Pepy I and his queens at South Saqqara. Since 2000, he is responsible for the IFAO Mapping Project of South Saqqara and director of the IFAO Mission at Tabbet al-Guesh (South Saqqara).

GÜNTER DREYER

Günter Dreyer studied Egyptology, Assyriology and Ancient Near Eastern Archaeology at Hamburg and Berlin, taking his PhD in 1978. He has led excavations at Elephantine (1973-1986) and Abydos (1980-present). Since 1998, he has been director of the German Institute of Archaeology in Cairo.

RENEE FRIEDMAN

Curator in the Egyptian Department of the British Museum and Director of the Hierakonpolis Expedition, she has excavated at a number of sites in Egypt, including Giza, Mendes, Tell el-Muqdam and Hierakonpolis, where she has worked since 1983.

AUDRAN LABROUSSE

Architect and Doctor of Literature and Human Sciences, Labrousse is a researcher at the CNRS. He carried out excavations in Iran, at Sedeinga, in the Sudan, and has worked in Egypt since 1973, where he is the director of the French Archaeological Mission of Saqqara.

MARK LEHNER

Mark Lehner has received several awards for his research from the American University in Cairo and Yale University. Author of many essays and articles, in 1999 he received the American Archaeological Society Book Award for his book *The Complete Pyramids*. He is a Research Associate at the Oriental Institute, University of Chicago, and Harvard Semitic Museum.

PETER DER MANUELIAN

Giza Archives Project Director at the Museum of Fine Arts, Boston, and Lecturer in Egyptology at Tufts University. His Giza Archives Project, an international collaboration, supports a scholarly website (www.gizapyramids.org) of archaeological images and archival materials from the Giza Necropolis.

KAROL MYŚLIWIEC

Director of the Research Center at the Polish Academy of Sciences and professor of Ancient Egyptian Archaeology at the Warsaw University, he is also the director of Polish-Egyptian excavations at Saqqara. Excavating in Egypt on various sites since 1969, he also directed the Polish-Egyptian rescue excavations at Tell Atrib (Nile Delta) in 1985-1995.

DAVID O'CONNOR

Professor of Egyptian Art and Archaeology at the Institute of Fine Arts, New York University, Professor Emeritus of the University of Pennsylvania and Curator Emeritus of the Egyptian Section, University of Pennsylvania Museum of Anthropology and Archaeology, David O'Connor has excavated extensively in Egypt and the Sudan, and he is author and co-author of several monographs.

ALI RADWAN

Ali Radwan is a professor at Cairo University and teaches Egyptian art and archaeology. He was the former dean of Cairo University and excavated at Abusir.

DAVID P. SILVERMAN

He is the Eckley B. Coxe, Jr., Professor of Egyptology and the Curator-in-Charge of the Egyptian Section of the University of Pennsylvania Museum of Archaeology and Anthropology in Philadelphia. He has curated several major exhibitions, including the *Treasures of Tutankhamen*. He has conducted fieldwork at a number of sites in Egypt, including Abydos, Bersheh, the Delta, and Giza, and, since 1990, he has led an ongoing expedition to Saqqara

HOURIG SOUROUZIAN

Egyptologist and Art Historian. Was guest professor in the American University in Cairo as W.K. Simpson Professor and in the University of Munich, she has participated in several archaeological missions at Karnak, Dahshur, Tanis, and Thebes-West, where she was entrusted with the study of the temple statuary and currently directs the excavations on the temple of Amenhotep III.

RAINER STADELMANN

Retired in 1999 and was Honorary Professor at the University of Heidelberg, and former First Director of the German Institute of Archaeology in Cairo, he has excavated at Elephantine Island and the mortuary temple of Seti I at Gurna and the pyramids of Sneferu at Dahshur. The several books and articles he has written include many monographs on the pyramids.

MICHEL VALLOGGIA

Professor of Egyptology at the University of Geneva and field Director of the Archaeological Mission at Abu Rawash, he has been in charge of archaeological excavations between 1976 and 1993 in the Kharga Oasis (Douch) and the Dakhla Oasis (Balat); he is also consultant for UNESCO.

MIROSLAV VERNER

Born in 1941, Miroslav Verner graduated in Egyptology and Prehistory at Charles University in Prague. He directed the Czech Institute of Egyptology for twenty-five years and since 1976, has led the excavations of Czech archaeologists in Abusir, Egypt. He is a professor at Charles University in Prague and also serves as guest professor at the universities of Vienna and Hamburg and at the American University in Cairo.

ARALDO DE LUCA

Born in Rome in 1952. He lived in the Italian capital and became involved in the photography of art at a very early age, and later won the prestigious Ilford Prize "Spazi ed immagini del Barocco Romano" (1980). Since 1995 his 90,000 or more renowned art pictures are catalogued in an archive which has won worldwide acclaim. Considered one of the world's greatest photographers of statuary and jewelry, De Luca has developed sophisticated lighting techniques that heighten the power of his seductive images to communicate the passion that the artists invested in their work. De Luca's great skill in the use of light, acquired while photographing wonderful statuary, enables him to work freely in other fields with amazing effects – as his portraits of dogs presented in this volume demonstrate. White Star Publishers has worked with De Luca on many volumes, including *Egyptian Treasures from the Egyptian Museum in Cairo* (1999), *Tutankhamun: the Eternal Splendor of the Boy Pharaoh* (2000), *Illustrated Guide to the Egyptian Museum in Cairo* (2003), *Valley of the Kings* (2002), *Ramesses II* (2002), *The Treasures of the Pyramids* (2003), *Pompeii* (2004), *The Eternal Army* (2005), *A Dog's Life* (2008) and *L for Labrador* (2010).

Contents

10-11
Scene showing the 'Meidum geese,' Egyptian
Museum Cairo, Old Kingdom.

The Pyramids

by Zahi Hawass

The pyramids of Egypt have long been my greatest passion. When I first came to Giza in 1974, I lived in a rest house facing the Great Pyramid of Khufu. Every morning I would watch the sun rise over the pyramids, long before anyone else set foot on the plateau. Every day I would sit and watch the pyramids from my veranda, and experience first-hand the magic spell that these great monuments cast, the ageless mystery that has enraptured so many.

I started my first excavation at Giza in 1974, in cooperation with my good friend and colleague Mark Lehner. We worked on a mound located just north of the Great Sphinx, within the eastern cemetery that was associated with Khufu's pyramid. This area had not been disturbed by previous excavations; our findings helped confirm an Old Kingdom date for the Sphinx.

At the beginning of my time at Giza, I became fascinated by an odd collection of people who would now qualify as 'pyramidiots.' Some of them would come to my office at the Giza plateau and ask me for permission to meditate inside the pyramids. On occasion, the pyramids echoed with the collective wail that marked the end of their sessions. One man asked me for permission to make a film about the pyramids. He believed that they had been used as giant granaries during the time of the Prophet Joseph. Once my dear friend, the late Gamal Mokhtar, sent a lady to me who had come from Hawaii with her child to meditate in front of the Sphinx. She stayed in front of it all night and in the morning she told me that the Sphinx had directed her to go south. I have met many of these people over the years, and some of them have even become my friends.

On my first trip to the United States, I was alarmed to find a number of books on the pyramids with no scientific basis. Many authors believe that the pyramids possess a mystical power. Others are convinced that the Great Pyramid and the Sphinx were built some 10,000 years ago by an ancient civilization, now lost in the mists of time, from which the Egyptians inherited their later greatness. The fact is that the Great Pyramid is only one of many royal pyramids, built over the course of almost nine hundred years, and all of the pyramids are part of an extremely well-documented culture. I have always maintained that if you do not study ancient Egypt's history and archaeology you leave your mind open to idle speculation. 'Pyramidiots' make the mistake of focusing only on pyramids, and willfully ignore the evidence that modern archeologists have found: the tombs, statues, bakeries, towns, and inscriptions that link these wonders to the ancient Egyptians themselves.

Or, if they are forced to look at the evidence, they try to twist it or discount it. For example, there are ancient graffiti inside the Great Pyramid that prove beyond any reasonable doubt that this pyramid was built for and by Khufu. In order to shift the massive weight of the pyramid's structure from the king's granite burial chamber, Khufu's engineers devised one of the most astounding features of any pyramid. They added three granite ceilings, each spaced one course of stone apart, to form four stress-relieving chambers. Above those, they added a fifth relieving chamber topped with pitched limestone beams. The first of the five chambers was entered in antiquity by way of a little crawl space from the top end of the Grand Gallery (the corridor that leads to the burial chamber). Workmen probably entered it to smear gypsum in cracks that had appeared in the huge granite roofing beams of the King's Chamber (each beam weighs some five tons).

The upper chambers were first entered in modern times in 1837, when the English explorer Howard Vyse blasted his way in with dynamite. On the walls he found red leveling lines, axis markers, and the names of work gangs compounded with the cartouche of the king. One beautifully preserved graffito on the uppermost limestone beam reads, "Friends of Khufu," the name of one of the gangs who worked on the pyramid. This inscription confirms that Khufu built the Great Pyramid, but 'New-Agers' and alternative pyramid theorists argue heatedly that Howard Vyse himself forged the graffito to enhance his fame as an archaeologist. These marks, however, lie deep in the space between the blocks and are far beyond the reach of any would-be forger. They were undoubtedly written before the blocks were set into the pyramid.

The reality is that there are thirty-five known major pyramids, most of which are securely attributed to the reigns of specific kings; there are many more smaller pyramids, some for the burial of queens, and others that served ritual functions associated with the royal cult.

The first pyramid, the Step Pyramid at Saqqara, was built by the Third Dynasty king Djoser Netjerikhet, who reigned around 2650 BC. Less than one hundred years later, the Great Pyramid of the Fourth Dynasty king Khufu was built at Giza; this extraordinary monument, and its companions on the plateau, represent the pinnacle of pyramid-building. Each successive king of the Old Kingdom, which lasted for about another four hundred years, built his own pyramid complex in a stretch of desert on the west bank of the Nile, reaching from Abu Rawash in the north to Dahshur in the south (with the early Fourth Dynasty pyramid of Sneferu at Meidum forming a southern outlier). Almost all of these have been identified and excavated, and, in conjunction with the elite tombs and other archaeological traces that surround them, have yielded enormous quantities of important information about ancient Egyptian culture.

Very few pyramids from the late Old Kingdom and First Intermediate Period have been identified, and these are relatively small. At the beginning of the Twelfth Dynasty (c. 985 BC), with the reign of Amenemhet I, colossal pyramids once again served to mark the burials of Egyptian kings. The rulers of the Middle Kingdom built their complexes in the region of the Fayum, with some kings revisiting the Old Kingdom site of Dahshur. A second mortuary complex belonging to Senusret III has also been found recently at Abydos. With the fall of the Middle Kingdom, the era of monumental pyramid building comes to an end.

This book comes at a good time. The contributors to this volume are the men and women who are most active in the field of pyramid studies today. They are the archaeologists now exploring these royal tombs of the Old and Middle Kingdoms, and the experts in the religion, art, and administration of these periods. These men and women have a first-hand understanding of these monuments, and have dedicated their lives to this work. All of the scholars represented in this book have made major discoveries in the field, and have contributed in significant ways to our understanding of these structures. In this volume, eminent Egyptologists share their most significant discoveries and thought-provoking theories. This text will not only be useful to scholars but also of interest to the general public.

The Pyramids

The book opens with an essay on the religious significance of the pyramids, including a discussion of the reasons why the ancient Egyptians chose this particular shape, by James Allen. Through his work with the Pyramid Texts, magical spells that were inscribed in the interior chambers of pyramids of the late Fifth and Sixth Dynasties, he illuminates the spiritual beliefs that motivated the construction of these monuments.

An elaborate and stable administrative system was necessary to implement the building of the pyramids, and this subject is treated by Vassil Dobrev, who shares the important work he has done on the graffiti left by workmen inside and outside the pyramids. These graffiti shed light on the organization of the gangs who built the pyramids, and help us to reconstruct the larger administration.

Very advanced engineering and architectural techniques were key to pyramid building; that is addressed in an essay by Mark Lehner. We are constantly learning new things about this fascinating subject. For example, we are now sure that the base of the pyramid of Khufu is of solid rock and is about 60 centimeters high. Therefore, there is no scientific evidence that the Great Pyramid is comprised of 2,300,000 stone blocks, as has been previously calculated. A team from Helwan University counted the stones of the Great Pyramid and concluded that the number is closer to 1,300,000. They also determined that these stones weigh about 1.6 tons on average.

Next, I contribute two chapters. The first is on the development of the royal tomb and the pyramidal shape, from its origins at the ancient cemeteries of the early dynasties through pharaonic history. The second is on the architectural elements of the typical pyramid complex: how they develop and change over the course of almost a thousand years of pyramid building.

The following chapter takes us back to the misty beginnings of Egyptian history, with an essay by Renee Friedman. This scholar is working at the key Early Dynastic site of Hierakonpolis, the location of some of the most important artifacts belonging to the first kings of Egypt, and where the remains of what many believe to be an Early Dynastic temple were found. This site is crucial to our understanding of the foundations of the architecture, art, and religion of ancient Egypt. Friedman's successes there follow the work of the late Michael Hoffman.

Günter Dreyer and David O'Connor have dedicated themselves to excavation at Abydos, another important site containing remains from the Early Dynastic Period. Dreyer has re-excavated the tombs of the First Dynasty and late Second Dynasty in Umm al-Qa'ab at Abydos, and has made a number of significant discoveries. He has identified what he believes to be the tomb of King Scorpion, the earliest king attested in the archaeological record, and Dreyer has also given us an exciting new date for the origin of writing, placing it before the beginning of the First Dynasty. In addition, he has found evidence that confirms the position of Djoser, builder of the Step Pyramid, as first king of the Third Dynasty. He is now cooperating with the Supreme Council of Antiquities (SCA) at the Memphite site of Saqqara and with Ali Radwan to re-excavate and document the tombs of the kings of the Second Dynasty under the funerary temple of Unas at Saqqara.

David O'Connor has contributed a great deal to the field of Egyptology. One of his most valuable contributions has come through the opportunity he has given his students to work at Abydos. His protégés have unearthed important archaeological information while working in different areas of the site. O'Connor's work in the area of the Shunet al-Zebib, an ancient mud brick enclosure that still towers over the surrounding desert, is especially significant. In this area are funerary enclosures (including the Shunet) that date to the First and late Second Dynasties, corresponding to the tombs in Umm al-Qa'ab farther out in the desert. O'Connor has clarified our understanding of these structures and has made important new discoveries, including, with Matthew Adams, a fleet of twelve boats, encased in mud brick and moored in the desert nearby. The SCA is also pleased to announce that it has agreed to work with O'Connor to effect a restoration of the walls of the Shunet. O'Connor's contribution to this book, co-authored with Matthew Adams, deals with royal funerary enclosures at both Abydos and Hierakonpolis.

Ali Radwan has spent much time excavating an Early Dynastic cemetery at Abusir and has made some remarkable archaeological discoveries there. His contribution to this book concerning early pyramids in general, and the Step Pyramid of Djoser in particular, traces the extraordinary achievements of the early pyramid builders. These early monuments are the first in the world to be built entirely of the enduring material of stone.

I have asked Rainer Stadelmann to write about the pyramids of the Fourth Dynasty because of his magnificent work at the two pyramids of the first king of this dynasty, Sneferu, at Dahshur: the Red Pyramid, and the Bent Pyramid, where he has continued the work of Ahmed Fakhry. I also felt it was important that he write about Giza in anticipation of the detailed book Mark Lehner and I are now finishing on that site and its extraordinary pyramids. Stadelmann has reconstructed a convincing outline of the reign of this long-lived and prolific king, demonstrating that he reigned for over fifty years and began and ended his pyramid building with his monument at Meidum.

To the material on the Fourth Dynasty, I have contributed a chapter on the queens' pyramids at Giza, an essay on my exciting discovery of the newly-found satellite pyramid of Khufu, a discussion of the pyramidion, and a chapter on the royal boats of Khufu.

Mark Lehner, one of the foremost living experts on the Great Sphinx, has written a chapter about this extraordinary sculpture. One of the things that makes pyramid studies, and Egyptology in general, so lively and fascinating is that scholars do not always agree with one another. Take, for example, the Great Sphinx of Giza. Egyptologists are all completely in agreement that it dates to the Fourth Dynasty, about 2500 BC; the evidence for this is overwhelming, and completely disproves the claim that it was built much earlier, as some researchers would like to believe. However, Stadelmann, who presents his theory in this book, is convinced that it was carved as a representation of the builder of the Great Pyramid, King Khufu. I, on the other hand, and my friend Mark Lehner, agree with the many scholars who believe that it was carved a generation later as an image of Khufu's son, Khafre, since it appears from an architectural point of view to be an integral part of Khafre's complex.

As evidence for this, we cite these facts: the south side of the Sphinx ditch forms the northern edge of Khafre's causeway as it runs past the Sphinx and enters Khafre's valley temple, and the drainage channel along the north side of Khafre's causeway opens into the southwestern corner at the back of the Sphinx ditch. This suggests that the quarry that forms the Sphinx ditch was dug after Khafre's causeway was built. If this were not the case, the ancient quarrymen would not have constructed the drain to empty into the ditch. In addition, Khafre's valley temple is set on the same terrace as the Sphinx temple. The fronts and the backs of the temples are nearly aligned and the walls of both are built in the same style: large limestone blocks with hard red granite added as casing; the stones in the south wall of the valley temple of Khafre are exactly the same as in the façade wall of the Sphinx temple. Moreover, although Stadelmann argues otherwise, most people agree (and computer-generated models have confirmed) that the features of the Sphinx resemble most closely the features of Khafre, as we know them from his statuary.

In 1978, Lehner and I found other evidence that Khafre's builders had not quite finished the Sphinx complex. By cutting the temple terrace lower than the Sphinx floor, the builders left a tall vertical bedrock ledge. To the west, the ledge forms the north side of the ditch, but the quarrymen did not finish cutting the line here. The point at which they stopped is just opposite the left forepaw. From here to the back of the ditch, the unfinished part is a rock shelf of decreasing width. Behind the Sphinx, the workmen were very far from completing the outline of the ditch. When they stopped working they left a huge massif of hard rock only a few yards from the rear of the Sphinx.

Khafre built the Sphinx to serve a specific function. It was meant to represent him as Horus giving offerings with his two paws to the sun god, to his father, Khufu, identified during both life and after death with the sun god, Re, who rises directly in front of the Sphinx temple each morning. To date any monument we must use art, archaeology, architecture, and all other related evidence. Given all of these considerations, I cannot find a reason to believe that Khufu carved the Sphinx.

Nearby, my Egyptian team is excavating two Old Kingdom cemeteries. The lower cemetery was for construction supervisors and the workmen who moved the limestone blocks that formed the pyramids; the workmen were temporary conscripts provided by households all over Egypt. The tombs in this cemetery are built of mud brick and come in many different shapes: *mastabas*, beehives, even a stepped pyramid tomb. Some of the owners are identified on limestone false doors and offering basins; a number of unique statues were also found. The upper cemetery was reserved for artisans and officials and contains higher-quality tombs built of limestone and mud brick, full of inscriptions and beautiful statues. The tomb of Nefertheith, for example, a man with two wives and eighteen children, has beautiful scenes on one of its three false doors of people grinding grain and baking bread. The tomb of Petety is notable for the unique threat inscribed on it, which ends, ". . . if anyone touches my tomb, he will be eaten by a crocodile, a hippopotamus, and a lion." Several of the tombs in this cemetery are approached by ramps, evoking the causeways of the nearby pyramid complexes.

We recently found the tomb of a man named Nesut-weret in this cemetery. It is approached by a ramp, and we found an intact sarcophagus in the burial chamber. The sarcophagus is made of limestone and sealed with mortar, and inside we were fortunate enough to find the fingerprints of the workmen who handled the burial. In another shaft within this tomb, we found the skeleton of a man with a dog buried beside him. On September 17, 2002, we opened the limestone sarcophagus live on a television program for National Geographic and found a skeleton inside of a man aged 35–40 years old. This show was very exciting, as it was devoted not only to the serious advancement of archaeological knowledge, but was also intended to educate the public, to tell them the true story of the pyramid builders, and to show them, first-hand, that there is no such thing as a lost civilization. The overwhelming majority of our profession was both pleased and proud at the astounding number of people viewing the program worldwide.

The upper cemetery at Giza has also revealed to us many of the titles of those who built the pyramid, including: Inspector of the building tombs, Overseer of the craftsmen, Overseer of the linen, Overseer of the draftsmen, Overseer who stands behind the officials, Overseer of the harbor, Overseer of the administrative district, Overseer of the workmen who drag the stones, and Overseer of the side of the pyramid. These titles give us a great deal of information about the administration and organization of the pyramid builders.

To the east of our excavations, under the village of Nazlet al-Samman, we found the remains of a settlement spanning some six square kilometers, including the mud-brick walls of workmen's huts *in situ*; plant pollen; bones of domesticated animals such as cows, sheep, and pigs; and pottery trays from Upper Egypt. The cemetery, the institutional area, and the settlement were separated from the pyramids by a monumental wall called 'The Wall of the Crow,' which is about 10 meters high and 200 meters long and has a massive gateway in the middle. I believe that the number of workmen involved in building the pyramids was on the order of 10,000 people at a time. (Herodotus claims that there were 100,000 workmen, but no government project at that time could have involved that number of workmen.)

We cannot understand pyramids without having an idea about the people who maintained the cults of the pyramid builders. These priests, and other high officials in the royal administration, built tombs around the pyramids of their kings. They were careful to write their titles on the false doors within and to leave statues inside as eternal homes for their souls. In regard to the Fourth Dynasty, Peter Der Manuelian discusses the tombs at Giza and the development of the cemeteries around each pyramid.

Michel Valloggia works at the pyramid of Djedefre, son and successor of Khufu, at Abu Rawash on a joint Egyptian-French-Swiss expedition. Among other things, he has discovered a queen's pyramid that contains a burial chamber with unique artifacts, such as a weight and a large alabaster vessel that displays the Horus name of Khufu. It is likely then, that the queen buried within this pyramid was a daughter of Khufu. His chapter discusses the unfinished pyramids of the Fourth Dynasty.

Miroslav Verner, the author of an excellent book on pyramids, is working at the site of Abusir, where the pyramids date primarily to the Fifth Dynasty. I like to call Abusir "The Forgotten Site" because the public is not aware of its significance. Verner has made very important discoveries near the pyramids there, such as papyri that relate the organization of the royal cult and the daily records of the temple of King Neferirkare, which cover two hundred years of history—from the reign of Neferirkare to the time of Pepy II, the last king of the Sixth Dynasty. Verner has also found important information about pyramid construction in one of the subsidiary pyramids at Abusir, underlining for us that we cannot take evidence from one pyramid and apply it to all: the layout and construction of each pyramid was treated as a unique problem to be solved, and a great deal depended on the topography of the site. I was very fortunate to participate with Verner in the discovery of the intact tomb of Iwf-aa, a director of the palace during the Twenty-sixth Dynasty. Verner's contribution to this book focuses on the pyramids of the Fifth and Sixth Dynasties at Saqqara and Abusir.

We are in the process of opening the site of Abusir to the public for the first time. During preparation of the site we discovered some unique blocks from the causeway of the Fifth Dynasty king Sahure, which are decorated with fascinating scenes. Verner and I have co-authored a chapter on these blocks.

Audran Labrousse is one of the foremost experts on pyramids of the Sixth Dynasty, and he has written the chapter that discusses these monuments. He has assisted my friend Jean Leclant in his work at Saqqara, where they have been working in the pyramid complexes of Pepy I, Merenre, and Pepy II. They have done extraordinary work in reconstructing the Pyramid Texts inscribed on the walls of these pyramids, and have also found new small pyramids around the

16-17
The author examining a skeleton inside a recently discovered sarcophagus in the tomb of Nesut-weret, Cemetery of the Pyramid Builders, Old Kingdom.

17 bottom
This photo shows a section of the Cemetery of the Pyramid Builders.

pyramid of Pepy I. As a result, we now know the names of queens that had heretofore been lost to history.

I have contributed here a chapter on the decoration of the pyramid complex, and the significance of the scenic programs with which the pyramids and their associated complexes were adorned. Karol Mysliwiec, who discovered a unique tomb next to the Step Pyramid containing beautiful scenes, writes about the tombs of the nobles at Saqqara dating from the Fifth and Sixth Dynasties.

There is no archaeologist who knows the pyramids of the Middle Kingdom better than Dieter

Arnold, who has written a chapter on these monuments. He has been excavating the pyramid of Amenemhet I at Lisht and the pyramids of Amenemhet III and Senusret III at Dahshur, and has made many interesting discoveries at Lisht, including information about reused blocks from the Old Kingdom that were used as fill in Amenemhet I's pyramid. Furthermore, he has found that the seven tombs in this complex originally believed to be *mastabas* were in fact pyramids. He also found the intact tomb of Weret, the mother of Senusret III, which contained fabulous pieces of jewelry. I visited Dahshur while Arnold was excavating there, and

vividly remember the maze of corridors that lay below the pyramid of Amenemhet III, as well as the magnificent interior of the pyramid of Senusret III.

David Silverman tells us about the noble and priestly tombs of the Middle Kingdom. Silverman is working on recording the Middle Kingdom burials at Saqqara, and in working on the site of a previous excavation, he has been able to make a great discovery that he explains in this book. This book also includes an excellent essay by art historian Hourig Sourouzian on the royal and private statues of the Old and Middle Kingdoms.

The site of the Giza pyramids, where I have

worked since 1974, is very important to me. I would like to add two further points before I leave you to follow the adventures of each of these great scholars. First, I would like to relate the story of my exciting last visit inside the Step Pyramid of King Djoser. There are perhaps only one or two scholars in our field who have had this opportunity. I entered the Step Pyramid at nine-thirty in the morning and left at five in the evening. I went through three-and-a-half miles of corridors and along the way saw the beautiful alabaster sarcophagi of Djoser's daughter, the reliefs that show his titles and scenes from his *sed* festival, and of course, visited his magnificent burial chamber. You will be able to vicariously experience the magic of the interior of this awesome monument through the description written by my dear friend Ali Radwan.

The second point is that I have seen many of the over fifty modern pyramids that have been built in Canada, Europe, and America, but no one today can build a pyramid like the ancient Egyptians did. We just do not have their dedication. The pyramid was the national project of each king. Every household contributed to its construction by sending temporary workers, food, or supplies to aid their king. For the workers, it must have been rather like enlisting in the army, as a way to honor your country and contribute to your society. The pyramids were designed to ensure the rebirth of the king and his deification, all of which served to ensure the proper functioning of the Egyptian cosmos.

Some say that the pyramids built Egypt, as each pyramid project unified the country for a common cause. In order to successfully design and construct these marvels of ancient technology, the Egyptians had to develop extraordinary skills in art, architecture, astronomy, and engineering.

This book not only tells us the story of the Egyptian pyramids and how they were built, but also of the passion and commitment of those scholars who have dedicated their lives to their work, to excavation, and to the translation of the texts t hey uncover.

The pyramids are slow to give up their secrets, but by carefully mapping and studying the ancient traces and clues that they contain, we are gaining a better idea of the solutions to the riddles they offer to the world.

New Discoveries at Giza and Saqqara

The major pyramid sites of Egypt have revealed not only great pyramids, but also many other fascinating secrets, including spectacular tombs and important artifacts. Since the ancient Egyptians used pyramid sites for burials during the Middle Kingdom, New Kingdom, and the Late Period, these discoveries date not only to the Old Kingdom, but to the entire span of pharaonic history. Over the past few years, scholars from all over the world have announced new excavations that tell us more of the stories of these sites. Giza and Saqqara are the most important pyramid sites to have yielded unique recent discoveries.

GIZA

In 2005, we discovered that the ancient Egyptians shored up Menkaure's causeway with stone rubble. Sometime during the Fourth Dynasty (c. 2575-2450 BC), a tomb was cut into the rock to the north of where this causeway was built. The stone rubble that Menkaure's workers used in the causeway closed the entrance of this tomb completely. At the moment, we can only see a slab of worked limestone at the top, indicating the existence of this tomb. We hope that it will be an intact Old Kingdom tomb and plan to excavate it soon. To the north of this tomb are many other interesting tombs from the reign of Menkaure that were excavated in the early 20th century by George Reisner from the Harvard University-Boston Museum of Fine Arts Excavations. One of these is the famous tomb of Debehen, Director of the king's toilette, who met the king during his inspection of his pyramid. Debehen asked Menkaure for a tomb, and the king ordered that stones be brought for him from the royal quarry at Tura and carved in the royal workshop.

My recent discoveries at Giza in the necropolis of the Pyramid Builders continue to provide us with important evidence concerning the lives of the workmen who were involved in the construction of the pyramids. We continue to discover and map new tombs in this area. I have focused, in my publications of these tombs, on the fascinating statuary found in this necropolis. My favorite of these are the statues of Inty-shedu, four limestone images of a man with the title Overseer of the boats of Neith. We found these hidden inside a serdab (closed statue chamber) in his tomb in the Upper Cemetery. There was also a fifth statue, of wood, but this had disintegrated. Another official, Kaihep, had three figurines hidden in a small box made of three stone slabs set against the west face of his mastaba in the Lower Cemetery. One is of Kaihep himself, striding forward; another is of his wife, Hepnykawes; the third is of either a servant or Hepnykawes herself grinding grain. One of my favorite statues is of a royal tenant farmer named Wenenemniut. This had once been set up in his serdab, but was found outside his tomb in the Upper Cemetery. These statues are wonderful, made from scraps of fine limestone probably left over from the construction of the pyramids and elite tombs on the plateau. They demonstrate for us that these lower-level workers and officials had access to, and probably included among their number, excellent artisans. The high regard in which the pyramid builders were held is also demonstrated by the medical care that they received, which we were able to illuminate through study of their skeletons. We found that all the skeletons of the men and women exhibit stress in their spinal columns, from moving the stones and carrying heavy burdens. However, one person had a leg amputated, and lived for about 14 years afterward. Another worker had an operation on his brain.

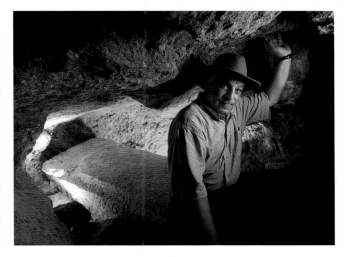

18-19
Mamdouh Taha, an archaeologist on Zahi Hawass's team, examines pottery in the tomb of Weser-Ptah, a large tomb in the Pyramid Builders' Cemetery at Giza.

18 bottom
The entrance and the rich inscriptions in the tomb of Debehen can be seen in these images. Debehen was a Director of the king's toilette and lived during the reign of Menkaure.

19 top
SCA workers excavate a site where a 4,500-year-old tomb was discovered in 2002. The tomb is at the top right of the image.

19 center and bottom
Zahi Hawass shows the inscriptions at the entrance of the 4,500-year-old tomb discovered in 2002 in the Upper Cemetery of the Pyramid Builders. In the lower image, the Secretary General of the SCA analyzes the sarcophagus found inside the tomb.

20 top
Students examine artifacts in the royal installation at Giza.

20-21
Excavations near the gateway in the Wall of the Crow at Giza.

20 bottom and 21 top
Mark Lehner, who found the Lost City of the Pyramid Builders to the east of the tombs of the pyramid builders, reviews the excavations.

21 center
Excavations in the Lost City of the Pyramid Builders, where many industrial areas have been found.

To the east of the tombs of the pyramid builders, Mark Lehner has found the Lost City of the Pyramid Builders. This was the workmen's installation, or as it was called by the ancient Egyptians, *per shena*. This rich settlement site includes an Eastern Town, perhaps occupied by the people who prepared the food and drink for the workmen, and the Western Town, in which, according to Mark, the pyramid administrators lived. I would suggest that the bigger houses in this area were for the overseers and artisans who built their tombs in the Upper Cemetery. One area contains a series of workmen's barracks, where temporary workers slept. Around the barracks were bakeries; these contain molds and jars similar to those illustrated in the tomb of Ti at Saqqara, where all the steps of bread-making are depicted.

I believe there were about 10,000 workmen at a time involved in the construction of the pyramid. This number includes the artisans as well as the workmen who dragged the stones. Some of these workmen came from the provinces, sent by their villages in lieu of royal taxes. Based on a new text found in the Western Desert, Khufu reigned for 30-32 years, and the construction of his pyramid may have occupied his entire period on the throne. The pyramid of Khafre may have taken about 25 years to build, and the pyramid of Menkaure 28 years. After these pyramids were completed, the pyramid builders were apparently involved in the construction of the tombs of high officials and nobles of the Fifth Dynasty at Giza.

MAP OF THE LOST CITY OF THE PYRAMID BUILDERS

A *WALL OF THE CROW*
B *ENCLOSURE WALL*
C *GALLERIES*
D *SOUTH STREET MAGAZINES*
E *WESTERN TOWN*
F *ROYAL BUILDING*
G *EASTERN TOWN*
H *MODERN SOCCER FIELD*

Another Old Kingdom tomb was found near the famous tomb of Tjery of the Twenty-sixth Dynasty, south of the pyramid of Menkaure. The new tomb was found about 250 meters to the northwest of Tjery, to the east of an area excavated by Karl Kromer and near the site of some Early Dynastic tombs. Built of reddish limestone in the lower part and white limestone above, the newly discovered tomb measures about 12 meters long from north to south, 4.35 meters from east to west, and 1.30 meters in height. A false door was found on the far north of the eastern façade; in association with this door were a number of pottery vessels on different levels. The false door, of fine white limestone, is in excellent condition. It has two drums, on which are images of the sons and daughters of the tomb owner making offerings to their father, along with other offering scenes and images of animals being butchered for the funerary cult. Each person depicted is labeled with their name, but the name and titles of the tomb owner were not present. This tomb includes three burial shafts; however, we found no evidence of burials.

The area between the Great Sphinx and the pyramid of Khafre, to the west of the famous Campbell's Tomb, is a very interesting site because it contains tombs for the priests who maintained the cults of Khufu and Khafre during the Twenty-sixth Dynasty. In 2004, we first excavated a rock-cut tomb, which we numbered T306. We went down for about 9 meters and discovered six rooms cut into the rock, one of which contained a decayed wooden box with 400 shabtis inside. These statuettes were put beside the sarcophagus to serve the deceased in the afterlife by answering questions and doing work in his or her place. One intact tomb from this period at Abusir held a full complement of 408 statuettes: one for each of the 365 days of the year, 35 overseers, and 8 directors. The excavation went down a further 2 meters but then we hit the water table.

Northwest of T306 is T307. At a depth of 3.9 meters is a burial chamber filled with sand, its floor covered with bones. In the floor of this chamber are a number of shafts, which were closed with limestone blocks. The first of these had a sarcophagus cut into the rock on the north side of the shaft. The sarcophagus measures about 2.20 meters and contained bones mixed with debris, along with a number of shabtis, amulets, and scarabs. Another sarcophagus was discovered on the west side, also cut into the rock. This was about 2.15 meters in length and contained bones, shabtis, amulets, and scarabs.

The area west of the Sphinx also holds many important tombs that date to the Twenty-sixth Dynasty. The study of these tombs may reveal important evidence concerning Giza during that period. As we excavate these tombs, we hope to find out more about how the cults of Khufu, Khafre, and Menkaure were maintained by priests during this period, and why they chose Giza as the site of their burial.

22 top
Elegant reliefs appear on the white limestone false door of the tomb recently found near the tomb of Tjery.

22 bottom
General view of the area near the tomb of Tjay.

22-23
Zahi Hawass exits the rock-cut tomb named T306, recently discovered in the area between th Great Sphinx and the pyramid of Khafre.

23 bottom
Tomb T307 was filled with sand and bones, but the archaeologists also found a large number of shabtis.

The Pyramids

SAQQARA

Although countless burials have already been uncovered at Saqqara, it is still almost a virgin site—much of it remains unexcavated, and almost every week there is a new discovery. The site was used from the Early Dynastic Period through the end of pharaonic history, with the heaviest use during the New Kingdom and Late Period. In recent years, many important excavations have been carried out, both under my supervision and by colleagues.

The Rediscovery of the Headless Pyramid

First mapped by Karl Lepsius in 1843, and labeled Pyramid no. 29, the pyramid to the east of the complex of Teti has been nicknamed the Headless Pyramid because its superstructure is missing. Gaston Maspero investigated this pyramid in 1881, searching for Pyramid Texts, but left no documentation other than a rough sketch. In 1930, Cecil Firth found red granite blocks and the lid of a sarcophagus made of black basalt, and suggested that this pyramid was built by a king who ruled for a short period. Through their study of the pyramid complex of Teti, J.-Ph. Lauer and Jean Leclant came to believe that the pyramid belonged to the Fifth Dynasty king Menkauhor: Teti's causeway bends to avoid the site of the Headless Pyramid, suggesting that this pyramid is older than Teti's.

Maragioglio and Rinaldi studied the remains of the Headless Pyramid and found that the passage that leads to the burial chamber bends to the east. This is a regular feature of the pyramids of the Fifth Dynasty, especially during the era from the reign of Neferirkare until the reign of Djedkare-Isesi. Other scholars, such as J. Berlandini, studied the pyramid and found that written evidence indicating that Menkauhor's worship existed in North Saqqara. However, other scholars have suggested that this pyramid should be assigned to Merykare of the Ninth Dynasty.

Since the pyramid had never been systematically excavated, we decided it was an important project to tackle. We began our work by clearing the passage that leads to the burial chamber. In this area we found huge blocks of limestone; to the south we discovered a large block of granite. Preceding the burial chambers was a small hall leading to a granite passage. A part of the satellite pyramid associated with the main pyramid was also found.

It seems to me from the study of the architecture of this substructure that it fits the Fifth Dynasty model well, and therefore Menkauhor is a good candidate for its owner. However, we have not entered the burial chamber yet; we hope we will find the name of a king inside.

Cemetery of the Dentists

My excavations at Saqqara recently uncovered three unusual tombs belonging to ancient dentists. The discovery happened by accident, after the Antiquities Police caught thieves digging in the area north of the pyramid of Userkaf, west of the elite tombs of the First and Second Dynasties, and east of the tomb of Ti. We excavated in this area, and found the tombs of three men, all belonging to the same family and holding the title: Dentist of the king.

The first tomb belongs to Iy-mery, who was an Overseer of the dentists and also a Priest of Soped. The tomb has two chapels. The northern one contains scenes of daily life and offering bearers; there are also unusual scenes of baboons. The southern chapel contains scenes of offerings and offering bearers and an image of the deceased in front of an offering table. Behind the chapel was found a serdab, but there was no statue.

The second tomb was built for Ka-em-mesu, also a Dentist of the king. This tomb is very small. It does, however, have a niche, containing a beautifully crafted statue of the deceased and his son; unfortunately, the upper part of the figure of the tomb owner is missing.

The last tomb belongs to Sekhem-ka, also a royal dentist. It is the smallest of the three and is built of mud brick.

The Pyramids

26-27 and 26 bottom
Zahi Hawass unveils a 2,500-year-old
mummy at Saqqara in 2005.

27 top
A superb alabaster headrest and tablet
for the sacred oils were found inside the
tomb of Tetiankhkem.

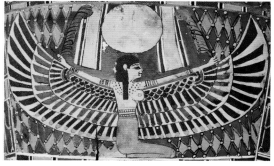

27 bottom left
SCA excavations led by Zahi Hawass
in 2002-2003 close to Teti's funerary
complex discovered, among other things,
a Sixth Dynasty tomb: here is its false
door.

27 bottom right
This image shows the area northeast of
the pyramid of Teti, where the tomb of
Tetiankhkem was found.

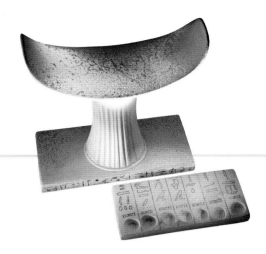

Teti and his Queens

Over the last decade or so, we have also carried out excavations in the complex of Teti, first king of the Sixth Dynasty. We began work on the east side of the pyramid of Queen Iput I, wife of Teti and also the mother of Pepy I, in order to fully document the pyramid and its temple. During excavations in this area, we discovered two pyramidions that had been excavated previously but never published. We also found additional two pyramidions; one was in the area between the pyramid temple and pyramid of Queen Iput I and the temple of Teti's other queen, Khuit. The pyramidion does not have any inscriptions, and its top was destroyed.

Northeast of the pyramid of Teti and east of the pyramid of Iput I, we found the tomb of a son of Teti's named Tetiankhkem. This tomb consists of an entrance, a horizontal hall, and a long hall. The offering chapel contains a false door that has the following titles: the Eldest son of the king of his body, the Hereditary prince, the Count, the King's son, the Seal bearer of the god, the Chief lector priest, Scribe of the divine words, Overseer of Upper Egypt, Sole friend, and Overseer of the two granaries.

A deep shaft led from the chapel to burial chamber, where we found a limestone sarcophagus about 3.25 meters in length. Inside the sarcophagus was a mummy in very poor condition, of a young man who died at about the age of 25. Inside the burial chamber was a headrest made of alabaster with

the titles of Tetiankhkem and also a tablet for the seven sacred oils.

Firth and Gunn, working in the area in 1922, had excavated the temple of Teti's principal queen, Khuit, but had left her pyramid untouched. We re-excavated the temple, and also explored the pyramid. We discovered that it had originally been 20 meters high, with an entrance on the north side. The interior passage was closed with blocks of limestone, with a block forming part of a *hetep* sign on top. We were not able to reach the interior of the pyramid from the main entrance, so we followed the breach made by ancient tomb robbers. We found a granite sarcophagus on the western side of the burial chamber, with its lid thrown to one side.

The study of the architecture of the two queen's pyramids shows that Khuit's monument was built first. We also concluded that in both pyramids, the rod appears to have been used as the standard unit of measurement rather than the royal cubit. Our work also shows that Iput I was a secondary wife and was originally buried in a *mastaba*, perhaps during the lifetime of Tetiankhkem, who was apparently the eldest son, perhaps of the principal queen, Khuit.

Events at the death of Teti, who is said by ancient records to have been killed in a conspiracy, are murky. After the death of Tetiankhkem, a shadowy king named Userkare appears to have ascended the throne and ruled for a short time. Then Pepy I, son of Iput, claimed the throne. To honor his mother as Isis, mother of Horus, Pepy I changed her *mastaba* to a pyramid, and cased it in fine white limestone.

More New Discoveries

I always say that until now we have only discovered 30 percent of our monuments, and recent discoveries at Saqqara prove this to be true. I wrote most of the text of this chapter at my resthouse at Saqqara. During this period, I was able in one day to announce several new discoveries.

Sakuji Yoshimura, of Waseda University in Japan, is excavating at two sites. North of Saqqara, his team has discovered a wonderful intact burial dating to the Middle Kingdom. He found three intact coffins decorated with very high quality scenes and texts. Two coffins are from the Middle Kingdom: one is for Sobekhat; and the other is for a woman named Senetites. Both are rectangular, and decorated with wedjat eyes. These prove that there was an elite workshop in the area during this era, a period for which there have been few finds in the Saqqara area. The third coffin is anthropoid, of wood covered with a black substance and is decorated with the four sons of Horus along with the name and titles of the deceased. It belonged to a person named Wia, and dates to the Nineteenth Dynasty.

The second discovery was made by Naguib Kanawati, head of the Australian expedition of Macquarie University, in the northwest corner of the Teti Pyramid cemetery, where many tombs have been found. Kanawati's team has cleared about 26 shafts. North of the tomb of Iunmin, in the process of clearing debris, the expedition discovered part of a New Kingdom tomb chapel. In the level below this, several new tombs were found. One does not contain any inscriptions that help to date it, but its architecture is similar to the Fifth Dynasty tomb of Kaemheset. Another of the tombs is built of mud brick and measures about 10.5 meters long. It contains a corridor-style chapel and has four niches of different sizes set into its western wall. Two of the niches are larger and appear to be more important than the others. The northern of these belongs to Seperi-ankh, wife of the tomb owner, while the southern and the largest niche belongs to Kahai, who held the title Scribe of the house of the divine documents. Kahai's niche has a long wooden panel, inscribed with an offering formula and offering list, embedded into its central recess. In front of each of the larger niches was an inscribed offering basin. In front of the northern niche were three wooden statues, two male and one female, and before the niche to the south of this were two more wooden statues, a standing man and a seated couple.

29 top
The Australian expedition of Macquarie University found wooden statues in the niches of the tomb of Kahai.

29 center
View of the area of the tomb of Kahai.

29 bottom
Special tape has been used to hold the fragile paintwork of one of the two wooden coffins found by the Japanese team of Waseda University at Saqqara in 2007. Right is an anthropoid coffin belonging to the Nineteenth Dynasty.

Maarten Raven from the Leiden Museum has been excavating at Saqqara for many years. His most recent find, a mud-brick tomb, is to the east of the tomb of Meryneith. This consists of an open courtyard surrounded by a columned portico, with three cult chapels to the west. The reliefs decorating this tomb date it stylistically and through its content to the reign of Akhenaten. The tomb was built for Ptahemwia, whose titles have been translated by Raven as: Greatly praised one of the perfect god, Beloved of the lord of the Two Lands, Royal seal-bearer, First courtier, Great one in the palace whom his master loves, Royal butler, Clean of hands. His wife Maia was a "Songstress of Amun." The scenes on the walls include the couple seated, receiving offerings (with pet monkeys playing beneath Maia's chair); Ptahemwia, with his Nubian bodyguards, his charioteer, and his sandal-bearer, arriving at his home, where his wife is upstairs enjoying a drink; and agricultural work.

Just before I was closing this chapter another discovery came that captured the hearts of the public. This was in the area of the many Late Period burial shafts located to the north of the causeway of the pyramid of Unas. Christiane Ziegler of the Louvre Museum has discovered many mummies in these shafts. Most recently, she discovered a limestone sarcophagus. When it was opened a mummy was found inside wearing a beautiful golden mask. The mummy was covered with colored linen decorated with scenes of the goddess Nut and the four children of Horus. On the chest of the mummy was a wide collar and an inscription with a prayer to Osiris. This mummy is dated to the 3rd century BC.

The Secret Doors at Giza

The most important project that we are preparing now is to reveal the secrets of the Great Pyramid of Khufu at Giza finding out what is behind the secret doors.

As explained later in this book, there are three "doors" inside the shafts of the so-called Queen's Chamber. Using robots we discovered two doors in the southern shaft, one with two copper handles at 63 meters and the other found at a distance of approximately 21 centimeters beyond the first one. A third door was found in the northern shaft. We also discovered that the northern shaft bent for 7.3 meters after a distance of 16.2 meters.

What is new? I appointed a committee of archaeologists and engineers to review the two proposals that we have received concerning the construction of a new robot: the first one from Singapore University and the second from the University of Hong Kong in cooperation with Manchester University. The committee reviewed each proposal.

Also in 2007, we built a tunnel similar to those inside the Great Pyramid, and we put this replica in the desert in the shadow of the Giza pyramids. We allowed each team to show us how they intended to use the robot inside the shaft.

We will conduct another experiment to see how each team will be able to get through the hole in the first door in the southern shaft and then drill through the second door. Then the robot will be placed in the northern shaft in order to drill through its door.

The legend of Khufu continued after his reign, as indicated by the story of Khufu and the Magician. In this story, he searches for the secret of Thoth, god of wisdom so he could find out how to build his burial chamber properly. I believe that Khufu's real burial chamber was still hidden inside his pyramid, and these doors (measuring 20 x 20 centimeters) may be the key that hides the king's treasure.

We will soon select the team that will work with us on revealing the secrets of the doors in the Great Pyramid, and we will do the most fascinating work ever done in archaeology.

30 top
This beautiful golden mask belongs to a Late Period mummy recently found inside a limestone sarcophagus located in a shaft in Saqqara.

Chronology

PREHISTORIC PERIOD: TO 3000 BC
BEFORE 10,000
Paleolithic period; nomadic food gatherers.

CIRCA 4500-3000
Neolithic period; farming and domestication of animals and first settlements; simple pottery; copper and gold working; local rulers.

EARLY DYNASTIC PERIOD: CIRCA 3000-2650 BC
CIRCA 3000-2650   FIRST AND SECOND DYNASTIES
Narmer
Aha
Hetepsekhemwy
Raneb (Nebre)
Ninetjer
Peribsen
Khasekhemwy
Unification under one ruler; capital at Memphis and royal tombs at Abydos and Saqqara.

OLD KINGDOM: CIRCA 2650-2150 BC
CIRCA 2650-2575   THIRD DYNASTY
Djoser
Step Pyramid at Saqqara
....
Huni

CIRCA 2575-2465   FOURTH DYNASTY
Sneferu
Khufu
Strong centralized government; pyramids at Dahshur and Giza.
....
Khafre
Menkaure
Shepseskaf
Queen Khentkaus

CIRCA 2465-2325   FIFTH DYNASTY
Userkaf
Sahure
Neferirkare
Pyramids and sun temples at Abusir and Saqqara;
Pyramid Texts.
...
Unas

CIRCA 2325-2150   SIXTH DYNASTY
Teti
...
Pepy I
...
Pepy II
Queen Nitokerty
Strong beginning but decline during long reign of Pepy II;
pyramids at Saqqara; last ruler probably Queen Nitokerty.

FIRST INTERMEDIATE PERIOD: CIRCA 2150-2040 BC
CIRCA 2150-2040   SEVENTH THROUGH TENTH DYNASTIES
Collapse of central government; country divided among local rulers; famine and poverty.

MIDDLE KINGDOM: CIRCA 1640-1550 BC
CIRCA 2040-1991   ELEVENTH DYNASTY
Mentuhotep II
Reunification of Egypt by Theban rulers.

CIRCA 1991-1783   TWELFTH DYNASTY
Amenembet I
Senusret I
Amenembet II
Senusret III
Amenembet III
Amenembet IV
Queen Sobekneferu
Powerful central government; expansion into Nubia (Sudan). Capital at Lisht, near Memphis.

CIRCA 1783-1640   THIRTEENTH DYNASTY
Rapid succession of rulers; country in decline.

SECOND INTERMEDIATE PERIOD: CIRCA 1640-1550 BC

CIRCA 1640-1580   FOURTEENTH DYNASTY
CIRCA 1585-1530   FIFTEENTH AND SIXTEENTH DYNASTIES
CIRCA 1640-1550   SEVENTEENTH DYNASTY
Country divided with Asiatics ruling in the Delta.
Theban dynasty begins reunification process.
...
Seqenenre Tao I
Seqenenre Tao II
Kamose

NEW KINGDOM: CIRCA 1550-1070 BC
CIRCA 1550-1307   EIGHTEENTH DYNASTY
Ahmose
Amenhotep I
Thutmose I
Thutmose II
Thutmose III
Queen Hatshepsut
Amenhotep II
Amenhotep III
Akhenaten
Tutankhamun
Ay
Horemheb
Reunification and expulsion of Asiatics in north, annexation of Nubia in south.
Period of greatest expansion and prosperity.
Thebes (Luxor) became main residence.

CIRCA 1307-1196 NINETEENTH DYNASTY
Ramesses I
Seti I
Ramesses II
Merenptah
…
Siptah
Queen Twosret
After glorious reign of Ramesses II, prosperity threatened by incursions of "Sea Peoples" in north. Residence in Delta.

CIRCA 1196-1070 TWENTIETH DYNASTY
Setnakht
Ramesses III–XI
Economic decline and weak kings ruling from the Delta. Civil disturbances and workers' strikes. Royal tombs robbed.

THIRD INTERMEDIATE PERIOD:
CIRCA 1070-712 BC
CIRCA 1070-945 TWENTY-FIRST DYNASTY
Smendes
…
Siamun
…
Egypt in decline. Siamun may be the pharaoh who gave his daughter in marriage to Solomon.

CIRCA 945-828 TWENTY-SECOND DYNASTY
Shoshenq I
Osorkon I
Shoshenq II
…
Osorkon IV
…
"Shishak" of the Bible. Egypt fragmented and politically divided.

CIRCA 828-712 TWENTY-THIRD AND TWENTY-FOURTH DYNASTYIES
Egypt divided among local rulers.

LATE PERIOD: CIRCA 712-332 BC
CIRCA 712-657 TWENTY-FIFTH DYNASTY
Kashta
Piankhy (Py)
Shabaka
Shebitku
Taharqa
Tantamani

Rulers from Kush (Sudan) united Egypt and started cultural revival. Threatened by Assyrians who invaded in 671, 667, and 663 BC. Last king fled south.

664-525 TWENTY-SIXTH DYNASTY (SAITE)
Psamtek I
Necho II
Psamtek I
…
Dynasty from Sais in Delta. Defeated Kushite kings and continued rebuilding program after Assyrians left.

525-404 TWENTY-SEVENTH DYNASTY
Cambyses
…
Egypt annexed into Persian Empire.

404-343 TWENTY-EIGHTH THROUGH THIRTIETH DYNASTIES
Amyrtaios
…
Nectanebo I
Nectanebo II
Last native rulers of Egypt. Cultural renaissance and nationalism but political decline

343-332 THIRTY-FIRST DYNASTY
Artaxerxes III
Persian reconquest.

GRECO-ROMAN PERIOD: 332 BC – AD 642
332-304 MACEDONIAN DYNASTY
Alexander the Great
Macedonian rulers after death of Alexander in Babylon (323).

304-30 PTOLEMAIC DYNASTY
Ptolemy I–XV
Last ruler, Cleopatra VII, allied with Mark Anthony against Rome. Defeated by Octavian at the Battle of Actium.

30 BC–AD 642 ROMAN PROVINCE
Egypt becomes a Roman province. Heavy taxation drains wealth from country. Christianity spreads and eliminates ancient religion.

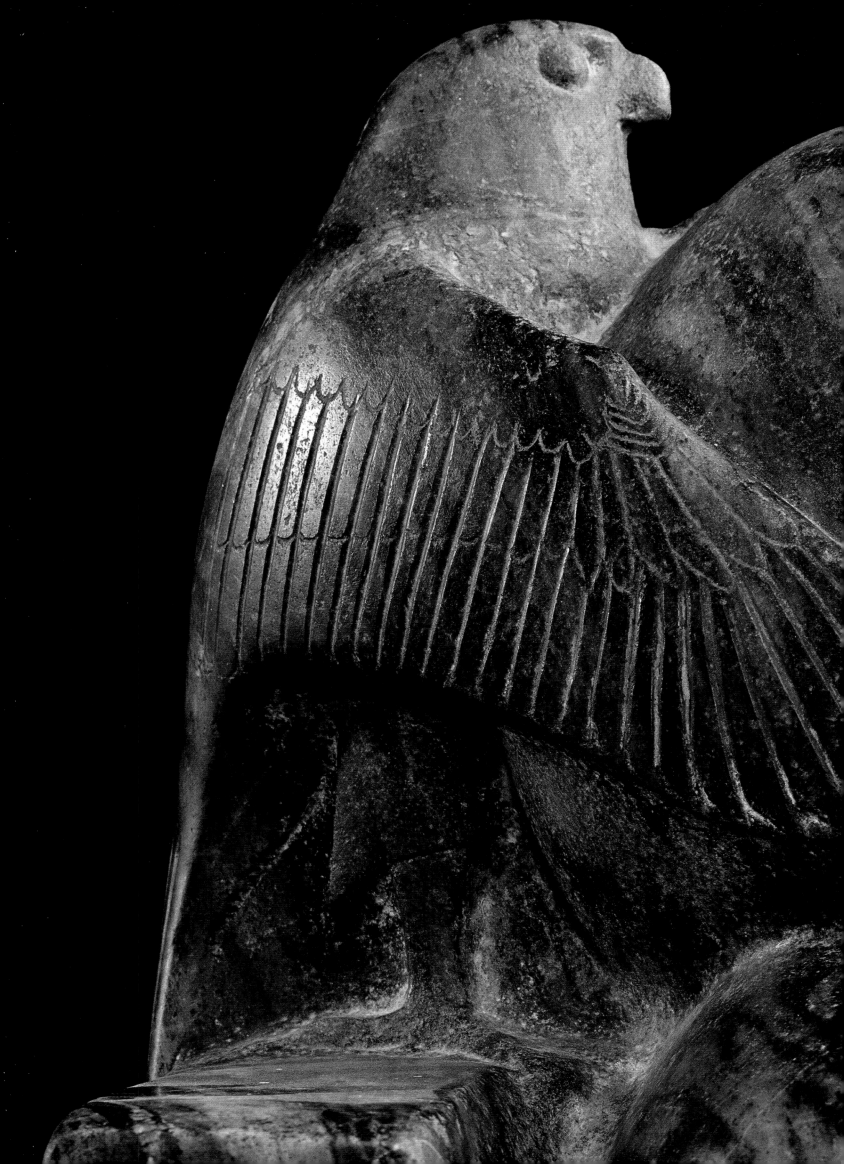

Chapter 1

Why a Pyramid?
Pyramid Religion

by James P. Allen

From simple piles of children's blocks to monuments erected by civilizations around the world, the pyramid is one of the most common of all architectural forms. Structurally, it is also one of the most stable. It is not surprising, then, that the ancient Egyptians should have chosen to create their most imposing architectural achievements in this shape. But the pyramids of ancient Egypt were more than huge piles of stone. They were also concrete expressions of specific beliefs about life in this world and the next. To understand why the Egyptians built pyramids in the first place, we have to look at the meaning and force of these beliefs.

Ancient Egypt was an agrarian society, and the Egyptians' view of the world was largely determined by agricultural life along the Nile. Each year, spring rains in the Ethiopian highlands fed the source of the Nile, raising the level of the river in Egypt above its banks and flooding the land on either side from June to October. Ancient records from the earliest Egyptian dynasties show that this annual inundation could rise as much as 4.4 m above the river's normal level, turning much of the Egyptian countryside into vast lakes. As the flood receded, leaving behind fertile silt, new plants would spring to life on the highest mounds of earth as they began to emerge from the waters of these lakes.

From this annual experience, the beginning of life was linked in the Egyptian mind to the vision of a mound of earth emerging from a vast expanse of water. The Egyptians extended this notion to their understanding of how the world itself had come into being. One of the earliest Egyptian creation accounts envisioned the first place in the world as a mound of earth emerging from the waters of a universal ocean, and the first life form as a lily growing on the peak of this primeval mound. In Egyptian thought the lily was

a god, Nefertum, whose name means 'perfect and complete.' Nefertum was honored as a harbinger of the sun, which rose from the lily's petals to bring life to the newly created world. The mound itself was also worshipped as a god, called Tatjenen, meaning 'the emerging land.'

Early temples sometimes incorporated a mound of earth as an icon of the original site of all life. This could be a hill of earth or sand, but it also took the more permanent shape of a small pyramid carved from a single block of stone. A miniature pyramid of this kind was called a *bnbn* ('benben'), a name that derives from the root *bn*, meaning 'swell up' or 'swell forth.' The *benben* was a concrete image of the first mound of land 'swelling up' from the waters of the pre-creation universe. As such, it was an icon not only of the primeval mound but also of the sun, which first rose from it; the Egyptian word for the rising of the sun is *wbn*, which comes from the same root as *benben*.

From the beginning, therefore, the pyramid shape represented the notion of new life, emerging both from a mound of earth and in the light and warmth of the sunrise. To the Egyptians, however, the *benben* was more than just an image. Like the primeval mound, it somehow incorporated the very power of life itself, the force that made it possible for new life to emerge after a period of dormancy. It is not surprising, then, that the Egyptians should also have associated mounds and pyramids with their funerary monuments. In the ancient Egyptian mind, death was not an end to life but the beginning of a new form of existence.

During life, each human being was thought to consist of three basic entities: body, *ba*, and *ka*. The body was the physical form, the material shell that a living being inhabited. The *ba* was somewhat like the modern notion of the soul: it was the unique essence of each individual, the person that inhabited the

36 bottom right
Head of Tutankhamun emerging as the sun from the lily on the primeval mound. Placed outside the sealed antechamber to his tomb, this image incorporated the king's reborn spirit as it left the tomb each morning.

36-37
The pyramid of King Sneferu at Meidum. This view, across the cultivated fields, evokes the ancient Egyptian concept of the pyramid as a mound of earth above the king's body that was planted beneath it.

physical body during life. The *ka* was the energy of life itself, a force transmitted from the creator to each living person; death occurred when this force was separated from the *ba* and its body. After death, the *ba* was thought to reunite with its life force, its *ka*; the deceased were called 'those who have gone to their *kas*.' This union allowed the individual, the *ba*, to continue living, but in a spiritual rather than physical form. The Egyptians called this new form of life *akh*, meaning an 'effective' mode of existence. Since it no longer had a physical component, it was not subject to aging or death: unlike the temporary form of life on earth, the *akh* was essentially eternal.

Incorporated within the structure of the tomb, the mound or *benben* provided the power for this spiritual rebirth to take place. Early Egyptian tombs were usually surmounted by the rectangular structure of mud brick known as a *mastaba*, but mounds of earth have also been found within these buildings above the burial chamber. The earliest pyramid tomb, that of the Third Dynasty king Djoser at Saqqara, began as a *mastaba* but was converted to a pyramid of six steps by the construction of five successively smaller *mastabas* on top of the original one. The resulting form seems to have been a variant of the primeval mound, envisioned as a series of steps rather than a hill with smooth sides; the same form has been found within earlier *mastabas* at Saqqara. The true pyramids that first appeared in the Fourth Dynasty were derived from this shape by filling in the steps to create four smooth faces, but they are also representations of the more common pyramidal *benben* on a monumental scale. Some of the newly discovered tombs of officials from the same period, to the south of the three Great Pyramids of Giza, were surmounted by conical mounds; these undoubtedly served the same purpose as the royal pyramids and represent yet another architectural manifestation of the primeval mound.

Apart from their incorporation of the power

of new life, not much is known about the role the earliest pyramids were thought to play in the king's afterlife. The great pyramids of the Third and Fourth Dynasties show a series of changes and innovations in their architecture and plan, which suggests an evolution in Egyptian thinking about their function.

In the Fifth Dynasty, however, the layout of the chambers within the royal pyramid became standardized. This new form reflects a vision of the afterlife that characterized Egyptian thought from then on. The typical interior plan of these later Old Kingdom pyramids consists of three main elements: 1.) an antechamber beneath the

apex of the pyramid, connected to the outside by an entrance corridor that opens in the pyramid's north face; 2.) a burial chamber to the west of the antechamber; and 3.) a stone sarcophagus at the west end of the burial chamber. Some of these features were introduced in the Fourth Dynasty. The stone sarcophagus is first seen in the pyramid of Khufu, and the separate antechamber beneath the pyramid's apex appears first in the pyramid of Menkaure. The standard

layout of all three elements, however, did not appear until the end of the Fourth Dynasty, in the royal tomb built for King Shepseskaf, Menkaure's successor. This was a *mastaba* rather than a pyramid, suggesting a break with the funerary traditions that had characterized royal burials since the time of Djoser, 150 years earlier.

Shepseskaf's tomb may have been designed to reflect the *mastabas* of Egypt's first kings at the site of Abydos in Upper Egypt. Abydos was a cult center of Osiris, the god most associated with the afterlife in Egyptian mythology. Like the primeval mound, Osiris represented the force of new life. His power was manifested in the transmission of life from one generation to the next and in the growth of new plants, the mysterious process that produced a living entity from an apparently dormant seed planted in the ground.

Osiris was also integral to the Egyptian understanding of the daily solar cycle. Each night the sun seemed to sink beneath the ground and die, yet in the morning it emerged again into the world, reborn to live once more during the day. To the Egyptians, this was possible only because during the night, the 'dead' sun had somehow received the power of new life. Two explanations of that process existed concurrently in Egyptian thought. In one, the sun reentered the womb of Nut, the goddess of the sky, each night, and was born from between her thighs again at dawn. In the other, the sun entered a netherworld, known as the Duat; there, in the middle of the night, it merged with the mummy of Osiris, lying in the depths of the Duat, and received from this union the ability to come to life once more. Together, these two explanations combined the role of mother and father in the production of new life.

Both of these concepts are reflected in the standardized layout of interior chambers

38
The union of Re with Osiris in the Netherworld, assisted by Isis and Nephthys, from the tomb of Ramesses II's queen, Nefertari. The sun god is represented by the disk and ram's head, Osiris by the mummified body.

39
Osiris, the god of rebirth, represented both as a mummy and as king of the afterlife. From the mortuary temple of Ramesses III at Medinet Habu, now in the Egyptian Museum in Cairo.

introduced by Shepseskaf and adopted in the pyramids of his successors during the Fifth and Sixth Dynasties. We know this because of the Pyramid Texts, a collection of funerary rituals and spells that were inscribed on the walls of these chambers and the sarcophagi in the pyramids of Unas, last king of the Fifth Dynasty, and his Sixth-Dynasty successors. These texts show that the king's afterlife was thought to parallel the daily solar cycle.

Each night, as the sun entered the body of Nut and the Duat, the king's spirit would come back to the interior of his tomb. The stone sarcophagus in the west end of the burial chamber was an analogue of Nut's womb. Within it, the king's mummy was both a fetus and an analogue of the mummy of Osiris lying in the Duat. The Pyramid Texts refer to the burial chamber itself as the Duat, and the spells inscribed on the walls of this room refer to the king not only by name but also as Osiris: for example, 'Osiris Unas.' As the sun united with Osiris's mummy in the Duat, the king's spirit was thought to join with his own mummy in the Duat of his tomb and, like the sun, receive through this union the power of new life.

The texts inscribed in the burial chamber are those of two rites performed at the funeral. They begin with a ritual of offerings, always inscribed on the north wall of the burial chamber. This may have accompanied the actual presentation of offerings at the funeral, but it was also meant to be repeated each day in the pyramid's mortuary temple; inscribed within the burial chamber, it would continue to provide the king's ba with the necessities of daily life. The offering ritual was followed by a second rite, whose words are always inscribed on the south wall of the burial chamber. This was a resurrection ritual, intended to release the king's ba from its attachment to the body so that it could rejoin its ka and enjoy life again. It begins by assuring the king that "you have not gone away dead: you have gone away alive," encourages him to "go and follow your sun . . . and be beside the god, and leave your house to your son of your begetting," and ends by reassuring him that "you shall not perish, you shall not end: your identity will remain among the people even as it comes to be among the gods."

As the sun left the womb of Nut and the Duat, the king's revitalized spirit proceeded from the pyramid's burial chamber to the antechamber. In Egyptian thought this room corresponded to the Akhet, a liminal zone between the Duat and the day sky (in practical terms, the Akhet was the Egyptian explanation for why the sun's light appears in the morning before the sun itself has risen above the horizon). The name Akhet means 'place of becoming effective' and refers to the process through which the ba—of the sun and the deceased alike—took on an 'effective' form of new life, as an akh: the Pyramid Texts tell the sun that he and the dead king "shall rise (wbn) from the Akhet, from the place in which the two of you have become akh." The texts on the walls of the burial chamber represent rituals performed by the living on behalf of the deceased king, but those inscribed in the antechamber were mostly intended to be recited by the king himself. They gave him the proper words and instructions he needed to overcome the hazards of his journey between the Duat and the world of the living: spells to surmount physical obstacles, to control and vanquish inimical forces, to persuade the celestial ferryman to accept him as a passenger, and to encourage the gods to accept him in their company. At this point the king was no longer identified with Osiris, and the texts of the antechamber refer to him only by his royal name.

Finally, as Nut gave birth to the morning sun, the king's akh left his tomb. In the earliest pyramids it was apparently thought to do so through the long corridor connecting the antechamber to the outside on the north of the pyramid, an analogue of the birth canal. From the Fourth Dynasty onward, however, the pyramid complex included a mortuary temple on the east of the pyramid, with a false door through which the akh could also emerge more appropriately in the direction of the rising sun. In either case, the reborn king was then free to enjoy life during the day, journeying across the sky with the sun and visiting the world of the living.

At least from the time of Shepseskaf onward, therefore, the afterlife was envisioned as a daily cycle of spiritual rebirth. Since Shepseskaf himself was buried beneath a mastaba rather than a pyramid, the function of the tomb's interior chambers—as Duat and Akhet—was apparently more important to this cycle than the shape of its superstructure. The kings of the Fifth and Sixth Dynasties, however, reverted to

the pyramid form while retaining Shepseskaf's layout of the interior chambers. In doing so, they combined Osiris's subterranean power of new life with the life-giving force of the primeval hill above the earth. The result was an evocative metaphor of rebirth: beneath the pyramid, the king's mummy lay like a seed planted in a mound of earth, waiting each night to transmit Osiris's power of new life to his spirit. Pyramids were not merely monumental tombs erected to perpetuate the memory of Egypt's kings: they were also—and more fundamentally—resurrection machines, designed to produce and ensure eternal life.

We have less information about the way in which the king's subjects envisioned their own afterlives in the Old Kingdom, but there is no reason to believe that it was any different. During this period, non-royal tombs were not inscribed with Pyramid Texts, but they do contain lists of the same offerings presented in the royal offering ritual. Some of them were also decorated with scenes of funerary rites corresponding to the king's resurrection ritual, and their owners

claim to be a "capable *akh*" and to know spells and "everything by which an *akh* becomes *akh*." Though these tombs were usually *mastabas* with a single burial chamber, they also contained sarcophagi, and the newly discovered mounds above some of them at Giza clearly served the same purpose as the royal pyramids.

All of these features point to a common vision of the afterlife for kings and commoners alike. After the Old Kingdom, non-royal tombs, sarcophagi, and coffins were also inscribed with Pyramid Texts—in some cases, direct copies of the corpus first inscribed in the pyramid of Unas—and with new spells of the same kind, known as the Coffin Texts. These eventually became the Book of the Dead and other funerary texts used in both royal and non-royal burials from the New Kingdom onward. Some non-royal tombs in the New Kingdom were also surmounted by small pyramids. Like the great pyramids themselves, these monuments and their texts bear witness to the hope for eternal life that all Egyptians shared.

40-41
The night sky represented as the goddess Nut, from the tomb of Ramesses VI. The upper figure shows the sun proceeding through Nut's body toward rebirth at dawn; the lower figure shows the stars on the surface of her body.

41 right
Detail of the night sky from the tomb of Ramesses VI, showing Nut's body receiving the sun as it disappears from the day-time sky at dusk.

Chapter 2

Administration of the Pyramid

by Vassil Dobrev

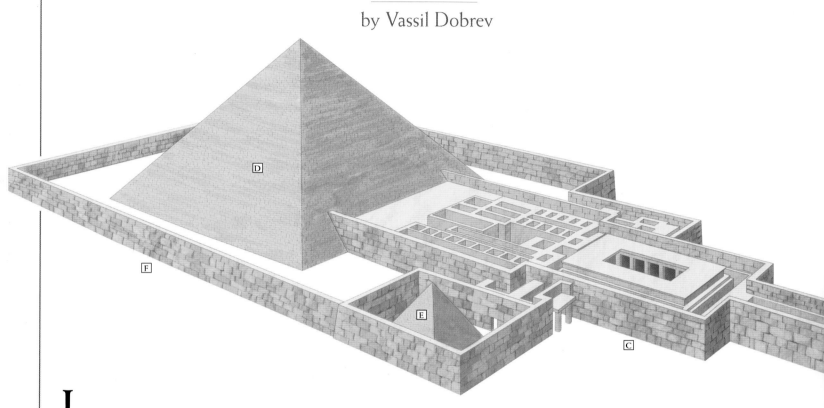

In ancient Egypt, after the death of a king, his successor had one idea in mind: to build a tomb that would help him, after his own death, to be resurrected and gain entry to the world of Eternity. For more than 1000 years (from the Third to the Thirteenth Dynasty, during the historical periods that we call the Old and Middle Kingdoms), the Egyptians built stone pyramids under which to bury their pharaohs. This is the so-called 'Pyramid Age' of Egypt, when more than a hundred pyramids were built. In the beginning, the Egyptians constructed step pyramids. Then, from the Fourth Dynasty on, they built true pyramids, the biggest of which is the Great Pyramid at Giza.

Building a pyramid was the major event during the reign of any king, but the pyramid was not the only monument that had to be erected for the royal funerary cult. It was surrounded by a protective wall and was supplemented by several other structures: a spacious mortuary temple (where the priests performed rituals), a small cult pyramid (which served as a cenotaph: a kind of secondary tomb but without the king's mummy), a long causeway (along which the mummy of the king was transported), and a valley

temple where the body of the king was mummified. The valley temple was accessible by a large harbor built on a canal connected to the Nile. All of these structures, with the pyramid as the major structure, made up the royal funerary complex.

At the beginning of his reign, the new king's first order of business was to choose an appropriate location for his funerary complex. He was helped by a number of people (priests, architects, and scribes among others) who belonged to his administration. Most of these people had already been working for years on the funerary complex of the king who had just died. Sometimes, his pyramid was not yet finished at his death, and his successor (generally one of the royal sons) had to complete the work and bury the dead ruler. At the same time, the new king had to start the work on his own pyramid. It is clear that most of the administrators attached to the funerary complex of the dead king had to come to serve the new king and organize the work on the new funerary complex. Nevertheless, a certain number of priests had to stay at the funerary complex of the deceased king, who was already considered a god, in order to perpetuate his

mortuary cult. The duties of this type of priest were recorded on numerous papyri. Some fragments of these papyri, dating from the Fifth Dynasty, are known as the Abusir archives. This archive is our main source of information about the organization of the administration of funerary complexes during the Pyramid Age. We would like to have similar archives from a funerary complex under construction, but nothing of the kind has so far been found. The quarrymen, the stone haulers, and the builders of the pyramids left numerous inscriptions on the stones, however generally painted in red, black, and ochre (very rarely were they carved). These inscriptions are another important source of information about the administration of pyramids.

The Egyptian administration existed long before the Pyramid Age. It can even be said that the creation of a well-organized administration was vital for the country. The question is: why did it come into being in the first place?

It started between 10,000–5000 BC, when nomadic tribes began to settle on the banks of the Nile. Immediately, they had to face an important natural phenomenon: the strong periodic flood of the river, which reached its zenith at the end of July. If the flood was not controlled, the country would have faced destroyed agriculture and a starving population. The Egyptians had no choice; they had to organize themselves and dig canals and basins in order to control and store the waters of the flood. It is not by chance that one of the first known representations of an Egyptian king shows him digging canals. An elaborate administration emerged to organize and direct the work in the country. The result was a fertile land that was irrigated permanently. Egypt became prosperous and was even considered the granary of the ancient world.

What we actually know about pharaonic administration may be quite far from the ancient Egyptian reality. Nevertheless, the sources of information that we have in our possession depict a certain image of this administration and how it was organized during the Pyramid Age.

There is a word in the pharaonic language, pronounced za, that might have been used to designate the most important groups of people in the administration. The earliest evidence of the hieroglyph za, which represents a looped cord serving as hobble for cattle, comes from First Dynasty inscriptions on royal stone jars (3100 BC). One of the latest is on a bilingual decree of King Ptolemy III (237 BC), where za was translated as the Greek word 'phyle' which means 'a tribe.' The fact that phyles were mentioned regularly throughout the three millennia of ancient Egyptian history, shows clearly that they were the skeleton of the Egyptian administration. The phyles were composed mainly of priests. An Egyptian priest could have many other functions at the same time: a scribe, a controller of works, an architect, a judge, a vizier, a king's son, and so on. Therefore, some of the members of the phyles were already high-ranking officials. They were the leaders of the phyles,

and, together with the other priests, served the pharaoh. The priests lived in a city next to the pyramid complex of the ruling king, called the 'pyramid town,' but some of them had their living place inside the royal temples where they worked. These temples were the storage places for the enormous quantities of offerings that came from all around Egypt to celebrate the royal mortuary cult. In fact, these offerings were also used after the ceremonies to provide the income of the priests. It is obvious that when a new king came into power, the priests would not let someone else plan and direct the building of his pyramid and its adjacent structures that were their main working place. From laying of the first stone of the future pyramid until the completion of the royal funerary complex, the priests' phyles were there to organize and control the work, then provide the necessary services for the mortuary cult of the king, even after his death.

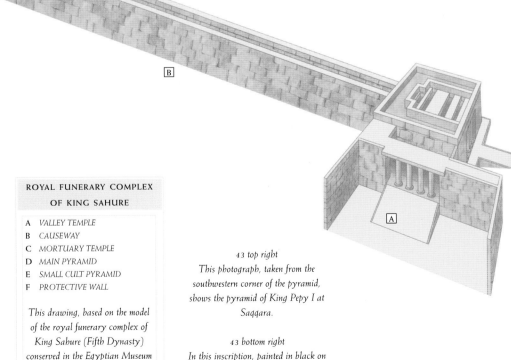

ROYAL FUNERARY COMPLEX
OF KING SAHURE

A   *VALLEY TEMPLE*
B   *CAUSEWAY*
C   *MORTUARY TEMPLE*
D   *MAIN PYRAMID*
E   *SMALL CULT PYRAMID*
F   *PROTECTIVE WALL*

This drawing, based on the model of the royal funerary complex of King Sahure (Fifth Dynasty) conserved in the Egyptian Museum in Cairo, shows the structures characteristic to a pyramid complex.

43 top right
This photograph, taken from the southwestern corner of the pyramid, shows the pyramid of King Pepy I at Saqqara.

43 bottom right
In this inscription, painted in black on one of the inner stones from the pyramid of Pepy I, the name of Inti, the pyramid's architect can be read.

The system of phyles was not exactly the same throughout the Pyramid Age. During the Old Kingdom, according to the Abusir papyri mentioned above, there were five phyles designated by adjectival names, such as 'great,' 'green,' and 'small.' Each phyle was divided into two divisions, bearing names like 'the living,' 'the strong,' 'the noble,' 'the favored,' 'the one in front,' 'the first,' or 'the rising one.' The members of a division were engaged in a ten-month cycle of rotating service, i.e. they worked one month in a temple, the next month in another temple, then after ten months they served again in the first temple. This rotation did not concern the persons that were employed permanently (lector and purification priests, scribes, guards, artisans, potters, handymen, and others in similar positions).

During the Middle Kingdom, the system of phyles was somewhat different: according to the papyri found at the pyramid town of Kahun (al-Lahun in the Fayum), there were four phyles named 'first,' 'second,' 'third,' and 'fourth' (a 'fifth' phyle was added later). Each phyle provided a one-month service, rotating with the other phyles in numerical order. This system was apparently in use for many centuries, until the Ptolemaic Period.

It was noticed long ago that some variant names of the phyles during the Old Kingdom are similar to four nautical terms that correspond to the right and the left sides of a ship (starboard and larboard), and to its front and rear parts (bow and stern). In a country like ancient Egypt, where the river Nile was the political and the economic axis, it was natural that fluvial activities should have been organized early on. The conclusion was therefore drawn that this nautical organization was later adapted to the other activities,

with nautical terms used as names for priests' phyles. In fact, the analysis of all phyle names shows that they did not originate from nautical terms but from several characteristic signs. These signs, or emblems, could have designated certain groups of people that might have existed long before the first military or commercial ships ever sailed on the Nile. In this case, the organization of ship crews could have been influenced by the organization of priests' phyles rather than vice versa.

There is a generally accepted idea that the administration of a pyramid was led by big crews or teams, incorporating the five phyles and their divisions (we have evidence of two divisions per phyle from the Abusir papyri, four from the mortuary temple of Menkaure, and even more from the pyramid of Pepy I). This idea should be reviewed, because large teams of several hundred persons, designated by the hieroglyph $\mathring{\text{o}}$ aper, were recruited when needed, especially when the pyramid was begun. Furthermore, it seems that they were not permanently in existence as the phyles were. The names of the aper-teams, known from the inscriptions of pyramid builders, often included one of the pharaohs' names. From the inside of the Great Pyramid at Giza, we have evidence of some aper-team names, like 'The Two-Lands (Egypt) Purifiers of Horus Medjedu (Khufu)' (team name A), 'The Purifiers of Horus Medjedu' (team name B), 'The Friends of Khufu' (team name C) and 'The Followers of the Powerful White Crown of Khufu' (team name D). Some elements of these names, like 'friends,' for example, could persist through different reigns, as illustrated by 'The Friends of Menkaure.' The name of another aper-team from the time of Menkaure has been

completely misunderstood for almost a century; the translation 'The Drunkards of Menkaure' is not logical and could be replaced by 'The Laborers of Menkaure,' which sounds much more appropriate for a group of people constructing a pyramid. The large aper-teams had to be guided and controlled by other people, permanently employed by the pharaoh: most probably these people were the members of a phyle. The fact that the name of the aper-team has been written before the name of a phyle, as is seen on some stones from the mortuary temple of Menkaure did not mean that this team was leading the work, with the members of the priests' phyle under its control. The names of these aper-teams included an important word—the royal cartouche—which had to be written at the beginning of the inscription, like the god's name Re (the Sun, illustrated by a circle in the cartouche of Menkaure), which was the most important element of the name. Even though pronounced last (Men-kau-Re), it was written at the beginning of the cartouche (this is the well-known Egyptian rule of the so-called honorific anteposition).

It is now preferable to think that it was the phyles, composed of several divisions, who were administrating the work of the big teams, like the aper-teams, but also the ges-teams and maybe others. These teams with numerous members were doing the heavy and demanding tasks like quarrying, hauling, and lifting stones, while smaller groups of persons, the divisions of the phyles, were doing the very precise and specialized tasks. The professionalism of these smaller groups made possible the miracle of the Pyramid Age of ancient Egypt.

One of the papyri from the Abusir archives

44 left
The Step Pyramid of Djoser at Saqqara seen from its southeastern corner.

44 and 45 bottom
Builders' inscriptions painted on some of the stones from the pyramid of Khufu and from the mortuary temple of Menkaure (Fourth Dynasty, Giza).

Old Kingdom phyle names					Nautical terms	Characteristic signs
from the Abusir Papyri		variant names from other documents				
wr	pronounced "ur"	*jmy-wr*	*jmy-wr.t*	pronounced "imi-uret"	*jmy-wr.t* = starboard	*wr* = great, big
t3	pronounced "ta"		*t3 -wr*	pronounced "ta-ur"	*t3 -wr* = larboard	*t3* = shrouded, hidden
w3ḏ	pronounced "uadj"		*w3ḏ.t*	pronounced "uadjet"	*w3ḏ.t* = bow	*w3ḏ* = green, fresh
nḏs	pronounced "nedjes"		*nḏs.t*	pronounced "nedjeset"	*nḏs.t* = stern	*nḏs* = small, little
jmy-nfr.t	pronounced "imi-neferet"		*nfr.t*	pronounced "neferet"	—	*nfr* = perfect, beautiful

45 top
The hieroglyph za *(a looped cord serving as hobble for cattle) designates the word "phyle."*

shows that a phyle's division consisted of ten priests, whose names were clearly written on the papyrus. These priests, called *hemiu-netjer* ('Servants of God') and *khentiu-she* (literally translated 'Those in Front of the Basin'), were assigned to daily and nightly rituals inside the mortuary temple or on its roof, as well as around the pyramid and on its surrounding wall (these rituals could have taken place even during the construction of the pyramid complex). They prepared and presented the ritual meals for the king; performed libation and fumigation rituals (with incense, for example); unveiled, cleaned, dressied, and adorned statues; guarded the monuments overnight, and so on. The accomplishment of each assignment was strictly controlled by noting the presence or the absence of the priests (a black vertical stroke when the priest fulfilled the task, a red stroke when he was absent).

We must always keep in mind, however, that the Abusir papyri gave account of the work of approximately 200–250 persons serving the mortuary cult of a dead king. During the whole reign of a king, the administration had to govern many more people. Herodotus mentions that 100,000 persons had been involved in the construction of the pyramid of Khufu, but modern Egyptologists' estimates reduce this number to 30,000. The majority of the Egyptian pyramids were not as big as the Great Pyramid, so one could imagine that 10,000–20,000 people would have been enough for the construction of these pyramids. Such figures show that the number of persons that had to be organized on the necropolis of a living king, during the construction of his pyramid, was about a hundred times higher than the number of

persons serving the cult of a dead king. Consequently, the information available from the Abusir papyri must be quite far from the real scope of the administration of a pyramid under construction.

In order to come nearer to the Egyptian reality, we must turn to the inscriptions left by the pyramid builders, a direct source on the administration of a pyramid. There is a serious problem however in using this source since the great majority of the stones with these inscriptions are still under sand and debris; the lower stone courses of the four sides of the commonly-known pyramids are generally not cleaned. The reason for this is most probably a lack of financial means to finish the job of clearing, but reluctance to do this work could also be a factor. Otherwise, it is hard to explain that out of more than a hundred pyramids, and after more than 150 years of modern excavations in Egypt, only the pyramids of Khufu and Khafre at Giza, the pyramid of Pepy I at South Saqqara, and to a certain extent, the pyramid of Unas at Saqqara, have been systematically cleaned, and the sand removed from their sides down to their foundations. The enormous potential of the pyramid builders' inscriptions is far from being completely explored. Some examples of inscribed stones from the pyramid of Pepy I show clearly how fertile this source of information could be.

When we see the essential information that has already been collected from builders' inscriptions (information about pyramid construction, the administration of the pyramid, and the persons

leading this administration), it is clearly a pity not to try to enrich the corpus of these documents. Archaeologists have to start thinking about systematically cleaning the lowest parts of some of the pyramids in Saqqara, Dahshur, Abusir, and Giza. Some prime subjects would be the pyramid of Djedkare (Fifth Dynasty) at South Saqqara; the pyramid of Teti (Sixth Dynasty) at Saqqara; the pyramids of the two half-brothers Merenre and Pepy II (Sixth Dynasty) at South Saqqara; the pyramid of Menkaure (Fourth Dynasty) at Giza; and the two big pyramids of Sneferu (Fourth Dynasty) at Dahshur, the Red Pyramid and the Bent Pyramid, which is the best preserved pyramid in Egypt. The monument of Sneferu at Meidum, where the clearing of its northwestern angle (work done in 1984–86) has produced hundreds of inscriptions, bears further investigation as well. Even the step pyramid of Djoser at Saqqara, one of the most famous and most visited monuments in Egypt, has the lower part of its western side still under sand.

The destruction of the Egyptian pyramids during the three to five millennia that separate us from the Pyramid Age leaves little or no chance for even the greatest optimist to imagine that one day treasures like those from the tomb of Tutankhamun could be found in an intact pyramid tomb. Instead, what we may find in the future, if we are willing to invest in cleaning some of the pyramids, are more and more inscriptions from their builders that will give us genuine information about how the pyramids were constructed and administered. In fact, these inscriptions would be the real 'treasures of the pyramids'!

Team names from the pyramid of Khufu

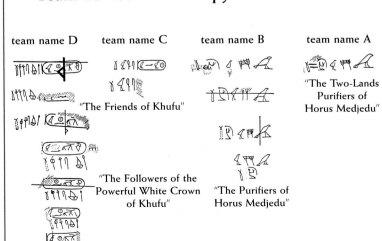

team name D   team name C   team name B   team name A

"The Two-Lands Purifiers of Horus Medjedu"

"The Friends of Khufu"

"The Followers of the Powerful White Crown of Khufu"

"The Purifiers of Horus Medjedu"

Phyle *uadjet*

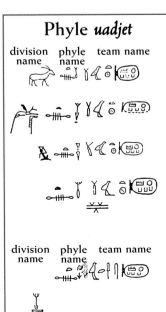

division name	phyle name	team name

Phyle *ur*

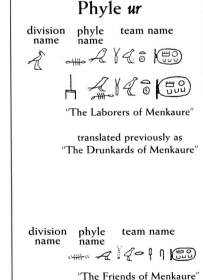

division name	phyle name	team name

"The Laborers of Menkaure"

translated previously as "The Drunkards of Menkaure"

"The Friends of Menkaure"

Building an Old Kingdom Pyramid

by Mark Lehner

How did the Egyptians build the Pyramids?" This question commonly comes to mind as people think of these gigantic stone structures, and it begs for a standard answer. There are only five or six pyramids that qualify as truly gigantic, all built within only three or four generations. It is ironic that these very examples, which belong to the experimental phase of pyramid construction, display the greatest variation in construction materials, sizes, and methods.

Such colossal pyramids provoke a variety of "how-to" questions. How did the Egyptians survey such a perfect square across so many acres of land? How did they level the base? How did they maintain control of slope and square as they built upward, surrounded by debris and ramps? Many more questions demand answers. How did they choose a site, select a quarry, quarry and haul the blocks, lift the blocks, and put them in place? What did they use as mortar? How much hard granite did they use, and how did they dress it, as well as the acres of pyramid face that had to be shaped into smooth, even sides?

Mundane operations, not to be taken for granted, included loading and off-loading multi-ton blocks on a transport sled or boat and turning corners with heavy blocks as laborers ran out of space near the top of the pyramid. Acres of casing stones had to be smoothed with small chisels. All these operations had to proceed in harmony to ensure that the crew completed the pyramid within the lifetime of the king. The sum total of all these tools, techniques, and operations was the *technical system* of pyramid building.

With most of the questions, we have the Great Pyramid of Khufu in mind—the apogee of pyramid construction. Many of the answers might have little to do with the construction of a Sixth Dynasty pyramid, or a mud-brick pyramid of the Middle Kingdom, but some of the answers will be the same (dressing the outer face, for example). On the other hand, much of what has been written assumes a generic pyramid on a level surface.

STONE TRANSPORT

Tomb scenes rarely show transport or other operations of pyramid building (and why that is the case is an intriguing question that would take us too far afield here). However, the tomb artists did render coffins, possibly of stone, transported on small boats. The coffin is raised off the deck by a series of supports. The relief scenes in the causeway of the Unas Pyramid show the transport, end to end on a single barge, of two granite columns with capitals in the form of palms such as were actually set up in the pyramid temple. They ranged from 5.5 to 6.5 meters in height. The columns in the scene rest on hauling sledges which, like the coffins, are raised off the deck by a support framework of beams or girders. These could have been used to relieve the weight of the load on the deck. The supports could also have had played a role in the loading and unloading, critical operations considering that a 50-ton block of granite, like those in the Khufu Pyramid, would readily capsize any boat if rolled too far to one side.

We must look ahead a millennium, to the New Kingdom, for further pictorial information (with the question in mind of how much that operation could have changed in the interim). Reginald Engelbach thought that in the Eighteenth Dynasty, Hatshepsut's builders loaded and off-loaded her great granite obelisks from the large barges shown on the walls of her Deir al-Bahri temple by building an earthen embankment all around the barge and right up to the deck. Once the obelisk was removed, the barge could be excavated from the embankment. Another possibility is that the barge was brought into a narrow canal so that a series of great cedar beams could be thrust underneath the load between the supports. The ends of the beams rested on supports set up on the banks of the canal. The transport barge could have been weighted with ballast and slipped out from under the load.

Whether or not this is feasible (obelisks weigh up to hundreds of tons, a weight that might stress any number of cross beams), no transport crews wanted to 'flat bed' their load, whether on ground or on barge. Contact between one face of a multi-ton block and deck or ground gives it inertia of rest, hard to maneuver and get on the move again. Modern stone workers always keep their load on pivots, supports, or levers until they are ready to set it into place.

The inscription above the scene of transporting Unas's granite columns reads ". . . the coming of these barges from Elephantine, laden with [granite] columns of twenty cubits" or 10.46 m, probably the total length of both columns. A fragment of inscription belonging to the unnamed official responsible for the delivery claims to have made the journey (back?) in seven days, indicating a round-the-clock speed of 5.5 kilometers per hour. The inscription actually reads "four days in transit"!

A Sixth Dynasty official named Weni fetched an offering table from the alabaster quarry at Hatnub, and granite from Aswan for a false door and other parts of King Merenre's pyramid. He says that he traveled north with them to the pyramid 'Merenre-appears-in-splendor' in six barges and three tow boats of eight ribs in a single expedition.

"His majesty sent me to Hatnub to bring a great altar of alabaster of Hatnub. I brought this altar down for him in seventeen days. After it was quarried from Hatnub, I had it go downstream in this barge I had built for it, a barge of acacia wood of sixty cubits (31.5 m) in length and thirty cubits (15.75 m) in width. Assembled in seventeen days, in the third month of summer, when there was no water on the sandbanks, it landed at the pyramid 'Merenre-appears-in-splendor' in safety...

"His majesty sent me to dig canals in Upper Egypt, and to build three barges and four tow-boats of acacia wood of Wawat (Lower Nubia). Then the foreign chiefs of Irtjet, Wawat, Yam, and Medja cut the timber for them. I did it all in one year. Floated, they were loaded with very large granite blocks for the pyramid, 'Merenre-appears-in-splendor.'"

Weni's boasts about these achievements in the Sixth Dynasty contrast with the silence of the officials responsible for far greater and more numerous loads of granite and alabaster for the gigantic pyramids of the Fourth Dynasty. We have only names, like Hemiunu and Ankh-khaf, who bore the title 'Overseer of All the King's Works.'

Ships were built of pieces stitched together with rope, so that they could be taken apart and reassembled. When the pieces wore out, the pyramid builders might use them like railroad ties in tracks for dragging heavy stones overland to the actual building site. Excavators from the Metropolitan Museum in

New York have found such hauling tracks around the
Twelfth Dynasty pyramids of Lisht.

Transport teams used hauling tracks to get the
load from the quarry to the river or canal, and from
the waterway to the building site. These tracks
needed to be hard and solid; nothing stops a two-ton
stone block quicker than when it comes to rest on soft
sand. At Lisht, the transport roads were five meters
wide and composed of limestone chips and mortar.
The wood beams were inserted so that their upper
faces were buried in the fill. The beams provided a
solid bedding. Thin layers of wet mud or gypsum
served as lubricant for the runners of the sledge.
Construction embankments and ramps that remain
intact from the Pyramid Age to this day at Giza are
composed of limestone chips, gypsum, and *tafla*,
which is a fine, calcareous, tan desert clay as opposed
to the gray alluvial clay of the Nile Valley. This
mixture occurs in millions of cubic meters at Giza,
filling the vast quarried areas along the southeast of
the plateau. There is *tafla* between and underneath
large building blocks in the Giza Temples, so it was
used as packing material *and* as lubricant.

Tomb scenes show teams pulling statues of wood
or stone on sledges. One worker usually pours liquid,
probably water, under the front of the runner of the
sledge. The most cited of these scenes is in the
Middle Kingdom tomb of Djehutihotep. One
hundred seventy-two men pull what is estimated to
have been (if it existed in reality) a 58 ton statue of
this local ruler. This amounts to one-third of a ton per
man. This might have been possible on a nearly
friction-free surface. In his work at the Karnak
Temple, the French engineer, Chevrier used a sledge
and a water-lubricated track to move a five or six ton
block with only six workers. In 1991, during the
experimental building of a small pyramid for the
American scientific documentary television program
NOVA, 10 to 12 men could easily pull two-ton blocks
mounted on sledges up an inclined roadway.

We have an ancient scene where the Egyptians
employ cattle to drag stone or assist humans in
pulling. At the Eleventh Dynasty complex of
Mentuhotep in Luxor, excavators found the carcasses
of draft cattle in the builders' debris. Dieter Arnold
pointed out that cattle allow "greater force to be
distributed over a smaller area," with one ox being
equivalent to five men.

47 top
*This 19th century lithograph shows an
imagined scheme in which the pyramids
were constructed of well-squared blocks,
levered into place in regular steps wide
enough to serve as working platforms.
The reality of the construction of the
largest pyramids was quite different.*

47 bottom
*The pyramid builders must have brought
much of their support materials (gypsum,
wood, grain, copper, and cattle) on small
transport boats with truncated prows and
hooded sterns. Detail from Egyptian
Museum relief, Sixth Dynasty tomb of Ibi.*

Building a Pyramid

QUARRIES: MASS AND MATERIAL

The size of the base set the goal for the mass of material that the builders had to compose into a pyramid before the king died. Base areas like those of Khafre or Khufu (around 53,000 square meters), demanded, therefore, completion of a pyramid as high as 146.5 meters and 2,600,000 cubic meters of material in the case of Khufu. Surely this reflects the supreme confidence of the royal house in marshalling human and natural resources. Most of the stone for the three Giza Pyramids was probably quarried directly from the plateau, down slope from the great northeast-southwest diagonal on which the pyramids are aligned.

Massive amounts of fine white homogenous limestone, a quality that is not found at Giza, did come into Giza from the eastern quarries of Muqqatam, Maasara, and principally, Tura, for the outer pyramid casings. Supply teams brought granite, the other major type of non-local stone in the

basalt from a variety of places for temple pavements. They used alabaster, granite, and gneiss for statuary, and diorite and quartzite for pounding and polishing tools.

It would have been most advantageous for the builders to quarry the bulk of the core material near the site of the pyramid. We should expect, perhaps, a hole in the ground of an order of magnitude equal to the sizes of the respective pyramids. Some of the large Middle Kingdom pyramids were built of mud brick, and we should expect that a tremendous amount of mud was scooped from the nearby valley floor.

The location of the quarry must have been a major consideration for the pyramid builders. The quality of local bedrock may have been one of the primary reasons for the various kinds of masonry that make up the cores of pyramids. The large 'moat' or depression that is suspected of surrounding the Djoser complex may in fact be the source for much of the filler stone and clay in the pyramid and the massive 'dummy' architecture that surrounds it. At Giza, the geological bedding along the low southeast part of the plateau consists of thick layers interspersed with softer thin layers perfect for the extraction of large blocks. Here the quarries for the Khufu and Menkaure pyramids are rather clearly delimited, in the form of great horseshoe-shaped basins.

About 300 meters due south of Khufu's pyramid is the quarry that must have furnished the bulk of its core stone. The deepest part of the quarry is 30 meters below the original surface, so the Fourth Dynasty quarrymen removed close to 2,760,000 cubic meters of stone. Although this is slightly more than the volume of the Khufu pyramid, it is still not sufficient since as much as thirty percent of the stone would have been wasted in the quarry channels. The quarry extends an unknown distance to the south beyond the line of the Menkaure causeway, where Abd al-Aziz Saleh cleared part of the western quarry face for Cairo University in 1980. Much stone was taken from the Central Wadi itself, which represents a volume of 4,400,000 cubic meters. With a combined volume of 5,220,000 cubic meters for the Giza Pyramid complexes, there is enough stone in the quarries at Giza for the cores of the three pyramids, without even considering the quarries specific to the Khafre and Menkaure projects.

Until the excavations in this century, millions of cubic meters of limestone chips, gypsum, sand, and *tafla* filled the quarry south of the Khafre causeway.

48
Blocks at the base of Khufu's pyramid, while not of modular sizes, are enormous, weighing up to 15 tons. The stones get progressively smaller toward the top. This pyramid is founded on a platform of fine limestone.

49 top
Granite casing on Khafre's valley temple. Rather than modular sizes laid in level ashlar courses, the blocks are custom cut and fitted to one another in trapezoidal patterns.

pyramid complexes, from Aswan, 933 kilometers south of the pyramid capital zone. Giza builders used red granite extensively for the burial chambers of Khufu and Menkaure, the lower seventeen courses of Menkaure's casing, and for the lowest pyramid casing course and the lining of the temples of Khafre. As much as 45,000 cubic meters of granite was quarried from the Aswan quarries during the course of the Old Kingdom. Pyramid builders imported alabaster and

Much of this material could be the remains of the ramp that the workers pushed back into the quarry as they completed the Khufu pyramid. The western edge always showed above surface, but the fact that most of the quarry was buried led pyramid explorers, like Sir Flinders Petrie, to believe that the stone for the pyramids was mostly brought from across the river. When Egyptian archaeologist Selim Hassan carted away much of this debris in the 1920s and 1930s, he exposed rock shelves, about 1.5 m high, that the quarrymen left when they separated blocks the size of those in the core of the pyramid. On the surface behind the shelves are long narrow channels that they cut to define the width of the blocks they would cut away.

Between the basin quarry directly south of Khufu's pyramid and the Sphinx, there is a triangular area that is honey-combed with tombs cut out of the bedrock. Some tombs are burrowed in and are under rectangles of bedrock the size of several railroad boxcars or small houses, separated by yawning corridors. These rectangles are mapped as *mastaba* tombs in Egyptology reference books, but the Fourth Dynasty workmen originally created them in the earlier stages of organizing the surface for quarrying building blocks. In the older Khufu quarry, the rectangles were exhausted, and the quarrymen continued to take out blocks along open banks or terraces. But here, southwest of the Sphinx, they did not exploit the rock as deeply, so one can wander through silent corridors that once resonated with the clink-chink of stone hammers, chisels, and the chanting of workers who pulled away the blocks. The large bedrock blocks are subdivided with narrower channels, just wide enough for one man to fit inside swinging a pick to cut the channel clear through a rock massif that is about one story tall and a few score meters across. There are a few places where the quarrymen separated and then abandoned a block about the size of the great multi-ton blocks in the core walls of Khafre's temples.

The Menkaure quarry, also horseshoe shaped, with the deep end toward the pyramid, lies just southeast of the third pyramid. One can still see here large sockets for wooden levers the size of railroad ties cut in rows along a softer limestone layer. Having separated the block around three sides, the quarrymen had only to pry it up and crack it free.

Quarries at Tura for the fine casing became galleries that followed the best layers of stone deep into the escarpment. To follow the beds of highest quality, the ancient quarrymen tunneled in and under the overburden of poorer stone, creating cavernous, rectilinear, covered quarries. They began with a 'lead' shelf cut along what would become the ceiling of the gallery. They then extracted the stone in terraces or banks, as they did in the bottom of the Giza quarry.

The quarries at Aswan, some 933 kilometers south of Giza, yielded the granite blocks for lining Khufu's burial chamber, for encasing Khafre's pyramid temples and Menkaure's pyramid, for the columns of the Fifth and Sixth Dynasty pyramids, false doors, offering tables, and some pyramid capstones. It has been said the Old Kingdom builders simply took away and then shaped the numerous natural granite boulders found along the First Cataract of the Nile. Given that granite is so much harder to work than limestone, this may be largely true. The longer granite pieces that the Egyptians worked into the ceiling beams of Khufu's burial vault and of four of the five stress-relieving compartments above it, however, and the temple columns throughout the Old Kingdom, were up to 5.5 m long and weighed as much as 60 tons. It is likely that these were separated, like the limestone blocks, by channeling out the mother rock. With granite, however, the channels had to be formed by excruciating pounding with dolerite hammer stones, a technique of quarrying granite that lasted for most of the Pharaonic period. 'Being sent to the granite' must have been the most painful task of all in pyramid building.

PUZZLES OF PYRAMID BUILDING

Pyramid construction was far less regular and standardized than our mental templates have led us to believe or allowed us to see. If the blocks are not of modular sizes, the tools for hauling, such as wooden sledges or cradles, could not be standardized. It is hard to imagine the builders using levers, fulcrums, and cribbing supports to raise 'blocks' that are not square, but trapezoidal or oval or irregular. Given that much of the fill is little more than rubble, it is far more likely that ramps and embankments, rather than fulcrums and levers, were used for lifting material. We even have to wonder if the builders sometimes used the same stony stuff for both ramps and pyramid fill. There was probably no manual for building the early pyramids. Rather, using some basic masonry techniques, the builders varied layout methods, blocks, courses, and other features in an *ad hoc* approach to building one pyramid after another.

SURVEYING THE BASE SQUARE

Many assume that finding true north to orient the pyramid, laying out the square of the base, and leveling, were one-time discrete operations. Once the ancient surveyors had drawn the gigantic square on the ground, the builders could receive trains of stone-laden sledges and start setting the blocks. This may have been true for some pyramids—those that were built on the natural desert surface. For the giant pyramids at Giza, however, the builders started with a natural stone surface that they carved away, down to the level they chose for the base. They left an irregular patch of natural rock protruding in the middle of the square, up to a height of seven meters in Khufu's pyramid and five meters in the northwest corner of Khafre's pyramid. They built this rock protrusion into the core of the pyramid.

The builders leveled an area approximately the width of a city street around the base of this core. In fact, their best leveling in bedrock was only about as wide as a modern sidewalk. Their finest leveling of Khufu's pyramid, off by only 2.5 cm in the entire perimeter, was on a platform built of fine Tura-limestone slabs. The baseline of Khafre's pyramid was simply a vertical cut in the foot of the bottom course of casing stone, where the slope of the pyramid would meet the top surface of the pavement of the pyramid court. The natural rock was cut into sockets of various depths to receive the granite casing blocks and to bring them flush at the top, as it was easier to cut away the natural limestone base than the much harder granite. The layout and leveling of these pyramids thus presents a 'chicken and the egg' situation. In order to know approximately where to level, the builders had to lay out the square. But the accuracy of the square, with the mass of natural rock protruding in the center, needed a surface that was as level as possible.

The builders, therefore, had to proceed in steps of *successive approximation*. They took aim on true north and laid out their reference lines at several stages as they worked the rock down to the broad terrace on which they would build the pyramid, its surrounding court and enclosure wall, and the mortuary temple. At various stages they refined their orientation to the cardinal directions, and to the perpendicularity of the corners, which became hidden from one another behind the core massif as they quarried away the rock for the final baseline.

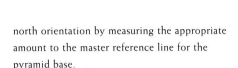

Building a Pyramid

FINDING TRUE NORTH

Ancient texts call the circumpolar stars 'the Imperishable Ones' because they neither rise nor set as they circle around the celestial pole about 26 degrees up in the northern sky. In a fragment of a scene from the Fifth Dynasty sun temple of Niuserre, the king and the goddess Seshat pound long stakes connected by a looping cord. A wall in the temple of Edfu dating two millennia after the Old Kingdom pyramids shows the king performing foundation ceremonies with Seshat and Thoth, the divine couple associated with writing and science. An inscription from the Temple of Dendera has the king "looking at the sky, observing the stars, and turning his gaze toward the Great Bear."

In his book, *The Pyramids*, I.E.S. Edwards suggested that the ancient surveyors could have constructed a circular wall, "with a diameter of a few feet on the already leveled rock-bed of the pyramid." Standing in the center of the circle and facing north, the observer could mark the point at which a star rose above the wall on his right (east) and where it set below the wall on his left (west). The bisection of the angle between rising and setting points (plumbed down to the base of the wall) and the center of the circle would give true north.

KOCHAB, MIZAR, AND 2467 BC

Kate Spence suggested that the pyramid surveyors could have found north by observing the circumpolar stars Kochab, in the bowl of the Little Dipper, and Mizar, in the handle of the Big Dipper. Since the celestial North Pole was only aligned exactly with these stars in 2467 BC, she takes that as the date of the founding of the Great Pyramid. Again the theory may work out mentally, but there are practical concerns. Her method requires that the Egyptians find the alignment of the two stars above and below the celestial pole and project it onto the ground with a plumb line. Anyone who has used a plumb line extensively in mapping or building knows how much harder it is to keep the line from swinging, the higher above the head it is held. The celestial pole is some 26 degrees above the horizon, and so we must envision some kind of large wooden frame to hold the plumb line. It is also hard to imagine how any stellar method could have been carried out in the darkness of night without the aid of modern illumination. Spence envisions a ring of "torches everywhere." If so, the trick must have been to illuminate the desired line on the ground, and the plumb line hanging from the frame, without obscuring the light of the distant stars. Finally, all this would have to be done in the very brief time that Kochab and Mizar align with the pole.

SUN AND SHADOW

The same scenes and texts of building foundations also speak of 'the shadow' and the 'stride of Ra' in connection with cord-stretching ceremonies. Martin Isler maintains that the Egyptians could have accomplished the astonishing precision of north alignment with a simple pole, or *gnomon*, "a stick in the ground, a bit of cord, and a shadow." The shadow method is based on the awareness that the sun rises and sets at equal and opposite angles to the meridian (true north). A pole is plumbed to vertical. The length of its shadow on a level surface is measured about two to three hours before noon. This becomes the diameter of a circle that is scribed with a cord and stick with the pole as its center. As the sun rises in the sky toward noon, the shadow withdraws from the circle. In the afternoon the shadow lengthens again at an angle with the morning shadow. When its end reaches the circle, the bisection of the angle between morning and afternoon corresponds to the meridian. The method is most accurate if carried out during the solstices.

EXTENDING AND MEASURING LINE

However they found true north, the ancient surveyors had next to extend the resulting north line. Their north line was only a few feet long if they used the circle and star method. Had they extended it the more than 230 meters (755 feet) from Khufu's pyramid base, the slightest inaccuracy would have vastly increased what surveyors call 'the traverse error.'

Along the extended line, they had to measure the distance of one side of the pyramid base. They then had to turn good right angles to make the corners. Finally, they had to measure the perpendicular sides to the opposite corners and turn another set of right angles.

The different suggestions for finding north all assume an initial starting point—the center of the circle in both Edwards' north star and in Isler's sun/shadow method. Using the shadow method, they might have used a series of gnomons, arrayed roughly north to south, but staggered slightly east to west. By performing the bisection of the morning and afternoon shadow on each gnomon circle, they would end up with a series of short north lines that paralleled and partially overlapped down the north-south direction. They could use each line as a check for extending the

north orientation by measuring the appropriate amount to the master reference line for the pyramid base.

Isler suggested another method, inspired by the scenes of the king with the goddess Seshat, holding stakes with a cord looped double around each stake. A double cord is pulled tangent to either side of round stakes. The line is off when one cord bends on the last stake while the other cord passes without touching the stake. The line is pulled accurately when both cords are exactly tangent to the stake. The exact line is the split between the parallel cords.

This last method may have required poles of exactly the same diameter. While ancient carpenters could have achieved this, we cannot take this kind of standardization for granted in a technology that did not know the lathe. The parallel line-pole method also requires that the stakes be embedded in the ground. The builders could have simply pounded them in when staking out a temple down on the valley floor or pyramids that were built on the desert clays and gravel. But the *final* layout (after a series of ever-closer approximations) of the pyramids of Khufu and Khafre was on prepared limestone bedrock. Here the builders either had to etch or paint lines on the rock floor, or they had to quarry out small holes in which to set the stakes.

MARKS OF THE ANCIENT SURVEYORS

The bottom casing blocks of both these pyramids weighed up to several tons. Moving them into position must have obscured the temporarily drawn baseline. It is likely that the ancient surveyors would have set a reference line *outside* the actual baseline of the pyramid, which would have been scrapped, scratched, pounded, and covered with debris as they began to build the bottom of the pyramid.

In fact, around the bases of the pyramids of Khufu and Khafre we *do* find lines of holes at regular spaces. A series of holes runs along the eastern side of Khufu's pyramid, and partly along the other three sides. The holes are rectangular, with sides varying from 35 to 68 centimeters, from 45 to 85 centimeters deep, spaced from 3.5 to 3.8 m apart (center to center) on line about three meters from the base of the pyramid. The builders fitted many of these holes with slabs of limestone, and obliterated others when they laid the limestone pavement of the pyramid court at the end of the building project. At Khafre's pyramid there are three separate lines of holes, possibly from the final stages of layout. The holes here are round, from 30 to 50 centimeters in diameter and spaced from 5.1 to 5.9 meters apart. There is a double line of staggered holes along the outside line of the pyramid enclosure wall 13.5 meters from the pyramid base, and another two lines of staggered holes along the inside line of the enclosure wall, from 9.1 to 9.9 meters from the pyramid base. At both pyramids, the holes are wide enough to allow a

finer adjusted line of posts which might have carried the final line in cord running over the tops of the posts.

The spacing of the holes, varying within a certain range, is certainly not for measuring distance, but just for carrying line. Egyptian tomb scenes show measuring cords with knots to mark increments. This might have been fine for measuring fields, but probably not for an accurate line as long as 230 meters. Cords stretch and sag, so Khufu's surveyors might have achieved their amazing results with rods.

Ancient Egyptian cubit rods have been found from later times. The royal cubit used in building was 0.525 meters. Joseph Dorner, a modern surveyor and Egyptologist, has shown that the Egyptians could have achieved the length and accuracy of Khufu's baseline with rods of 4 or 8 cubits (2.1 to 4.2 meters).

CONSTRUCTING A RIGHT ANGLE

By the time Khufu and Khafre's builders cut the bedrock down to the level of the pyramid base and were ready to scribe the actual baseline, they had already repeatedly performed the extension of the line and turning the right angles for the corners. They began these operations at the original surface of the plateau, some five to ten meters higher. They refined the base square in *successive stages* as they worked the surface down.

For the final layout of the pyramid base, the protrusion of natural rock would have prevented the builders from measuring the diagonals to check the accuracy of their square. At the northeast corner of Khufu's pyramid, enough core stones are missing to expose the natural rock rising in four steps to a height of four meters. Here, the bottom of the bedrock massif is six to seven meters back from the series of holes that may mark the external reference lines for setting and cutting the casing stones to make the base.

For the corners, the ancient surveyors could have achieved a right angle in three ways. They could have used the 'Sacred' or Pythagorean triangle—three of any unit on one side, four on the other and five on the hypotenuse. Such triangles seem to be present in the design and layout of the Old Kingdom mortuary temples attached to pyramids, but the evidence is not conclusive. They could have also used the Egyptian set square—an A-shaped tool with perpendicular legs set at right angles and a cross brace. One leg is placed on the already established line and the perpendicular

is taken from the other leg. The square is then flipped and the operation repeated. The exact perpendicular is taken from the small angle of error between the two positions. Thirdly, they could have used a measuring cord to pull two intersecting arcs of the same radius from two points on the same line. A line connecting the points of intersection will be at a right angle to the original line.

LAYING THE FOUNDATION PLATFORM

The extraordinarily accurate leveling of Khufu's pyramid, so admired by all, is actually on the surface of the foundation platform, not the bedrock

floor. The masons formed the corners of the platform from extraordinarily large slabs, still marked on all but the southwest corner by seats, or sockets, cut several centimeters into the bedrock floor. The setting line of the foundation platform would have been scuffed and scratched as the large slabs were laid in. The line would also have been covered by the extra stock of stone left on the front face of the platform slabs, a practice in evidence on unfinished masonry throughout ancient Egypt. An outside reference line would therefore have been required, which may have now been marked by stakes, cord, and pins set into the holes forming a line three meters from the platform. The lines of the front face and upper edge of the platform were marked on each slab as it was laid in by measuring inward from the reference line.

When it was required to cross the reference line to drag in more slabs on a hauling sled, parts of the staked line could have been removed and later re-established by sighting along the line from either side.

52 top

52 top
Casing and backing stones near the top
of Khafre's pyramid. The fine outer
casing hid tremendous irregularity in the
core, packing, and backing masonry.

52 bottom
Looking out across the casing on upper
east side of Khafre's pyramid. The
slabs are slightly out of flush,
indicating they may have been trimmed
before setting.

RAISING THE PYRAMID BODY

The bulk of most pyramids consists of core stones. The cores of some, if not all, pyramids have tiers or steps forming, in other words an internal step pyramid. The masonry that filled in the steps we could call 'packing stone.' The pyramid was finished off with a smooth outer casing of limestone or granite. The softer stone that the builders set between the core and casing, we might call 'backing stone.'

THE FABRIC OF THE PYRAMIDS: CORE STONE

It has often been written that Khufu's pyramid contains an estimated 2,300,000 blocks of stone, weighing on average about 2.5 tons. Theorists, both professional and amateur, assume that the pyramids are composed of generic two-and-a-half-ton blocks. They then set about solving the puzzles of how the builders raised and set the blocks. If we take the giant Giza Pyramids as the starting point, we should look carefully at their composition rather than assuming regular courses of modular stone blocks.

At first glance, the Giza Pyramids, stripped of most of the smooth outer casing in the Middle Ages, look like regular steps. These are the courses of 'backing stones,' so called because they once filled the space between the pyramid core and outer casing. A closer look will reveal that the steps are not at all regular. Here is a step more than a meter wide, over there almost nothing! The idea of regular steps is a mental template, one assumed by most theorists. However, instead of regular, modular, squared blocks of stone neatly stacked, there is a considerable 'slop factor' even in the Great Pyramid of Khufu.

The outer backing stones are not only irregular, but are also progressively smaller toward the top. Behind them, the core stones are even more irregular. During the 1830s, Howard Vyse blasted a hole in the center of the south side of Khufu's pyramid while looking for another entrance. In this wound we can see how the builders dumped great globs of mortar and stone rubble in wide spaces between the stones. There are big blocks, small chunks of rock, wedge-shaped pieces, oval and trapezoidal pieces, as well as smaller stone fragments jammed into spaces as wide

as 22 centimeters between larger blocks.

At the base of Khafre's pyramid, the coursing of the core stones is not uniformly horizontal. The builders tailored blocks to fit the sloping bedrock that they left protruding in the core as they leveled the surrounding court and terrace. In the northeast and southeast corners, where the downward slope of the plateau left no bedrock in the core, the builders used enormous limestone blocks, two courses thick, to level the perimeter.

Higher above the base, the pyramid core is made up of very rough, irregular stones. Covering more than the lower third of the pyramid, this rubble layer could be backing between core and casing, left after the casing stones were ripped away. The upper third of the pyramid core appears to be stone blocks in regular stepped courses. On closer inspection, it can be seen that the heights of these steps range from ninety centimeters to 1.20 meters and their widths varied from 23 centimeters to a meter.

Like Khufu's pyramid, Khafre's core is composed of loose, irregular fill. Through seams and gaps in the stepped core blocks, limestone chips and rubble are visible. In 1818, when Giovanni Belzoni cleared out a tunnel that robbers had forced through the center of the north side of the pyramid, the core fabric of the pyramid kept collapsing. Vito Maragioglio and Celeste Rinaldi, who surveyed the pyramids between 1963 and 1975, wrote, ". . . this was due without doubt to the incompactness of the internal masonry and the lack of mortar, so that the blocks are not always in contact at the sides, and cannot mutually support each other."

In spite of the irregularity of their cores, the Giza Pyramids have the most massive large-block masonry of all pyramids. The first pyramid, Djoser's Step Pyramid, began as a *mastaba* built with small, gray limestone blocks of a size that one man could carry, set along roughly horizontal courses in gravel and desert clay (*tafla*) and encased with fine white limestone. The builders twice expanded the *mastaba* before they conceived the idea of a pyramid, built in six steps from roughly shaped, larger core stones, directly over the fine Tura limestone casing of the earlier *mastaba*. They built the core as a series of accretions that lean inward about 74°, an effect achieved by tilting each course toward the core of the pyramid. This kind of core masonry is found in all

53

*Sneferu's Bent Pyramid at Dahshur,
with much of the smooth outer casing
covering the cruder core masonry. We
know little about the structure of the
inner core of the gigantic pyramids of the
early Fourth Dynasty.*

later step pyramids: Sekhemkhet; the Zawiyet al-Aryan Layer Pyramid; seven small 'provincial pyramids' located at or near Elephantine, Edfu, Hierakonpolis, Ombos, Abydos, Zawiyet al-Meitin, and Seila; and the two step-pyramid building stages (E1 and E2) inside the Meidum Pyramid.

During the reign of Sneferu, in the pyramid of Meidum and the lower part of the Bent Pyramid at Dahshur, builders still set core blocks at a tilt toward the center of the pyramid rather than on horizontal beds. They built upon the desert gravel and clay, but at Dahshur, the softer surface, and the steep slope of some 60 degrees that they attempted, soon threatened the pyramid with settling and collapse. They added a girdle around the base of the pyramid, reducing its slope to 54° 31′ 13″, and then, at about half its height, built up at the reduced slope of 43° 21′, creating the Bent Pyramid. At this point they began to lay core blocks along horizontal, rather than tilted, beds.

Sneferu's builders raised the North Pyramid at Dahshur with a uniform 43° slope. They filled out the steps of his Meidum pyramid with packing stones and Tura casing, laid on horizontal beds, to create a true pyramid (E3) of 51° 50′ 35″, practically the same slope as Khufu's pyramid and within the 52–53° range of the classic Old Kingdom pyramid.

The gigantic stone pyramids, the classic pyramids of popular imagination, were built in only three generations. All other kings pyramids combined, including those of the Middle Kingdom (but excluding queens' and other satellite pyramids), contain only 54 percent of the total mass of the pyramids of Sneferu, his son Khufu, and grandson, Khafre.

Until the Giza Pyramids, builders set blocks more in natural desert clay, *tafla*, than gypsum. *Tafla* can be simply mixed with water, while to use it as mortar, gypsum needs to be heated from 100° to 200°C (212° to 392°F), so the Giza builders needed much fuel for many fires to prepare their pyramid mortar. The size of stone blocks and the quantity of gypsum mortar, as opposed to *tafla*, increased from the Dahshur to Giza pyramids. Khufu's was the largest and most accurately built and aligned of all Egyptian pyramids, rising more than 146 m from a base 230 meters square and containing about 2.3 million blocks. Menkaure still used multi-toned stone blocks for the Third Pyramid

of Giza, but the total mass was less than that of Djoser's Step Pyramid.

Fifth and Sixth Dynasty builders composed pyramid cores of small stones, rubble, and sometimes clay binding in the retaining wall—the kind of material their predecessors had used for the construction ramps on the large stone pyramids of the Fourth Dynasty. In effect, it became more convenient to put the ramp inside and cover it with fine limestone casing! Middle Kingdom builders used stone retaining walls, debris fill, and, eventually, mud brick for the core.

THE INNER STEP PYRAMID

Although considerable irregularity shows in the inner core of even the largest and finest pyramids at Giza, the builders did not simply pile up rubble as, in all probability, they built the core slightly ahead of the casing. The evidence is that they built up in large chunks of structure, like the *mastaba* (Arabic for 'bench') tombs that surround the pyramids.

Pyramid theorists have suggested that a stepped core makes up the bulk of every pyramid. Some believe that the rise and run of the steps have a specific relationship to the slope of the outer casing. These ideas are inspired by the Pyramid of Meidum, where the steps of the inner seven-step pyramid, superseded by the eight-step pyramid, have fine sharp corners and faces that might have served as references for measuring set amounts out to the slope of the enlarged true pyramid.

We do not know if the largest pyramids of the Fourth Dynasty, from Sneferu to Khafre, are built with an inner step pyramid.

Howard-Vyse blasted a gash more than nine meters deep into the south side of Khufu's pyramid, about eighteen courses above the base and rising up to the thirty-first course. In this wound we see nothing close to the regular stairs that Martin Isler envisions in the core structure (see below). Not a single vertical joint corresponds with another. None of the blocks are the same size, and there are no clear impressions of regular rising joints. There are only horizontal joints, and these are not very clear; in places, two stones make up a single 'course.' In the eastern face of the cut, the courses are not regular, but there could be two crude steps, 1 and 1.2 m, of a

large inner structure, perhaps the tier of a crude stepped core.

Similar crude structure is to be seen in the cores of the partially destroyed or unfinished queens pyramids of Khufu and Menkaure, and in the gash in the north face of Menkaure's pyramid. It seems likely that the cores of these pyramids are composed of great rectangular blocks of crude masonry similar in form to *mastabas*—a kind of 'chunk approach' to assembling an inner step pyramid that lacks the beautifully finished faces and corners of Meidum. On queen's pyramid GI-c, the *mastaba* pattern is obscured by packing stones, of almost equal size to those forming the *mastaba*-like chunks, that filled in the broad steps and by smaller backing stones that filled the space between the core and the casing.

At this height, the reference lines on the ground would have been inaccessible, covered with ramps and building debris, but the builders could have transferred measurement and control up onto the top of the truncated pyramid. Above the mass of natural rock that the builders left in the base of Khufu's and Khafre's pyramids, the masons could have measured across the truncated pyramid to insure that its diagonals and sides were of equal length. If the core masonry rose ahead of the fine outer casing, the masons could have measured from reference points and lines on the core out to the facial lines of the pyramid as they brought up the casing.

Built in crude rectangular parts with irregular fill, the core masonry must have risen a good height above the casing. The three-tiered step pyramid in the queens pyramids was certainly not in itself a reference for the rise and run of the outer casing, but the core could have carried reference lines and points with paint, pegs, and cord. On the southernmost pyramid of Khufu's queens, there are small holes, about five centimeters diameter, near the corners of the tiers of the inner step pyramid. Some of these align with the sharp corners still preserved in the fine casing down near the base of the pyramid. The holes might be the sockets for small pegs that carried temporary cord reference lines from which the masons measured out the appropriate amount to mark the line of the outer pyramid face when the setting crews built up the casing.

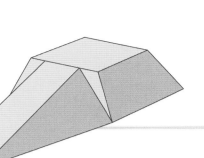

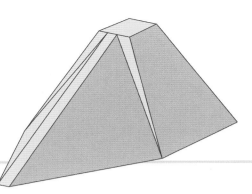

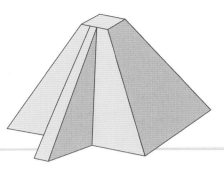

Building a Pyramid

RAISING STONES: RAMPS OR LEVERING?

There are only three basic techniques that the ancient Egyptians could have used for lifting blocks: the inclined plane (ramp), levering, and some assembly using rope, wood, and stone. To raise most of the stone, the builders probably used ramps that, however they were shaped, must have been enormous structures in their own right.

RAMP MATERIAL

It has often been suggested that the ramps would have been made of mud brick. Indeed, ramps found at the Middle Kingdom pyramids at Lisht have mud-brick retaining walls with fill of Nile alluvial mud and bricks. However, at Giza, there are no signs of the great deposits and stains of mud rubble that a gigantic construction ramp of mud would have left behind, even if the builders removed most of the ramps. Millions of cubic meters of limestone chips, plus gypsum and *tafla*, fill the quarries south of the Giza pyramids. This must be the material that the builders used to make the pyramid ramp. But would a ramp composed of this material have been able to make an ascent more than a hundred meters skyward, leaning against the ever narrowing faces of the pyramid?

In Khufu's time, as today, there must have been specialists for construction in broken stone and clay. Today, they build very quickly in this material. An advantage of this mixture is that when the walls, ramps, or embankments need to be dismantled, it easily picks apart into its constituent chips, gypsum, and clay.

ARCHAEOLOGICAL RAMP REMNANTS

At Giza, there still remain small ramps attached to certain *mastaba* tombs. East of Khufu's pyramid and south of the queens' pyramids and *mastabas* in the Eastern Field, archaeologists from Cairo University excavated two parallel walls formed of broken stone and *tafla*. One of the walls is thicker and composed of segments 10 cubits long (5.25 m). These must be retaining walls, which, when filled with debris, formed a ramp or embankment that leads in the direction of the *mastabas* and queens' pyramids east of the Great Pyramid.

North of Khafre's pyramid, the modern paved road runs up onto an ancient construction embankment where tour buses now park. The embankment runs along a colossal unfinished wall of large limestone blocks. The sides of the embankment have collapsed into a sandy slope, but in 1881 Petrie saw a series of cross-walls that formed compartments for retaining debris fill. The pyramid ramps must have been similarly composed, at least at Giza. In 1993, Zahi Hawass excavated trial pits in thick deposits of debris similar to that forming the above-mentioned walls and embankments. At the bottom of a point off the southwest corner of Khufu's pyramid, and south of the modern road, he found foundations of broken stone walls oriented in the direction of the southwest corner of the pyramid. These may be vestiges of the kind of ramp leading from the southern quarry to the pyramid's southwest corner.

The form of the construction ramps, or whether they were used at all, is one of the thorniest problems of pyramid building. The numerous theories can be reduced to two major proposals, a ramp that ascends one face of the pyramid by sloping up in a straight line from some distance away, and one or more ramps that begin near the base and wrap around the pyramid as it rises during construction.

STRAIGHT-ON RAMPS

The straight-on ramp must be lengthened each time its height against the pyramid is increased in order to maintain a low functional slope of about one unit of rise per ten units of length. Either work stops during these enlargements, or the ramp is built in halves and one side serves for builder traffic while the ramp crew raises and lengthens the other half. But the biggest problem is that the ramp would need to be extremely long in order to maintain a functional slope up to the highest part of the pyramid. At Giza, this slope would take the ramp for the Great Pyramid far beyond the quarry to the south, where Khufu's builders took most of the stone for the core of his pyramid.

WRAP-AROUND RAMPS

The wrap-around ramp either had to be supported on the slope of the pyramid or on the ground, in which case it would have leaned against the faces of the pyramid like a giant envelope with a rising roadbed. If it cloaked the entire pyramid, it might have presented a problem for controlling square and slope as the pyramid rose. If it was supported on the 52 degree slope of the pyramid, the extra stock of stone on the casing blocks would have to protrude step-like enough to support the weight of the ramp. The unfinished granite casing blocks on Menkaure's pyramid do not fill this requirement. But recently, Zahi Hawass has excavated at the bases of Khufu's queens' pyramids to reveal that the builders here left a great deal of extra stock in rough steps protruding beyond the plane of the pyramid. These may be unusual because they are part of the foundation, but if this much extra stock was left on higher casing stones, it might well have supported a spiral ramp.

If the ancient builders had opted for this solution, it would have been necessary to leave the protruding casing stones staggered diagonally up across the pyramid face in order to allow the roadbed to rise.

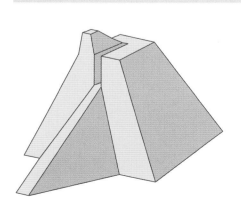

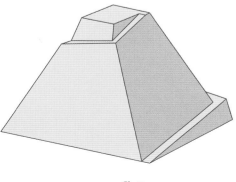

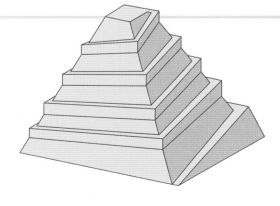

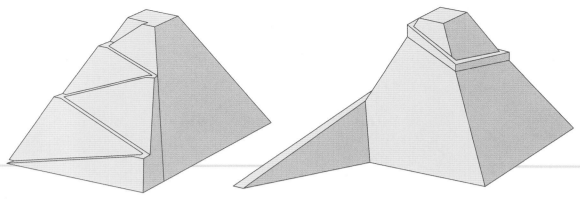

Or, they could have left horizontal courses protruding at certain intervals so that the foundation wall of the ramp would be level but step up at intervals, while the roadbed rose at a gradient.

All ramp suggestions run into trouble near the top of the pyramid, where the slope becomes increasingly steep, and where the faces of the pyramid become too narrow to support a ramp from one corner to the next.

QUARRY DELIVERY RAMP

When the pyramid was at its lower levels of construction, the builders could have delivered stone over many short ramps. As the pyramid rose, the ramp builders would have wanted to gain some height in the course of the approach from the quarry. If the Khufu delivery ramp began at the north mouth of the southern basin quarry, where the quarrymen left a bedrock incline down to the quarry floor, it would have extended 320 m to the southwest base of the pyramid. If it connected to the pyramid 37 meters above the base, it would have sloped 6° 36´. A roadbed 30 meters wide would have easily accommodated two-way traffic. A ramp of similar dimensions was posited by a scribe in Papyrus Anastasi I: 383 m (730 cubits) long, 29 meters (55 cubits) wide, 31 meters (60 cubits) high, and a side slope of eight meters (15 cubits).

LEVERING

While pyramid theorists have proposed that the ancient builders raised most of the stones by levering, all indications are that levering was used for sideways movements and for final adjustments. Loads can be see-sawed up by levering up one side, putting supports underneath, and then levering up the other side. But as it becomes clear to any reasonable person who climbs the Khufu or the Khafre pyramids, it is inconceivable that this lever lifting took place on the stepped courses of the core

stone or the undressed casing stone. Those who think so have in mind very regular wide courses, like a stairway rather than the actual fabric and structure of the pyramid core. Many of the 'blocks' are odd shapes and sizes that would be unwieldy to lever. The sheer slope itself precludes levering many tons of stone for the higher courses.

Martin Isler proposed that the builders used massive stone stairways ascending the center of each face of the pyramid core, later covered by the casing and packing stone. Isler imagines small stones and rubble, "passed up the steps by hand; larger stones moved on two-, four-, or six-man litters . . . sledges with runners can be used for the smaller blocks; made to span two or more steps, sledges can be dragged up a few courses at a time or boards made to span several steps can be used as slides over which blocks are pulled . . . ." (*Sticks, Stones, and Shadows*, p. 250) Furthermore, he imagines the builders levering even larger blocks up these steps, rocking the stones up and tumbling them over each step of the supply stairway.

Isler's only evidence of these steps embedded into the pyramid core is the presence of stepped courses showing on the upper third of Khafre's pyramid. Isler quotes Maragioglio and Rinaldi in saying that these courses, "formed an actual flight of steps." But when one measures the widths of these very steps, they range from 58 to 86 centimeters! A meter is just too narrow to lever the ends of heavy stone blocks up a 53 degree slope, yet Isler has the huge granite beams of Khufu's burial chamber being levered up similar steps. In his drawings, only two men stand on steps and lever up the ends of these beams, which weigh several tens of tons, but he admits it would have taken ten levers at each end. There is simply no room for ten men on a step a meter wide, to say nothing of a step with a width of only 58 centimeters; there are many, many other very particular problems with raising pyramid stones by levering.

When he tested his method with a 1,500 lb stone on the experimental NOVA tv show pyramid, Isler

asked the masons to carve two lever sockets on the lower edge of the sides of his block. Right here is a bit of a hitch in his theory, since the core stones of the pyramids do not show side sockets although casing stones sometimes do, presumably for side adjustments. The men used two levers on each side of the block, with two men per lever. Two additional men worked in front of the block (they actually stood on the ground), inserting supports. Each pull of the levers raised the side of the block just enough to slip in a well-planed flat board. Again, there is a problem.

How much flat-planed lumber would be required to construct Khufu's pyramid? The amount of wood for levers and sledges alone must have been enormous; raising all the blocks on lumber supports vastly increases the amount of wood. In our age, we take machine-planed boards for granted. But in the third millennium BC, the fact that the supports must be planed smooth vastly increases the amount of labor. If the supports were not planed smooth, the stack that supports the block is not at all stable. Even with our machine-planed boards, the support stack, 12 layers of board per 72 centimeter rise, was becoming a little unwieldy. In order to get purchase (good leverage), the fulcrum—a stack of stone—had to be raised as the block went up. However, the fulcrums were also becoming unwieldy. Isler answers for this by conveniently drawing solid masonry platforms under the ends of the blocks, raising the fulcrum. But in practice, such sturdy platforms cannot be built under a heavy load that rises by small increments. If not well-planed lumber, all that can be inserted are small stones that result in another unwieldy pile.

It is doubtful whether most of the stones of the pyramid were raised this way. However, it is very possible that levering was the only means to raise the blocks of the highest courses, near the apex, once the builders had brought them as high as they could on ramps. In general, these are much smaller blocks than those of the lower courses.

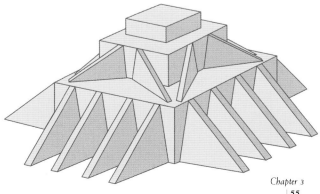

54 and 55
The many different theories about building ramps can be grouped into two major variations: a straight sloping ramp up one face of the pyramid (drawings top left); or one or more ramps starting close to the base of the pyramid and wrapping around the building (drawings top right and bottom left). Alternatives include a zigzag ramp up one face or an internal ramp.

Building △ a Pyramid

BUILDING KHUFU'S FIRST COURSE

Khufu's masons built the first course of his pyramid of casing, backing, and core blocks about 1.5 m thick. They set the foot of the sloping casing back 38 centimeters from the line marking the upper edge of the foundation platform. Leaving extra stock of stone on the front faces of the platform and on the faces of the casing stones would have ensured that the final smooth surfaces would not have been damaged as the stones were moved into their positions. We see extra stock and handling bosses on the casing stones in the undressed lower part of the pyramid, GI-c, built for one of Khufu's queens. There could not have been much extra stock on the lower front of Khufu's casing stones because the platform did not extend out very far.

After they had set all the casing stones, the masons could have trimmed the front face and top edge of the foundation platform. Then the ancient builders could have measured the setting line, or baseline, of the casing from the line of the platform's upper edge, or from the reference line marked by stakes in the holes. Once again, segments of the staked reference line could have been taken up when large casing blocks needed to be brought in, and then later replaced. The casing blocks were probably brought in rough on sledges; then, while the block was parked on rollers or wedges, each join-side was custom-dressed to fit into position with its mates in the pyramid casing. Once the join faces were finished, the masons drew the lines of the sloping pyramid face at the front of each block. The marked pyramid slope defined the extra stock on their fronts.

INCORPORATING SLOPE AND ALIGNMENT: CASING STONE

The core stone in pyramids was irregular because it was only fill for the gleaming shell. It was in this outer casing, formed of blocks of homogeneous fine white limestone from eastern quarries at Tura, that the builders achieved the great precision in the pyramids. Khufu's builders required about 67,390 cubic meters of Tura-quality limestone to cover the Great Pyramid. From the very few of these casing stones that remain at the base, we can see with what skill and care the builders placed them to form the foot of the pyramid. Joints between large blocks, some weighing as much as 15 tons, are often so fine that one cannot even insert a razor blade, and these fine seams sometimes run back from the outer face for more than a meter.

The evidence of unfinished pyramids indicates

that the masons shaved off the extra stock of rough stone after the entire pyramid had been built, starting from the top and working down to the baseline as they removed the construction ramps and embankments. How did they make certain that under all the extra rough stone they had four straight corners and four good, flat faces that would sweep up evenly to a point? How could they dress the acres of fine limestone without chiseling away too much stone and so creating waves and undulations across the acres of the pyramid faces?

Masons incorporated guidelines for the final pyramid trim into each and every casing block as they joined one block to another. We know this from the unfinished limestone casing on the bottom of the pyramids of Khufu's queens, and from the unfinished granite casing at the bottom of Menkaure's pyramid. They probably began, like modern masons, by setting 'leader' casing blocks at the corners and in the middle of each side of the pyramid. The rough extra stock on the front of each block stuck out beyond the intended plane of the pyramid face. The masons parked the blocks to be joined beside one another, hoisted on wooden wedges or rollers just above their intended positions on the pyramid. They then custom dressed the join-faces to be parallel. The join-faces were not necessarily at right angles to the horizontal bedding planes; they could be angled laterally and vertically. Before they concealed the joint side on each block by setting the next block against it, they had to draw the line of slope of the pyramid face—the lines along which that gigantic cut would shave away the extra stock at the end of the building project. For the first course, the masons measured a set amount from an outside reference line, then marked the point where the baseline of the pyramid would intersect with the smoothly dressed join-sides of the block. They then etched the slope line of the pyramid face on the join-sides.

The ancient Egyptians determined the slopes of walls with a measurement called *seqed*, the amount that the face of the wall is set back for a rise of one cubit (.525 of a meter). A set back of one cubit for a rise of one cubit results in a 45° slope. The nearly 52° angle of Khufu's pyramid could be obtained from a set back, or run, of 11 to a rise of 14.

We are not certain how they laid out the *seqed* angle. Khufu's builders could have measured in 11 and up 14 units from the already determined baseline with a plumb line to mark the top of the slope. Perhaps they drew the slope by placing wooden set squares made to the desired angle against the join-face of each block. However, in order to use a triangle, one should ideally have a surface that is absolutely parallel

to the ground. In modern drafting, angles are extremely sensitive to a T-square that is not perfectly perpendicular to the side of the drafting board. Using a plumb line against the vertical side of the triangle may have helped, but plumb lines move. At best, the error in each block would have been compensating, not cumulative, over hundreds and thousands of blocks. The pyramid builders probably also had long distance markers to sight to as checks on the cumulative slope.

Next, the masons beveled or chamfered away the extra stock of stone on the outer face of each block from the lines where all four join-faces (top, bottom, and two sides) intersected with the plane of the pyramid face. This beveling was a lead, created block by block, for the final dressing of the pyramid casing. When the masons brought up the next block in sequence and set it down, creating the side join with its neighbor, the new stone had extra stock on the non-joining front face, and extra dressed join face, extending out beyond the beveled sloping side joint of its older partner. The masons beveled away the extra stock on the newest block along the slope of its neighbor. On the opposite free join face, they repeated the procedure, marking the slope and beveling away the extra stock along this line and along the top and bottom where these sides intersected the sloping plane of the pyramid face.

Block by block, the ancient masons created the sloping planes of the pyramid faces, leaving them hidden behind the extra stock of stone. If the slope as marked on one block was a little off in one direction, the others might deviate in another direction so that the errors averaged out.

REACHING FOR PERFECTION: THE APEX

As the four sides of the pyramid narrowed toward closure at the top of the pyramid, the builders ran out of room for ramps and for men to pull on ropes. They could have used levering to raise some of the last few blocks. It is clear that they were using smaller blocks, and that they could no longer use the loose core masonry as the finished edges came together. They needed a finer grade of stone for edges and the final point. Careful observation of the backing stone now showing on Khufu's pyramid shows that all along the arris lines, and toward the now truncated top, the builders used a finer grade of limestone, even if not Tura-quality. The masonry that remains of the tops of pyramids shows that the builders dispensed with core stone altogether, and came to the point with fine casing-quality limestone.

57

The Giza Pyramids from the south.
Menkaure's horseshoe-shaped quarry
(lower right) lies southeast of his
pyramid (left). Fieldstone walls form
great rectangular precincts around each
of the main pyramids.

THE APEX OF SNEFERU'S NORTH AND KHUFU'S SATELLITE PYRAMID

Rainer Stadelmann found the pieces of the oldest pyramid capstone, also called a pyramidion, on the east side of Sneferu's North Dahshur pyramids. This was a simple culmination of the casing, a plain capstone of good quality limestone.

Zahi Hawass found the second oldest pyramid capstone, a large piece of fine Tura-quality limestone that once crowned Khufu's satellite pyramid off the southeastern corner of the Great Pyramid. He also found a large piece with three exterior sloping faces of the pyramid that once formed a little more than half of

block(s) forming the second course down from the top. Obviously, here the pyramid superstructure is all casing, with no fill or core material, as it narrows to the apex.

The second course down from the top is missing, but Zahi Hawass found the actual apex stone of the satellite pyramid, a single piece of fine, Tura-quality limestone. The underside of the pyramidion is convex, with four triangular faces sloping slightly to the raised center point of the base. This convex, protruding base was meant to fit into the concavity of the top of the second course from the top, just as the convex underside of the second course had evidently fitted into the concave top surface of the third course down. The mean slope of the faces is 51° 45′, almost exactly that of Khufu's main pyramid (51° 51′).

below it on the pyramid. Such slabs once formed the final upper courses that the builders composed entirely of fine casing stone, since the pyramid was now too narrow for any loose and irregular core masonry. The raised and rebated undersides and tops of these pieces of the pyramid corners and top once fitted into one another like Lego blocks.

Peter Jánosi described the remains of a capstone that might have been the crowning stone of GIII-a on the south side of the queen's pyramid. He reported that the broken capstone retained parts of three smoothly finished sides, and that its original width was 1.125 m (15 'palms').

the south side of the third course below the apex. The underside of the block is flat, but the top surface was shaped as a concavity. When it completed the square of the top of the third course down from the top, there were four triangular planes sloping 2.6 meters (five cubits) to the center and forming the lines of the diagonals. The diagonal lines must have helped the builders square the top of the pyramid so that the sides met at a point. This concavity of the top surface was also intended to receive the convex underside of the

THE APEX OF MENKAURE'S QUEEN'S PYRAMID GIII-A

Excavations in recent years have turned up numerous fragments of Tura-quality casing stones around the northeastern corners and eastern side of GIII-a. Certain pieces show how the masons gave the corner special treatment to ensure firm joins. The undersides of large corner slabs are rebated, or recessed, to fit a raised edge of the casing course

A square rebated or sunken panel, about 7.5 centimeters (one palm) deep, on the underside measured 1 x 1 cubit (about .525 meter). The sunken panel would have fitted over a raised panel of nearly equal size on the course below as a way to fix the capstone. With an angle of 52 degrees, the pyramidion was originally about ten palms (75 centimeters) high.

Building a Pyramid

KHAFRE'S POINT

The capstone of Khafre's pyramid is missing, but 40 to 45 meters down from the top of the pyramid, fine limestone casing remains intact. The truncated top shows the socle, or anchoring, of the last blocks that would receive the pyramidion, which could have been granite to match the base.

I measured the thickness of the casing courses where I could reach them on the overhang of the northeast corner. From lower to upper they are: 82, 67, 35, 45, 66, 44, and 45 cm thick. These courses are from one-third to two-thirds the thickness of the lowest course of casing stone, which was granite, 1.05 m thick.

Looking out across the expanse of casing, one sees that the slabs are not flush, but stagger by a few millimeters. We would expect the faces to be flush if the masons had trimmed them in place on the pyramid, a practice well in evidence in the lower parts of unfinished pyramids. Perhaps they were unable to do so in the tight working space of the upper reaches, and this is one indication that working methods had to change as the pyramid grew toward the top. Perhaps the slope was cut into the casing blocks of the highest courses before they were laid. (It is also possible that the stones shifted after the casing farther down was removed.)

When the builders completed the body of the pyramid, masons began to free, from the top down, the smooth, sloping faces hidden in the rough extra stock of stone on the lower part of the pyramid.

FIRST AND LAST: THE PYRAMID BASELINE

There is a certain irony in the Giza Pyramids that the baseline was the both the first and last thing the builders did. This is certainly indicated at Menkaure's pyramid, where the builders never completed the base.

Petrie dug down to the foot of the casing at some points on the Menkaure pyramid. There is no clean baseline. The builders left the pyramid base without trimming the granite casing on the lower part of the pyramid. The lowest course rests on the rough limestone foundation. The builders had smoothed the sides of the individual granite blocks to join them together. As they set each block, they beveled the rough extra stock of stone on the outer face away from the smooth side where the block would eventually join the next block. This beveling, or chamfering, followed the intended slope line of the pyramid face (about 51 degrees) which ended about six to 18 inches above the foundation. Menkaure's builders probably intended to dress the bottom of the lowest casing course into a vertical foot that would have met the pavement of the court—had it ever been finished—to finally form the true baseline. This is the configuration at Khafre's pyramid where the only baseline is the top of that cut at the bottom of the lowest course of casing. The masons truly completed the baseline when they laid the pavement of the court up to that cut. Paving the court was one of the last operations, which is also indicated at Menkaure's pyramid. It may seem odd to form the clean baseline as the last, rather than the first task of creating the pyramid, but such was their procedure.

Since Menkaure's builders did not get to that end, what should we consider as the true baseline of this pyramid? The answer is that there isn't any—the bottom of the slope chamfered or beveled into the side joins of the granite blocks stops at different levels. If there is no true base line, how did the ancient builders control its square? Petrie took the average height of all the granite courses, which are all nearly the same—"a rather short two cubits each"—except for the bottom course being four to eight inches thicker. He reckoned the base as the height of one course below the top of the first course.

For their purposes, the builders could certainly not have used the actual bottom of the lowest course as their base reference because the thickness of the blocks of this course vary from 1.11 to 1.40 m. For this lowest course of casing, they shaved the tops of blocks even and flush, while leaving the bottoms at different levels upon the rough foundation. As we saw at Khafre's pyramid, the ancient builders must have used the top of the first course as a level reference, similar to the way Petrie used it to obtain a theoretical baseline. For laying in the bottom course, they must have used a temporary outside reference line that may or may not have left traces, such as the lines of post holes around the bases of the Khufu and Khafre pyramids.

Khufu's builders proceeded differently. They had already prepared a good level baseline—the contact of the lowest course of large limestone casing blocks with the foundation platform. But it is still likely that they left the baseline obscured under extra stock of stone until they shaved down the casing at the end of building the pyramid.

THE HUMAN HAND: IMPERFECTIONS

As good as they were, the Giza Pyramid builders were not perfect. The pyramids are very human, not supernatural, monuments. The square of Khafre's pyramid, completed by the casing, is not perfect. In 1881, Petrie determined the square of the pyramid base by extrapolating the corners from the casing socle, the bedding of the lowest course. He then checked the angles of the casing at the top of the pyramid in relation to the square of the base and discovered a slight twist to the pyramid of 3° 50'. The builders had to bend the corner angles slightly to make them meet at the apex. Even with such discrepancies, pyramid builders never again attained the accuracy of the Giza Pyramids. As Petrie did with the Fourth Dynasty Giza Pyramids, Borchardt used modern instruments to survey Sahure's Fifth Dynasty pyramid at Abusir. He found the southeastern corner shifted 1.58 m farther east than the northeastern corner, making a rhombus or trapezoid base instead of a perfect square. Sahure's builders compensated in the upward slope of the pyramid and hid the imperfection of the base under the back end of the pyramid temple. Seeing the imperfections of the human hand only increases our admiration for the astonishing achievements of the people who built the pyramids and helps us relate to the sense of accomplishment and community that they must have felt when the pyramid was completed. Recently, Zahi Hawass discovered a scene carved in fine limestone relief from the causeway of Sahure's pyramid. It shows the dancing, singing, and celebration that broke out with the setting of the capstone.

59
The fine limestone top of Khafre's pyramid. The masonry below the casing appears regular and stepped, but widths of steps and block sizes vary greatly. Lower rubbly backing masonry adheres after the casing was ripped away.

The Architectural Development of the Egyptian Royal Tomb

by Zahi Hawass

The kings of the First Dynasty were buried in their ancestral cemetery at Abydos. There is also a group of large, elaborate First Dynasty tombs at Saqqara, near the Early Dynastic capital of Ineb-hedj; the current Egyptological consensus is that these tombs belong to high officials, but it is also possible that these are royal cenotaphs or cult centers.

The tombs of the First Dynasty at Abydos are located in an area called the Umm al-Qa'ab, which means 'mother of pots.' These Early Dynastic tombs mark a significant change in construction from those of the Predynastic Period, when tombs were simple oval or rectangular graves. The tombs become more and more elaborate, with pits and chambers lined with mud brick or, in some cases, wood. In addition to the burial chamber, there were also chambers for grave goods. Surrounding the tombs of the First Dynasty were small subsidiary tombs for attendants thought to have been sacrificed to accompany each king into the afterlife.

Set on the east side of each tomb were limestone stelae bearing the name of the king in a *serekh* (a rectangle bounded at the bottom by the representation of a niched palace façade). Most of the kings of the Second Dynasty were buried at Saqqara, but the last two kings of this dynasty, Peribsen and Khasekhemwy, were buried at Abydos.

At a distance of about two kilometers from the Early Dynastic tombs in Umm al-Qa'ab, closer to the floodplain, is a group of large enclosures associated with the funerary cults of the kings; the earlier enclosures also had subsidiary burials associated with them. These are thought to have once contained ritual structures built of perishable materials. David O'Connor of the Pennsylvania-Yale Expedition recently found a fleet of twelve boats moored neared the complex of the Second Dynasty king, Khasekhemwy (although not necessarily belonging to this king). The funerary complexes associated with the Second Dynasty tombs at Saqqara have not yet been located. We are now making a new plan of these tombs, in cooperation with Günter Dreyer of the German Institute, and we have already begun to clean these tombs in preparation for this new plan.

Through study of the royal tombs and associated enclosures at Abydos, one can identify their basic architectural components, and correlate them with the elements of later complexes: the tomb, enclosure wall, the stelae (corresponding to the upper temple), the funerary/valley complex (lower temple), and boats. Thus, the basic elements of the royal tombs, which continued to develop throughout Egyptian history, were already in existence at this time.

A number of the Early Dynastic tombs at Saqqara have mounds, and in one case a stepped platform, over the burial shafts. The tombs at Abydos are also thought to have been covered with mounds. These are thought to represent the primeval mound on which the creator god stood to bring the universe into being.

The Step Pyramid complex of Djoser represents a major step forward in royal funerary architecture. Djoser and his chief architect, Imhotep, brought the two elements of the Early Dynastic complex, tomb and valley enclosure, together into one monumental complex, and translated the mud brick and perishable materials into stone. The mound above the burial shaft became a towering step pyramid, rising in six stages to a height of 60 meters.

The components of Djoser's complex are:
1. The enclosure wall with the colonnaded entrance
2. The pyramid
3. The northern temple
4. The south tomb
5. The south court
6. The *heb-sed* court
7. The southern altar
8. Temple 'T'
9. The northern temple
10. The northern altar
11. Pavilion of the south
12. Pavilion of the north
13. Boundary markers

Over the course of the next hundred years, the major elements of the step pyramid complex evolved into the standardized elements of the Old Kingdom pyramid complex. Much of this development can be traced in the complexes of Sneferu, first king of the Fourth Dynasty, at Meidum and Dahshur. Sneferu built four pyramids: one each at Seila and Meidum, and two at Dahshur. He probably built the Seila pyramid as a representation of the primeval mound associated with a royal residence in the area, not as a tomb. The Meidum pyramid was built as a step pyramid in the beginning of his reign and left unfinished for reasons we do not know. Sneferu started a new pyramid complex at Dahshur in about the fifteenth year of his reign; this was designed to be the first true pyramid. However, for structural reasons, the angle of slope had to be modified part way up, which gave the pyramid its distinctive 'bent' profile. This complex was then abandoned, and a new true-pyramid complex in North Dahshur was completed and used for the king's burial.

The complex at Meidum contains some of the basic elements of the pyramid complex: a wall, which encloses a small satellite pyramid to the south and an offering chapel to the east, and a causeway leading toward the flood plain. There are also tombs of officials and family members near the pyramid.

The Bent Pyramid complex contains all of these elements, plus a lower temple at the eastern end of the causeway. These elements now become standard, and can also be seen in Sneferu's Northern Pyramid complex at Dahshur. We also have evidence for a pyramid city associated with this complex.

Thus by the time of Seneferu's son and successor, Khufu, the basic elements of the pyramid complex were in place. The Early Dynastic mound has become a straight-sided pyramid. The royal stelae have become the upper, or mortuary, temple. Djoser's south tomb, *sed*-festival court, and Temple 'T' become the satellite (ritual) pyramid and its court. Djoser's complex also contains *sed*-festival chapels, altars, and the pavilions of the north and south. These separate buildings develop into rooms and niches inside later pyramid temples. Khufu adds three queens' pyramids and an elaborate, planned cemetery for royal relatives and officials to the elements of the pyramid complex. Evidence for harbors associated with the complexes of

60 bottom
General view of Djoser's Step
Pyramid complex at Saqqara,
Third Dynasty.

61
The imposing structure of the pyramid of
King Khufu of the Fourth Dynasty
dominates the Giza plateau and represents
an engineering feat never again reached
during the following dynasties.

both Khufu and his son Khafre have also been found, and traces of Khufu's palace have recently been uncovered. Ongoing excavations at Giza are yielding traces of the workers who built the pyramids: the tombs of the pyramid builders, and the Lost City, where the temporary workers who built the pyramids received tools and rations, perhaps slept, and the permanent staff probably lived.

The current work at Giza is clarifying the issue of where the king lived while his pyramid was being built. It used to be thought that the capital, the royal residence, of the king was at Memphis itself. However, The Egypt Exploration Society excavations at Memphis under David Jeffreys have found no evidence for a settlement dated to the Archaic Period or the Old Kingdom. They have, however, found traces of an Archaic settlement at the foot of the

Saqqara plateau, near the First Dynasty tombs there.

At Giza, in addition to the remains of a monumental building which may be Khufu's palace, we have found traces of an Old Kingdom settlement under the modern village that lies at the foot of the plateau. This settlement was about five square kilometers, and I believe that this is where the royal administration was based. Textual evidence from the Fifth Dynasty also supports this interpretation: the Abusir Papyri, found in the pyramid complex of Neferirkare, mention a palace of Djedkare Isesi that was located near his pyramid.

The pyramid was the national project of the nation; every household participated in this monumental task by sending workers and food to help the king. The construction of the pyramid and its complex magically provided for the rebirth and

divinity of the king, and thus assured the safety and prosperity of the country. It has been said that the pyramids built Egypt: the complex administration needed to manage these enormous projects helped to create this ancient civilization. The king would have had his primary residence near the pyramid site so that he could supervise the most important project of his reign.

Khufu's pyramid required a large number of men to move and place over 2,600,000 cubic meters of stone, yet the number of artisans required was relatively few. This ratio of stone-movers to artisans would change, however, over the next two dynasties as architects decreased the volume of stone by making the pyramids smaller and using smaller stones, mud brick, or loose rubble fill, while they increased the number of beautiful wall reliefs with which the temples were decorated. For example, it is estimated that the pyramid of the Fifth Dynasty's first king, Userkaf, contains only one-thirteenth of the bulk of Khufu's pyramid. Indeed, the 2,600,000 cubic meters of raw stone in Khufu's pyramid is almost equal to all the raw stone of all the pyramids of the Fifth and Sixth Dynasties combined. On the other hand, the Fifth Dynasty pyramid of Sahure at Abusir had, according to German Egyptologist Ludwig Borchardt, 10,000 square meters of wall reliefs. The decreasing size of the pyramids, and hence the reduced need for workmen, was probably not economically motivated

62

The pyramid of Amenembet III at Dahshur, Middle Kingdom.

because the increasing number of reliefs would have necessitated hiring many more skilled artisans who commanded a higher wage than the workmen who moved the stones.

It is at the end of the Fifth Dynasty that the so-called 'Pyramid Texts' appear on the inside walls of the royal burial of suites—the first example being in the pyramid of Unas at Saqqara. The Pyramid Texts are magical spells inscribed in vertical columns on the walls of the antechamber and burial chamber of the pyramid. The spells are designed to help the king ascend to the sky, to illuminate the relationship of the king to the gods, and to ensure the divinity of the king. In the following dynasty these precise carvings grace the subterranean chambers of both kings and queens.

The pyramid complexes of the Fifth Dynasty, in addition to their expanded decorative repertoire,

make some changes to the specific details of the Fourth Dynasty complex. Neferirkare and Niuserre all have their entrances at ground level, and the interior layout is different. The royal sarcophagus is placed near the west end of the chamber and the chamber walls are decorated with designs of a palace façade, an alabaster veneer, and later, the Pyramid Texts. The temples become larger (providing more wall surface for the reliefs), and contain numerous rooms and magazines. The courts of the upper temple, which are oriented north to south in the Fourth Dynasty, are now oriented east to west.

The kings of the Fifth Dynasty also built sun temples in an area about one kilometer north of Abusir. These complexes consist of a large, squat obelisk and an altar in an open court, an upper temple, causeway, and lower temple. These temples were dedicated to the worship of the sun god, Re. Two of these temples have been found and excavated so far; we have textual evidence for six of them.

After the chaos of the First Intermediate Period, the kings of the Middle Kingdom were once again buried in pyramids. The first king of the Twelfth Dynasty, Amenemhet I, built his pyramid at Lisht, near the entrance to the Fayum. In the core of his pyramid, he used rough blocks of limestone and a fill of mud brick and debris. Included in this debris, and also in the lining and blocking of the substructure, were inscribed blocks from the pyramid complexes of Khufu, Khafre, and Unas. These blocks may have served to magically link this king with his divine predecessors.

Amenemhet I's complex is clearly based on the Old Kingdom prototype, with, however, some details that reveal the Theban origin of the family. Some of the standard features are present: upper temple, causeway, and lower temple, but the causeway was unroofed, like the processional ways of the Theban tombs of the kings who preceded him. Another Theban element is the fact that the pyramid and its temple are on terraces. There was no satellite pyramid, and family members were buried in *mastabas* or shaft tombs within the pyramid enclosure. A small chapel lay in front of the entrance to the substructure in the north face of the pyramid, and the king was buried in a chamber that lay at the bottom of a shaft on the vertical axis of the pyramid—this shaft is another Theban element. The Middle Kingdom decoration that has been retrieved from the complex is difficult to tell from Old Kingdom intrusive fragments, as the later artists appear to have tried to copy the older models as faithfully as possible. The causeway was decorated with scenes of foreigners, funerary estates, royal officials, and gods.

Amenemhet I's son and successor, Senusret I, built his pyramid near that of his father. For the core of the pyramid itself, his architects used an ingenious system of spines and cross-walls, but the pyramid was unstable, and only a ruined mound remains today. Like his father, he placed an entrance chapel against the north face, from which a descending passage leads to the burial chamber far beneath the ground (and now under the water table). All the Twelfth Dynasty kings placed their burial chambers deep in the earth as part of an effort to link themselves with Osiris, king of the underworld.

Senusret I's complex contains most of the elements that had become standard by the end of the Old Kingdom: upper temple, causeway (originally uncovered but later roofed), lower temple (which has never been found), and a satellite pyramid in the southeast corner of the inner enclosure. Nine queens' pyramids lie inside the outer enclosure wall surrounding the main pyramid. Large statues of the king in the red and white crowns were placed in niches along the inside of the causeway. Another decorative innovation found in this complex is the addition of monumental *serekhs* containing the king's names to both faces of the inner enclosure wall. The wall was also niched, harkening back to the Third Dynasty enclosure of Djoser and the Early Dynastic walls at Abydos and Saqqara.

The succeeding kings, Amenemhet II and Senusret II, built pyramid complexes that are significantly different, referring perhaps more to the Third Dynasty step pyramid enclosures than to the late Old Kingdom models. In any event, each of the next kings built a unique complex which incorporates some of the standard elements with experimental features. Amenemhet II's pyramid is at Dahshur, and is set in a rectangular, east-west enclosure. The pyramid itself was built as a skeleton of stone filled with sand and then cased with fine white limestone; it is now in ruins. The entrance to the substructure is in the north face and leads to a burial chamber which contains a sarcophagus of sandstone. This complex has been neglected by archaeologists: little is known about the layout of the upper temple, and the lower temple has never been found, although an open causeway leads down to the edge of the floodplain.

Senusret II moved back to the Fayum, and built a pyramid primarily of mud brick within a square enclosure. The substructure of this pyramid is very unusual, and is the first to try to hide the entrance in an attempt to foil tomb robbers. This substructure is entered via a shaft on the south side of the pyramid.

A horizontal passage at the bottom of the shaft leads to a vaulted chamber, at one end of which is a deep well whose bottom has never been reached. The horizontal passage continues through an antechamber to the burial chamber cased in granite, in which was found a red granite sarcophagus and an alabaster offering table. A passageway runs around the burial chamber, providing for the symbolic journey of the king's spirit and also helping to associate him with Osiris, whose cult was becoming increasingly more important during this period.

In this complex are a number of *mastabas* and one subsidiary pyramid which may be a ritual pyramid. The enclosure wall of the complex was niched, like Senusret I's. Included in the complex were an upper temple, causeway, and lower temple, none of which have been adequately explored. At the foot of the plateau is Senusret II's pyramid town, a planned settlement which tells us a great deal about daily life, at least under royal protection, in the Middle Kingdom.

Senusret III moved back to Dahshur, and built his pyramid again of mud brick with limestone casing. The substructure consists of a hidden entrance to the west, a descending passage leading to an antechamber, magazines, and a burial chamber of granite containing a granite sarcophagus. Against the northern face of the pyramid is an entrance chapel, and to the east is a small upper temple. The pyramid enclosure was expanded later in the reign, and a second temple was added to the south. A causeway leads from the southeastern corner of the expanded enclosure, but no lower temple has yet been found. Surrounding the main pyramid are the superstructures of seven small pyramids; underneath are the shaft tombs of a number of royal women, in which a number of inscribed artifacts and jewels were found. Just outside the southwest corner of the pyramid enclosure is a building of mud brick and a fleet of six wooden boats, each six meters long.

Fragments of relief from the upper temple include the king at an offering table, a funerary menu, offering bearers, scenes of gods, officials, and the butchering of sacred cattle. Bits of relief from the southern temple show the king in his *sed*-festival robe. Josef Wegner has recently discovered a second tomb for Senusret III at Abydos, which may have been the king's actual burial place.

Amenemhet III built two pyramids, one at Dahshur and the other in the Fayum. The Dahshur pyramid was built of mud brick. Underneath is a maze of corridors cased in white limestone that includes the king's burial chamber, a number of small chapels, and the chambers used for the burial and equipment of several queens. There are two entrances, and the corridors are quite complex. They may, in addition to their practical purposes, model the underworld. In 1997, I was able to visit this pyramid with Dieter Arnold. It was amazing to explore these labyrinthine corridors myself.

Amenemhet III's Dahshur complex had an upper temple, causeway, and lower temple. Structural problems, however, caused the king to leave this site and build a second pyramid at Hawara in the Fayum. The layout of this pyramid and its enclosure is very different from its predecessor at Dahshur. The substructure here is truly a labyrinth, with dead-end corridors and passageways hidden in the ceiling. The burial chamber itself is carved from a single piece of quartzite. Inside was the king's quartzite sarcophagus, a second, smaller sarcophagus, and two canopic chests.

The pyramid complex of Amenemhet III at Hawara is the largest of the Middle Kingdom enclosures. It is oriented north to south. It was approached via an open causeway from the east. The upper temple is completely unique, and was called 'The Labyrinth' by visitors in ancient times. Unfortunately, most of this structure has now been destroyed; enough remains only to tell us that it was a vast complex of small courts and shrines. Petrie found the remains of a large granite statue of the king close to the pyramid. Other statue fragments of gods, the king, and offering bearers, were recovered from this area.

The kings of the New Kingdom were aware that neither the huge monuments of the Fourth Dynasty nor the maze corridors of the late Twelfth Dynasty had protected the royal burials. Thus, beginning with Thutmose I of the Eighteenth Dynasty, the kings built only their mortuary temples in the open, in the floodplain along the west bank. In place of a valley, or lower temple, they used the temples at Karnak. In a vain effort to protect their mummies and treasures, they hid their actual tombs in a remote valley further to the west, the Valley of the Kings. Towering above this series of desert wadis is a pyramid-shaped peak, known as the Qurn. Thus, the royal burials continued to be surmounted by the powerful symbol of the pyramid. In one sense, the New Kingdom came full circle, back again to the tombs separated from their cult centers that were seen in the First Dynasty. Each period introduced changes in the funerary cult, but the primary importance of the pyramid remained, from its beginnings as a mound of sand over the first royal tombs, to the towering peak that protected the last.

The Architectural Components of the Pyramid Complex

by Zahi Hawass

Many people approach the royal pyramids of the Old and Middle Kingdom as if they were isolated monuments. But in fact, each major pyramid forms the centerpiece of an elaborate complex consisting of fourteen distinct elements, each crucial in its own right to the successful afterlife of the king and the proper functioning of the Egyptian cosmos.

THE PYRAMID

The most important component of each complex is the pyramid itself, which marked the burial place of the king. In the Old Kingdom, these were built mainly of local limestone cased with finer white limestone from the site of Tura; in the Middle Kingdom, the core was of limestone rubble or mud brick and the casing of limestone. In the Old Kingdom, the entrance to the pyramid was in the north face, with some exceptions. For example, the Bent Pyramid at Dahshur has two entrances, one from the north and the other from the west. The architects of the later Middle Kingdom tried to hide the entrance to the pyramid in an attempt to outwit tomb robbers, so its location is variable. The burial chamber is always located under the pyramid, except for in the pyramids of Khufu at Giza and Sneferu at Dahshur, where the burial chambers are within the pyramid core, above ground level.

THE UPPER TEMPLE

The upper temple, also called the funerary temple or mortuary temple, was where the cult of the deceased king was celebrated. It was usually located on the east side of the pyramid, unless the topography of the area caused the temple to be moved, such as in the Third Dynasty complex of Djoser and the Fifth Dynasty complex of Userkaf. In the Third and early Fourth Dynasties, the temple plan was very simple, generally a small offering area marked by royal stelae. Later, the upper temple became larger and more elaborate. From the reign of Sneferu onward, the walls of the upper temple were decorated with scenes and texts.

THE ENCLOSURE WALL AND PYRAMID COURT

Each pyramid was surrounded by a wall about three meters high, built of stone rubble. A second wall was built around the first. A well-preserved example of these enclosure walls can be seen in the complex of Menkaure. These walls served to limit access to the pyramid and its inner court to the priests directly responsible for the cult of the king. During the Old Kingdom, the enclosure walls were left undecorated; during the Twelfth Dynasty, kings began to carve their names in monumental hieroglyphs on these walls.

THE CAUSEWAY

The causeway leads east from the upper temple to the lower temple. Our recent work at Giza found some decorated blocks *in situ*, suggesting that causeways were roofed as early as the reign of Khufu. Most causeways were built of limestone, although some, like the causeway of Menkaure, were of mud brick. Causeways were decorated with scenes depicting activities of the king and events such as the capping of the pyramid with its pyramidion. The average length of the causeway was about one and a half kilometers.

THE SUBSIDIARY PYRAMIDS

Two kinds of subsidiary pyramids appear as part of pyramid complexes: queens' pyramids, and cult, or ritual pyramids. These smaller pyramids usually stand about 50 to 60 meters high, were cased with fine white limestone, and can be located to the east or south of the main pyramid. Small chapels often lie to the east of these pyramids. Queens' pyramids usually contain evidence for a burial, such as a sarcophagus, bones, or funerary equipment.

In early Old Kingdom complexes, the position of the ritual pyramid is somewhat variable, but eventually takes up a standard position at the southeast corner of the main pyramid (where it is seen, for example, in the complex of Khufu). The substructure can be T-shaped or echo the interior of the main pyramid on a smaller scale; cult pyramids do not contain evidence for burial. The prototype for the ritual pyramid is the south tomb of Djoser. Scholars are still debating the function of these structures

BOAT PITS

Boat pits have been associated with royal mortuary complexes since the Early Dynastic period: David O'Connor and the Pennsylvania-Yale Expedition to Abydos recently found thirteen wooden boats cased with mud brick near some massive enclosures associated with the mortuary cults of the kings of the First and Second Dynasties. Some other Early Dynastic funerary monuments also have model boats or boat pits as parts of their complexes.

The pyramid complex of Khufu has five boat pits cut into the rock around the pyramid. Three are on the east side, and are shaped like boats. The fourth and fifth are south of the pyramid and are rectangular in shape; a full-size wooden boat had been dismantled and buried inside each of these pits. One of these boats has been excavated and restored; it is now exhibited in a museum just south of the pyramid. The pyramid complex of Khafre also includes five boat pits, all to the east of the pyramid.

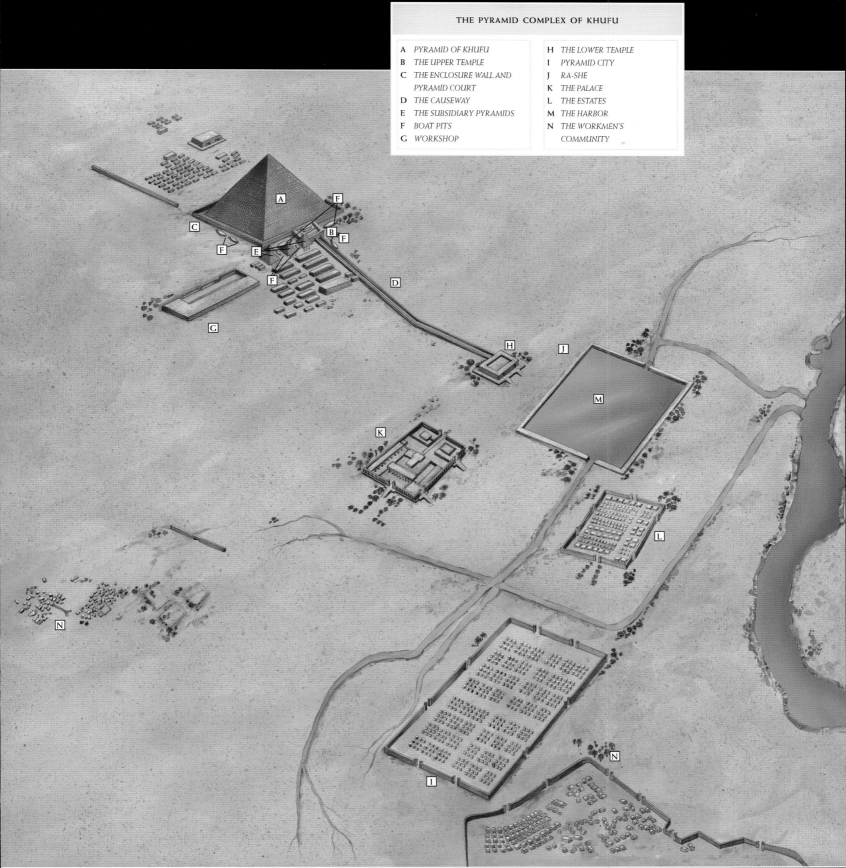

THE PYRAMID COMPLEX OF KHUFU

A PYRAMID OF KHUFU
B THE UPPER TEMPLE
C THE ENCLOSURE WALL AND
    PYRAMID COURT
D THE CAUSEWAY
E THE SUBSIDIARY PYRAMIDS
F BOAT PITS
G WORKSHOP

H THE LOWER TEMPLE
I PYRAMID CITY
J RA-SHE
K THE PALACE
L THE ESTATES
M THE HARBOR
N THE WORKMEN'S
    COMMUNITY

Architectural ▲ Components

WORKSHOP

There is no specific location for the pyramid workshop, where cult objects such as small statues were produced and stored, where the process of mummification was carried out, and where kitchens for the preparation of fresh offerings were located. Evidence for what could be Khufu's workshop was found to the south of his causeway. Our recent work at Giza has demonstrated that the so-called 'Workmen's Barracks' located to the west of Khafre's pyramid were actually workshops and storage magazines. Menkaure's workshop was to the south of his causeway. No workshops have yet been found around the pyramids of the later Old Kingdom, but this is primarily due to lack of sufficient excavation.

THE LOWER TEMPLE

The lower temple, or valley temple, is invariably located to the east of the pyramid complex, generally at the edge of the floodplain. Scholars have suggested that the temple was used for mummification and also for the people who attended festivals and feasts after the death of the king. I believe the temple was used for the worship of the king as Horus.

Plans have been recovered for eight Old Kingdom lower temples. The temple of Khafre is the best-preserved of these, although the temple of Unas at Saqqara is also in relatively good condition, and is now being restored. The lower temple of Khufu was recently discovered during the construction of a sewage system for the village at the foot of the Giza plateau. Due to the presence of a modern villa on the site, we were not able to excavate the entire temple, but we collected some of the basalt blocks, found *in situ*, that formed part of its pavement.

THE PYRAMID CITY

Each pyramid had a pyramid city associated with it, always located to the south of the lower temple and bearing the same name as the pyramid itself. During the Fourth Dynasty, only the priests who maintained the cult of the king, all of whom were royal relatives, lived in the pyramid city; in the later Fifth and Sixth Dynasties, the pyramid city expanded in size. We recently found evidence for the pyramid city of Khufu south of his lower temple, stretching for about five square kilometres, under the modern village of Nazlet al-Samman. Other known pyramid cities are that of Khentkaus at Giza and Senusret II in the Fayum area.

RA-SHE

Ra-she means the mouth of the lake or pool. This area is referred to in texts, and seems to be the place where goods from royal estates around the country were delivered to the pyramid for use in the maintenance of the king's cult and for the living king. It was the area where the boundary between the mundane world outside the pyramid complex and the sacred world within was located. Only one *Ra-she* has been found and excavated, in front of the lower temple of Khafre's pyramid. This area has two ramps sloping up from the harbor area to the east and leading to the two entrances of the temple, one to the north and one to the south. Beneath each of the ramps is a boat-shaped tunnel, perhaps representing boats used by the king for the day and night trips, or perhaps built so that people could pass through without entering the sacred space of the complex.

THE PALACE

It was once thought that the king's palace was located at Memphis, but we now know that each king had a palace at his pyramid site. The pyramid was the national project of the country, and every household in the entire land, from the Delta to Aswan, participated in building the pyramid by sending workers and food. Therefore, the king needed to be on hand to unite the nation, and the pyramid site itself was the most logical place from which he could control his most important project.

Recent excavations at Memphis by David Jefferys demonstrates that there was no major settlement in the area dating to the Archaic Period or Old Kingdom. Instead, he found evidence for the Archaic capital of Inb-hedj near the tombs of the First and Second Dynasties at Saqqara. The papyri found in the tomb of Senedjemib-Inty at Giza state that the Fifth Dynasty king Djedkare Isesi lived in a palace near the site of his pyramid. In addition, we have recently found evidence for a palace to the south of Khufu's valley temple.

THE ESTATES

We know of the existence of royal estates from offering lists and scenes representing personified estates used to decorate the pyramid temples and associated private tombs. These were scattered along the length of the Nile. The estates were agricultural units which provided food offerings of grains, fruits, vegetables, and animals for the maintenance of the living king and for the royal cult; relatives and priests were granted materials from these royal estates as a mark of favor. We have no archaeological evidence for these estates.

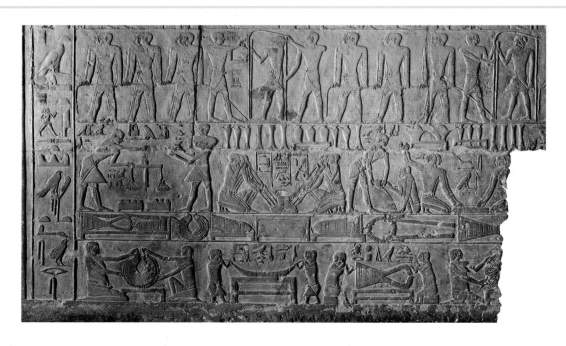

THE HARBOR

The harbor is always located near the lower temple. We have evidence at Giza for harbors of both Khufu and Khafre. It is believed that a large canal was cut parallel to the Nile, and additional canals were built to connect to these harbors. The harbor was used for the delivery of non-local stone, such as granite, basalt, alabaster, and white fine limestone, as well as offerings from the royal estates, to the site. It was also used by the workers who lived nearby and traveled to the worksite every morning, and by people attending feasts of the gods.

THE WORKMEN'S COMMUNITY

The only well-excavated example of a workmen's community is at Giza, located southeast of the main plateau. This was discovered recently and is still being excavated. The workmen's community consists of the following areas:

1. The tombs of the pyramid builders. The lower cemetery contains the tombs of supervisors and the workmen who moved the stones, and the upper cemetery contains the tombs of the more skilled artisans, such as craftsmen, draftsmen, and artists, as well as minor officials.

2. The industrial area. In this area are bakeries, an area for sorting salted fish, metal and faience-working shops, and also dormitories where the workmen slept during the work week.

3. The settlement of the workmen. The Old

Kingdom settlement in this area, of which we have caught only glimpses, seems to include a camp for the workmen who moved the stones and a village for the permanent artisans.

4. The 'Wall of the Crow.' This separates the workmen's area from the royal tombs themselves. It is built of limestone, and is about ten meters high and two hundred meters long. A doorway in the center leads from the workmen's community to the sacred pyramid site.

There are very few complexes for which we have found all of these components, and modern excavations are constantly finding new pieces of the individual pyramid complexes that were missed by earlier excavators. Much important information is buried under the shifting sands of the Egyptian desert or hidden by the new buildings that are constantly being erected in the Memphite region to serve the exploding Egyptian population.

66 bottom
Scene showing jewelry workshop, Tomb of Mereruka, Saqqara, Old Kingdom.

67 top left
Scene showing furniture workshop, Tomb of Niankhkhnum and Khnumhotep, Saqqara, Old Kingdom.

67 top right
Steps of sculpting of a statue, Tomb of Niankhkhnum and Khnumhotep, Saqqara, Old Kingdom.

67 center right
A wooden statuette of a man tending a fire, Egyptian Museum Cairo, Old Kingdom.

67 bottom
A wooden statue of two men preparing bread and beer, Egyptian Museum Cairo, Old Kingdom.

The Predynastic Period

by Renee Friedman

Unlike other periods of Egyptian history, the prehistoric, or Predynastic, period left no soaring monuments or written documents. Ancient annals provide a sequence of kings stretching back to the First Dynasty, but the time before was ascribed to the spirits of the dead—rulers whose names, but not existence, had been long forgotten. The reality of this ancient memory was proved only a little over a century ago. In 1895, while investigating the temple of the god Seth at Naqada in Upper Egypt, W.M.F. Petrie came across a cemetery of over two thousand graves containing pottery and objects unlike anything he had seen before. Although it was his archrival Jacques De Morgan who realized their actual date, Petrie continued to study the material. He worked out an ingenious relative dating system to put this Predynastic (and thus preliterate) society in order, long before the advent of absolute dating techniques such as Carbon-14. Following this discovery, there was a flurry of interest and over sixty-five Predynastic cemeteries throughout Upper Egypt were explored. These excavations revealed, among other things, an evolving idea of the afterlife and its material requirements. The burials developed from sandy pits, to large tombs containing wicker coffins, to tombs lined with mud bricks. However, cemetery excavations did not make clear how these Predynastic farmers and traders came to be the founders of one of the world's first nation-states and the builders of the pyramids. The pottery, tools, and jewelry in the graves offer little evidence to explain the origin of the religious, economic, and architectural traditions that flowered in the Pharaonic age. This scarcity of information led some to suggest that an invading 'Dynastic Race' must have been responsible for the appearance of these traditions, or even today this idea lingers on in fantastic theories of spacemen and lost civilizations from Atlantis as the founders of ancient Egyptian civilization.

68 and 69
The palette of King Narmer graphically signals the end of the Predynastic Period with its use of writing to identify people and places and also its subject matter—the unification of the Two Lands. Narmer, wearing the White Crown of Upper Egypt, smites an enemy in the presence of the falcon god Horus, patron of kingship, who holds captive the people of the papyrus plant, the Delta. On the obverse of the Palette of Narmer (detail left), the king, wearing the Red Crown of Lower Egypt, marches in a victory procession to inspect the decapitated enemy. Now in the Egyptian Museum, Cairo.

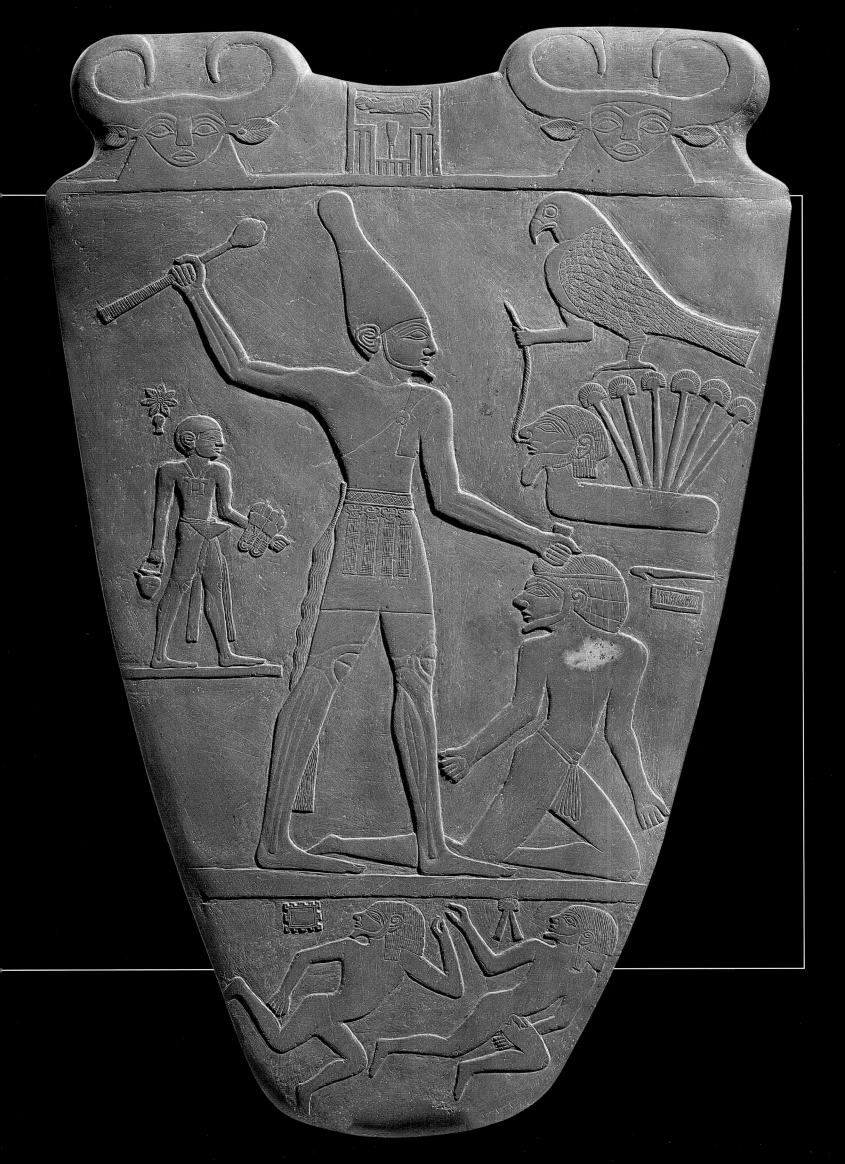

Over the last thirty years, new excavations in cemeteries and, more importantly, in settlements in Upper Egypt, the Nile Delta, and deep in the Sahara Desert have begun to fill in the blanks. These new discoveries have revealed a rich background of indigenous cultural development. They have also pushed the origins of Egyptian civilization much farther back in time than anyone could have anticipated.

Remarkably, early evidence for the innovation that may have served as a springboard for Egyptian civilization is found in the Sahara Desert, about one hundred kilometers due west of Abu Simbel, at a place called Nabta Playa. Here, Fred Wendorf and Romuald Schild have been investigating the scattered remains of people who may be the very first Egyptians. Athough it is now one of the most arid places on earth, its climate was wetter between 8500 and 4500 BC. This climate nourished grassy savannas and seasonal lakes, or playas. Although their existence was precarious, depending on the summer rains, societies of cattle-herders lived in this area off and on for four thousand years. Investigations there have yielded evidence, so far lacking in the Nile Valley itself, for the development of an indigenous Neolithic (food producing rather than only food gathering) way of life, and for the independent invention of pottery. More impressive still are the stone monuments these desert dwellers built to express their religious beliefs. These structures suggest that they had already achieved a

previously unsuspected level of social organization by 5000 BC. The earliest glimpses of ritual behavior on a major scale can be seen at Nabta in what must have been a regional ceremonial center where various groups gathered each year to celebrate the coming of the life-giving rains. A calendar circle of sandstone slabs, arranged like a miniature Stonehenge, was created to sight the sunrise at the summer solstice, the all-important day when the rainy season began. The desert dwellers also constructed lines of megaliths, large standing stones, some up to 2.5 m high, that were brought from quarries at least a kilometer away. Radiating out from a central point, these stones were set up in three groups, possibly aligned with stars, such as Sothis and Orion, which were later to have a prominent position in Egyptian cosmology.

This ceremonial center also included eight large stone mounds, or tumuli, that contained the remains of sacrificial cattle, as well as thirty enigmatic 'complex structures' composed of a large ring of upright stones surrounding a central slab. These structures were built above deep pits. Buried in one of them was a carefully shaped stone: with smooth sides and sharp edges, it may well be Egypt's earliest sculpture.

The size of these stones, some of which weighed several tons, shows that a considerable amount of muscle, time, and skill was invested in the creation of these monuments. They also indicate the presence of leaders who controlled human resources, and, more

70 top left
Weighing about four tons, this statue, perhaps of a stylized cow, was found buried beneath a stone structure at Nabta Playa. With its sharp edges and two carefully smoothed faces, it is an impressive piece of stone working and may mark the very beginnings of the Egyptian fascination with the manipulation of large stone.

70 bottom left
The purpose of the 'complex structures' at Nabta is obscure. Were they shrines, memorials to those who died elsewhere, cenotaphs for spirits, or used for astronomical observations? Whatever the case, considerable effort was invested in quarrying and positioning the large, originally upright stones used to create the ensemble.

Predynastic ▲ *Period*

importantly, felt the need to create public architecture to ensure the running of their cosmos in a way perhaps not far different from the builders of massive pyramids two thousand years later.

It is unlikely that these surprisingly early developments occurred in a cultural vacuum. The recent discovery of the burials at Nabta, some richly endowed with pottery, jewelry, and stone palettes, similar to those belonging to the earliest settled inhabitants in the Nile Valley, leaves little doubt that these desert pastoralists were in contact with their neighbors. What form their interaction took as the deteriorating climate made the desert uninhabitable is still unknown. When we first meet those settled along the Nile, they have already melded the various influences, and perhaps immigrants, from all around them into a culture distinctly their own.

In the Delta of Lower Egypt, different influences and different climatic conditions led to the creation of a culture with distinct pottery, architecture, and beliefs, suggesting that the ancient conception of Egypt as the 'Two Lands' was based on more than geography and a love of symmetry. Evidence for the Delta religion is scanty and limited mainly to the intriguing clay head found in the settlement of Merimde in the Western Delta. However, it is clear from the few cemeteries that have been found that in the north of Egypt the afterlife did not require extensive and lavish grave goods—a few pots and a shell would do. As a result, it is difficult to distinguish levels of wealth and form an idea of Delta society. On the other hand, along the Nile Valley in Upper Egypt, the inhabitants were already strong subscribers to the belief that the dead could and should take with them both their wealth and their status. The conspicuous consumption evident in the rich graves of the elite minority shows that by 4000 BC society had already divided into the rulers and the ruled. This is graphically illustrated on a decorated pot recently discovered by the German expedition at Abydos, which shows the large and ornately attired ruler threatening groups of smaller bound captives with a deadly mace. This is the earliest example of the smiting of the enemy, a long-running theme in Egyptian art, perhaps best known from the famous Palette of Narmer.

When the Palette of Narmer was discovered in 1897 in the midst of the sleepy hamlet at Hierakonpolis, it caused an immediate sensation. An icon of the birth of Egyptian civilization, it depicts a battle, if not the definitive one, in the war to unify the Two Lands, led by Narmer, who is generally considered to be the first king of the First Dynasty. This magnificent object, found along with hundreds of other early temple furnishings, put Hierakonpolis on the map as a capital of early Egypt. The discovery of the exquisite golden head of the falcon god Horus and the remarkable copper statues of King Pepy of the Old Kingdom attest to the long and continued veneration of the site and its patron god, Horus.

70 bottom right
The calendar circle at Nabta Playa, less than 4 m in diameter, is the oldest solar calendar ever found. Four pairs of taller and narrower slabs form two sets of gates. One set is aligned north-south, while the other sights the position of the rising sun on the summer solstice of 6000 years ago.

71 left
Investigations at Nabta Playa provide evidence for the development of a Neolithic way of life based on cattle raising and the collection of wild and cultivated grasses. Sorghum and millet were ground into flour with grinding stones like these and then cooked as porridge with milk or blood.

71 right
Originally mounted on a staff or a wooden body, this expressive clay head from the Delta site of Merimde is one of the oldest human representations from Egypt. Feathers were placed in the small holes around the face and head to provide hair and a beard. Now in the Egyptian Museum, Cairo.

However, an understanding of the true significance of the site would have to wait another seventy years until the Hierakonpolis Expedition under the direction of Walter Fairservis and Michael Hoffman began investigations not in the temple mound, but in the desert behind it. Here, stretching for over four kilometers, they found the largest Predynastic settlement still extant along the Nile, clearly a regional center of power and capital of an early kingdom, but one at its peak some five-hundred years before Narmer was born. By 3600 BC it was already a vibrant, bustling, and sophisticated town and in it can be seen the first beginnings of many aspects that were to come to typify Egyptian civilization. Hierakonpolis is still preserved as a unit containing all the component parts that made up a city: houses, cemeteries, temples, industrial zones, administrative buildings, trash mounds and more, and can tell us more about developments in this formative period than any other place.

Excavation and survey at selected locations across this vast site provide a snapshot of life at this time. In the cliffs on the outskirts of town, special craftsmen created the elegant black-topped red ware, arguably some of the most beautiful pottery Egypt ever produced, for home use and the burgeoning funerary needs. Other potters fashioned everyday cooking wares for their neighborhood clientele. It is due to the hazards of this trade that a considerable portion of one house and workshop could be examined. Substantial remains of houses from any phase within the Predynastic Period are rare, and it is thanks to a stray spark from the nearby pottery kiln that the potter's rectangular, semi-subterranean dwelling was burned to the ground, thereby ensuring its fine preservation including charred roof beams and the cooking hearth. The house, roughly 3.5 x 4 meters in size, had walls originally composed of mud-coated wattle and daub reinforced with the oldest mud bricks in Egypt still in place.

The process of brewing seems to have been more specialized, and appears on a far larger scale. Evidence for Egypt's first industrial-scale brewery comes in the form of huge pottery vats in which the mash was brewed. The residue on the interior of the vats has made it possible to reconstruct the recipe for this nutritious, if only mildly alcoholic beer. It was wheat-based with dates and grapes added to provide the sugars necessary for fermentation. Nearby, another pottery kiln manufactured standardized jars in which to package it. It is estimated that the eight vats uncovered in this brewery could produce about 300 gallons of beer a day, an amount far in excess of one family's needs. In fact, at that rate, it could supply a daily ration

72 left
Four gigantic post holes once held the tall posts that formed the façade of the monumental shrine in the Predynastic temple at Hierakonpolis. Composed of timber and matting, its design and style can be compared to buildings at the Step Pyramid complex where such structures were imitated in stone.

72 right
A large oval courtyard, post holes, and trenches are all that remain of the Predynastic temple at Hierakonpolis, but the nature of the finds leaves no doubt that it was an early ceremonial complex that anticipates the royal ritual precincts of the Early Dynastic Period, especially the heb-sed *complex of Djoser at Saqqara.*

73 left
Some of the most elegant pottery ever produced in Egypt was made during the Predynastic Period by specialists who may have traveled throughout the Nile Valley plying their trade. Such fine pottery was used as the 'fine china' in the home and in the grave.

73 right
Large vats coated with a blackened residue are the remnants of Egypt's earliest industrial-scale brewery. Capable of producing a daily ration of beer for over 200 people, it may be evidence of a royal estate at Hierakonpolis already at 3500 BC.

for over two hundred people, and so far, only a small fraction of this quarter has been investigated. Thus, much of Hierakonpolis's greatness may stem from this early organization of the redistributive economy, as known in Pharaonic times, in which agricultural produce was centrally collected and then distributed, perhaps as wages. It is too early to know if this brewery was part of a 'royal' estate or whether this pooling of resources developed voluntarily as a hedge against drought years or the increasingly drier climate, since the fuel necessary to sustain the heat was probably the most expensive part of the brewing process. Whatever the case, the control of the food supply is certainly a key step in the concentration of power in a small number of hands, and there can be no better way to cement that power than by appeal to the gods.

Located in the center of the Predynastic town, an extensive temple complex was discovered in 1985. Although little remains above ground to attest to its former importance, both the scale and the nature of the finds indicate that the complex was an early ceremonial center. Excavations have revealed a large, oval courtyard surrounded by wooden and mud-brick walls. Four enormous post holes on the west side of the court once held tall wooden columns that formed the façade of a monumental building, no doubt a main shrine composed of mats and poles. Shallow furrows in the soil indicate that the rear part of this building had three chambers, as in later temples. The preserved remains accord well with Early Dynastic representations of the archetypal shrine of Upper Egypt, which portray a vaulted structure composed of posts and lattice work shaped in the silhouette of a crouching animal complete with tail and horns. The home of the great shrine of the Upper Egyptian crown was traditionally believed to be at Hierakonpolis, and it is possible that this complex may indeed be that very shrine. Later destined to be recreated in stone at the Step Pyramid complex at Saqqara, it remained a prototype for temple architecture for millennia to come.

It is not just the architectural remains that suggest that this is a cultic center. Finds from the courtyard indicate lavish ceremonies took place here, during which new-born sheep or goats were offered, perhaps as 'first fruits.' Sacrifices also included gazelles, crocodiles, and hippopotami—large and dangerous wild fauna later identified with the chaotic elements of the universe that temples were built to control. Fine stone vessels and other offerings were produced in a series of workshops just beyond the temple walls, showing that the association of craftsmen and temples is not a new feature in dynastic Egypt.

Predynastic Period

Hierakonpolis is one of the few sites at which widely separated and distinct cemeteries for the different segments of society have been found. Along the southern side of the site stretches the large cemetery of the working class, who were buried in mat-lined pits with what grave goods they could afford, rarely more than a pot or two. Nevertheless, they were dressed in their best, as the evidence of henna dyes to cover gray hair and the use of hair extensions and even a sheep-skin toupée make clear. The discovery of resins, and in a few cases linen wrappings around the head, hands, and some internal organs, indicates a growing concern with the preservation of the body and may represent the first steps in the development of artificial mummification.

On the other side of town, back along the main wadi that provided seasonal water to the town, lay the cemetery of the elite. The wealth of these elite burials is evident in the quality of objects still to be found within their highly plundered graves—fine flints, some expertly knapped into animal form; exotic materials like obsidian from Ethiopia; ivory figurines; and, unique to this cemetery, expressive clay masks. Curved to fit over the human head, they were attached by means of thongs passed through the holes along the side. They are probably funerary masks, Egypt's earliest, and stand at the beginning of a long tradition whose origin had previously been unknown.

Not satisfied with taking a wide array of precious and expertly fashioned materials with them to the grave, the most important among the elite were also accompanied by an entourage of human and animal companions, including exotic elephants, wild cattle, baboons, wild cats, hippopotami, and even a collection of seashells. The purpose of these companions is not entirely clear. Nevertheless this practice reveals the vast wealth and power of these individuals; a status also displayed in the size and elaborate construction of their graves.

Recent excavation in Hierakonpolis by Barbara Adams has uncovered the largest tomb yet known from the period, dating to about 3600 BC. Measuring over three meters wide and five meters long, it was set within the earliest funerary complex ever discovered. One and possibly two large wooden fences surround the tomb, creating a rectangular enclosure that forms the prototype for later funerary architecture constructed in mud brick on a massive scale at Abydos. Immediately above the tomb, stout wooden beams are all that remain of the substantial structure marking the spot. A small, square building along the eastern side, however, indicates that service to the ruler did not end with his death. These fragments of Egypt's first life-size human sculpture, including a beautifully carved nose and ear, found within and around this structure suggest that the tomb was already equipped with a shrine or *serdab* to serve as a focal point for offerings and ceremonial activities under the recipient's eternal gaze. Thus, long before the pyramid, the funerary cult of the ruler was a well-established feature of society.

Some idea of the elaborate ceremonies surrounding the death of a Predynastic king can be gleaned from the decorated walls of the 'Painted Tomb,' also from Hierakonpolis. The paintings depict an extensive funerary flotilla, mourners and dancers, the capture and slaughter of animals, and the smiting of enemies—motifs that were to become standard parts of royal and non-royal funerary symbolism throughout dynastic history. However, by the time this tomb was painted at about 3300 BC, the power and status of Hierakonpolis was about to change. From a variety of sources we know that there were at least three main centers of power in Predynastic Upper Egypt (Hierakonpolis, Nagada, and Abydos), along with an untold number of others in Lower Egypt. At the close of the Predynastic Period, in a time now called Dynasty 0, the political position of Hierakonpolis gradually began to diminish for unknown reasons. The bellicose nature of many of the documents of this period, such as the Battlefield Palette, makes it clear that warfare was an important aspect, both literally and symbolically, of the acquisition and retention of power. Environmental and geographical factors, however, as well as a good deal of politics and diplomacy, certainly also played a role.

Carved onto a rock high in the desert behind ancient Thebes at a place called Gebel Tjauty, an elaborate scene recently discovered by John and Deborah Darnell provides new evidence for this turbulent time. The tableau depicts a triumphal procession and may well celebrate the conquest of Naqada by a coalition of rulers from Abydos and Hierakonpolis, who used the desert roads to outflank their enemy. Once Naqada was out of the way and Upper Egypt united, the stage was now set to take control of Lower Egypt, although archaeological evidence for this is limited to the replacement of the distinct Delta culture with Upper Egyptian forms of architecture, pottery, and religion.

In whatever way the unification of the Two Lands was actually achieved, it was an event etched permanently on the Egyptian psyche. The coronation of every pharaoh involved the ritual reenactment of the unification. Although the names may have been lost in the mists of time, the legacy of very real ancestors spanning back over two millennia was never forgotten. The foundation laid in the Predynastic Period would remain at the heart of Egyptian civilization and forms the base for its future development.

74

The Hunters Palette, now at the British Museum, is among the earliest of the elaborately-carved ceremonial palettes that were made as dedications to the gods. Warriors outfitted with the gear and weapons of the late Predynastic Period hunt wild animals, especially lions. This pursuit of the lion, a dangerous but empowering act, will become a symbol of the victorious pharaoh.

75

This clay mask, now in the Egyptian Museum in Cairo, may be the earliest actual funerary mask in Egypt and is one of at least four found in the elite cemetery at Hierakonpolis. Funerary masks were intended to transform the deceased into a glorified spirit in the afterlife, a belief that appears to have lasted over 4000 years.

The Tombs of the First and Second Dynasties at Abydos and Saqqara

by Günter Dreyer

After the unification of Upper and Lower Egypt, the royal residence was established at Memphis, but following tradition of their Predynastic ancestors, the kings of the First Dynasty were still buried at Abydos. The sequence of their rule is shown on seal impressions from the tombs of Den and Qa'a.

The Second Dynasty is still one of the most obscure periods in Egyptian history. The Horus-names (so-called because the king's name is shown inside a representation of a *serekh* surmounted by a falcon) of the first three kings—Hetepsekhemwy, Raneb, and Ninetjer—are incised on a statue of a priest found at Mit Rahina. Seal impressions of

Hetepsekhemwy from the tomb of Qa'a at Abydos prove that he was responsible for the burial of the last king of the First Dynasty and that there was no break between the two dynasties, although Hetepsekhemwy was the first king to be buried at Saqqara. During the later part of the Second Dynasty, the unity of Upper and Lower Egypt was temporarily broken and the last two kings, Peribsen and Khasekhemwy, built their tombs at Abydos. Inscriptions on statues of Khasekhem (later Khasekhemwy) tell of the suppression of an uprising in Lower Egypt. Khasekhemwy was succeeded by Netjerikhet (also called Djoser), who shifted the royal burial place back to Saqqara.

76

Hetepdief, kneeling, with a curly wig and a short skirt has his name is written on the base of the statue. On his right shoulder the names of the Horus-names of first three kings of the Second Dynasty are carved: Hetepsekhemwy, Raneb, and Ninetjer. He probably served in the cult of these kings during the Third Dynasty.

77 top

An impression of an earlier version of the seal from the time of Den mentions Narmer, Den and also Den's mother Merneith, omitted in the later edition. This impression was discovered at the staircase of Den's tomb.

77 bottom

The text of the reconstructed cylinder seal gives the names of the jackal god of the necropolis, Khentiamentiu (the First of the Westerners, i.e. the dead) and the kings buried at Umm al-Qa'ab in reverse chronological order (from left to right): Qa'a, Semerkhet, Anedjib, Den, Djet, Djer, Aha, and Narmer. Impressions of this seal were found at the tomb of Qa'a on lumps of clay used as stoppers of boxes and other containers.

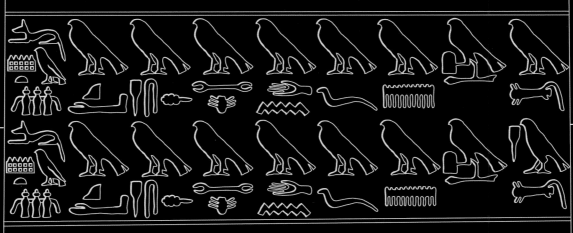

Horus-name of Djet on a stela (now in the Louvre) from his tomb at Abydos. The stela shows the façade of the royal palace, the Horus-falcon as title of the king, and his name-snake.

78 top and center left

These photographs show the subsidiary graves and the main chambers of Aha's tomb. The tomb of Aha/Menes, the first king of the First Dynasty, is built on a much larger scale than those of his predecessors. For the first time it comprises rows of subsidiary burials. Around the chambers, bones of young people were found, probably they were killed to serve the king in his afterlife. The large chambers contained wooden shrines, the king probably was buried in the middle one.

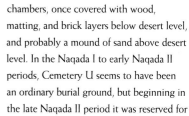

THE ROYAL TOMBS OF THE FIRST DYNASTY AT ABYDOS

The archaic royal necropolis of Abydos, called Umm al-Qa'ab (Arabic for 'mother of pots'), is located in the desert about 1.5 km from the cultivated land in front of impressive limestone cliffs and to the east of a large wadi. This wadi ends near the ancient settlement area and beside the great funerary enclosures of the First and Second Dynasties.

The cemeteries were first excavated by E. Amélineau in 1895–98 and again by W.M.F. Petrie in 1899–1901, who revealed eight large complexes from the First Dynasty, two from the Second Dynasty, and a few Predynastic tombs. Petrie also excavated at the large enclosures which are constituent parts of these funerary installations. Since 1973, the German Institute of Archaeology has been re-examining the entire cemetery, and the enclosures are under re-investigation by an American mission from Pennsylvania State University and Yale University.

The necropolis seems to have developed along the course of the wadi from north to south and consists of three parts:

1. Cemetery U: tombs from the Naqada I period and elite tombs of the late Predynastic period to the north;

2. Cemetery B: royal tombs of Dynasty Zero and the early First Dynasty in the middle part of the cemetery;

3. Tomb complexes of six kings and one queen of the First Dynasty and two kings of the Second Dynasty to the south.

Apart from the earliest Predynastic burials in simple pits and some graves with wood linings, the smaller as well as the very large tombs are rectangular brick-lined chambers, once covered with wood, matting, and brick layers below desert level, and probably a mound of sand above desert level. In the Naqada I to early Naqada II periods, Cemetery U seems to have been an ordinary burial ground, but beginning in the late Naqada II period it was reserved for the elite only. The large single-chamber tombs and multiple-chamber tombs are probably to be ascribed to chieftains and a sequence of rulers preceeding the kings of Dynasty Zero, who were buried in Cemetery B.

Of particular importance is the large tomb called U-j, discovered in 1988. According to Carbon-14 samples it dates to approximately 150 years before the First Dynasty. It is divided into twelve chambers and measures 9.10 x 7.30 m; the brick lining has a depth of 1.55 m, and its top layer lies about 0.50 m below desert level. The tomb was built in two stages. Originally there were nine small chambers to the east of the large burial chamber, probably modeled on a house with a central hall or court. Two long chambers were later added to the south. All chambers are connected to one or two of their neighboring chambers by small slits.

Although robbed in antiquity and partly excavated by Amélineau, the tomb still contained a lot of the funerary equipment: many ivory and bone objects, about 150 small labels with short inscriptions, large amounts of different kinds of Egyptian pottery, and more than 200 wine jars imported from Canaan/Palestine. Inside the burial chamber, traces of a wooden shrine and a complete crook-scepter made of ivory were found, leaving no doubt that the owner of the tomb was a ruler.

The small labels, incised with numbers or up to four hieroglyphic signs, show writing at a rather developed stage. The numbers seem to indicate sizes of pieces of cloth, the signs presumably the provenance of

78 bottom

Small labels of bone and ivory with early hieroglyphs from tomb U-j were fixed to containers to indicate the origin of various commodities. The incised signs are the earliest examples of hieroglyphic writing.
The stork and the chair represent the phonetic values ba + st, the name of a city (Basta) in the delta. The tree and the animal indicate the provenance from an agricultural estate (tree) founded by a ruler, whose name was dog/jackal.

79 bottom left

A reconstruction drawing of a Predynastic palace. According to the ground plan of U-j, the most elaborate tomb of the Predynastic Period, a palace of a Predynastic ruler consisted of an entrance room, a central hall with a higher roof, store chambers to the left, and private apartments in the rear part.
A servant's room or kitchen was accessible via a separate entrance.

different goods. Some of them are readable (with phonetic values), mentioning administrative institutions, royal estates, or localities such as Buto and Bubastis in the Delta. Many of the wavy-handled pots are also 'inscribed' with one or two large signs in black ink. Most frequent is a scorpion, sometimes together with a plant. This is probably to be read as "estate (plantation) of Scorpion." Considering the high frequency of pots with this indication of origin, it can be concluded that a king named Scorpion was buried in the tomb.

In the later Predynastic tombs the element of a model house is missing. The reason could be that it was separated from the tomb and built somewhere else. The most likely place would be the area of the funerary enclosures, and the small brick buildings in the southwestern corner of the enclosures of Khasekhemwy and Peribsen may originate from such model houses.

Cemetery B comprises three double-chamber tombs of the last rulers of Dynasty 0: Iryhor (B 1/2), Ka (7/9), Narmer (17/18), as well as the tomb complexes of the first two kings of the First Dynasty, Aha (B 10/15/19 + 16), and the ephemeral Athotis (B 40/50).

Whereas the modest double-chamber tombs still belong to the predynastic tradition of tomb building, the complex of Aha with three very large chambers and rows of subsidiary burials, marks the transition to monumental architecture, reflecting the beginning of a new era with the unification of Upper and Lower Egypt under one ruler.

The chambers measure about 7.50 x 4.50 m and have a depth of about 3.60 m, and each contained a large wooden shrine supported by wooden posts. The king was probably buried in the middle chamber (B 15), the roof of which seems to have been slightly vaulted while the others are flat. This feature is quite important, and may be understood as a first attempt to have a 'back-up copy' of the traditional mound of sand above the burial, which—originally a marker only—was considered to

represent the primeval mound of creation.

Around the rows of subsidiary chambers (B 16), many human bones were found, most of them from young males who died at about twenty years of age, with none older than twenty-five, meaning they must have been killed when the king was buried. Near the long easternmost chamber, the bones of at least seven young lions were collected; obviously the king wanted to enjoy hunting in his afterlife.

The seven tomb complexes of Djer, Djet, Queen Merneith, Den, Anedjib, Semerkhet, and Qa'a of the First Dynasty generally have the same layout: a large royal burial chamber surrounded by magazines and up to more than 200 subsidiary burial chambers. The royal chambers all contained a large wooden shrine (like U-j and B 10/15/19). From the time of Den, a staircase leads into the king's chamber, which was blocked after the burial. This innovation allowed the roof (and superstructure) to be built before the funeral took place.

From Djer to Den, the subsidiary burial chambers are arranged in separate rows around the royal chamber; only in Semerkhet's and Qa'a's complexes are they attached to it. Except for two high officials (in subsidiary burial chambers at the tombs of Den and Qa'a) who perhaps died at the same time as the king, the subsidiary burials are of lower-ranking people (men, women, dwarves), as well as dogs. In all probability they were killed (see description of Aha's tomb above) to serve the king in his afterlife. This custom ceased at the end of the First Dynasty.

At each tomb, two large stelae indicated the owner's name. There were also small stelae for the occupants of the subsidiary chambers, including those of the dogs. Unfortunately, none of the royal or private stelae were found *in situ*, so their original position (perhaps on top of the chambers?) is uncertain.

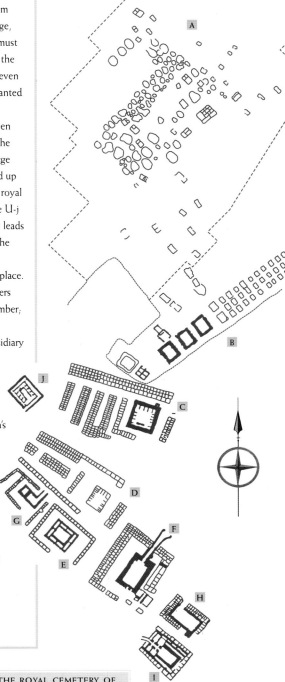

THE ROYAL CEMETERY OF ABYDOS: UMM AL-QA'AB

A CEMETERY U, PREDYNASTIC
B AHA, FIRST DYNASTY
C DJER, FIRST DYNASTY (OSIRIS)
D DJET, FIRST DYNASTY
E QUEEN MERNEITH, FIRST DYN.
F DEN, FIRST DYNASTY
G ANEDJIB, FIRST DYNASTY
H SEMERKHET, FIRST DYNASTY
I QA'A, FIRST DYNASTY
J PERIBSEN, SECOND DYNASTY
K KHASEKHEMWY, SECOND DYNASTY

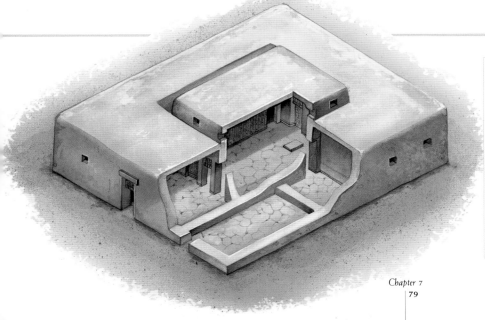

Tombs of the First and Second Dynasties

Since the Middle Kingdom, the tomb of Djer was regarded as the tomb of the god Osiris. Here an Osiris bed made of black granite is depicted, from the Egyptian Museum, Cairo. King Khendjer (Thirteenth Dynasty) equipped the burial chamber with a sculpture showing the procreation of Horus by Osiris and Isis (as a sparrow-hawk).

81 top and bottom left
The subsidiary burials were all marked by small stelae with the occupant's name and a sign indicating whether a man, woman, dwarf (bottom), or dog (top) was buried in the chamber.

The largest tomb complex is that of Djer, which covers an area of 70 x 40 m and comprises more than 200 subsidiary chambers in single, double, and triple rows. A small single chamber attached to the king's chamber near the southeast corner perhaps served for a (buried) guard. The wooden shrine in the central chamber, which has a depth of about 2.60 m, was supported by cross walls of store rooms to the north, east, and south. During the Middle Kingdom the tomb was converted into a cenotaph of Osiris with a staircase leading into it. In the chamber, an Osiris-bier (with erased inscription of Khendjer, Thirteenth Dynasty) was found by Amélineau. Behind the staircase, Petrie discovered an arm with some precious bracelets, which in all probability belonged to the original burial and had been hidden by robbers.

No remains of superstructures have been found, but it is likely that the royal chambers were covered by a mound of sand. On top of the massive brick lining of the royal chamber of Djet's tomb, Petrie revealed the remains of a "retaining wall for sand covering" above the roofing beams, plastered on the outside but rough on the inside. This artificial tumulus was generally considered to be a superstructure, but a re-examination in 1985 has shown that it was built within the tomb pit below desert level. It may be explained (as in the tomb of Aha above) as a 'back-up' of the usual tumulus above a tomb, linked with the religious belief in the primeval mound of creation. Inside the tomb it guaranteed resurrection of the dead.

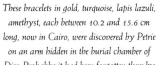

81 center
These bracelets in gold, turquoise, lapis lazuli, amethyst, each between 10.2 and 15.6 cm long, now in Cairo, were discovered by Petrie on an arm hidden in the burial chamber of Djer. Probably it had been forgotten there by robbers. In all likelihood, the arm belonged to the mummy of the king, as one of the bracelets consists of plaquettes showing the Horus-falcon on the façade of the royal palace.

81 bottom right
At each royal tomb there were two large stelae with the name of the owner. Merneith ('beloved of Neith'), the mother of King Den, acted as regent when he was still a minor. Her role as ruler entitled her to build a tomb at Umm al-Qa'ab. Now in the Egyptian Museum, Cairo.

| A | CHAMBER WITH A STATUE OF THE KING | C | SUBSIDIARY BURIALS |
| B | STAIRCASE | D | COURT |

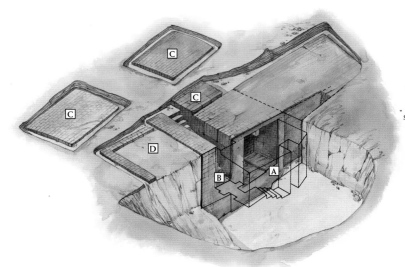

82-83
The tomb complex of Den, here looking west, covers an area of 40 x 55 m. The central burial chamber of the king is surrounded by 144 subsidiary graves for servants and dogs and three storage chambers for wine jars.

83 top
Remains of wood on the floor of the burial chamber of the tomb of Qa'a indicate the position of a large shrine. The staircase was blocked by a portcullis stone.

The tomb of Den is the most elaborate of the First Dynasty tombs at Umm al-Qa'ab. The king's chamber measures 9 x 15 m and has a depth of about 6 m; its floor had been paved with slabs of red and black granite, the earliest known use of stone on a large scale. The walls were covered by reed matting. Based on impressions and post holes in a layer of bricks on the stone pavement, and holes for fixing beams in the walls, the size of the wooden shrine in this chamber was 24 x 12 x 6 cubits. Around this shrine, many stone vessels and imported Canaanite pottery were piled up. The king's chamber was accessible from the east by a long descending stairway. There were wooden doors midway down the staircase and at the chamber's entrance, which was blocked by a portcullis.

The tomb is of special interest because of an annex to the southwest, which can be explained as a *serdab* (statue chamber). In all probability, the small staircase to this annex was to serve as an exit for the rising king represented by his statue. The idea of such a way out is present in all the other First Dynasty tombs since Djer. There is always a gap in the

surrounding rows of subsidiary tombs near the southeastern corner and all these 'potential exits' point toward the impressive wadi opening in the cliffs behind the cemetery. This seems to have been regarded as the entrance to the other world, the tombs being 'through stations' on the way there.

From their construction, the tombs were plundered time and again. A passage in the "Instruction for Merikare" may refer to a destruction of the royal tombs at Abydos during the First Intermediate period. In fact, most of the First Dynasty tombs show traces of immense fires. Although partly destroyed and deprived of most of their contents, the tombs and the remaining objects, including much inscribed material, are a major source for the archaic period.

Beginning in the Middle Kingdom, the site gained new importance through being associated with the cult of Osiris, who was believed to have been buried

there. It thus became the most sacred place in Egypt. During the New Kingdom and the Late Period, thousands of pilgrims left large amounts of offering pottery, mostly small bowls (in Arabic, *qa'ab*, hence the modern name Umm al-Qa'ab). Amélineau estimated the total number of pots to be about eight million.

Several indications point to excavations already occurring during the Twelfth Dynasty, probably in order to identify the burial place of Osiris. In Qa'a's tomb some Middle Kingdom pottery was found on the floor of the burial chamber and a staircase made of large bricks was built over the remaining lower part of the portcullis stone. The entrance to the royal chamber in Den's tomb is also partly restored in large (unburnt) bricks and the entire staircase shows traces of a secondary white wash. The conversion of Djer's tomb into a cenotaph of Osiris may have taken place at the same time.

83 bottom
Such inscribed labels like these, found in the tomb of Qa'a by the German excavation team, were attached to oil containers indicating the date of the delivery, quality, amount, origin, and the name of an official. The date is given by the name of the year which mentions important events.

PLAN OF THE TOMB OF DEN

A   *KING'S CHAMBER*
B   *MAIN STAIRCASE*
C   *SUBSIDIARY GRAVES*
D   *STORAGE CHAMBERS S 8, 11, 12*
E   *ANNEX WITH STATUE*
F   *CHAMBER S 4*

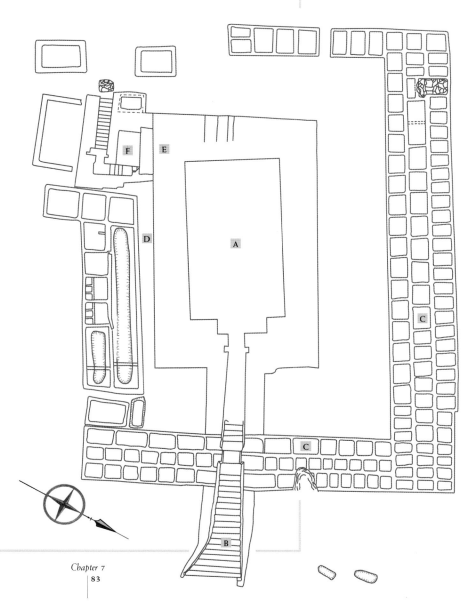

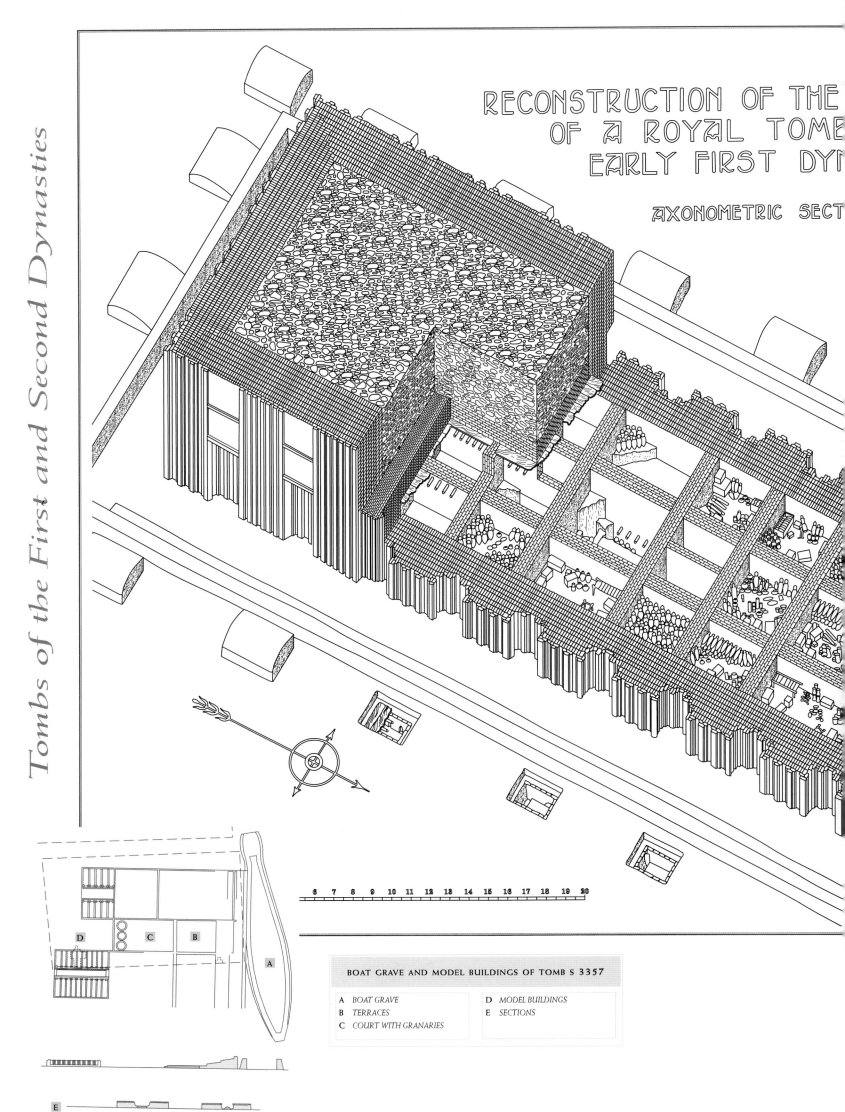

RECONSTRUCTION OF THE
OF A ROYAL TOMB
EARLY FIRST DYN

AXONOMETRIC SECT

6 7 8 9 10 11 12 13 14 15 16 17 18 19 20

BOAT GRAVE AND MODEL BUILDINGS OF TOMB S 3357

A BOAT GRAVE
B TERRACES
C COURT WITH GRANARIES

D MODEL BUILDINGS
E SECTIONS

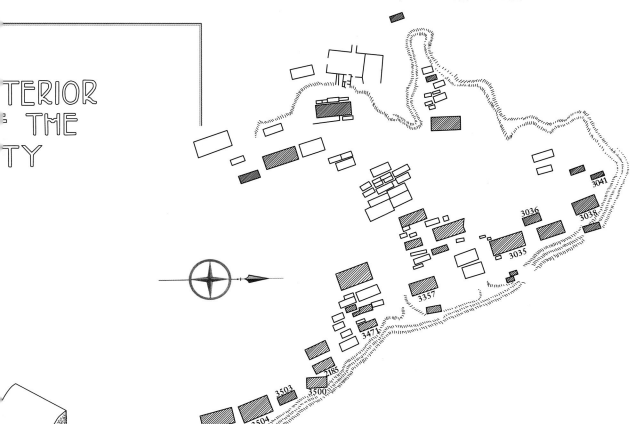

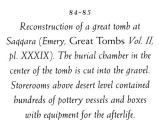

84–85
Reconstruction of a great tomb at Saqqara (Emery, Great Tombs *Vol. II, pl. XXXIX). The burial chamber in the center of the tomb is cut into the gravel. Storerooms above desert level contained hundreds of pottery vessels and boxes with equipment for the afterlife.*

EMERY'S EXCAVATION OF THE GREAT TOMBS AT SAQQARA

The archaic necropolis of Saqqara is located on an escarpment of the Western Desert southwest of the modern village of Abusir. Between 1936 and 1956, at the edge of the cliff overlooking the ancient site of Memphis, W. B. Emery revealed a series of approximately fifteen large tombs of the First Dynasty, each with impressive rectangular superstructures. The exterior façades of these *mastabas* (*mastaba* is an Arabic word meaning bench) had recessed niches on all four sides, similar to the palace façade hieroglyph representing the king's Horus name on the stelae of Djet. This architectural feature demonstrates that the tomb was regarded as a palace where the dead were believed to dwell. The size of the *mastabas* range from 24 to 57 m (length) by 12 to 26 m (width); some are preserved up to a height of 2.5 m, however, their original height was estimated to be about 3 to 5 m.

The substructures cut into the gravel and/or rock show many variations, but in general they consist of a large rectangular pit with brick lining, a single burial chamber or a burial chamber and magazines. The burial chambers probably each contained a large wooden shrine. Since the time of Den the substructure was accessible by a staircase similar to those which occurs at Abydos at the same time. After the funeral the passage was blocked with one or more portcullis stones. Some tombs are surrounded by enclosure walls and a few have subsidiary burials and various other structures associated with them.

The oldest *mastaba* (S 3357) dates to the reign of Aha. The superstructure has an overall measurement of 48.2 x 22 m and is subdivided into twenty-seven magazines for funerary equipment such as wine jars, food vessels, and so on. Below ground level are five compartments in a shallow brick-lined pit, roofed with timber. The middle chamber probably contained the burial, while the others held the most important possessions of the dead person. About 35 meters to the north of the double enclosure wall, the remains of a wooden boat were found in a large boat-shaped pit with a brick lining. This boat, like those discovered near the pyramids, was to be used by the owner in the afterlife. Between the *mastaba* and boat grave were two groups of small, bench-like false buildings made of rubble and cased with mud plaster, and two model terraces adjoining the boat pit and several courts, one of which had three round structures, perhaps granaries. Whether these installations are to be regarded as a model estate (Emery), a quay or dock (Lehner), or an offering place, including a slaughterhouse (Stadelmann) is not quite clear, but somehow they must have served for food supply.

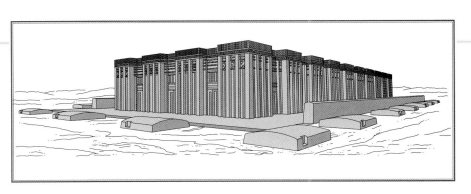

Tombs of the First and Second Dynasties

The importance of provisions for eternal life is indicated at Tomb 3504, which dates from the time of Djet. Hundreds of clay ox heads with real horns are attached on the bench of the façade. Such heads or skulls, or other offerings, have been found at several *mastabas*, especially in the broader niches, which—like the later false doors—were contact points between the living and the netherworld.

Like the tombs of Abydos, some of the *mastabas* at Saqqara have subsidiary burials, but their number is much smaller and they occur only from the time of Djer to Qa'a. At Tomb S 3504 sixty-two graves for servants with offerings are arranged in rows to the east, south, and west. In some cases the superstructures, low brick *mastabas* with a convex top, have survived. At Tomb S 3500 (reign of Qa'a) the superstructures are higher, and built with the earliest known brick vaults. On one side is a small false door niche.

Five large tombs can be dated to the reign of Den, which seems to have been the culmination of the First Dynasty. One of them (S 3035), which belonged to the most important official, the chancellor Hemaka, provided many important finds: flint implements, ivory objects, weapons, stone vessels, beautifully carved disks, and the first preserved roll of papyrus.

In some *mastabas*, remains of a hidden brick-cased tumulus of sand and rubble over the burial pit were recovered and it is quite likely that most, if not all tombs, contained such a feature, which is also an integral part of the Abydos tombs (see above).

At Tomb S 3038 (reign of Anedjib) the tumulus has a stepped form, similar to the Step Pyramid of Netjerikhet/Djoser. This tumulus was covered by gravel within the niched façade, but two staircases from the north and south allowed access to the top.

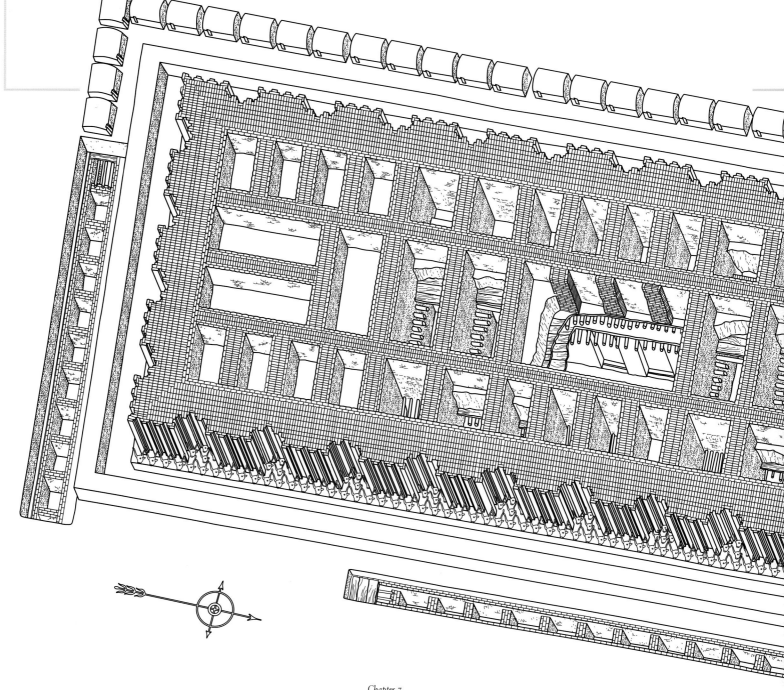

The latest of the great tombs (S 3505) dates from the reign of Qa'a. On the niched superstructure, colored frescoes were preserved, showing geometric patterns imitating matting. According to a stela found near a niche in the eastern façade, it belonged to a high official called Merka.

Within the massive enclosure wall, a remarkable funerary temple composed of several rooms and corridors is associated with the tomb on its north side. The remains of two large wooden statues were found there; most likely they represented Merka.

Until the discovery of these large *mastabas* no one doubted that the tombs at Abydos were the actual burial places of the early kings. Impressed by the size of the Saqqara superstructures, however, Emery suggested that the kings in fact were buried there, the smaller Abydos tombs being cenotaphs only.

Despite the discrepancy between the number of tombs at Saqqara, which considerably exceeds the number of kings (e.g. five tombs from the time of Den but none from that of Semerkhet), this does not account for the large enclosures at Abydos, situated some distance away from the tombs at the end of the wadi, which are part of the funerary installations. Furthermore, the pottery and seal impressions from at least some of the Abydos tombs indicate that the equipment is of a later date than their Saqqara counterparts, which are probably the tombs of high officials (and possibly queens) who died earlier than their respective kings. The much larger number of subsidiary burials, the presence of royal stelae (missing at Saqqara), the skeletal remains in the tombs of Djer and Khasekhemwy, and last but not least, the fact that the ancient Egyptians thought Osiris had been buried at Abydos, also support the theory of Abydos being the true burial place of the pharaohs.

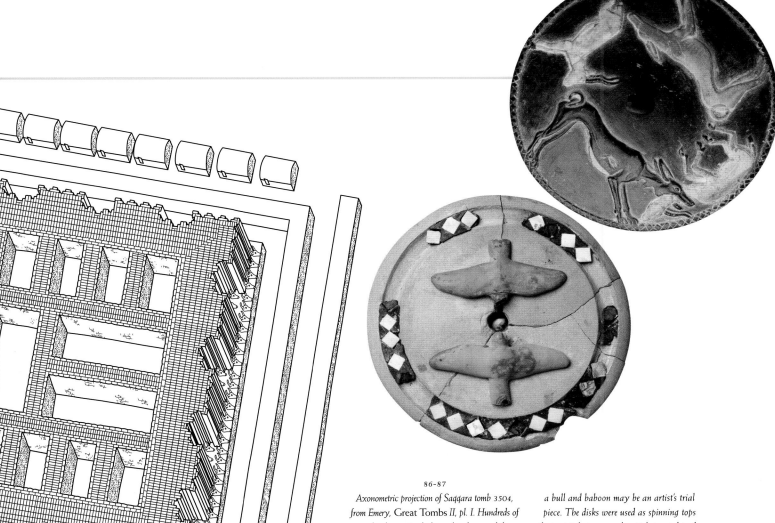

86-87
Axonometric projection of Saqqara tomb 3504, from Emery, Great Tombs II, *pl. I. Hundreds of ox heads are attached on a bench around the superstructure, which is subdivided into 46 storage chambers. The tomb is surrounded by a wall and 62 small subsidiary burials of servants.*

87 *top and bottom right*
The tomb of Hemaka, chancellor during the time of Den, was rich in various finds. The limestone ostracon (top) bearing a painting of a bull and baboon may be an artist's trial piece. The disks were used as spinning tops that rotated via a wooden stick inserted in the central hole. The one of black steatite inlaid in pink veined alabaster shows a dog hunting and catching a gazelle (diameter 8.7 cm). The other is made of limestone with inlaid pieces of alabaster at the border, the two attached doves are of pink limestone, their eyes are of ivory (diameter 9.7 cm). Egyptian Museum in Cairo.

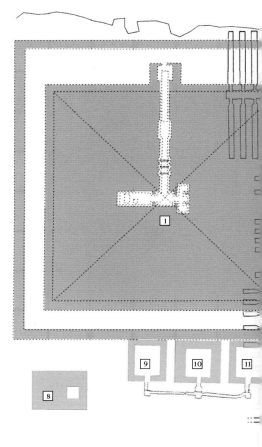

THE ROYAL TOMBS
OF THE SECOND DYNASTY
AT SAQQARA AND ABYDOS

Saqqara

So far only three large sets of underground galleries of royal tombs from the Second Dynasty are known at Saqqara, all in the area to the south of the Step Pyramid complex. The most elaborate and largest (about 130 x 46 m) is the one underneath the pyramid temple of Unas. It was discovered by Barsanti in 1901 but only partly cleared. A long north-south corridor, entered from the north by a staircase passage, is carefully cut into the rock five meters below the surface. The corridor, with four portcullis stones, leads to the burial chamber and some lateral rooms in the south and gives access to more than eighty storage chambers on both sides. These chambers were blocked with mud-brick walls; some still contain wine jars and animal bones. According to seal impressions, the tomb belongs either to Hetepsekhemwy, the first ruler of the Second Dynasty, or his successor Raneb.

Ninetjer, the 3rd king of the Second Dynasty was buried a little farther to the east. His tomb, overbuilt by the causeway of Unas, was first excavated by S. Hassan in 1937–38. It is now being reexamined by a German mission.

At present the tomb can only be entered via a shaft between the mastaba of Neb-kau-Hor and the causeway of Unas. In this shaft there are still two large limestone portcullis-stones in situ (height ca. 3.20 m, width 1.70 m), blocking a passage that is now covered by the mastaba of Neb-kau-Hor. The original entrance starts with a ramp about 25 m farther north.

The substructure covers an area of about 60 m x 50 m. It consists of a central N-S corridor N-S, leading to the burial chamber and more than 150 passages along which are smaller rooms of different sizes, all cut from the bedrock 3.5 m – 6 m below the present desert surface.

The ground plan of the northern and the southwestern part looks quite irregular and forms a kind of a labyrinth. Altogether, the layout seems not very suitable for the storage of goods as the corridors and passages cover much more space than the chambers.

Several details of the southeastern part, which is more regular and structured, indicate that there was a special meaning behind the design of the whole tomb. To the east of the king's chamber, a second corridor of 18 m length gives access to six large chambers to the west and a group of 12 narrow chambers to the east. Another group of three small rooms is located at the end of corridor. The chambers to the west and east are quite different. In the western chambers there are large benches (mastabas) of 1.5 m in width and 50-65 cm in height on one side. The eastern chambers are rather narrow (in width ca. 0.70-0.80 m only) and on both sides, there are very small benches (width 20 cm, height 30-40 cm) cut from the rock which are more suitable as seats for people than for the storing of goods. Altogether it seems likely that all the chambers in the southeastern part of the tomb can be understood as model architecture: those with the large benches represent living/sleeping rooms and those to the east copy dining halls for a larger group of people. The group of three small rooms at the end of corridor would fit neatly into such a model of living quarters, and can be explained as lavatories. In some private tombs of the Second Dynasty, there are toilets carved from the rock in exactly the same position at the end of a corridor. In the vicinity of the king's chamber, this part of the tomb in all probability can be understood as a simplified model of the royal palace (or harim) that would be used in the king's afterlife. Likewise, the northern and the southeastern part of the tomb seem to represent a settlement, with small roads, open places/areas, and façades of buildings with dummy entrances. Thus the king was equipped with a complete residence for eternity. The same idea found its ultimate expression in the complex of Djoser.

88 left
Tomb of Ninetjer, southeastern part. Several chambers with a large bench (mastaba) represent living and sleeping rooms.

88 right
Tomb of Ninetjer, southeastern part. Small benches on both sides of narrow chambers indicate dining rooms. To the right, there is an elevated seat for a high ranking person.

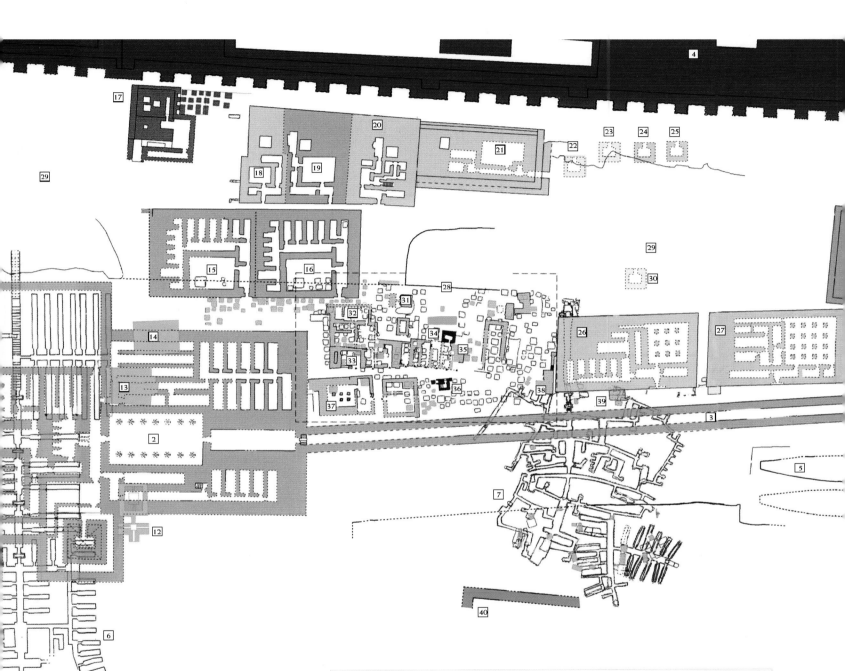

SAQQARA, ROYAL TOMBS OF THE SECOND DYNASTY UNDERNEATH THE MORTUARY TEMPLE AND CAUSEWAY OF UNAS.

1	PYRAMID OF UNAS	14	TOMB OF AMEN-TEF-NACHT	28	STRUCTURES OF THE 5TH AND 6TH DYNASTIES
2	MORTUARY TEMPLE OF UNAS	15	MASTABA OF KHENUT	29	DRY MOAT OF DJOSER'S COMPLEX
3	CAUSEWAY OF UNAS	16	MASTABA OF NEBET	30	TOMB OF BIA IRERY
4	DJOSER'S STEP PYRAMID COMPLEX	17	MASTABA OF NEFER-SECHEM-PTAH	31	TOMB OF III
5	BOAT PITS	18	MASTABA OF II-NEFERT	32	TOMB OF IDU
6	TOMB OF HETEPSEKHEMWY/RANEB	19	MASTABA OF UNAS-ANCH	33	TOMB OF KHENU
7	TOMB OF NINETJER	20	MASTABA USURPED BY IDUT	34	TOMB OF NI-ANCH-PEPI
8	TOMB OF ESBANEBDED	21	MASTABA OF MEHU	35	TOMB OF NI-ANCH-KHENU
9	TOMB OF THANENHEBU	22	TOMB OF IRATI	36	TOMB OF NI-ANCH-PTAH
10	TOMB OF PSAMMETHEK	23	TOMB OF ANCHI	37	TOMB OF PTAH-SHEPSES-IMPII
11	TOMB OF PEDENESI	24	TOMB OF SNEFRUHOTEP	38	TOMB OF HOR-MERU
12	TOMB OF PEDENEIT	25	TOMB OF NENGEM	39	TOMB OF IY-N-HOR
13	TOMB OF HEKAEM-SAF	26	MASTABA OF NEB-KAU-HOR	40	WALL DATED TO REIGN OF HOREMHEB
		27	MASTABA OF NO-ANCH-BA		

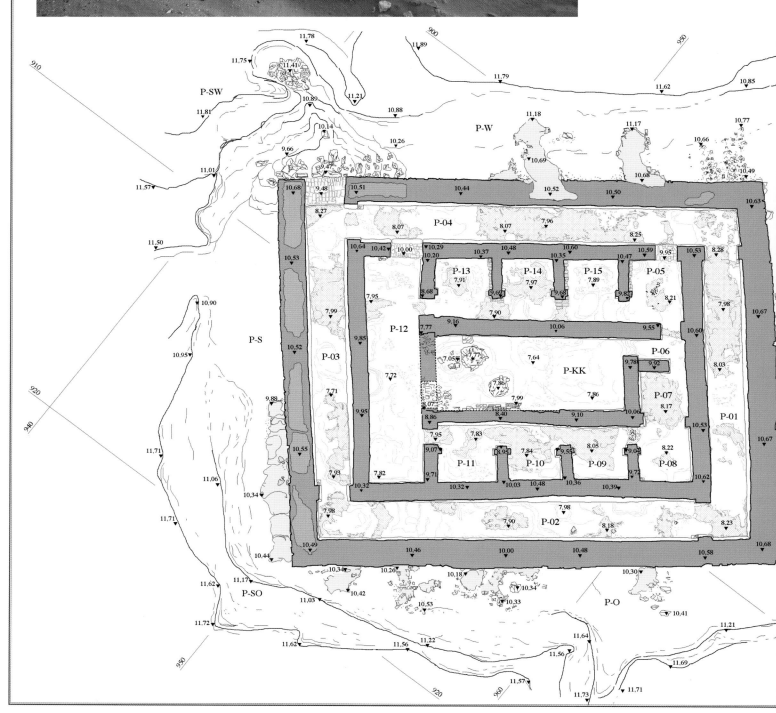

90 top and 90-91
*View and map of thet tomb of Peribsen,
after recent reexcavation.*

91 left
*Bowl inscribed with the name of Horus
(Seth) Peribsen, now conserved at the
Saint-Germain-en-Laye Museum.*

Abydos

In comparison with the large complexes of the First Dynasty kings at Abydos and the vast Second Dynasty substructures at Saqqara, Peribsen's tomb is rather small and simple. It seems to revert to the earlier tomb type of Djer and Djet, but the central wooden shrine is replaced by a brick chamber with a passage around it, giving access to the storage chambers. The ground plan is reminiscent of the model house in tomb U-j. The new feature of a continuous passage around the tomb also points to a house for the afterlife. This idea is still present in the subterranean king's apartments or model palace of Djoser (the blue chambers). The entrance or exit is to the southwest of the tomb. From Peribsen's tomb, two stelae bearing his name are preserved.

GRAVE

CORNICE

PLASTER

FOUNDATION LAYERS

ADDITIONS

REMAINS OF PAVEMENT

GEBEL

LIMESTONE

REMAINS OF NILE RIVER SILT

WOOD

CHANGES IN COLOR

POTTERY

91 right
The stela of Peribsen, now conserved in the Egyptian Museum in Cairo, is made of black granite and it is 1.54 m high. In his name, Peribsen did not employ the Horus-falcon. Instead, the Seth-animal is above the palace facade. This probably reflects a conflict between Upper and Lower Egypt. In a later period the Seth-animal was erased.

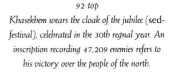

The large tomb of Khasekhemwy shows a great change in form and is built much deeper into the ground, its roof being about five meters below desert level. Re-investigation proved that the tomb was built in different stages. At first, it consisted of a central burial chamber, an anteroom to the south, and a backroom to the north between rows of five storage rooms on either side that were accessible from corridors. This plan is very similar to that of Peribsen's tomb.

In two or three enlargements, forty-three chambers were added, to the north and to the south, arranged in galleries like those in the Saqqara tombs. In a later phase a limestone-lined burial chamber was installed below floor level in the central room. The chamber has a depth of 1.80 m and measures approximately 5.25 x 3.20 m (10 x 6 cubits), and its longitudinal axis is about one meter to the west of the old chamber's axis. In all probability, the chamber was covered with small stone slabs, some of which were found loose inside the chamber. They must have rested on the roof of a wooden shrine inside the chamber. When the stone chamber was closed after the burial, it was then covered by a mud floor and was no longer visible.

In the southern extension of the tomb pit, probably prepared for another enlargement, a small ramp in the southwest corner leads up to the desert surface. The orientation of this ramp seems to reflect the idea of a way out for the reviving king, heading toward the opening of the wadi like the gap in the surrounding rows of subsidiary burials (as with the staircase at the tomb of Den) to the southwest of the king's chamber.

Although nothing is left of a superstructure, some details allow the reconstruction of a very large tumulus or *mastaba* above desert level. Whereas the northern and southern chambers are preserved up to their original height of about 2.35 m and do not show any deformation, the chambers of the middle part have a very irregular appearance: they have shrunk from about 2.30 m in height to 1.20–1.50 m, but are up to two times their original breadth, as indicated by the lowest courses of masonry. Certainly, they yielded to enormous pressure from above the roof and flowed sideways when they were wet. According to Petrie the walls were built of freshly made (not yet dried) bricks. This explanation, however, is unlikely as they belong to different building phases. The reason must be that there was an extra pressure above the middle chambers, most probably an artificial mound above desert level on top of the five meters of sand filling of the pit. The weight of this mound may have had its effect quite some time after the tomb was built, when—as a result of a heavy rainfall—descending moisture reached the masonry. The extension of the tumulus can be reconstructed accordingly. Limestone blocks found scattered around the site, with the same kind of dressing as the stone blocks of the king's chamber, indicate that this tumulus had a stone casing.

With its increased number of store rooms, the tomb must have contained an enormous amount of goods, above all thousands of pottery jars containing wine, beer, and oil; copper and stone vessels (some with gold caps); baskets and boxes for bread; and meat, fruits, and vegetables. In the chambers to the east of the king's chamber Amélineau found remains of two skeletons. Since there are no subsidiary burials in the whole complex, they are very likely to have come from the original burial.

92 top
Khasekhem wears the cloak of the jubilee (sed-festival), celebrated in the 30th regnal year. An inscription recording 47,209 enemies refers to his victory over the people of the north.

92 bottom
The storage chambers of Khasekhemwy's tomb contained thousands of pottery and stone vessels. Some vessels with gold caps were discovered by Petrie under collapsed walls where they had escaped tomb robbers. Egyptian Museum, Cairo.

92-93
The tomb of Khasekhemwy, here looking south, was enlarged in several building stages and finally comprised 56 storage chambers. The king's chamber is the first chamber built in stone. To the southwest, a ramp led toward the wadi opening, which was regarded to be the entrance to the other world.

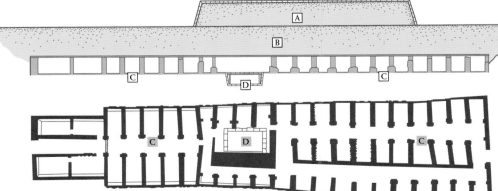

**SECTION AND PLAN OF THE
TOMB OF KHASEKHEMWY**

A TUMULUS WITH STONE
   CASING
B PIT WITH SAND FILLING
C STORAGE CHAMBERS
D BURIAL CHAMBER

The Royal Mortuary Enclosures of Abydos and Hierakonpolis

by Matthew Adams and David O'Connor

The royal tombs of the First and Second Dynasties at Umm al-Qa'ab, a site at Abydos, were completely excavated by Petrie in 1900–1902. Their significance as early royal monuments has been clear from the outset, although current excavations by Günter Dreyer are adding to Petrie's discoveries, as well as locating even earlier royal tombs. However, the royal enclosures of Abydos, located together about 1.4 km north of the tombs, still remain puzzling to many Egyptologists. Although one of them had already been explored fifty years before the discoveries at Umm al-Qa'ab, the enclosures have been excavated sporadically over many years, and not all those built have yet been located.

Since 1982, these enclosures have been coming into much sharper focus. Under the aegis of the Pennsylvania-Yale-Institute of Fine Arts, New York University Abydos Expedition (co-directed by W. K. Simpson and D. O'Connor), an Abydos Early Dynastic Project co-directed by David O'Connor and Matthew Adams has been systematically excavating and re-excavating these monuments. The Project plans, with the aid of magnetic survey, to ultimately locate and excavate all those yet undiscovered.

The Abydos royal enclosures are mortuary structures built for the First and Second Dynasty kings buried at Umm al-Qa'ab. Scholars sometimes call them *Talbezirke* ('valley places') or 'funerary

palaces.' Their importance is two-fold: the enclosures are as essential a component of the early royal mortuary monument as the tombs themselves; and in combination, tomb and enclosure can be plausibly seen as the direct ancestor of the step and true pyramid complexes of the later times.

One enclosure, the latest (built for king Khasekhemwy at the end of the Second Dynasty), survives as an impressive standing monument today and is called locally Shunet al-Zebib. Its mud-brick walls, in some parts, rise close to an original height of perhaps 11 meters and its total area is one hectare. All other enclosures, clustered nearby and also of mud brick, are severely denuded and can only be revealed and studied via excavation. Khasekhemwy's is the largest standing monument to survive from Early Dynastic times, although another enclosure of his, at Hierakonpolis, also still stands but is about half the size.

Khasekhemwy's enclosure was explored on behalf of Auguste Mariette in the 1860s, but he could not determine its date or function. However, in 1903 the English archaeologist E. R. Ayrton dated it to Khasekhemwy, located an enclosure for Peribsen (Khasekhemwy's predecessor) nearby, and suggested that a third enclosure, surrounding a Coptic village (still thriving today) might also be Early Dynastic. However, the extant brickwork of the latter suggests a much later date.

The northeast (local east) external face of Khasekhemwy's enclosure (Shunet al-Zebib): its recessing is still well preserved.

The south corner of Shunet al-Zebib, the perimeter wall is partially visible. The damage endured by this enclosure over the millennia is evident, and is now being addressed by a conservation program.

ABYDOS AND ITS ENVIRONS
IN THE EARLY DYNASTIC
PERIOD

A UMM AL-QA'AB
B EARLY DYNASTIC
   ENCLOSURES
C KHENTIAMENTIU TEMPLE
D MODERN VILLAGES

96 top
Shunet al-Zebib seen from the south.

96-97
Detail of the southwest main and
perimeter walls of Shunet al-Zebib.

97 top
The enclosure of Aha, seen from the
northwest. The walls and interior have
been heavily pitted in later, though still
ancient, times. The interior chapel is
visible in the far portion of the interior.
Shunet al-Zebib is seen in the distance,
and the wall of a modern Christian
cemetery on the right has overbuilt the
west corner of the enclosure.

Between 1911 and 1914, T. E. Peet found traces of another enclosure, associated with sacrificial subsidiary burials like those surrounding the First Dynasty royal tombs at Umm al-Qa'ab. Subsequently, in 1922 Petrie confirmed that it was an enclosure for queen mother Merneith, and discovered to its northwest two huge hollow rectangles (average area, .86 hectares) of subsidiary graves dating to kings Djer and Djet (First Dynasty). Finally, southwest of Merneith's enclosure, Petrie found another possible enclosure, but—uncertain of its nature—cautiously named it the 'Western Mastaba.'

No further fieldwork occurred until 1986, but in 1966 Barry Kemp suggested that the Western Mastaba was indeed an enclosure, and further mud-brick enclosures could be predicted within the Djer and Djet grave rectangles. Generally concurring, Werner Kaiser (in 1969) noted the predicted enclosures might have been of wood and matting, rather than brick. However, both scholars, along with Günter Dryer, felt sure that the enclosures showed the related if distant royal tombs at Umm al-Qa'ab were genuine tombs, and not cenotaphs—with the real tombs at Saqqara—as some, even now, suggest.

The Abydos Early Dynastic Project has much expanded our understanding of the Abydos enclosures. The northwest wall (with a monumental gateway) of Peribsen's enclosure, missed by earlier excavators, has been located; and we have confirmed that Djer's (brick) enclosure, and hence implicitly Djet's, exists. The Western Mastaba has been shown to be definitely an enclosure and, in 2001, we initiated a magnetic survey of the entire area, which has already resulted in the exciting discovery of two hitherto unknown enclosures. It is clear that for every royal tomb at Umm al-Qa'ab an enclosure was built far away in what today is called the North Cemetery. This location places the enclosures much closer to the ancient town at flood plain edge than the actual tombs, set far out in the desert. However, while the two late Second

Dynasty enclosures are identified, only six of the predicted eight First Dynasty ones are yet located. Of the enclosures found in 2001–2002, one belongs to Aha, and is the earliest known. At Hierakonpolis, the enclosure of Khasekhem (Khasekhemwy's earlier name), sporadically explored earlier, is being systematically studied by Renee Friedman. Square, rather than rectangular in plan like the Abydos enclosures, the Hierakonpolis example (including its external, peripheral wall) occupies about 0.49 hectares and in parts still stands 11 meters high. Whatever its purpose, it was unlikely to have serviced a tomb of Khasekhemwy at Hierakonpolis, evidence for which has never been found.

Second Dynasty kings prior to Peribsen were buried at Saqqara, not Abydos, and it has been suggested their tombs were also complemented by enclosures separate from them. The relevant archaeological remains, however, have not been definitively dated, and may be of Third Dynasty step pyramid complexes built subsequent to King Djoser's, which is the earliest one.

The survival of Khasekhemwy's enclosure at Abydos is amazing but now, at over 4600 years old, much of it threatens to collapse. Supported by a grant from the United States Agency for International Development funds via the Egyptian Antiquities Project of the American Research Center in Egypt, we have undertaken to document, stabilize, and conserve this great monument, and to work further on one of our most surprising discoveries at Abydos.

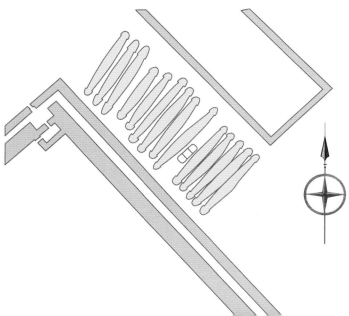

98-99
*Some of the boat graves northeast
of Shunet al-Zebib, which can be seen
in the background.*

98 bottom
*This map represents the fourteen boat
graves that were dedicated to the as yet
anonymous royal owner of the 'Western
Mastaba' enclosure.*

99 top left
*Conservator Deborah Schorsh
(Metropolitan Museum of Art,
New York) treats exposed planking
in Boat Grave 10.*

99 top right
*In this image can be observed Boat
Grave 10, partially excavated; part
of the boat's planking is still* in situ
*although intrusive pits have destroyed
it on either side.*

99 center right
Two of the boat graves, showing their
buttress-like prows or sterns. Note the
small boulder on the left-hand grave:
this probably represented an anchor or
mooring stone.

THE ARCHAIC FLEET OF ABYDOS

In 1991, we found—to our great surprise—twelve enormous boat graves (two more were located in 2000) arranged in a row outside the northeast side of Khasekhemwy's enclosure. They date to the First Dynasty and establish another important link between Abydos and Early Dynastic royal monuments and the pyramid complexes of later times. The latter too sometimes had boat graves, or boat pits shaped so as to resemble a boat.

The boat graves of Abydos are, so far as we can tell, similar if not completely identical in shape and content. In each case, an actual wooden boat (averaging 23 meters in length) was supported upright by a shallow trench dug in the desert surface. Each boat rose about 50 centimeters above the latter, and was carefully encased in well-built mud-brick masonry. Once the top of the boat was reached, it was filled solid with mud brick. At each end, a buttress-like mass of brickwork had been added so that the grave (averaging 26.23 m long) was considerably longer than the boat. The entire superstructure of the grave was plastered and whitewashed.

These superstructures naturally reflected the outline of the boat they contained, while the buttresses seem to represent a prow and stern. The row of fourteen boat graves must have looked like a fleet 'moored' out in the desert, an impression reinforced by the small boulder (an anchor or mooring device) placed on some of them.

Boat graves are also found with some First Dynasty elite tombs at Saqqara and Helwan, but only one occurs per tomb and they are usually smaller and less complex in form than the Abydos examples. The boat graves are contemporary with the "Western Mastaba" enclosure, but the royal owner of the latter is not yet identified. The boat graves are definitely earlier than Khasekhemwy's enclosure, which was built at least 200 years later, and probably more.

We have already (in 2000) excavated part of a boat, in order to study the associated excavation and conservation problems and also to start understanding the structure of the boats themselves. Ultimately, we plan to excavate fully and conserve one or more of them.

The excavated segment showed that much wood planking survives *in situ*, but it is fragile; much else has been reduced to frass, the dried excrement of wood-eating insects. Nevertheless, our expert consultant, Professor Cheryl Ward, could easily observe that the boat's planks were 'sewn' together by woven straps passing through lashing channels cut into the wood. There was no decking or framing, but she believes the boats were functional, not merely gigantic models. Low-lying, sleek shells, each would have been propelled rapidly along by as many as thirty rowers.

In themselves, the Abydos boats are tremendously important for nautical archaeologists. They more than double the number of ancient wooden vessels surviving in Egypt, and are by far the earliest. Moreover, they are the oldest surviving built boats anywhere in the world.

99 bottom
Plan of a typical boat grave
(unexcavated). Although cut into by
later pits, the grave retains its boat-like
shape, while the outline of the wooden
hull within it is visible (bold, dark line).

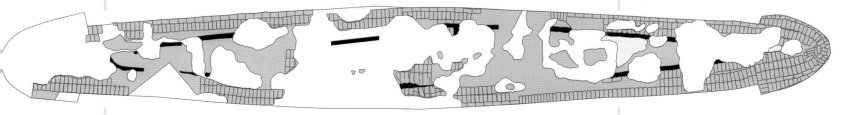

THE ABYDOS ENCLOSURES: ARCHAEOLOGY AND FUNCTIONS

Available evidence, though still very incomplete, indicates that the Abydos enclosures are essentially mortuary in function and changed relatively little in plan and appearance over the more than 300 year-long span of the Early Dynastic Period. Their mortuary function is indicated by their obvious connections to the contemporary royal tombs at Umm al-Qa'ab, and especially by the sacrificial subsidiary burials associated with both in the First Dynasty. These sacrificed courtiers and retainers (like the buried boats) were intended to serve the dead king in the afterlife, in the context of tomb and enclosure alike.

The First and late Second Dynasty tombs at Umm al-Qa'ab varied in plan, but each was probably capped by a surface mound of sand and gravel with brick or stone (Khasekhemwy) retaining walls. A chapel may have stood southeast of each mound. As each tomb was built, so was an enclosure in the North Cemetery; some, and probably all contained a chapel, used for the cult on behalf of the dead king.

Over time, the enclosures spread over a wide area (perhaps 10 hectares) which was kept free of contemporary graves, except the subsidiary burials noted above. These subsidiary burials were laid out neatly around some, and probably all of the First Dynasty enclosures. All the enclosures follow the same basic template, although some significant changes in architectural detail probably indicate changes in ritual use.

The enclosures vary in size, but not very much in plan. Smallest is the enclosure of Aha found in 2001, at 0.07 hectares; Merneith's and the 'Western Mastaba' average 0.18 hectares; Djer's and Peribsen's, 0.55 hectares. Khasekhemwy's, covering 1.07 hectares is the largest. However, in their rectangular plans and in their orientation (long axis always northwest to southeast) the enclosures are very

similar, as they are in significant details as well.

All external façades are niched, following a virtually identical pattern, with simple niching on three faces, and more complex on the northeastern, or local east, face. All wall faces are mud plastered; Khasekhemwy's enclosure had an additional coat of white plaster. Each enclosure had a gateway near the north and east corners respectively, and some had additional gateways. A chapel has been located in Aha's enclosure, and in those of Djer, Peribsen, and Khasekhemwy. These chapels are always in the southeastern half of the enclosure. So far no evidence has been found for any other substantial surface feature within the enclosures, including Aha's fully excavated enclosure. In 1988 we thought traces of a surface mound were identifiable in the west quadrant of Khasekhemwy's enclosure, but subsequently (in 2001) these remains were shown to belong to a basin, used during the construction of the enclosure.

The east corner gateway was always relatively elaborate, with an inner room providing access to the enclosure interior. This gateway was left open through the life span of the enclosure and was relatively close to the chapel. The gateway's importance in the First Dynasty was indicated by the fact that subsidiary graves left a large gap in its vicinity, and the largest, presumably most prestigious burials clustered nearby.

Other details suggest ritual changes over time may have caused changes in architectural form. In the First Dynasty the north corner gateway was relatively simple in plan. Moreover, it was sealed off soon after the enclosure was completed, to become a deep, externally oriented niche. The gateway was in use for only a short period, and perhaps related to rituals performed in the northwestern half of the enclosure. However, in the late Second Dynasty enclosures, the north corner gateway became more elaborate. It was deeply recessed and had an inner room; it was apparently not sealed off. These changes suggest the north corner gateway had

become more important and now perhaps was used for repeated ritual entries, still related to the northwestern half of the enclosure.

Throughout most of the Early Dynastic period, the chapel, located near the east corner gateway, was relatively simple and small. The chapel of Aha's enclosure and that of Peribsen's contained only three chambers, of almost identical plan. In size they and Djer's chapel average 86.5 square meters. However, Khasekhemwy's chapel was much larger (290.7 square meters) and contained eleven or more rooms. Thus, it seems to have provided for more elaborate ritual than any of the preceding chapels. In all the chapels, ritual probably focused on an image of the deceased king.

Khasekhemwy also had a perimeter wall (unique for Abydos) surrounding his enclosure. Of lower height than the main enclosure wall, it created an unroofed corridor around the entire monument, perhaps also used for rituals.

Perhaps most surprisingly, we have found evidence that each Abydos enclosure may have been pulled down, perhaps as the final act of the funerary ritual for its royal owner or as the enclosure of the next king was being built. This demolition seems to have been a kind of 'burial,' ensuring that the enclosure and its chapel—like the literally buried retainers and boats— would be fully and eternally available to its deceased owner. Khasekhemwy's, however, was left intact, perhaps because it was so much more massive than earlier enclosures, this being thought sufficient to guarantee its usefulness to the dead king.

Khasekhemwy's Hierakonpolis enclosure is different from the one at Abydos. It has a similar perimeter wall, but its chapel is centrally located, not placed toward the south end of the enclosure. Moreover, the Hierakonpolis enclosure has only one, not two gateways and is square, not rectangular, in plan. Inscriptions show that it housed a cult dedicated to Khasekhemwy, but not a specifically mortuary one.

ABYDOS ENCLOSURES AND PYRAMID ORIGINS

The true pyramid complexes of ancient Egypt clearly derive from the Step Pyramid complex built for king Djoser at Saqqara at the beginning of the Third Dynasty; but how does Djoser's complex—constructed immediately after Khasekhemwy's monuments—relate to the Early Dynastic royal tombs and separate enclosures of Abydos?

The differences are obvious. Djoser's complex, in its final form, was enormous compared to its Abydos predecessors, occupying about 15 hectares—fourteen times the size of Khasekhemwy's enclosure—and built entirely of stone rather than mud brick. Djoser's complex was surrounded by an enclosure, within which stood not a chapel and empty space, but a dense mass of buildings and courts with a tomb at their center, capped by a huge stepped pyramid, 62 meters high.

Djoser's complex was initially smaller, however, simpler in plan, and more obviously related to Early Dynastic prototypes. It consisted of an enclosure, with gateways near the northeast and southeast corners as at Abydos, although its external niching was much more elaborate. The interior space contained a tomb capped by a low, stone-built mound (very reminiscent of the royal tombs of Umm al-Qa'ab) and only a few other structures. It was this initial layout that was elaborated into the Step Pyramid complex as we know it today.

However, the immediate inspiration for Djoser's first phase may not be the Early Dynastic royal tombs and enclosures at Abydos, but rather the royal mortuary monuments of the earlier Second Dynasty located at Saqqara, close to the eventual site of Djoser's Step Pyramid complex. Two of the Second Dynasty royal tombs of Saqqara are definitively identified, and each consists of a large network of subterranean, rock-cut magazines with a burial chamber and associated rooms and galleries to the south. What stood on the surface above the tomb is unknown but is likely to have followed the same basic plan as the Abydos royal enclosures, albeit with certain important modifications.

At Abydos, tomb and enclosure were separate, the former set far out in the desert to be near tombs of even earlier rulers, while the enclosures are set close to the flood plain. At Saqqara there was no reason to keep tomb and enclosure separate (as Kemp noted), and perhaps the surface above the entire, subterranean tomb was defined by an enclosure, presumably in brick. The extent of the tomb indicates that the enclosure would be similar in size to Peribsen's at Abydos. The actual burial chamber would be in the south half of the enclosure, and capped by a surface mound with perhaps a chapel on its south, as at Umm al-Qa'ab. Much of the rest of the enclosed space might be empty, but the tomb entrance would be in the extreme north. The burial procession might then enter the enclosure via a gateway near the northeast corner, while the mound and chapel above the tomb were served by another gateway near the southeast corner of the enclosure.

The Second Dynasty royal monuments of Saqqara would, as hypothesized here, be very similar in appearance to the first phase of Djoser's complex, except the latter's tomb and surface mound have been moved further north. However, the non-functional 'South Tomb' of Djoser's complex, and the nearby, equally non-functional chapel, might commemorate the real tomb and chapel which stood in approximately these positions in the Second Dynasty enclosures at Saqqara, as reconstructed above. Even the final phase of Djoser's monument, with its fully developed step pyramid, still has important relationships with Early Dynastic prototypes. These include the continued use of an enclosure of rectangular plan, while the mound above the Early Dynastic tomb is transformed into the Step Pyramid, itself a mound in elevated form. The pyramidal shape was necessary to stabilize this great mass of stone masonry which was subject to severe internal stress.

Finally, most of the many cultic structures of the final phase of Djoser's complex are non-functional; they are filled solid with rubble except for a small, nominal chamber or two. In other words, just as the Early Dynastic enclosures of Abydos were provided with sacrificed retainers and demolished so as to pass fully into the afterworld, so Djoser's complex is largely intended for the afterworld use of the dead king. The activities of the living are restricted to only a few locales, such as the mortuary temple.

Even the Abydos boat graves connect the Early Dynastic monuments with later pyramid complexes. They are the ancestors of the boat graves and boat-shaped pits that were sporadically provided for Fourth Dynasty and later pyramids.

Each Early Dynastic royal mortuary monument at Abydos consisted of two separate parts—the tomb at Umm al-Qa'ab and the enclosure about 1.4 km to its north, in the North Cemetery. Thus, the royal enclosures of Abydos were an integral part of each king's mortuary complex. Increasingly, new discoveries and the re-examination of earlier excavations are beginning to suggest what were the specific ritual functions and symbolic meanings of these enclosures. Equally important, the royal enclosures and tombs of Abydos, taken together, are the prototypes for the Step Pyramid complex of king Djoser at Saqqara, with the Second Dynasty royal mortuary monuments of Saqqara playing a vital mediating role. The Early Dynastic royal monuments of Abydos are therefore the source of the main stream of development that leads on to the pyramid complexes, and ultimately to the royal tombs of the New Kingdom.

100
Part of the southwest face of Shunet al-Zebib; the deep recesses were cut to house hermitages for Coptic monks in medieval times and now threaten Shunet al-Zebib's stability.

101
The south corner of Shunet al-Zebib. Damage inflicted upon it by human agency has been compounded by the hundreds of birds who have created nests within its fabric.

The Step Pyramids

by Ali Radwan

According to Herodotus, the founding of Memphis (the 'white wall') as the capital of the 'Two Lands' was one of the main achievements of Menes. It is now generally accepted that this legendary king was Horus-Aha, the founder of the First Dynasty. Memphis, being at the main strategic point between Upper and Lower Egypt, was an ideal location for the centralized administration of Egypt. To the west of Memphis, on the northern edge of the Saqqara plateau (not far away from the later Step Pyramid complex of Djoser), Horus-Aha erected a *mastaba* tomb (no. 3357) with a niched superstructure, model estate, and boat-grave. All his successors in the First Dynasty followed his example, and thus a new national necropolis, North Saqqara, was established. This was the first official cemetery of the Memphite region, and the second royal necropolis after Umm al-Qa'ab at Abydos. The late Hans Wolfgang Müller has argued convincingly that the great Saqqara *mastabas* (with the Lower Egyptian niched-paneling system) are to be considered cenotaphs (empty tombs) of the kings of the First Dynasty, while other tombs nearby were the tombs of members of the royal family and high-ranking officials. The actual tombs of these kings were at Abydos, in Umm al-Qa'ab. According to Erik Hornung, "The kings of the First Dynasty had a secondary tomb in Saqqara, the necropolis of the new residence in Memphis."

The funerary equipment that had been left in these Saqqara *mastabas* offers important information about the well-established organizations and systematic methods with which Egypt of the First Dynasty was ruled. The titles on the stela of Merka (from the reign of Qa'a, the last king of the First Dynasty) provide concrete evidence of this administration. This stela was certainly a mark of special favor and great honor from the king, who allowed his high official to place it on the eastern side of his royal *mastaba*. Sabef, another dignitary of the same king, was similarly honored and permitted to erect his stela within the Abydos tomb of his monarch.

Throughout their history, the ancient Egyptians recognized the great value of the written word. Consequently, inscribed (i.e. documented) works of art form the majority of the Egyptian heritage. The tombs of the first kings of the Second Dynasty have never been precisely located, but an inscription incised on the shoulder of the statue of a cult-priest from the Third Dynasty named Hetepdief lists the Horus names of the first three kings of the Second Dynasty: Hetepsekhemwy, Raneb (Neb[i]re), and Ninetjer. This statue was recovered from the Memphite area, and can be considered evidence that these three kings were buried in the Saqqara necropolis. Indeed, the subterranean galleries of two large tombs have been discovered just to the south of the Third Dynasty Djoser complex, in the area of the pyramid of King Unas, last king of the Fifth Dynasty. These could be assigned, based on inscribed clay sealings, to Hetepsekhemwy (or Raneb) and Ninetjer. In addition, the funerary stela of King Raneb (from Saqqara) should be taken as another indication that this king was most likely buried in the Saqqara necropolis.

102 bottom

One of the so-called boundary stelae from the southern court of Djoser's complex. It shows the Horus-name of the king facing the Anubis fetish and the names and titles of the two royal ladies Hetephernebty and Inetkaes. The signs above mention Anubis as the "foremost of the sacred land (necropolis)." Chicago, Oriental Institute Museum.

103

The features of the famous seated figure of Djoser (painted limestone), found in his closed stone room (serdab) beside his mortuary temple at Saqqara. The inlaid eyes are lost. Nevertheless, his majestic appearance is expressed through the heavy wig, the ceremonial beard, and the royal headcloth (nemes). Egyptian Museum, Cairo.

104
*One of the typical figures of the legendary
architect Imhotep, who is seated unrolling a
papyrus to emphasize his status as a wise
man. The skull-cap gives him the appearance
of the god Ptah, who was considered to be
his father. Egyptian Museum, Cairo.*

The Third Dynasty was the 'Age of the Step
Pyramid.' During this period when accelerated
progress was made toward achieving real and
everlasting greatness for ancient Egypt. The architects
of Djoser and his successors laid the foundation for
the great pyramid builders of the dynasties of the
Old Kingdom. This was the first 'Golden Age' of
ancient Egyptian history. On the artifacts that have
survived from his lifetime, King Djoser is known as
Netjerikhet, the name found on his statues and on the
reliefs found under his Step Pyramid and its associated
south tomb. (The south tomb is an enigmatic
structure in the southern part of the pyramid precinct
whose subterranean galleries resemble those under the
Step Pyramid itself, but with a square burial chamber
too small for an actual burial; see below.) His personal
name, Djoser, is first found in the famous Westcar
Papyrus, which dates from the Middle Kingdom.
Senusret II (Twelfth Dynasty) dedicated a statue
to King Djoser, thus commemorating his great
predecessor.

From the Ramesside king lists (from Abydos,
Saqqara, and Turin) onward, Netjerikhet is only
known as Djoser. Manetho, the Egyptian priest and
historian who lived in the third century BC, refers to
him as 'Tosorthros.' That those who had compiled the
names of the kings on the Turin Papyrus had written
the name of Djoser in red ink (indicating the
beginning of a new dynasty) instead of black ink
could mean that his reign was considered the starting
point of a new era, as it actually was. In the Saqqara
list, Djoser is the first king of the Third Dynasty, but
the lists of Abydos and Turin both have Nebka as the
predecessor of Djoser and therefore as the founder of
the dynasty. However, the recent discovery of clay

105
*The base of a statue of Djoser with the feet
of the king upon the so-called 'Nine Bows'
(the enemies of Egypt). The three rḥyt-birds
are to represent the humble subjects of
his majesty. To the left of the Horus-name
of Djoser are given the name and the titles
of his architect Imhotep. Egyptian
Museum, Cairo.*

sealings with the Horus-name 'Netjerikhet' by Günter Dreyer in the tomb of Khasekhemwy, last king of the Second Dynasty, at Abydos, lends credence to the theory that Djoser was the founder of the Third Dynasty. Nebka can perhaps be identified with a king whose Horus name was Sanakht, who appears on two reliefs carved into the cliffs near the turquoise mines at Wadi al-Maghara in the Sinai Peninsula and on clay sealings from the mortuary temple of Djoser. The clay sealings suggest that he ruled after Djoser, and the style of his Sinai reliefs (standing in front of a sanctuary), as compared to reliefs in the same area left by Djoser and his immediate successor, Sekhemkhet (both shown in the so-called smiting position), confirm this theory. In addition, a mention of Nebka in the Westcar Papyrus indicates clearly that he came between Djoser and Sneferu (the founder of the Fourth Dynasty). According to Dreyer, the kings of the Third Dynasty ruled in the following order:

1. *Djoser*	*dsr*	Horus	*ntry-ht*
2. *Sekhemkhet*	*dsr-tti/dsr-ti*	Horus	*shm-ht*
3. *Khaba*	*(nfr-k3-rꜥ)??*	Horus	*ḥꜥi-b3*
4. *Nebka*	*nb-k3-rꜥ/nb-k3*	Horus	*z3-nht*
5. *Huni*	*hwni*	Horus	*k3i-ḥdt?*

The most important queen of the Third Dynasty was without doubt the queen mother, Nymaathep. She was the wife of Khasekhemwy, the last king of the Second Dynasty, as she is mentioned on a jar-sealing from the burial chamber of this king as 'the Mother of the King's Children.' In Mastaba K1 at Beit Khallaf, which has been dated to the reign of her son

Djoser, she is called 'The Mother of the King of Upper and Lower Egypt.' Three royal women are shown kneeling at the feet of their king on a fragment from a shrine of Djoser found at Heliopolis. The two ladies in front of Djoser are identified as Queen Hetephernebty and Princess Inetkaes; the label of the third lady, who embraces the king's leg from behind, has been lost, but it is very probably Nymaathep. Her cult-chapel, which must be located in North Saqqara, is referred to in the tomb biography of Metjen, who lived from the end of the Third to the beginning of the Fourth Dynasty.

Imhotep, who, according to Manetho, "invented building with hewn stone," stands at the beginning of the Third Dynasty as the symbol of an age of high creativity, development, and progress. He was Djoser's chief architect and primary counselor. In addition, he held the extremely powerful position of High Priest of Heliopolis. His dominance in the reign of Djoser is attested by the fact that he was allowed the unique privilege of inscribing his name and titles on the base of a statue of his monarch.

Later on, in the reign of Hatshepsut (Eighteenth Dynasty), the famous architect Sen(en)mut was given the exclusive right to dig his tomb beneath the lower courtyard of the temple of Deir al-Bahari, which he himself had designed and built as his architectural wonder for Her Majesty. The third great architect of

Egyptian history was Amenhotep son of Hapu, who was the 'Overseer of All Works' for Amenhotep III (Eighteenth Dynasty). This great man was the only Egyptian official who was given permission to build his funerary temple beside those of the kings in the Theban necropolis.

According to Dietrich Wildung, Imhotep could have begun working as an architect under the last king of the Second Dynasty, Khasekhemwy, and died in the reign of Huni (last king of the Third Dynasty). Imhotep was not a prince, and he was never raised to the high office of vizier, although we know that the office existed by this time, since two fragments of stone vessels from one of the storage galleries in the complex of Djoser (these stone vessels were heirlooms by the time of the Third Dynasty) mention a high official called Menka who bore the titles of judge and vizier. Nevertheless, it was Imhotep, the sage and writer, who was considered the patron of the scribes during the New Kingdom. On the Turin Papyrus he is called "The Son of Ptah." This is the first indication of his early reputation as a demigod; his deification came later, in the Saite period. In the Ptolemaic Period, an inscription on the island of Sehel (to the south of Aswan) mentions the names of Djoser and his famous architect, Imhotep. Imhotep's genius lay both in his novel use of stone for large-scale building (although the Palermo Stone refers to the erection of a stone temple at the end of the Second Dynasty, there is no evidence that this was ever completed), and in his juxtaposition of traditional forms with new ones to create Djoser's unique burial complex.

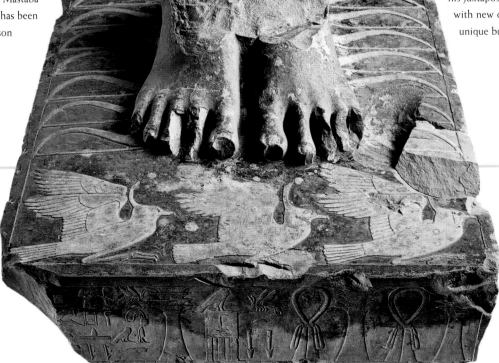

ART, ARCHITECTURE, AND RELIGION

Owing to their deep belief in an afterlife, ancient Egyptians made it a priority to prepare their 'House of Eternity' (the tomb) and provide it with all they would require for life in the next world. In fact, religion was the only motivation for almost all their artistic achievements—sculpture, painting, reliefs, and building projects like tombs, chapels, shrines, and temples. It is obvious that stone was the most suitable material, not only for building but also for works of art that were destined for eternity. In broad outline the religious doctrine of the ancient Egyptians, which was fixed in its basic points throughout pharaonic history, can be traced in the following table:

Heaven	Underworld
Day	Night
Light and air	Darkness and silence
Cycle of Rebirth	Cycle of Death
Sunrise (east)	Sunset (west)
Re-Horakhty	Osiris
Day course of the sun	Night course of the sun
mꜥndt	*msktt*
(day-barque of the sun god)	(night-barque of the sun god)

In ancient Egypt, the integral concept of duality was not only related to the geographic nature of the land and consequently its monarchy, but also to the religious beliefs of its inhabitants. According to their invariable concepts, the components of every deceased human being could be defined in the following manner:

Heaven	Earth
b3-soul	dead body (mummy)
3ḫ-spirit	*k3*-soul
Shadow of the dead	Name of the dead

In hieroglyphics the tomb was sometimes called *ḥwt-k3* ('House of the *ka*'). This term could also be used to refer to the above-ground cult-chapel of the tomb in which funerary rituals were to be performed; or even to the 'statue chamber' (in Arabic, *serdab*). The well-being of any dead person was dependent on the preservation of his/her body to make it possible for

them to come back to life again during the daily revival. Offerings were made to the *ka*, and it was important that the body always be prepared to receive its *ba*, which was the part of the soul that could travel outside the tomb. The proper performance of the cult rituals enabled the deceased to become an *akh* and travel to the sky (like the circumpolar stars), with a living name and shadow everywhere. In the Pyramid Texts of the Old Kingdom the whole matter is summarized in the following words: ". . . the *akh*-spirit belongs to the sky, the corpse belongs to the earth."

The spells of the Pyramid Texts, which were collected and inscribed for the first time on the walls of the royal burial chambers under the pyramid of King Unas, the last king of the Fifth Dynasty, were designed to help the dead king to find his way easily in the Netherworld and be raised to the status of an eternal great god. Hermann Kees argued that the priests of the Third Dynasty were the first compilers of the Pyramid Texts. The so-called 'snake pillar' of Djoser, which was discovered and published by Zahi Hawass in 1994, could be considered good evidence for Kees's argument. It is a free-standing pillar made of limestone, measuring 211 cm in total (it is incomplete and the preserved portion is in two pieces). The front is decorated, beginning (from the top) with the Horus-name of the king on the top of twelve divisions that contain the alternating figures of a jackal and a lion or lioness. This sequence is partially repeated below, but is incomplete. The back of the pillar was left plain and unfinished. On both sides of the pillar, there are raised carvings of two undulating snakes. The length of each snake corresponds to the decoration of the front (Horus name plus twelve divisions), thus they could be interpreted as the two goddesses who help and protect the dead king during the twelve hours of the day (the upper part of the pillar) and the twelve hours of the night (the lower part of the pillar). Snake goddesses serving similar functions can also be found in the Pyramid Texts: ". . . may it [the Red Crown in its capacity as the Eye of Horus] set your power, O King, at the head of the Two Enneads as the two serpent-goddesses who are on your brow [in other words, in front of you], that they may raise you up, O King; that they may guide you to your mother Nut that she may take your hand" (Pyr. 902).

The Step Pyramid of Djoser was the first attempt to build a monumental tomb for an Egyptian king in order to raise him to the position of a god in the afterlife. There is no need to refer, as has often been done (after Herbert Ricke), to the tumulus above the royal tombs at Abydos as the prototype of the step pyramid. This so-called 'Grabhügel' (grave mound) was not a purely Upper Egyptian particularity, but was related to the Heliopolitan concept of the so-called 'Primeval Hill' (a sacred mound of sand). As is attested in several spells from the Pyramid Texts, a strong influence of the solar cult of Heliopolis was evident with respect to the step pyramid as a royal tomb. These spells stress that the dead king (as a transfigured spirit) must ascend to the sky to be among the gods. This act of climbing or going up to the sky was certainly connected with the pyramid as a stairway. In two spells, Pyr. 209 and 210, the king is instructed to 'ascend and descend' four times. He has to join the sun god once in the Night-barque (an act of descending) and the other time in the Day-barque (an act of ascending). As the dead king was "the possessor of five meals, three in the sky and two on earth" (Pyr. 717), he must ascend to the sky and descend to the earth daily. The hieroglyph of a pyramid of four steps is seen as the determinative of the following words: *iꜥr* 'ascend' – *k33* 'primeval hill' – *k3y* 'ascent.'

If the true pyramid could be taken as a 'ladder of rays' for climbing up and down from the heavens, the step pyramid is certainly a suitable staircase to the sky. In three depictions from later periods, the step pyramid form is seen as a stand for the sun-barque, for the enthroned Osiris, and for a reclining mummy. All these images have only one meaning, and that is the resurrection, or the beginning of a new life.

One of the reliefs from a fragmentary Heliopolitan chapel of Djoser (now in Turin) shows the god Geb (as usual, in his human form), thus we can expect that Osiris (the son of Geb) and other members of the Heliopolitan Ennead would also have been depicted on this monument. According to Alexander Scharff, there are some indications even from the Archaic Period that the Osirian cult originated at that time. It is unrealistic and illogical to deny the god Osiris a direct connection with the solar cult of Heliopolis. Throughout the Pyramid Texts the Horus–Osiris relationship is prevalent, but direct linkage between Re and Osiris is also present.

It is well known that the *djed*-pillar is the main symbol of Osiris. Depictions of this pillar can be found in several places within Djoser's pyramid complex: as part of the tiled decoration in blue faience under the south tomb and in the Step Pyramid. The *djed*-pillar is also found on the wall of the statue-chamber in Temple 'T and together with the so-called 'Isis knot' on the base of the famous Djoser statue. According to Hourig Sourouzian, the three unfinished statues of Djoser from his *heb-sed* court can be interpreted as the first attempt to give the king the Osirian shape.

During the Third Dynasty, the artistic heritage of the Archaic Period had already been completely developed into the forms, patterns, and techniques of the conventional Egyptian 'style.' The royal statues of Djoser, especially the famous one in the Egyptian Museum made of painted limestone from the *serdab*, stressed the truly majestic appearance of the king through his heavy wig with its *nemes* headdress, the clenched fist on his breast, and the close-fitting robe he wears for the *sed*-festival. The name and titles of the king on the base end with *R𝑐-nwb* ('the golden Re'), which could only be his golden-Horus name. The statue of a princess in Turin, whose features are similar to those of Djoser, and the backrest of whose seat is like the throne of the king, could also belong to the beginning of the Third Dynasty.

A fragmentary standing figure of Djoser, which could have come from the so-called 'oblique' temple to the south of the colonnade hall, is important because its base is inscribed with the name and titles of Imhotep, Djoser's architect. However, the following things should be kept in mind regarding this inscription:

1. It is not the 'signature' of the famous Imhotep.

2. It is the only mention of Imhotep's name from within the whole complex of Djoser.

3. The last title of Imhotep on this statue refers to him as the 'sculptor' (*gnwty*). This could mean that he himself was responsible for carving this statue or even all other statues of his monarch.

4. Stadelmann's assertion that Imhotep was the son of Djoser is quite uncertain and can hardly be accepted. Even sons of a king would not have been granted such a privilege.

5. At any rate, it is an exceptional case, which denotes the great mark of honor given to Imhotep for his unprecedented achievement.

As for private statues of the Third Dynasty, we can refer to those of Ankh (Louvre and Leiden), the lady in Brussels, the artisan Ankhwa (British

106 bottom and 107
The so-called 'Snake Pillar' (in two blocks about 211 cm high), discovered by Zahi Hawass, was an important element in the funerary complex of Djoser. It is decorated with the two Horus-names of the king with divisions showing alternately the figures of a jackal (Anubis) and a lion. Two snakes are depicted on each side to symbolize the guardian deity of the day (upper half) and night (lower half). The back of this pillar is left undecorated. Egyptian Museum, Cairo.

Museum), and of course the standing figures of Seba and his wife Nesa (Louvre). The statue of Metjen (Berlin) can be assigned to the very end of the Third or the beginning of the Fourth Dynasty. The kneeling priest, Hetepdief, in the Egyptian Museum in Cairo, dated to the first half of the Third Dynasty, is a unique piece, not only because of his attitude of putting both hands flat upon the knees, but because the incised inscription on his shoulder shows that he might have been the cult priest of the first three kings of the Second Dynasty. Dietrich Wildung and Matthias Seidel once assigned the lion in the Ashmolean, Oxford (made of baked clay and colored red; h. 42.5 cm) from the temple enclosure of Hierakonpolis to the very beginning of the Third Dynasty, while Hans Wolfgang Müller was inclined to date it to the Sixth Dynasty. The standing god in Brooklyn Museum with the knife in his right hand was associated by Wildung with the *heb-sed* court of Djoser.

The reliefs on the 'false-door' panels under the Step Pyramid and the south tomb of Djoser are of fine quality and had a special function. They show the king performing royal rituals while visiting shrines of the deities of Upper and Lower Egypt. Through the magical power of the written word and the actions depicted, these reliefs served to provide for the needs of the dead king in his afterlife.

The mud-brick *mastaba* of the Chief of Dentists and Physicians, Hesire (to the north of Djoser's complex) is dated by a jar-sealing from its burial chamber to the reign of Djoser. The funerary furniture, and for the first time some scenes of daily life, were depicted in painting on one of the walls of the two corridors of this famous tomb (which has a remarkable *serdab* looking northward, like that of Djoser). The wooden panels of Hesire in the Egyptian Museum in Cairo show the figure of the deceased in a formal style that resembles some of the determinative signs for a man in hieroglyphic writing. Hesire is represented in both a sitting and a

standing position. Those are the conventional stages of the half and then complete resurrection, according to Wolfhart Westendorf. It is amazing that the *mastaba* of Hesire had eleven niches to hold his wooden panels. This reminds us of the eleven galleries under the Djoser Pyramid. The reliefs from the chapel of Khabawsokar (Egyptian Museum, Cairo) could be dated to the middle of the Third Dynasty, while those of the official Akhetaa (Louvre and Berlin) should belong to the end of the Third Dynasty.

A relief of Horus Qahedjet (King Huni?) clearly illustrates the equal status and strong relationship between the king and the sun god of Heliopolis ('Horus who is [presiding] in the Great House [the Sun-temple of Heliopolis]'). Even the two hieroglyphs of the word 'Horus,' which refer here to the king and the god respectively, are depicted facing each other on an equal level. Not only Djoser, but also Huni, the last king of the Third Dynasty, placed great emphasis on the solar religion.

The inscription of Metjen reflects a *new development*, especially in administrative and economic affairs. The scenes from his tomb-chapel (built in stone), as well as his granite statue (both in Berlin), belong to the transitional period at the end of the Third and the very beginning of the Fourth Dynasty.

UNSOLVED PROBLEMS

Apart from the step pyramids of Djoser and his successor Sekhemkhet, one cannot speak precisely of any dated step pyramid of the Third Dynasty. The name of King Khaba, found on some stone vessels from a mud-brick *mastaba* (Z-500) just to the north of the unfinished structure at Zawiyet al-Aryan is our only evidence for assigning this step pyramid to this king, who must have been one of the successors of Sekhemkhet (see discussion below). Following the general acceptance that Nebka (Sanakht) was one of

the kings in the second half of the Third Dynasty (see above), there is no place for Lauer's theory that this king was buried in one of the galleries under the Step Pyramid of Djoser. Likewise, it is quite uncertain if the enclosure of al-Deir at Abu Rawash, or one of the two unfinished enclosures to the west of the Djoser's complex was intended to be the afterlife residence of this king. In the opinion of other scholars, those funerary enclosures belong to kings of the transitional period between the end of the Second Dynasty and the beginning of the Third (e.g., Khasekhemwy). Such a funerary enclosure, at North Saqqara, had already been dated to the reign of King Dewen of the First Dynasty. The unfinished mud-brick complex at Abu Rawash (al-Deir) could be assigned to the second half of the Second Dynasty also. It is hard to understand how Huni, the last and after Djoser the most significant king of the Third Dynasty, could be left without any associated tomb. It is supposed that he could be the builder of all the provincial step pyramids (except Seila), as we shall discuss below.

In 1985, Rainer Stadelmann proposed that the pyramid to the northeastern side of the Pyramid of Teti at Saqqara (Lepsius XXIX) be assigned to Huni. Later, this proposal was rejected, even by Stadelmann himself, in favor of a later king. Once it was thought that Khaba was Huni himself, in which case he might be the possessor of the unfinished step pyramid of Zawiyet al-Aryan. Furthermore, it has been argued by Stadelmann that Huni's presently unknown pyramid could be located in the region of Herakleopolis Magna (Ihnasya al-Medina), as the name of this king could refer to this town (according to Helck). For many years, the pyramid of Meidum was attributed to Huni in its first stage and assigned to Sneferu in its last stage of completion; this position is still held by some scholars today. At any rate, the small cult-pyramid to the south of the Meidum Pyramid was one of the last step pyramids of ancient Egypt, although the form survived in later periods.

108 and 109
One wooden panel and details of two others from the mastaba of the 'Chief Dentist' Hesire, who lived during the reign of Djoser. The fine reliefs show the great official in two positions (sitting and standing). Each time he is represented with his staff and scepter *together with the equipment of a scribe. His wigs and personal features are elaborately carved. Such panels were originally put in the eleven niches of the western wall of the long corridor of his mastaba-tomb. Egyptian Museum, Cairo.*

Chapter 9
109

110 bottom
Model of the Step Pyramid of Djoser.

111 top
In this view, the Step Pyramid of Djoser
can be clearly observed.

THE STEP PYRAMID OF DJOSER AND ITS COMPLEX

The dominant appearance of the Step Pyramid itself inside the complex of Djoser is designed to denote the divine position of the dead king. This complex shows us clearly that the unification of the 'Two Lands' was firmly established. Different architectural elements from Upper and Lower Egypt have been put together in a simple and nicely harmonized order. The different structures inside this complex represent a selection of units that were essential for the existence of the king in the afterlife: the south tomb and its mortuary chapel, the *heb-sed* chapels and Temple 'T,' the mortuary temple and *serdab*, the Pavilions of the South and North, and the Step Pyramid itself. Underground galleries beneath the Step Pyramid, the so-called 'Western Massifs' (or Mounds), the northern granaries, and the two altars were meant to ensure the *provisioning* of the dead king for eternity. The entrance colonnade, and every other element of this huge enclosure, has its own function: for example, the two markers in the south court mark the route of the ceremonial run of the king, who must eternally repeat the celebrations of his *sed*-festival. Simply put, the entire complex was the place where the dead king was to take up residence in the netherworld. It was also where he was expected to perform all his official duties as a lord of the 'Two Lands' forever.

The sense of tradition that distinguished the ancient Egyptian character underwent a marked development during the Third Dynasty. The spectacular achievements of Djoser's reign were important steps in the development of this sense. The royal tomb in the form of a step pyramid was the distinctive mark of this dynasty. This remarkable stage in the development of the royal tomb was doubtless the result of strong religious beliefs. I cannot easily accept Kaiser's proposal that most of the elements of Djoser's complex were built in a purely Upper Egyptian tradition, after the model of the valley enclosures at Abydos. No one can tell what the origin of the so-called 'Abydos tradition' was. Even the 'dummy mound' itself, seen inside the enclosures of Peribsen and Khasekhemwy at Abydos, are most probably linked with the 'Primeval Hill' in the Heliopolitan myths of creation. Also, as Müller points out, the niched paneling system of some walls of Upper Egyptian enclosures at Abydos or at Hierakonpolis from the reign of Khasekhemwy can be attributed to the Lower Egyptian tradition seen at Saqqara and everywhere in the north. Djoser's complex, at the threshold of the Old Kingdom, is the evident result of the steady cultural unification of ancient Egypt. From this point on, there is only one Egyptian tradition.

The name of Djoser's complex, *ḳbḥw-ntrw* ('libation of the deities'), suggests that the colonnaded hall, with its forty engaged columns, might have contained representations of the deities of the nomes of Upper and Lower Egypt. If not, those same deities are represented in the chapels of Upper and Lower Egypt in the *heb-sed* court.

The Saqqara Tomb of Anedjib (3038) has been proposed as a forerunner of the Step Pyramid of Djoser. In fact, we have discovered small *mastabas* with three steps at Abusir. These have been dated to the second half of the First Dynasty. Like the enclosure wall of Djoser's complex, all the large *mastabas* at Abusir have their only true entrance on the southeastern side. Although Mastaba IV at Abusir (from the reign of Den) has its offering place on the eastern side, there is a small projection in the north wall of the *mastaba* that could be taken to be a special cult-niche, which can be compared with the northern altar in Djoser's enclosure. As a matter of fact, there is a similarity between the ground plan of the mortuary temple of Djoser and the cult place attached to the northern side of Mastaba 3505 at Saqqara, which belongs to Qa'a, the last king of the First Dynasty, and not to one of his nomarchs or officials.

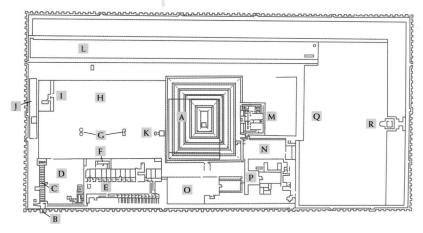

THE STEP PYRAMID COMPLEX

A STEP PYRAMID	K ALTAR
B ACTUAL ENTRANCE	L WESTERN STOREROOMS
C ENTRANCE COLONNADE	AND GALLERIES
D ROOMS AND GALLERIES	M MORTUARY TEMPLE
ATTACHED TO THE HEB-SED	N SERDAB WITH ITS COURT
COURT AND COLONNADE	O PAVILION OF THE SOUTH
E HEB-SED COURT	AND ITS COURT
F ROYAL PAVILION (TEMPLE 'T')	P PAVILION OF THE NORTH
G MARKERS	AND ITS COURT
H THE SOUTH COURT	Q THE NORTH COURT
I CHAPEL	R THE NORTH ALTAR
J SOUTH TOMB	

The reasons for the multiple changes in the building plan of Djoser's Step Pyramid are still under debate. Even the stages of these changes are not definitely accepted by all scholars. At first, a solid *mastaba* with a square ground-plan roughly facing the four cardinal points was built. It would seem that the architect already intended to build a step *mastaba*, as this first solid structure was enlarged on all four sides with a somewhat lower extension (or addition). Another addition along the eastern side (to cover the eleven shafts of the substructure) is also lower than the previous one. The next change in the design of the royal tomb was to transform it into a four-stepped pyramid, with a small mortuary temple just to the north. A small statue-chamber (*serdab*) was also planned to be attached to this temple on its eastern side. The final building stage transformed this small step pyramid into a pyramid of six steps (with a height of 62.5 m) with a much larger ground plan (121 x 109 m following two extensions to the north and the west) and an outer casing of fine Tura limestone. The unique group of galleries and small chambers under the Step Pyramid of Djoser is a puzzling complex. According to Zahi Hawass, it is about 5635 meters in total length with a 27-meter-deep shaft containing a granite burial chamber in the center. This is rectangular in shape, built to have the function of a sarcophagus, and measures 1.6 x 2.9 meters. It was proposed earlier that there was also a limestone chamber, but Stadelmann has proved that this was not the case. The eastern gallery still retains its decoration of small blue-glazed tiles which imitate hanging reed-mats, along with three limestone reliefs framed by inscriptions giving the name and titles of the king.

112 top
The Step Pyramid of Djoser with some of the surrounding buildings.

112-113
This drawing shows the central shaft of the Step Pyramid of Djoser with its granite burial chamber and the other underground galleries and rooms.

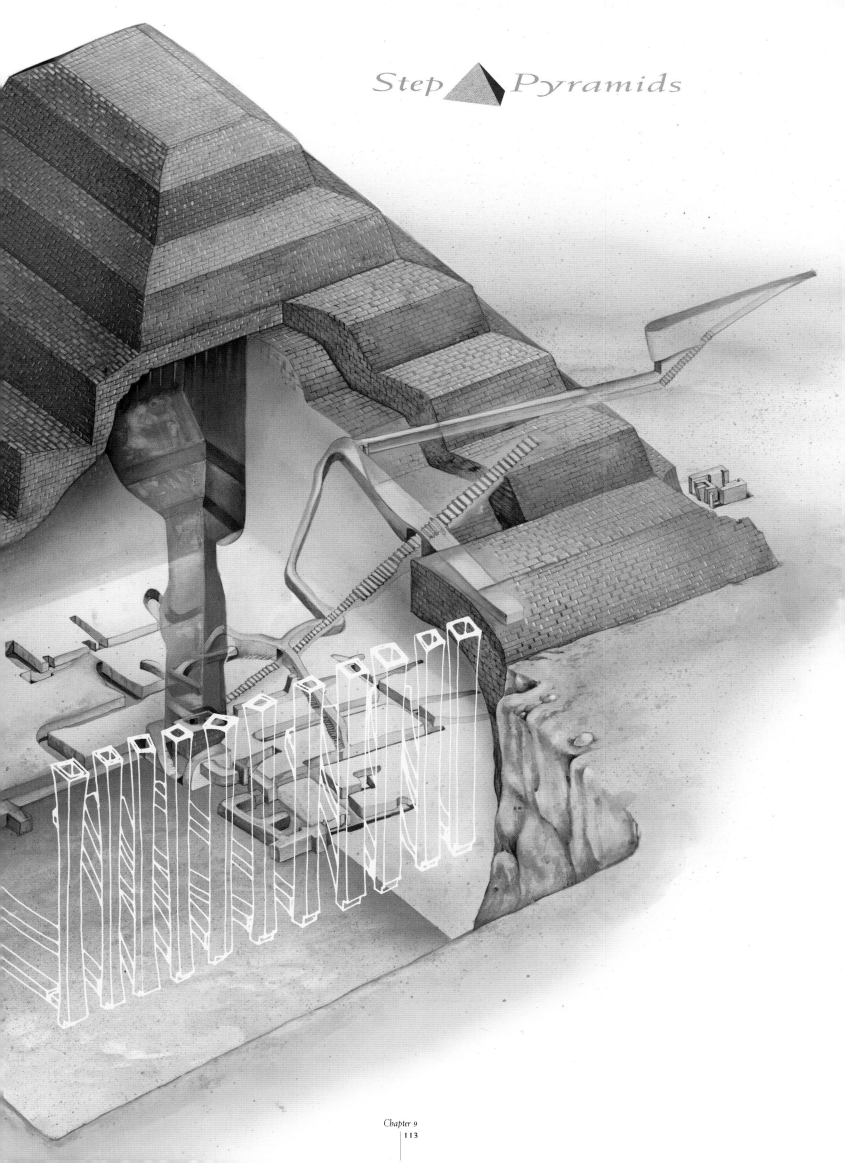

A stairway leads down from the western court of the northern mortuary temple to the substructure of this pyramid. This specific orientation of the pyramid entrance is noteworthy and must have been done intentionally. The *ba* of the dead king had its permanent abode in the northern part of the sky. The location of a mortuary temple, or a small chapel instead of it, allowed the priests in the performance of their rituals the opportunity of communicating with this vital aspect of the royal soul.

Some of the eleven shafts under the pyramid were actually used as burial places for members of the royal family, as several alabaster sarcophagi and the burial of a boy (about eight years old) in a wooden coffin were found there. This was the reason that the eastern side of the *mastaba* (M3), in front of the five northern shafts, was furnished with a pair of blank stelae for each shaft. More than 40,000 stone vessels were stored in the galleries of the other shafts to guarantee the constant and eternal supply of offerings for the king in the afterlife. Nearly all the names of the kings of the First and Second Dynasty were found inscribed on many of these vessels. In some instances, a group of royal names is arranged in the order of their actual succession. Even the name of Narmer was found on a stone bowl from one of these magazines. This shows how important it was for Djoser to possess such inscribed objects, thought to refer to the continuation of the divine kingship of the pharaohs on earth and in the underworld. Djoser was the first king who was keen to legitimize his sovereignty by gathering such a king-list in his eternal abode. It is interesting to note, however, that Djoser's name was not written on a single one of these artifacts. Only a clay-sealing bearing the Horus-name (Netjerikhet) of the king was found in these galleries.

114 top left
The so-called heb-sed *vase (made of alabaster, 38 cm high) was found in the underground galleries of the Step Pyramid of Djoser. The body and the handle of this vase show a stepped platform with the double pavilion of the royal jubilee (heb-sed) and two thrones on it. The whole group is supported by the* heh-*figure which symbolizes millions of years. Egyptian Museum, Cairo.*

114 top right
One of the tall alabaster vases with the waved cord decoration on its body, from one of the Djoser's underground galleries. Egyptian Museum, Cairo.

114-115
One of the two alabaster altars which had been found by Mariette to the north of the mortuary temple of Djoser. It is said that they belong to

the Second Dynasty. They could belong to the funerary cult of Djoser himself. The two lions are a pure Egyptian motif. Egyptian Museum, Cairo.

115 right
Three different types of funerary vases, which could be dated to the Third Dynasty, found under the Step Pyramid of Djoser. Egyptian Museum, Cairo.

The south tomb is the forerunner of the cult pyramid found beside the main pyramid begun in the Fourth Dynasty and continuing throughout the Old and Middle Kingdoms. The south tomb has its own cult chapel, built to the north of the superstructure. This chapel has a frieze of cobras to protect its top or, according to Robert K. Ritner, to illuminate it, as they were used to "shoot flame… in the darkness." The granite burial chamber of the south tomb was built, like its counterpart under the Step Pyramid, at the bottom of a shaft (7 x 7 x 28 m). However, it is smaller (1.60 x 1.60 m), and could not have been the burial of an adult. This indicates that this tomb was for a symbolic, rather than actual burial of the

king. I believe that it was the tomb of the divine *ka* of the king, for which a royal statue may have served as a substitute. The cobras symbolize new life, as they are the manifestation of the shining eye of the sun god ('*irt-R*ᶜ'). That the south tomb belongs to the so-called 'Abydos tradition' is simply unproved. It has also been suggested by Herbert Ricke that this tomb represented the Lower Egyptian tomb of the king, while the Step Pyramid itself represented his Upper Egyptian burial. It is also possible that the south tomb burial was connected with the renewal ceremonies of the jubilee festival (*heb-sed*), as the royal *ka* was the focus of this celebration in the afterlife. The subterranean chambers in this tomb, decorated with blue faience tiles and thus equivalent to the royal apartments, are of special importance.

116 and 117
The funerary chapel that belongs to the south tomb has a paneled wall and its top is decorated with the figures of the sacred cobras to symbolize hope in a new life.

Step ▲ Pyramids

It had been proposed several times that the niche-paneled enclosure wall of Djoser's complex was simply an imitation of the walls of Memphis. It could also be taken as the enclosure wall of a Lower Egyptian palace of mud brick from the Archaic Period. In fact, the stone blocks of this impressive wall (which reaches a height of 10.5 m) are the same size as the mud bricks of the Archaic Period. It is not easy to explain why, in addition to its true entrance, this enclosure wall has exactly fourteen dummy doorways. The sun god Re, with whom the dead king could be identified in the afterlife, has fourteen *kas*. Likewise, the number of the so-called sacred *iat*-places—niches destined for the sacred or blessed in the afterlife—of the netherworld is also fourteen. The dead body of Osiris was cut into fourteen pieces by his evil brother Seth. Those relics of Osiris were scattered and later buried in fourteen different places throughout Egypt. Could it mean, in the case of the fourteen dummy gates of Djoser's enclosure wall, that the dead king is the equal of Re in the afterlife? Thus, he would also have fourteen *kas*, which would each need their own false doors. Seven was always considered a sacred number (for example, Re has seven *bas*), and its multiples must have the same connotation. Oddly enough, the superstructure of Mastaba XVII at Abusir (from the second half of the First Dynasty) has exactly fourteen niches (or false doors).

I believe that the rectangular hall with eight engaged columns which marks the end of the Entrance Colonnade is connected with the practice of dividing visitors into classes according to status: The most important person (the living king) or persons should pass through the middle (or main) passage, while the less important must make their way to the right or the left.

That E. Otto sees in the *heb-sed* a pure Memphite ceremony, could mean that the Lower Egyptian influence was great within the Djoser's complex. The coronation in Memphis was in all periods essential, even up to the time of Alexander the Great.

The so-called Temple 'T' is a special building that could be interpreted as a small palace or even a 'sacristy' in which the king would have the chance to change his insignia (especially the white and the red crowns) during the *sed*-festival. Otherwise, one could

see in it the so-called 'Statuen-palast' (palace for the statue of the king) which resembles the archaic structure to the south of the entrance colonnade, the so-called 'oblique building'.

At the northwestern end of the *heb-sed* court, in a small chapel, there is a pedestal on which the feet of four statues have been preserved. The following identifications of the four people represented here have been proposed:

1. The king and the queen mother (Nymaathep) beside the two ladies Queen Hetephernebty and Princess Inetkaes. This theory is accepted by most scholars (for example, see the relief fragment in Turin).

2. The king with Anubis and two royal women, Hetephernebty and Inetkaes. This theory is advocated by Stadelmann.

3. Jean-Philippe Lauer has proposed that the king is represented by two statues, one in the white and the second in the red crown; beside him are Hetephernebty and Inetkaes.

4. Matthias Seidel also believes the king is represented twice (once with the crown of Upper Egypt and once in the crown of Lower Egypt); beside him are the two national goddesses of coronation, Nekhbet and Wadjet.

5. My own proposal is that the king is shown with the double crown beside the goddess Hathor, Queen Hetephernebty, and Princess Inetkaes.

The anthropomorphic representation of Egyptian deities can be traced back to the very beginning of Egyptian history. Even in the reign of Djoser, as has been mentioned above, some fragments from his small chapel at Heliopolis show the god Geb in a human form. As Hathor was identified with the mother and wife of the Egyptian king, she played an important role during the ceremonies of the jubilee.

The small temple or chapel on the northwestern corner of the *heb-sed* court was seen by Ricke as a temple for the early god of the Abydos necropolis, Khentiamentiu ('the foremost of the Westerners'), while Lauer believed this to be a chapel of the king and the two royal ladies, Hetephernebty and Inetkaes. This small temple could also have served the cult of the dead king in his capacity as the foremost of his subjects in the afterlife.

118 left
This side view of the upper steps of the Step Pyramid of Djoser gives the impression that it was a suitable staircase to the sky, enabling the dead king to 'ascend and descend' daily to and from the heavens.

118-119
General view from southeast showing the Step Pyramid of Djoser with all the surrounding buildings.

119 bottom left
The Step Pyramid of Djoser (seen from the north) with the Southern Court (with the two markers), the massifs of the western galleries, the south tomb, temple 'T' and the colonnade of the entrance.

119 bottom right
In this photograph can be observed the detail of one of the corners of the Step Pyramid of Djoser; the image clearly shows the remains of some casing stones.

120 top
At the end of the entrance colonnade is a rectangular hall with eight engaged columns to give visitors the chance to enter through different passages, according to status.

120-121
The main entrance leading to the colonnade and a small part of the niched enclosure wall of Djoser's complex which could represent the façade of a Lower Egyptian palace of mud brick.

122-123
*This view shows the heb-sed court with all
its elements: the platform (on the southern end)
and the remains of the chapels of the South
(western wall) and those of the North (eastern
wall). The royal pavilion (Temple 'T') is
shown in the southwestern corner of this court.*

123 right
*A detail (top) and a general view of the
reconstructed chapels of the south on the
western wall of the heb-sed court with
the platform on which Djoser was
enthroned during his ritual coronation as
king of Upper and Lower Egypt.*

The two 'Pavilions of the South and the North' represent, in the opinion of I.E.S. Edwards, the two national sanctuaries of Upper Egypt (at Hierakonpolis) and Lower Egypt (at Buto). The hoof-shaped altar which was found in the court of the southern pavilion clearly shows that a kind of ceremony was to be performed in both buildings. I would like to see them as the tombs of the pre-dynastic rulers of Upper Egypt (the 'Bas of Nekhen') and Lower Egypt (the 'Bas of Buto'), the mythical ancestors of every Egyptian king. The *kheker* frieze, which was used as a method of decoration on the façades of those two buildings, can be traced back to the reign of Aha, to a small ivory label from Naqqada which depicts a *kheker* frieze on the top of a small building in which three officials stand.

As the *serdab* has its own court and was not built inside the nearby mortuary temple, it seems plausible to me that the statue inside it functioned as a substitute for the dead king and was meant to stress the divine nature of his majesty as a monarch in the afterlife. This would then be one of the earliest signs of the deification of the Egyptian king. Djoser, within his step pyramid, was no doubt raised to the position of the sun god. The golden name (**R^c-nwb**) clearly inscribed on the base of this statue indicates that this statue functioned as a representative of the supreme ruler of Egypt.

A separate chapel was built into the northern enclosure wall. It faces the Step Pyramid and includes an altar cut out of the bedrock. This was once explained as a sun-temple, or as a stage or podium which would have held a canopy with two thrones for the ceremonies of Djoser. It now seems that it was only used for offering purposes and was linked with the northern part of the enclosure. It resembles the small projection of Mastaba IV at Abusir (from the reign of Den).

In Djoser's complex one can still admire the great achievements of Imhotep, whose primary and most difficult task was to create a new stone architecture that exactly mimicked previous building materials such as mud brick, wood, reeds, mats, and so on. Although there are no free-standing columns in the complex, the engaged ones, ribbed or fluted, and especially the engaged papyrus columns, are the first examples of their kind in Egyptian architecture. It is not only the use of stone as the only building material, but also the perfection of achievement, introducing a new technique but still utilizing traditional designs, that made this complex exemplary for generations to come. For example, the reliefs under the south tomb were copied in the Saite Period.

The scientific efforts begun by C. M. Firth and J. E. Quibell were continued, and to a great extent were completed by Lauer. The main, and for many years, painstaking task for Lauer was to restore the different architectural elements which had been found scattered around the site to their original positions. This is the most important and successful reconstruction project in the history of fieldwork in Egypt. Indeed, King Djoser was very fortunate to have two extremely devoted architects in his service: Imhotep in his lifetime and Lauer in our modern times.

124 top
The serdab *chapel just to the east of the mortuary temple of Djoser with its court, which means that the ceremonies were performed here in front of the enclosed statue of the deified monarch.*

124-125 and 125 bottom left
In the general view above the Pavilion of the North can be admired; below is a detail of its façade and the entrance to the short, curved passage with niches.

125 bottom right
This photograph shows the façade of the Pavilion of the South with the remains of the fluted columns and the so-called 'kheker' frieze on the top of the entrance.

THE STEP PYRAMID OF SEKHEMKHET AND ITS UNFINISHED COMPLEX

Sekhemkhet was Djoser's successor, if not his son, he left three reliefs in Wadi al-Maghara (Sinai) next to those of Djoser and Sanakht. It was through the efforts of the Egyptian archaeologist, Zakaria Ghoneim, that the complex of this king was discovered just to the southwest of that of his predecessor. It seems that Imhotep, the famous architect of Djoser, was also behind this project, as his name and titles were found written on the enclosure wall, which has the same niched-paneling system as that of Djoser's complex. Everything at this site was left unfinished. The step pyramid (120 x 120 m) should presumably, if completed, have reached a height of approximately 70 meters with seven steps. Its current height is not more than seven meters. Its mortuary temple (as yet unexcavated) must lie just to the north of the pyramid. From this area, a tunnel goes under the pyramid and gives access to a burial chamber. At the halfway point, a shaft was found to be blocking the sloping passage to the burial rooms. There, Ghoneim found a large number of stone vessels from the Third Dynasty and a small treasure consisting of the following pieces: twenty-one gold bracelets and rings; a small golden container in the form of a seashell; necklaces of gold, faience, and carnelian beads; and a small tablet inscribed with the name of a queen (Djosernebtyankhty). From this point, another passage curves around to reach a group of 132 magazines laid out in the shape of the letter 'U.' The sloping tunnel leads to the burial chamber (in the center of the ground-plan of the pyramid) with some corridors or galleries around it. A unique alabaster sarcophagus, with a sliding panel at one end, was sealed and had some dried plants on it (perhaps a funeral bouquet). When it was opened, it was found to be empty. It was once supposed that an empty burial had been made, but such an interpretation cannot be accepted without sufficient proof.

At any rate, this is a curious and unexplained discovery. Lauer thought once that the king was buried in his south tomb, which lies to the south of the pyramid, since the premature death of the king must have stopped the work on the pyramid. However, only a wooden coffin, containing remains of the skeleton of a child about two years old, was found in the burial chamber of this south tomb. The stone vases which were found beside this coffin show clearly that it was not of a later date than the Third Dynasty. The whole enclosure must be re-excavated.

THE STEP PYRAMID OF ZAWIYET AL-ARYAN (THE LAYER PYRAMID)

At the site of Zawiyet al-Aryan, between Giza and Abusir (about seven kilometers to the north of Saqqara), there are the remains of another unfinished step pyramid of the Third Dynasty. The plan is similar to Sekhemkhet's, but on a smaller scale (84 x 84 m), and even less had been completed here. The pyramid stands to almost 18 meters, and the subterranean corridors lead to a burial chamber with no sarcophagus and no sign of a burial. A. Barsanti, the first excavator of the site, believed that the pyramid had never been used.

The most interesting feature here is the group of thirty-two magazines, which takes the shape of the letter 'U,' like those of Sekhemkhet. In my opinion, this U-shaped arrangement of the subterranean magazines, which embraces the burial chamber of both pyramids from beneath, resembles the *ka* hieroglyph (⊔) which means, in addition to other translations: food, nourishment, or means of living (life force). Should this remarkable array have been done on purpose, it could give the hidden storerooms the power to supply the dead king—practically and magically—with his 'life-force,' his *ka*. The same aspect of 'giving' through the *ka*-sign can be traced in the shape of the Archaic ritual vessel in the Metropolitan Museum of New York or a cosmetic palette from Helwan. In verse 1653 of the Pyramid Texts, one can read the following wish: "O Atum, set your arms about the king, about this construction, and about this pyramid *as the arms of a ka-symbol*, that the king's essence may be in it, enduring forever." (Italics are the author's emphasis.)

There is no doubt that the 'Layer Pyramid' is one of the step pyramids of the Third Dynasty. The name of the owner could be Horus-Khaba, as his name was found on some stone vases in a *mastaba* (Z-500) to the north of his structure. Nabil Swelim proposed that this *mastaba* (made of mud brick) was the mortuary temple of this pyramid, although other remains of mud-brick walls had been traced to the east of the pyramid, and they could also be the mortuary temple. Swelim also sees in other traces, a distance to the east, the valley temple of this pyramid. All of this area must be investigated further.

126 top left
View of the unfinished step pyramid of Sekhemkhet; its remains are only seven meters high.

126 center
The step pyramid at Zawiyet al-Aryan, which now stands 18 meters high, had probably never been used.

126 bottom
This sectional view is a hypothetical reconstruction of the step pyramid at Zawiyet al-Aryan. In evidence are the subterranean corridors that lead to the burial chamber, and the current dimensions of the pyramid.

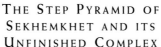

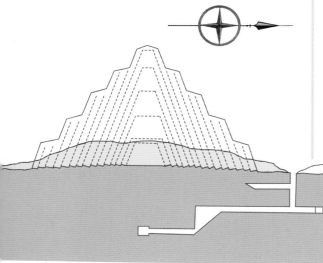

THE PROVINCIAL STEP PYRAMIDS

The (provincial pyramids) are a group of seven very similar small step pyramids found scattered from Elephantine in the south to Seila in the north. Each is a solid structure of three, or sometimes four, steps, built with local stone, without any indication of a substructure or chambers at all.

Seila	*4 steps*	*H. 6.8 m*
Zawiyet al-Meitin	*3–4 steps*	*H. 4.75 m*
Sinki (Abydos)	*3 steps*	*H. c. 4 m*
Ombos (Naqqada)	*3? steps*	*H. c. 4.5 m*
al-Kula	*3 steps*	*H. 8.25 m*
Edfu (South)	*3 steps*	*H. 5.5 m*
Elephantine	*3 steps*	*H. 5.1 m*

It is quite difficult to interpret this group of minor pyramids without more evidence. A gray granite cone was found near the pyramid of Elephantine, which could have the same function as the so-called boundary stelae of Djoser's complex. On the bottom of the cone is the cartouche of Huni and the word 'palace-window,' alternatively read as 'palace-shrine.' This identifies the entire structure as the 'palace-window or palace-shrine of Huni.' Dreyer and Kaiser have, based on this evidence, suggested that this small pyramid was attached to a provincial royal residence in Elephantine, and that the other small step pyramids served similar functions. They have also concluded that all seven of these pyramid belong to a single building program carried out in the reign of Huni. Huni was the first king to use a cartouche to surround his name. This cartouche was connected with the *shen* ring, which symbolized the endless circle of the universe. The use of the cartouche implies that the authority of the king was boundless, like the sun god Re. These pyramids might be another expression of this concept.

The appearance of minor step pyramids in the provinces could express the first attempt by the central government toward achieving an official religion (the solar doctrine) for the whole land. Imhotep, the great thinker of the Third Dynasty, was himself the head of the priesthood in Heliopolis. Indeed, according to Andrzej Ćwiek, the step pyramid, with or without a burial chamber, could resemble the 'Primeval Hill,' and 'the stairway to heaven,' i.e. "the transition point between the earth and the sky." Ćwiek proposed that all the provincial step pyramids were built by Sneferu in his early years. For Lauer, they are cenotaphs for the queens in their own provinces.

At Seila, two limestone stelae, one inscribed with the names of Sneferu, were found on the eastern side of the pyramid, together with an offering table (typical elements of an offering place). Fragments of a shrine and a seated statue were found on the northern side of the same pyramid. Stadelmann has proposed that the statue was placed on the flat top of the pyramid to demonstrate the actual presence of the mighty king in the province. Lauer suggests that this small pyramid was the first tomb of Queen Hetepheres (mother of Khufu) with a burial chamber in the core of the pyramid (inside the upper step). This is pure speculation without any solid basis in fact.

In my opinion, the step pyramid became a symbol of the eternal unity of the Two Lands, not only politically, but also in terms of religion. Its appearance in the provinces was to demonstrate this very principle.

The Sixteenth Upper Egyptian Nome (*m3-ḥḏ*), the nome of the gazelle, was the only attested nome in the reign of the Djoser. It is therefore possible that this king was the possessor of the Step Pyramid of Zawiyet al-Meitin, the oldest cemetery in the region of this nome.

126 top right
A small golden container in the form of a seashell together with a group of gold bracelets and other objects had been discovered by Zakaria Ghoneim inside the shaft near the burial chamber of Sekhemkhet. This small, fine quality treasure can only be dated to the Third Dynasty. Egyptian Museum, Cairo.

127 top and bottom
In these images can be observed two of the seven provincial pyramids and more precisely the 3-step, 8.25 meter-high pyramid of al-Khula (bottom), and the northernmost 4-step, 6.8 meter-high pyramid of Seila (top).

Chapter 10

The Pyramids of the Fourth Dynasty

by Rainer Stadelmann

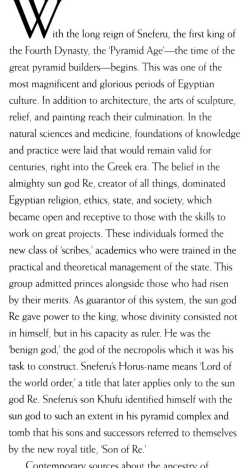

With the long reign of Sneferu, the first king of the Fourth Dynasty, the 'Pyramid Age'—the time of the great pyramid builders—begins. This was one of the most magnificent and glorious periods of Egyptian culture. In addition to architecture, the arts of sculpture, relief, and painting reach their culmination. In the natural sciences and medicine, foundations of knowledge and practice were laid that would remain valid for centuries, right into the Greek era. The belief in the almighty sun god Re, creator of all things, dominated Egyptian religion, ethics, state, and society, which became open and receptive to those with the skills to work on great projects. These individuals formed the new class of 'scribes,' academics who were trained in the practical and theoretical management of the state. This group admitted princes alongside those who had risen by their merits. As guarantor of this system, the sun god Re gave power to the king, whose divinity consisted not in himself, but in his capacity as ruler. He was the 'benign god,' the god of the necropolis which it was his task to construct. Sneferu's Horus-name means 'Lord of the world order,' a title that later applies only to the sun god Re. Sneferu's son Khufu identified himself with the sun god to such an extent in his pyramid complex and tomb that his sons and successors referred to themselves by the new royal title, 'Son of Re.'

Contemporary sources about the ancestry of Sneferu are rare. His mother Meresankh was probably a secondary queen of Huni, last king of the Third Dynasty, but the royal ancestors of kings of the Old Kingdom are never mentioned directly because the king was by nature of divine parentage. Besides his large pyramid structures, the principal achievements of the reign of Sneferu were the campaigns in Nubia and Libya that brought substantial booty in both cattle and men, who were settled in thirty-five new royal estates in the Fayum and in the Delta. Additional achievements that

can be linked to this period include the construction of a new royal palace, possibly near Dahshur, with large gateways of cedar wood; intensive ship building; the manufacture of life-sized royal statues in copper and gold; and an extremely large and precious wooden harp.

It is astonishing that the building of the pyramids is never mentioned in inscriptions of contemporaries, kings, or high functionaries, although it must have been the main event that took place during the reign of any king. The building of a pyramid was, however, like the performance of daily rituals in the temples—the ceremonies that guaranteed the rising and setting of the sun, the passage of the seasons, and the arrival of the Nile floods. All these rituals were such a fundamental part of the king's natural lifetime assignments that they hardly needed mentioning. Sneferu was without doubt the most outstanding builder of the ancient world, having constructed three large and two smaller pyramids in his long reign, using more than 3.6 million cubic meters of stone: one million more than his son Khufu used in his Great Pyramid at Giza. Nonetheless, he is known in Egyptian tradition as the good king *par excellence*, who addressed, according to folk tales, his subordinates as 'friend' or even 'brother.'

The shape of the pyramid complex changed under the influence of the sun god and his worship, from a north-south–oriented rectangle into a square east-west complex, following the course of the rising sun. The east-west orientation emphasized a new element in the layout of the pyramid complex: the long causeway, which led from the east, the land of the living, up to the pyramid tomb, finally ending at the mortuary temple, which from this time forward lay on the east side of the pyramid. The entrance gate to the causeway developed into a valley temple, the cult center of the pyramid town, in which the goddess Hathor and the king were worshipped as local deities.

The stela of Sneferu from the cult pyramid at Dahshur South, now in the court of the Egyptian Museum, Cairo, represents the king as Lord of the Two Lands and Lord of the Divine World Order.

This life-size statue of Sneferu with the white crown of Upper Egypt once was inserted in the niche of one of the six chapels of his valley temple at Dahshur. Now restored and in the Egyptian Museum, Cairo.

130-131

The pyramid of Sneferu at Meidum was originally built as a towering step pyramid but it was 'modernized' into a true pyramid at the end of Sneferu's reign. The picturesque form of the pyramid is due to stone quarrying from Greco-Roman to modern times.

130 bottom

This wall fragment from Mastaba M 16 of Prince Nefermaat and his wife Atet shows the catching of birds with the clap net, two pecking geese, and farmers plowing with oxen. For this relief, a technique of inlaid color pastes was used, but the inlays fell out when they dried. Now in the Egyptian Museum, Cairo.

MEIDUM PYRAMID PRECINCT

A ENCLOSURE WALL
B PYRAMID WITH CORRIDOR AND BURIAL APARTMENTS
C OFFERING TEMPLE WITH ROYAL STELAE
D SOUTH OR CULT PYRAMID
E TOMB SHAFT, PERHAPS THE TOMB OF THE KING'S MOTHER MERESANKH (?)
F MASTABA M 17 TOMB OF A CROWN PRINCE WHO DIED YOUNG
G CEREMONIAL CAUSEWAY WITH THE REMAINS OF A VALLEY TEMPLE

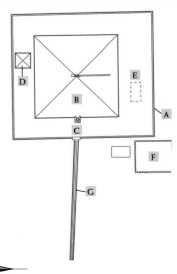

131 top
In this view from the pyramid of
Meidum, the offering temple with the two
stelae and the ceremonial causeway
leading to the valley temple in the east
can be observed.

Sneferu built his first two pyramids, still in the form of step pyramids, at Meidum. A small, solid step pyramid formed a towering landmark above the royal palace at Seila, on the eastern edge of the Fayum. His first pyramid complex, 10 kilometers to the east, overlooking the Nile valley, included a huge step pyramid, which was enlarged in a second building phase to the tremendous height of 85 meters. It still dominates the view of the Nile Valley today. Toward the end of his long reign Sneferu 'modernized' this step pyramid, changing its form into that of a true pyramid.

The form of the step pyramid had its roots in the preceding Third Dynasty. There were now, however, important innovations influenced by the orientation of the pyramid complex following the course of the sun, and also in the system of tomb chambers. From the older cult buildings of the Third Dynasty complexes, only the mortuary temple and the south tomb remained in the new pyramid complex of the Fourth Dynasty. The south tomb was adapted to the king's tomb as a small step pyramid directly to the south of the main pyramid. At Meidum the mortuary temple was a small sanctuary to the east of the pyramid with two large, high stelae which replaced and physically represented the king, who was not buried at Meidum. The tomb-chamber system in the pyramid also differs from those of the Third Dynasty. The burial chamber was no longer situated deep in a shaft in the subterranean rock, but was constructed above ground in the center of the

pyramid. During the Old Kingdom, the entrance into or exit out of the pyramid was always situated on the north flank. Through the tomb corridor leading up from the burial chamber, the king would ascend to the everlasting stars in the northern sky, in order to meet the sun god in his barque there. The beginnings of a three-chamber system can already be recognized in the tombs of the First Dynasty: it included the tomb chamber proper, as well as two subsidiary chambers, which initially served to store the most important offerings for the deceased king. In the pyramid of Djoser, the ante- and side-chambers were already conceived of as having religious functions. Thus, the ascent to the stars began from the antechamber, it is for this reason that the portcullis stones there were decorated with stars. The eastern corridors and the so-called 'Blue Chambers' are the model palace for the king's afterlife. In the Fourth Dynasty, the horizontal arrangement of the chambers is replaced by a vertical system, of which the Pyramid of Khufu provides the ultimate example. At Meidum a trend was set by laying out a royal cemetery in regular rows to the northeast of the pyramids with the double *mastabas* of Sneferu's sons and their wives. A huge single *mastaba* stands right by the northeast corner of the pyramid complex and thus in an important position. This was apparently built in a hurry and contains the burial of a nameless prince, probably a crown prince who died young in the early years of Sneferu's reign.

Meidum Pyramid

MEIDUM PYRAMID: THE CONSTRUCTION PHASES

A	FIRST STEP PYRAMID OF SEVEN STEPS	APPARENTLY NEVER COMPLETED
B	SECOND PHASE, WITH EIGHT STEPS REACHING 85 M	a ENTRANCE
C	THIRD PHASE, TRUE PYRAMID	b DESCENDING CORRIDOR
		c FUNERARY APARTMENTS

MEIDUM STEP PYRAMID

A	ENTRANCE	D RUBBLE FROM ANCIENT
B	DESCENDING CORRIDOR	AND MODERN STONE
C	FUNERARY APARTMENTS	QUARRYING

Bent  Pyramid

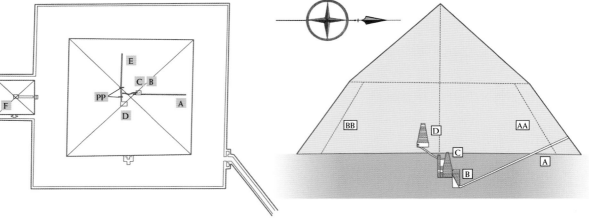

We can only speculate as to the reasons why, in the fifteenth year of his reign, Sneferu should have abandoned his palace and the nearly complete pyramid at Meidum, and begun again nearly fifty kilometers north, constructing a new residence with a royal palace and a pyramid near Dahshur. Possibly, it proved difficult to control the colonization of the Nile Delta and the trade routes from far away in Middle Egypt. The new site near Dahshur, on the other hand, was very convenient. A natural basin for the harbor ensured the development of the region. To the east, a trade route led to Sinai, and a wadi led to the western oases and the Fayum. Conveniently sited limestone quarries for building material lay on both sides of the Nile. There, a new opportunity was found for the now idle workers and specialists, in a bold undertaking: to build a towering pyramid without steps, and with an inclination almost as steep as that of the step pyramids, which should have reached the extraordinary height of about 150 meters.

It needs emphasizing that the development from a step pyramid to the pure geometrical form of the pyramid proper was certainly not inevitable. None of the other ancient cultures that built step pyramids made this advance. The progression from assembling step-shaped masses to form an artificial hill to the abstract geometrical form of the pyramid is a remarkable intellectual achievement that was the result of an extraordinary and unique venture in the time of Sneferu. Bold improvements were also made in the tomb chambers in the new pyramid, which, because of its present form, is known as the 'Bent Pyramid.' These chambers were to have corbeled vaults, conceived at Meidum but perfected here, up to a height of 15 meters. The ensuing alterations, necessitated by subsidence and damage during construction, resulted in a chamber system in this pyramid that is extraordinarily complicated and difficult to follow.

According to earlier religious descriptions of the royal hereafter, this mystical place was situated deep in the underworld. For this reason, the lowest of the three tomb chambers had to lie deep in the rock, as in the tomb of Djoser. The upward slope of the tomb corridor is also determined by the requirement for an undeviating passage up to the circumpolar stars. It therefore needed to begin deep in the rock below ground in order to lead to the desired exit, a short distance up the north face of the pyramid. The middle chamber is connected with the king's ascent to heaven, which is in turn represented by the tomb chamber above, although the ascent also lies in the direction followed by the tomb corridor.

In order to facilitate the excavation of a shaft about 7 x 7 m and 22.5 m deep, an underground layer constituted of mixed layers of marl and slate as at Saqqara was chosen; this was not, however, adequate to support the weight of the stone masses. As the pyramid grew upwards, sizeable cracks appeared in the three chambers and in the corridor. Initially it was thought sufficient to repair these by fillings. Soon, however, it became evident that both the lower chambers and the entrance corridor were seriously damaged and could not be saved by any further repairs. Eventually all attempts to save the project— even giving up the lower chamber and reducing the pyramid's angle of slope—proved to be in vain. After fifteen years of construction work, the boldest of all pyramid projects had to be abandoned. Sneferu began work on building a third pyramid. At the same time, the step pyramid at Meidum was modernized and altered into a true pyramid. This was surely in order to secure a burial place for the king if he should die before completing the new pyramid.

132-133
The Bent Pyramid at Dahshur with its cult constructions. To the east, a small offering temple with two stelae, and to the south, the cult pyramid with the remains of two stelae of Sneferu.

133 top
In the pyramid field of Dahshur, the Bent Pyramid is in the center with its enclosure wall and the small south or cult pyramid. About two kilometers farther to the north the Northern or 'Red Pyramid' is visible.

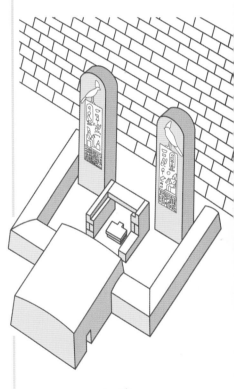

133 center right
This isometric reconstruction shows the offering chapel with a vestibule, the offering plate in form of the hieroglyph Hetep, which means 'offering,' and two 9 meter-high rounded stelae with the name of Sneferu.

133 bottom
The small offering chapel with two royal stelae and an offering table under a massive limestone shelter is surrounded by brick walls.

CROSS SECTION OF THE BENT PYRAMID

A *NORTHERN ENTRANCE AND CORRIDOR*
B *LOWER CHAMBER WITH STAIRCASE*
C *ANTECHAMBER WITH 'CHIMNEY'*
D *UPPER BURIAL CHAMBER*
AA, BB *INNER CORE*

Red △ Pyramid

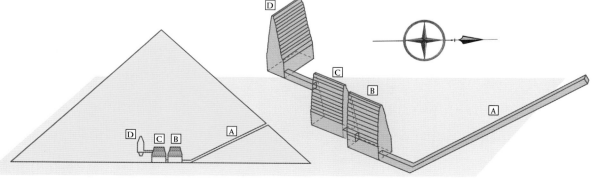

For the third of Sneferu's great pyramids, the 'Red Pyramid' at north Dahshur, the underground layers were properly tested. The base of the pyramid was increased to 220 meters along all sides, and it was decided to lower the angle of inclination to 45°. The method of construction in layers which was in use for the step pyramids was now abandoned. It proved to bring no saving of labor in building steeper pyramids, and was therefore replaced by laying horizontal courses of stone.

With a height of 105 meters, the 'Red Pyramid' is the third largest and highest after the pyramids of Khufu and Khafre. Everything about this building contributes to a harmonious and majestic effect. The system of chambers is harmonious and congruent because they are laid out one behind the other. They are set just below ground, and reached by an exit in the north side of the pyramid nearly 30 meters above ground, which must have been very inconvenient for the introduction of the royal mummy during the funeral ceremony and the final blocking off of the corridor.

The foundations of a hastily completed mortuary temple in front of the east side of the pyramid, and the sad remains of a mummified corpse that were found in the burial chamber, suggest that Sneferu was eventually buried in this pyramid. The princes and princesses of the later years of Sneferu's reign at Dahshur are buried in great stone *mastabas* in the eastern area in front of the two pyramids at Dahshur. Theses mastabas are massive rectangles of stone with a smooth casing.

Only the east side originally had two niches; the southern one bore the names of the deceased and perhaps a false door panel. In a small court to the front were possibly displayed two stelae with names and titles of the princes. Even the principal queen of this period, probably the famous queen Hetepheres, had only a modest undecorated *mastaba*. She was, however, not buried in Dahshur but later in Giza in the cemetery of her son Khufu.

Nearly fifty years of continuous construction work under Sneferu brought about remarkable advances in building techniques: in masonry, tunneling, the transport of stone, and in structural engineering. The bitter experience of a catastrophic collapse due to an unstable underground led to extreme caution in the choice of sites. The organization and logistics of a building site profited from the experience of twice relocating the pyramid-building towns.

The need for building materials, special types of stone, wood, and copper for tools and equipment stimulated expeditions and trade with countries to the north and the east. This brought a greater awareness of the world around the Nile Valley. The officials also gained experience through their varied tasks and became an efficient instrument of central government.

134-135
The Northern or 'Red Pyramid' of Sneferu at Dahshur can be observed in this spectacular aerial view from north. The entrance, nearly 30 meters high, is on the north side. It is the red color of the core stones which gave the name 'red' to the pyramid. The shining white-limestone casing of the pyramid was quarried off in the Middle Ages.

135 top
The first antechamber of the Northern Pyramid of Sneferu presents, as is easily seen here, a perfectly corbelled roof 12.30 meters high.

136 and 137
The Northern Pyramid of Sneferu was originally 105 meters high. Today, the top is flattened by the work of stone robbers of the Middle Ages and the pyramid is now only about 92 meters high.

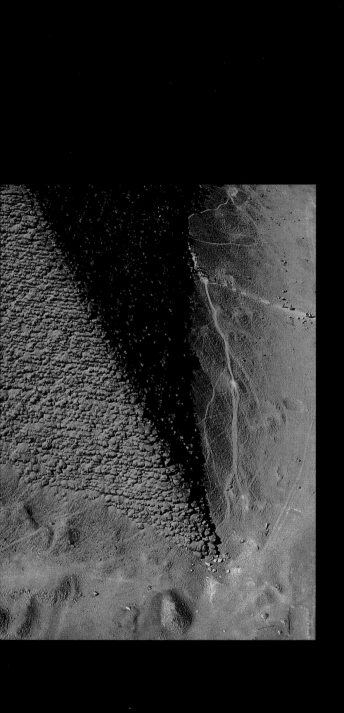

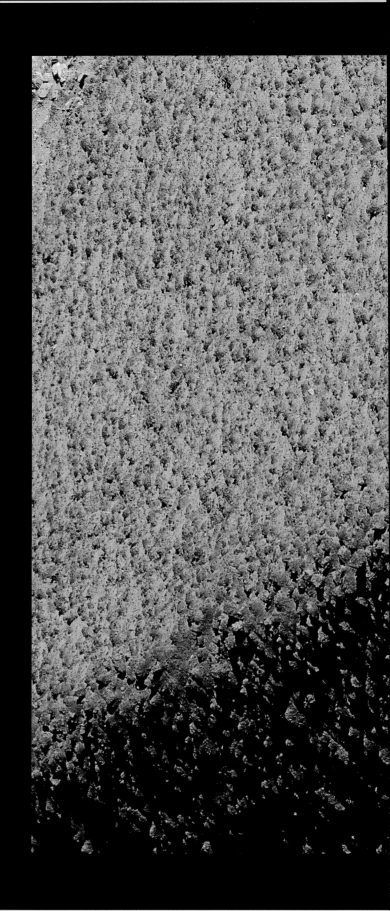

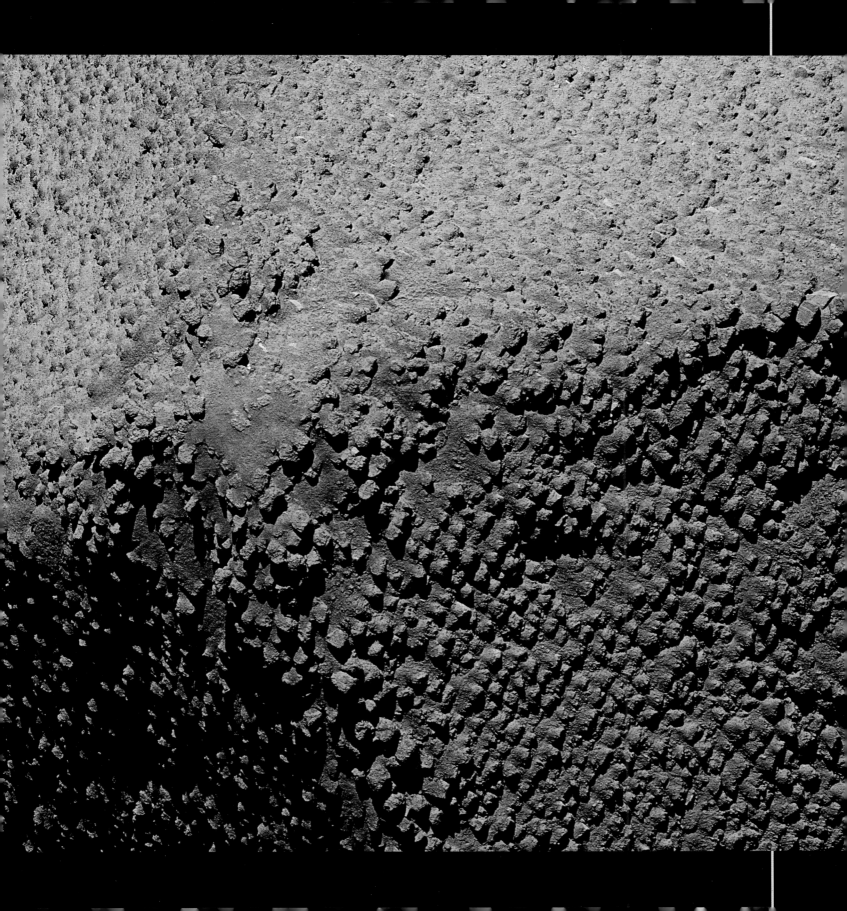

The Giza Plateau seen from northwest
with the Great Pyramid of Khufu, the
large Western Cemetery, Khafre's
pyramid, and the pyramid of Menkaure
with two of its satellite pyramids.

138 bottom
In this view of the Giza Plateau,
the northeast corner of Khafre's
pyramid and Khufu's pyramid
can be observed.

139 top
The ivory statue of Khufu wearing the
crown of Lower Egypt was found at
Abydos. This small figure, only 7.6 cm
tall, is the only complete effigy of the
great king who built the largest
monument and 'Wonder of the World.'

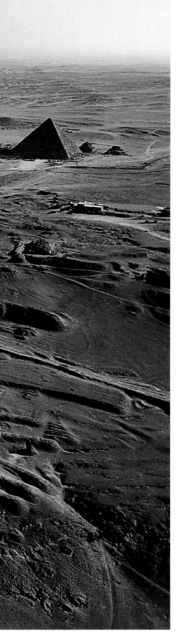

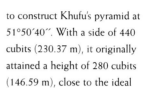

Sneferu's son and successor thus benefited from the best examples he could have in order to plan an even more ambitious pyramid for his own tomb. In order to avoid another ruined building, he settled on a solid rock foundation, which he found in a commanding position on the ridge above what is now Giza.

Since the time of the step pyramids, the alignment of the pyramids to the cardinal points had been a substantial concern. Khufu's pyramid is oriented almost exactly to true north, with a minor deviation of only five degrees. The pyramids of Khafre and Menkaure are seemingly aligned by a diagonal which touches, in each case, the corners of Khufu, Khafre, and Menkaure's pyramids. Most other alignments between the three pyramids and temples are only inspired by the fantasy of pyramid enthusiasts. This is undoubtedly the case concerning the theory that the layout of the Giza pyramids has a celestial origin, and that it follows the stars in the Belt of Orion, which in the Pyramid Texts is associated with Osiris on earth.

The technical perfection of Khufu's pyramid demands maximum admiration: the accurate orientation toward the north; the leveling of the corners, which do not differ more than 2.1 cm; the minute difference in length between the sides of only 4.4 cm; and the variation of the angles of only 2´48° all seem incredible, considering the simple tools available at the time. In contrast to the low 45° angle of slope of Sneferu's last pyramid, the builders dared

to construct Khufu's pyramid at 51°50´40´´. With a side of 440 cubits (230.37 m), it originally attained a height of 280 cubits (146.59 m), close to the ideal height of 300 cubits. Today the pyramid is still 138.75 m high. The perfection of the proportions and construction of the superstructure exactly matches the planning of the system of corridors and chambers inside.

To the present day, scholars have tried in a broadly positive spirit to attribute the pyramid's three chambers to three successive changes in the design. It does not do justice, however, to the architects who designed and executed this unique building so perfectly to suggest that in the essential element of the pyramid's construction, the system of tomb chambers, they had proceeded without concept or design. A conclusive argument against this view is that the exterior construction and the layout of the chamber system work in perfect accord, and that neither inside nor out is there any suggestion of a change of plan. Recent research has shown that since the Thinite era, royal tombs have had not just a single burial chamber but a series of three rooms or spaces, whose function has so far been only partially understood.

Recently, this realization has also provided evidence against pyramid mysticism, an epidemic of which is again breaking out, which suggests that hidden secrets, or even further treasure chambers, the 'chambers of knowledge,' were built into the chamber system of the pyramid of Khufu.

Khufu

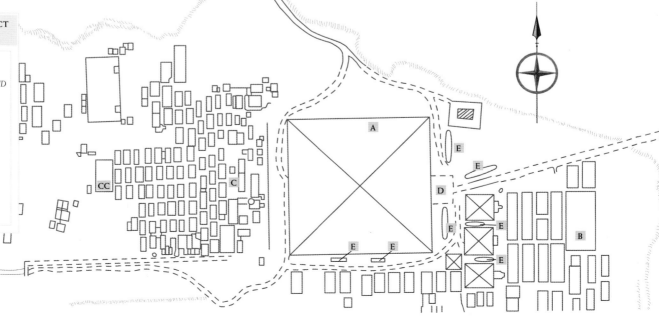

MAP OF KHUFU'S PRECINCT 'HORIZON OF KHUFU'

A   GREAT PYRAMID
B   EASTERN CEMETERY WITH THE QUEENS' PYRAMIDS AND THE MASTABA TOMBS OF KHUFU'S SONS AND DAUGHTERS
C   WESTERN CEMETERY
CC MASTABA OF HEMIUNU, MASTER BUILDER OF THE PYRAMID
D   MORTUARY TEMPLE AND CAUSEWAY
E   BOAT PITS

The upper granite burial chamber stands more or less isolated in the interior of the pyramid. Five relief chambers with granite beams weighing up to forty tons serve to relieve the pressure. The uppermost relieving chamber has a gabled roof of magnificent limestone blocks that rest on the stones of the core construction. In the upper relieving chambers, graffiti written by the ancient construction workers can be found that name Khufu as builder of the pyramid. This is the only authentic evidence of Khufu found in his pyramid. From the middle of the south and north walls of the burial chamber—and in the same way from the middle chamber—narrow model corridors with a diameter of 20 x 20 cm lead toward the southern and northern skies. They

provide a direct route up to heaven for the deceased king's soul. Previously these had been seen as ventilation shafts or telescopes for observing the skies; but it is certain that these corridors were originally sealed off and could only have served for the ascent to heaven of the deceased king's soul. During recent examinations of the southern shaft in the middle chamber, a small limestone block obstructing the end of the shaft was discovered that shows two copper fittings on its well-polished surface. These fittings were most probably hieroglyphic signs, symbols of magic power which enable the soul of the king to pass through the blockage. In the newest investigations, an opening was drilled through this small limestone block and

an endoscopic camera inserted. The first pictures show a narrow empty space behind the first blocking and another less smoothed limestone that shows faint quarry marks on its surface, which means that this stone is from the core of the pyramid. This would definitely confirm the theory developed after our first examination in 1992 that these shafts are model corridors sealed with model blocking stones. The first well-polished stone might well be a model portcullis stone. The examination of the model corridor leading out from the north side of the chamber presented more or less the same results. The corridor ends in front of a white limestone block. On its smoothed surface, the traces of two copper fittings of the same kind as those on the

140 top
The original entrance in the north side of the pyramid of Khufu. Below it is the entrance cut by the ancient tomb robbers.

140 bottom left
The Great Gallery of the pyramid of Khufu is 47 meters long and 8.50 meters high with a perfectly corbelled roof.

140 bottom center
The antechamber of Khufu's pyramid, the so-called Queen's Chamber, has a statue niche in the east wall.

140 bottom right
The king's burial chamber, with the red granite sarcophagus, is completely built of granite; the roof consists of nine enormous granite beams, weighing each about 40 tons.

141 left
Giza, Khufu's pyramid: cross section through the burial apartment with the King's Chamber (J), a corridor chamber (I) with the room for the

portcullis blocking stones, and five stress-relieving chambers (K). A roughly hewn corridor connects the top of the Great Gallery with the first of the relieving chambers.

142-143
The pyramid of Khufu with the Great Sphinx.

southern blocking or porticullis stone are visible. These are surely not handles, but magic hieroglyphic signs for the soul of the king. On the surface, faint traces of quarry marks are detectable, the sign of the work-gang *wadj* ('the green one'), and probably the hieroglyph *prjj*, 'to come out' (of the tomb). One can be absolutely sure that these corridors served only the ascent of the soul of the dead king to the northern and southern sky and that there were definitely no hidden chambers behind these blocks.

It is characteristic of the conservative beliefs and traditions of the ancient Egyptians that alongside the predominant theology, centered on worship of the sun, older ideas about an underworld afterlife in the depths of the earth were tolerated. This 'chthonic' or netherworld aspect is manifested in the rock chamber cut thirty meters deep into the solid ground underneath. The corridor on the east side of the rock chamber, which might have led to a southern tomb underneath the pyramid, was never completed; perhaps the workmen did not have enough air to breathe at this extreme depth. Khufu later built a small southern pyramid on the southeast corner of his pyramid enclosure, only discovered and excavated a few years ago. The middle chamber has a statue niche on the east side for a *ka* statue of the king and, like the granite chamber, has model corridors leading to heaven. This chamber cannot ever have served as an actual burial chamber since it was not provided with a stone sarcophagus or a sealing by portcullises (stone plugs released from above in the entrance corridors). Through the inclusion of a closed cult area in the body of the pyramid, the precinct outside was reduced to the mortuary temple of which only the basalt paving remains today. From the pattern of markings in the paving it is evident that the temple once consisted of a broad court surrounded by columns and a chapel for mortuary offerings. Also added later, and only after the south tomb in the rock beneath the pyramid had been abandoned, was a small cult pyramid in the southeast corner of the complex. Fragments of statues made of limestone and other materials are evidence of the rich decoration of the mortuary temple.

Khufu

AXONOMETRIC VIEW OF THE PYRAMID OF KHUFU

A	ENTRANCE	G	HORIZONTAL CORRIDOR
B	DESCENDING CORRIDOR	H	GREAT GALLERY
C	SUBTERRANEAN ROCK CHAMBER	I	CORRIDOR CHAMBER WITH PORTCULLISES
D	SERVICE CORRIDOR	J	KING'S CHAMBER
E	ASCENDING CORRIDOR	JJ	AIR SHAFTS
F	ANTECHAMBER	K	STRESS RELIEVING CHAMBERS
FF	AIR SHAFTS		

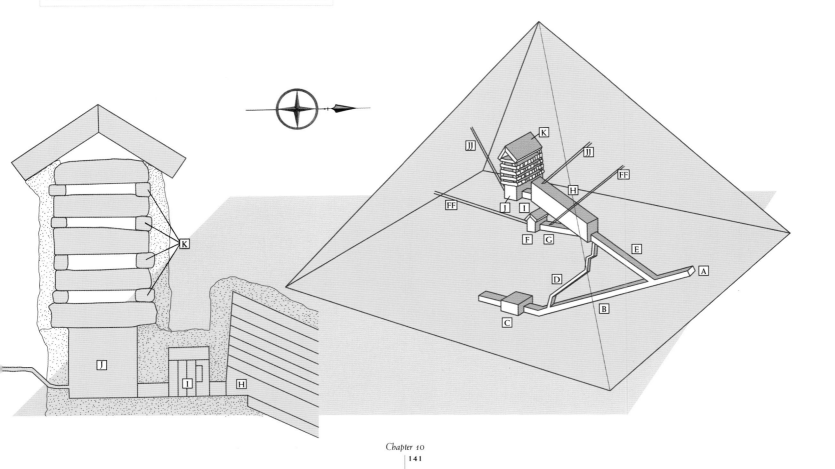

The necropolis was planned just as precisely and carefully as the pyramid complex itself. Five shafts in the rock to the east and south of the pyramid once contained funerary barques—not solar barques—for Khufu. The two shafts to the south of the pyramid were originally found sealed. The eastern shaft contained a royal ship complete with all its oars and cords, dismantled into over 1,200 pieces. Now reassembled, it measures 43.40 m long. The other barque burial has not yet been opened, although recent video images taken through a drill hole showed that the ship it contains has been badly damaged by the environmental impact of the underground rock and the construction of the Boat Museum above the eastern shaft. Undoubtedly both ships provided transport for the king while he was alive and were to be at his disposal in the afterlife. These are not the only ships found in a royal necropolis. As early

as the First and Second Dynasties, kings were provided with ships for the afterlife. To the east of the Great Pyramid lie three small pyramids. One belongs to the king's mother Hetepheres, main consort of Sneferu, who outlived her husband and died in her son's palace at Giza and was buried there. The other two pyramids belong to the two chief queens, Meretites and Henutsen, mothers of Khufu's sons and successors, Djedefre and Khafre. The genuine sons and daughters of the king were given huge, solid double *mastabas* to the east of the queens' pyramids. High court officials, the architects, and even prince Hemiunu, the influential building manager of the king's pyramid, were given tombs in the western cemetery. To the east, down in the valley and near to his palace, Khufu carved one of the greatest statues ever created, the Great Sphinx, now recognized as a genuine *chef-d'oeuvre* of Khufu. The

tradional assignment of the Great Sphinx to Khafre has no archaeological, epigraphic, or stylistic basis. On the contrary, all pieces of evidence point firmly to Khufu. The sphinx is hewn out of a large rock formation inside the quarries of Khufu. The stylistic and iconographic features are those of Khufu. The overall form of the Sphinx's face is broad, almost square, with a broad chin, whereas the features of Khafre are long, noticeably narrower and the chin almost pointed. The Sphinx has the earlier, old fashioned, fully-pleated type of *nemes* headcloth, like that of Djoser's statue. The same *nemes*, fully pleated, can be seen on the fragment of a statue of Khufu in the Museum of Fine Arts, Boston, which comes from Khufu's pyramid temple. It is remarkable that the *nemes* has no band in the form of a raised hem over the brow. This is again the older type, like Djoser's. From Djedefre and Khafre onward, the raised hem band

over the brows becomes the norm. Under Khafre, only the lappets of the *nemes* headcloth are pleated but never the *nemes* head or the *nemes* wings. The side wings of the *nemes* headcloth of the Sphinx are deeply hollowed, but with Khafre hardly at all. With Khafre the headcloth corners curl up, but they do not do so with the Sphinx. The Sphinx has a uraeus cobra placed on the lower edge of the headcloth. In contrast to those of Khafre and Menkaure, it shows high relief with naturalistic detailing of the serpent's neck and the scales of its hood. The eyebrows of the Sphinx bulge powerfully forward, and they are pitched high and slope down toward the temples. The monumentality of the head owes something, perhaps, to the large, wide-open eyes, which are deep-set and strongly modeled. These wide-open eyes are absolutely typical of sculptured reserve heads from the time of Khufu. The ears are fundamentally

different from those of the statue of Khafre. The ears of the Sphinx are very broad and folded forward, those of Khafre elongated and situated closer to the temples. A decisive criterion is the absence of a beard. The sphinx has no indications of hair on its chin. There is also no trace of a break under the chin. Consequently, there would not have been a beard on the Sphinx in the Old Kingdom. The fragments of a plaited god's beard which are now in the British Museum in London and in the Cairo Museum are certainly of New Kingdom origin, and were added to the Sphinx when it was identified with and adored as god Harmachis. Certainly, the rounded god's beard is an innovation of the New Kingdom and did not exist in the Old Kingdom or the Middle Kingdom. When this beard was added, a small platform was carved out of the Sphinx's chest on which the beard and a royal statue rested. The beard is a royal

attribute. Some kings wear a beard, others do not. In the Old Kingdom it is an absolute and strict rule that if a king wears the beard, it appears in all representations, sculpture and relief, in Upper Egypt and in Lower Egypt—there is no exception. In the Fourth Dynasty one can observe that Sneferu never has a beard, nor does Khufu, neither on his small ivory statue nor on the Brooklyn Museum or the Munich Museum heads. From Djedefre on, however, all kings, including Khafre and Menkaure, wear the ceremonial beard in relief and in sculpture. Userkaf, the first king of the Fifth Dynasty, however, abandons the beard again, but has a moustache. In the recent excavations of a Japanese mission, a small sphinx was discovered. It bears the name of Khufu and Pepy I. This proves that in the Sixth Dynasty, the awareness was still alive that it was Khufu who created the Great Sphinx.

King Khufu himself influenced the form of the tomb chapels and their decoration, which is limited only to scenes of the most important offerings. In this way, state and society were included, in a unique and monumental way, in the strict hierarchy of the royal necropolis and in the imaginary world of the king's afterlife, in order that they might serve him forever. They also became recipients of royal donations and offerings from the central royal mortuary temple.

We know as little about the person of Khufu as we do of other kings of the Old Kingdom. The critique of his reign and achievements handed down by Herodotus is a purely Greek reaction to the superb architecture that towers above everything on a human scale, which for a Greek could only signal human hubris. That Khufu was Sneferu's son we know only from the chance find of the tomb equipment of his mother Hetepheres in a shaft burial at Giza. When Queen Hetepheres died, she was initially buried in this shaft tomb, until her pyramid, the northernmost of the queens' pyramids, was completed to the east of the pyramid of Khufu. Khufu must have been one of the younger sons of Sneferu,

probably born at Dahshur, in about the twentieth year of Sneferu's reign, which would mean that Khufu came to the throne when he was about twenty-five to thirty years old. By this time, his older brothers, the princes Nefermaat and Rahotep, who were the architects of the pyramids at Meidum and Dahshur, had already died. Never before or ever again in Egyptian history are the claims of divine kingship so powerfully expressed. That this could be completed in the twenty-three to twenty-six, or more likely thirty, years of his reign, is the result of the remarkable training of the managers, architects, and workers engaged in undertakings that had now continued for half a century. This enabled the participants to accomplish astonishing achievements: the hollowing out of a 100 m shaft into a deep and solid rock bed; the preparation and storage of incredibly heavy stones to provide a constant supply for the teams of workmen; the design of ramps and transport routes that cost a minimum in time and materials and which still did not hinder the continuing process of surveying as the pyramids rose upward. The details of how this was done are still largely unknown.

Recent research into pyramid building by architects, construction engineers, and archaeologists of the German Institute of Archaeology in Cairo examining different models has resulted in the proposition of a new theory that the transport of the stones was achieved by initially using a number of small ramps on all sides of the pyramid. When they reached a height of about 20 to 25 meters—by this time nearly 40 percent of the stone had been laid—the small ramps had to be abandoned, as their inclination would have become too steep. Therefore, another method of transport had to be used. A single direct ramp sloping up against one side of the pyramid must be excluded; it would have been about 1,500 m long and would enclose more than seven times the material of the pyramid. Similarly, a double spiral ramp, starting at two or even all four corners of the pyramid and spiraling upward while resting on the unfinished casing of the pyramid, would have posed enormous difficulties during construction as it would have been nearly impossible to constantly control the correct inclination by means of beams. It is therefore proposed that an inclining ramp was built on one side

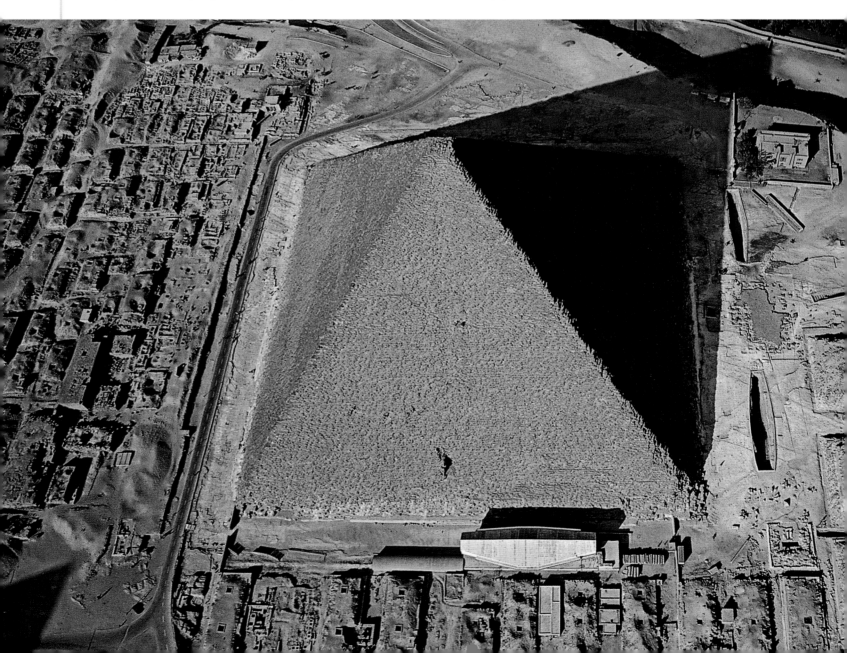

of the pyramid. At first, this inclining ramp could have used the material of the small ramps. After reaching a height of about 100 meters—then already 97 percent of all building material was put in place—even the inclining ramp would have become too steep to still be useful. For the last 40 meters, stepped ramps and combined mechanics, levers, and even pulleys might have been used. The top stone of the pyramid, the pyramidion, might have been brought up already in an earlier stage via the ramp and constantly raised from level to level during construction until it could be placed on the top. At a much later time, Egyptian priests reported strange stories on pyramid construction to the Greek historian Herodotus. They told him about a workforce of hundreds of thousands of workers, slaves, and bonded laborers working during the inundation season using wooden levers and machines to lift the stones. These fanciful stories are still repeated in our time. It is, however, evident, that the narrow building sites did not leave sufficient room for such large numbers of people. According to quarry marks which were found and registered during the excavations

at the northern pyramid of Sneferu at Dahshur, a highly specialized troop of workmen, a kind of pioneer army, worked all year round, not only during one season. Our calculations suggest a number of workers not exceeding 20–25,000: quarrymen and stonemasons, sappers and carriers, bricklayers and plasterers, suppliers and servers of food, and by then many engineers and architects. With the estimated total population of Egypt at around two million people, their numbers would have lain just below one percent of the total population of the country. They were hardly affected by the pyramid-building program. Even the costs and material assets for the building and its teams of workers remain within reason with this percentage. A new class of men and their families, professional members of the court, administrators, and craftsmen, occupied the towns that surrounded the palace and pyramids. They were employed as priests and officers of the mortuary temple. It is these people who shaped the state, and enabled it to achieve ever greater accomplishments. For a better understanding of the Pyramid Age we must distance ourselves once and for all from the positivist

viewpoint of the nineteenth and early twentieth centuries, and remember that the construction of the pyramids, the layout of the tomb chambers, and the form and size of the mortuary temple were not only an architectural achievement and a technical progress, but that they were determined by religious ceremonies and the needs of the cult. These, and nothing else, were the real motives. The burial chamber system inside the pyramid and the form of the mortuary temple outside are interrelated. A sophisticated arrangement of the burial chambers corresponds to simple architecture in the mortuary temple and vice versa. The size of a pyramid is in no way a measure of the power and position of its builder. For example, Djedefre, the son and successor of Khufu, began building his pyramid on a much smaller scale, but in such a commanding position at Abu Rawash (north of Giza) that it dominates the landscape because of its location in just the same way that Khufu's pyramid does at Giza. Although unfinished, the mortuary temple of Djedefre was nevertheless adorned with many statues of the king of the highest quality.

144-145
The pyramid of Khufu with boat pits, the Solar Boat Museum, the satellite pyramid in the southeast corner, the mortuary temple, and the cemeteries of the queens and high officials.

145 top
The portico of the mastaba tomb of the Seshemnefer family, high officials of the Fifth Dynasty and residents of Khufu's pyramid town.

145 bottom
The Giza Plateau seen from the east with the Eastern Cemetery and the small pyramids of Khufu's queens and the large double mastabas of Khufu's sons and daughters.

This can be demonstrated even more clearly by the examples of the complexes of Khafre and Menkaure. Khafre was one of Khufu's younger sons. He came to the throne unexpectedly after the sudden and early death of his brother Djedefre. Khafre's pyramid was intended to equal the height of that of his father, which he achieved, in fact, through the choice of a slightly higher site and a steeper angle of slope. He therefore named his pyramid "Khafre is the Greatest." For the first time the base of the pyramid was cased with blocks of beautiful red granite. At the top of the pyramid the original casing is still preserved. On the other hand, the system of chambers is so simple that in the 1960s serious attempts were made by a team of prominent American scientists using the most modern technical equipment to locate additional rooms in the pyramid, without success. The burial chamber is quite large and impressive with its high gabled roof, and a marvelous sarcophagus was discovered only in 1818 by Giovanni Battista Belzoni, but of course it was already ravaged in antiquity. The funeral temple and the valley temple of Khafre are very lavishly constructed using enormous blocks for the core masonry and granite for the casing. They, too, were cased with smoothly polished red granite blocks, as were the huge square pillars of the valley temple. The rooms of the valley temple are surrounded by massive cyclopean stone walls, creating the impression either that the temple was enclosed in a solid cliff, or that it was carved from the heart of the pyramid and set down outside it. More than seventy majestic hard-stone statues that once decorated the funerary and valley temples contributed to this effect by depicting the king as the visible image of the gods, among them the famous seated statue of Khafre protected by the falcon god Horus. Recent excavations in front of the valley temple brought important cult installations to light, connected with the cult of Sokaris. This was certainly part of Rosetau, perhaps the first stage of this famous cult location which is reported from the Fourth Dynasty to the Roman Period. To the south of the main pyramid, the outline and some casing blocks of the south pyramid are still in place. In a separate shaft slightly to the west of this pyramid, a wooden box was hidden which contained an enigmatic scaffolding, probably a carrying shrine for the *ka* statue buried in the south pyramid.

146
This diorite statue of Khafre, 168 cm high, with the falcon god Horus protecting the king, was found in the valley temple. It is now in the Egyptian Museum, Cairo.

147
Aerial view of the complex of surrounding the pyramid of Khafre.

 *Khafre*

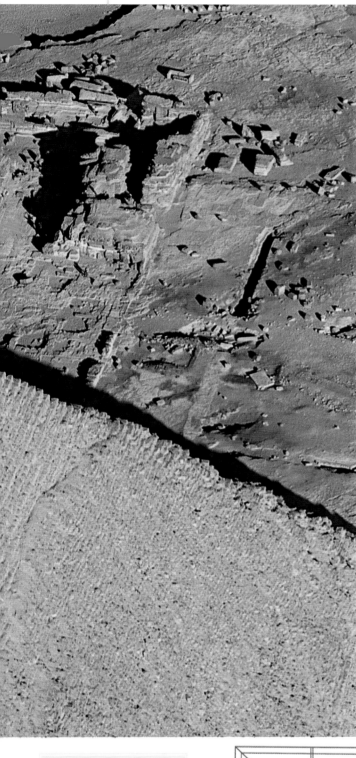

148-149
The top of the pyramid of Khafre presents well-preserved casing stones. To the right are the remains of Khafre's mortuary temple.

148 bottom right
The burial chamber of the pyramid of Khafre presents a magnificent black granite sarcophagus, which is embedded in the floor of the chamber.

148 bottom left
The valley temple of Khafre was completely built in shining red granite.

149
This view from north shows the Western Cemetery looking toward the pyramids of Khafre and Menkaure.

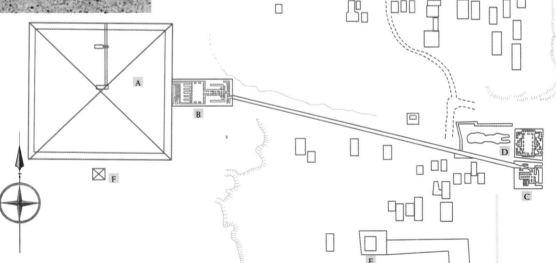

MAP OF KHAFRE'S
PYRAMID PRECINCT

A PYRAMID
B MORTUARY TEMPLE
C VALLEY TEMPLE
D SPHINX DITCH
E TOMB OF QUEEN
   KHENTKAUS
F SATELLITE PYRAMID

Menkaure

The third pyramid at Giza, the pyramid of Menkaure, is remarkably small. It had, however, a casing of sixteen courses of wonderful red Aswan granite. Menkaure had a long and peaceful reign of twenty-eight years, and there is no reason to assign the reduction of the height and mass of his pyramid to an economic crisis.

The explanation must be sought elsewhere. We must reconsider our understanding of the pyramids as royal monuments representing power only, and think of them also as religious monuments comparable to the cathedrals of the European Middle Ages and Renaissance. It was not only their size but their religious significance that determined their form and style. The system of the corridors and funerary apartments in the pyramid of Menkaure is characterized by an extraordinary succession of rooms comparable only with those of Khufu's pyramid, except that those of Menkaure lead down into the rock whereas those of Khufu are ascending. Certainly this different design was not

the result of secondary architectural corrections; it may already attest to the new concept of the underworld god Osiris. His funerary temple is, however, more like that of Khufu, consisting of a broad, open courtyard with a large and deep offering chapel. Within this temple itself and in the valley temple, a large number of statues of different materials—limestone, alabaster, and granite—were discovered.

With the three pyramids in Giza, the development of the pyramid complexes reached its apogee. Already the kings of the Eighteenth Dynasty showed a deep respect for the pyramids, the monuments of their ancestors at Giza. Greek travelers from the sixth century onward admired these enormous monuments even if they did not understand their religious meaning.

A Greek poet of the second century BC included the pyramids of Giza within the 'Seven Wonders of the World.' They are now the only ones that survive.

150
This triad of Menkaure in green-grey schist, 95.5 cm high, with the goddess Hathor and Bat, the goddess of the 7th Upper-Egyptian nome, belongs to a group of statues, numbering at least eight, which at one time were standing in the valley temple of Menkaure. Now in Egyptian Museum, Cairo.

151
This head from a seated statue, found in the valley temple of Menkaure, is now conserved in the Egyptian Museum in Cairo. The statue, which is made of alabaster and is 161 cm high, portrays a pharaoh in all his majesty.

152-153
This aerial photograph clearly shows
the pyramid of Menkaure with the
remains of his mortuary temple.

152 bottom right
Inside the pyramid of Menkaure is a
rock chamber with six niches, perhaps
for storage of offerings.

152 bottom left
The corridor chamber of the pyramid
of Menkaure still presents fine,
panelled decoration.

153
The pyramid of Menkaure seen from the
north with part of its granite casing, the
entrance, and a great gash reportedly made
by Caliph Othman in the 12th century.

AXONOMETRIC PLAN OF THE PYRAMID OF MENKAURE

A	MAIN PYRAMID		FOR THE CASEMENT OF		ONCE IT CONTAINED
B	CULT PYRAMID		THE BURIAL CHAMBER		A BEAUTIFULLY DECORATED
C, D	QUEENS' PYRAMIDS	**c**	CORRIDOR CHAMBER AND		SARCOPHAGUS OF
E	MORTUARY TEMPLE		HORIZONTAL CORRIDOR		DARK GRANITE REMOVED
a	ENTRANCE AND DESCENDING	**d**	ANTECHAMBER		BY VYSE AND LOST IN A
	CORRIDOR	**dd**	STATUE NICHE		SHIP WRECK OFF THE COAST
b	SHAFT USED TO PULL IN	**e**	BURIAL CHAMBER CASED		OF SPAIN
	THE GRANITE BLOCKS		WITH DARK GRANITE, IT		

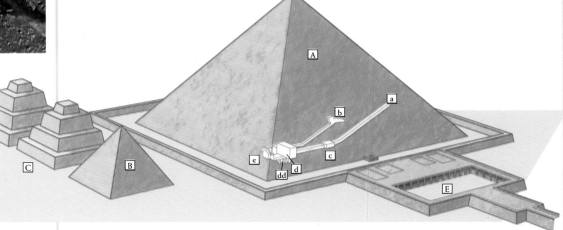

Chapter 11

The Queens' Pyramids of the Fourth Dynasty at Giza

by Zahi Hawass

The Giza kings each had a number of queens associated with them. Some of these queens were buried in the *mastaba* cemeteries that cover the plateau; others were given their own small pyramids in the complexes of their husbands or sons.

There are seven queens' pyramids at Giza: three in the complex of Khufu, one in the complex of Khafre, and three in the complex of Menkaure.

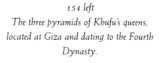

154 left
The three pyramids of Khufu's queens, located at Giza and dating to the Fourth Dynasty.

154-155
Menkaure's three queens' pyramids, dating to the Fourth Dynasty, in front of the pyramids of Menkaure, Khafre, and Khufu, at Giza.

156-157
This aerial view, taken from the eastern
side, shows the three queens' pyramids
of King Khufu, the Great Pyramid of
Khufu, and the pyramids of Khafre
and Menkaure at Giza, Fourth
Dynasty.

157 top right
This photograph shows the area
surrounding the Pyramid of Khufu: two
of the solar boat pits of Khufu, the
satellite pyramid, and the three pyramids
of Khufu's queens are visible, Fourth
Dynasty.

THE QUEENS' PYRAMIDS IN THE COMPLEX OF KHUFU

Three small pyramids, generally attributed to queens of Khufu, lie in a north-south row just outside the east enclosure wall of the Great Pyramid and to the south of the causeway. Archaeological evidence for a small chapel exists on the eastern side of each pyramid; two boat pits were also found, one each on the southern sides of the northernmost and the central pyramids.

These pyramids were first explored in modern times by Vyse in 1837; the area was excavated again early in the 1900s by George Reisner, who recorded most of the architectural components. As part of my site management plan, our Egyptian team did some clearance work around these pyramids, which added to the understanding of these monuments.

The pyramids are not part of the inner complex of Khufu since they are outside the inner enclosure wall which surrounds the Great Pyramid. Instead, they seem to be part of the eastern field containing the *mastabas* of Khufu's closest relatives. Access from the north of the plateau would have been through a tunnel cut under the causeway.

157 bottom
These plans and sections refer to King Khufu's queens' pyramids: GI-c, GI-b, and GI-a (from left to right). The top drawing depicts the reconstruction of the three pyramids; the lower drawings illustrate the design of the pyramids, showing each with a sloping passage leading to a chamber, with a right-angle turn that leads into the burial chamber.

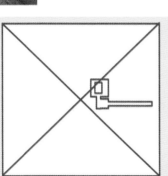
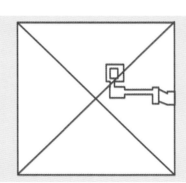
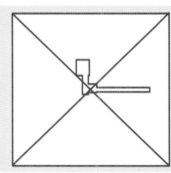

THE NORTHERN PYRAMID: GI-A

This pyramid lies 61 meters from the base of Khufu's pyramid. Its base measures 49.5 m, and it would originally have stood 30.25 m high. It has been stripped of most of its casing and has lost almost two-thirds of its height. The entrance is just east of the center of the north face, slightly above ground level.

The interior chambers were cut into the bedrock of the plateau. The burial chamber was lined with limestone, and Reisner believed that it originally housed a sarcophagus made of limestone or granite. A shallow recess, within which several fragments of basalt were found, was carved into the west wall of this chamber. Vyse believed that these were fragments of a basalt sarcophagus that once stood there, but Italian scholars Maragioglio and Rinaldi suggested instead that the basalt fragments were from the pavement of the upper temple of Khufu. This latter

explanation is reasonable, since other fragments of this pavement have been found scattered all over the area east of Khufu's pyramid.

The area just east of pyramid GI-a was cleared to the level of the bedrock, in which cuttings forming a rectangle can be seen. These cuttings are thought to be emplacements for a platform on which a cult chapel would have been built; unfortunately, these traces in the bedrock are all that remain of the chapel. A boat pit was found cut into the bedrock on the southern side of the pyramid. There is a ledge near the upper edge of the walls of this pit on which roofing slabs would have been laid.

Due to the proximity of GI-a to the *mastaba* of Khufu's crown prince, Kawab, Reisner assigns this pyramid to Kawab's mother, who would have been the main queen of Khufu. An inscription in Kawab's *mastaba* reads: "Her son, her beloved, Kawab, the daughter of her God, [she who is in charge] of the affairs [of the

im3t], Meritites [his mother] who bore [him] to Khufu." A stela found by Mariette, for which there is no exact provenance, but which was presumably found in the eastern field, calls Meritites "The great officiant of Sneferu and Khufu, revered by Khafre." Meritites was clearly important enough to merit a pyramid tomb, and the position of Kawab's tomb nearby makes it likely GI-a was indeed her monument.

An alternative suggestion has been made by Mark Lehner, who proposes that GI-a was originally built as the tomb of Hetepheres I, Khufu's mother. He interprets one particular group of cuttings in the bedrock as evidence that GI-a was begun farther to the east, and notes that the shaft in which her burial equipment, but not her body, was found is aligned with the original position of GI-a on the north. Later, after GI-a in its modified position was completed, her body was moved to its burial chamber with a new set of burial equipment.

The Middle Pyramid: GI-b

This pyramid is about 10 meters south of GI-a and lies on the same north-south axis. Its base is 49 meters square and its original height would have been 30 meters. It is also in poor condition, having lost most of its casing and almost half its height. Its entrance is located in the center of its north face, just above ground level. As is the case for GI-a, all of the subterranean passages were cut from bedrock, and the burial chamber is lined with limestone.

It is certain that a simple cult chapel stood against the east face of GI-b. A boat pit similar to the one alongside GI-a was found on the south side of GI-b by Kamal El Mallakh in 1953. It was filled with stone and rubble by the excavator because it projected into the area where the modern road was to be built, and thus is not visible today.

Reisner proposed that GI-b be assigned to an unknown queen of Libyan origin. She would have been the mother of a secondary group of Khufu's children, including Djedefre. He cited the facts that Djedefre built his pyramid at Abu Rawash rather than Giza and that the tomb of Djedefhor, also possibly a son of this queen (although other scholars believe he was a son of Meritites), was purposefully destroyed, as evidence that there was disagreement between various branches of the family after the death of Khufu. More recent work at both Giza and Abu Rawash tends to contradict the theory of a family feud, and Reisner's idea of a Libyan origin for this queen has also been disproved. However, GI-b might still have been designed for the burial of the unknown queen who bore Djedefre. Lehner suggests, alternatively, that this pyramid was built for Meritites; Stadelmann agrees with this interpretation.

158
The northern queens' pyramid of Khufu, the Great Pyramid, and the pyramid of Khafre in the background. Giza, Fourth Dynasty.

159
The middle pyramid of Khufu's queens' pyramids. Giza, Fourth Dynasty.

THE SOUTHERN PYRAMID: GI-C

This is the best preserved of the three small pyramids; it retains much of its core and several courses of its casing. It lies about 3.8 m south of GI-b, and is offset slightly to the east. The length of its base is 46.25 m and its original height was 29.62 m. Its entrance, like that of the others, is located on the north face, approximately in the center and just above ground level. Several casing blocks remain *in situ* around the entrance. Just west of the entrance are blocks of limestone at a right angle to the face of the pyramid; Maragioglio and Rinaldi think that these represent a later addition. The layout of the underground chambers is similar to the other queens' pyramids; the burial chamber is again lined with limestone. There is a four centimeter-deep niche in the south wall of the burial chamber; Maragioglio and Rinaldi suggest that this served an unspecified ritual purpose.

On the eastern side of the pyramid, a later temple to Isis incorporates the remains of the Fourth Dynasty cult chapel. The Fourth Dynasty chapel was built on a platform of colossal limestone blocks that abutted the eastern face of the pyramid. The original entrance was in the east wall, the outer face of which was decorated with a design of matting carved in shallow relief. On the west wall of the chapel, only one block of limestone from the south end remains. This block has a niched design carved on it. Later additions and modifications have destroyed the original interior plan of the chapel.

Since both of the other queens' pyramids had boat pits on their southern sides, I wanted to see whether GI-c might also have a boat pit associated with it. We did not find a pit, but the area to the south had been prepared for a pit that was never cut. We also found evidence that the pyramid superstructure had been left unfinished—two perpendicular lines carved into the bedrock, which indicated where the corner would have

been set. GI-c is generally attributed to Henutsen on the basis of a stela, usually referred to as the 'Inventory Stela,' which was found by Mariette in the Isis temple that was built onto the eastern chapel. The relevant part of this stela reads: "Live Horus Medju Hor, king of Upper and Lower Egypt, Khufu, given life. It was beside the house of the Sphinx on the northwest of the house of Osiris, lord of Rostaw, that he established the house of Isis. It was beside the temple of this goddess that he built his pyramid. It was beside this temple that he built a pyramid for the king's daughter, Henutsen."

This stela is dated to the Eighteenth Dynasty, but may be a modified copy of an earlier inscription. If it were an exact copy, it would mean that the Sphinx had been carved before the reign of Khufu, which we know to be incorrect. In any case, Henutsen is an Old Kingdom name, and in the absence of any other evidence for or against this attribution, it seems reasonable to let it stand.

THE DECORATION
OF THE CHAPELS

Decorated fragments that may have come from the chapels of the three pyramids discussed above have been found in several areas. These fragments are comparable in artistic style, quality, and subject matter to other reliefs from funerary temples of the Old Kingdom. The subject matter of the relief fragments can be sorted into six categories: queens' titles, names of royal children, palace façades, boats being paddled with oars, the bringing of offerings and offering lists, and miscellaneous fragments of inscription.

POST-OLD KINGDOM
HISTORY

At some point, presumably after the fall of the Old Kingdom, the small pyramids and their chapels were badly damaged. As mentioned above, all of the pyramids have lost most of their casing blocks, and GI-a and GI-b have lost much of their cores. The chapels of GI-a and GI-b have left only very meager traces.

As is generally the case at Giza, there is no archaeological or textual evidence of cultic activity at any of these pyramids during the Middle Kingdom. It is not until the Eighteenth Dynasty that any interest was taken in these monuments. During this period, the chapel of GI-c was used as a temple to Isis, probably in connection with the worship of the Sphinx. The name, Henutsen, which is given to the owner of GI-c contains the hieroglyph *Henwt*, which means 'mistress,' providing a link to the cult of Isis as Mistress of the Pyramids. The chapel was added to in the Twenty-first and Twenty-sixth Dynasties, and eventually spanned the area from the east face of GI-c to the west face of the *mastabas* of Khufukhaf and his wife (G 7130–71400).

At some point, the boat pits of GI-a and GI-b were divided by walls into compartments. It has been suggested that they were used in later periods for burials, or possibly as magazines in the Twenty-sixth Dynasty.

THE SUBSIDIARY PYRAMID
OF KHAFRE GII-A

A single subsidiary pyramid (GII-a) lies to the south of Khafre's pyramid, in the area between the inner and outer enclosure walls. It is on the north-south axis of the pyramid, about 29 meters from its base. Very little of the superstructure remains, but blocks of local limestone found on the site indicate that it was built of this material, and show that the inclination of the faces was between 53 and 54 degrees.

There are two entrances to the rock-cut substructure of this pyramid. The first is a series of steps leading downward in the center of the pyramid's north side; a second descending passage leads into the pyramid from a point beyond the northern base. The walls of the burial chamber were plastered and numerous reference lines, whose purpose is unclear, can

be seen. Pieces of wood, ox bones, fragments of stoppers from jars or vases and two carnelian necklaces were found inside the burial chamber. One of the stoppers bears an inscription which reads: "The eldest royal son of his body, beloved by him, the sole friend." No trace of a stone sarcophagus was found in the substructure of this pyramid. The wood fragments have been reassembled by Ahmed Youssef; they once formed a type of shrine known as a 'divine booth,' the sort of structure which is shown in tomb scenes with a statue inside. There are traces of what may be part of an altar on the north side of the entrance; if there was a chapel on the east, it is now completely destroyed and no traces remain. Some scholars believe that GII-a belonged to a queen of Khafre, citing its location, the size of its burial chamber, and the necklaces found inside. Others think that, since no stone fragments that could have belonged to a sarcophagus were found, it was a ritual pyramid, or even a temporary burial place for the king's body while the main pyramid was being completed. Lehner supports the identification as a ritual pyramid, citing the wood pieces from a statue shrine as evidence that is was used for the burial of a statue dedicated to the *ka* of Khafre. I believe that it was a queens' pyramid. The tombs of two of Khafre's queens, Khamerernebty I (mother of Menkaure) and Meresankh III, are known to us, but there are at least two other queens whose tombs are still unidentified.

160-161
The southern queens' pyramid from the east side with the Isis temple, and the pyramids of Khufu, Khafre, and Menkaure in the background. Giza, Fourth Dynasty.

161 left
In this aerial view, just behind the summit of the pyramid of Khafre, one can recognize the structure of the subsidiary pyramid of Khafre. Giza, Fourth Dynasty.

161 right
The base of the subsidiary pyramid of Khafre from the southern side. Giza, Fourth Dynasty.

QUEENS' PYRAMIDS IN THE COMPLEX OF MENKAURE

Three subsidiary pyramids lie to the south of the pyramid of Menkaure. They are located just outside the inner enclosure wall of the pyramid and inside the outer enclosure wall. The three pyramids were first recorded by Lepsius, and then investigated by Vyse. Reisner was the last to enter and describe them until recently, when I entered the burial chamber of the easternmost of the three.

The three pyramids lie on the same east-west axis. On the east side of each is a mud-brick temple. An 80 centimeter-thick wall of stone rubble surrounds the three pyramids; this wall can be entered via the northwest corner of the temple of the easternmost of the pyramids, by a road lined on either side by a thick wall that connects to the upper temple of Menkaure. The fact that this is the only access to the temples of the small pyramids suggests that the priests who performed the daily rite for Menkaure also performed them for the occupants of the small pyramids.

THE EASTERN PYRAMID: GIII-A

This pyramid is the largest of the three and is the only one built as a true pyramid; it is sometimes referred to as the fourth pyramid of Giza. The pyramid was built of local limestone and the lowermost course was cased with granite. It is thought that the rest of the pyramid was cased with Tura limestone, but there is no evidence for this; the casing could also have been constructed completely in granite.

Pyramid GIII-a measures 44 meters on each side, and it originally stood at a height of 28.4 meters. The main entrance to the interior chambers is located in the north face. The subterranean apartments consist of a narrow descending corridor cased with limestone, which opens into a roughly square area closed by a portcullis; then a short corridor leading to the burial chamber. I recently explored these apartments during a live television special, and got stuck while squeezing

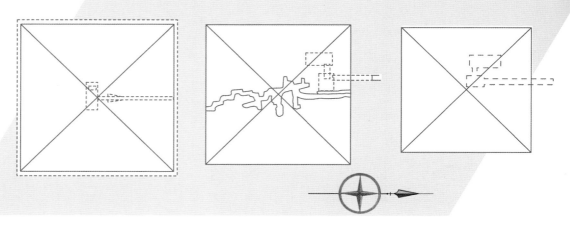

162-163
The queens' pyramids of Menkaure, dating to the Fourth Dynasty, stand in the desert area of the Giza Plateau.

162 bottom
These plans show the queens' pyramids of Menkaure: GIII-c, GIII-b, and GIII-a (from left to right).

163
The cross sections, which refer to the queens' pyramids of Menkaure GIII-c, GIII-b, and GIII-a (from left to right), clearly illustrate the different constructions of the three structures.

under this portcullis because of the camera on my back!

The burial chamber was unlined, and a granite sarcophagus was found embedded in a hole in the western side of the floor. This sarcophagus contained fragments of red pottery, green glazed pottery, and remains of burnt wood and reeds. The name of Menkaure was written in red ink on the ceiling of the burial chamber.

The temple to the east was built of mud brick on a platform of local limestone, which suggests that it was planned by Menkaure and built by his son and successor, Shepseskaf. Restoration was done in the temple in the Fifth and Sixth Dynasties, indicating that the cult of this queen was maintained at least to the end of the Old Kingdom.

The entrance to the temple is the at northeast corner. It is considerably more complex than the chapels associated with the pyramids of Khufu's queens. The temple can be divided into two sections: exterior spaces, which include a courtyard; and interior chambers, including a sanctuary. A number of finds were made in the exterior rooms: the remains of an altar of stone slabs; coal and ashes; and eight offering jars.

place, consisting of seven slabs of stone, was set into the floor. In one of the horizontal slabs is a small depression which could hold a small stone or pottery bowl. A rectangular basin rested on the floor beside the offering bench. In the debris, before the bench was found, about fifty to sixty small offering jars and red brown pottery saucers were discovered.

A mud-brick base north of the doorway may have supported a small obelisk, connected with the worship of Re, and was possibly added to the room during the Fifth or Sixth Dynasties. Fragments of an alabaster statue of a queen, fragments of other statues, a small pot containing five alabaster model cups bearing the name of the "King's son Kay," and a slate cup with no inscription were found in this hall.

A doorway in the center of the west wall of this room leads to the sanctuary. There is a niche in the center of the western wall, in which a statue of Hathor or Neith might have been placed. Another possibility is that the niche contained a false door for the queen, and that an altar was placed in front.

The sarcophagus found in the burial chamber of GIII-a leaves little room for doubt that this pyramid was

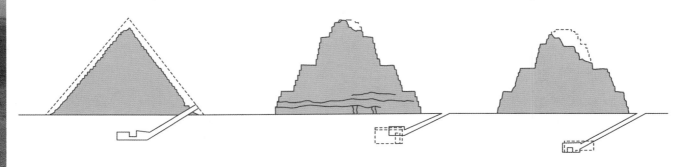

Reisner believes that some of these rooms were used as kitchens, and Maragioglio and Rinaldi suggest that the animals used for sacrifice in the courtyard were cooked in this area. However, these rooms are paved, and most kitchens were unpaved; it also seems to me inappropriate to place a kitchen inside the temple itself—the cooking should have been done elsewhere. Instead, I believe that these rooms were used as storage magazines during the Old Kingdom and that they were not converted into kitchens until the Roman period, when many tombs and temples in Egypt were used for this purpose.

The private part of the temple includes a long hall called the 'Hall of Niches.' The west wall of this hall is decorated with two large complex niches, one to each side of the door leading to what I believe was the sanctuary, and each was flanked by a total of six smaller niches. In the northwest corner of this room, an offering

used for burial. That the owner was a queen is strongly suggested by the statue fragments found in the temple, and by the arrangement of the compound niches in the inner offering room, which parallels the arrangement found in private chapels of the Fourth Dynasty. In private chapels, there are usually two inches, one for the tomb owner and one for his or her spouse. In the temple of GIII-a, the niches should be for the queen and Menkaure.

Reisner has suggested that GIII-a belonged to Khamerernebty II, the main queen of Menkaure, who is portrayed with him in several of the group statues found in the king's lower temple. He suggests that 'Kay,' whose name was found on five model cups, was the son of the queen who was buried here. This does seem the most likely attribution; however, both Ricke and Stadelmann believe that this pyramid was originally built as the satellite pyramid of Menkaure.

THE MIDDLE PYRAMID: GIII-B

This pyramid is located about 10.15 m west of GIII-a; it is a stepped pyramid of local limestone built in four stages. It measures 36 meters square and now stands to a height of nine meters. No casing blocks have been found, but it has been suggested that it was cased with fine limestone in such a way that the casing would have converted it into a straight-sided pyramid.

From an entrance in the north side of the pyramid, a rock-cut passage leads to an antechamber, in which an inscribed stone fragment reading "giving life" was found. This epithet usually follows a royal cartouche, which indicates that the person buried here was from the royal

The temple east of GIII-b was filled with debris of decayed mud brick mixed with sand, ashes, dust, and coal. The temple foundation was built of massive stones, and the temple itself was completed, presumably by Shepseskaf, in mud brick. It is not as large as the temple associated with GIII-a. The temple entrance is just east of the center of the north side, and is entered via the road from Menkaure's upper temple. The entrance leads to a rectangular room which is thought to have been a kitchen, magazine, or an anteroom. A doorway in the west wall of this room leads to a square chamber, thought to be a guardroom by Reisner; I believe it held temple equipment. In the eastern corner of the southern wall of the anteroom, a doorway leads to an open court,

was probably a magazine. I believe that the precious objects of the temple were stored here, and that it would have been closed and sealed with official seals. There is a compound niche in the southeast corner of the northern room; there was probably a matching niche on the north side, and a base or niche in the center on which, a statue of Hathor or Neith would have stood to represent the queen who was buried in the pyramid. This room is opposite the burial chamber, thus I believe that this room functioned as the temple sanctuary. Since skeletal remains of a young woman were found buried in a sarcophagus in GIII-b, its designation as a queen's pyramid seems fully justifiable. This attribution is also supported by the fragments of a

family. In the anteroom were also found pottery fragments, a piece of a green statuette, and a stick of uncertain date.

Beyond the anteroom is a burial chamber lined with granite. In this chamber, an undecorated sarcophagus of a size to fit a smallish person was found; inside were some bones and teeth belonging to a young woman. Quarry marks in red ink on the roof of this chamber contain the name Menkaure in a cartouche.

the floor and walls of which were plastered with mud.

A doorway in the southern wall of the court leads to a long north-south hall. In its northeast corner is an altar built of limestone slabs under which is a basin; the altar is of the sort seen in the temple of GIII-a. Sacrifices were probably performed in front of the altar and the basin. Two doorways in the western wall of this hall lead to rectangular rooms. The southernmost of these rooms had walls covered with thick plaster; this room

statue found inside the temple which indicate that the cult was kept up after the queen's death. The name of Menkaure found in a cartouche inside the pyramid, along with the fact that she is buried in his complex, supports the theory that this queen was related to Menkaure. It is likely that this queen was the mother of Shepseskaf. However, Reisner suggests that the queen who was buried in this pyramid was a secondary wife of Menkaure, who died after the king.

The Western Pyramid: GIII-c

This pyramid lies about 13.6 m west of GIII-b. It was built as a step pyramid of local limestone in four stages, and, as in the case of GIII-b, may have been intended to be cased so that it formed a true pyramid. It is in very poor condition, and only three of the stages are now visible. It is 36 meters square and stands at a height of nine meters.

An entrance in the north face leads through a descending corridor to an unfinished antechamber, and then through a short passage to the burial chamber, which was also left unfinished. Decayed wood, from something other than a coffin, and stones were found in all of the subterranean apartments, but no sarcophagus was found in the burial chamber.

The temple against the east face of GIII-c was built of mud-brick walls placed into trenches cut in the rock of the plateau. The temple underwent at least one change of plan; the walls were plastered and white washed and the floor was made of gravel and paved with mud. The temple entrance is located on the north side and consists of a doorway closed by a two-leaved door leading to a room east of the temple axis. A door in a cross-wall made of brick on the west side of the room gives access to a smaller room to the west. An offering jar, four rough-ware trays, six small model jars, two model bowls, and part of the neck of a jar were found in this room, suggesting that it was used for storage. The east room may have been a guardroom.

The temple also includes a large open court. The east, west, and north walls of this court are decorated with a series of simple and compound niches; on the south side was a portico. A great many objects were found in the area of the portico, including 620 small model offering bowls, 278 small offering models of various types, the lower part of the stand of a low bowl, and fragments of several bowls.

The temple contains a number of other chambers, including storage rooms and a hall lined with niches that appears to have been the sanctuary. A rectangular base of mud brick lies on the floor in the southwest corner of this hall; in front of this is an uninscribed basin of limestone. Among the finds from this hall were a small bag-shaped jar without a neck; 34 model offering jars, and 76 model offering bowls. The door in the west wall leads to another long hall, which may have functioned as the inner offering room, or possibly as a magazine for the precious objects of the cult.

The attribution of GIII-c is very difficult, as there is no evidence of a burial. The burial chamber was not lined, and there is no sarcophagus. Vyse believed that GIII-c was never used as a tomb in the Fourth Dynasty. However, his excavations in this pyramid and its temple convinced Reisner that a burial had been made in GIII-c during the Fourth Dynasty. He believes that statue fragments found in the temple, along with the fact that a cult was maintained in the temple after the Fourth Dynasty, prove that the pyramid was used for a royal burial. Maragioglio and Rinaldi add their observation that the temple had been replastered many times in the Old Kingdom, indicating that a cult was practiced here for a considerable amount of time. They comment that even if the temple had not been completed, the pyramid could have been used for a burial.

However, the evidence only proves that there was an active cult here; the temple could have been used for something other than the cult of a queen buried in the pyramid. The fact that the burial chamber was found empty and unfinished supports Vyse's contention that the pyramid was never used as a tomb. The owner of the pyramid has not been identified, and nothing was found inside or outside the pyramid, or inside the temple of GIII-c to indicate the name or the rank of the owner of this pyramid. We have no records giving us the name of a third queen of Menkaure.

I suggest that this was the cult pyramid of Menkaure, and that the cult practiced here was a cult of Menkaure himself. It seems reasonable to expect that Menkaure would have a ritual pyramid, in keeping with the cult layouts of the other Old Kingdom pyramids. As discussed above, some scholars assign the function of ritual pyramid to GIII-a, since it is the only true pyramid of the three, was partially or wholly cased with granite, and lies on the north-south axis of the main pyramid. It would then have been used afterward for a burial. This reasoning is not convincing for several reasons. First, there is cause to believe that both GIII-b and GIII-c would have been cased so that they acquired the forms of true pyramids. The partial granite casing of GIII-a could reflect the importance of the tomb's owner rather than a ritual function. The fact that GIII-a was undoubtedly used for a burial is good evidence that it was not the ritual pyramid.

The ritual pyramids of the Fifth and Sixth Dynasties are located east of the main pyramids' axis and Menkaure's complex contains many parallels to the Fifth and Sixth Dynasty complexes. Pyramid GIII-c is the only one of the three pyramids that did not contain a burial. Thus, it is the most likely candidate for ritual pyramid. However, the fact that it has a temple associated with it is a problem, since none of the known ritual pyramids have temples. Despite this difficulty, GIII-c remains the best possibility for the ritual pyramid of Menkaure.

The royal family of the Fourth Dynasty included many fascinating people. We have records of a number of powerful queens who would have been considered incarnations of the goddess Hathor, and thus fit mothers and consorts for their respective kings. The fact that so many of these queens were honored by burial in their own pyramids stands as tribute to their importance to the royal cult and the high honor in which they were held by their sons and husbands.

164-165
Menkaure's queens' pyramids seen from the east side. Giza, Fourth Dynasty.

165 top
Aerial view of the western pyramid of Menkaure's queens' pyramids, also known as GIII-c. Giza, Fourth Dynasty.

165 bottom
The middle pyramid of Menkaure's queens, also known as GIII-b. Giza, Fourth Dynasty.

Chapter 12

The Satellite Pyramid of Khufu

by Zahi Hawass

In 1991, my team at Giza was working to the east of the Great Pyramid of Khufu, clearing the area as part of our site management plan. The area had been explored before by George Reisner, and by the Antiquities Department under Selim Hassan who moved many meters of sand and excavated Khufu's upper temple. After Hassan's excavations were complete, the Antiquities Department prepared the site for visitors, and in the process built a paved road running north-south along the east face of the pyramid. We decided to move this road in 1991, in order to prevent cars and buses from driving on the basalt pavement of the upper temple. During this work, we made a startling discovery: a new subsidiary pyramid, the satellite pyramid of Khufu, lay under a mound of sand at the southeast corner of the Great Pyramid.

This pyramid is located about 25.5 m southeast of the corner of Khufu's pyramid. Its ruins cover an area approximately 24 meters square. The remains include fine, Tura-quality limestone blocks from the pyramid's outer casing and perimeter foundation, some of which remained *in situ*, large blocks of cruder limestone and debris that filled the core of the pyramid, and a T-shaped substructure.

When we first found the pyramid, all that remained of the superstructure was a U-shaped block of crude masonry and debris fill that surrounded the substructure on the west, south, and east. The east and south sides had the greatest number of preserved foundation slabs and casing blocks of fine, Tura-quality limestone. On the south side of the pyramid, we found an inscription in red paint on the north side of a core block, which reads: *"imy rsy gs,"* 'which is on the south [back] side.'

We recovered several blocks of the outer casing that were not in their original position. One of these was a casing block from the southeast corner, probably from the second course above the foundation platform. We found many casing blocks that had toppled out of place along the south side and lay scattered on the ground.

The original baseline, or setting line, marking the foot of the lowest course of casing blocks, is preserved on five foundation slabs on the east side and seven foundation blocks on the south side. We found no remains of the original baseline on the north side, where most of the foundation slabs were missing. We could see sockets or emplacements cut into the rock floor to receive the individual slabs, but these do not help determine the exact position of the original pyramid baseline. On the west side, there is only one foundation block *in situ* that carried the baseline. By measuring from the preserved baseline on the east to the single block on the west, we have ascertained the original base length of the pyramid as 21.75 m.

In the debris south of the pyramid, we found a large trapezoidal piece of Tura-quality limestone with three exterior sloping faces. This formed a little more than the south half of the third course below the apex of the pyramid. It is 2.7 m long and 0.56 m thick. Exposure has coated the exterior faces with a light brown patina. The average slope of the preserved faces is 52.4 degrees. The underside of the block is flat, but the top surface was concave. This concavity was intended to receive the convex underside of the block(s) forming the second course down from the top. Here, as it narrows to the apex, the pyramid superstructure is all casing, with no fill or core material.

The block or blocks of the second course down from the top are missing, but later we found the actual apex stone of the satellite pyramid: a single piece of fine limestone. It is the second oldest pyramidion ever found; the earliest belongs to the North Pyramid of Sneferu and was discovered by Rainer Stadelmann at Dahshur. The underside of the pyramidion was convex, with four triangular faces sloping outward. We know, from the decorated blocks we recently found at Abusir that the setting of the capstone atop the main pyramid was a major event, and marked the official completion of the pyramid complex.

The substructure of GI-d consists of a sloping entrance passage, approximately one meter wide, entered from the north, and leading downward for 5.35 m to a rectangular chamber, oriented east-west and measuring about eight meters by three and a half meters. We found this substructure unroofed, completely open to the sky. There is a cutting in the floor of the rectangular chamber, one meter wide, immediately in front of the opening into the chamber from the entrance passage. The walls of this chamber were cut to a depth of 2.85 m; the north and south walls slope inward slightly as they go up.

At the west end of the chamber there are four small holes, a pair each in the north and south walls respectively. The backs of the holes are round. They are about ten meters deep, and the holes of each pair are spaced about 1.45 m apart. These appear to be sockets for wood cross-beams, perhaps for lowering or covering an object in the west end of the chamber.

Since the upper part of the burial chamber is no longer extant, and no ceiling blocks remain, the original shape of the chamber remains a mystery. There are traces of red mortar on the floor of the burial chamber and on the south side. This mortar could indicate that the chamber was originally paved with limestone.

So that visitors to Giza can get an idea of the original appearance of this pyramid, and to preserve the loose and crumbling core material, we replaced some of the fallen blocks and restored parts of the satellite pyramid with new masonry. We also reconstructed the apex of the pyramid, incorporating the pyramidion and the trapezoidal block from the third course down with newly constructed blocks.

The satellite pyramid was an important feature of the standard Old Kingdom pyramid complex, and the discovery of this pyramid is extremely important to our understanding of these structures. Many scholars believe that the subsidiary pyramid can be traced back to a mysterious structure in the first pyramid complex, that of the Third Dynasty king, Djoser, called the 'south tomb.' This is a *mastaba* that lies south of the main pyramid, and has a square burial chamber, too small to hold a body. Decorating the walls of the substructure of this tomb are images of Djoser performing rituals associated with an important royal event called the *sed* festival. Scholars are still studying this festival, but many believe that it was a sort of jubilee, celebrated for the first time after the king had been on the throne for about thirty years, and designed to symbolically rejuvenate him and renew his right to rule. I believe that this festival was held when the royal mortuary complex was completed, to celebrate the fact that the king had completed all that the gods had asked him to do.

The unfinished pyramid complex of Djoser's successor, Sekhemkhet, also included a south tomb, which contained in the passageway the mysterious skeleton of a two-year old boy in a Third Dynasty wooden coffin. Two of the three major pyramids of Sneferu each have subsidiary pyramids associated with

them that do not seem to have served as burial places for queens, but instead were connected with the cult of the king, and thus qualify as ritual pyramids.

The lack of a satellite pyramid in Khufu's complex has always been a stumbling block in the discussion of these ritual structures, and now we have filled in this gap. Khafre may have had a ritual pyramid, placed directly south of his main pyramid and on the same north-south axis. Inside this subsidiary pyramid were wooden fragments that have been reconstructed as belonging to a statue shrine; ox bones; fragments of stoppers from jars or vases, one of which reads, "The eldest royal son of his body, beloved by him, the sole friend"; and two carnelian necklaces. However, this might also be a queen's pyramid, in which case we do not have a ritual pyramid for Khafre. Menkaure does

not seem to have had a ritual pyramid; it is interesting to note that he also had no boat pits. We know he died before his complex was finished, so it may be that his ritual pyramid and boat pits were never built because of his early death.

The standard pyramid complex of the Fifth and Sixth Dynasties includes a satellite pyramid, usually located at the southeastern corner of the complex (like Khufu's). There is still a great deal of discussion among scholars about the function of these structures. Some believe that they were for the royal *ka*, one aspect of the king's soul, or to store his canopic equipment (the viscera, which were removed and packaged separately) or placenta. Others suggest that they were built to house the royal crowns, as provisional tombs to store the king's body while he was being embalmed, or as

solar symbols for the storage of offerings. I believe that the satellite pyramids were used during the *sed* festival, perhaps as a changing room where the king removed his jubilee cloak and put on the kilt and bull's tail in which he would perform his ritual dance.

I believe that Khufu originally planned to place his satellite pyramid north of the three queens' pyramids, and that the so-called 'trial passage' that lies north of the causeway was cut as the substructure of this pyramid. After Year 5 of his reign, when Khufu changed his cult and took on the role of the sun god Re, he enlarged the upper temple and abandoned the original satellite pyramid. GI-d, the new satellite pyramid, appears to have been built in a hurry near the end of Khufu's reign, or perhaps even a few days after his death.

The Mystery of Hetepheres

by Zahi Hawass

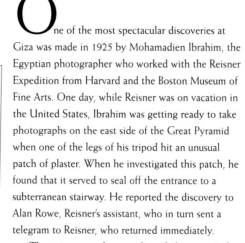

One of the most spectacular discoveries at Giza was made in 1925 by Mohamadien Ibrahim, the Egyptian photographer who worked with the Reisner Expedition from Harvard and the Boston Museum of Fine Arts. One day, while Reisner was on vacation in the United States, Ibrahim was getting ready to take photographs on the east side of the Great Pyramid when one of the legs of his tripod hit an unusual patch of plaster. When he investigated this patch, he found that it served to seal off the entrance to a subterranean stairway. He reported the discovery to Alan Rowe, Reisner's assistant, who in turn sent a telegram to Reisner, who returned immediately.

The stairway, twelve steps long, led to a vertical shaft, about 27.5 m deep, which was filled to the top with limestone plaster blocking. This shaft, labeled G 7000x, took ten years to excavate. The shaft follows two vertical fissures in the rock; its walls were left rough. Various artifacts and pottery sherds were mixed with the fill, and near the bottom was a sealing bearing the name of Khufu's mortuary workshop. A niche in the west wall of the shaft, which had been blocked with plaster masonry, contained the remains of an offering: three leg bones of a bull wrapped in a reed mat; a horned skull that had been crushed; and two wine jars. Also mixed in with these remains was a limestone boulder, two chips of basalt, and some charcoal, which were probably not part of the original offering.

In the burial chamber at the bottom of the shaft, also left unfinished, were many beautiful objects. There were several items made of gilded wood, including a portable pavilion, a bed, two armchairs, and a carrying chair. There were also a curtain box, a leather case for walking sticks, several wooden boxes, some copper tools, and numerous other small objects, including twenty silver bracelets inlaid with turquoise, lapis lazuli, and carnelian. An alabaster sarcophagus lay against one wall of the chamber, but to everyone's great disappointment, it was empty.

Various inscribed objects from the tomb bore the names and titles of Sneferu and of Hetepheres, whose principal title was 'Mother of the King of Upper and Lower Egypt.' Mud sealings bearing the name of Khufu were also found in some of the boxes; the obvious conclusion is that Hetepheres was the wife of Sneferu and the mother of Khufu.

A sealed recess in the west wall of the burial chamber contained an alabaster canopic chest on a small wooden sledge. It was divided into four compartments, three of which contained packages lying in a solution of natron and water; the fourth compartment contained dried organic material. A mud sealing, protected by a small pottery lid, was found on the lid of this box.

The style of the objects found in the tomb, including many fragments of pottery found scattered throughout the chamber, confirmed a Fourth Dynasty date. After the artifacts were restored by Hagg Ahmed Youssef, our great Egyptian conservator, they went to the Cairo Museum, where they now form one of the Museum's most important collections. Although at that time excavators were usually given "duplicate" artifacts as partage, the tomb of Hetepheres was found intact, and according to Egyptian law all of its objects were kept in Egypt. However, the Egyptian Antiquities Service gave Reisner a beautiful bust of the architect Ankhhaf instead, and the Boston Museum was permitted to display replicas of some of the queen's furniture.

Reisner attempted to account for the condition of the burial chamber, the broken and scattered pottery, the chips from the sarcophagus found strewn about the

168
Plan of the funeral equipment found inside the shaft of Hetepheres. Giza, Old Kingdom. Drawing from Reisner and Smith.

169 top
Gilded wooden carrying chair, part of the funeral furniture found in the shaft of Hetepheres, Egyptian Museum, Cairo, Old Kingdom.

169 bottom
Gilded wooden chair from the shaft of Hetepheres, Egyptian Museum, Cairo, Old Kingdom.

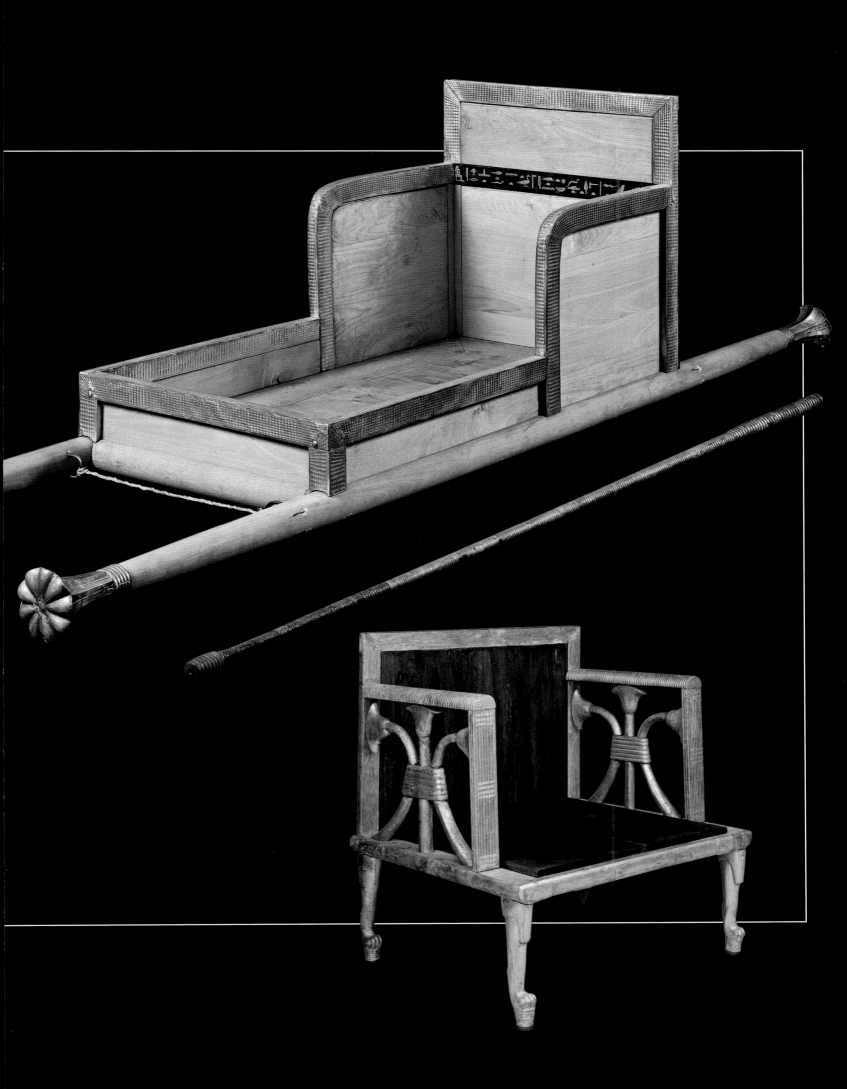

170-171
*Gilded wooden bed from the tomb of
Hetepheres, Egyptian Museum, Cairo,
Old Kingdom.*

170 bottom
*Wooden box with beautiful inscriptions
from the tomb of Hetepheres, Egyptian
Museum, Cairo, Old Kingdom.*

Queen Hetepheres

chamber, the lack of a superstructure, and the lack of a body, with the following hypothesis: Hetepheres died during the first part of Khufu's reign (as indicated by sealings from his mortuary service) and was originally buried by him at Dahshur, near her husband Sneferu. At some point in Khufu's reign, her tomb was broken into and her body was stolen. Khufu found out that the tomb had been disturbed and had the burial dismantled and the remaining contents moved secretly to Giza, where shaft G 7000x was hastily dug to receive it. As further support for his theory, Reisner notes that the side of the alabaster sarcophagus against the wall of the burial chamber was damaged, which he believes could not have happened in G 7000x. He also believes that the contents of the Giza tomb were in the reverse order of their original positions at Dahshur. The equipment found in the body of the shaft would represent items that were forgotten and then thrown into the shaft at the last minute. Since an offering was made at this new tomb, Khufu presumably did not know that the body of the queen was missing. These events would have occurred while Khufu's upper temple was in the process of being paved, accounting for basalt fragments found in the offering niche.

Mark Lehner objects to this interpretation on a number of grounds. He thinks that robbers would have smashed the lid of the sarcophagus rather than lifting it carefully, and that they are unlikely to have missed easily portable valuables such as the silver bracelets. He believes that if Hetepheres had originally been buried at Dahshur (a theory for which there is absolutely no evidence), the reburial should also have been made there. He also objects to the idea that such a deep shaft could have been dug in secret, and points out that it is hard to imagine Khufu knowingly allowing his mother to be reburied with broken pottery and violated equipment.

As an alternative scenario, Lehner has suggested that Hetepheres died early in her son's reign and was buried in this hastily dug shaft. It was dug in the style of the Third Dynasty, then still current. A superstructure that would have overlain this shaft was started, again in the style of the Third Dynasty, but then abandoned when Khufu's cult was changed and the plan of the eastern field was modified because Khufu's upper temple would have interfered with it. Instead, the three small pyramids, GI-a, b, and c, were built. The queen mother's body was then taken from G 7000x and reburied with new funerary equipment inside either GI-a or GI-b.

Lehner deals with each of the points raised by Reisner, and comes up with alternative explanations that fit his new theory. For example, he suggests that the basalt fragments found in the offering niche might be tools, and proposes that the limestone boulder might have been thrown into the niche to crush the skull and invalidate the offering. Lehner suggests that the copper tools found in the burial chamber were left by the workmen, who pried off the lid of the sarcophagus and removed the body of the queen. He disagrees with Reisner's assessment of the damage to the sarcophagus, noting that the chipping of the lid is not just on the east side, but runs all the way around, and could easily have been done in G 7000x.

Both of these theories are very attractive, but neither accounts for all of the evidence. If the queen was originally buried at Dahshur, where is her first tomb? How could her burial equipment have been moved all the way from Dahshur to Giza in secret? If G 7000x represents the original burial, why was it left in such disorder? Why was the queen mother buried in such haste? Why would Khufu's officials have needed a completely new set of funerary equipment? Most importantly, why would Khufu's mortuary officials take the queen's body but leave her canopic material behind?

I believe that Hetepheres was originally buried in Gl-a, the northernmost of the small pyramids. Lehner has pointed out that the portable canopy and furniture found in G 7000x would have fit almost perfectly into the burial chamber of Gl-a, which makes more sense if it was originally designed to go there rather than thrown hurriedly into G 7000x. But how and when was it moved into its final resting place?

We know that a great deal of vandalism was carried out on the Giza plateau during the upheaval of the First Intermediate Period—there is a lot of evidence suggesting that much of Khufu's complex was destroyed during this tumultuous time. It is likely that Hetepheres' burial was disturbed at this time, and perhaps her body was taken by thieves looking for jewels. Priests loyal to Khufu's cult might then have moved what remained of the burial equipment to hide it from pillagers. The architectural style of G 7000x points to a date in the Second or Third Dynasty, and this shaft could easily have been dug much earlier and abandoned before Khufu's complex was begun. Thus the priests would have found and used this ancient shaft to protect what was left of the burial of this important queen.

If my theory is correct, it accounts for a number of problems. As Reisner himself pointed out, the objects in G 7000x were reversed, as if the equipment had been moved from one place to another. This reversal makes more sense if those responsible for the reburial were moving the equipment over a short distance, such as the distance between the burial chamber of Gl-a and G 7000x. The offering in the niche would have been transferred hastily from its original location, and would have been disturbed in the process. The basalt chips found with this offering are most likely fragments from the destroyed pavement of Khufu's upper temple, and the limestone debris is probably residue from his vandalized temples. A later reburial would also account for the lack of an official seal over the entrance to the shaft.

This hypothesis still does not completely account for the fact that the queen's body is missing. As Lehner has pointed out, robbers are more likely to have broken the lid open than to have chipped around the edges. The priests responsible for the reburial must have known that the body was missing, yet they still took the trouble to move the queen's equipment, including her empty sarcophagus. Perhaps future discoveries on the Giza plateau will someday shed more light on this ancient mystery.

171 top
Bracelets discovered with the funeral equipment of Hetepheres, Egyptian Museum, Cairo, Old Kingdom.

171 bottom
Gold bowls, part of the funeral goods found in the shaft of Hetepheres, Egyptian Museum, Cairo, Old Kingdom.

Chapter 14

The Secret Doors Inside the Great Pyramid

by Zahi Hawass

The Great Pyramid of Khufu has fascinated people since ancient times; in fact, it is the only wonder of the ancient world that still exists today. Although most people today know that it was built as the tomb of the second king of the Fourth Dynasty, Khufu, alternative theories about its construction and purpose still circulate. The interior chambers of this extraordinary structure are very complex, adding to its mystery, and scholars are still debating their exact functions.

The modern entrance to the pyramid was created in the ninth century AD by al-Mamoun, son of Haroun al-Rashid. They just missed the true entrance, which lies about a third of the way up the north face. From the original entrance, a passage descends through the body of the pyramid, leading to an unfinished chamber carved into the bedrock under the pyramid. From a point partway along the descending passage, a second passage leads upward to a horizontal passage that leads in turn to a second chamber, misnamed the 'Queen's Chamber' (in fact, it was certainly not for any of Khufu's queens, who had their own small pyramids). From the point where the first ascending passage meets the horizontal passage, an incredible corbelled corridor, the Grand Gallery, ascends to a third chamber, the 'King's Chamber,' where the granite sarcophagus of Khufu was found, empty. Scholarly discussion about the building sequence and purpose of these corridors and chambers is ongoing: many Egyptologists believe that the three chambers represent three changes in the interior plan, reflecting changes in Khufu's cult, but others believe that all three chambers were part of the original plan.

A number of early adventurers explored the chambers inside the Great Pyramid, and various Egyptologists have made contributions to our understanding of their layout and purpose. Serious modern scientific work on the Great Pyramid began in 1993, when, for the first time, we closed the pyramid for a full year. This was part of a plan to institute a rotation system at Giza, closing one pyramid for a year while leaving the other two open,

in order to balance conservation with tourism. During our conservation work, we found that the humidity level inside the Great Pyramid was at 85 percent. Most of this was due to tourism, as each person who enters the pyramid breathes out approximately 20 grams of water. This water evaporates and leaves behind salt. The salt leeches into the stone and slowly destroys it: in 1993, we found the surface of the Grand Gallery encrusted with salt, and many cracks could be seen.

We needed to clean the pyramid, and also to develop a system to permanently lower the humidity. One idea was to clean two narrow conduits, each about 20 cm square, known as airshafts, that lead outward and upward to the exterior of the pyramid from the north and south walls of the highest chamber (the King's Chamber) and put machines inside them to create a ventilation system. I talked to Rainer Stadelmann, the director of the German Archaeological Institute in Cairo at that time, who in turn arranged for a robotic expert, Rudolf Gantenbrink, to come and work under the auspices of the Institute. Gantenbrink designed a robot called Wepwawet (an ancient Egyptian god of the dead) to investigate the airshafts in the third chamber. Using the robot, we cleared the shafts and set up fans inside to circulate the air and keep down the humidity.

The robot was also sent inside similar shafts in the second chamber (the Queen's Chamber). These shafts were originally discovered in September of 1872 by British engineer Waynman Dixon. Dixon had pushed a wire through the joints of the masonry of the south wall, and realized there was a hollow space behind it. He then chiseled through the wall and found the southern shaft. He looked for a shaft in the equivalent area of the north wall and found one. When he lit a candle and placed it in the southern shaft, it flickered, telling him that there was a slight draft.

In the northern shaft, Dixon and his associate James Grant found a small bronze hook, a granite ball, and a portion of cedar-like wood. These objects became known as the Dixon Relics. They were taken to England, recorded by the Astronomer Royal of

172-173
Members of the National Geographic staff check the robot that is going to explore the southern shaft in the so-called 'Queen's Chamber.' The Great Pyramid, Giza, Fourth Dynasty.

174 top
*The first secret 'door' in the southern
shaft of the Queen's Chamber.*

174 bottom
*The National Geographic team
exploring the southern shaft in the
Queen's Chamber. The Great Pyramid,
Giza, Fourth Dynasty.*

Scotland, and returned to Dixon—after which they disappeared. Fortunately, drawings were published in the journal *Nature* of December 26, 1872.

In 1993 a concerted search led to the discovery of the ball and hook in the British Museum, where they remain today. The piece of cedar-like wood remained missing until 2001, when it was traced to the Marischal Museum, Aberdeen. (Although they are sure it is in their collection, they haven't yet located it, as they are currently in the process of moving.)

During the 1993 explorations of the Queen's Chamber shafts, Gantenbrink made some intriguing finds. The northern shaft turned sharply to the west after approximately eight meters, and the robot could go no farther. In the southern shaft, Wepwawet was stopped after 63.4 m by a door or small slab with two copper handles that blocked the entire shaft. The left handle had lost a piece sometime in antiquity, which

was lying about two meters in front of the 'door.'

Gantenbrink also found a long piece of wood and a modern metal pole lying in the sloping portion of the northern shaft. Its cross-sectional area and general appearance are similar to the piece of wood found by Dixon. No mention of the pole is made in Dixon's reports, but it is now thought to have been lost when Dixon and his colleagues were 'treasure-hunting' in the shaft. They probably broke the small piece of wood from the longer piece while they were manipulating the metal pole, but did not report this accident. Some suggest that carbon dating the wood would allow accurate dating of the pyramid because they assume that the wood must have been left in the shaft when the pyramid was constructed (given that the shaft was sealed). I do not believe that this is necessarily the case: the wood may also have been placed in the shaft after construction via the shaft's exit, if one exists. He also found a piece of wood

with two holes drilled into it that might be the handle into which the bronze hook found by Dixon might once have been set. Gantenbrink has published his information on the web at *www.cheops.org* (see also *www.guardians.net/hawass*).

Egyptologists have multiple explanations for these 'airshafts.' Some believe that they were used for ventilation. This is possible for the shafts in the King's Chamber, which lead all the way to the outside (although they might have been covered by the casing stones), but there are no openings on the outside of the pyramid that might correspond to the shafts in the Queen's Chamber so this theory is very unlikely. More likely is that they have a religious and astronomical function: the southern shaft aligned with the star Sirius (Orion), and the northern shaft pointed to the circumpolar stars Minoris, Ursa, and Beta. Stadelmann believes that these shafts are tunnels through which the king's soul would ascend to join the divine stars.

I believe that the shafts from the so-called Queen's Chamber are likely to have no function, as they were blocked from the inside. If they had a religious function, they should have been left open, as were the shafts of the third chamber (the King's Chamber). Since these open outside of the pyramid, I believe that Khufu's soul was meant to travel through them. The southern shaft was intended for Khufu to use as the sun god Re. It opens exactly between the two boat pits to the south of the pyramid. Khufu would take the two boats and use them as solar boats—one for the day trip, one for the evening trip. The northern shaft was made for the soul of Khufu as Horus to travel to join the stars.

In order to discover more about the purpose of the shafts of the so-called Queen's Chamber, further work had to be done. The German Institute in Cairo had the concession to the Great Pyramid, and I could see that they were not interested in completing the work on the shafts. It was impossible to assign the concession to Gantenbrink as he is an individual, and the antiquities law in Egypt only allows for concessions to be granted to institutions. So I decided that the Supreme Council of Antiquities (SCA) would do the work instead. I asked Tim Kelly of National Geographic Television to design a robot to probe the shafts, and I would head the expedition. I believed there was nothing behind this door at all but that it was very important for both scholars and

the general public alike to know the truth. Archaeologists know that even empty space can be important.

The National Geographic Society designed a robot and called it the Pyramid Rover, and the Permanent Committee of the SCA acknowledged the project as an Egyptian endeavor. We decided to look behind the 'door' on live television, and set the date for September 17, 2002. I, as well as my colleagues at National Geographic, wanted to be sure that we were honest and that people were prepared for whatever find (or lack thereof) we might make. Before the show, I went to Hong Kong and Singapore to publicize it, and my colleague Mark Lehner went to Australia, India, and Spain right afterward.

One of the main goals of the documentary was to show the public evidence about the people who built the pyramids. I was to talk about tombs, show graffiti which names the work gangs that built these monuments, and even go inside the Step Pyramid of Djoser for the first time. The substructure of this pyramid consists of tunnels and passages and rooms with a total length of just over five and a half kilometers. I believe that the interior had never been shown in a film before, and that no living Egyptologist had entered this maze of corridors and chambers.

One day before the show, we used ultrasound to determine that the 'door' in the southern shaft of the Queen's Chamber was about six centimeters thick, and that there was something behind it. We decided to drill a hole, three millimeters in diameter, through the door so we could send a camera behind it. In the last minute of the show, the camera was sent in, and we found a second door 21 centimeters behind the first. It is not similar to the first, in that it looks as if it is screening or covering something. There were also cracks all over the surface. I was very happy to see it, but also very surprised.

The show was well received all over the world, and was rated 'great' by Fox Television in the United States. Half a billion people in China watched the show. Newspapers all over the world covered it to a degree that had never been done for any television program before.

A few days after the show, we sent the new robot into the northern shaft of the Queen's Chamber. Gantenbrink and Dixon both were only able to probe a little more than eight meters because of a turn in

the shaft. After further investigation, we determined that the turn was made in order to avoid intersecting the Grand Gallery, implying that the shafts were cut after the Grand Gallery's construction. The Pyramid Rover turned and continued through the shaft, only to be stopped in front of another door with copper handles. This is 63.4 m into the shaft, the exact same distance as the door in the southern shaft, and it is very similar to it. Behind this door there is probably another door 0.21 m away from the first, as we found in the southern shaft.

The copper handles in the first doors in both the north and south shafts are similar to those on the box that held the canopic jars of Tutankhamun, now at the Egyptian Museum in Cairo. Ropes used to pull the box were threaded through these handles. The doors in the Queen's Chamber shafts are made of fine white limestone from Tura, and it seems as if their handles allowed them to be pulled inside the shafts.

The presence of these doors in the Great Pyramid raises many questions. One idea is that the doors are challenges that the king must face during his journey to the afterlife. It is written in the Pyramid Texts that the king will face bolts before he travels; perhaps this is a reference to the doors' copper handles. Yet if this is true, why is Khufu's pyramid the only one with such doors? Also, why are there no doors in the shafts of the third chamber? Logically, they should be where the king's body was buried. It is possible that these doors are evidence that Khufu's actual burial chamber might be hidden somewhere inside of his pyramid. An ancient story from the Westcar Papyrus tells of how Khufu searched for the secret documents of the god Thoth in order to design the chambers of his pyramid; we are still trying to understand the complex he and his architects left behind.

We are planning to search again for openings on the outside of the Great Pyramid that correlate with the shafts in the Queen's Chamber. If we find them, then it is possible that these were symbolic doors for the king to use in crossing to the Netherworld. We will also, as soon as we have decided the best and safest way to proceed, look behind the second door in the southern shaft. If the shafts are truly sealed, we will have to consider other theories. Only further research into the shafts and the doors that block them can reveal their function, and help us to solve one of the many remaining mysteries of the Great Pyramid.

The Pyramidion

by Zahi Hawass

The term 'pyramidion' refers to a miniature pyramid that was placed on the top of the larger pyramid to serve as its apex. It was made of a special type of stone; in the Old Kingdom, either diorite, granite, or a very fine limestone which was then cased with gold or electrum was used. In the Middle Kingdom, the pyramidion was usually granite, which was then inscribed with texts and symbols.

A number of examples of pyramidions, or capstones, have been discovered around Old and Middle Kingdom pyramids. The oldest pyramidion ever discovered was found by Rainer Stadelmann in 1982 in the area of the Red Pyramid of Sneferu at Dahshur. It is made of fine, white Tura limestone and is uninscribed. The pyramidion was found in pieces; it has now been reconstructed, and stands at a height of about three quarters of a meter. It has been placed on a stand located on the east side of the Red Pyramid at Dahshur.

The second oldest pyramidion was found east of the Great Pyramid of Khufu in 1991, near the recently discovered satellite pyramid that it once surmounted. The east side of Khufu's pyramid had been explored before, but all previous excavators had missed this small pyramid. The pyramidion was found to the south of the satellite pyramid; its top and base had been destroyed and were reconstructed by Josef Dorner. A trapezoidal block from the third course from the top was also found near the satellite pyramid; this block and the pyramidion have been set up just to the north of the satellite pyramid.

Many people believed that the pyramid of Khafre never had a pyramidion because they thought that the casing of white limestone continued to the top of the pyramid. However, Italian scholars Maragioglio and Rinaldi surveyed the top of this pyramid and pointed out that the summit of the pyramid had been destroyed and now ended in a small platform. Another Italian expedition recently surveyed this pyramid to assess damage from an earthquake. They discovered that the casing stone of the top is only five centimeters thick,

which is different from all the other pyramids at Giza. Nabil Swelim believes that two pieces of polished diorite, discovered by Selim Hassan, could be part of the pyramidion of Khafre. He reconstructs this pyramid as having a whitish-gold outer facing with a course of rose granite below a dark green, diorite pyramidion.

The only other Fourth Dynasty pyramidion discovered was found near one of the subsidiary pyramids of Menkaure. Only the square base of this pyramidion has been preserved; a second piece that would have been on top is missing. The lower surface is smooth and pierced with holes that could have been used to secure the stone to the pyramid. This base is made of limestone; I believe that the upper part was made of a different type of stone, otherwise it would most likely have been made in one piece.

The pyramids of the Fifth Dynasty were also surmounted by special pyramidions. A relief found within the pyramid complex of Djedkare Isesi shows that his pyramid once had a pyramidion: one scene shows King Isesi standing with a staff in his hand; in front of him is an inscription that reads: "Following the pyramidion to the pyramid of Isesi." The actual pyramidion of this pyramid has not been found. The Czech expedition under the direction of Mirsolav Verner found a fragment of a basalt pyramidion from the pyramid of Khentkaus II, a consort of Neferirkare, that was originally cased with metal (copper and gold?). Blocks from the causeway of Sahure at Abusir, discovered recently when work was being done to prepare the site for the public, are decorated with scenes related to the installation of the pyramidion. One unique scene shows the pyramidion being dragged toward the pyramid. Workmen pull a rope connected to the pyramidion (depicted on the next block to the right, which has not been found). In this scene, one can see part of the sledge on which the pyramidion rested, as well as the workmen who pull the

177

The black granite pyramidion dating from the reign of Amenemhet III, Twelfth Dynasty, was found at Lisht. Now in the Egyptian Museum, Cairo.

sledge and pour water in front of the runners to reduce friction with the ground. Other scenes show women, labeled as members of the *khener*, wearing a special uniform, standing with their right hand upraised and their left hand on their waist. The word *khener* has traditionally been translated as 'harem,' but has recently been reinterpreted as 'musical troop.' However, this meaning seems rather narrow and does not express the nuance that the original word conveyed. It is more likely that this refers mainly to an administrative and economic establishment. Whatever the interpretation, entertainers, musicians, singers, and dancers were clearly an important part of the king's female entourage, and part of the celebration of the pyramidion installation. It is clear from these scenes that an expedition was sent into the desert to quarry special stone for the pyramidion. The presence of a group of emaciated Bedouin, perhaps being brought to the royal court to be tried for attacking the quarrying party, indicates that the area into which the royal team ventured was barren and desolate, inhabited only by wandering tribes. In 1996, while we were carrying out excavations at Saqqara in the complex of Teti, the first king of the Sixth Dynasty, we rediscovered a pyramidion which had originally discovered in 1930 by Firth and Gunn near the southeast corner of the pyramid of Queen Iput I, one of Teti's wives. When we found it, it was lying in the area between the pyramid temples of this queen and another, Khuit. It is uninscribed and its top is destroyed. It is of polished limestone and has a rectangular base. Its total height is 47 centimeters. Maragioglio and Rinaldi suggested that it might be part of an obelisk, similar to one found in the upper temple of Pepy II, rather than the pyramidion for Iput I's pyramid. However, the style of this pyramidion is of the New Kingdom, and I do not believe it comes from an obelisk.

We found three additional pyramidions during our recent work at Saqqara. One was inside the storage magazine of Firth and Gunn, the original excavators of the complex of Teti. They had not published this discovery, so it was a surprise to find it in the

magazine. The surface of this pyramidion is polished and is pierced with three holes. These holes would have been used to attach a plating of electrum to the pyramidion. We found the second and third pyramidions in the area of the Teti complex in 1992–93. Both were made of limestone: one has a square base, is unpolished and has broken edges; the other is 46 centimeters high and its base is 53 by 37 centimeters.

The French expedition at South Saqqara recently found pieces of the pyramidion of the subsidiary pyramid of Queen Meretites, wife of Pepy I of the Sixth Dynasty. And finally, there is evidence for the existence of a pyramidion connected with the subsidiary pyramid of Queen Wedjebten of Pepy II, which is located at the northeast corner of the main pyramid. An inscribed block was found here by Jéquier in 1925–26; the text included a phrase which he translated as "pyramidion of electrum." This interpretation is supported by the work of other scholars; there is no other reasonable way to understand this text. Most of the Old Kingdom pyramidions found were in poor condition. There is no direct evidence that pyramidions were cased in the Fourth Dynasty. However, it is likely that these pyramids had pyramidions encased in gold, connecting them to the sun cult. The inscriptions from Abusir and Saqqara, coupled with the example from the complex of Khuit, all support the theory that pyramidions of the

Fifth and Sixth Dynasties were coated with electrum. Several pyramidions have also been found that date from the Middle Kingdom. Fragments of pyramidions made of red granite have been found near two of the queens' pyramids in the complex of Senusret I, second king of the Twelfth Dynasty, at Lisht. From Amenemhet III's pyramid at Dahshur comes a pyramidion of black granite, with a band of hieroglyphs running around its base and the image of wings and a sun disk protecting the eyes, names, and titles of the king. This was found in good condition. It may never have been set at the apex of the pyramid, since Amenemhet left Dahshur and built a second pyramid at Hawara. Numerous fragments of a black granite pyramidion belonging to Thirteenth Dynasty king, Khendjer, were found in his complex at South Saqqara. These were covered with hieroglyphic inscriptions and have now been reconstructed. Two additional pyramidions of black granite were found at South Saqqara, in association with an unfinished and unattributed pyramid of the Middle Kingdom. One of these was polished and the other was left rough; both were uninscribed. The fact that these pyramidions were found on the site of an unfinished pyramid suggests that they were brought to the site early on in the construction process. The scenes on the blocks found at Abusir illustrate the importance of the king's search for special stone for the pyramidion: a military escort was even sent along to protect the quarrying expedition. The pyramidion, like the pyramid itself, was a representation of the *benben* stone—in fact, the word in Egyptian for pyramidion is *benbenet*. The original *benben* was kept in the sun temple at Heliopolis, and was a potent symbol of the sun god.

The scenes from Abusir suggest that the pyramidion was the last architectural component to be installed as part of the pyramid. It was probably done during a festival in the presence of the king, and marked the moment when the king became a god. When the workmen put the pyramidion on the top of the pyramid, it meant that the pyramid was officially finished, and everyone in Egypt would have danced and sung in celebration of its completion.

178
The fine white limestone pyramidion from the cult pyramid of Khufu, with the Great Pyramid of Khufu behind. Giza, Fourth Dynasty.

179
The pyramidion of the Red Pyramid at Dahshur dates from the reign of Sneferu, Khufu's father. Dahshur, Fourth Dynasty.

The Royal Boats at Giza

by Zahi Hawass

Five boat pits have been discovered in the pyramid complex of Khufu. The three to the east of the pyramid are boat-shaped, with narrowed prow and stern, the remaining two, to the south, are rectangular in shape, and were cut to house full-size wooden boats that had been dismantled. There is a great deal of scholarly argument about the purpose and symbolism of these pits, which are the descendants of boat pits found associated with a number of Early Dynastic royal tombs.

Two of the eastern boat pits lie parallel to the east face of the pyramid, and were dug into the rock of the plateau to the north and south of the upper temple. These are very large: for example, the southern pit is 51.5 m long, seven meters wide at its midpoint, and eight meters deep. They were originally paved with limestone blocks, traces of which were found *in situ* in the southern pit by Petrie. Petrie also found some roofing blocks covering the west end of the southern trench, although other scholars believe that the pit was never covered, since pillars would have been needed to help span its width.

The southern pit was cleared of debris long ago; we recently cleared the debris from the northern pit as part of our site management plan. Various artifacts were found in the fill of these pits. One was a fragment of limestone with the word *akhet* written on it in hieroglyphs. This was probably part of the name *akhet-khufu*, the 'Horizon of Khufu,' which was the name of the Great Pyramid. A sherd from a red pot was also found, as well as a fragment of limestone

with the hieroglyph for life on it, and a fragment of a granite statue. The inscriptions and the statue fragments may originally have come from Khufu's temple; they would, of course, have been deposited in the boat pit at a time after the reign of Khufu, possibly later than the Old Kingdom.

The Egyptian scholar Selim Hassan, who did a great deal of work at Giza, noted the presence of a shallow cutting in the bottom of the southern pit, and suggested that it might indicate the original presence of a rectangular cabin, or that it may have formed a bed to support casing stones. There is argument about the orientation of both of these pits: some scholars think the prow of the southern pit was to the south and the prow of the northern pit was to the north, but others feel that the opposite was the case.

The third boat pit lies parallel to the causeway at a point several meters from the eastern wall of the upper temple. It measures 45.4 m in length and 3.75 m at its widest point. The vertical prow, representing a curtained bow post, is to the east, and is shaped like a cradle. The shape of this pit has been compared to boats from the Archaic Period. A stairway containing eighteen steps was found inside the pit, filled with masonry rubble; it is difficult to tell whether or not the pit was roofed originally. Holes cut in the sides of the pit have been interpreted as sockets for small transverse beams. George Reisner found cordage and pieces of gilded wood inside the pit, indicating that a boat had once been inside.

180
Khufu's extraordinary wooden solar boat was found by Kamal El Mallakh and now is conserved in a museum close to the pyramid of Khufu.

181
This wooden model of a solar boat is now conserved in the Egyptian Museum in Cairo.

182 top left
Aerial view of the three boat pits that were discovered on the east side of the Great Pyramid of Khufu. Giza, Fourth Dynasty.

182 center left
The eastern boat pit can be easily discerned in this photograph. Giza, Fourth Dynasty.

182-183
The cabin of the solar boat of Khufu, discovered in 1954, has been completely reassembled in an accurate restoration.

183 top
The first boat pit of Khufu: in particular, one can observe the limestone covering stones.

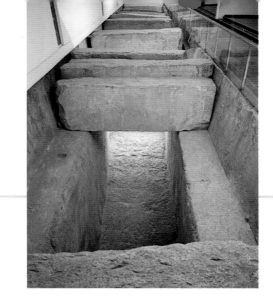

In 1954, while excavating the southern side of the Great Pyramid between the base of the pyramid and the southern *mastabas*, Egyptian archaeologist Kamal El Mallakh discovered two new boat pits. These two pits lie outside the great *temenos* wall of the pyramid, and they were covered by the debris of the enclosure wall. The two pits are separated by a north-south wall of rocks which lies on the north-south axis of the pyramid. The eastern pit was opened and found to contain a large wooden boat; the western is yet to be excavated, and is still covered by twenty limestone slabs. When the eastern pit was discovered, it was covered by forty-one slabs of limestone (nine of which bore quarry marks in red and black ink) that were resting on a ledge around the upper edge of the pit. These blocks weigh about 15 tons each; the largest is about 4.8 m long. The three westernmost of these stones were much smaller than the others and have been interpreted as keystones.

The pit itself is rectangular in shape and measures 32.5 m in length; its sides are vertical and tool marks on the sides and bottom show that they were dressed using copper chisels. Among the quarry inscriptions found on many of the roofing blocks were eighteen cartouches of Djedefre, Khufu's son and successor, showing that he was responsible for the funeral of his father. On the southern wall of the pit are signs in red ink that list measurements which, as yet, have not been studied.

Inside the pit were found the dismantled pieces of a very large wooden boat. On top of the wood was a layer of mats and ropes, an instrument made of flint, and some small pieces of white plaster. The prow of the boat, a wooden column topped by a round wooden disk, was found at the western end of the pit. This column was connected to two long wooden pieces that extended along the bottom of the pit. Most of the wooden parts had been tied together with ropes. Also found inside the pit were many other items, such as twelve oars, each of which was made of a single piece of wood; fifty-eight poles; three cylindrical columns; and five doors. In total, there were thirteen layers of materials consisting of 651 artifacts ranging in size from 10 centimeters to 23 meters.

183 bottom
In this plan of Khufu's pyramid complex, one can see the location of the five boat pits. The three to the east are boat-shaped, the two to the south are rectangular. The two boat pits between the queens' pyramids are also present.

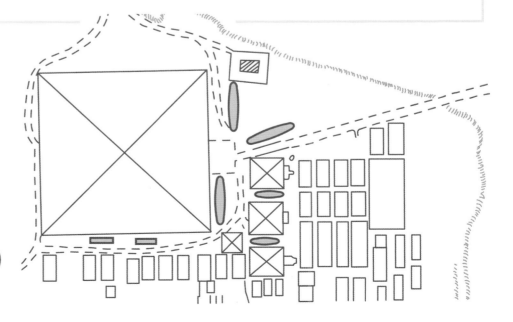

184 top left
This archival photograph shows
the location of the first boat pit
before discovery.

184 top right
The photographer has captured the
moment that the blocks of the boat pit
were excavated.

184 center
In these images one can see the
different steps taken to collect the
pieces of the boat and put them
together with ropes. In a more
advanced phase of the reconstruction
(below) the boat starts to return
to its original shape.

184 bottom
The drawing on the left gives
a cross section of the planking
of the boat. The drawing on the
right shows the final stage of the
restoration of the boat.

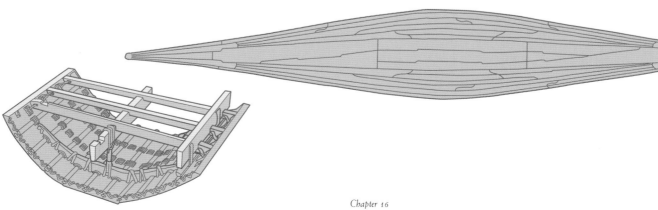

Royal ▲ Boats

The expert conservationist Hag Ahmed Youssef spent many years preserving each individual piece found in the pit and reconstructing the ancient boat. The rebuilt boat measures about 43.4 m long and 5.9 m wide in the beam. The woods used in its construction were cedar and acacia.

Many scholars believe that the three boat pits found to the east of the Great Pyramid were cut during the reign of Khufu and that the two southern pits were built during the reign of Djedefre, as indicated by the cartouches bearing his name found in the eastern pit. It is likely that the main building ramp leading from the southern quarry covered the area directly south of Khufu's pyramid, so these boat pits would certainly have been some of the last elements of the complex constructed. That the pits were built no later than the end of the Fourth Dynasty is demonstrated by the fact that they lie partially under the pyramid's southern enclosure wall, which is dated to the end of the Fourth Dynasty.

184-185 and 185 top right Hag Ahmed Youssef is shown here with Khufu's boat during restoration. The image on the left shows the workers during the rebuilding of the boat.

Boat pits are found associated with royal and high elite mortuary complexes from the First through the Fifth Dynasties. There is no standard number for these; Khufu's five pits are matched only by Khafre, who also had five pits, all east of his pyramid. The earliest boats of this sort were found recently at Abydos by David O'Connor: a fleet of twelve full-size wooden ships encased in mud plaster lie in the desert near the funerary enclosures of the Early Dynastic kings.

There are three main schools of thought concerning the function of Khufu's pits and the boats that they contained. The first, propounded by Jaroslav Černy, is that four of the boats were ritual boats for carrying the king to the four cardinal points, and that the fifth was the boat in which the body of the king was transported to Giza. The second school, originally expressed by Walter Emery in reference to the First Dynasty *mastabas* at Saqqara, and then adopted by Selim Hassan, holds that the boats were solar boats, and thus carried the king to visit the sun god, Re, or to accompany him in his voyage across the sky. The third concept, expounded principally by Abubakr, suggests that all the boats were originally used in the king's lifetime for pilgrimages and other ceremonies. Kamal El Mallakh, the discoverer of the two southern boat pits, thought, like Hassan, that the boats were solar boats for the soul of the dead king: the boat found in the easternmost southern pit would have traveled to the west, parallel to the daily course of the sun. A fourth theory that could be suggested is that the southern pits contained solar boats, the pits flanking the upper temple contained the boats of Horus, and the pit by the causeway contained either the funerary boat used to carry the body of the king,

or was meant to be used symbolically by Hathor.

Černy notes that four of the boat pits (excluding the one parallel to the causeway) are oriented so that each faces a different cardinal point. Thus, he suggests that the king could depart at any time for any destination. As support for his theory, he refers to a passage in the Pyramid Texts that states that the western, eastern, southern, and northern gods give the king four reed mats to use when he goes into the sky. Thus, the boats would be later developments of these reed mats. He goes on to suggest that the fifth pit held the boat that transported the body of the king to Giza.

In his study of boats in Old Kingdom period complexes, Hassan identifies boat pits as receptacles for conventional solar boats regardless of their number in a particular complex. According to his theory, the king was identified with the polar stars in the northern sky, and under their influence, flew southward in the day boat to reach the west, and northward in the night boat to reach the east. The crew of the night boat was the 'Indefatigable Stars,' and the king acted as the boat's commander.

Hassan uses evidence from the Pyramid Texts and the Palermo Stone to support his theory. The Pyramid Texts contain several passages mentioning the use of solar boats. In one spell: "The king comes to Re and is proclaimed king of earth. He ascends with Atum, rises and sets with Re and the solar barges." Another spell proclaims: "Ye Gods of the west, ye gods of the east, ye gods of the south, ye gods of the north, these four boats which you placed for Osiris when he ascended towards heaven." Another spell tells us that the king's *ka* will become a star and join the northern stars, and yet another one associates the king with four cardinal points, stating that he will sail to the sky like Horus and Re.

Abubakr originally argued that the two southern boats represented solar boats used by the king and the sun god, and also quoted from the Pyramid Texts, referring to a passage where Re uses boats to make his daily journey across the sky. The float, or boat, that he used during the day, was called *mandjet*, and the one for the night was called *mesketet*. Since the king represented the sun god on earth and after his death, he also would need similar boats. According to the Pyramid Texts, the king needs such boats to travel across the sky and reach his father Re.

In the second to fifth registers of the Palermo Stone, there are representations of several different kinds of boats, that have been studied by Hassan. One line contains the information that King Neferirkare erected a large 'day' boat at the southern corner of his sun temple. Another inscription of the same king refers to a day and night boat belonging to Re. In 1900–1901, Borchardt discovered a mud-brick boat built for King Niuserre beside his sun temple in Abusir. Because of their association with this temple, these boats are clearly 'solar' boats.

However, there are few pyramid complexes from the Fifth Dynasty, those of Unas and Neferirkare, that were found to contain boat pits. There are two pits in this complex, both lying parallel to the southern side of the causeway. The two boats of Unas probably represent the night and the day boats of Re referred to in the Palermo Stone. No boat pits have been found yet around the pyramids of the Sixth Dynasty, which may be due to lack of sufficient excavations; another possibility is that for economic or cultic reasons, the Sixth Dynasty rulers made do with representations of boats in scenes on the walls of their funerary complexes, or with model boats such as were

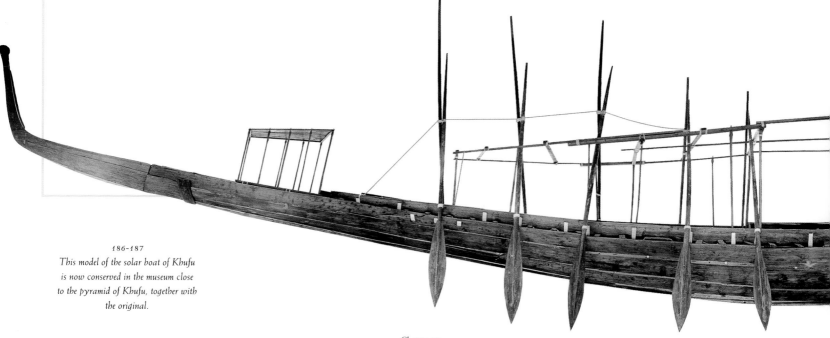

186-187
This model of the solar boat of Khufu
is now conserved in the museum close
to the pyramid of Khufu, together with
the original.

found near the pyramid of Pepy II's queen, Neith, rather than cutting pits and burying actual boats. In support of this conclusion are fragments bearing representations of two boats found within the pyramid of Pepy II.

In a later article, Abubakr and Mustafa state that the reconstructed boat from the first of the southern boat pits is not a solar boat. Their analysis is based on a scene from the wall of the tomb of Kaninisut that shows a sailing boat, above which a text reads: "The coming from Buto and the sailing to the fields of the great beautiful offerings." A second text reads: "Sailing to Heliopolis." On this piece of textual evidence, which is not even royal in character, they label the five boats of Khufu as follows: one for the pilgrimage to Heliopolis; the second for the pilgrimage to Sais; the third for the pilgrimage to Buto; the fourth for various rites of coronation; and the last one for the sons of Horus who participated in the rites of coronation. The king would certainly have used boats during his lifetime to visit these cult centers, but there is no proof that he needed them beside his pyramid.

The reasons that Abubakr and Mustafa cite in their claim that the reconstructed boat could not be a solar boat are each easily refuted. They begin by arguing that the kings of the Fourth Dynasty did not officially adopt the dogma of the cult of Re. Most scholars believe just the opposite, that the cult of Re was very strong in the Fourth Dynasty, especially during the reign of Khufu. His son and successor, Djedefre, who buried this boat and its companion, was the first to hold the title 'son of Re.' The cult of Re is attested as early as the First Dynasty, and there was a man who held the title 'high priest of Re' from

the reign of Khufu's father, Sneferu, indicating that the cult was active. Stadelmannn has even suggested that both Sneferu and Khufu were considered to be embodiments of Re himself during their lifetimes.

Abubakr and Mustafa state that the Pyramid Texts do not claim that the kings had solar boats for themselves. This is not true; there are a number of Utterances in these texts, which were recorded first at the end of the Fifth Dynasty but thought to be based on material dating back in to the Early Dynastic Period, stating that the kings traveled in solar boats.

Abubakr and Mustafa are joined by Černy and Jenkins in some of their arguments against a solar-boat designation for the reconstructed boat. They argue that the form of the boat is considerably different from a solar boat. For example, it does not have a ram or hawk-headed prow. However, the hull is similar to the hulls described in the Pyramid Texts. Khufu's boat may differ in other features from those mentioned for the solar boats of the Pyramid Texts, such as the large deckhouse and the hut for the captain, but this does not prove that it is not a solar boat.

Abubakr and Mustafa argue that not a single one of the characteristic emblems of the solar boat was found in the pit which contained all the parts of Khufu's boat. However, Hassan lists all the determinatives that occur with boats in the Pyramid Texts. Two of these symbols are flint tools and reed mats, and both of these symbols were found in Khufu's boat. These could well be considered solar symbols, thus disproving Abubakr and Mustafa's statement.

The fact that Khufu's boat was provided with ten rowing oars and two steering oars suggests to Abubakr and Mustafa that it was a real, rather than a symbolic,

boat. However, these oars could be considered symbolic oars. In the mind of the ancient Egyptians, the stars would row and the king would steer the boat. This identification is supported by Paul Lipke, who writes that the oars are too heavy to be used, therefore, they must have been symbolic.

Abubakr and Mustafa believe that there is some proof that the boat was once used, and therefore must have been funerary rather than solar; they cite, for example, the impressions of the tightly fitting ropes are still visible on some of the logs, which would have assured the water tightness of the boat. However, there is much evidence that the boat was never used. Traces of white color on the surface of some pieces of the boat and a complete absence of water marks on the hull suggest it was never used on the Nile. Zaki Iskandar, who was in charge of the scientific study and conservation of the objects and materials found in the pit, found remains of cedar and acacia wood on the site, along with traces of mud and plaster covering the blocks of the pits. He concluded that it had been built near where it had been buried. Another boat expert, Björn Landström, states that the boat was never painted or decorated, indicating that the boat was built in a hurry.

I believe that the boats to the south of the pyramid are solar boats in which the soul of the king symbolically traveled through the heavens with the sun god. The boats in the pits by the upper temple were used by the king as Horus to travel throughout Egypt and maintain order in his realm. The pit that lies parallel to the causeway might have contained the funerary boat which was used to bring the king's body to its final resting place, or might have been used symbolically by the goddess Hathor.

Chapter 17

The Sphinx

by Mark Lehner

HOW OLD IS THE SPHINX?
WHO BUILT IT AND WHY?

The Sphinx of Giza has inspired a wealth of speculation about its age. Popular writers have proposed that the Sphinx is a remnant of an advanced civilization, mostly lost to archaeology, and that it dates to thousands of years before the Fourth Dynasty pharaoh Khafre, who built the Second Pyramid at Giza around 2500 BC. Most Egyptologists accept that Khafre had the Sphinx created as part of his pyramid complex. Recently, however, it has been argued that Khufu built the Sphinx.

The Sphinx is the first truly colossal royal sculpture in ancient Egypt, 72.55 m long and 20.22 m tall. Other larger-than-life-size statues preceded it, but none of them come close to the scale of the Sphinx. The human head is on a scale of about 30:1 and the lion body is of the smaller scale of 22:1. Except for a sphinx head of the pharaoh Djedefre, now in the Louvre, and one small limestone sphinx, both from Abu Rawash, the Giza Sphinx is the earliest complete Sphinx to wear the distinctive royal *nemes* scarf.

The Sphinx is the single instance of colossal sculpture carved in the round directly out of the natural rock (Ramesses II's colossi at Abu Simbel come close, but they are more high relief than sculpture in the round).

The fabric of the Sphinx, the limestone bedrock of what geologists call the Muqqatam Formation, originated fifty million years ago from sediments deposited at the bottom of sea waters that engulfed northeast Africa in the Middle Eocene period. An embankment formed along what is now the north-northwest side of the plateau. Nummulites packed the embankment. Each of these small, disk-shaped fossils, named after the Latin word for 'coin,' were once the shells of extinct planktonic organisms. They range from the size of a lentil to that of an American quarter or fifty-cent Euro coin. A shoal and coral reef grew over the southern slope of the embankment. As the sea retreated northward, a shallow lagoon formed above what is now the south-southeast part of the plateau. Carbonate mud deposited in the lagoon petrified into the layers from which the ancient builders, fifty million years later, but 4,500 years before our time, quarried their limestone blocks. They hauled them from quarries dug into the low southern zone, up the slope, to build the pyramids on the northeast-southwest diagonal of the embankment.

The layers that originated as an Eocene lagoon at the bottom of the southeastern slope of the Muqqatam Formation were ideal for quarrying the large blocks that the Fourth Dynasty builders used in the pyramids and temples of Giza. The layers alternated between hard and soft, which allowed the quarrymen to cut the softer clay-like layers and extract the intervening harder layers in blocks of various sizes. They carved the Sphinx out of the very lowest of these layers in the Muqqatam Formation.

The builders trenched out a deep, U-shaped ditch that isolated a huge rectangular bedrock block for carving the Sphinx. The ditch opens to the east where they had already cut out a broad terrace (Terrace I) from the hard and brittle reef limestone. On the south end of this terrace the builders constructed Khafre's valley temple from huge blocks of limestone weighing many tons. On the north end, immediately below the Sphinx's outstretched paws, they built the Sphinx temple, also from huge limestone blocks that they quarried very nearby.

The bedrock body of the Sphinx became a standing section of the deeper limestone layers of the Giza Plateau (restoration work of the 1980s now conceals much of the bedrock body). The lowest stratum of the Sphinx is the hard brittle rock of the reef (Member I). Since all the geological layers slope about three degrees from northwest to southeast, they are higher at the rump of the Sphinx and lower at the front paws. The surface of Member I has not appreciably weathered compared to the layers above it. Tool marks and small cuttings left by the original Sphinx builders still show in the Member I surface on the floor of the Sphinx and on the north side of the Sphinx ditch.

Most of the Sphinx's lion body and the south wall and the upper part of the ditch were carved in Member II, seven soft layers near the bottom, becoming progressively harder near the top, but that generally alternate hard and soft. The head and neck are composed of Member III. The neck is carved in

the base of Member III, which is softer than the upper part from which the head is sculpted. Member III is good building stone and that is why the ancient Egyptians probably quarried most of it away in the area around the Sphinx. The durability of Member III is also why the details of the face are so well preserved after thousands of years, while the bedrock surface of the lion body has been ravaged by weathering.

The Fourth Dynasty builders seem to have been good geologists in their own right. They carefully reserved the good building stone of Member III for the head, which would be the most vulnerable part of the statue. They accommodated the softer and fissured rock of Member II in the massive lion body. They utilized the solid bed of Member I as the base of their colossal sculpture.

THE QUARRY CONSTRUCTION SEQUENCE

It is not a new idea that the Fourth Dynasty builders created the Sphinx, Khafre's valley temple, and the Sphinx temple as one continuous project. As early as 1910, when the Sphinx temple was still buried under 15 meters of debris, Uvo Hölscher, the excavator of Khafre's pyramid temples, already perceived that the Sphinx and valley temple were built concurrently. He came to this conclusion from the obvious similarity between the colossal core blocks of Khafre's temple walls and the bedrock layers showing in the upper part of the Sphinx. The limestone blocks formed the cores of the massive walls that the builders sheathed with red granite from Aswan. When the Swiss architect-Egyptologist Herbert Ricke carried out a detailed study of the Sphinx temple between 1967 and 1970, he suggested that the Fourth Dynasty builders worked on it along with the Sphinx and Khafre's valley temple as part of the same quarry and construction process. The limestone core blocks in the Sphinx temple are so big

that they can have three or more geological layers running through them. These layers are very similar to the layers running through the body of the Sphinx.

In 1980, Thomas Aigner, a geologist from the University of Tübingen, did a detailed study of the geological layers in the Sphinx, the surrounding ditch, more distant quarries at Giza, and each of the 173 core blocks in the Sphinx temple. As part of the Sphinx Project of the American Research Center in Egypt (ARCE), Aigner noted the qualities of the stone in each layer, including the fossilized life forms. The petrified sea ecology of fifty million years ago includes sponges, oysters, bivalves, urchins, sharks' teeth, and corals in life position. With such geological clues, Aigner's study supports what Hölscher and Ricke suspected.

The Fourth Dynasty builders created the Sphinx, Khafre's valley temple, and the Sphinx temple as a continuous architectural landscaping project (see map). When they quarried out the U-shaped ditch around an elongated block of bedrock from which they carved the Sphinx, they took the stone away in huge blocks that they used to form the cores of the walls of the temples. The builders used the blocks that they quarried from the upper layers of rock, corresponding to those of the Sphinx head and possibly higher, to build Khafre's valley temple. These blocks are less layered and more homogeneous, like the layers at the top of the Sphinx's chest, neck, and head. As they quarried deeper and created the Sphinx ditch, they dragged the blocks directly east to build the Sphinx temple. Most of these stones have a characteristic yellow band running through them, just like the layers around chest and shoulder height on the Sphinx. In fact, the geological layers run continuously through adjacent but separate blocks around much of the temple. As they hauled stone away from the Sphinx quarry and down to Terrace I for making the temple, there was not a lot of opportunity to mix up blocks weighing up to 100 tons!

191
The Sphinx sanctuary, Sphinx temple ruins, and (upper left) Amenhotep II's temple of the 18th Dynasty.

The causeway of Khafre's pyramid (lower right) forms the south side of the Sphinx sanctuary.

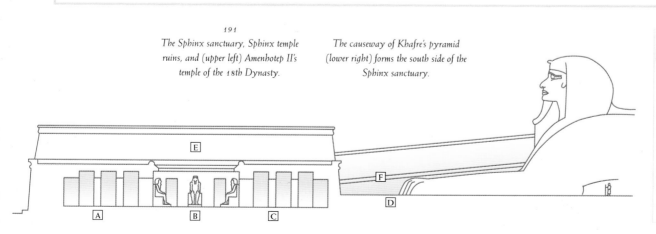

RECONSTRUCTED PROFILE OF THE SPHINX AND SPHINX TEMPLE

- **A** *EASTERN SANCTUARY*
- **B** *STATUES AROUND OPEN COURT*
- **C** *WESTERN SANCTUARY*
- **D** *HIGHER TERRACE OF SPHINX*
- **E** *TALLER KHAFRE VALLEY TEMPLE TO SOUTH*
- **F** *WALLS OF KHAFRE'S CAUSEWAY ALONG SOUTH SIDE OF SPHINX DITCH*

WHICH CAME FIRST? KHAFRE'S VALLEY TEMPLE OR THE SPHINX TEMPLE?

There is striking and clear evidence that the Fourth Dynasty builders made Khafre's valley temple before the Sphinx temple. In 1970, Herbert Ricke noted this sequence by pointing to an early enclosure wall around the valley temple.

A low wall composed of a single course of locally quarried, monolithic limestone blocks runs parallel to the south side of the valley temple. At the western end, two blocks make a corner and attach to the southwest corner of the valley temple. The end block is fitted over a small granite block that remains *in situ* from a low granite bench, 75 centimeters wide, that ran along the base of the south, east, and north sides of the valley temple. Ricke recognized that the builders had completed the 'bench' and probably the entire granite casing of the valley temple before they built the wall of large limestone blocks.

This wall runs 8.5 m south of the south side of Khafre's valley temple. It turns 90° at the edge of the bedrock terrace in front of the valley temple, where one large block remains of the eastern part after the turn. In front of this block to the north, the rock floor is cut as an emplacement bed for an additional long block that must have been removed. This missing block would have brought the wall to within

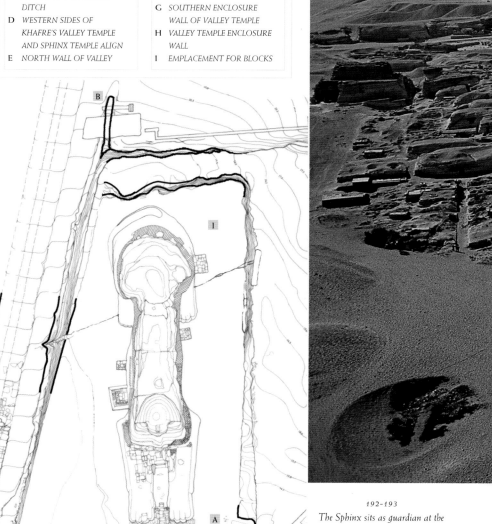

MAP OF THE SPHINX, SPHINX TEMPLE, AND KHAFRE VALLEY TEMPLE

A QUARRY WORK ABANDONED IN SPHINX DITCH
B CHANNEL IN UPPER SOUTHWEST CORNER OF SPHINX DITCH
C KHAFRE'S CAUSEWAY FORMS SOUTH SIDE OF SPHINX DITCH
D WESTERN SIDES OF KHAFRE'S VALLEY TEMPLE AND SPHINX TEMPLE ALIGN
E NORTH WALL OF VALLEY TEMPLE AND SOUTH WALL OF SPHINX TEMPLE PARALLEL
F SPHINX TEMPLE SOUTHEAST CORNER BUILT OVER TRACK OF OLD NORTHERN ENCLOSURE WALL OF VALLEY TEMPLE
G SOUTHERN ENCLOSURE WALL OF VALLEY TEMPLE
H VALLEY TEMPLE ENCLOSURE WALL
I EMPLACEMENT FOR BLOCKS

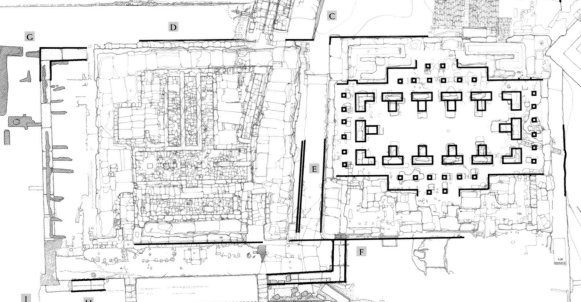

192-193
The Sphinx sits as guardian at the eastern base of the Giza Necropolis, as part of Khafre's valley temple complex. Pyramids of Khufu (right) and Menkaure (left).

five meters of the southern entrance ramp of the valley temple.

In front of the opposite, northeast, corner of the valley temple, the foundation track of a similar wall is sunk into the bedrock. This northern wall also ran parallel to the valley temple and was 8.5 m north of the north wall. Exactly like that of the wall on the south, the track on the north wall is close to 2.6 m (five cubits) wide. And just like the wall on the south, the foundation cutting of the wall on the north shows that it turned a corner to run along the front edge of the terrace in front of the valley temple. Like the southern arrangement, the wall on the north stopped five meters from the northern stone entrance ramp. The northern wall also attached to the back end of the temple, six meters east of the northwest corner. As on the south, this connection is marked by a single

granite block remaining of the bench along the base of the valley temple.

The northern and southern walls once formed an enclosure, like two arms, attached to the back western corners of Khafre's valley temple and reached out to enclose the front eastern corners, leaving a wide space for the approach ramps and front terrace. However, the Fourth Dynasty builders removed most of the wall to the north, leaving only its track cut into the rock floor. They removed the northern enclosure wall of Khafre's valley temple to build the south wall of the Sphinx temple directly over the path. Ricke pointed to one block of the northern enclosure wall still in its track because the builders incorporated it into the core of the southeast corner of the Sphinx temple. This block is very close in size and shape to the blocks of the valley temple's southern enclosure wall.

On top of all the other relationships that tie the Sphinx and Sphinx temple to the final phases of building Khafre's valley complex (see map and list), the path of the missing northern enclosure wall makes it as certain as we can be that Khafre's builders:

- completed Khafre's valley temple with its granite casing;
- built the northern and southern enclosure walls;
- removed the northern wall;
- built the Sphinx Temple where the northern wall had been;
- used huge blocks from the Sphinx quarry for the Sphinx temple walls.

Who made the Sphinx? The facts of the bedrock, the monumental architecture, and the quarry-construction history at the Sphinx precinct point to Khafre as the Sphinx builder.

The granite 'Dream Stela' of the 18th Dynasty pharaoh Thutmose IV sits in the Sphinx's embrace. The stela is what remains of a chapel between the paws where kings were ordained by a revitalized Sphinx already more than a millennium old.

Bedrock layers in alternating hard-soft sequence comprise the Member II stone of the Sphinx's body (before covering by recent restoration work). The head is carved from the stone of Member III, with gaps from erosion filled in by 1926 restoration work.

WHAT DID THE SPHINX MEAN?

By the middle of the Fourth Dynasty, a trend toward gigantic stone architecture had been underway for nearly a century, as expressed by the pyramid superstructure of the royal tomb, which was the focus of a temple complex designed to merge the king with the power of the sun god. Khafre took the trend toward gigantism further. He began using limestone core blocks weighing hundreds of tons in his temples. His craftsmen fashioned more than fifty-eight, and perhaps as many as one to two hundred, statues of hard stone; twenty-two of these were at least three times life size. The largest statue of all, the Great Sphinx, would remain unique for its size and for the fact that it was hewn directly from the living rock.

Given its immensity, it is surprising that the Sphinx appears suddenly, without much precedent. Its form, in better proportions, remained a classic image of kingship down to the close of antiquity. Preceding it, however, there was no continuum of lion figures that became more human in the face, first the eyes and nose, then the ears, and finally the mane giving way to the *nemes* scarf. Such half-sphinxes exist, but as far as we know, they do not represent a developmental step toward the *nemes*-coiffed Sphinx. Rather, the complete form appears all at once as the Giza Sphinx, even though the detached Djedefre head in the Louvre may suggest that the form had been executed in stone a few years earlier. The Giza Sphinx, therefore, may be a prototype. It is an excellent example of the ability of ancient Egyptian designers to come up with new combinations of 'formal visual culture.'

Its sheer size must have conveyed tremendous importance and, like the gigantic serpent in the ancient Egyptian fantasy, the *Shipwrecked Sailor*, otherworldliness. The fact this earliest super-colossal image of the king was a mixed form, animal and human, is also significant. In mixed forms it is the head that conveys the essential identity, and with the *nemes* scarf, this must be the king. But in its attachment to the lion body there is, as Henry Fischer put it, "a suggestion of shape-shifting, of metamorphosis, that is appropriate to the king who is, uniquely, the link between mankind and the gods, and stands constantly on the threshold of these two worlds."

Alan Gardiner suggested that the Egyptian phrase, *shesep ankh Atum*, 'Living Image of Atum,' which was associated with sphinxes in later times, signified the pharaoh in the form of the primeval sun and creator god. *Shesep ankh* as a word for statue, perhaps of a particular kind, is known from the Old Kingdom. Fischer suggested that it derives from *shesep*, 'to receive.' Fischer goes on to say that a statue is "'one who receives' offerings and other ministrations." Both primeval creator and recipient of offerings fit the Great Sphinx and its temple.

Hewn from living rock, the Giza Sphinx is an apt symbol for the god Atum (or the king as Atum), particularly in Atum's aspect of chthonic creator god. James Allen points out that Atum's name means 'completed one,' and that the entire physical world came forth from Atum as the 'primeval mass.' An obscure notion in the Pyramid Texts, Coffin Texts, and Book of the Dead has it that that the lion was the earliest form to emerge from the primeval mass within the primeval waters. Karol Myśliwiec pointed to an association between the birth of Atum and the lion—that Atum appeared on earth as a lion. The idea is expressed in the association between Atum and Ruti, the double lion god who is somewhat like a cell that has doubled its elements and begun to divide, before the actual split has occurred. The double lion also alludes to Shu and Tefnut, the first differentiation of Atum's being. But Ruti says 'I am the double lion, older than Atum,' appearing even before the actual birth of the next primordial generation.

We cannot be certain that the Fourth Dynasty Egyptians thought of the Sphinx as an image of Atum. But even if the Sphinx was an image of the king, according to the Pyramid Texts, kingship descended from Atum, through Shu, Geb, and Osiris to Horus, and thus the reigning king. The pyramid was more assuredly associated with Atum in Atum's capacity of the primeval mound and the *benben* stone, sacred icon of Heliopolis. So the Sphinx, hewn from the living rock, could have been associated with Atum as the primeval king in lion form, emerging from the formless mass, the royal head rising just above the earthy pit.

It would be perverse to think the Sphinx and the temple immediately in front of it were not connected, especially since they were part of the same quarry-construction sequence. The Sphinx temple suggests a cult that had something to do with the solar cycle, which would include Atum and the sun in its other phases—Khepri, the rising sun; Re, at its zenith; and Atum, its setting.

The Sphinx temple had an open central court surrounded by ten colossal statues of Khafre against piers. The court is an almost exact copy of the one in Khafre's pyramid temple, but here there were ten instead of twelve statues. This is yet another link between the Sphinx and Khafre. A covered colonnade whose roof was supported by twenty-four square granite pillars surrounded the court. Two sanctuaries, one on the east and another on the west, aligned on the center axis of the temple at the far back of recessed bays. Herbert Ricke understood the arrangement as symbolic of the sun's circuit, the eastern sanctuary for the rising sun (*Khepri*), the western for the setting sun (*Atum*), with each colonnade pillar symbolizing one of the twenty-four hours of the day and night.

Working at the Sphinx over the seasons, I was intrigued to discover that the east-west axis of the temple aligns, over the Sphinx's shoulder, with the sun's setting point at the south foot of Khafre's pyramid on both the vernal and autumnal equinox. This alignment is yet another element tying the Sphinx to Khafre's pyramid complex. If the temple had been completed, at the equinoxes, the sun would have passed over the western colonnade, across the court and into the eastern sanctuary. As the sun sets as Atum, the silhouettes of the Sphinx and Khafre's pyramid merge.

The builders positioned the Sphinx temple on Terrace I, 2.5 m lower than the floor of the Sphinx (Terrace II). This made an altar in the open court, which was paved with white alabaster, ideal for the presentations of offerings as the Sphinx looked down from above the western colonnade. It is impossible to say whether the Sphinx is the sun god *receiving* offerings, or the king as Horus, presenting the offerings. (Some later sphinxes have outstretched hands holding offering jars.)

Surely, the Sphinx relates to an advancement of the royal sun cult in the Fourth Dynasty. It was in the reign of Djedefre, who ruled briefly between Khufu and Khafre, that pharaohs adapted the title, 'Son of Re.' As Horus, the presenter of offerings, the Sphinx might represent a sublimation of kingly power to a higher deity. At the same time, it would be hard for anyone familiar with ancient Egyptian thought not to admit that the Sphinx could have been both the king as Horus, presenting offerings to the sun god, and at the same time, identified with the sun god.

Finally, its designers must have intended an apotropaic role for the Great Sphinx, that is, to avert evil. Situated at the very entrance to the sacred necropolis, alongside Khafre's causeway, the Sphinx, like the sphinxes and griffins in the relief decorations of the valley temple of Sahure's Fifth Dynasty pyramid or the lower causeway of Pepy II's Sixth Dynasty pyramid, must have been a repellent to dangerous forces.

SPHINX AND TEMPLE: AN UNFINISHED ROYAL PROJECT

It is a striking fact that from the hundreds of Old Kingdom tombs at Giza, Egyptologists cannot recognize any titles of priests or priestesses that clearly belong to the Sphinx temple. It is very possible that service was never activated because the builders left the temple unfinished. Although someone stripped the Sphinx temple of its granite casing and alabaster flooring in antiquity, anyone visiting the temple today can see the seats or emplacements for individual blocks at the base of the walls where the builders had finished covering the gigantic limestone core blocks with red granite casing. (It was easier to trim away the softer limestone than the hard granite in adjusting each block.) Since the builders only made sockets and cuttings at the time that they set up the granite pillars, statues, and casing blocks, these features track how much of the temple they had finished.

Ricke believed that they had completed the interior of the temple. They were just about to begin on the exterior when they quit the job. Their sockets for the granite wall casing stop just outside the entrance doorways. The builders left an extra stock of stone protruding from the huge core blocks forming the front corner hubs of the temple. At the base of the exterior northeast corner, channels in the bedrock show exactly where a team stopped leveling the floor in advance of the crew just behind them that was setting up the granite casing.

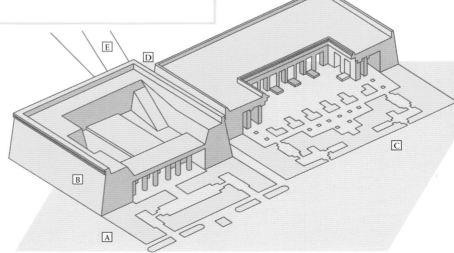

KHAFRE VALLEY TEMPLE AND SPHINX TEMPLE

A   KHAFRE'S VALLEY TEMPLE
B   SOUTHERN ENCLOSURE WALL AS RICKE RECONSTRUCTED
C   SPHINX TEMPLE
D   NORTH LEDGE OF TERRACE I

(SPHINX TEMPLE) AND SPHINX DITCH (TERRACE II)
E   KHAFRE'S CAUSEWAY CONNECTING VALLEY TEMPLE AND UPPER PYRAMID TEMPLE

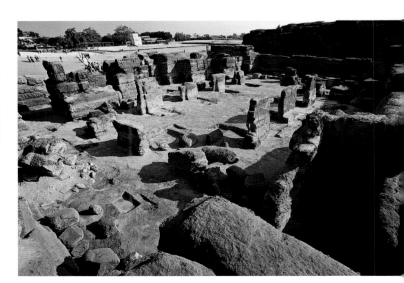

197 bottom left
View to the northwest across the open
court of the Sphinx temple. The pyramids
of Khufu (right) and Khafre (left) frame
the Sphinx's head like the two mountains
flanking the sun disk in the hieroglyph
for 'horizon.'

197 bottom right
This view to southeast clearly shows
the Sphinx temple court. Colossal
royal statues once fronted the limestone
cores of piers that were originally
clad in granite.

196–197
Aerial view looking down into Khafre's
valley temple, with the Sphinx temple
and the Sphinx sanctuary from
the east.

TOOLS OF THE SPHINX BUILDERS

There is also clear and definite evidence that Khafre's builders had not finished carving out the Sphinx ditch. By cutting the temple terrace lower than the Sphinx floor, the builders left a tall vertical bedrock ledge that forms a corridor with the north wall of the Sphinx temple (see map). On the east end, the ledge runs under the modern road that comes down from the Great Pyramid. To the west, the ledge forms the north side of the Sphinx ditch, but here the quarrymen did not finish cutting the line. The point at which they stopped is just opposite the Sphinx's left (north) forepaw and below the entrance of the Eighteenth Dynasty mud-brick temple of Amenhotep II, built 1,100 years after Khafre when the Sphinx temple was buried. From here to the back of the Sphinx ditch, the unfinished part is a rock shelf of decreasing width. Behind the Sphinx, the workmen were nowhere near finishing the outline of the ditch. When they stopped work, they left a huge massif of hard Member I rock jutting out to within a few meters from the rear of the Sphinx.

In 1978 a project directed by Zahi Hawass cleared off the top of the ledge along the north side of the Sphinx and discovered rectangular humps, depressions, and channels. This kind of pattern is found in many places at Giza where work was left unfinished. The ancient quarrymen removed bedrock by channeling to isolate humps that they would then knock away with heavy hammer stones. Very compact sand and gypsum, removed with small pick hammers, filled the channels and depressions. Embedded in the fill were fragments of pottery, including half of a common Fourth Dynasty jar used for beer or water, and hammer stones, one of which still had copper flecks on the percussion end where it was used to strike a chisel. The Sphinx builders must have abandoned these tools when they stopped work while cutting the north side of the Sphinx ditch.

The 1978 project found more evidence of the Sphinx builders in a small mound of debris in the northeast corner of the Sphinx ditch. Left by previous excavators, this mound supports the southwest corner of the Eighteenth Dynasty temple of Amenhotep II where it juts out over the north ledge of the Sphinx ditch and over the northwest corner of the Sphinx temple. Three large, limestone core blocks lie at the base of the mound where the Sphinx builders seem to have abandoned them while they were dragging the blocks over to complete the work on the northwest corner of the Sphinx temple. One block rested upon debris containing numerous pieces of Fourth Dynasty pottery. The other two rested on a layer of desert clay, or *tafla*, that the builders used as a lubricant for dragging blocks and sledges. Just under the clay layer, cuttings in the rock floor were used as sockets for thick wooden levers used to maneuver the ends of the blocks.

This little archaeological tableau, preserved under the Eighteenth Dynasty temple, is the tail-end of the quarry-construction process that created the Sphinx and the stone temples immediately to the east. These preserved 'frozen moments' in the ancient building project add to the conclusion that the builders walked off the job before finishing the Sphinx ditch and temple. The Sphinx and its temple were the last major project of Khafre's pyramid complex.

THE SPHINX AT THE END OF KHAFRE'S REIGN

If the Sphinx temple and Khafre's valley temple had been excavated according to modern archaeological standards, we would know far more about the state in which the builders left the site. Unfortunately, the large-scale clearing and the poor recording left us scant stratigraphic clues about the temple's history. I am convinced, though, that the complete archaeological tableau would have shown that the Sphinx temple was the last major item, left unfinished at the end of Khafre's reign. It is even possible that the builders left the whole interior of the Sphinx temple filled with the construction debris. Centuries later, those who systematically stripped the Sphinx temple of its granite casing and colossal statues must have turned over the construction embankments and debris that the original builders left inside the temple. Ricke thought there had been two periods of stone-robbing in Khafre's valley complex, the first in the Twelfth Dynasty reign of Amenemhet I when the Sphinx temple interior was stripped, and the second when the granite was removed from the valley temple exterior, possibly in the Eighteenth Dynasty.

The fact that the builders left the Sphinx ditch and the Sphinx temple unfinished is itself suggestive that they were the last items under construction in the reign of Khafre. Would Khafre have erected his beautifully finished valley temple smack beside the unfinished Sphinx temple and its messy construction yard without cleaning it up? No, the general picture we have been able to salvage from the large-scale expeditions that cleared out the Sphinx and the two temples suggests that all three monuments originated from the same long-term project.

STATE OF THE STATUE IN THE FOURTH DYNASTY

In what condition did the Sphinx builders leave the Sphinx itself? The relief-carved features we see today on the head—the body of the royal cobra on the forehead, the stripes of the headdress, eyes, eyebrows, and mouth—are those left in the natural rock of Member III by the original Sphinx builders.

The Sphinx builders also completed the mass and general contours of the lion body in bedrock. The bedrock body weathered in an undulating pattern of recessed softer layers and protruding harder geological layers of Member II. However, with all the recesses filled in, there would be a complete lion body. The 1926 restoration under Emile Baraize, and the work of the Egyptian Antiquities Organization ([EAO], now the Supreme Council of Antiquities [SCA]), in the 1980s exposed parts of the original bedrock body of the Sphinx, carved out of Member I, which weathers relatively little. Although the surface of the Member I bedrock is rough and gnarled, the toes of the north hind paw and front paws have relief-carved claws. Such details suggest that, like the head, the sculptors finished the paws in the natural rock without a coating of masonry. On the other hand, when Baraize, and again recently the EAO restoration team, treated the south hind paw, they found an enormous gap in the natural rock (part of what we call the Major Fissure that cuts through the entire Sphinx). The greater part of this paw was built almost entirely of large masonry blocks. However, the bottoms of the toes are finished, each with a claw in the sound rock of Member I, which here rises only a couple of feet above the Sphinx floor.

Would the Sphinx builders have left serious gaps in the left hind paw and the fissure cutting through the body without filling or covering the flaws with masonry? It is possible that some of the larger blocks encasing the lower parts of the Sphinx may represent the beginning of a Fourth Dynasty casing that masked these flaws. It is also possible that the Sphinx builders never got around to masking these flaws, considering the evidence that they quit before completing work on the sides of the ditch and on the temple. The details of the claws suggest that when they stopped work, the builders did not intend to finish the lion body with a casing of fine limestone, as they did they with *mastaba* tombs and pyramids.

SPHINX BEARD

Captain Giovanni Battista Caviglia, a Genoese merchant turned Giza explorer, found several fragments of the beard at the base of the chest in 1817, the earliest recorded modern excavation of the Sphinx. The fragments were part of a long, braided 'divine beard,' curled at the end, such as gods and deified kings wore, as opposed to the short square beard sported by statues of living kings. Egyptologists have questioned whether the beard was original to the Sphinx or a later addition. Relief-carved figures of a kneeling pharaoh offering up a gold collar toward the Sphinx's chin once adorned both sides of the flat limestone that connected the outward thrusting beard to the Sphinx chest. The figures are certainly New Kingdom in style (1550–1070 BC).

One of these connecting pieces is lost, but an examination of the other, in the Egyptian Museum in Cairo, shows that it is like a broad plate, only about 30 centimeters thick, with the backside roughed up to assist a bonding with gypsum mortar. So the beard seems to be a later addition. On the other hand, the limestone of the beard fragments seems to match the natural limestone layers of the monument's chest and neck, as though the beard was once carved from the natural rock like the rest of the Sphinx. It is possible that the beard was originally carved from the bedrock along with the Sphinx head, and that it had detached, fallen, and broken to pieces. During a later restoration, the pieces that connected to the chest were recut as thin slabs and worked on the backside for reattaching them.

Another feature that suggests the divine beard may be original is the prominent boss or bump formed in the bedrock near the bottom center of the Sphinx's chest. The boss only makes sense as a support for a long divine beard. The sculptors could not extend the thin supporting plate below the curl all the way to the base of the chest, nor could they simply leave the beard and its plate suspended. Both options would have left the beard even more fragile. So they left a thicker column of natural rock from the bottom of the beard down to the base of the chest. Once again, the study of the beard suggests that the original Sphinx sculptors did attempt to finish their work in the natural rock.

It appears certain that where bedrock was sound enough, at the head, the north hind paw, and the bottoms of the other paws for example, the Sphinx builders did finish the sculpture in the natural rock. They probably intended to fill in flaws, like the Major Fissure. They may have intended and begun to build over weaker rock with a casing.

At the northwest rear haunch, the SCA restoration work exposed, under more recent casing-stone veneer, very large blocks of fine limestone that appear to be set into some kind of gap in the bedrock-core body of the Sphinx. Unless we get better exposures of the lower part of the Sphinx-core body, there is just not enough evidence to answer conclusively whether the Fourth Dynasty builders began, or how far along they had progressed, filling in and building up with masonry the weak spots in their massive sculpture. It is clear that, as they did with so many other royal monuments, the builders simply stopped work shortly after the king's death to turn their attention to the monuments planned for his successor.

Again, it was most likely Khafre's, not Khufu's, builders who left the Sphinx almost, but not quite, finished. They stopped work when Menkaure, the new king, came to the throne. In fact, he wasn't able to finish his own pyramid complex, located away to the south at Giza.

199 bottom
Fragments of the Sphinx's beard found
by Caviglia in 1816. The upper piece
is in the Egyptian Museum, Cairo.
The lower piece is a cast from the
original, now in the British Museum.

200

The Great Sphinx looking west.
In 1816, Caviglia found a horned
limestone table on the granite altar.
The granite stela of Thutmose IV
remains from a royal chapel at the
base of the Sphinx's chest.

201

The Stela of Thutmose IV tells a
story of the Sphinx speaking to the
prince in a dream. As king,
Thutmose makes offerings to the
Sphinx shown high on a pedestal.
The slab is a lintel from Khafre's
pyramid temple.

ANCIENT RESTORATIONS OF THE SPHINX

It was probably the Eighteenth Dynasty pharaoh Thutmose IV who undertook the oldest restoration of the Sphinx, about 1,100 years after Khafre. His craftsmen covered the body with large limestone casing slabs (Phase I). By this time, the surface of the core body formed from Member II bedrock had eroded drastically into a profile of deep recesses and rounded protrusions, as indicated by the fact that Phase I fills in the recesses. Large chunks of natural rock were about to fall off the Sphinx. At the upper part of the rump and at the Sphinx's rear left haunch, huge boulders of bedrock had detached from the Sphinx body in ancient times and were held in position by the Phase I restoration slabs.

Another major restoration of the Sphinx, most probably, in the Twenty-sixth Dynasty, ca. 664–525 BC (Phase II), filled in patches or covered the Phase I cladding. The limestone used in Phase II is the same fine-grained, homogeneous limestone employed in the first restoration. Phase III, of Greco-Roman date (332 BC–395 AD) patched and replaced parts of the Phase I and II veneer using small blocks of white, relatively soft and friable limestone.

THE CHAPEL OF THE SPHINX

Prior to the recent restorations, we could trace the Phase I cladding from the rump all the way to the front of the Sphinx where it wraps around both of the Sphinx's shoulders. A wide gap at the center of the chest corresponds to the remains of a small open-air chapel tucked between the forepaws. Thutmose IV erected the centerpiece of this chapel, a granite stele, 3.6 meter tall and weighing 15 tons. Thutmose IV was the son of Amenhotep II, who built a mud-brick temple dedicated to the Sphinx as the god Horemakhet, 'Horus in the Horizon,' at the northeast corner of the Sphinx ditch. Ramesses II placed smaller stelae that show him worshipping the Sphinx on the

side walls of the chapel. Much of the chapel was stripped away soon after Caviglia first cleared it in 1817. The two Ramesses stelae were taken to the Louvre. What remains today are the lower part of the south wall and the granite stele of Thutmose IV.

The 'Dream Stela' is named for the hieroglyphic story it tells. Thutmose was a prince, but apparently not the crown prince, when he went on a hunting expedition in the vicinity of Giza. Thutmose calls the Sphinx "this very great statue of Khepri," the god of the rising sun; and *Khepri-Ra-Atum*, that is, the sun god in all its aspects—rising, zenith, and setting. Thutmose also calls the Sphinx *Horemakhet*, 'Horus-in-the-Horizon,' as do the inscriptions on Amenhotep II's temple, and on numerous smaller New Kingdom stelae of private persons.

Toward noon, Thutmose slept in shadow of the Sphinx. The Sphinx appeared to the prince in a dream and offered him the throne in exchange for clearing the sand from the godly body, which had fallen into a ruinous state. Thutmose did clear the sand, and did indeed become king in the year 1401 BC. At the top of the stele, he etched a double scene of himself giving offerings and libations to the Sphinx, dated to the first year of his reign.

NEW KINGDOM RENAISSANCE

The evidence allows us to recreate a picture of the Sphinx as a restored national monument in the fifteenth century BC. A statue of a standing king may have stood against the chest of the Sphinx. A large block of masonry behind the Dream Stele would have been the base. Salt's drawings of Caviglia's excavations show a stack of stones against the Sphinx—possibly a back support for the statue. Several of the smaller New Kingdom stelae that Selim Hassan found near the Sphinx depict a royal statue at the chest of the Sphinx. One of these stelae labels the statue with the name of Amenhotep II.

Statues of animal-form deities with a king striding forth from the chest of the god are well known in the

early New Kingdom. The arrangement symbolized the god's protection of, and merger with, the king. In fact, the inscription on the side plates of the Sphinx beard read, "life and protection [of the Sphinx] around and behind him [i.e., the king]."

A complete Phase I reconstruction of the Sphinx in the Eighteenth Dynasty fits with the picture of the site that emerges from the major excavations of the Sphinx from 1925–38. The documentation includes the unpublished Baraize photographs and notes of Pierre Lacau, Director General of the Antiquities Service, along with Selim Hassan's published record of his excavations from 1936–38. Numerous stelae, votive falcons, and small sphinxes attest to a robust cult of the Sphinx as the god Horemakhet ('Horus in the Horizon'), an amalgamation of the primeval sun god and Horus, god of kingship. This rich evidence of attention paid the Sphinx is in marked contrast to the cultic silence about the monument in the Fourth Dynasty. Princes at the administrative capital, Memphis, and newly ascended kings, recorded their homage to the Sphinx. Amenhotep II, Thutmose IV, and Ramesses II dedicated stelae to the Sphinx in the first year of their reigns.

The New Kingdom inscriptions call the Sphinx enclosure *Setepet*, 'The Chosen,' or 'Select.' The Sphinx had become an image of ancient authority that could ordain and confirm the privileged position of princes and kings. The New Kingdom administration of Memphis built terraces, enclosures, rest houses, and temples as a kind of royal national park upon and around the ruins of Khafre's Fourth Dynasty stone temples.

Amenhotep II's temple in the northeast corner of the Sphinx ditch was only a part of this arrangement. Thutmose IV covered the sides of the Sphinx ditch with massive mud-brick walls, more than eight meters tall, that encircled the Sphinx like a giant cartouche and held back the sea of sand. Baraize removed most of this covering in 1926, but he left a section along the north ledge of the Sphinx ditch. When Selim Hassan continued excavations in 1936, he removed

more of these walls, and recorded the fact that some of the bricks were stamped with the name of Thutmose IV. A broad viewing platform and stairway fronted the Sphinx, the first and lowest of several platforms, each with shrines and podiums, built one on top of another, until the latest in the Roman Period. A royal villa was attached to the front of Khafre's valley temple. Tutankhamen built a kind of rest house in back of the valley temple that Ramesses II took over, superimposing his name over those of Tutankhamen and his queen, Ankhesenamen, on the doorway. In addition to the massive enclosure walls around the Sphinx ditch, Thutmose IV built a bastioned wall forming a enclosure that encompassed a much wider area around the Sphinx.

Emerging from their rest houses over by Khafre's old valley temple, royalty descended a stairway to the broad viewing platform that covered the Sphinx temple. After ritual stops at shrines and podiums, another stairway led down into the heart of the cult—the small chapel at the chest of the giant statue. Standing there, a newly ascended king like Thutmose or Ramesses might feel that he could trace his descent back to far more ancient kings like Khufu and Khafre,

indeed, back to the primeval god king, Horus in the Horizon, whose image towered above him.

As they restored, or completed, the Sphinx, the New Kingdom pharaohs quarried stone from Khafre's pyramid complex. The foundations of an Eighteenth Dynasty royal villa built onto the front of Khafre's valley temple rested on the bottom course of granite casing. The rest of the casing might well have been stripped not long before the villa was founded. Granite casing blocks, probably from Khafre's pyramid, have been found in the New Kingdom Ptah temple at Memphis. The Overseer of Works for Ramesses II, May, etched his name into the rock walls beside the northwest corner of Khafre's pyramid. In 1909, Uvo Hölscher found a New Kingdom mud-brick ramp on the south side of Khafre's mortuary temple that was probably used for hauling away its granite pillars and sheathing.

The 15-ton Dream Stela of Thutmose IV is itself a reused lintel from a doorway in one of Khafre's temples. Anyone who looks at the lintels still intact in Khafre's valley temple cannot doubt this. The back of the Dream Stela has the same ledge that forms the top of the door frame, and the same two sockets and

pivot-holes for a standard Egyptian double-leaf swinging door. The bottom turning sockets of such doors were set into the thresholds, and cut right into the bedrock floor of the temples. By measuring the space between these, we can determine where Thutmose got the lintel. The space between the sockets on the back of the stelae only fit three doors in Khafre's mortuary temple, one being the entrance to that temple from the causeway.

This suggests an explanation for the similarity of the Phase I Sphinx restoration blocks to Old Kingdom masonry. The range of thickness of the Phase I slabs very closely match those slabs that form the walls of Khafre's causeway. Only a small part of these original walls are left near the exit of the causeway from the valley temple. It is very possible that Thutmose had his workmen utilize Khafre's causeway blocks to restore the Sphinx. After they had worked their way up the causeway taking blocks for the Sphinx, Thutmose had them drag the lintel from the mortuary temple down between the forepaws, where he erected it to commemorate the story of his selection by the Sphinx for the throne of Egypt.

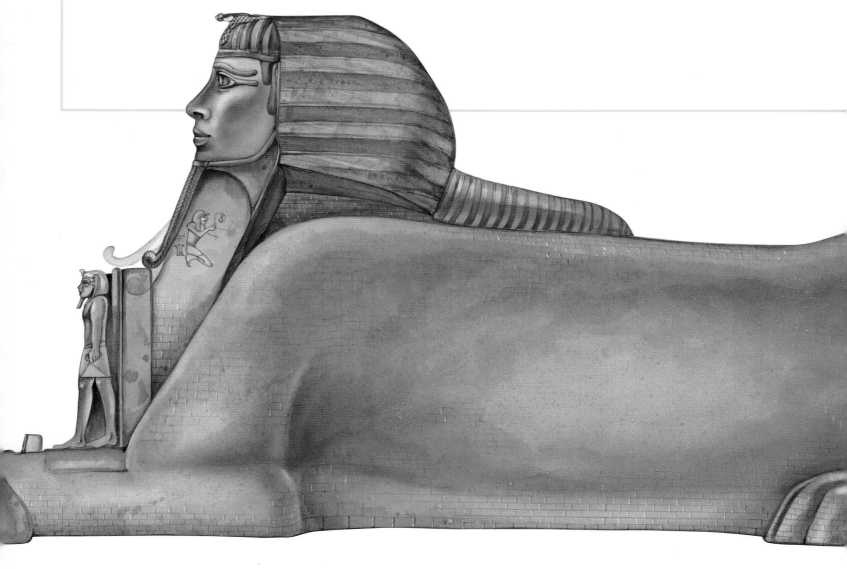

CONCLUSION

After they erected and modified the valley temple of Khafre's pyramid, the Fourth Dynasty builders created the Sphinx and the temple in front of it as a continuation of the same quarry-construction project. In spite of the gigantic size and grand new concept of the Sphinx, they did not finish the temple, and so religious services never began in the Fourth Dynasty. Archaeological evidence suggests that after the Old Kingdom, the Sphinx was abandoned for nearly a millennium. During the New Kingdom period of empire, nearby Memphis emerged as a second capital, and old shrines and temples were unearthed and rebuilt throughout Egypt, including the Sphinx. In terms of an active cult and its popularity, the Sphinx was as much a New Kingdom as a Fourth Dynasty monument. For it was in the New Kingdom that the Sphinx became a popular sacred image, under the name Horemakhet, a union of king and god, a super-deity on earth. The chapel between its paws was a select place for princes and newly ascended kings. In Pharaonic times, the Sphinx was already an ancient and restored national symbol of Egypt.

202 and 203
The revitalized and restored Sphinx of the New Kingdom. The royal statue against the chest might have been Amenhotep II.

204-205
The battered face of time. The nose has been snapped off, the eyes pecked, and the beard cleaved from the chin. Erosion has revealed the original geological bedding, but the hard bedrock of the head has preserved enough detail that the majesty of the god shines through.

The Tombs of the High Officials at Giza

by Peter Der Manuelian

Perhaps the greatness of an achievement may be defined by the degree of difficulty we have in imagining the world without it. Can we conceive of ancient Egypt without the Pyramids of Giza? Over four millennia have passed since anyone gazed upon the now famous plateau and saw only bedrock and sand, devoid of towering mortuary edifices and surrounding cemeteries. So imposing is the image of the Great Pyramid and Sphinx on the collective memory of humanity that to consider its absence, its pre-existence, strikes us as a highly unnatural and arduous task.

The pyramids themselves are the subject of other chapters in this volume. This chapter emphasizes that the three pyramids that catch the eye and dominate the horizon west of modern Cairo are merely the tip of a vast funerary 'iceberg.' The Giza plateau consists of hundreds of tombs of the governing classes carefully placed around three royal pyramid complexes. They were conceived as an integral part of the cemetery, and their proximity to the royal monuments was no accident. The owners of these sepulchers represent the uppermost echelons of Old Kingdom society, the literate few who administered the country on behalf of the royal court. They were architects, scribes, physicians, tax-gatherers, priests and temple officials, doctors, manicurists, musicians, princes and princesses. The tombs testify to every aspect of ancient Egyptian society, often containing frozen glimpses into the lives of thousands of individuals (not just the tomb-owners themselves) at the height of the Old Kingdom. This was Egypt's

first—and some would say greatest—era of prosperous stability, centralized under the authority of the semi-divine pharaoh. To compound the Giza story further, the modern archaeological history of the plateau, most of it occurring in the twentieth century, is no less fascinating than the ancient monuments themselves.

The development of the Giza necropolis followed the almost incomprehensible feat of the construction of four pyramids by a single pharaoh. Sneferu, first king of the Old Kingdom's Fourth Dynasty, solidified the transition from earlier step pyramids to the true pyramid, culminating in the north or 'Red Pyramid' at Dahshur, which might actually have held the king's remains. The sprawling cemeteries of the Memphite capital stretched by this time from Meidum in the south to Dahshur and Saqqara in the north. Recent excavations are even painting a picture of one long, connected necropolis, suggesting that its differentiation into discrete sites is a modern and artificial one. Sneferu's son and successor, Khufu, sought out a new portion of the desert's edge for his own sepulcher. Just beyond the arable floodplain west of the Nile, a few kilometers west of what is now modern Cairo, Khufu located a natural promontory. Composed of a limestone geological surface known as the Muqattam formation, it slopes gently from the northwest to the southeast in three primary alternating layers of hard and soft stone (Members I, II, and III). When the Nile's annual inundation reached the Memphite region, the floodwaters stretched all the way to the edge of the

plateau. This was doubtless a consideration in Khufu's selection of the site, for the transport of limestone blocks could be greatly facilitated by barges across the flooded riverbanks.

The area was probably not completely virgin territory upon Khufu's accession, for some evidence of cemeteries prior to the Fourth Dynasty exists; but nothing would be allowed to stand in the king's, or his necropolis architects', way. Khufu's vision far exceeded anything the country, indeed the entire ancient world, had ever experienced before, for he set in motion the most ambitious construction project ever undertaken. He prepared the largest, most accurately conceived pyramid complex to date. It included a porticoed mortuary temple abutting the pyramid's east face, a long causeway stretching eastwards off the plateau to a valley temple below, and four subsidiary or satellite pyramids on the eastern side. In addition, he engaged in 'urban planning' for the dead on an unprecedented scale. The pyramids were reserved for royalty; non-royal Egyptians, as well as certain royal family members, were buried in traditional *mastaba* tombs, low rectangular superstructures with sloping sides. While the majority of the Giza tomb owners were male, there is clear evidence of a number of major *mastaba* tombs housing exclusively the burials of women. Taken as a unit, the site came to encompass almost the entire corps of the elite members of Egyptian society in the Fourth Dynasty. Fully developed Old Kingdom provincial cemeteries were still a dynasty or two away.

206 bottom
This scene of boating (above) and statue manufacture (below) comes from the rock-cut mastaba chapel of Queen Meresankh III, G 7530sub, main room, east wall, upper registers, and dates from the Fourth Dynasty.

207
This polychrome relief shows the deceased, Iasen, seated before a table of offering loaves. From the rock-cut mastaba chapel of Iasen, G 2196, west wall, southern section. Sixth Dynasty.

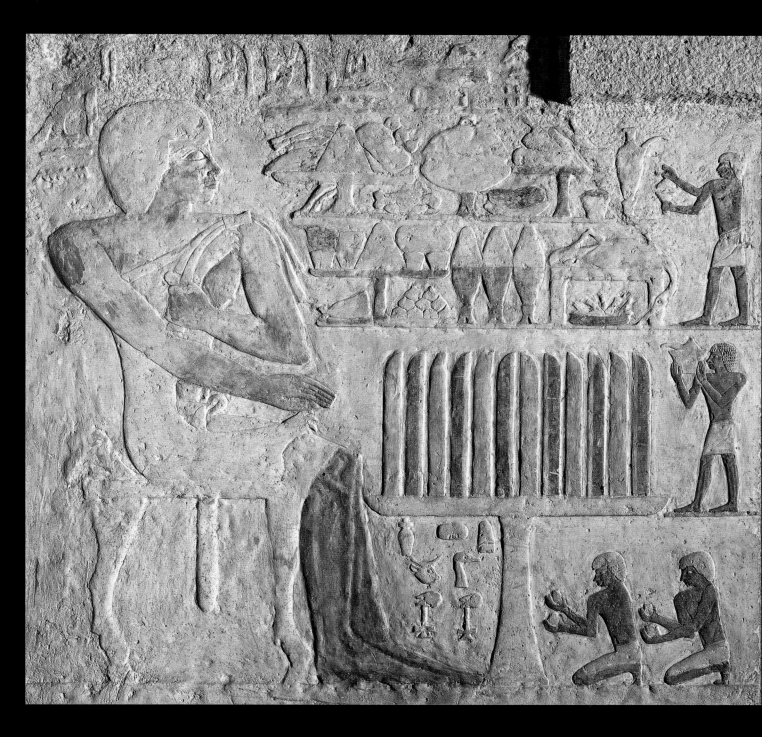

208-209
This aerial photograph shows the Giza plateau, looking west, with the pyramids (from right to left) of Khufu, Khafre, and Menkaure. The Eastern Cemetery is in the foreground, while the Western Cemetery lies behind the Great Pyramid. The Central Field and Sphinx are visible toward the lower left.

208 bottom
In this view of the Great Pyramid, looking southeast, Khufu's queens' pyramids (top) and the Solar Boat Museum are visible, and southern mastaba field is to the right.

Attempts at organized necropolis development had been undertaken previously, but Khufu expanded the pattern to include vast arrays of *mastabas*, all laid out methodically in 'streets' and 'avenues,' and aligned to the axis of the king's pyramid complex. It is staggering to consider the sheer metric tonnage of limestone that required preparation, transport (from either local quarries or from Tura, on the east bank, across the river), dressing, and placement during the several decades of the king's reign. Thousands of laborers must have covered the site, working on both royal and private construction projects, probably simultaneously. The scaffolding, dust, and cacophony must, at times, have been disorienting at best, and downright dangerous at worst. How these workers were managed, where they lived, and how they were compensated is only just coming to light, thanks to recent excavations to the south of the plateau. Far from brutally enforced slave labor, the image made famous by the Hollywood film industry, the construction at Giza is now seen rather as massive public works projects, religiously motivated, and carried through to completion by and for the benefit of the entire nation. To the average Egyptian, the pyramid was most likely much more than just the pharaoh's 'mansion of eternity.'

Excavations from the first half of the twentieth century unearthed the vast cemeteries surrounding the Pyramids. In 1902, the Egyptian antiquities authorities, decrying the unscientific treasure hunters at Giza, invited several archaeological missions to excavate the site responsibly. Among the candidates were three foreign missions: an American team headed by George A. Reisner (1867–1942), a German expedition by Georg Steindorff (1861–1951), and an Italian team led by Ernesto Schiaparelli (1856–1928). The necropolis was divided into equal portions and the colleagues drew lots to determine their shares. This historic division was later revised as the Italian mission abandoned Giza for other sites, and Steindorff traded his concession to Hermann Junker (1877–1962) of the University of Vienna, in order to excavate in the Sudan. The only excavator to work almost continuously at Giza was Reisner. From his early years under the sponsorship of Phoebe Apperson Hearst (1842–1919) and the University of California (1902–1905), through the transfer of his expedition to Harvard University and the Museum of Fine Arts, Boston (1905–1947), Reisner settled into his beloved 'Harvard Camp' west of the pyramid of Khafre and based all his archaeological activity from this landmark location. Physically exhausted and nearly blind after forty-three years of excavations in Egypt and the Sudan, with a short interlude in Palestine, he died at Giza in June 1942. His concession came to include two-thirds of the vast cemetery west of the Great Pyramid, the entire cemetery east of it, and the pyramid and valley temples of Menkaure, builder of the third and smallest pyramid. The Steindorff/Junker expeditions excavated the central third of the Western Cemetery and the row of *mastabas* just south of the Great Pyramid. Important later excavations by Selim Hassan (1886–1961), on behalf of Cairo University, revealed the so-called Central Field, west of the Sphinx and south of the causeway to Khafre's pyramid. Abdel-Moneim Abu Bakr (1907–1976) worked in the far Western Cemetery in the 1940s and 1950s, also for Cairo University. All these scholars, and several others in recent years, have produced a total of about thirty monographs on their work at Giza, and these remain fundamental secondary sources for the study of Old Kingdom mortuary tradition, and indeed most aspects of ancient Egyptian civilization.

209 top
The so-called 'Cemetery en Echelon' looking south, with the large mastabas of Babaef (G 5230) and Duaenre (G 5110) visible toward the top.

209 bottom
This reconstruction illustrates a typical portion of the Western Cemetery, showing mastaba superstructures, chapels, and burial shafts.

210 top
Four giants of Egyptology (from left to right): Herrmann Junker, George Reisner, James H. Breasted, and Ludwig Borchardt, in the garden of the Continental Hotel, Cairo, November 15, 1935.

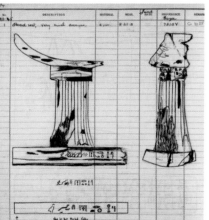

What were the basic funerary needs of the average high official of the Old Kingdom? Most tombs of this era consisted of two discrete elements. The first of which was a substructure that could house and protect the deceased's mummy, which had to survive intact in the next world as a point of reunification for the various aspects of the persona. While the art of mummification was still in its early stages in the Fourth Dynasty, high-ranking individuals were interred in stone sarcophagi or wooden coffins deep within a burial chamber sunk into the bedrock off of a vertical shaft. The second element was a superstructure that could house the cult focus, the offering place where the living provided food offerings and recited invocation spells on behalf of the tomb owner. The various forms of equipment needed for the cult focus developed and changed at Giza, sometimes with surprising results.

It seems clear that Khufu laid out the orderly cemeteries to the east and west of his pyramid in what may be the world's first example of 'prefabricated' construction, with the assignment of specific tombs to specific individuals following later. The construction process consisted of laying exterior courses of limestone blocks around the perimeter of the *mastaba* 'core,' which was then filled with rubble or debris. (Only a few *mastabas* contained a core of solid limestone blocks.) Additional courses were added, with the blocks set back from the preceding course, to form a battered or stepped exterior. The burial shaft (or shafts) was sunk through the core of the *mastaba's* superstructure deep down into the bedrock below. A short corridor connected the shaft to the actual burial chamber, which housed the sarcophagus and canopic equipment. Some *mastaba* superstructures later received an additional exterior casing consisting of blocks of smooth white limestone, quarried, for those whose resources allowed, from across the river at Tura. One of the more interesting challenges for scholars of Egyptian

archaeology is disentangling the architectural history of the Giza mastabas, distinguishing the originally intended structures from the various subsequent additions and determining the degree of completion attained.

Another challenge is unraveling the events of Khufu's early reign that led to the form and content of the Giza *mastabas*. It is perhaps a modern prejudice to expect a linear development of cultural expression. Prior to the Fourth Dynasty, tomb development does indeed appear to follow such a course, with ever-higher pyramids, larger temples, and an expanded repertoire of decoration appearing over time. At Giza, however, this development suddenly stops in favor of a simplicity and austerity whose explanation remains the subject of scholarly debate. In place of elaborate tombs with multiple chambers, in the superstructure and so-called 'false doors' serving as the focal point for offerings and contact between the realms of living and of the dead, the earliest Giza *mastabas* under Khufu are solid buildings. Gone are the interior chambers, and the decorated wall surfaces known from earlier tombs at other sites. With very few exceptions, the early Fourth Dynasty Giza tombs show only a simple niche at the south end of the east wall where an inscribed rectangular slab stela, a sort of ancient tombstone, was installed. Carved on the stela was just about everything needed for a successful afterlife: a scene of the deceased seated at a table of offerings, his/her name and administrative titles, various offerings both spelled out in hieroglyphs and represented ideographically, and a list of different types of linen needed for the burial. In some cases a mud-brick exterior chapel was added around the stela; in others, the stela was later walled up and the area refitted with a stone exterior chapel and a monolithic false door. Clearly, changes crept into the design process, and the pace accelerated towards the end of the reign of Khufu and beyond.

210 center
The American Egyptologist George Andrew Reisner on June 26, 1933, photographed by Bob Davies. He was the only excavator to work continuously at Giza at the beginning of the twentieth century.

210 bottom
This page, now conserved in the Harvard University–Museum of Fine Arts, Boston Expedition's Object Register books, shows an Old Kingdom headrest found in Giza tomb G 7215.

211 left
In this detailed map showing the Western Cemetery at Giza, all the tombs are color-coded by expedition, with the indication of the expedition dates. Drawing by Peter Der Manuelian.

211 right
View of the courtyard of 'Harvard Camp,' headquarters of the Harvard University–Museum of Fine Arts, Boston Expedition from 1902–47. Fragments of a colossal seated calcite statue of Menkaure are visible.

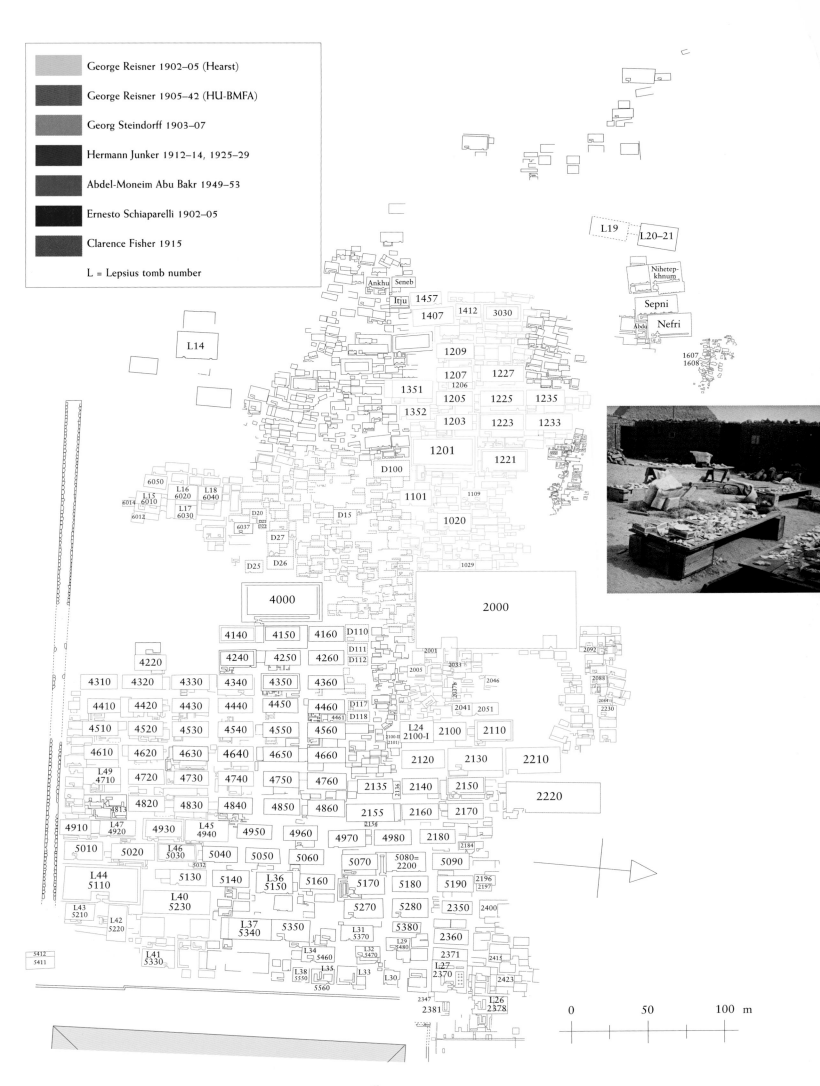

George Reisner 1902–05 (Hearst)

George Reisner 1905–42 (HU-BMFA)

Georg Steindorff 1903–07

Hermann Junker 1912–14, 1925–29

Abdel-Moneim Abu Bakr 1949–53

Ernesto Schiaparelli 1902–05

Clarence Fisher 1915

L = Lepsius tomb number

What accounts for this reductionist royal policy? Did Khufu perceive a threat from the administrative classes and attempt to refocus attention solely on the monarchy? Were the state's resources simply stretched too thin with the construction all over the site, resulting in a dearth of craftsmen to decorate tomb walls as in earlier times? Or were the slab stelae merely 'placeholders,' a temporary solution prior to the intended expansion and completion of the tomb and its decoration? Did the tomb owner's premature death play a role in the use of a slab stela over more traditional forms of decoration, as has recently been suggested? We may never know the real answer, but systematic research into these questions is only now receiving detailed scrutiny as the archaeological finds from the 1900s are processed with the fresh eyes of a new archaeological generation. But one fact is clear: the dearth of private tomb decoration under Khufu was certainly not caused by a lack of talent. The famous slab stela of Wepemnefret, with its masterful polychromy and exquisite low-relief carving attests to a sophistication and stylistic refinement that can only be the product of the finest royal workshops. The stela was the only decorated element from its *mastaba*, no. G 1201, located in the cemetery far to the west of the Great Pyramid, and it survived in such pristine condition because the ancient craftsmen lovingly covered it up as they reworked the tomb's offering chapel in limestone and mud brick, shifting the cult focus from the slab stela to a monolithic false door. Some of the archaic elements on the stela, such as the raised ground line for the table of offering loaves, the stool carved in imitation of bull's legs, and the small linen list, indicate that Wepemnefret may have been one of the first occupants of Khufu's new Western Cemetery.

212-213
This painted limestone 'slab stela' from the mastaba of Wepemnefret (G 1201), dates to the Fourth Dynasty reign of Khufu, and is 45.7 cm high, 66 cm wide, and 7.6 cm thick; it is conserved in the Phoebe A. Hearst Museum of Anthropology, University of California, Berkeley. At bottom is a detail of three Horus falcons from the slab stela of Nefret-iabet from Giza tomb G 1225; Musée du Louvre E 15591.

213 bottom
This short end of the painted limestone sarcophagus of a high official presents a 'palace façade' decoration. From mastaba G 7340. Ht. 110 cm; width 97.5 cm; length 210 cm. Fourth Dynasty. Egyptian Museum, Cairo.

214
*Limestone 'reserve head' of a high official,
from mastaba G 4340. Height 26 cm;
Fourth Dynasty, reign of Khufu. Now in
the Egyptian Museum, Cairo.*

215 top
*Another limestone 'reserve head' of a high
official, found in mastaba G 4640, shaft A.
Height 25.5 cm, width 18 cm; Fourth
Dynasty, reign of Khufu. Now in the
Egyptian Museum, Cairo.*

215 bottom
*Limestone relief fragment from the
mastaba chapel of Hemiunu, G 4000.
Height 12.1 cm, width 39.5 cm,
thickness 7 cm; Fourth Dynasty, reign of
Khufu. Now in the Museum of Fine
Arts, Boston.*

Along with the slab stelae, many of the early Fourth Dynasty Giza tombs contained another unique item: the so-called 'reserve heads.' Most unusual in Egyptian art, which prefers complete statuary, these limestone heads were never part of composite or complete sculptures. They were found, not in the *mastaba* superstructure in a *serdab* (statue chamber), but in disturbed contexts at the bottom of the burial shafts. No two heads are alike, and their highly individual features also set them apart from the rest of Egyptian sculpture. The last word remains to be written about the reserve heads; they are commonly taken as stand-ins should a substitute home for the deceased's spirit be needed in the event of damage to the mummy, but alternative theories abound (sculptor's models? templates for funerary masks? ritually mutilated effigies?). The absence of accompanying inscriptions, the curious incisions running down the center of the skull on some heads, the apparently removed or mutilated ears, and the range in quality, from crude visages to polished and finished masterpieces, have only fueled speculation as to the original function of these mysterious heads. They clearly belong, like the owners of the slab stelae, to the high officials of Khufu's reign, the original *mastaba* owners as per Khufu's commands; they are not found in later dynasties.

A powerful official named Hemiunu, one of the Western Cemetery tomb owners during the era of slab stelae and reserve heads, is justly famous today

as the architect who probably oversaw the Great Pyramid's construction. As vizier (second in command to the pharaoh), royal seal bearer, and overseer of all royal construction projects, Hemiunu was the eldest son of the vizier Nefermaat, who in turn was Sneferu's eldest son, and whose beautifully painted tomb is located at Meidum. Under Khufu, Hemiunu obtained one of the three largest *mastabas* at Giza. The owner of the largest tomb, mastaba G 2000, remains unidentified but must have been a favored prince; the tomb is so monumental that one might even construe some of the surrounding *mastaba* fields as oriented to it rather than to the Great Pyramid. To the south of mastaba G 2000, Hemiunu extended the simple *mastaba* layout described above to include two chapels in his tomb, connected by a long corridor added to the east face of the superstructure. The cut of these limestone blocks is so precise that the corners retain their joins and sharpness even today, some 4,600 years after the tomb's construction. In the northern chapel, an over-life-sized seated statue of the corpulent (to the ancient Egyptians corpulence was equated with the prosperity and success) Hemiunu gazed eastwards towards the pyramid of his sovereign. We can only guess at the logistical challenges Hemiunu faced as the pyramid slowly rose to dominate the surrounding landscape, raising the national psyche with it in an unprecedented public works project to secure the immortality of the pharaoh and thereby

the cosmic order and prosperity of the country.

By the end of Khufu's reign, the original layout of the great *mastaba* fields had undergone significant changes. Simple core *mastabas* with nothing but a slab stela as the cult focus were expanded with exterior chapels, sometimes in limestone, sometimes in mud brick. Additional burial shafts were sometimes added, probably for additional family members. In the Eastern Cemetery, reserved primarily for the royal family, what began as four rows of twelve *mastabas* was completely remodeled. Some of these tombs were joined together while others received extensions; the result was four rows of eight great double-*mastabas*. Most of these were badly plundered before the arrival of the twentieth-century archaeologists, but they once contained the burials of the ruling elite of the land, and perhaps some of Khufu's successors on the throne. His own mother, the wife of Sneferu, Queen Hetepheres, may also have been buried in the Eastern Cemetery, either in one of the three queens' pyramids, or in the hundred-foot deep burial chamber just to the north, which was accidentally discovered in 1925. Some of the oldest examples of furniture from the ancient world were found here, along with a mysteriously empty sarcophagus and the queen's viscera in canopic jars, containing a solution still in liquid form after more than four millennia. This royal mystery—a burial without a body—continues to contradict what we think we know about Egyptian burial traditions.

Giza Tombs

Khufukhaf I

216 left
The entrance façade to the limestone chapel of Khufukhaf I—prince and son of Khufu—mastaba G 7140, looking southwest. Fourth Dynasty.

216-217
On the south side of the entrance to the limestone chapel of Khufukhaf I, looking west, one can clearly admire the tomb owner's mother and son.

217 right
Large-scale figures of the prince and his wife Nefret-kau on the northern and eastern walls, looking northeast, in the chapel of Khufukhaf I (top). On the west wall, north end, looking west, there is a large-scale figure of Khufukhaf I embraced by his wife Nefret-kau.

Tomb decoration began to expand again later in Khufu's reign, into the succeeding reigns of the Fourth Dynasty and beyond. Chapels bearing carved and painted scenes and inscriptions on interior walls of limestone were now added inside the core of the *mastaba* superstructure. One such tomb in the Eastern Cemetery, belonging to a priest of Khufu named Khufukhaf I, shows remarkably well-crafted, large-scale figures of the deceased and his wife Nefretkau in a variety of poses and costumes, as well as countless offerings, magically available for all eternity by virtue of being carved in stone. Size did not matter in terms of providing equipment for the afterlife: a model beer vessel, just a few centimeters in height, bore the same ritual potency as a carved or painted two-dimensional representation, or indeed an actual beer vessel interred in the tomb itself. Mortuary ceramics

abound in the Giza *mastabas*, and form a corpus that still awaits detailed study, not to mention comparison with ceramics from secular (that is, non-mortuary) contexts of the Old Kingdom. On the back of one of Khufukhaf's casing stones displaced from the east face of the *mastaba*, quarry marks seem to contain a date indicating Khufu's twenty-third regnal year.

The largest tomb in the Eastern Cemetery belonged to Ankhhaf, possibly a vizier under Khafre if not under Khufu himself. While fragments from Ankhhaf's destroyed chapel remain to be published, the tomb owner is justly famous for a striking bust found on a plinth in one of the exterior mud-brick chapel rooms east of the *mastaba*. That the bust lay on top of a heap of shattered ceramics indicates that it was the 'recipient' of offerings from the living. Carved in limestone with modeling added in plaster, the bust portrays the careworn expression of a burdened official, and departs radically from the more idealized sculpture that was the norm during the Old Kingdom.

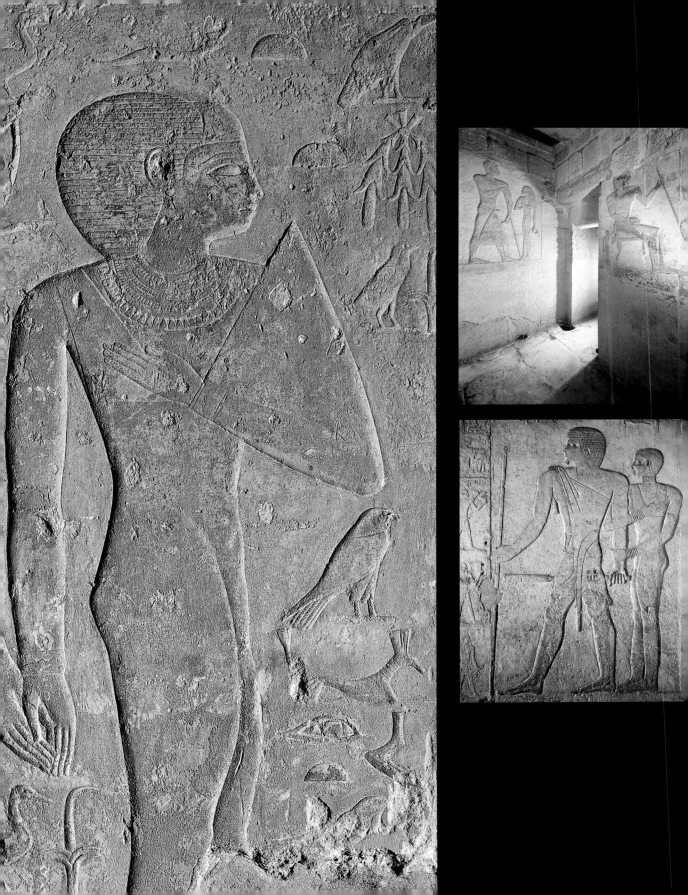

Meresankh

219 top
Engaged statues of Meresankh III
and her family on the north wall
of the main room of the rock-cut
mastaba of Queen Meresankh III,
looking northeast.

218-219
The north and east walls, looking
northeast, in the rock-cut mastaba
chapel of Queen Meresankh III: the
reliefs depict the daughter of Kawab
and Hetepheres II and royal wife of
Khafre. G 7530sub, main room.
Fourth Dynasty.

218 bottom
Reliefs with the figures of Hetepheres,
Meresankh III, and her son
Nebemakhet on the west wall of the
main room of the chapel of Queen
Meresankh III.

Engaged statues in scribal pose in the
main room of the rock-cut mastaba
chapel of Queen Meresankh III,
on the east and south walls,
looking southeast.

Along with increasingly elaborate chapels in the *mastaba* superstructures, a new type of burial place developed at Giza, most likely late in Khafre's reign: the rock-cut tomb. Carved out of the bedrock and lacking a superstructure, these tombs foreshadowed the type of burial place that was later to dominate Egyptian cemeteries through the Middle and New Kingdoms at sites such as Beni Hasan, Aswan, and Thebes. An unusual early example of a rock-cut tomb belongs to Queen Meresankh III, daughter of crown prince Kawab, the eldest son of Khufu, and wife of Khafre. Located in the Eastern Cemetery, Meresankh's decorated chapel rooms were actually hewn beneath a *mastaba* superstructure in a most unusual combination of the two tomb forms. Her decorated chambers contain some of the most vibrant wall paintings ever found at Giza, and expand the scene repertoire to include boating scenes, offering

bearers, scribes, craftsmen and agricultural production. The tomb even boasts a number of engaged statues of Meresankh and other family members and officials, set into niches in the chapel walls. Statues of the deceased, his or her family, and even of servants immortalized in the act of producing the staples of daily existence began to turn up in the serdabs, or statue chambers, in the mastaba superstructures. Hundreds of statues and statuettes from Giza, if not a few thousand, now in collections the world over, would form a veritable 'who's who' of the necropolis if they could be united, for the inscriptions carved on their bases and back pillars tell us their names and administrative titles. While it is probably impractical to bring them all together physically, the potential exists today for a 'virtual' gathering via digital images, databases and the Internet.

220-221
Scenes with offering-bearers, a scene of
fowling with a the clapnet, and
presentation of livestock from the east
wall of the main room of the rock-cut
mastaba chapel of Queen Meresankh III.

Rawer

The Fifth Dynasty at Giza saw the beginnings of the eventual breakdown of Khufu's ordered system of *mastaba* streets and avenues. Intrusive burials, additional shafts and new areas all added to the complexity of this urban city of the dead. Officials under Khafre had begun to exploit the quarry area west of the Sphinx, which became available for the construction of both *mastabas* and rock-cut tombs after the removal of all that stone to build the first two Giza pyramids. With additional chambers came an increased repertoire of wall scenes, and longer hieroglyphic texts. During the Fifth and Sixth Dynasties, we can read for the first time extensive narratives containing records of the exploits of the tomb owners, their biographies, interactions with the pharaoh, and even legal decrees concerning the means of providing for their mortuary cults.

In the Central Field, between the Sphinx and the second pyramid of Khafre, is a labyrinthine *mastaba* belonging to the vizier Rawer. Dating to the second half of the Fifth Dynasty, the tomb contained, in addition to columned porticoes borrowed stylistically, perhaps, from royal mortuary architecture, a unique account of an accident that took place in the reign of Neferirkare. The hieroglyphic inscription tells us that Rawer bumped up against the king's staff during a particular ceremony, and feared not just corporal, but divine punishment for disturbing the proceedings. The king, however, sided with Rawer, forgiving his indiscretion and avoiding an unpleasant incident. Rawer was so proud of this event that he had the account carved in a raised relief inscription in his tomb.

Other tombs in the Western Cemetery testify to the elegance of the polychromy that originally adorned the increasingly elaborate chapel areas. Processions of offering bearers, scenes of daily life, boating scenes, and a wide variety of produce from the tomb-owner's estate all appear over and over, but each time with subtle personal touches and unique features. The all-important 'false doors' set into the chapel's west wall (the west being traditionally the land of the setting sun, and hence of death and resurrection) now graced the elite burials at Giza, and reveal their own line of development. Some of the decorated chapels are still preserved at Giza, while others are housed in several Egyptian collections in European museums (Kaninisut in Vienna, Seshem-nefer III in Tübingen, Wehemka in Hildesheim).

222-223
This limestone raised-relief inscription from the tomb of Rawer, Central Field, details the 'accident' with the king and a staff during an important ceremony. Height 57 cm; width 1.25 m; thickness 25 cm. First half of the Fifth Dynasty. Now in the Egyptian Museum, Cairo.

224
General view looking north, showing the chapel of Nisut-nefer, mastaba G 4970. Early Fifth Dynasty.

225 top left
The ka-priest and scribe Tjenti presents accounts to the tomb owner on the west wall of the chapel of Nisut-nefer.

225 top right
On the east wall of the mastaba of Nisut-nefer, offering-bearers personify the estates that provide produce for the mortuary cult of the tomb owner.

225 bottom
A scene of ushering a young oryx before the tomb owner from the west wall of the chapel of Nisut-nefer.

Seshat–hetep

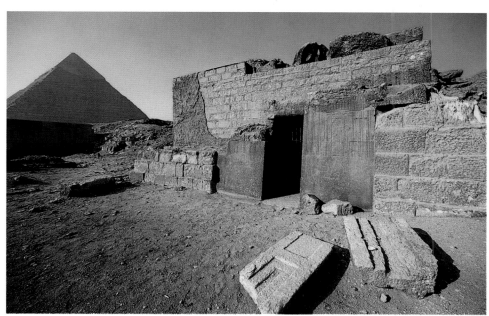

226-227
The tomb owner seated at a table of
offering loaves, on the northern entrance
to the chapel of Seshat-hetep, mastaba G
5150, looking north. End of the Fourth
Dynasty–early Fifth Dynasty.

227 top left
The entrance to the chapel of
Seshat-hetep, looking southwest.

227 bottom left
Detail of the 'palace façade' decoration
on the exterior of the mastaba of Seshat-
hetep, looking west.

227 right
General view inside the chapel of
Seshat-hetep, looking north.

Iasen

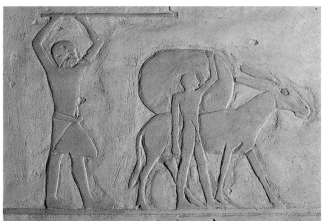

228-229
*Detail of relief with livestock from the
north wall, bottom register of the rock-
cut chapel of Iasen, mastaba G 2196.
Sixth Dynasty.*

228 bottom
*The tomb owner and his wife and son at
right, overseeing processions of livestock
and accounts on the east wall of the
rock-cut chapel of Iasen. The vertical
text reads: "Viewing the document of the
gifts brought from an invocation offering
(consisting of) bread, beer, and cakes
every day."*

229 bottom
*Relief detail from the rock-cut chapel of
Iasen showing a donkey driver. From the
north wall, middle register.*

230-231
*This relief from the south wall of the
rock-cut chapel of Iasen shows the tomb
owner seated on a high-backed chair
within a booth.*

231 bottom
*An engaged niche statue stands in
the west wall of the chapel (right)
of Iasen's mastaba.*

Iymery

232 top
A banquet scene from chamber 2, south wall, middle section of the chapel of Iymery, G 6020. Fifth Dynasty, reign of Niuserre.

232-233 top
A scene depicting jousting in the papyrus marshes from the north wall of chamber 2, eastern section of the chapel of Iymery.

232-233 bottom
This calving scene is conserved in chamber 2, south wall, eastern section of the chapel of Iymery.

233 top
General view of the vaulted chamber 2 of the chapel of Iymery.

One complex of *mastabas*, located at the northwest corner of the Great Pyramid, belonged to a family of chief architects in the Fifth and Sixth Dynasties. Senedjemib Inti inscribed letters of praise from his sovereign, King Isesi (also called Djedkare), on the façade of his tomb, while his son, Senedjemib Mehi, wrote that he completed the construction of his father's *mastaba*, "which I made for him in one year and three months, while he was in the embalming place in his mansion which is in (the necropolis of) the pyramid 'Isesi is perfect.'" This is one of very few Egyptian references to the amount of time needed for a particular construction project. A Sixth Dynasty-related burial, belonging to a man named Ptahshepses Impi, produced seemingly countless miniature copper vessels, placed in a box on top of the tomb-owner's cedar coffin. Broad collars and other items of jewelry accompanied the burial, testifying to the prosperity of the Senedjemib family.

The legal aspects of tomb building and the care of the mortuary cult, sometimes for generations after the tomb-owner's death, were major contributing factors to the longevity of a necropolis. A number of tombs at Giza bear inscriptions designating individuals for mortuary service and exempting them from various taxes or forced labor. One Penmeru, an 'overseer of *ka*-priests, royal acquaintance, and priest of Menkaure,' carved a decree on the wall of his small Western Cemetery tomb chapel, stating: ". . . as for my brother of my funerary estate, Neferhotep, and those born to him by either father (or) mother, they are the *ka*-priests of (my) funerary estate for the invocation offering in (my) tomb . . . which is in the cemetery of Akhet-Khufu . . . I have not empowered any persons to have authority over it . . . ." Another small tomb, sandwiched during the Sixth Dynasty in between the major *mastabas* of the near Western Cemetery, contained a small niche belonging to

Redines, who took pains to assure his peers that "Never did I do anything evil against people . . . I have constructed this (tomb) of mine by means of my own resources. It is the god who will judge (my) case along with him who does anything against it."

As the Sixth Dynasty progressed, Giza cemeteries were overrun by intrusive tombs and burial shafts choking the streets and avenues between the major *mastabas* of the Fourth and Fifth Dynasties. Khufu would probably not have recognized the site, for the ordered layout of his Eastern and Western Cemeteries became overpopulated with many hundreds of additional burials. Rock-cut tombs lined the edge of the plateau at the Eastern Cemetery, forming a complex warren of interlocking subterranean chambers that still await final analysis and publication. Tombs filled the rest of the quarry area between the Sphinx and the pyramid of Khafre, and even a smaller quarry east of Menkaure's pyramid had by this time already received its share of rock-cut tombs. A second style of representing the human figure, including wide eyes, pinched torsos, and minimal musculature separated many Sixth Dynasty monuments from those of the earlier Old Kingdom, as evidenced by the Sixth Dynasty tombs of Qar and Idu in the Eastern Cemetery, or the uniquely painted burial chamber of Kayemankh in the Western Cemetery. The royal necropolis had moved on to other sites, such as Saqqara, after the close of the Fourth Dynasty, but high officials, many of them employed by the mortuary cults of the Fourth Dynasty pharaohs Khufu, Khafre, or Menkaure, or desiring to join their ancestors in family tomb complexes, continued to be buried at Giza. One of Qar's titles was 'Overseer of the Pyramid Towns of Khufu and Menkaure.' Although little survives of his superstructure, his numerous rock-cut chambers were enhanced by a number of engaged statues.

234 top
Detail of two processions of men towing the funerary boat containing Qar's sarcophagus toward his tomb; in court C, north wall, lower half of the subterranean chapel of Qar, G 7101. Sixth Dynasty, reign of Pepy I or later.

234 center
Sunk relief depicting the seated figure of Qar. From his subterranean chapel, room D, west wall, with entrance to room E, looking southwest.

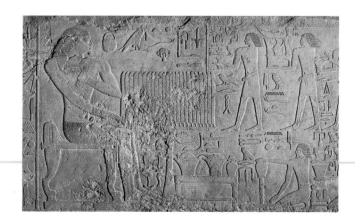

Idu

236
Engaged statue positioned in the east wall of the subterranean chapel of Idu, looking southeast. Idu, a royal scribe, was probably the father or the son of Qar. Sixth Dynasty, reign of Pepy I or later.

237 top
The subterranean chapel of Idu looking south.

237 bottom left
Raised relief depicting Idu seated at a table of tall, stylized offering loaves, with his wife Meretites kneeling beside him, from the west wall of his subterranean chapel.

237 bottom right
This partial statue of Idu emerging from the netherworld to receive offerings is located in the false-door niche on the west wall of his subterranean chapel.

Kai

238-239
General view of the chapel of Kapunisut Kai, recently discovered by Zahi Hawass in the Western Cemetery. Mid-Fifth Dynasty.

239 top
The northern false door on the west wall of the chapel of Kapunisut Kai is richly decorated with polychrome bas-reliefs.

239 bottom left
On the north wall, bottom register of the chapel of Kapunisut Kai, the tomb owner stands in the center of his hedgehog-prowed henet-boat.

239 bottom right
This seated statue of Kapunisut Kai and his family, was recently discovered by Zahi Hawass in Kai's tomb. Now in the Egyptian Museum Cairo.

Although much of the Giza plateau has been excavated over the past century, new discoveries continue to surprise us. Additional *mastabas* have been unearthed in recent years, a 'new' workmen's cemetery and a possible palace (or at least state building complexes) south of the site are under investigation, and even the ruins of one more pyramid were unearthed to the southeast of Khufu's monument in the 1990s. Additional statuary has accompanied many of these new finds. New excavations by Zahi Hawass, Mark Lehner, and others are helping us understand the construction and management process behind all the Giza edifices, and new technologies are allowing for more efficient methods of documentation and ever-greater access to

them, primarily over the Internet. Due to its archaeological history, the Giza legacy today is shared by many museums and institutions around the world, as well as the Egyptian Museum in Cairo and, of course, the site itself. The potential now exists to unite these disparate objects along with their archaeological documentation into vast, integrated digital archives on the Internet that will 'reconstruct' the site and its history in ways unimaginable to the original excavators from the early twentieth century. In future years, we can expect to solve many of Giza's remaining puzzles, and make the site ever more accessible to new generations of researchers curious about this great testament to the first of Egypt's many golden ages.

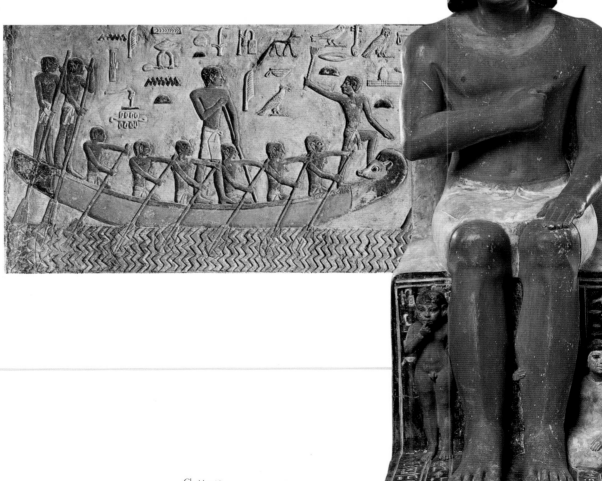

Chapter 19

The 'Unfinished' Pyramids of the Fourth Dynasty

by Michel Valloggia

Witnesses to centuries past, archeological remains invariably preserve imprints of the historical events that shaped their present aspect. Consequently, certain sites reveal the existence of projects begun and then abandoned. There are many possible reasons for such abandonment. It could have resulted from the early disappearance of the project's initiator, as well as from natural events such as hydrological or geological phenomena. It is not unusual for the present appearance of a site to be the result of demolition in later times. The disappearance of ancient monuments can sometimes be explained by a desire to reuse the construction stone for new buildings, or by either positive or negative attitudes toward the memory of a predecessor. It may be remembered that Amenemhet I of the Twelfth Dynasty, anxious for official recognition, inserted into his pyramid at Lisht inscribed blocks bearing the names of his remote predecessors Khufu, Khafre, Unas, and Pepy II from the Fourth to the Sixth dynasties. Later, at the end of the Amarna period, adherents of the orthodox cult of Amun worked unceasingly to destroy all traces of the city that Akhenaten (Amenhotep IV of the Eighteenth Dynasty) had built at what is now Tell-el-Amarna. Mention must also be made of the lime burners and quarrymen, who from Roman times up to the nineteenth century intensively exploited all the archeological sites of Egypt. The huge Memphite necropolis was not spared: for over a thousand years it supplied the large medieval and modern building sites of the Cairo metropolis. While working on the pyramid of Abu Rawash in 1882, W.M.F. Petrie complained in his journal about the progressive disappearance of the monument: the stones were being taken away at the rate of three hundred camel-loads a day.

Fortunately, the situation has improved. Nowadays it is up to the archeologists who explore the sites to protect and restore this universal heritage, which must be transmitted to future generations. Within this context, it falls to the specialists to visualize the state of a structure at the time of its completion and determine its original condition prior to the injuries wrought by time and human depredations. Once this is accomplished, the present state of the project—whether incomplete, or demolished in ancient times—offers excellent opportunities for analysis. In either case, an abandoned or destroyed project bears an uncanny resemblance to a building site; this makes it very easy to study the procedures used to build these structures.

Studied in this way, the numerous 'unfinished' pyramids of the Memphite Cemetery shed new light on our knowledge of the Fourth Dynasty. It is a great paradox that this "Age of Builders", dazzling in its command of the arts and in the virtuosity of its techniques, was so parsimonious in its use of writing to record the originality of its message. The historian, anxious to understand the remote past, must therefore meticulously examine what remains in the archeological record. Thus the "unfinished" monuments of Abu Rawash, Zawiyet-el-Aryan, Giza, and Saqqara South have sometimes been the subject of over-interpretation, despite the lack of information about them.

240-241
The Central Field of Giza Cemetery and the superstructure of the tomb of Queen Khentkaus I.

The Pyramid of Djedefre at Abu Rawash

The mortuary complex of Djedefre, third ruler of the Fourth Dynasty, is located atop an escarpment that overlooks the archeological area of Abu Rawash at the northern end of the Memphis necropolis, eight kilometers north of the pyramids of Giza and fifteen kilometers west of Cairo. The French Institute of Oriental Archeology conducted excavations on this site, and the pyramid there, from 1900 to 1902. Emile Chassinat discovered the remains of a worship settlement, a boat pit, and a great number of statuary fragments that bore the name of the king and thus allowed the monument's owner to be identified. This funerary complex had been mishandled since the Roman period, actually having been used as a quarry up to modern times. The resulting lack of information explains why attempts at reconstruction of the Fourth Dynasty's history have deliberately ignored the site of Abu Rawash and its owner. The discovery of royal statuary broken into small fragments led Chassinat to suspect a *damnatio memoriae* connected with the presumed illegitimacy of Djedefre's power. From this point of view, the transfer of the royal pyramid site from Giza to Abu Rawash could in some way have been the expression of a usurping pharaoh's desire for a break with the past. Djedefre, who mother was Libyan, is even supposed to have killed his eldest brother in order to accede to the throne. This pyramid has raised numerous questions. The fact that it has been preserved only to a height of ten to twelve meters has been attributed to the short duration of Djedefre's reign, which lasted only eight years according to the Turin Papyrus. It was always thought that this pyramid remained unfinished, like the entire mortuary complex, whose chapel would have been quickly built of mud brick.

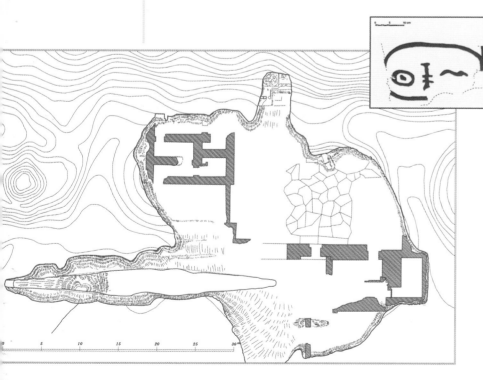

ARCHITECTURAL RECONSTRUCTION OF THE ROYAL CHAMBER OF DJEDEFRE AND HIS COFFIN

A   BURIAL CHAMBER IN PINK GRANITE

B   NATURAL ROCK

C   LIMESTONE FILLING

D   GRANITE COFFIN

244-245
The recently-discovered satellite pyramid of Abu Rawash is situated in front of the southeast corner of what remains of the royal pyramid of Djedefre.

244 bottom right
The cross section of the royal and the satellite pyramids of Abu Rawash.

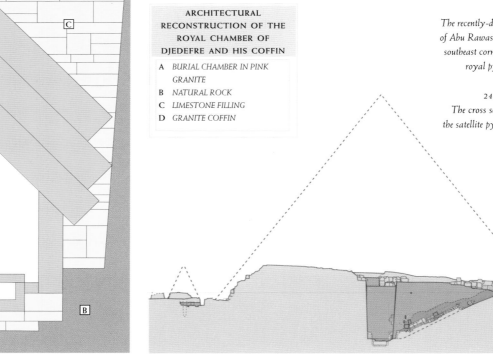

Since 1995 a joint mission of the University of Geneva and the French Institute, with the cooperation of the Supreme Council of Antiquities, has undertaken new investigations on the site with the objective of reevaluating Djedefre's reign. Stratigraphic study of trenches cut during the first season proved that the destruction of the statues occurred while the site was occupied during the Roman period, in the second century. Remains found on the eastern portion of the site attest to a long Roman occupation, explained by the site's strategic position overlooking a crossroads and its convenience as a source of construction material. As for the historical aspect, it can now be established that assumptions about Djedefre's usurpation of royal power and of a posthumous revenge must be discounted.

Examination of the pyramid itself shows that its dimensions were close to those of Menkaure's: 106.20 meters square, with a height of 66.0 meters at a slope of 51 degrees, 57 minutes. The base of Djedefre's pyramid revealed a foundation bed with a slope of 12 degrees, becoming gradually more horizontal toward the corners of the tetrahedron. This arrangement, running around the entire pyramid, prevented it from sliding toward the outermost of the backing stones and off the surface of the rocky pinnacle, or *inselberg*, which forms the nucleus of the tetrahedron and occupies 44 percent of its total volume.

The interior of this "open pyramid" revealed a T-shaped plan, consisting of a north-south sloped passage and a large pit identified as the royal tomb. The destruction of the pyramid's superstructure caused huge monoliths to fall, making it impossible for the excavators at the beginning of the twentieth century to clear the underlying material and reach the burial chamber. In order to remove these huge blocks, the recent excavators found it necessary to build a causeway to provide access, and allow room for a mobile crane to operate from the top of the funerary pit. Graffiti painted in hematite by the quarrymen were found *in situ* in the descending corridor, mentioning the king's name and the first year of his reign and thus offering evidence that work on a new pharaoh's royal pyramid began immediately after his accession to the throne. In the central pit, only the solid platform of the foundation escaped the stone-hewers of later ages. Nevertheless, the discovery of numerous architectonic fragments inscribed *wabet*—"tomb"—allowed the mortuary tomb to be located and theoretically reconstructed.

245 bottom
General map of the archaeological area of the funerary complex of Djedefre in Abu Rawash, completed in summer 2002.

245 top
The northeast corner of the royal pyramid of Djedefre.

245 center, top
This entrance leads to the descending corridor of the pyramid of Djedefre in Abu Rawash.

245 center, bottom
The enclosures of the royal pyramid with the satellite pyramid; in the background are the Pyramids of Giza.

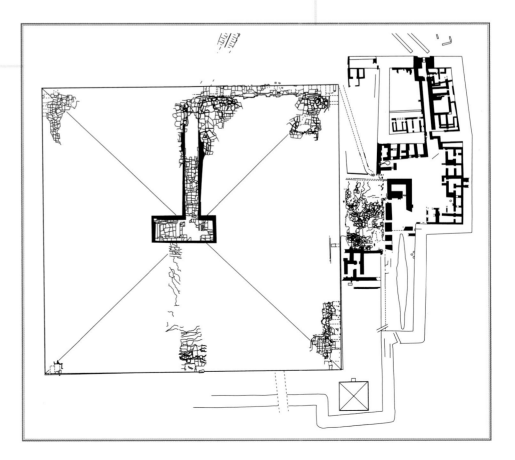

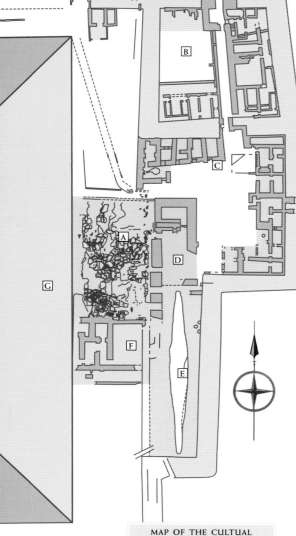

**MAP OF THE CULTUAL
INSTALLATIONS ON THE EAST
SIDE OF THE PYRAMID**

A *COURTYARD OF THE HIGH
  TEMPLE*
B *SERVICE AREAS (BAKERY
  AND BREWERY)*
C *AREAS FOR THE PRIESTS
  DEDICATED TO THE
  FUNERARY CULT*
D *EAST CHAPEL OF THE
  TEMPLE*
E *BOAT–SHAPED PIT*
F *MAIN CHAPEL OF THE HIGH
  TEMPLE*
G *MAIN PYRAMID*

Clearing operations have been undertaken on the east and south sides of the tetrahedron with a view to completing the information gained from the exploration of the pyramid's surroundings. These investigations have revealed that five independent structures can be associated with the mortuary temple. On the northeast corner, a passageway opened onto an inner enclosure of dry stone assigned to workshops and dwellings; the stored materials and places for light shelters here suggest bakery and brewery fittings. To the south, there was an esplanade surrounded by buildings on each of its three sides whose function has not yet been defined. On the west side of this courtyard there was a chapel intended for the near relations of the king; this building was next to another structure that contained a boat-pit in its basement. This boat has been observed to be quite similar to that of Khufu, which was discovered in 1954 and is now on exhibit in Giza. At Abu Rawash the cutting of the rock shows that the boat had its prow to the south in accordance with the ancient traditions of the Egyptians, who oriented themselves to the source of the Nile. Close by to the west was the mortuary chapel of the king, where a clay seal impression was found. This seal, which belonged to an official attached to the royal cult, mentions the name of the pyramid in the phrase "The Director of the Firmament of Djedefre". Finally the interior court of the upper temple, built right next to the east side of the pyramid, was closely connected with each of these other structures.

Continuing excavations to the south of the royal pyramid in 2002 led to the uncovering of a small, square satellite pyramid measuring 10.5 meters on each side. Beneath this newly discovered tetrahedron, which was aligned with the cardinal points and with the axis of the mortuary temple, was a tomb in the hypogeum style. Its shaft contained a broken sarcophagus, in front of which was a niche apparently meant to hold canopic vessels. Although this tomb had been plundered in antiquity, it still yielded a large, deep alabaster bowl bearing the name of *Horus Medjedu* ("the good shooter")—*King Khufu* (Khufu), as well as a canopic vessel with its seal, and a quantity of ceramics. All of this material is typologically close to the furniture discovered earlier at Giza in the tomb of Queen Hetepheres I, the mother of Khufu.

It appears that this new satellite structure could have at first been a cult pyramid, but its subterranean arrangement argues more strongly for a queen's pyramid. Not least importantly, the name of Khufu on an alabaster vessel suggests a direct relationship with the monument's owner, namely one of the daughters of the builders of the Great Pyramid: Hetepheres II or Khetetenkai. In final analysis, this monument seems to represent a project that was originally planned as a cult pyramid and then evolved into a queenly burial place.

With regard to the mortuary complex as a whole, the clearing of the inner enclosures surrounding both pyramids and the presence of this satellite building clearly prove that the king's pyramid had been completed *prior* to the construction of these adventitious elements. Consequently, this new inquiry on the site leads to the conclusion that the pyramid of Djedefre at Abu Rawash should no longer be considered an unfinished monument that was abandoned in the course of its construction.

THE PYRAMID OF BAKA AT ZAWIYET AL-ARYAN

The unfinished pyramid of Zawiyet al-Aryan, known as the 'Great Pit,' belonging to the successor of Djedefre, King Baka, is located six kilometers south of Giza. The site was excavated by A. Barsanti between 1905 and 1912, but the First World War and the death of the excavator put an untimely end to this exploration. Subsequently, sand re-covered these remains until they were uncovered for the last time in 1954 for the occasion of a full-length film by Howard Hawks, 'Land of the Pharaohs.'

On the surface, Barsanti found the remains of a huge rectangular enclosure measuring 465 x 420 m. In the middle of it, there was probably a pyramid 210 m square. However, only a few foundation blocks, dug out of the substructure, seem to have been laid against the nucleus of the pyramid. Inside the pyramid, from the center of the north side, a long sloping passage of 106 x 6 m leads down into the rock with two slopes separated by a horizontal landing, down to 24.5 m. As in the substructure of Abu Rawash, this descending passage leads to a deep pit (27.0 x 11.7 m). In the west part of its approximately 4.5 m thick foundation, which is paved with granite and limestone blocks, an oval sarcophagus with its cover in red granite was found. This tub, hidden in antiquity by a thick clay layer, was entirely covered by a limestone pavement. The sarcophagus was empty and it obviously never held the intended owner.

This funerary complex is lacking in documentation and therefore remains enigmatic, as much as for the historian as for the archaeologist. The traces of painted inscriptions on the blocks show the mark of a royal cartouche variously assigned to several kings of the Third Dynasty. However, a few archaeological clues speak in favor of a Fourth Dynasty construction: the size of the blocks used, unknown previous to Khufu; the embedding of the sarcophagus within the pavement, which reminds one of the pyramid of Khafre; and, finally, the similarity of the plan with the substructure of Abu Rawash, appear in conjunction with the habit of inscribing the royal names within a cartouche from the Fourth Dynasty onwards. Furthermore, the discovery by Barsanti of a schist tablet with the name of King Djedefre in a workers' settlement of the 'Great Pit' establishes a likely historical link. In these conditions, the discovery of the name of Baka, eldest son of Djedefre, seems to provide a possible identification for the owner of the pyramid of Zawiyet al-Aryan. The incomplete state of the superstructure work is confirmed by the clay protection and the pavement laid on top of the sarcophagus in the substructure. This could well indicate either the completion of a stage in the work or the renunciation of the final project.

Be that as it may, new investigations in the field are absolutely necessary, especially as this archaeological area is now threatened by the extension of the southwest Ring Road of Cairo and the unavoidable urbanization which will follow in this region.

247 top
This archival photograph focuses on the Great Pit of the pyramid of Baka, at Zawiyet al-Aryan.

247 center
General plan of the infrastructures of the pyramid of Baka, in Zawiyet al-Aryan: in particular notice the descending ramp and the funerary pits. (Drawing by V. Maragioglio and C. Rinaldi.)

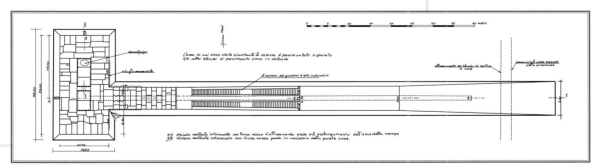

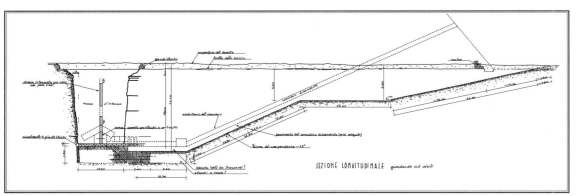

247 bottom
General section of the infrastructures of the pyramid of Baka, in Zawiyet al-Aryan; the descending ramp and the funerary pits are shown clearly. (Drawing by V. Maragioglio and C. Rinaldi.)

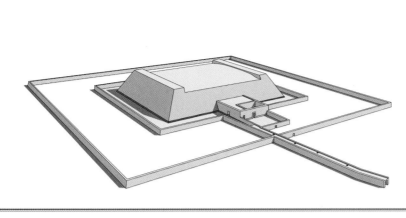

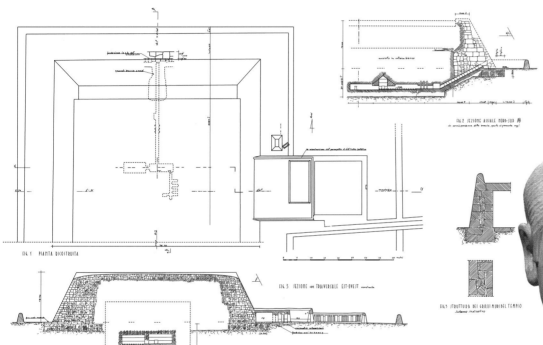

FIG. 1 PIANTA RICOSTRUITA

FIG. 2 SEZIONE ASSIALE NORD-SUD AB

FIG. 3 SEZIONE TRASVERSALE EST-OVEST

FIG. 4 STRUTTURA DEI GROSSI MURI DEL TEMPIO

248 top
Reconstruction of the funerary complex of Shepseskaf (Mastabat Faraun) in South Saqqara by H. Ricke.

248 center left
Plan and section of the funerary complex of Shepseskaf (Mastabat Faraun) by V. Maragioglio and C. Rinaldi.

248 center right
Calcite head of king Shepseskaf, 28.5 cm high, now in the Museum of Fine Arts of Boston.

248 bottom
Plan and sections of the infrastructures of Mastabat Faraun by G. Jéquier, after the work of J.-Ph. Lauer.

248-249
This aerial view of Mastabat Faraun shows the rounded shape of the structure. The same shape is typical of coffin covers.

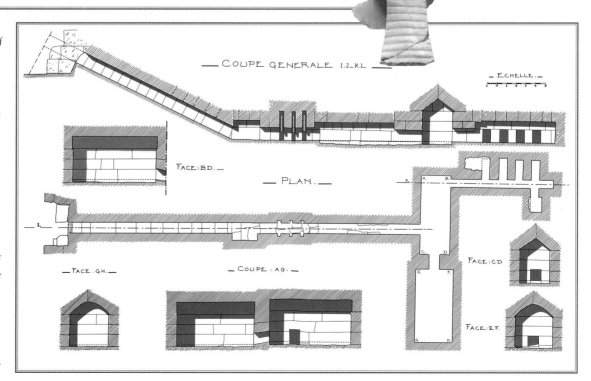

COUPE GENERALE I.J.K.L.

ECHELLE.

FACE.BD.

PLAN.

FACE.GH.

COUPE:AG.

FACE:CD

FACE:EF.

THE GIANT *MASTABA*
OF SHEPSESKAF
(MASTABAT FARAUN)

The funerary complex of Shepseskaf, penultimate
king of the Fourth Dynasty, stands in the southern
part of Saqqara, halfway between the Step Pyramid
of Djoser and the site of Dahshur, and is known by
the name of Mastabat Faraun ('bench of the
pharaoh') due to its present form. The monument
was partly explored by A. Mariette in 1858, and
investigations were left unpublished until the work
of G. Jéquier in 1924–25. Previously, J. Perring had
noticed the huge dimensions, 95.0 m long by 67.0
m broad, with a height of 18.0 m. The peculiar
shape of its superstructure has been identified by
R. Lepsius: he thought of a huge sarcophagus with
a vaulted top between vertical ends. The clearing
undertaken by Jéquier confirmed this identification
and revealed the presence of a huge foundation
platform on which this edifice is built. At the
beginning, its shape was that of sloped faces
encased with fine limestone and granite for a
bottom course.

The plan of the subterranean burial chamber is
in the form of a T, as at the pyramid of Abu Rawash.
After the descending corridor there is a horizontal
corridor, followed by three portcullis slots and a
passage to an antechamber opening west on the
burial chamber. However, the architect added a
series of five small rooms opening onto the
antechamber in a southeasterly direction. They
were obviously magazines for the royal mortuary
furniture.

The general organization of this plan shows an
important innovation in the general concept of the
plan of the burial chamber of the pyramids, which
was systematically taken over and applied to the
pyramids of the Fifth and Sixth Dynasties, from the
time of Djedkare Isesi.

In the construction of the substructure, Jéquier
observed that the burial chamber, which is entirely
built of granite, had been built in the open air. At
the end of his work, the architect covered the whole
underground building with a first limestone masonry
envelope. The final shape in form of a huge
sarcophagus, was created in a second phase covering
the first one. This original style of construction,
clearly shows that this project differed entirely from
the traditional system of pyramid building.

The incompleteness of the rough-cast and
buffing work in the burial chamber, in association
with the total lack of furniture pieces, led Jéquier
to state that Shepseskaf had never been buried in
the tomb he had ordered for himself.

One of the major problems that remains
unexplained is the shape of this amazing
superstructure in form of a sarcophagus. For
what reasons was the choice of a pyramid
abandoned here? According to Jéquier, this new
architectural choice proceeded from opposition
to the Heliopolitan dogma. The adoption of a
tetrahedron, as well as the insertion of the name
of Re within the royal cartouches of this dynasty,
actually emphasized the great influence of the
solar cult on the royalty. The new shape of this
superstructure expressed the reservations that the
king may have held against the Heliopolitan
priesthood. However, it could also have shown
some ties to Lower Egypt and to the archaic
sanctuaries of Buto, the hieroglyphic writing of
which retains the symbolic form visible on the
royal sarcophagi of the Middle Kingdom. Finally,
let us stress the fact that the incompleteness of the
archaeological excavation, namely that of the valley
temple and of the causeway, does not allow a
complete assessment of this mortuary complex
at this time.

THE TOMB OF KHENTKAUS AT GIZA

Queen Mother Khentkaus, a relative of Khufu through her father, Prince Hordjedef, is an enigmatic character from the end of the Fourth Dynasty. Based on the Westcar papyrus, she is considered to be the mother of the first rulers of the Fifth Dynasty; however, up to now, the name of her royal husband is unknown. Furthermore, contrary to the customs of this ancient period, the location of Khentkaus's tomb, within the central field of Giza, is not associated with any royal pyramid.

This monument, in the past considered by R. Vyse and J. Perring to be an unfinished pyramid, was nevertheless also called 'the fourth pyramid of Giza.' Selim Hassan, the excavator of the site, proved that this atypical building did not show a pyramidal shape. More recently, V. Maragioglio and C. Rinaldi, in their architectural study of the Memphite pyramids, came to the conclusion that the superstructure of this tomb had been executed in two distinct stages. In the first phase, there was work on the limestone core resembling a *mastaba* (43.7 x 45.8 m), which was cleared and its south side ornamented by a niched decoration. Around this core, the quarrymen had lowered the soil level by about 10 meters. Later on, a constructed volume about eight meters high may have been added onto the first structure. This new shape built on the aforesaid plateau looked like a huge sarcophagus, like Mastabat Faraun. It is precisely because of the similarity of these superstructures that a great number of historians have suggested that Khentkaus could well have been Shepseskaf's wife.

During the second phase of construction the whole volume was encased in limestone. A chapel was constructed to the east and was found to be cut within the rock above the burial itself. There are three chambers which were decorated in the past, based on the evidence of wall fragments discovered by the excavator. A short sloping passage leads down from the offering room to the burial chamber constructed of granite.

On the outside, an enclosure surrounded the funerary complex; in its southwest corner was a boat pit and on the opposite side was a rectangular basin with a flight of steps.

In this monument, the causeway with its exceptional right angle does not seem to have been associated with a valley temple, as is the case with the royal complexes of that period. On the other hand, a series of houses, arranged in a linear settlement and meant for the funerary priests of Khentkaus were built quite early on, in accordance with an extremely precise town-planning scheme.

This monument, in its conception and most original setting, seems to illustrate the final stage of development of the Fourth Dynasty cemetery at Giza. The funerary complexes of the following dynasty, including in their layout a solar temple, were actually located to the south, in the Abusir necropolis.

Having reached the end of this short presentation of the 'unfinished' pyramids of the Fourth Dynasty, we can see that despite the huge amount of archaeological work already accomplished, our present knowledge of the royal monuments of that time is limited. If ups and downs have shaped the picture of buildings abandoned in the course of their construction or partly demolished over time, it is now up to the archaeologists to re-examine their earlier assumptions in the light of actual progress. The development of the methods of investigation in the field, comparison with preserved monuments, and, last but not least, analysis of new historical data allow unquestionable progress as shown by the recent excavations on the funerary complex of King Djedefre at Abu Rawash. In the future, new surveys of the sites of Zawiyet al-Aryan, of Mastabat Faraun, and of Giza should open the way to innovative interpretations, thus allowing the historical re-evaluation of a period that aroused the admiration of the ancient Egyptians, and by its perfection, still fascinates the specialists as much as the modern visitors to the Nile Valley.

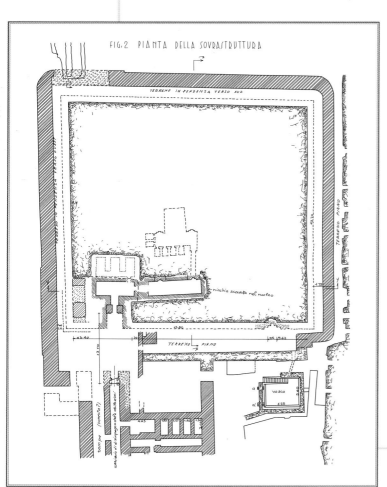

FIG. 2 PIANTA DELLA SOVRASTRUTTURA

250 top
Detail of a granite pillar at the entrance to the chapel of the superstructure of the tomb, in the central cemetery at Giza, showing the inscription of the name of Queen Khentkaus I.

250 bottom
Plan of the superstructures of the tomb of Queen Khentkaus with a cross section of the buildings used by the funerary priests as a house, and the sacred lake, by V. Maragioglio and C. Rinaldi.

Unfinished Pyramids

250-251
This aerial view clearly shows the superstructure of the tomb of Queen Khentkaus, with its two levels.

251 bottom
This section of the superstructure shows the inferior level dug into the local limestone, while the upper level has been built. The drawing also shows the room of the chapel for the offerings and the entrance.

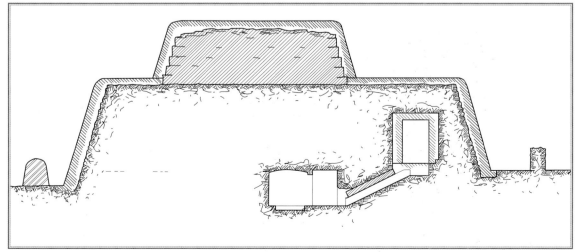

The Pyramids of the Fifth Dynasty

by Miroslav Verner

Dismissing the fairy tale of the Westcar papyrus regarding the divine birth of the first kings of the Fifth Dynasty, the ascension of Userkaf to the throne and the foundation of the dynasty largely remains shrouded in mystery. Despite this mystery about the origins of Userkaf, we *do* know that two of the king's earliest decisions were to profoundly influence the rule of the entire newly-founded dynasty. He ordered the building of a sun temple in the Memphite necropolis and, moreover, for the construction of this monument he chose Abusir, a place between Giza and Saqqara—an area thus far neglected by his predecessors. Five of his successors—Sahure, Neferirkare Kakai, Neferefre, Niuserre, and Menkauhor—followed him and built their sun temples somewhere in this same region. At the same time, all of them except for Menkauhor decided to be buried at Abusir. Though the size of their pyramids cannot match those of their predecessors in Giza, more attention was paid in the former to the mortuary temples –especially in the volume and quality of the relief decoration.

Interestingly, Userkaf himself built his pyramid complex—named 'Pure are the (Cult) Places of Userkaf'—in Saqqara, in immediate proximity to the Step Pyramid. Behind this wish of his to be buried in the shadow of Djoser's pyramid may have been hidden efforts to enhance the legitimacy of his claim of the throne.

252
This head of Userkaf, the first pharaoh of the Heliopolitan Fifth Dynasty in Abusir, is in red granite and belonged to colossal statue of the pharaoh. Now it is conserved in the Egyptian Museum, Cairo.

253
This limestone relief with birds and papyrus plants was found in Userkaf's mortuary temple by the expedition of C. M. Firth (1928–29). Now in the Egyptian Museum, Cairo.

254-255 and 255 bottom
Userkaf's pyramid complex seen from above.

255 top
In the foreground, Userkaf's mortuary temple with the royal pyramid in the background.

255 bottom left
Reconstruction of Userkaf's pyramid complex without the causeway or valley temple by H. Ricke.

USERKAF´S PYRAMID COMPLEX
WITHOUT CAUSEWAY
OR VALLEY TEMPLE
(AFTER V. MARAGIOGLIO
AND C. RINALDI)

A	ENTRANCE HALL
B	STORAGE ROOMS
C	FIVE-NICHED CHAPEL
D	PILLARED COURT
E	CULT PYRAMID
F	OFFERING HALL
G	MAIN PYRAMID

Userkaf

The ground plan of Userkaf's pyramid was designed in such a way that if divided axially, its plan would consist of two right triangles whose sides were in a ratio of 3:4:5. In contrast to the pyramids of his Fourth Dynasty predecessors, the entrance to Userkaf's pyramid was not located in the north wall, but was hidden in the pavement of the courtyard. About 10 meters under the pyramid's base, the descending corridor opened out into the antichambre lying directly on the pyramid's vertical axis. The burial chamber lay to the west of the antichambre. Both chambers, already plundered by robbers in antiquity, are cased in fine white limestone. Their gabled ceilings are made of enormous blocks of the same material.

The mortuary temple was located neither on the east side (as was common in the Fourth Dynasty), nor on the north side (as usual in the Third Dynasty), but on the south side of the pyramid. Its unusual position was probably influenced on the one hand by Userkaf's obvious wish to be buried near the Step Pyramid and, on the other hand, by the restricted area of the solid ground between the northeast corner of Djoser's pyramid enclosure and the so-called 'Great Trench' surrounding the latter.

Though the scanty remains which survived from the temple do not allow us to reconstruct its original plan in all details, it is obvious that its central part was formed by an open pillared courtyard. The black color of the basalt pavement of the courtyard must have once perfectly harmonized with the pink granite pillars and, behind them, the white limestone walls decorated with fine polychrome reliefs. On the south side of the courtyard stood a pink granite statue of Userkaf. It was about five meters high and is the oldest known colossal statue—besides the Great Sphinx—of an Egyptian king (its head is now in the Egyptian Museum, Cairo). In the southern part of the temple there also lay a chapel with five niches for other statues of the king. West of the mortuary temple, in front of the southeast corner of the pyramid, stood a small cult pyramid.

The offering hall, the most important cult place in the whole pyramid complex, was in a little temple built on the eastern side of the pyramid, at the very edge of the Great Trench. The false door was embedded in the western wall of the hall, i.e. directly adjacent to the pyramid.

The causeway opening in the southeast corner of the mortuary temple, and the valley temple on the other side of the causeway, remain unexcavated so far.

South of the mortuary temple stood a small pyramid complex of Queen Neferhetepes, Userkaf's consort. Both the pyramid and the mortuary temple were so severely damaged by stone robbers that the exact reconstruction of the original plan of this complex is impossible.

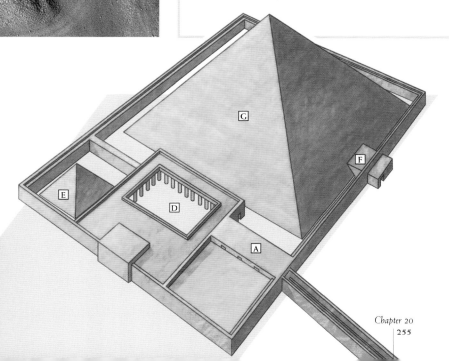

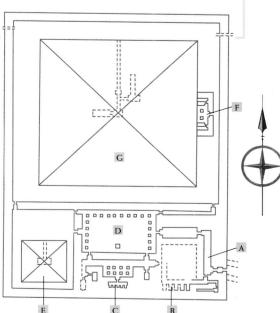

Also largely devastated by stone robbers was Userkaf's sun temple complex in Abusir, previously mentioned above. The complex, named 'Re's Nekhen' ('Re's fortress,' or 'storeroom'), consisted of a valley temple linked by means of a causeway to a temple built on a hillock above the Nile Valley. The dominant feature of the latter temple was the large obelisk of limestone and red granite. On an altar at the obelisk's foot, offerings were presented daily to the sun god. From here, the offerings were transported to Userkaf's mortuary temple. The sun temple thus made an important contribution to the king's mortuary cult. One of the unique finds made by the Swiss-German archaeological team in the valley temple is the head of Userkaf's black schist statue wearing the Lower Egyptian crown (now in the Egyptian Museum, Cairo).

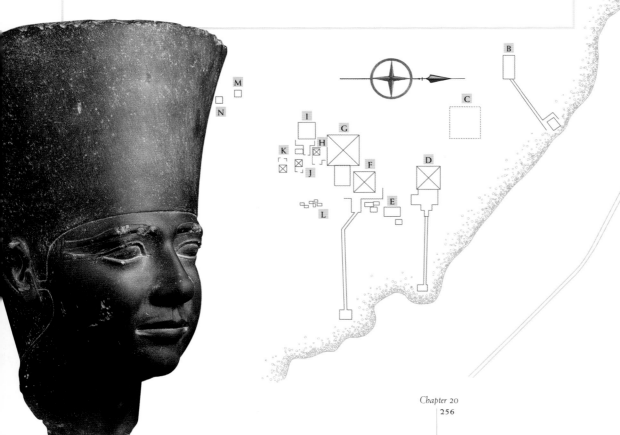

256 top
Aerial view of the sun temple of Userkaf from the northwest with the pyramids of Abusir in the distance.

256 bottom left
Head of Userkaf's schist statue, wearing the Lower Egyptian crown. The statue was found in the solar temple of Abusir and is now in the Egyptian Museum in Cairo.

256-257
Aerial view of the pyramid field at Abusir from southeast.

PLAN OF THE PYRAMID NECROPOLIS NEAR ABUSIR (BY J. MALÁTKOVÁ) AND RECONSTRUCTION (BY J. KREJČÍ)

A   *NIUSERRE'S SUN TEMPLE*
B   *USERKAF'S SUN TEMPLE*
C   *SHEPSESKAF'S (?) UNFINISHED PYRAMID*
D   *SAHURE'S PYRAMID*
E   *PTAHSHEPSES'S MASTABA*
F   *NIUSERRE'S PYRAMID*
G   *NEFERIRKARE'S PYRAMID*
H   *KHENTKAUS II'S PYRAMID*
I   *NEFEREFRE'S (UNFINISHED) PYRAMID*
J   *PYRAMID LEPSIUS NO. XXIV*
K   *PYRAMID LEPSIUS NO. XXV*
L   *NECROPOLIS WITH MASTABAS BELONGING TO KHEKERETNEBTI, HEDJETNEBU, MERNEFU, IDU, KHENIT AND ANONYMOUS MASTABA 'L'*
M   *UDJAHORRESNET'S SHAFT TOMB*
N   *IUFAA'S SHAFT TOMB*

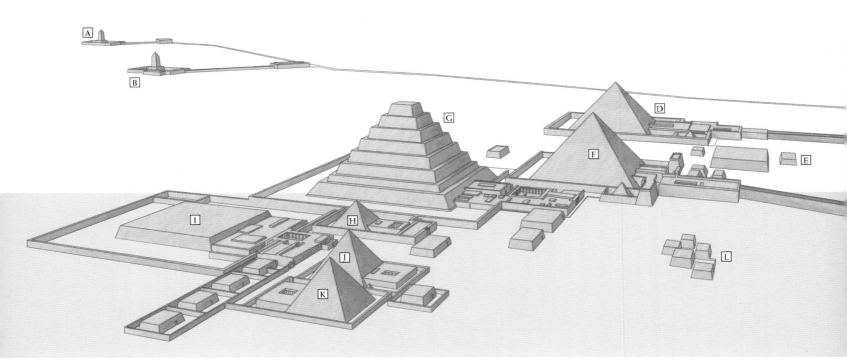

Sahure

Sahure, possibly a son of Userkaf, erected his pyramid complex, 'Sahure's Soul Shines,' near his predecessor's sun temple in Abusir. The monument was excavated by the German expedition led by Ludwig Borchardt at the beginning of the twentieth century. It is considered to be another milestone in the development of the Old Kingdom royal tomb, especially in regard to the new and harmoniously balanced layout of the whole pyramid complex, the variety of different kinds of stones used in its construction, and the thematically rich relief decoration of high workmanship.

Unfortunately, the same cannot be said about the pyramid. Stripped of its casing, the pyramid's core, consisting presumably of horizontal layers of inferior quality limestone blocks, today resembles a mere mound of rubble. The entrance to the pyramid lies at the foot of the north wall, in the axis of the monument. The corridor, provided originally with three strong points of pink granite, opened in the antechamber lying at ground level, just on the vertical axis of the pyramid. The burial chamber lay,

as in Userkaf's pyramid, to the west of the antechamber. The gabled ceiling of both chambers consisted of three layers of huge limestone blocks. In the plundered burial chamber, only fragments of the king's sarcophagus survived.

The plan of the mortuary temple consisted of six basic elements: an entrance hall, an open courtyard surrounded by a row of pink granite palm columns, a transverse corridor (separating the western, more intimate part of the temple from the eastern one), a five-niched chapel for the king's statues, an offering hall, and, eventually, two groups of magazines. The pavement of the courtyard was of basalt. The walls of the temple were of fine white limestone. In some places in the temple, black granite, alabaster, and quartzite were also used; however, only fragments of the temple's original relief decoration have survived. Among them can be seen fragments of splendid scenes of the king defeating a Libyan chieftain and bringing rich bounty from a military campaign, the king hunting in the desert, sea battles, and trading ships returning

from Asia. Adjacent to the south of the temple was a small cult pyramid. The valley temple at the edge of the desert was linked to the mortuary temple with a causeway—originally a corridor built of limestone blocks. The causeway's inner walls were once richly decorated with fine reliefs representing, as indicated by several recently found blocks, the ceremonies accompanying the conclusion of the pyramid's construction, the bringing of captured emaciated Bedouins to the royal court, and other courtly events.

The floor of the valley temple today lies several meters below the desert ground. The temple, built of the same materials as the mortuary temple, was conceived as a sort of gateway to the whole pyramid complex—the king's eternal residence in the netherworld. The temple had two porticos with pink granite palm columns, and two landing ramps, one on the eastern and the other on the southern side. Some themes of the relief decoration of the temple were linked with the magical protection of the entrance to the pyramid complex.

258
This statue of Sahure with a figure personifying the province of Coptos is now conserved at the Metropolitan Museum of Art, New York.

259
Aerial photograph of Sahure's mortuary temple and his pyramid from the east.

Sahure

260-261
Aerial view showing the pyramid field at Abusir from the northeast; in the foreground is the pyramid of King Sahure.

260 bottom left
The columned court of Sahure's mortuary temple presents many interesting subjects for archaeologists working in the field.

260 bottom right
View of Sahure's mortuary temple from the summit of his pyramid.

261 top
Fragment of a red granite palm column, located in the southern portico of Sahure's mortuary temple.

261 center
Procession of Lower Egyptian deities bringing offerings to Sahure from the low reliefs in Sahure's mortuary temple; now in the Egyptian Museum in Cairo.

261 bottom left
Drawing reproducing the model of Sahure's pyramid complex, without the causeway or valley temple (after L. Borchardt).

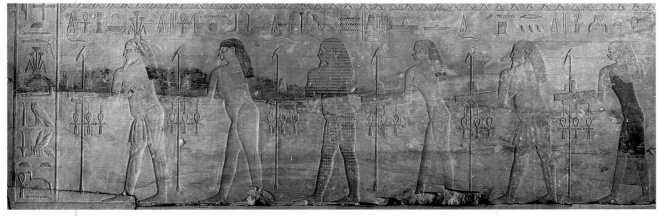

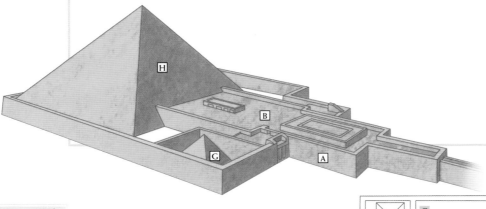

GROUND PLAN OF SAHURE'S PYRAMID COMPLEX WITHOUT CAUSEWAY (AFTER H. RICKE)	
A	ENTRANCE HALL
B	COLUMNED COURTYARD
C	TRANSVERSAL CORRIDOR
D	FIVE-NICHED CHAPEL
E	STORAGE ROOMS
F	OFFERING HALL
G	CULT PYRAMID
H	MAIN PYRAMID

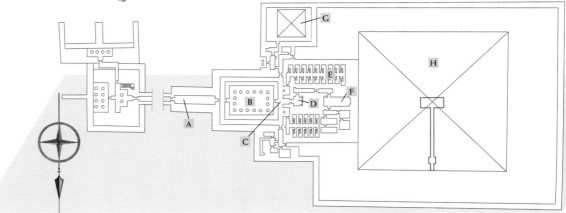

262-263
Aerial view of the pyramid complexes of Khentkaus II and Neferirkare from the south.

262 bottom left
Reconstruction of the hypothetical building stages of Neferirkare's pyramid, by M. Verner.

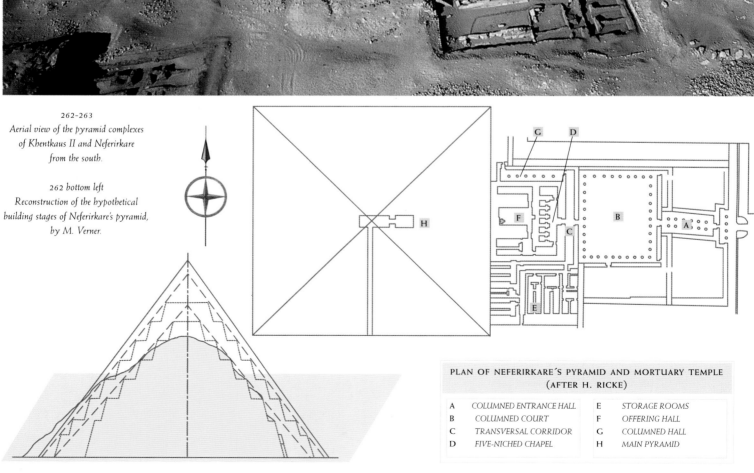

PLAN OF NEFERIRKARE'S PYRAMID AND MORTUARY TEMPLE
(AFTER H. RICKE)

A	COLUMNED ENTRANCE HALL	E	STORAGE ROOMS
B	COLUMNED COURT	F	OFFERING HALL
C	TRANSVERSAL CORRIDOR	G	COLUMNED HALL
D	FIVE-NICHED CHAPEL	H	MAIN PYRAMID

Neferirkare  Kakai

In some further alterations to the reliefs in his predecessor's mortuary temple, Sahure's successor Neferirkare Kakai (often referred to as Neferirkare only) was represented as a king. This unusual decision is considered by some scholars as evidence that the two men were brothers. Be that as it may, Neferirkare began to build his pyramid complex, 'Neferirkare is a Soul,' on a hillock south of Sahure's monument. Surprisingly, Neferirkare's monument was originally planned, more than one and a half centuries after the end of the era of step pyramids, as another step pyramid. But the plan was later changed. The six-step monument, with only its lowest step cased, was expanded in order to be eventually converted into a true pyramid, about 73 meters high. The king, however, died prematurely and his pyramid project remained unfinished.

The substructure of Neferirkare's pyramid does not basically differ from Sahure's. One minor modification occurred in the plan, however, namely a slight deviation of the southern part of the descending corridor to the east. As a matter of fact, the corridor was to open in the antechamber, which lay slightly to the east of the vertical axis of the pyramid. This deviation of the corridor is characteristic of the Fifth Dynasty pyramids until Djedkare's time; it was to occur in the future only once more, at the beginning of the Twelfth Dynasty in Senusret I's pyramid. Owing to its severe destruction by stone robbers, the substructure was left by Borchardt largely unexplored.

Of the two large wooden funerary boats of the king, one presumably on the northern and the other on the southern side of the pyramid, only the southern one was unearthed by Czech archaeologists in the 1980s. Lamentably, the boat was found to be completely decayed.

Neferirkare's sons and successors, Neferefre and after him Niuserre, decided to drastically alter their father's pyramid project. The plans for the valley temple and the causeway were canceled and only Neferirkare's mortuary temple was hastily finished in mud brick and wood—except for the offering hall and several rooms in its vicinity which were built in limestone. In the center of the temple, there was an open courtyard with wooden lotus columns. The temple was also provided with a columned portico and a columned entrance hall. In the ruins of magazines in the southwest part of the temple, the remnants of the temple papyrus archive were discovered by robbers in the early 1890s. Other fragments of papyri were later found in this place by Borchardt. The papyri, translated and edited in the 1970s by P. Posener-Kriéger, offered us a completely new and surprisingly detailed view of the economic and religious background of the royal mortuary cults at the Abusir necropolis.

Highly surprising, and at the same time of great historical importance, was the discovery by Czech archaeologists of a small pyramid complex of Neferirkare's consort Khentkaus II at the southern wing of the mud-brick perimeter wall of the king's pyramid. Inscriptions revealed in the ruins of the queen's mortuary temple showed that Khentkaus II bore the same very unusual title of 'Mother of Two Kings of Upper and Lower Egypt' (interpreted by some Egyptologists as 'King of Upper and Lower Egypt and Mother of the King of Upper and Lower Egypt') as her earlier namesake, Khentkaus I, buried in the so-called 'Fourth Pyramid' in Giza. The two queens may have been related and may also have played the same key role in the enhancement of the legitimacy of their obviously underage sons—successors to the throne. Khentkaus II's sons were Neferefre and Niuserre and her title might reflect her support of an immature Niuserre's claim to the throne after the premature death of his elder brother. The identity of the sons of Khentkaus I, however, remains so far unknown.

263 bottom left
View of the pyramid complexes of Neferefre, Khentkaus II, (Lepsius no. XXIV, and Lepsius no. XXV) from the summit of Neferirkare's pyramid.

PLAN OF KHENTKAUES II'S PYRAMID COMPLEX IN ABUSIR (AFTER P. JÁNOSI)

A	PILLARED PORTICO (I)
B	PORTER'S LODGE
C	STORAGE ROOMS
D	CULT PYRAMID
E	PILLARED PORTICO (II)
F	PILLARED COURT
G	OFFERING HALL
H	ENTRANCE CHAPEL
I	MAIN PYRAMID

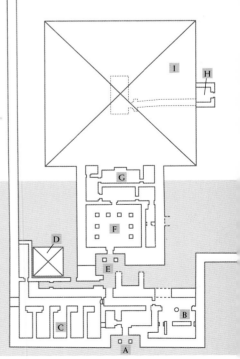

The remnants of the first step of the core of an unfinished pyramid, lying only few dozen meters southwest of Neferirkare's complex, never attracted much attention from archaeologists who worked in Abusir. Some took it for the unfinished funerary monument, never used as the tomb, of the short-lived King Neferefre, or the monument of the ephemeral King Shepsekare. Borchardt's short trial digging in the ruins of the monument brought negative results. Only the systematic archaeological research by the Czech team, begun in the late 1970s, confirmed that the monument was the tomb of Neferefre. Moreover, it eventually led to the unearthing of a large burial complex, named originally 'Divine is Neferefre's Power,' and to the discovery of a number of invaluable archaeological artifacts. Neferefre died in about the second year of his reign, at the time when only the first step of his pyramid's core was under construction. Therefore, the original pyramid project must have been completely altered in order to ensure the standard royal burial within the stress of the time limit of about seventy days needed for the mummification of the dead body. The unfinished first step of the pyramid's core was converted into a *mastaba*-like structure imitating the primeval mound. Though executed in roughly dressed white limestone, the substructure of the tomb respected in principle the standard plan of a royal funerary apartment as known from other pyramids of that time. It consisted of the descending corridor with a portcullis in pink granite, the antechamber, and the burial chamber. Above the entrance to the corridor, opening in the middle of the northern side of the monument, a small mud-brick chapel was built. This so-called northern chapel is supposed to have been an integral part of the standard plan of a royal pyramid. Unfortunately, in some earlier excavations (e.g. in Sahure's or Neferirkare's case) the archaeologists failed to search for this chapel. In the ruins of the pyramid's substructure, largely devastated by stone robbers, the remnants of the royal burial were found; namely, fragments of a red granite sarcophagus, fragments of alabaster canopic jars, and most importantly, tiny pieces of the king's mummy. Forensic examination of the latter fragments proved that Neferefre died between the ages of twenty to twenty-two years. Simultaneously with the construction of the funerary apartment, a small mortuary temple, mostly in mud brick, was built on the eastern side of the tomb. The temple was of an unusual north-south orientation. Its plan, too, largely differed from the standard royal mortuary temples of that time. Only the actual cult center of the temple, the offering hall, and a few rooms in its close vicinity were built in fine white limestone; the walls were left undecorated. Most of this limestone structure, including the false door once set in the western wall of the offering hall, was taken away by stone robbers. The northern part of the temple involved ten two-storied magazines, the southern one an unique hypostyle hall—the first to be accounted in ancient Egyptian architecture. The hall, whose blue-painted ceiling, decorated with golden stars, was supported by twenty polychrome six-stemmed wooden lotus columns. The hall was probably to be the dead king's throne hall in the afterlife. The temple lacked a five-niched chapel. In the main portico was a pair of polychrome four-stemmed lotus columns in limestone. Southeast of the temple a large slaughterhouse, called the 'Sanctuary of the Knife,' was constructed in mud brick. It is the earliest archaeological evidence of a slaughterhouse known so far from ancient Egypt.

A little later, under the rule of Niuserre, the initial temple was expanded to the east. A newly-added, large open courtyard with wooden palm columns and a monumental entrance with a pair of six-stemmed papyrus columns in limestone completed the mortuary temple to contemporaneous standard. Importantly, however, the valley temple and the causeway were omitted. Among a great number of invaluable archaeological finds made in Neferefre's mortuary temple were, for example, a papyrus archive comparable with Neferirkare's, a set of royal sculptures which are now on display in the Egyptian Museum in Cairo, inscribed faience and frit tablets and ornaments, beautiful stone vessels used in the temple cult, and many other objects.

Neferefre

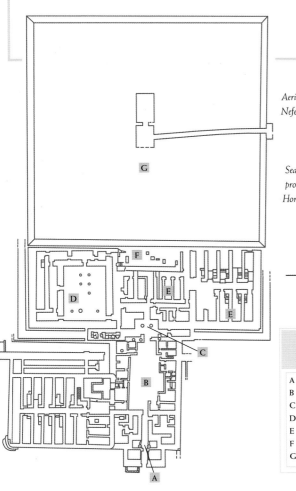

264
Aerial view of the pyramid complexes of Neferefre, Khentkaus II, and Neferirkare from southwest.

265 right
Seated statue of Neferefre, whose head is protected by the wings of the falcon god Horus, in pink limestone, conserved at the Egyptian Museum in Cairo.

PLAN OF NEFEREFRE'S
PYRAMID COMPLEX
(AFTER M. VERNER)

A	COLUMNED PORTICO (I)
B	COURT
C	COLUMNED PORTICO (II)
D	HYPOSTYLE HALL
E	STORAGE ROOMS
F	OFFERING HALL
G	MAIN PYRAMID

Neferefre

266-267
Bust of basalt seated statue of Neferefre
with nemes-headcloth, now in the
Egyptian Museum, Cairo.

267 top
View of the northern storage rooms of
Neferefre's mortuary temple (in the
foreground), and Neferirkare's pyramid
(in the background).

267 bottom
Fragment of a frit tablet with gold foil;
now conserved in the Egyptian
Museum, Cairo.

Niuserre

Regardless of the relatively restricted free area in the cemetery, Neferefre's successor, Niuserre, apparently wished to be buried as close to his parents and elder brother as possible. At the same time, he was obliged to complete the largely unfinished funerary monuments of his royal ancestors in Abusir. He resolved the problem by founding his mortuary temple and pyramid on the ground adjacent to the north of his father's mortuary temple. At the same time, he used the ground reserved for Neferirkare's valley temple and the eastern half of the latter's causeway. This decision thus essentially influenced the plan of both the causeway and the mortuary temple of Niuserre's pyramid complex, called 'The (Cult) Places of Niuserre are Enduring.'

Though its core consists of seven steps, Niuserre's pyramid is the smallest royal pyramid in Abusir. Its substructure's plan does not, in principle, differ from that of Sahure or Neferirkare. However, its large-scale devastation by stone robbers prevented Borchardt from thoroughly investigating the king's funerary apartment.

As previously mentioned, the topographical and dynastic circumstances essentially influenced the plan of the mortuary temple. The standard plan of that time resembled a letter 'T,' whereas Niuserre's temple resembles an inverted letter 'L.' Nevertheless, it involved the same basic elements as, for example, Sahure's mortuary temple; only their arrangement was different. The entrance hall, flanked by storage rooms, was followed by an open courtyard with basalt pavement and six-stemmed papyrus columns in red granite. The courtyard thus resembled a marshy papyrus thicket, the place where, according to ancient

Egyptians, life was constantly renewed. In the western, intimate part of the temple, for the first time there appeared, between the five-niched chapel and the offering hall, a small room with a square-shaped ground plan. Its ceiling was supported by a column. This room, known as the *antichambre carrée*, became from this time until the reign of Senusret I a standard component of all royal mortuary temples. Another innovation of Niuserre's temple was a deep niche, between the antichambre carrée and the five-niched chapel, with a large statue of a recumbent lion in pink granite (now in the Egyptian Museum, Cairo). Finally, the last major architectonic innovation were large, tower-like structures in the northeast and southeast corners of the temple. They are considered as precursors of pylons—the monumental gateways of Egyptian temples.

For the aforesaid reasons, the causeway which linked the valley temple with the mortuary temple has an atypical, bent ground plan. As in the case of Sahure's complex, Borchardt also left Niuserre's causeway largely unexplored and, therefore, in future times, it would not be surprising if further archaeological discoveries were to be made in its neighborhood.

The plan of the valley temple did not basically differ from Sahure's valley temple. It also had two porticos with landing ramps. In Niuserre's temple, however, one of the porticos was on the eastern side, whereas the second one was on the western side. The columns in pink granite imitated a six-stemmed bundle of papyrus flowers.

On the northern outskirts of the Abusir cemetery, not far from Userkaf's sun temple, Niuserre built his sun temple and named it 'Re's Delight.'

The monumental gateway to the temple lay at the edge of the Nile Valley and was surrounded, as in the case of the royal valley temples, by a town in which lived mostly the priests, officials, and workmen professionally connected with the local royal mortuary or sun cults. A short open causeway linked it with the upper temple founded on an artificially constructed terrace on a low hillock. The eastern part of the temple formed a large open courtyard dominated by a 36 meter-high obelisk built of limestone blocks. The base of the obelisk was cased with pink granite blocks.

At the eastern foot of the obelisk, in the courtyard, stood an altar made of four huge alabaster blocks, facing the cardinal points and having surfaces making up the hieroglyphic sign *hetep* meaning 'offering' or 'offering table.' A rounded block in the middle of the altar imitated the sign *re* ('sun' or 'sun god'). The meaning of the altar was obvious: 'The sun god's offering table.' Before their presentation on the altar, the offerings were ritually purified in large alabaster basins placed around the walls of the courtyard. On the walls of a ramp leading through the base to the obelisk, splendid reliefs survived. These depict the changing natural background during the three ancient Egyptian seasons of inundation, emergence (of crops), and harvest. Called the 'Chamber of Seasons,' the reliefs are now on display in the Egyptian Museum in Berlin. At the southern side of the temple, a large symbolic solar boat made of mud brick and wood was revealed.

Userkaf's and Niuserre's sun temples are the only ones which have been found by archaeologists so far.

268-269
Aerial view of the pyramids and mortuary temples of Niuserre and Neferirkare.

269 top
Aerial view of the pyramid complexes of Khentkaus II, Neferirkare, and Niuserre.

269 bottom left
North-south section through the burial chamber of Niuserre's pyramid, after V. Maragioglio and C. Rinaldi.

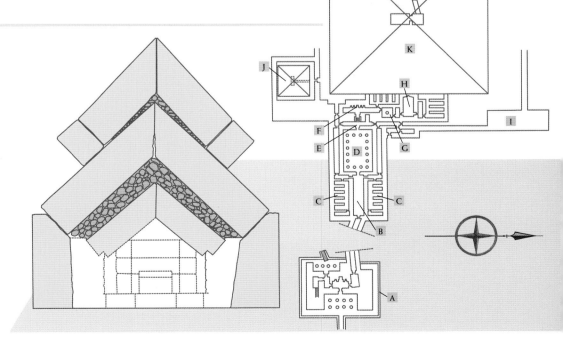

PLAN OF NIUSERRE'S MORTUARY AND VALLEY TEMPLE (AFTER H. RICKE)

A *VALLEY TEMPLE*
B *ENTRANCE HALL*
C *STORAGE ROOMS*
D *COLUMNED COURT*
E *TRANSVERSAL CORRIDOR*
F *FIVE NICHE CHAPEL*
G *"ANTICHAMBRE CARRÉE"*
H *OFFERING HALL*
I *"ECKBAU" (CORNER BUILDING)*
J *CULT PYRAMID*
K *MAIN PYRAMID*

270 top left
Photograph showing the entrance, the open court, and the remains of the obelisk of the sun temple of Niuserre.

270 center left
Calcite basins used for ritual purification of offerings in the open court of Niuserre's sun temple.

270 bottom left
Alabaster altar located in Niuserre's sun temple.

The remaining four sun temples—Sahure's 'Offering Field of Re,' Neferirkare's 'Favorite Place of Re,' Neferefre's 'Offering Table of Re,' and Menkauhor's 'Horizon of Re'—are known from contemporary texts only.

Two small pyramid complexes, severely damaged by stone robbers, are to be dated to the time of Niuserre and were marked by Karl R. Lepsius on the archaeological map of Abusir as no. XXIV and no. XXV. They lie in the southern outskirts of the pyramid field. The pyramids belonged to queens, one possibly to Niuserre's and the second to Neferefre's consort. A mummy of a woman of about twenty-three years old was found, with the remnants of a pink granite sarcophagus, in the pyramid no. XXIV. The presence of an ancient female mummy in this burial chamber appears to corroborate this theory.

From approximately the same time as the two small pyramids also dates the splendid tomb of Niuserre's son-in-law, Ptahshepses. The monument, ranking among the largest of Old Kingdom *mastabas,*

he also became the vizier. Eventually, he married Niuserre's daughter, Princess Khamerernebty, and advanced to the rank of a king's son. His rising career found its reflection in the repeated expansions of his *mastaba;* not only the size and architecture, but also the relief decoration of the *mastaba* bear witness to Ptahshepses's high social standing. The entrance was ornamented with a pair of eight-stemmed lotus columns in limestone, the earliest example of this type of column. His large, open pillared courtyard bears comparison with those in contemporaneous royal mortuary temples as do his three-niched chapel and burial chamber with gabled ceiling built of huge limestone blocks. The extant reliefs in the *mastaba* rank among the best we know from Old Kingdom relief art.

Very little is known about the parentage and reign of Niuserre's successor Menkauhor. His pyramid, known from contemporary texts as 'Divine are the (Cult) Places of Menkauhor,' still remains to be found. It was certainly not built in Abusir. Some scholars

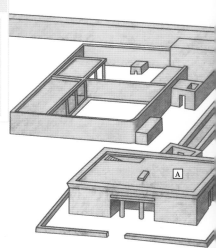

lies almost midway between the pyramid temples of Niuserre and Sahure. It had been discovered as early as the late 1890s by J. de Morgan, but was only fully excavated by the Czech team about eighty years later.

Ptahshepses began his career as a royal hairdresser and manicurist. Gradually, his position at the royal court rose and, in addition to many other functions,

would like to identify it with the ruins of a monument northeast of the Red Pyramid of Sneferu in Dahshur. The others identify it with the so-called 'Headless Pyramid' east of Teti's pyramid in North Saqqara. On the basis of some archaeological observations made so far on the two sites, the second option seems to be more plausible.

MAP AND RECONSTRUCTION
OF NIUSERRE'S SUN TEMPLE
(AFTER L. BORCHARDT)

A   *MONUMENTAL GATEWAY*
B   *CAUSEWAY*
C   *OPEN COURT*
D   *STORAGE ROOMS*
E   *ALTAR*
F   *OBELISK*
G   *SOLAR BOAT*

Niuserre

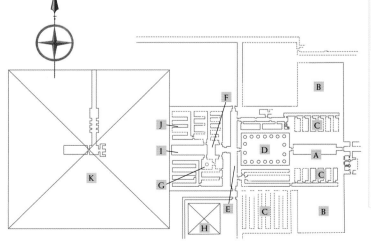

PLAN OF DJEDKARE'S PYRAMID
AND MORTUARY TEMPLE
(AFTER V. MARAGIOGLIO
AND C. RINALDI)

A ENTRANCE HALL
B PROTOPYLONS
C STORAGE ROOMS
D COLUMNED COURT
E TRANSVERSAL CORRIDOR
F FIVE-NICHED CHAPEL
G "ANTICHAMBRE CARRÉE"
H CULT PYRAMID
I OFFERING HALL
J STORAGE ROOMS
K MAIN PYRAMID

RECONSTRUCTION OF
DJEDKARE'S PYRAMID
(AFTER M. LEHNER)

A ENTRANCE CHAPEL
B DESCENDING CORRIDOR
C VESTIBULE
D PORTCULLIS
E ANTECHAMBER
F BURIAL CHAMBER
G THREE STORAGE ROOMS
H CULT PYRAMID

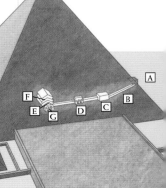

273 right
Polychrome wooden statue of Hedjetnebu,
a daughter of Djedkare. Now in the
Egyptian Museum, Cairo.

Djedkare

Either because of the lack of a convenient building site for a pyramid in Abusir or for some other reason, Djedkare (also called Djedkare Isesi) chose for the construction of his funerary monument a place at South Saqqara. His pyramid, which has suffered severe depredation by stone robbers, was archaeologically examined only in the middle of the twentieth century by Alexander Varille, Abdel Salam Hussein, and eventually, Ahmed Fakhry. Lamentably, the excavation documentation was lost and the results of the research were never fully published.

Basically, Djedkare's monument followed the concept of the preceding Fifth Dynasty pyramid complexes. From the casing of fine white limestone only remnants have survived in position. In contrast to the preceding pyramids, the descending corridor opened onto the pavement of the court in front of the north wall of the pyramid.

Another innovation appeared in the plan of the pyramid's substructure: a small room with three deep niches in its eastern wall. The room, adjacent from the east to the antechamber, was used for storage. In the ruins of the burial chamber the remnants of the king's burial were revealed: fragments of a dark graywacke sarcophagus, fragments of alabaster canopic vessels, and small pieces of the mummified body of an old (by ancient Egyptian standards) man of about fifty years of age.

Prior to the construction of the mortuary temple, the sharply sloping ground in front of the pyramid's east side had to be leveled by means of an artificial terrace. Basically, the plan of the temple followed the trend set by Sahure and Niuserre. The temple was entered from the east through a long, vaulted hall, flanked on each side by six magazines. The hall opened into a large courtyard surrounded with a row of palm columns in pink granite. The way continued

westward through the transverse corridor, five-niched chapel, and antichambre carrée, to the offering hall surrounded with other store rooms. The eastern façade of the temple was dominated by two tower-like structures resembling, in a way, similar structures in Niuserre's mortuary temple.

In front of the southeast corner of the pyramid stood a small cult pyramid surrounded with its own perimeter wall of limestone. The causeway, slightly deviating to the south, and the valley temple have not yet been excavated.

Adjacent to the northern wing of the enclosure wall of Djedkare's mortuary temple lies a smaller pyramid complex of an unknown queen, probably Djedkare's consort. The plan of the complex—consisting of a pyramid, a little cult pyramid, a mortuary temple, and a perimeter wall—is in many respects very original. The temple was entered from the west, from the courtyard around Djedkare's pyramid, through a long hall whose ceiling was supported by a row of six-stemmed papyrus columns in limestone. The same type of column ornamented the open-columned courtyard lying north of the entrance hall. To the north of the courtyard lay a group of ten magazines. The western, intimate part of the temple involved the antichambre carrée, the three-niched chapel for the queen's cult statues, and the offering hall. According to Fakhry, parts of the temple's relief decoration were additionally altered. These changes led some scholars to the hypothesis that after Djedkare's death, and prior to (her son?) Unas's accession to the throne, the queen herself ruled for some time. However, these and other questions surrounding Djedkare's pyramid complex can hardly be answered without a new and thorough examination of the whole monument, including the queen's pyramid.

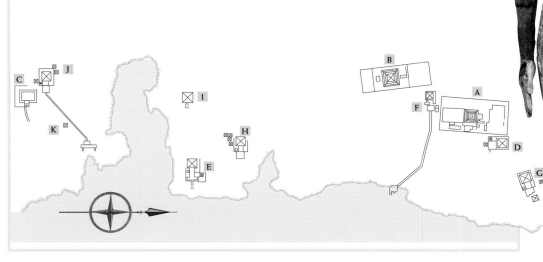

THE PYRAMID FIELD
AT SAQQARA
(AFTER A. LABROUSSE)

A DJOSER
B SEKHEMKHET
C SHEPSESKAF
D USERKAF
E DJEDKARE
F UNAS
G TETI
H PEPY I
I MERENRE
J PEPY II
K IB

Unas

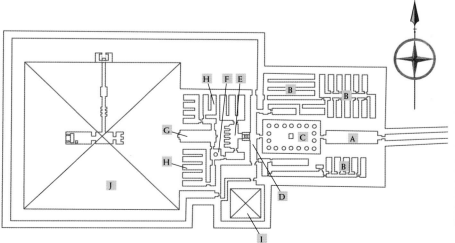

**PLAN OF UNAS'S PYRAMID
AND MORTUARY TEMPLE
(AFTER J.-PH. LAUER)**

A	ENTRANCE HALL
B	STORAGE ROOMS
C	COLUMNED COURT
D	TRANSVERSAL CORRIDOR
E	FIVE-NICHED CHAPEL
F	"ANTICHAMBRE CARRÉE"
G	OFFERING HALL
H	STORAGE ROOMS
I	CULT PYRAMID
J	MAIN PYRAMID

274-275
*Aerial view of the entire pyramid
complex of King Unas, seen from west.*

275 top
*Close-up detail of the Pyramid Texts
from the pyramid of Unas.*

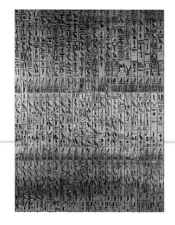

As did the founder of the Fifth Dynasty, its last king, Unas, returned to the 'shadow' of the Step Pyramid in his planning of his own pyramid. However, contrary to Userkaf, Unas built his monument next to the southern wing of the Great Trench. With its height of about 43 meters, Unas's pyramid, called 'Beautiful are the (Cult) Places of Unas,' is the smallest royal pyramid of the Fifth Dynasty. In spite of this, it represents another milestone in the development of ancient Egyptian royal tombs, since, on the walls of its underground chambers, there appeared for the first time the so-called Pyramid Texts—a compilation of various religious inscriptions (litanies, hymns, divine utterances, recitations, etc.) referring to the king's life in the beyond. The excavation of Unas's pyramid complex was gradually carried out by Alexandre Barsanti, Jean-Philippe Lauer, and Ahmed Moussa.

Except for the straight, no longer deviating descending corridor, the plan of the relatively well-preserved substructure of the pyramid resembled that of Djedkare. Just before the opening into the antechamber, the corridor was provided with a pink granite portcullis which did not, however, prevent the robbers from plundering the royal burial. On the west wall of the burial chamber, decorated with the representation of the stylized façade of the royal palace, stood a dark graywacke sarcophagus, already robbed in antiquity. The walls of the chamber were covered with the blue-greenish painted Pyramid Texts and its gabled ceiling depicted yellow stars on a blue background. The chamber thus represented the underworld out of which, according to the beliefs of ancient Egyptians, the mythically resurrected king ascended through the corridor up to the heavens to become one of the never-setting circumpolar stars.

The plan of the mortuary temple in front of the east side of the pyramid did not differ greatly from Djedkare's temple. However, the tower-like structures in the eastern façade were omitted. The ceiling of the open courtyard's ambulatory was supported by palm columns in pink granite. Some of the columns were later, in the Twenty-first and Twenty-second Dynasties, taken away and reused in buildings in Tanis in the Eastern Delta. The same type of column, but of brownish quartzite, supported the ceiling of the antichambre carrée. From the fine relief decoration on the limestone walls of the temple, only fragments were found (for example, a small part of the false door set in the western wall of the offering hall is still in position).

A causeway more than 720 meters long linked the mortuary temple with the valley temple. In order to build this causeway, some earlier tombs had to be dismantled (for instance, the *mastaba* of Khnumhotep and Niankhnum). Among the reliefs which survived from the original decoration of the inner walls of the causeway is the famous scene of starving Bedouins, which has long been considered by Egyptologists as evidence of the ecological stress in northeast Africa and the retreat of the desert nomads to the Nile Valley at the end of the Fifth Dynasty (see above, Sahure's causeway).

South of the upper end of the causeway, a pair of large boat pits, cased with limestone, was unearthed. Originally, they probably contained two wooden funerary boats. The latter were to be symbolically used by the dead king accompanying the sun god in his journey across the heavens of both day and night.

Palm columns in pink granite also ornamented the porticos of the valley temple. The main portico had eight columns and a landing ramp was on the eastern side of the temple. Two smaller porticos, each with a pair of columns and a landing ramp, were on the northern and southern sides of the temple. Among important finds made in this temple was, surprisingly, a dark graywacke sarcophagus with a mummy of 'the king's son Ptahshepses.' Unas' consorts, queens Nebet and Khenut, were not buried in the pyramids, but in *mastabas* north of the king's mortuary temple.

More than one thousand years later, Unas' pyramid complex became, for a while, a building site again. As attested to by his inscription on the southern wall of Unas' pyramid, Prince Khaemwaset, Ramesses II's son and the high priest of Ptah in Memphis, a great admirer of the pyramids of his royal predecessors, ordered the restoration of the damaged monument. His 'reconstruction inscriptions' have also been discovered on some other Old Kingdom pyramids.

275 center right
The walls of the antechamber in the pyramid of Unas are covered with Pyramid Texts.

275 bottom right
The burial chamber with the sarcophagus of king Unas.

The Surprising Abusir Blocks

by Zahi Hawass and Miroslav Verner

Recently, the Supreme Council of Antiquities decided to prepare the site of Abusir for tourists. Part of this plan was to restore the funerary temple of Sahure and install sidewalks for visitors. There were mounds of debris in the area left over from excavations carried out by Ludwig Borchardt, who had explored the complex of Sahure in the early twentieth century. I asked Mohammed Moselhy, the driver of our front-loader at Giza, to clear the area to the north of Sahure's causeway. He worked for a month carefully moving masses of sand. One day, his loader hit a limestone block, and he stopped immediately to investigate.

When he examined the block, he saw that it was carved with beautiful scenes. He took some photographs, and brought them to show me. I saw right away that these were important scenes connected with the building of the pyramid. We found three other inscribed blocks near the first one, and were able to determine that these blocks had originally lined the lower part of the northern wall of Sahure's causeway corridor. Similar blocks had been found by Borchardt in his excavations in the early twentieth century, and we were surprised to discover that he had not cleared the entire area. The four new blocks were clearly were from the same general area on the causeway wall, but did not join together.

The decorated surface on each block covers an area of about two square meters. At the bottom of each block are the remains of a geometric frieze. The relief decoration is of exceptionally high quality. The degree of delicacy of the relief made the photographic recording of the blocks so difficult that it had to be done at night with artificial illumination. Of the original color on the reliefs, only tiny pieces of paint have survived the passage of time.

276
Two of the recently discovered blocks from the causeway of King Sahure. Abusir, Fifth Dynasty.

276-277
Block from the ceiling of the causeway of Sahure depicting stars. Abusir, Fifth Dynasty.

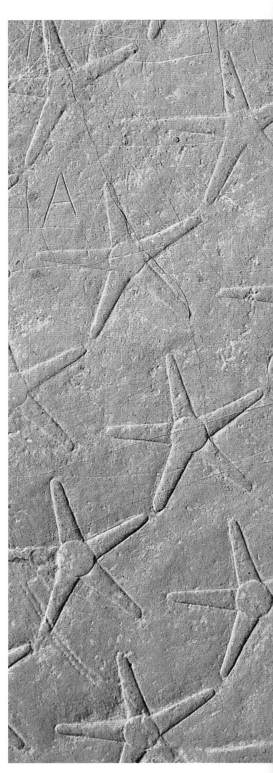

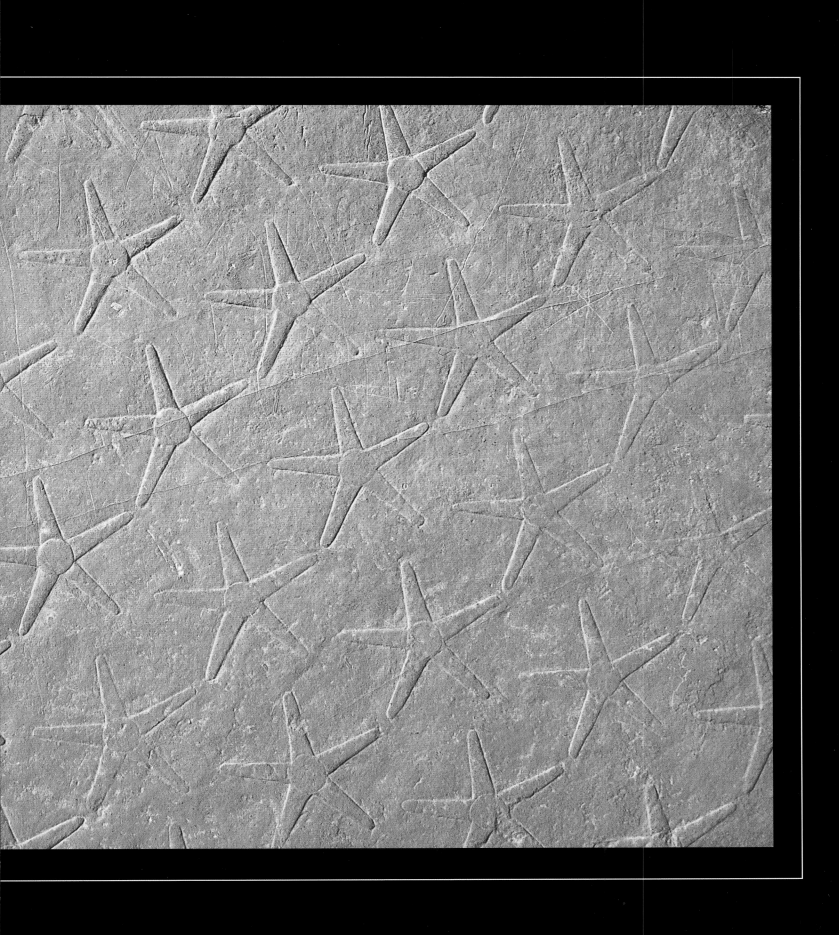

Line drawing after Z. Hawass of a relief showing workmen dragging the pyramidion for the pyramid of King Sahure. From a block from the causeway of the pyramid complex of Sahure, Abusir, Fifth Dynasty.

There are five registers of scenes on Block One. In the uppermost are scenes showing foodstuffs that would have been used for offerings, such as fruit, vegetables, and fish and meat that had been hung up to dry. In the second register, a row of men hold a rope. The object they are dragging is not preserved, but the inscription says: "[Bringing], the pyramidion [covered with] electrum to the pyramid." The pyramidion was dragged on a wooden sledge. A man bending in front of the sledge pours water on the ground to ease its passage. Standing behind him is the director of operations, who holds in his hand a scepter made in the shape of a human arm.

the reliefs could be carved. These reliefs are arranged—as in the previous instance—in five registers. The first register displays offering tables and baskets with fruit and vegetables, vessels containing wine and beer, and other similar items. The second register contains the remains of several scenes. At the left, a group of women bring trays of offerings; they are followed by a group of bowing men. On the right are two groups of men performing a dance with a rope. In the third register, to the right, a group of men brings boxes of funerary equipment. To the left is a group of courtiers bowing in the direction of the pyramid. The fourth register contains butchering

included royal wives and concubines, the *khener* was primarily an administrative and economic institution, an independent establishment connected with the royal palace.

In the third register, on the left, is a row of bending men, some of them carrying batons, others with long objects (perhaps rolled up mats, or linen); on the right, a group of young male dancers is performing. The inscriptions identify the men as members of two different crews, *Sahure shepesu* and *Sahure semsu*: the nobles of Sahure and the courtiers of Sahure. In the fourth register, on the left is again a row of men, members of the crews *Sahure...*[?] and

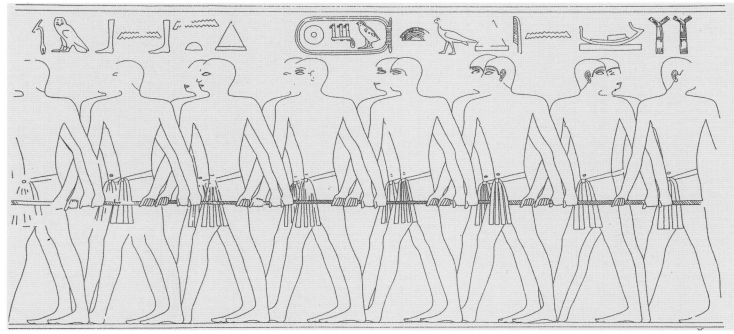

A tiny curiosity is the later graffito of an archer shooting at the pyramidion: he has been superimposed upon the figure of the man pouring the water. The author of the graffiti might have been inspired by a nearby scene of archers engaged in target practice, represented on Block Four. Also on Block One are a row of men advancing along the causeway while carrying chairs and staffs, all part of the funerary equipment; butchering scenes that depict different stages in the slaughtering of animals; and a row of men holding short batons in their hands. The inscriptions identify the men as 'the royal followers' and 'the royal tenants.'

The second block is the smallest and most eroded of the four: the poor quality of the stone is indicated by the fact that repairs had to be made to it before

scenes, showing again different episodes in the slaughtering of animals. The fifth register depicts another group of courtiers bowing in the direction of the pyramid.

The reliefs on Block Three are also arranged in five registers, and are organized into two halves within each register. In the first register offerings are displayed, as on previous blocks. To the left of the register, the legs of a row of offering-bearers can be seen. In the second register, a row of men—members of the royal suite—are bending and holding batons in their hands. On the right, a group of young female dancers are performing. These are labeled as members of the *khener*, which is usually translated as 'harem.' However, this translation can be misleading; although royal women who formed the *khener* almost certainly

nebty-neb-ha u-rehu, bending towards the pyramid. The men carry batons and rolled objects, as before. On the right, marching in the opposite direction, is a group of men bringing offerings.

In the fifth register, on the left, there is a group of men bending in the direction of the pyramid. A major portion of the register to the right of the vertical line is filled by a scene of courtiers and high officials who are facing away from the pyramid. The men, their hands placed on their knees, look in amazement at a group of squatting Bedouin. This group is arranged in two half-registers. The Bedouin are emaciated, and most of them have their arms raised in a gesture of supplication. One of them is so weak from hunger that he is unable even to raise his hands. Another one, at the end of the upper register, is so weak that he cannot even squat like the others, and he leans backward instead. Some of the Bedouin wear short kilts, the others are naked. Some of them wear wigs, the others have a mane of unkempt hair. Their emaciation is so extreme that their bellies are entirely shrunken, and their bones protrude. Above the group of Bedouin there are the remains of an inscription reading: " . . . [pyramidion?] in the Three Great Halls very much."

The figures of the Bedouin, especially their faces, were deliberately damaged with a sharp metal pick in a later age, presumably, at a time when the blocks were still *in situ*, probably because the Bedouin, the inhabitants of the desert, were considered as natural enemies of the inhabitants of the Nile Valley. The damage can possibly be dated to the New Kingdom, when the secondary cult of a goddess known as 'Sahure's Sakhmet' flourished in the eastern part of the mortuary temple. Clear traces of a red-painted grid indicate that the scene was later copied—probably in the Saite Period, although the later Fifth Dynasty cannot be excluded.

Though it is incomplete, and its inscription a little unclear, the scene of the Bedouin probably represents the most astounding episode among these newly discovered scenes. A similar scene from the causeway of Unas has long been known, and interpreted as evidence for famine during the late Fifth Dynasty. The discovery of this new scene takes from Unas's scene its claim to priority and originality. At the same time, it has opened up the possibility of an eventual revision of the hitherto-accepted interpretation of the scene.

It is certain that the scene from Sahure's causeway representing the Bedouin weakened by hunger represented an exotic attraction for the ancient Egyptian dignitaries who once viewed them. The inscription above the Bedouin, however, regardless of its being incomplete and questionable, almost certainly mentions the pyramidion. This puts the meaning of the scene into a different category from what was previously assumed: the scene is not just a simple piece of evidence for ecological stress and worsening of living conditions in the areas adjacent to the Nile Valley during this period. To judge from the context of all these newly discovered scenes, the episode with the Bedouin would indicate the hardships that had to be overcome when the ancient Egyptians searched for a stone pyramidion, rather than a general famine. To get the most suitable stone, the builders of the pyramid had to go to the

inhospitable mountains in the desert, where only the thirsty and hungry Bedouin lived—an unprecedented spectacle for the dignitaries of the pharaoh's court. To verify this assumption, however, the discovery of the missing part of this scene would be essential. It has also been suggested that these Bedouin are being brought back to Egypt to be tried for some sort of wrongdoing, perhaps for attacking the quarrying expedition, at the court of the king.

On the fourth block, found closest to the mortuary temple, sporting scenes predominate. As in the previous blocks, the decoration is arranged in five registers. In the first archers, each accompanied by an instructor, are shooting at targets. In the second register, two complete and two incomplete pairs of men are shown fighting with staffs. Short inscriptions beside each pair comment concisely upon the struggles. In the third register, six pairs of men are engaged in freestyle wrestling. The referee standing by carefully observes the contest. The inscriptions above the wrestlers identify them as members of Sahure's crews. The fourth register contains a large ship manned by rowers. Of a second ship, only a small portion remains. The scene is very dynamic, depicting the long line of rowers in different phases of stroking the oars. The rowers belong to Sahure's crew. In the lowest register, a row of men bows in the direction of the pyramid. One group of men represents the architects, who hold under their arms papyrus rolls undoubtedly containing the plans for the pyramid complex. Following the architects there are members of the crew *š3hw-r'- …,* holding batons.

In conclusion, let us briefly summarize the meaning of the above-mentioned scenes and emphasize some aspects of their discovery. The scenes surprise us by the variety of their subject matter, which forces us to reconsider long-held ideas about the monothematic decoration of the causeways of the Old Kingdom. This idea had already been challenged by Selim Hassan's discovery of the reliefs from the causeway of Unas, the meaning of which, however, remained neglected and unpublished. Apart from the variety, it seems that all the new scenes from Sahure's causeway have one common denominator: the termination of the building works for the pyramid, bringing reports about this event to the pharaoh, and, finally, the celebrations and offering ceremonies which accompanied that conclusion. It should be emphasized once again, however, that this discovery opens the way to a new consideration of the scenic

program of the Old Kingdom pyramid complex, its relation to the architecture of the complex, and its religious and historical aspects.

The scenes provide evidence that shows how important the construction of the royal tomb was to the lives of the ancient Egyptians. Without idealizing the evidence of these scenes, it seems that their meaning is far removed from the entrenched idea of the slave labor of anonymous masses of people engaged in the megalomaniac construction of the pharaohs' tombs.

Nevertheless, at present, the archaeological aspect of the problem seems to be the most urgent consideration. Around the causeway of Sahure we can expect to find further decorated blocks. In fact, several dozens of small fragments of relief have already been found on the spot, together with the blocks already mentioned. Many other fragments—several hundred, in fact—were found during the Czech excavation of the site. Many more are certain to lie beneath the surface, but recovering them will not be easy: according to preliminary estimates, about 30,000 cubic meters of sand and debris will have to be removed and checked for fragments. The end of the story still lies ahead.

There are three important points here that I would like to mention: the scene of dragging the capstone and the other scene showing the *khener* (dancing troupe) suggests that the capstone was the last architectural component added to the pyramid. Its placement signified that the pyramid was finished; after its installation, the whole country celebrated the national project of the land. The inscription associated with the scene showing the arrival of the pyramidion confirms that this object was cased with electrum.

Another important point clarified by the discovery of these new blocks has to do with the scene that depicts starving Bedouin. An identical scene had been discovered earlier in the twentieth century by Selim Hassan in the pyramid complex of Unas and was interpreted as evidence for the occurrence of a famine during the Fifth Dynasty. The additional information provided by the newly-discovered scene and its context on the new blocks suggests that these Bedouin are emaciated because they come from the inhospitable land where the stone for the pyramidion was quarried, and that they are shown here as prisoners brought back with the royal expedition to be judged in the pyramid court.

The Pyramids of the Sixth Dynasty

by Audran Labrousse

The Sixth and last dynasty of the Old Kingdom probably lasted a century and a half and numbered seven kings, originally from Memphis. Today we only know of four of their pyramids—those of Teti, Pepy I, Merenre I, and Pepy II. The tombs of Userkare, Merenre II, and Netjerkare Siptah ('Nitocris') have yet to be discovered.

Although the Sixth Dynasty has sometimes been presented as the harbinger of the weakening of the Old Kingdom, nothing in the architecture or decoration of the tombs of the period indicates the slightest sign of decline. Rather, after the classical apogee achieved during the Fifth Dynasty, the Sixth Dynasty marked the highlight of the development that had taken place since the beginning of the age of the pyramids. The result was architecture that associated form and symbolic function, even if its effect was to become repetitive. Before disappearing, the Old Kingdom under the Sixth Dynasty achieved a proud synthesis of its five centuries of artistic history.

The pyramids of the Sixth Dynasty kings all measure roughly 79 meters along the sides and 52 meters in height (the size of Sahure's pyramid) and have an inclination of 4/3 or 53°(the same as Khafre's pyramid, calculated using a 3:4:5 triangle). The funerary apartments are all laid out in the same manner (fixed under Djedkare Isesi), having a burial chamber and antechamber covered by inverted V-shaped vaults (in conformity with the prototype invented for Khufu's pyramid) and are decorated with inscriptions from the Pyramid Texts (which appeared for the first time in the funerary apartment of Unas). The funerary temples tend to archaism, with a return to the taste of the start of the Fourth Dynasty; for example, the reappearance of the pillar after the use of palm-shaped columns, or the prevalence in low reliefs of scenes characterized by large figures (as seen in Sneferu's funerary complex).

280
The inlayed eyes of this statue give extraordinary life to the gaze of King Pepy I. This full-size statue in hammered copper was found in 1897–98 on the site of Hierakonpolis. Now in the Egyptian Museum, Cairo.

281
The virtuosity of Sixth Dynasty craftsmen in the art of low relief is superbly illustrated by this detail of hunting ducks. One almost hears the cackle of the multitude of birds trapped in the hexagonal net.

As with most of the dynastic transitions during the Old Kingdom, the circumstances of the transmission of power from Unas to Teti remain obscure. The foundation of the Sixth Dynasty, whether by means of matrimonial succession or usurpation, seems to have occurred without difficulty. This is revealed by the stability of the administrative staff between the two governments.

Teti, who chose Seheteptauy ('He Who Pacifies the Two Lands') as his Horus name, seems to have effectively pursued a policy of conciliation. Although the royal monuments of Teti are rare, his activity as a legislator is fully documented in Abydos where he exempted the temple from the payment of taxes. He was also the first sovereign to link his name to the temple in Dendera. It was during Teti's reign that Uni first emerged, a model official whose brilliant career continued under three pharaohs. The beginning of his autobiography gives the bare details of what was a glittering life: "As soon as I left my adolescence behind me, under the Majesty of Teti, I was appointed Superintendent of the Store, then Inspector of the Palace staff. I was then made the ritualist, the elder in the old palace under the Majesty of Pepy: His Majesty placed me in the function of Friend, the superior of the priests of the city of his pyramid and […] he appointed me state attaché in Hierakonpolis, as he confided in me more than in any other of his servants."

According to Manetho, Teti, whose last documented year of rule was his thirteenth, was killed by his own guard. The incomplete decoration of his pyramid—called 'Longlasting are the Places of Teti' and in which the Pyramid Texts were never painted—seems to support this thesis. Alabaster was used profusely in the building and cult objects of his funerary temple; two inscriptions found in the quarries in Hatnub in Middle Egypt record expeditions organized by the king. Teti also pursued a policy of alliance with the nobility, marrying four of his daughters to viziers or other high officials.

Excavation work currently conducted by the Egyptian Supreme Council of Antiquities under the direction of Dr. Zahi Hawass has provided greater knowledge of the necropolis of the royal family: although Teti had his secondary consort, Iput II, buried in a *mastaba*, he restored, for the tomb of his principal wife, Khuit II, the pyramidal form abandoned for the queens of Unas; this model was to be copied throughout the rest of the Sixth Dynasty.

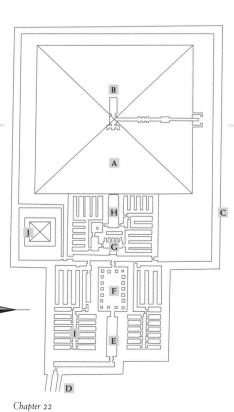

PLAN OF THE MORTUARY COMPLEX OF KING TETI ACCORDING TO J.-PH. LAUER

A *PYRAMID OF THE KING*
B *MORTUARY APARTMENT WITH THE SARCOPHAGUS*
C *ENCLOSURE WALL*
D *END OF THE CAUSEWAY FROM THE VALLEY TEMPLE*
E *ENTRANCE HALL*
F *COURTYARD*
G *ROOM WITH FIVE STATUE NICHES*
H *SANCTUARY*
I *STORAGE ROOMS FOR THE OBJECTS OF THE MORTUARY CULT*
J *SMALL SATELLITE PYRAMID*

Teti

282 left
Representation of the king wearing the
white crown of Upper Egypt in the
classical walking attitude, discovered in
the mortuary temple of Teti; although
uninscribed, the small granite statue, now
in the Egyptian Museum, has been
attributed to the sovereign.

282-283
For his tomb, King Teti choose a site
north of a diagonal formed by the
previous pyramids of Sekhemkhet, Djoser,
Unas, and Userkaf. The monument
stands just below that of Djoser, at the
highest point of the upland.

283 bottom left
In the burial chamber, above the
sarcophagus of King Teti, the depredations
of medieval stone-quarrying caused the
partial collapse of the enormous blocks of
the reverse V-shaped vault supporting the
mass of the pyramid.

283 bottom right
The Pyramid Texts in the burial
chamber were completely engraved,
but never painted. This may be
due to Teti's early death, perhaps by
murder. The color would have been
intended to enhance the magic power
of the texts.

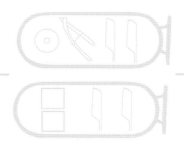

USERKARE

Although there is no supporting evidence for the hypothesis, it has been suggested that King Userkare, 'Powerful is the *ka* of Re,' was behind the assassination of Teti. Regardless, this king, mentioned between Teti and Pepy I in the 'King List' in the temple of Seti I in Abydos, seems to have reigned for a very short period, four years at most, as the recently identified annals of the Sixth Dynasty may record. No pyramid has been found that bears his name and no mention of him is made in the many autobiographical texts from the period. With the exception of some very rare documentation, Userkare's name is almost non-existent.

PEPY I

King Pepy changed his 'son of Re' name from Nefersahor, ('Perfect is the Protection of Horus'), to Merire, ('Beloved of Re'), for reasons that are not clear. It has been hypothesized that Userkare was a usurper whose territory was confined to the Delta, from where he governed at the same time as Pepy I, and that Pepy only changed his name after his rival had been definitively defeated.

Pepy I, who was to adopt Meritaui, 'Beloved of the Two Lands,' as his Horus name, reigned for at least fifty years. He raised the Old Kingdom to its highest point through his activities outside of Egypt, the many buildings he had constructed in the capital

and the rest of the country, and the reorganization of the administration. The name of the king's pyramid, Mennefer-Pepy, 'The Beauty of Pepy Abides,' was later to indicate the capital of Egypt and was transcribed as Memphis by the Greeks. At the end of his reign, Pepy I brought a legal action against one of his consorts. This extraordinary event, unique in the history of Egypt, was recorded by Uni in his autobiography: "A secret trial was held in the harem against the wife of the king, his great favorite. His Majesty asked me to judge, alone, without any vizier of the state, and no official other than myself being present [...] because his Majesty had faith in me. Being alone, I wrote down the proceedings myself [...]. Never in the past had someone of my rank ever come to know of a secret of the royal harem."

Having explored the funerary complex of the king for almost twenty years, the French archaeological mission in Saqqara has discovered many outstanding decorative elements in the funerary temple, including representations linked to the symbolic triumph of Egypt over known peoples. Large numbers of these images exist as low reliefs and as statues of prisoners. The Pyramid Texts were painted in the pyramid for the first time in a lovely green color to suggest a thriving and eternal rebirth beyond the tomb.

Excavation work in the royal necropolis has revealed the tombs of six royal consorts and that of a prince, Hornetjerikhet, who probably died before taking the throne. It was another of Pepy I's sons, Merenre, who succeeded him.

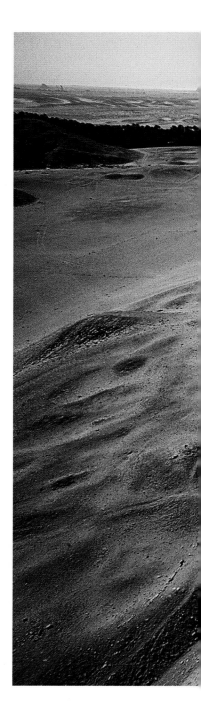

284 bottom left
Under the reverse V-shaped vault, which supported the weight of the pyramid, the restored walls surrounding the sarcophagus of Pepy I still show utterances of the Pyramid Texts.

284 bottom right
The Pyramid Texts are the oldest mortuary composition of mankind. Prayers, practical advice, even magic formulae, describe, in poetic language, the symbolic path of the king from death to life. The beautifully engraved hieroglyphs are painted in the pleasant green shade of young shoots in springtime; this color, made with ground malachite, symbolizes the rebirth of Pepy I in the eternity of the Beyond.

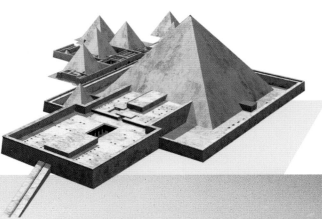

284-285

The ruins of the tombs of King Pepy I and the royal family are shown here from the same angle as the virtual restoration of the figure above. In spite of major restoration efforts, the vicissitudes of time have reduced the complex to a mere shell of its former majesty.

285 top

Restored in virtual reality, the geometry of Old Kingdom architectural forms can be seen here in their perfection. Besides the mass of the mortuary complex of King Pepy I, the pyramids of the queens appear, smaller as if satellites. Drawing by EDF/Labrousse.

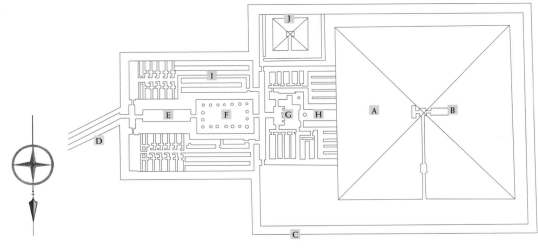

PLAN OF THE MORTUARY COMPLEX
OF KING PEPY I ACCORDING TO
A. LABROUSSE

A PYRAMID OF THE KING
B MORTUARY APARTMENT
   WITH THE SARCOPHAGUS
C ENCLOSURE WALL
D END OF THE CAUSEWAY
   FROM THE VALLEY TEMPLE
E ENTRANCE HALL
F COURTYARD
G ROOM WITH FIVE STATUE NICHES
H SANCTUARY
I STORAGE ROOMS FOR THE
   OBJECTS OF THE MORTUARY
   CULT
J SMALL SATELLITE PYRAMID

Merenre I

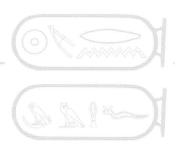

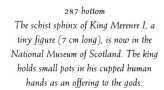

286 top
Although the texts on the lateral walls of the burial chamber of Merenre I have disappeared, the Pyramid Texts behind the sarcophagus are intact. The starry sky above revolved in the direction of the dead king to assist him in his resurrection.

286 bottom right
This unguent jar, of translucent calcite, is inscribed with the name of King Merenre I. A gift of the king, this type of jar, now in the Musée du Louvre, was valued more for its inscription than the perfume oil or unguent it contained.

286-287
This virtual reconstruction shows the entrance of the pyramid of Merenre I. Just before the three granite portcullises, shown here raised, an inscription reads: "As for anyone who shall lay a finger on this pyramid [...], his house will be nowhere; he will be one proscribed, one who eats himself." Drawing by EDF/Labrousse.

287 bottom
The schist sphinx of King Merenre I, a tiny figure (7 cm long), is now in the National Museum of Scotland. The king holds small pots in his cupped human hands as an offering to the gods.

Merenre, 'He Whom Re Loves,' adopted as his Horus-name Ankh-khau, 'The Living Apparition.' It seems that Merenre I's reign was brief—no more than eleven years were recorded—but it is widely documented.

The two most important events of his reign were a campaign in the south to subject Lower Nubia, and the construction of the king's pyramid, both of which were completed. Once again it was the irreplaceable Uni who provides the facts: "His Majesty sent me to Ibhat [a quarry in the Nubian desert between the first and second cataracts] to bring back a sarcophagus and its lid and the *pyramidion* to be used on the pyramid called 'The Beauty of Merenre Appears.'

[Then] His Majesty sent me to Elephantine to retrieve a false door made of granite with its offering table for the same pyramid. I then returned north with six goods ships, three rafts, three other boats, and a single warship. Never in the past had a journey been made to Ibhat and Elephantine with a single warship."

Despite Uni's efforts, the early death of the king marked the end of the work on the funerary temple, the decoration of which was still in its early stages.

Only one of Merenre's queens is known of with certainty: Ankhesenpepy II, the widow of Pepy I. It is probable that he also married his half-sister, Neit. After her husband's death, Neit was to marry Pepy II.

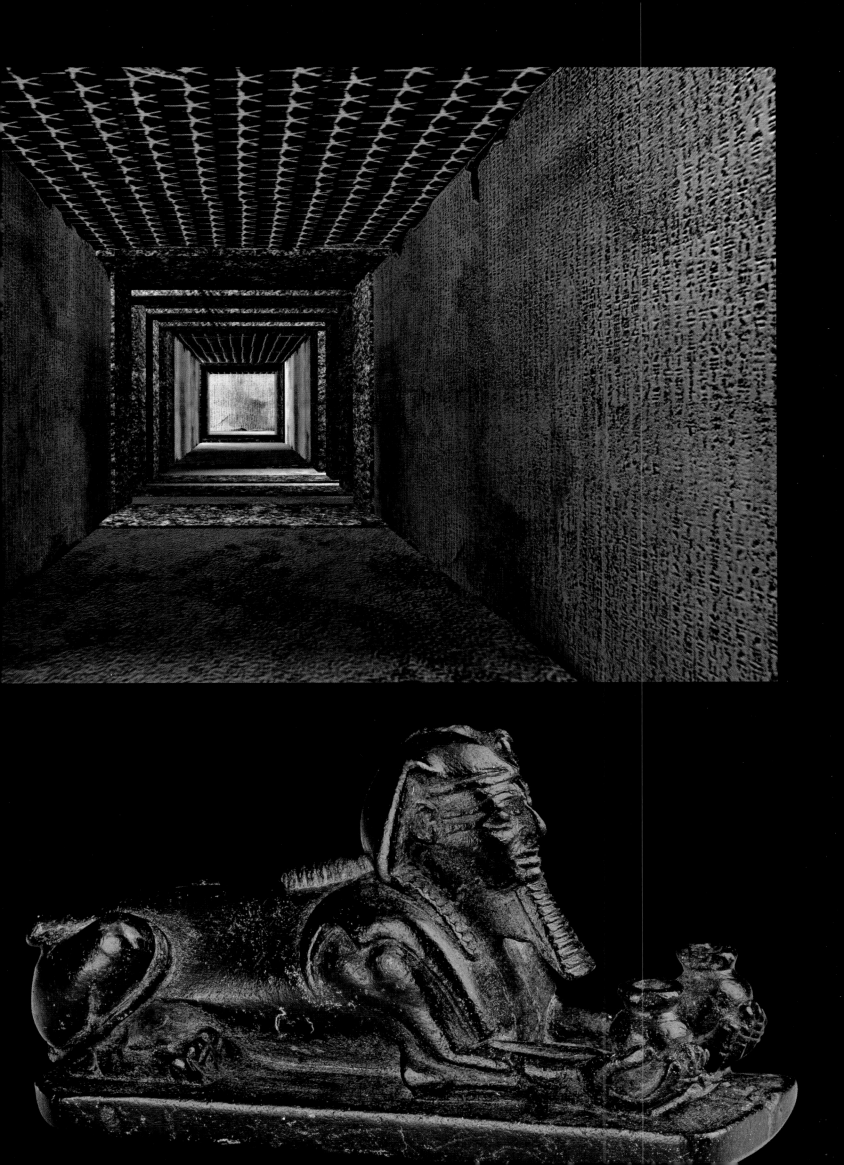

Pepy II

288 top
This charming calcite statuette of King
Pepy II as a child represents the king
naked, squatting, with one hand (now
broken) held to the mouth. The child
does not wear the side-lock of youth,
but short-cropped hair with a uraeus
on his forehead.

288-289
The last pyramid of the Old Kingdom to
be discovered was that of Pepy II, whose
over-long administration ended with the
disorder of the earliest revolution in
Egypt, called the First Intermediate
Period by Egyptologists.

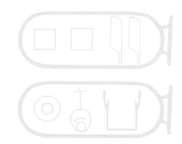

289 top and center
The antechamber and burial chamber
of the pyramid of Pepy II are covered
with Pyramid Texts: "The king's
lifetime is eternity, his limit is
everlastingness, in this his dignity of, if
he wishes, he does; if he dislikes, he
does not. He who is at the limits of the
horizon for ever and ever."

289 bottom
The drawing at left is a reconstruction
of the mortuary complex of Pepy II and
of three queens, by J.-Ph. Lauer, the
drawing on the right shows the
necropolis of Pepy II.

Pepy II took as his Horus name, Netjer-khau, 'Divine of Appearances.' According to Manetho, Pepy II "began to govern at the age of six and continued until his hundredth year," thus having the longest reign in history. This claim should be taken with a pinch of salt, as Queen Ankhesenpepy II, the widow of Merenre I, acted as regent until he came of age, and the last documented year of his reign is the sixty-sixth. It is reasonable, therefore, to suppose that the king died at seventy-two years of age.

Provincial high officials of this time left many autobiographical texts that document dangerous expeditions to the south. One of the most famous is that of Herkhuf, who reproduces a copy of a letter sent by Pepy II regarding a pygmy that was brought back for the pleasure of the king, who then was ten years old:

"You said [...] that you have brought back a pygmy from the land of the inhabitants of the eastern horizon for the dances of the god, like the dwarf that the treasurer of the god Urdjededba brought back from the country of Punt at the time of Isesi. You said to My Majesty that never before had one like him been brought back by anyone who had visited Iam [...]. Come quickly by boat to the Residence. Leave the others and bring with you this pygmy whom you report to be alive, healthy, and safe from the land of the inhabitants of the horizon for the dances of the god and to cheer the heart of the King of Upper and Lower Egypt, Neferkara, may he live forever! If he embarks with you, position able men that are with him on either side of the boat so he cannot fall in the water. If he sleeps, at night, let able men sleep next to him in his cabin. Check on him ten times each night.

THE NECROPOLIS OF KING PEPY II

A	VALLEY TEMPLE	F	PYRAMID OF QUEEN MOTHER NEIT
B	CAUSEWAY	G	PYRAMID OF QUEEN IPUT II
C	MORTUARY TEMPLE	H	PYRAMID OF QUEEN UDJEBTEN
D	PYRAMID OF PEPY II		
E	SATELLITE PYRAMID		

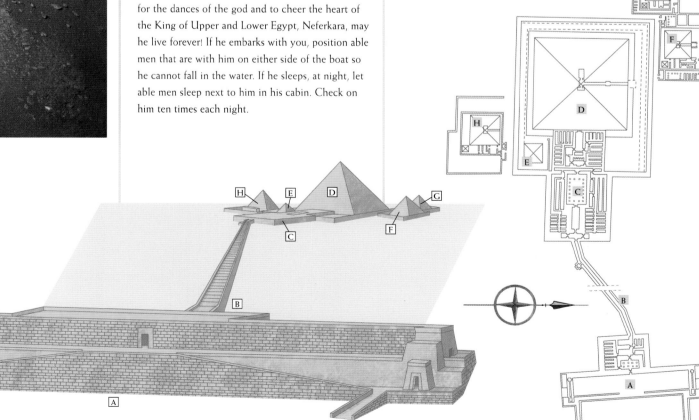

"My Majesty wishes to see this pygmy more than the products of the quarries of Punt. If you arrive at the Residence with this pygmy alive, healthy, and safe, My Majesty will give you a larger reward than was given to the treasurer of the god Urdjededba, at the time of Isesi, and equivalent to the desire of My Majesty to see this pygmy."

Another venture, which had the aim of importing African goods, was less successful. Its leader, Mekhu, died during the expedition. His remains were brought back to Egypt on a later journey, thanks to his son.

Pepy II's funerary complex was explored during the 1930s and published by the Swiss Egyptologist, G. Jéquier, to whom is owed the discovery and restoration of the most complete set of low reliefs from Sixth Dynasty. Three smaller pyramids that ringed Pepy II's pyramid, called 'The Life of Pepy Abides,' have been unearthed. They belonged to three of Pepy's wives: the queens Neit, Iput II, and Udjebten, and their funerary apartments are decorated with Pyramid Texts.

MERENRE II

Manetho and the Canon of Abydos give the king after Pepy II, as Merenre II. The ephemeral reign of Merenre lasted no longer than a year. In all probability he was the son of Pepy II and it has been hypothesized that his mother was Neit. His burial place is unknown.

NETJERKARE SIPTAH

It has been proposed that the king Netiqerty Siptah who appears in a new restoration of the king list in Turin as the successor to Merenre II, the king Netjerkare referred to in the Canon of Abydos, and the famous queen Nitocris referred to by Manetho and Herodotus are one and the same person. Although the Turin papyrus and the Abydos Canon are contemporary, the name Netjerkare found in the Abydos list may have been transformed into the Netiqerty of the Turin papyrus, and in turn become Nitocris during the Greek period.

This sovereign took the name Netjerkare, read incorrectly as Netiqerty, as a coronation name, but bore the name 'Siptah' at birth. The fact that the name 'Ṣiptah' is masculine means that the obscure 'Nitocris' must be regarded as a man, Netjerkare Siptah, in spite of the more than two thousand year-old belief perpetuated by the classical authors that the last pharaoh of the Sixth dynasty was a queen.

Netjerkare was the last king in the Sixth Dynasty, but to establish the precise end of the Old Kingdom is not easy. Should it, for example, be taken back to the middle of Pepy II's reign when the slow decline of regal authority set in? Or should it be the end of the Sixth Dynasty? And did the complex succession to King Netjerkare take place naturally without any break, or was it generated by the various crises experienced by Egypt during that period?

The five golden centuries of the pyramids of the Old Kingdom came to an end here. How could such a brilliant civilization, able to build for eternity and supported by a glorious succession of theological and royal successes, fade away into the dark period referred to as the First Intermediate Period? The causes of the decline of the Old Kingdom remain uncertain but were undoubtedly multiple. Associated with the impoverishment of the pharaonic administration as a result of donations and favors handed out since the pharaohs of the Fourth Dynasty, there was a diminishment in royal authority which originated during the long reign of Pepy II, and which was accompanied by an increase in the power of local governors and exacerbated by the climatic change that caused gradual desertification of the plateaus that lined the Nile valley.

The end of the Old Kingdom—one of the most glorious periods in the history of mankind—brought a marked alteration to the spirits and minds of the Egyptians. Its dramatic consequences were expressed in a famous document, the Ipuwer Papyrus:

"Events have taken place that had never occurred since the dawn of time: the King has been deposed by the rabble! He Who had been buried as a Falcon was brutally dragged out of his sarcophagus! The burial chamber in the pyramid was profaned! And now a handful of incompetent men in the government of the kingdom has managed to deprive the country of its royalty."

291 center and bottom
This headrest in ivory inscribed with the name of Pepy II is a rare example of a head support retaining the curve of the elephant tusk it is made from. The inscription says: "The King of Upper and Lower Egypt, Neferkare, the Horus, the One of the Two Ladies, Divine of Appearances, the Horus of Gold, given Life and Strength, like Re." Now in the Musée du Louvre.

290
In the courtyard of the mortuary temple of Pepy II, the decorated pillars are carved with double-figured groups showing the king embraced by gods, as here by Horus.

291 top left
The pyramid of Pepy II shows the details of its construction, with steps made of retaining walls of irregular stones set in mud and encased in blocks of limestone.

291 top right
The door of the mortuary temple of Queen Iput II is turned toward the pyramid of Pepy II.

The Architecture of the Pyramid Complexes of the Queens during the Sixth Dynasty

In the Sixth Dynasty, the evolution of pyramids built in honor of the queens came to a halt, fixing what might be termed a classical model The tomb of a queen was placed at the foot of that of her king-consort with the entrance generally facing the pyramid of the king. Lying east-west, in other words, progressing from the land of the living to that of the dead, a temple dedicated to the funerary cult was built against the small pyramid that held the mummy of the dead queen, but the monumental complex was given neither a temple down in the valley nor a processional ramp.

The queens' temples reflected on a smaller scale those of the kings, both in organization (function and layout) and architecture (doors and pillars). The funerary temple was divided into a front section, comprising an entrance hall and a courtyard with porticoes, and a smaller temple, consisting of a sanctuary and a room fitted with niches for statues. The sanctuary was the most important element of the temple and was aligned with the center of the pyramid and burial chamber. Any of the elements may have had a vestibule or an antechamber, or even a storage area. Finally, a miniature satellite pyramid stood in the southeastern corner of the enclosure wall.

The queens' pyramids measure roughly 21 meters on each side and in height (that is, with an inclination of 2/1 or 63°), and correspond to approximately one fourteenth of the surface area of the king's pyramids, and one tenth their volume. The entrance to the funerary apartment lies in the middle of the north face of the pyramid. A complex such as this was based on the kings', but it seems that no walls in the queens' complexes were decorated with Pyramid Texts before the end of the Sixth Dynasty.

The Decoration in the Funerary Temples of the Queens

The queens' funerary temples were usually decorated in the same manner as the temples of their husbands. The general theme of rituals and offerings was inspired by the idea of eternal life, but the decorations differed from those in the kings' temples in that the latter were more elaborate, further reinforcing the power of his sovereignty and his victory over chaos. Flanked by small obelisks, the representations on the queen's entrance doorway were accompanied by her titles and her name. The scenes in the entrance hall portray the queen standing on a small dais as she makes offerings to the goddesses Hathor and Bastet. In exchange, she is given the scepter that confirms her divinity and power. On the low reliefs in the court, the queen is present at the procession

The Queens' Pyramids

of her properties, which are personified by women bearing products of their lands and preceded by the name of the dominion in question. The queen also receives the homage of her servants, who present herds and offerings destined for the funerary cult in the sanctuary.

The room with the niches for the statues was the setting for a daily ritual. Openings in the east wall allow early morning sunlight to brush the statues, which infused them with life during the celebration. The central niche very probably held a statue of the queen, while the side niches held those of the goddesses. The low reliefs on the walls show the queen officiating over ceremonies in worship of these goddesses.

RECENT DISCOVERIES AT SOUTH SAQQARA

Since its creation in 1963 by Professor Jean Leclant, the French Archaeological Mission in Saqqara has investigated and studied the pyramids decorated with texts in the royal necropolis of Memphis. These are the same pyramids in whose funerary apartments Gaston Maspero had discovered the Pyramid Texts at the end of the nineteenth century, the purpose of which was to ensure the immortality of the sovereign.

After the pyramid complex of Pepy I in south Saqqara had been explored and restored, twelve hectares of land, in which the necropolis of the royal family was thought to lie, remained to be examined. The queens' pyramids built during the following reign of Pepy II—and which lay close to the burial place of the king at the extreme south of Saqqara—had already revealed a further series of Pyramid Texts in the 1930s. How had the queens of previous pharaohs been treated?

292 top
This papyrus thicket marked the transition between the Valley, the world of the living, and the arid upland, the world of the dead. This representation from the temple of Ankhesenpepy II culminates in a geometrical abstraction of timeless, even modern appearance.

292 center and bottom
Queen Mother Ankhesenpepy II, wearing the vulture crown, as represented on the low reliefs of the courtyard of her mortuary temple. This remarkable queen, wife of two kings, mother of a third, was regent during the childhood of her son.

292-293
In this virtual restoration of the necropolis of Pepy II, the comparison of the pyramid of the king with those of the queens seems modest: their surfaces and volumes represent about only one tenth of the pyramid of the pharaoh. Drawing by EDF/Labrousse.

THE NECROPOLIS OF THE ROYAL FAMILY OF PEPY I

Since the discovery of the two small pyramids to the south of the pyramid of Pepy I in 1988, the excavation work by the French Archaeological Mission in Saqqara has unearthed an incredibly closely-packed area reserved for members of the royal family. The places in the history of the Sixth Dynasty of five of the six currently-known queens of Pepy I are confirmed by the pyramids of Inenek/Inti, Nubunet, and Ankhesenpepy II and the inscriptions that mention queen Mehaa and a "wife of Pepy I, elder daughter of a king." To these can be added the pyramids of two later queens, Ankhesenpepy III (a wife of Pepy II) and Meretites II (a wife of a king Neferkare). In addition, inscriptions on various dispersed blocks make mention of another queen, Nedjeftet, whose consort remains unknown.

If an attempt is made to reconstruct the chronological evolution of the necropolis, the earliest tomb was very probably that of Inenek/Inti, a consort of Pepy I. The two granite uprights in the entrance to her temple, which stands opposite that of her husband, are inscribed with her name, alternately Inenek and Inti. The queen is shown seated as she sniffs a lotus flower. On either side of the entrance, two gray limestone obelisks, painted red to imitate the more highly valued granite, show the queen standing, accompanied by her name (either Inenek or Inti) and by some interesting elements that form part of her titles. The variety of her roles is evidence of her importance; she bore the title of vizier, an exceptional position for a woman.

So far, only the pyramid and part of the temple with the entrance to the complex have been excavated in the funerary complex of Pepy's consort Nubunet, which lies to the east, against that of Inenek/Inti. The entrance gate, of which almost all the components have been identified and repositioned, also faced the king's pyramid. The queen is shown on either upright of the gate, with her face framed by a voluminous three-part wig, wearing a sheath-like dress with shoulder straps and a large necklace. One hand lies naturally down her side while the other holds a lotus flower that the queen sniffs. Her main title and name are given: "Bride of the King, the One He Loves, Nubunet."

Heading west down 'Queens' Street,' one reaches the southwest corner of the enclosure wall of the king's pyramid, where there stands a building as yet uncleared. On the entrance, an inscription in columns lies over the name and representation of Hornetjerikhet, the son of Pepy I. The prince, who most probably died before ascending to the throne, is accompanied into the tomb by his mother, Queen Mehaa, another of Pepy's wives who, until the discovery of this inscription, had been unknown.

Near this tomb, but unfortunately outside the area of study, the tip of a small obelisk has been found, which, it is supposed, stood opposite its twin at the entrance to a queen's funerary complex. Carved in columns on the obelisk are three of the titles of one of Pepy I's wives—"Bride of the King"—a title associated with the name of the pyramid belonging to Merire/Pepy, "The Beauty of Merire Abides," followed by "First-born Daughter of the King" (or "of a king").

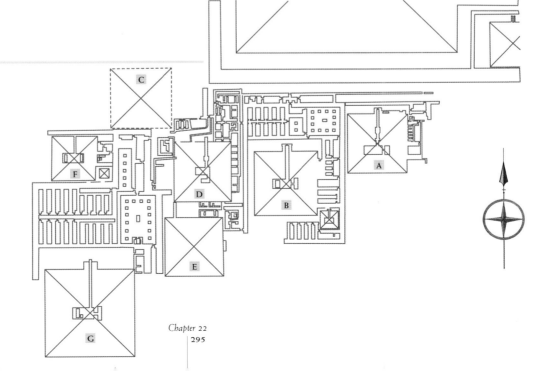

296 left
An extraordinary portrait of Queen
Mother Ankhesenpepy II represented as
regent, with her son Pepy II sitting on
her knees. It is the first known example
for this rare type of royal statuary: one
must wait more than eight centuries
before finding an equivalent in the New
Kingdom. Now in the Brooklyn
Museum of Art.

296 top right
The presence of the Pyramid Texts in the
pyramid of Queen Mother
Ankhesenpepy II is a major revelation.
For the first time, a queen receives this
great privilege, which opened the way to
eternity for her.

296 bottom right
The lintel of the entrance door
of the mortuary temple of the queen
mother Ankhesenpepy II is here shown
at the time of its discovery. This large
granite monolith, which weighs about
17 tons, is on the scale of a monument
made for a king.

The Queens' Pyramids

Also close to Hornetjerikhet's tomb lies a large granite architrave that weighs seventeen metric tons. It is inscribed with the titles of the famous queen mother, Ankhesenpepy II, the mother of Pepy II. The size of the architrave suggests that the funerary complex of the queen mother stood close by and indeed, much was revealed by further investigations.

So far only part of Ankhesenpepy II's monument has been cleared of sand. A few blocks belonging to the walls of the courtyard have been retrieved, which are carved with excellent decoration. Many of the blocks have been fitted together, thereby allowing the reconstruction of an important scene: the queen stands on a boat preceded by a small female named Neit. Although nothing exists to suggest that this figure is the same as Queen Neit, the wife of Pepy II (whose pyramid in south Saqqara is well known), it is an attractive hypothesis that the mother is shown here with her daughter.

Besides the aesthetic interest of the blocks found in the temple of the queen mother, their decoration has been of enormous historical value. One of the inscriptions is of fundamental importance to understanding the familial relationships of the kings at the end of the Sixth Dynasty: Queen Ankhesenpepy II must have married her nephew, Merenre I, who was the son of Ankhesenpepy I, her sister or half-sister. But who, then, was the father of Pepy II? Pepy I or Merenre I?

The survey of this sector reveals the original layout designed by the royal architects, who grouped the tombs of the king's family around his monument. However, the initial design seems to have been modified soon after: three pyramids, not in the original plan and belonging to figures from later than Pepy I's reign, have been forced into the composition of the necropolis; they are those of Ankhesenpepy III (a wife of Pepy II), Queen Meretites II (the wife of a King Neferkara), and an anonymous person.

Ankhesenpepy III's funerary complex is wedged into a narrow area to the east of the pyramid. The temple is as simple as possible, with a tiny satellite pyramid to the south. The pyramid itself is of modest size (30 cubits per side as opposed to the 40 of earlier queens) and it has a simplified layout inside. The sarcophagus was cut out of an enormous block of pudding stone sunk in the western side of the floor in the burial chamber; a line of shallow hieroglyphs runs inside the sarcophagus giving the queen's titles. The same banded configuration exists in the walls of the burial chamber. Both legends define the queen as the daughter of Merenre I and wife of Pepy II. However, there is no inscription of the Pyramid Texts in this monument. This absence creates confusion in that as far as is currently known, Ankhesenpepy III is the only one of Pepy II's consorts not to have benefited from the famous wall inscriptions in her tomb.

This discovery has raised more questions than it has solved. Why was Ankhesenpepy III not buried close to her consort Pepy II, as was the custom, but next to the queen mother, Ankhesenpepy II? Perhaps because the queen mother, then regent, held power? Perhaps because she was to be buried close to her mother, Ankhesenpepy II, who we know was a wife of Merenre I? Why are there no Pyramid Texts in Ankhesenpepy III's tomb? As Pepy II's last wife, Ankhesenpepy should have received the same treatment as the wives that preceded her. Did the brief phenomenon of the inscription of Pyramid Texts in the tombs of the queens die out during Pepy II's reign?

Two pyramid complexes lie between the tombs of queens Inenek/Inti and Ankhesenpepy II, occupying a transit area in the necropolis. One of these, temporarily called the 'West Pyramid,' constitutes the beginning of the series of discoveries that began in 1988. Sadly, the considerable material found in the pyramid—including a stuccoed and gilded wooden sandal—bore no name. The external funerary structure stretching northward, made from mud bricks, is unusually long and narrow and was subject to many modifications. Investigations in progress immediately to the south of the West Pyramid have revealed a further pyramid. An enormous funerary stela weighing more than 12 metric tons has been restored and stands once more in the sanctuary that lines the east side of the pyramid. Its inscription reveals the existence of a Queen Meretites II, the daughter (or more probably a descendant) of Pepy I and consort of a King Neferkare. Elements have also been found of a five-pillar court decorated with figures of the queen, with text giving her name and some of her titles.

Despite the exceptional historic value of the monuments so far uncovered, a new set of Pyramid Texts was not found; however, the discovery of the funerary complex of Queen Mother Ankhesenpepy II raised hopes once more. Soon the site of her ruined pyramid was identified and excavation of the immense crater of sand and detritus allowed the remains of the west and north walls of the queen's burial chamber to be reached. What a happy reward after so many years of patient work! Inscribed and painted in a beautiful green color that symbolized eternity, were passages taken from the Pyramid Texts. In a short time, roughly 1200 inscribed fragments were found on the site, and Ankhesenpepy II's sarcophagus was still in its place, though unfortunately it had been broken into by tomb robbers.

The discovery of this new pyramid bearing Pyramid Texts is an extraordinary one. Only the pyramids of the three queens of the last pharaoh of the Old Kingdom had been inscribed with them: those of queens Neit, Iput II, and Udjebten. The discovery of their existence in the previous generation (in the pyramid of Ankhesenpepy II, the mother of Pepy II) is a revelation. For the first time, a queen received the privilege of the Pyramid Texts, which were believed to allow her to pass on the road to eternity.

Was it her position as royal consort that brought Ankhesenpepy II this honor? The queen's extraordinary importance as the wife of two pharaohs, the mother of a third, and the regent during the childhood of her son made her an uncommon woman. The size of her funerary complex and many of the characteristics of her tomb suggest that she was buried as a king.

The excavations conducted in the necropolis of the royal family of Pepy I should provide further knowledge of a period of Egyptian history that is as yet little understood. The end of the Sixth Dynasty, the last dynasty of the Old Kingdom, occurred immediately prior to the First Intermediate Period and the collapse of centralized royal authority. At the end of the reign of Pepy II, son of Ankhesenpepy II, social and religious disorder put an end to the golden age of the pyramids. The continuation of the excavation of the tomb of the queen mother Ankhesenpepy II and the collection of funerary monuments in the necropolis of Pepy I is particularly promising. It will throw more light on this period of change in which a new social class won the right to express itself and to exercise power at the start of a new millennium.

The Decorative Program of Old Kingdom Pyramid Complexes

by Zahi Hawass

Simple stelae bearing a royal name that were erected outside the kings' tombs of the Early Dynastic Period developed, over the course of the Old Kingdom, into an elaborate decorative program, designed to both ensure a successful afterlife for the king and to maintain the proper order of the cosmos. This development can be traced from scenes of the royal *sed* festival seen in the Third Dynasty complex of Djoser, reliefs found in the early Fourth Dynasty complexes of Sneferu and fragments of relief from the temples of Khufu, to the standard decorative program of the pyramid complexes of the Fifth and Sixth Dynasties.

Decorative scenes appear in the earliest pyramid complex, that of the Third Dynasty king Djoser Netjerikhet. Niches under both the Step Pyramid itself and the south tomb depict the king wearing the white crown, a kilt, and the bull's tail and holding the flail while he performs. These represent ceremonies that were performed at the *sed* festival, where the king's right to rule was renewed and he celebrated the accomplishments of his reign.

Important wall reliefs were found in the lower temple of the Bent Pyramid complex of Sneferu, the first king of Fourth Dynasty, at Dahshur. The entryway into the temple is decorated with sculpted friezes on the eastern and western walls. The western frieze depicts the royal estates of Upper Egypt, which are represented as female offering bearers with the names of specific estates on their heads. The eastern frieze is similar, but the estates represented are in Lower Egypt. Above these registers are scenes representing the king in front of different gods. The

walls of the portico were also adorned with representations of personified royal estates. Some of the pillars of the portico were decorated with scenes of the *sed* festival, with the king wearing his *sed* robe and the crown of Upper Egypt while holding the flail, or wearing a kilt and dancing, again holding the flail. Other pillars depict the king making ceremonial visits to important religious sites, standing in front of the gods, or being embraced by a lioness-headed goddess. There are six niches within the temple. Above the opening to each niche are carved the names of the king, flanked by emblems and stars representing the night sky.

Fragmentary wall reliefs from the complex of Khufu have been found at Giza, and also at Lisht, where they were taken to be used as fill in a pyramid of the Twelfth Dynasty. The reliefs from Giza represent the *sed* festival; fragments from Lisht show processions of personified funerary estates, foreign captives, representations of ships, scenes including animals, and *sed* festival scenes. A fragmentary depiction of the *sed* festival from Khufu's complex, which includes a white hippopotamus, was discovered built into the wall of a staircase inside Bab al-Futuh in Cairo. According to Herodotus, the causeway of Khufu was carved with figures.

Few or no wall reliefs have been discovered from the complexes of Khufu's successors: Djedefre at Abu Rawash, and Khafre and Menkaure at Giza. It seems to me that the statues found in all of these pyramid complexes served the same purpose as the wall reliefs found in other complexes. In general, these statues represent the king in the company of various gods and goddesses.

298 bottom
This Fifth Dynasty relief in the tomb of Niankhkhnum and Khnumhotep at Saqqara shows a few artisans working on some funerary equipment.

299
Relief from the south tomb in the Step Pyramid complex of Djoser in Saqqara, showing King Djoser running in the sed-festival. Third Dynasty.

Decorative ▲ Program

Substantial quantities of wall relief have been found in the pyramid complexes of Sahure of the Fifth Dynasty and Pepy II of the Sixth Dynasty. These reliefs give us a good idea of the decorative scheme that became standard in the late Old Kingdom.

In the first portico of the lower temple of Sahure are a number of scenes. On the north wall, the king is shown hunting. On the south wall are scenes of the *sed* festival, with the king seated, wearing his robe, and holding a flail in his hand; in front of him are priests. There are also scenes of gods and goddesses, and depictions of the king in hunting and fishing, and the king giving offerings to the gods. The king is shown here in large scale, holding arrows. There are also scenes that show Asiatics with foreign pottery; animals and birds; the king, accompanied by his courtiers, witnessing the departure of twelve seafaring ships to a land whose name is not written; and scenes of the king and his courtiers watching the return of the ships laden with cargo and carrying a group of Asiatics, who are not prisoners, but are connected with trade or diplomacy. Additional scenes show the gods Horus and Anubis bringing gifts to the king.

appears again in the upper temple of Pepy II, even though the two kings are separated by a period of almost two hundred years.

Thus, the scenes did not necessarily record historical events from the lifetime of the king, but instead served a symbolic and religious purpose designed to ensure the divinity of the king and through him, ensure the proper functioning of the Egyptian world. The basic program, repeated from one complex to another, was designed to maintain the cosmos and provide for the afterlife of the king.

The wall decoration seen in Old Kingdom

the form of a great sphinx trampling Libyans and Asiatics.

Sahure's causeway repeats some of the scenes from the lower temple, but with different gods and goddess. Recently discovered blocks depict the celebrations associated with the placing of the pyramidion on top of the pyramid, and include dancers, wrestlers, and processions of priests and officials, as well as a group of emaciated Bedouin from the area where stone for the pyramidion was quarried being brought to court for judgment.

On the walls of the upper temple are processions of royal estates, depictions of the king

The same types of subjects are represented in the pyramid complex of Pepy II and in fragmentary reliefs from some of the other late Old Kingdom complexes. Each component, such as lower temple, causeway, and upper temple has its own repertoire of scenes, but the scenes themselves are repeated from one complex to another. Scenes could even be copied exactly from one complex to another. For example, one scene from the complex of Sahure shows the king smiting a captured Libyan chieftain on the head while the chieftain's two sons and wife watch and beg for forgiveness. Exactly the same scene, down to the names of the wife and sons,

pyramid complexes can be divided into several categories:

1. Scenes of domination

These portray the king imposing his will and might on disorderly elements of the universe, such as wild creatures or foreigners. Scenes that show the king hunting or fishing in the marshes, hunting in the desert, or smiting his enemies belong to this category. Also included here are scenes of ships sailing to visit foreign countries.

2. Scenes of the king's identification with the gods

The function of these scenes is to show the king

as Horus in the company of the gods and goddesses of Egypt. The king makes offerings to these divinities (one of his principal duties as ruler). They in turn reciprocate by offering affection and the right to rule.

3. *Sed*-festival scenes

In these scenes, the king can be in his palaces, with his officials and courtiers or in his *sed* chapel, wearing the crown of Upper and Lower Egypt. He wears a robe and carries the flail to show his kingship and his power over Upper and Lower Egypt. Other scenes show him performing a dance

shows the king receiving offerings and divinity from the gods. He is accepted by all the gods and becomes equal to them, because he has accomplished what they required for him to do on earth; he is now a god.

These scenes are repeated from one royal temple in the pyramid complex to another and can also be repeated within each temple as well. The decorative program in each complex, which also includes statuary, ritual objects, and architectural elements, was designed to confirm the perfect nature of each king's governance and the special

to celebrate his success and his good government, and to show that he has accomplished what the gods required of him.

4. Offering scenes

The guarantee of proper offerings was important to the success of the funerary cult. Many scenes show processions of offering-bearers, including personified estates from the royal domains in Upper and Lower Egypt. Many scenes also include courtiers and officials of the king.

5. Offerings from the gods to the king

This is the last scene in the sequence of the wall reliefs. It always occurs in the offering room and

relationship this created between the king and the gods, culminating in his deification.

The study of the wall reliefs and other elements in the pyramid complex demonstrates the fundamental purpose of the pyramid complex: to accommodate the worship of the king as Horus during his life and as the sun god Re after death. Associated with him in these complexes is the queen as the goddess Hathor. By performing the appropriate rites and accomplishing what was required of them both by the gods and as gods, the royal couple also assured the proper functioning of the Egyptian world.

300-301
This nautical scene showing men clapping and celebrating on a ship, comes from the causeway of the pyramid of Unas at Saqqara, Fifth Dynasty.

The Tombs of the Fifth and Sixth Dynasties at Saqqara

by Karol Myśliwiec

Essential changes occurred in the administrative structure of the pharaonic state during the Fourth Dynasty, when the greatest pyramids were built. This enormous technical and artistic effort, engaging the people of the entire country, required not only a high degree of human skill, but also perfect organization. As a result of this development, the Fifth Dynasty inherited thousands of specialized builders, artisans, scribes, and administrators of various rank. The highest positions in the social hierarchy, like that of the vizier, were more and more frequently occupied by people who did not belong to the royal family. Among the most important people of the Sixth Dynasty were the *nomarchs*, chief administrators of Egypt's many provinces (*nomes*). Their monumental, usually rock-hewn tombs,are found at such remote Upper Egyptian sites as Aswan, Akhmim, Edfu, and Dendera; elite tombs, in this case of mud brick, have also been found at Balat in the Dakhla Oasis. The walls of these tombs are decorated with hieroglyphic inscriptions, including biographic texts which are of primary importance to the history of the late Old Kingdom. These monuments bear witness to the decentralization of the Egyptian state at the end of the Old Kingdom. Scholars tend to interpret a centrifugal trend in the administration as the main factor leading to the fall of royal power at the end of the Sixth Dynasty. At the same time, diminishing humidity affected Egyptian agriculture, which was dependent on the annual inundation, and also caused a migration of nomads into the Nile Valley. This may have contributed to a general collapse of the country's economic prosperity, resulting in a loss of royal authority.

Whatever may be to blame for the disintegration of centralized power at the end of the Old Kingdom, one may observe a gradual weakening of the pharaoh and an increasing importance of his highest officials during the Fifth and Sixth Dynasties. This may be observed particularly well on their funerary monuments. Royal pyramids, i.e. the tombs of the pharaohs, become smaller and poorly constructed during this period, while the tombs of contemporary noblemen are often larger and more complex in plan and decoration than the non-royal burials of earlier times.

Like all earlier tombs of members of the upper classes, the sepulchres of Fifth and Sixth Dynasty

302 and 303 bottom
Details from the mastaba of Ti, who lived in the second half of Fifth Dynasty.

303 top
Long processions of offering bearers providing food and other items for the deceased are represented on the walls of late Old Kingdom mastabas. Two men depicted in the tomb of Ptahhotep bring lotus flowers, papyrus stems, a calf, and a ritual vase.

noblemen are essentially composed of two parts: a subterranean burial chamber and a superstructure having the shape of a bench (*mastaba* in Arabic). Both parts are connected by a rectangular vertical shaft varying in depth from tomb to tomb. Its upper part is built into the masonry of the superstructure, and its lower part is hewn into the rock. A sloping, descending corridor replacing the shaft in a few cases may be considered an archaizing feature, reminiscent of earlier Old Kingdom tombs. The *mastaba* is built of either limestone blocks or mud bricks, or else a combination of both materials. Another type of tomb popular in the second part of the Old Kingdom is a rock-hewn chapel with a mud-brick superstructure above it.

In the Memphite necropolis, the most important agglomerations of private tombs dating from the Fifth Dynasty are found at Abusir, Giza, Abu Rawash, and Saqqara. The courtiers of the following dynasty were mainly buried in various parts of Saqqara. Their *mastabas*, with unique reliefs decorating their walls, are today the greatest tourist attraction of the site. In general, the highest officials wanted to be buried close to the pyramid of the king they served. Their tombs, usually more sophisticated in their architecture and decoration than lesser *mastabas* found around this core cemetery, bear witness to a wealth and power without precedence in Egyptian history. This can be seen particularly in the funerary complex built for Ptahshepses, 'Overseer of All Construction Projects,' married to a daughter of King Niuserre (mid-Fifth Dynasty). This unique monument, found at Abusir in the vicinity of Niuserre's pyramid, constitutes a turning point in Egyptian tomb building. It became a model for generations of Old Kingdom noblemen and architects, particularly at Saqqara till the end of the Sixth Dynasty. Its dimensions (80 x 107 meters) are unprecedented. In addition, the most important elements of royal funerary monuments are found in its complex layout. From this moment on, imitations of royal architecture become a common feature of the *mastabas* built for the highest noblemen. Later tombs imitated not only the plan but also the decoration of royal tombs, incorporating many motifs invented in the royal workshops of the Fifth Dynasty for the funerary and solar temples of subsequent kings.

304 left
Another Ptahshepses was a prince who lived during the reign of Unas. His belt, made of gold, carnelian, obsidian, and turquoise, was found in a sarcophagus containing his mummy, near the valley temple of Unas's funerary complex. Egyptian Museum, Cairo.

304 right
The name Ptahshepses ('Ptah is noble') was popular among Memphite noblemen of the late Old Kingdom. One of them was a judge and inspector of bookkeepers, whose small statue (42 cm high), made of limestone, was found in his mastaba (C10) at Saqqara. The judge is represented as a scribe. His characteristic hairstyle denotes a sculpture from the Fifth Dynasty. Egyptian Museum, Cairo.

304-305
The huge mastaba of Ptahshepses at Abusir, a model for later tombs of the greatest noblemen at Saqqara, imitates the architecture of royal funerary complexes. It was built in three stages, and excavated by the Czechoslovak archaeological mission in the years 1960–74. In front of the entrance there is a pair of eight-stemmed lotus columns.

305 bottom
An altar court is the central element of Ptahshepses' mastaba. The rooms surrounding it include magazines, a chapel with statue niches, an offering room, and so on. Visible behind the mastaba is the pyramid of King Sahure.

306-307
*Harpooning hippopotami was a popular sport
for Egyptian men. It also conveyed the
symbolic meaning of victory over enemies. The
papyrus thicket represented in Mereruka's tomb
may be considered a handbook of Egyptian
zoology. Frogs and dragonflies cowering on
the weeds seem to follow the action.*

307 top
*Mereruka, chief justice and vizier in the reign
of Teti, has the largest of all the mastabas built
around this pharaoh's pyramid at Saqqara.
Two parts of his funerary complex are the
tombs of his wife Watetkhethor and son
Meryteti. The relief shows Mereruka wearing
a kilt, a short wig, and a broad collar, while
holding a staff and scepter in his hands.*

307 bottom
*Wit and humor are frequently found in the
work of the artists who decorated the
mastabas. Examining this aquatic scene in
Mereruka's tomb, the viewer is amused by
two unbelievable situations: the
hippopotamus devouring a crocodile and a
man catching the tail of a mongoose, one of
the fastest-moving animals in Egypt.*

Some architectural features of Ptahshepses'
funerary complex were later copied in the *mastabas*
of the highest officials at Saqqara. For exemple, a
room with a staircase leading to the roof of the
monument, inspired by similar structures of the
valley and pyramid temples, may be found in the
mastabas of Mereruka, Kagemni, Ankhmahor, and
Neferseshemre. Pillared courts, copies of similar
elements found in royal tombs until the reign of
Userkaf, appear in private tombs at Saqqara until
the middle of the Sixth Dynasty. Examples of this
kind of court are found in the *mastabas* of Ti,
Ptahhotep I, Akhtihotep, Kagemni, Mereruka, and

Khentika-Ikhekhi. Another feature reminiscent of
Ptahshepses' and royal funerary monuments are
multi-roomed magazine complexes found in
numerous *mastabas* at Saqqara, for example those
of Mereruka and Khentika-Ikhekhi. In spite of
these efforts to imitate the great Ptahshepses' tomb,
none of the noblemen buried at Saqqara till the end
of the Sixth Dynasty surpassed or even equaled his
architectural achievement, a complete and exact
miniature of royal funerary complexes. The largest
Old Kingdom *mastaba* at Saqqara, built for
Mereruka and containing twenty-nine rooms,
measures 'only' 48 x 81 m.

308-309 top
Scenes of fishing from papyrus skiffs with small nets and baskets, and netting fish with a dragnet occupy the lowest registers in a large tableau, where the deceased is represented with his wife, attendants, and scribes. The presentation of various fish species within the dragnet looks like an encyclopedia of Egyptian ichthyology.

308-309 bottom
Squatting scribes register on papyrus scrolls the offerings brought from estates across the entire land for the posthumous cult of Mereruka. Two men behind them conduct animals to the deceased, represented with his wife at the end of this scene.

309 top
The tender sensuality of the relationship between man and woman is rendered with simple gestures by the Egyptian artist.
The design of the body clearly differentiates the male and female beauty. Both genders could wear similar jewelry, bracelets for example. Noblemen are often represented with a piece of folded cloth held in one hand.

309 bottom
The lotus was associated with women from their earliest representations in the tombs of Egyptian noblemen. Seated in front of an offering table laden with half-loaves of bread, and smelling a lotus flower is the wife of Mereruka, who was of royal descent. An important part of his mastaba was reserved for her posthumous cult.

310 top
The burial chamber, accessible through a shaft hewn in the floor of a small room, contained the sarcophagus with the body of the deceased. The painted decoration of this room includes representations of offerings, as well as offering-lists and offering-texts.

310 center
Most of the decoration in the burial chamber is unfinished. The wall, where the artist left the figures and hieroglyphs in the preparatory drawing stage, contrasts with the final painting preserved above the entrance. Still visible in some places are traces of horizontal and vertical lines that guided the designer at the beginning of his work.

310 bottom left
Part of Mereruka's tomb was reserved for his son Meryteti, another chief justice and vizier. His monumental false door is accompanied by representations of Meryteti seated at a table, with offering lists, priests, and offering-bearers, sculpted on the lateral walls of his chapel.

310 bottom right
The long suite of rooms in the mastaba of Mereruka reminds one of a palace, but their irregular layout, supposed to fill a rectangular space, looks more like a labyrinth. Endless rows of offering bearers, as well as monotonous representations of the deceased, alternate with scenes of daily life in the reliefs decorating the walls.

311 top
On the north wall of the room with pillars, there is a niche containing a striding statue of Mereruka, sculpted in limestone. Thus he is supposed to approach the offering table placed in front of the niche, at the top of four steps. His two-dimensional figures decorate the walls and the pillars in this room.

311 bottom
Mereruka's brother Ihy has also been immortalized by the artist who decorated this tomb. The plump dignitary, seated in the middle of a papyrus skiff, enjoys a drink served by a male servant.

312-313
A long sequence of episodes shows the feeding and bringing of various animals. The lowest register shows the fattening of hyenas, while a group of artisans building boats is represented at the top. Watching the scenes are the vizier with his wife and his mother. On the left, he is escorted by his two sons.

Kagemni

314

The sledge was the vehicle used for transportation of heavy loads on land. Two teams, each consisting of four men, are shown dragging huge jars of oil and ointment on sledges while another man softens the ground by pouring water in front of each vehicle.

315 top

This representation of the tomb owner is a model example of the conventions characterizing the Egyptian artist's 'aspective' approach to nature. Some parts of the body are represented frontally and some in profile. The same attempt at 'objectivity' allowed him to represent the fingers and the position of the scepter in an utterly unnatural way. The male body was conventionally painted red.

315 bottom left

Kagemni, a chief justice and vizier, lived at the beginning of the Sixth Dynasty (reign of King Teti). His beautiful mastaba located near Teti's pyramid has a labyrinth of rooms. The west wall of one of them is a huge false door, missing its upper part.

315 bottom right

Kagemni standing in front of a long procession of offering bearers who occupy seven registers of the scene. The dignitary wears a panther skin whose tail is hanging between his legs.

Kagemni

Processions of offering-bearers walking
towards a false door are represented in
many registers on the long lateral walls
(here on the northern one) of the chapel.
They provide everything the deceased
needed in his afterlife: bread, meat,
poultry, baskets laden with fruit, and so
on, and they also lead various animals.

316 bottom left
Fragment of a marsh scene on the north
wall of the pillared hall, showing three
men in a papyrus skiff, one of whom is
netting fish wish a small net, while
another one is angling with a multi-
hooked line. The abundance and variety
of large fish is like a review of species,
typical of such scenes.

316-317
One of the favorite daily-life
scenes occurring in the decoration
of the mastabas was cattle fording
a canal. Young calves were carried
by men or attached to a papyrus
boat, as in the lower register of this
relief found in the tomb of
Kagemni.

318 left
This large statue of Ti (198 cm high), sculpted in limestone, was originally standing in his mastaba at Saqqara, and is now in the Egyptian Museum, Cairo. Its rigid shape contrasts with the fineness and naturalism of the reliefs decorating his tomb.

However, some architectural features found in the funerary complex of Ptahshepses became standard components of later *mastabas*. The tombs of the high officials all have a characteristic multi-roomed superstructure, but no two are exactly alike. Their layouts display many individualized solutions, often responding to the limits of available space. The large *mastabas* usually have an entrance portico, a pillared hall, a complex of storerooms, a *serdab* or hidden room for a statue of the deceased. An east-west oriented offering room, with a huge false door hewn into the room's western wall so that it faces east. This last element constitutes the most important part of a tomb's superstructure, even if that consists of only one room, for it connects the realm of the dead with that of the living.

The *mastabas* of the Fifth and Sixth Dynasties at Saqqara are concentrated in groups around the pyramids of the successive kings, but are also scattered all over the site. When the area surrounding the Step Pyramid of Djoser was re-adopted as a royal cemetery at the beginning of the Fifth Dynasty (the pyramid of Userkaf), some private tombs, partly of mud brick, were built at the western edge of the archaic necropolis. Further expansion of the cemetery continued in a southwesterly direction. The greatest

concentration of Fifth Dynasty *mastabas* is found to the northwest of the Step Pyramid enclosure (e.g. those of Ti, Ptahshepses (II), Ptahhotep, and Akhtihotep), and numerous late tombs of this dynasty are clustered around the pyramid complex of Unas. Many of these are rock-cut chapels or tombs partly hewn into the rock, like the 'Mastaba of Two Brothers' (Nyankhkhnum and Khnumhotep) from the second half of the Fifth Dynasty, or the tomb of the vizier Mehu dated to the first half of the Sixth Dynasty. The former still constitutes a puzzle to Egyptologists trying to fathom the nature of the relationship between the two 'overseers of manicurists of the Great House,' 'prophets of Re in the Sun-temple of Niuserre.' The symmetrical composition of certain scenes showing both of them, emphasizing their parallel social position, inspires some scholars to identify them as brothers (twins?) or close friends, but their intimate approach visible in some scenes leads other researchers to interpret the two men as lovers.

A number of small tombs, having only one or two rooms, are cut into the escarpment south of the causeway to Unas's pyramid or into the side of the 'dry moat' on the south of the Step Pyramid enclosure. Egyptian archaeologists started excavating

318 top right
Ti, an overseer of two pyramids and four sun temples, lived in the second half of the Fifth Dynasty. His gorgeous tomb, located northwest of the step pyramid, has an inner hall with two pillars and two false doors. One of these is visible in the photograph. Each side of both pillars is inscribed with the name and titles of the deceased.

318 center right
Unlike the burial chambers in other mastabas of the period concerned, the chamber housing the undecorated sarcophagus of Ti is accessible via a staircase leading from the floor of a pillared hall to a slanting passage.

318 bottom right
The bas-reliefs sculpted on the walls of Ti's mastaba belong to the masterpieces of ancient Egyptian art. They combine artistic elegance with technical perfection, as in this representation of a sail boat.

319
Leaning on a long staff and accompanied by his kneeling wife Neferhotepes, the chief hairdresser of the royal court, Ti, watches the animals led to him by his courtiers. The offerings are recorded by the scribes depicted in the lower register.

 *Ti*

320-321

Two standard motifs in agricultural scenes sculpted on the walls of the mastabas: a musician playing a long flute accompanies the men harvesting the crop (upper register), while a flock of sheep is guided across the sown area to trample the seed into the soft ground (lower register).

321 top

Two registers from a long sequence of harvest scenes depicted on the east wall of the offering chamber in the mastaba of Ti. Donkeys carrying wheat are seen in the lower register. Watching the scenes are Ti and his wife (not visible in the photograph).

321 bottom

Ti in papyrus thicket, standing in a papyrus skiff and watching the hippopotamus hunt performed by naked men from another skiff. Naturalistic features in the representation of the hunters, such as their frontal baldness and protruding bellies, characterize them as being from a lower class.

322 top
Ptahhotep II is here represented
as the eldest son of Akhtihotep,
and is busy registering the offerings
brought from the estates for the
posthumous cult of his father.
This relief can be admired on
the eastern wall in the hall of
Akhtihotep's tomb.

322 bottom
The mastaba of Ptahhotep, northwest of the
Step Pyramid, is a funerary complex built
for two Ptahhoteps and an Akhtihotep. The
latter was a son of Ptahhotep I, and the
father of Ptahhotep II. Each of them was a
chief justice and vizier at the end of the
Fifth Dynasty. Four pillars support
architraves in the tomb of Akhtihotep.

323
Ptahhotep ('Ptah is happy'), one of the
greatest noblemen of late Fifth
Dynasty, represented in bas-relief in
his mastaba at Saqqara. A broad
collar and a long necklace with an
amulet decorate his nude torso. His
name is written with hieroglyphs on the
wall in front of him.

Ptahotep

324 top

A kaleidoscope of genre scenes is represented
in seven registers on the east wall of the cult
chamber. Watching them is Ptahhotep with
his eldest son, also named Ptahhotep. Lively
episodes of fowling and fishing are depicted
in the two lowest registers.

324-325

The relief sculpted in the fourth register of
this panorama shows a hunt in the desert.
It surprises the viewer with its dynamism.
The fighting and copulating wild animals
are reminiscent of some scenes depicted in the
sun temples of the Fifth Dynasty.

325 top

At the right end of this scene, the hunter
lassoes one of two wild bulls running
beside an antelope. Represented in the
same register are also two hedgehogs,
one of which, leaving its abode,
devours a locust.

 *Irukaptah*

326-327
Irukaptah, the libationer and butcher of the king's repast, lived in the second half of the Fifth Dynasty. His rock-cut tomb, located immediately south of the causeway of Unas, has fourteen niches cut into three walls holding statues of the deceased.

327 top
Atop the east wall there is a sequence of scenes showing butchery. One of the

butchers skins an ox with a knife, another cuts into the entrails and uncovers the ribs, while a third holds the animal's rear legs.

327 bottom
Some of the statues, as well as the scenes and inscriptions decorating the walls, preserve their original polychromy. The group of hieroglyphs visible above this statue on the east wall belongs to a long inscription and reads ". . . in the western desert . . . ."

328 top left
Nefer ('The fair one') was an inspector of the singers in the reign of King Niuserre. Also buried in his tomb were his parents, Kahay and Meretites, for whom two false doors were sculpted in the west wall of the chapel. The inscriptions identify Kahay as a controller of the singers.

328 right
Some members of the household of Kahay are represented with their offering tables on the west wall of the chapel. The three men clad in leopard skin vestments and wearing short wigs are probably his sons. All of them are described as inspectors of the singers.

328 bottom left
Hewn into the rock of an ancient quarry facing the causeway of Unas, the tomb of Nefer, Meritites, and Kahay has a long L-shaped chapel and eleven shafts. One of these (the entrance of which is visible in the floor) leads to a burial chamber containing a sarcophagus with an intact male mummy.

329
Nefer and his wife approach their false door. The relief sculpted on the chapel's west wall shows the tomb owner holding a long staff and a scepter, while his consort holds a goose in her left hand. His name and titles may be read in the inscriptions framing the scene.

330 top
Four offering-bearers represented in relief above the false door of Meretites, on the chapel's west wall. The first burns incense, the next bearers bring a goose and a gazelle, the last one leads a calf.

330-331
A sequence of scenes depicting every day life occupies the east wall in the tomb chapel. It extends between large-size figures showing the tomb owner with his family members. Fishing with a seine and catching birds with the clap net are the motifs depicted in the lowest register.

331 top
One of the scenes in the marshes (upper register) shows the picking and carrying of papyrus by nude men with bald foreheads. They seem to carry this material for the construction of a papyrus boat that is represented in the next scene.

an important part of the necropolis, situated west of the pyramid of Unas, in 2001. Some recent discoveries are particularly worth mentioning: a small, but extremely interesting tomb built for Qar, the chief physician of the royal court at the end of Fifth Dynasty, and remains of two larger tombs. Although the wall paintings decorating the chapel in the doctor's tomb are badly damaged, an unusual discovery was made in its intact burial chamber. A set of medical instruments made of copper was found lying among some fifty vessels representing the highest quality of Old Kingdom pottery. Most of the vessels are inscribed with the name and title of the deceased, written with black ink on the smooth surface of a red slip. Some shapes are found in series of four similar types. Globular vessels, fired without a slip on the surface, are particularly numerous. These vessels may have contained liquid medicaments. Much bigger than these vessels is an amphora with two handles in the middle part of its body. Made of grayish-white marl clay, it represents the type of ware produced in Egypt, but imitating imports from Palestine.

Unique in their painted decoration are four round offering tables found in the same deposit. Preserved in many pieces that necessitated thorough conservation before any effort of reconstruction could be made, they are made of red clay having an almost metallic structure after firing. Each of them is provided with a small cylindrical foot, and the upper surface of each table bears an extremely fragile polychromatic painting representing various objects known from offering tables depicted on the walls of Egyptian tombs. Could it be one more register of the offerings connected with the posthumous diet of the deceased?

The Sixth Dynasty tombs are mainly grouped around the pyramids of the kings: Teti, located northeast of the Djoser pyramid enclosure, and the following Sixth Dynasty kings (for example Pepy I and Pepy II) in South Saqqara. Marking the beginning and the end of the dynasty, these two groups of *mastabas* are completely different in their shape. Thus, they illustrate the development of Egyptian society in the last century of the Old Kingdom. The Teti pyramid cemetery comprises many multi-roomed *mastabas* having a solid stone masonry superstructure with a rich and fine decoration on the walls. Among the tombs of this type are those of Mereruka, Kagemni, Neferseshemre, Ankhmahor, Khentka-Ikhekhi or Ptahshepses. They indicate a wealthy upper class, while the poor collective tombs found in South Saqqara, built of mud brick with a minimum of decoration, bear witness to a general impoverishment of Egyptian society at the end of the Old Kingdom. French archaeologists used to call these primitive *mastabas* 'tombes à fours' (tombs with furnaces), because their large brick vaults, used as relieving arches above stone roofing slabs, give them the appearance of bakers' ovens.

A new cemetery of Sixth Dynasty noblemen has recently been discovered by the Polish-Egyptian archaeological mission excavating west of the Djoser pyramid enclosure since 1987. Directly under a layer of sand housing hundreds of simple burials from the Ptolemaic Period, a sequence of broad terraces descending westward from the Djoser pyramid enclosure came to light. Hewn in the rock, their cliff ledges constitute long façades extending longitudinally and facing west, with entrances to many tombs of late Old Kingdom noblemen. The most beautiful of the funerary chapels unearthed so far belongs to vizier Merefnebef who lived in the first half of the Sixth Dynasty. Unlike other *mastabas* of the same period, the reliefs decorating this tomb preserve a great deal of their original polychromy. Many motifs, known from other tombs as well, have thus displayed their color for the first time. Unfortunately, this masterpiece of Egyptian art immediately provided a formidable challenge to the conservators. The local rock in which the reliefs are executed is extremely friable and contains a lot of salt that tends to concentrate on the surface of the painting. A team of conservators from the National Museum in Warsaw and Cracow has made every possible effort to save this unique decoration for posterity.

The tomb of Merefnebef, however, turned out to be an important historical source as well. Some unusual characteristics of the vizier and his tomb shed new light on turbulent times, where high officials increasingly usurped prerogatives of the king. First of all, the size of his mastaba was surprisingly small. It comprised only one cult room hewn in the rock, a mud-brick superstructure built partly of re-used bricks above the cult chapel, and a deep shaft hidden in the superstructure, behind the chapel's eastern wall, with a burial chamber at the bottom, more than ten meters below the chapel. This structure seems extremely modest when compared to the grand stone-built multi-roomed *mastabas* of other viziers at Saqqara. As Merefnebef's title of vizier is found almost exclusively in the façade of his cult chapel, one may presume that he ascended to this high function quite late in his career, when his modest tomb was almost finished. This promotion may have taken place as late as after the death of King Teti, perhaps in the short reign of his ephemeral successor Userkare, predecessor of Pepy I. In

this respect, the vizier's career would resemble that of the Great Judge Kagemni, whose biography is known from the inscription sculpted on the walls of his *mastaba* at Saqqara. After having served two subsequent kings, Djedkare-Isesi and Unas, he was promoted to the function of vizier by the next king, Teti I, at the latter's accession to throne. Some unfinished parts of the façade of the tomb of Merefnebef show that the ambitious, newly-rich noble feverishly started enlarging his tomb in order to make it more monumental, but death surprised him before he could fully satisfy his vanity.

The megalomania of Merefnebef may also be deduced from his three names, one of which (Unasankh) commemorates the last king of the Fifth Dynasty, while another one (Fefi) resembles that of the next dynasty's first ruler, Teti. Some titles of Merefnebef identify him as priest and administrator connected with the latter's pyramid.

Another unusual feature of his biography is the presence of at least four 'beloved wives,' who are repeatedly depicted as a quartet of harpists accompanying Merefnebef at various occasions. Still, his erotic appetite seems not to have been satisfied with this harem, since a fifth lady, depicted in large size at a most representative place, in the chapel's doorway, is shown in the same intimate position as one of the four wives in the parallel scene on the doorway's other wall. Since, very unusually, the beautiful lady is not labeled with any diagnostic title at all, and this scene possibly registers her only appearance in the tomb, it seems legitimate to think that she was a 'flame' who had passed away before the tomb was decorated.

But the joyful and frivolous atmosphere at Merefnebef's court must have changed dramatically after his death. Other scenes and texts decorating the walls of his cult chapel bear witness to a conflict that

ravaged his family, and particularly his progeny. Representations of his sons and the inscriptions accompanying them have purposefully been chiseled out, except for those of a younger son bearing his father's name, Fefi. He seems to have been the winner in the fight for heritage, and he was probably the iconoclast who ordered the figures and names of his brothers to be destroyed. It is presumably he and his wife who had a relief added later to the chapel's original decoration representations. This scene, executed on irregular stone slabs inserted into the wall and covered with a layer of gypsum, is completely different in style from the rest of the decoration. It represents a Merefnebef, probably the junior, whose wife Hemi does not appear in any other scene found in the tomb. Although it depicts a peaceful episode of fishery, this scene bears a silent witness to fervent fights between the sons of Merefnebef after his death.

This conflict seems to have had some political aspects as well, as may be suggested by another victim of the iconoclast's fury. This is a fragment of the inscription sculpted on both parallel walls of the doorway. Places where Merefnebef was described as "honored under the King" are thoroughly chiseled out, and one of the damaged reliefs preserves traces of a sarcastic epithet written later with black ink to replace the word 'King' with, 'The desert' (Honored under the desert). We do not know the identity of the king who favored this vizier, but the disgrace that became this monarch's share, possibly after his death, characterizes political and social unrest in the Egyptian capital toward the end of Old Kingdom. Similar damage is found in other tombs of the same period at Saqqara as well.

The multiplication of rooms in the *mastabas* of the Fifth and Sixth Dynasties has also increased the space on the walls decorated with reliefs and paintings. This created an unprecedented possibility for the artists to enlarge the repertoire of motifs that in earlier times were mainly limited to representations of the deceased and offering table scenes, as well as inscriptions enumerating the titles of the deceased and the offerings connected with his cult. Imitating the pattern invented for royal funerary and solar temples, Memphite sculptors of these two dynasties created a genuine world of naturalistic and lively scenes that, on one hand,

The cemetery located west of Djoser's pyramid has been excavated by the Polish-Egyptian mission since 1987. Remains of mud-brick superstructures belonging to late Old Kingdom mastabas were reused, two thousand years later, to house simple burials of the Ptolemaic Period.

The modest tomb of vizier Merefnebef, who lived in the first half of the Sixth Dynasty, has a rock-cut cult chapel with reliefs sculpted in the friable limestone. Represented on its south wall is the deceased with a lady watching the performance of half-nude female dancers.

336-337

offering-bearers, an offering table

336 bottom left

There are two false doors sculpted for
Merefnebef on his chapel's west wall.
Their spotted red-painted surface
imitates granite. Four registers of

represented in front of the deceased,
and an offering-list above the table,
preserve their brilliant original
polychromy.

Merefnebef fowling with a throw-
stick from a papyrus skiff is
represented on the chapel's east wall.

Particularly rich with colors and
full of dramatic tension is the
representation of animal life in front
of the vizier.

Merefnebef

336 bottom right
Here is a representation of fishing. The style and the technique of this tableau betray an addition to the original decoration. This relief may have been ordered by a son of the vizier, who was also named Merefnebef.

337 top
One of the natural life forms appearing in the papyrus thicket is a beautiful butterfly whose identity (Danaus chrysippus) remains beyond doubt.

register all possible details of daily life in those days, and, on the other, reflect Egyptian beliefs concerning life in the netherworld.

Although this art reveals thousands of individual solutions, and it would be difficult to find an exact copy of any motif, there are some strictly observed rules concerning the general concept of the decoration on the layout of particular scenes. On one hand, the motifs decorating the walls are connected with the function of certain rooms, and on the other, some elements are repeated in almost every room because of their magical meaning.

Among the motifs that fall into the latter category are the name of the deceased and his titles, as well as his representations. According to ancient Egyptian beliefs, each human being lived as long as his name and physical appearance were known, registered, and remembered. That is why, in the tomb of each important nobleman, his name and figure are repeated many times. The other scenes illustrate, sometimes in an extremely detailed way and often with a remarkable sense of humor, how the needs of the deceased were going to be satisfied in the netherworld. Of course, he had to be fed first of all. This required permanent offerings provided by priests of his funerary cult. Comprising all possible kinds of food—from bread, cakes, fruits, vegetables, meat and fowl, to various drinks, especially beer and wine—these offerings are listed and depicted together with other ritual items, for example sacred oils. Large-size representations of the deceased seated in front of an offering table that resembles a sumptuous 'still life,' usually accompany a false door, the most important place in each funerary chapel. This monumental stela, decorated with inscriptions containing names and titles of the deceased, as well as his representations, was always sculpted in or inserted into the western wall of the chapel. It was here that priests deposited offerings on a bench found in front of the stela, thus assuring the continuity of his life after death. Detailed lists of offerings, having the form of a square divided into small sections, each containing the name of one item, are usually sculpted above the 'still life.' Other scenes sculpted beside false doors often show long processions of offering-bearers bringing food, flowers and other,

mainly ritual objects. In multi-roomed *mastabas*, one also finds scenes representing various earlier stages of food preparation, such as hunting, fowling, fishing, harvesting, baking, as well as artisans and artists at work preparing jewelry, furniture, and other objects for the deceased.

Particularly interesting are the scenes showing a nobleman crossing the marshland in a papyrus boat. This was the very place where an artist could demonstrate his knowledge of Egyptian nature and deploy his creative imagination. Since he was trying to concentrate a maximum number of species in a single tableau, these representations often appear as a genuine encyclopedia of Nilotic zoology Sometimes, they were also masterpieces of sophisticated composition. With the deceased and his retinue shown on the background of a papyrus thicket, we participate in the tragedies of the birds whose nestlings are attacked by a mongoose or a common genet, but we laugh at the sight of hippopotami and crocodiles trying to defeat each other in combat. A classical work of this genre is the swamp scene in the *mastaba* of Ti from the late Fifth Dynasty. Natural in its composition, fine and precise in the execution of particular details, this tableau is a masterpiece of ancient Egyptian art. In later swamp scenes, found in the *mastabas* of the Sixth Dynasty, the composition tends to become more schematic, and particular motifs lack the elegance of the earlier reliefs. These scenes were also a kaleidoscope of colors, but their original polychrome painting has vanished in the majority of cases. In this respect, the miniature scene in the cult chapel of Merefnebef (early Sixth Dynasty) provides a unique chance to admire the skill of the period's painter and the richness of the shades in his palette.

Another scene, showing the vizier at a moment of leisure, occupies nearly entirely the southern wall in his funerary chapel. It represents him with a female companion, whose identity is lost with the inscription that had originally been an integral part of this relief. They enjoy an acrobatic performance of some half-nude female dancers and the play of four female harpists described as the vizier's wives. A narrow space left at the wall's eastern edge is filled with some small genre scenes showing various craftsmen at work.

Mehu

From the beginning of the Sixth Dynasty onward, rooms in the *mastabas'* superstructure, as well as the walls of the burial chamber, entered from the bottom of the shaft, could be decorated. Limited to lists and depictions of offerings, the decoration of burial chambers reflects some changes in the general concept of the tomb at the end of the Old Kingdom. The concern about the deceased's welfare in the afterlife is now centered in the burial chamber, rather than in the superstructure, which visibly shifts the latter's function from the house of the dead to a chapel of his cult.

Both the architectural shape and the decoration of the *mastabas* delineate their owners' social position. Many tombs built of mud bricks, presumably for owners of lower status, have a false door made of limestone, inserted into the chapel's western wall, as the only element decorated with hieroglyphic inscriptions and representations of the deceased. A dense agglomeration of such burials was recently discovered between the tomb of Merefnebef and the enclosure wall of the Djoser pyramid. In front of their eastern façade, there is usually a longitudinal chapel having palace-façade paneling on the west wall. One of this wall's niches housed the false door. Unfortunately, most of these stelae have been removed from their original place by tomb robbers. Some had been thrown into the shaft or even into the undecorated burial chamber. Their presence enables archaeologists to identify the tomb owner. Among the officers of lower rank than that of Merefnebef, there were two priestesses of the goddess Hathor (the ancient Egyptian goddess of love), sometimes described as 'the King's sole adornment.' Their function at the royal court is still a subject of

Egyptological disputes. The only false door so far found standing at its original place in this part of Saqqara is the limestone slab inscribed for a certain Pehenptah. The only missing section is its upper part, which contained the titles of the deceased.

Another characteristic feature of these *mastabas* is the occurrence of two shafts, a northern and a southern one, hidden in the masonry of the superstructure. The northern shaft usually has a burial chamber for the deceased, in which a skeleton or its remains are found. The southern one finishes with a plain bottom and usually contains lots of broken pottery, and sometimes remains of bandages, wooden boxes, and other objects that could have been used in the process of embalming. These shafts seem to have had a purely ritual function, connected with the funeral.

Changes in religious concepts of the afterlife, reflected in the architecture and decoration of the *mastabas*, seem to follow innovations concerning the deceased king. Particular elements of royal funerary complexes were imitated by noblemen in their tombs since the mid-Fifth Dynasty (the tomb of Ptahshepses at Abusir), and the decoration of their *mastabas* developed from the prototypes created for solar and funerary temples of that period. The Pyramid Texts, sculpted on the walls of the rooms inside royal pyramids since the time of Unas, became an additional source of inspiration. This influence is quite visible in the façade of Merefnebef's cult chapel. Hewn in the rock, the façade has the form of an oblong rectangular niche with two narrow lateral walls and a broad rear wall (being the outer face of the chapel's west wall). Its decoration is a masterpiece of sophisticated composition. The rear wall is divided into three

338 top left
A sequence of cliff ledges descends gradually westward from the girdle wall of Djoser's funerary complex to a deep 'dry moat.' Hewn in both faces of the latter are various subterranean structures, including this mysterious corridor leading to a chamber in which a grand ritual harpoon and a deposit of wild animal bones were found.

338 bottom left
A dense agglomeration of mastabas dating from the late Old Kingdom extends between the tomb of Merefnebef and the Step Pyramid enclosure. There are but poor remains of their mud-brick superstructures, destroyed by robbers in ancient times. Their once hidden subterranean parts, the vertical shafts leading to burial chambers, reveal the rest of their secrets to Egyptologists.

338 top right
Mehu, vizier and minister of justice in the reign of King Teti (early Sixth Dynasty), is shown seated at an offering table laden with half-loaves of bread. This scene is from a relief on the south wall of the offering chamber in his rock-hewn mastaba at Saqqara, south of the Step Pyramid's girdle wall.

339
A huge false door for the deceased occupies the entire west wall of the offering chamber in Mehu's tomb. Its architectural frame and its division into a sequence of recesses imitates the façade of a royal palace, while its red-brown color imitates quartzite.

Four of the numerous offering-bearers represented on the south wall of the offering chamber. Two of them wear collars decorated with lotus flowers. Worth attention is the boat-shaped basket with fruit carried by the third man, and the animals offered by the fourth: three gazelles on his shoulders, an ibex, and an oryx beside him.

340 bottom

The next three men represented in the same register carry various animals and baskets laden with fruit. The basket of the first man is covered with a lettuce, and that of the third one is in the shape of a papyrus boat.

341 bottom

The processions of offering-bearers depicted on the offering chamber's south wall are paralleled by rows of similar figures on the north wall. These are bringing geese and storks to Mehu. All of them stride in the direction of the false door and its offering table.

registers, with elements which contrast in their form but form a harmonious whole with respect to their contents. The upper one is filled with a hieroglyphic inscription composed in four horizontal lines that extend the entire length of the wall above the entrance, thus constituting a kind of frieze. It gives the most essential information about the vizier, including his three names, interspersed into a kind of 'ideal biography,' a conventional text presenting the libidinous Fefi almost as a saint. Completed with a small 'label' depicting the vizier with one of his wives and one of his sons, at the end of the inscription, this lintel has some features inspired by the Pyramid Texts. The hieroglyphic signs are sculpted in sunken relief and no detail except their outline is modeled. Their concave bodies were filled with a blue-greenish paste that is still preserved in a few places. Much better preserved is the original white paint of the space surrounding the hieroglyphs. Both the technique and the coloring imitate the shape of the Pyramid Texts, the oldest version of which is found in the pyramid of Unas, a few hundred meters south of the tomb. It seems that noblemen as well as artists were fascinated with this new invention and enjoyed its reflection in their own tombs.

The middle register, extending on both sides of the narrow entrance, contains another hieroglyphic text, an 'appeal to the living,' which, unlike the previous text, this one is written in more than fifty short vertical columns. Its form contrasts in every respect with that of the above inscription. The signs are modeled in high relief, and their convex surface bears a polychrome painting rendering the finest details of each hieroglyph; they stand out from a monochrome blue-gray background.

A kind of pictorial 'signature' under these texts closes the decoration of the façade in its lowest register. Here the vizier is depicted eight times, walking toward the entrance of his own chapel. As in the decoration of royal monuments, the imagination and skill of the artist reappears, engaged with personal propaganda using religion as its main instrument. Text and picture complete each other, considered by the artist as two integral parts of a harmonious creation.

Although several elements occur repeatedly in the architecture and decoration of late Old Kingdom *mastabas* at Saqqara, our knowledge of this necropolis is still far from complete. Every excavation brings surprises. Some of them came to light west of the tomb of Merefnebef. The cliff-ledge closing the sequence of terraces in this part of the necropolis recently yielded some unusual structures hewn in the rock. There is a long corridor ending with a chamber in which a unique deposit of wild animal skeletons was lying on the surface of a filling that contained an extraordinary ritual object—a huge harpoon decorated with representations of snakes in relief. The pottery found in this context dates the deposit to the Sixth Dynasty. Was this mysterious place connected with the cult of a king or that of a god? Another corridor contains several cult chapels and many shafts hewn in their floor. Was a family or another group of people buried at this place? How far north and southward do the rock terraces in West Saqqara extend?

Even before these and other questions are answered, it is beyond doubt that the Fifth and Sixth dynasties contributed much to the development of the Egyptian mastaba. During this period, the superstructures of private tombs were enlarged and their decoration enriched, in imitation of the multiroomed royal solar and funeral complexes of the Fifth Dynasty. The introduction of some decoration to the burial chambers at the beginning of the Sixth Dynasty reflects general changes in funeral imagery of the period. The superstructure becomes primarily a cult place, while material aspects of the afterlife are accentuated in the burial chamber, closer to the mummy. Egyptian reliefs and paintings reached the highest level of artistic refinement during this period, exhibiting a purity and variety of form that were rarely equaled, and never surpassed, in later times.

The Pyramids of
the Middle Kingdom

by Dieter Arnold

P olitical unrest, economic problems, and the decline of the concept of the divine character of the pharaoh at the end of the Old Kingdom were certainly reasons for the renouncement of building noteworthy royal pyramid complexes during the First Intermediate Period. With the restoration of royal power under the Theban ruler Mentuhotep Nebhepetre of the Eleventh Dynasty, the old concept of divine kingship was revived and contributed to the creation of a new Upper Egyptian type of royal funerary monument, the Mentuhotep temple of Deir

al-Bahari at Thebes. This formally and functionally innovative building would certainly have strongly influenced the funerary monuments of the succeeding kings—had they stayed at Thebes. With the transfer of the royal residence to Lower Egypt, however, the Upper Egyptian tradition was interrupted and the royal builders again fell under the spell of the Memphite tradition of pyramid building. The first Lower Egyptian pyramids of the Middle Kingdom, built by Amenemhet I and his son Senusret I, are preserved at Lisht.

342
This pillar or 'Osiride' statue of Senusret I, dating to the Twelfth Dynasty, was found by Gautier (1894–95) on the causeway leading to the pyramid of Senusret I at Lisht, painted limestone, height 239 cm. Now in the Egyptian Museum, Cairo.

343
This head of a female statuette, in painted wood with gilding, is 10.5 cm high and was found by the Metropolitan Museum of Art, New York Excavation in 1907. It dates to the Twelfth Dynasty, reign of Amenemhet I. Now in the Egyptian Museum, Cairo.

Pyramids of the  Middle Kingdom

344-345
Panoramic view of the pyramid of
Amenemhet I at Lisht, Twelfth Dynasty.

344 bottom
Map showing the pyramids of
Amenemhet I (right) and Senusret I
(left) at Lisht.

THE PYRAMIDS OF LISHT

The reign of King Amenemhet I seems to have been plagued by internal conflicts. Even his co-regency with his more powerful son and successor, Senusret I, could not prevent the final assassination of the older king by his bodyguards. One wonders why Amenemhet I could not build his tomb or establish his residence at the traditional capital, Memphis. What forced him to relocate to a place called *Ity-tawi* (meaning 'the grip on the two countries') near the modern town of Lisht, halfway between Cairo and the Fayum?

The cemetery of Lisht was first excavated by Gaston Maspero in 1882, then by the French Institute of Oriental Archaeology under Joseph Gautier in 1895–96, and then by the Egyptian Expedition of The Metropolitan Museum of Art, New York from 1906 to 1934, and again from 1990 to the present. The combined results of these efforts laid the cornerstone of our knowledge of the art and history of the Middle Kingdom.

The Pyramid Complex of Amenemhet I

The building at Lisht of a pyramid for a ruler with Upper Egyptian roots suggests a compromise between Upper and Lower Egyptian royal funerary customs. In addition, a number of architectural oddities and mistakes in the pyramid complex suggest that the builders no longer had the experience of pyramid building developed by the builders of the Old Kingdom. This pyramid complex is characterized by small dimensions, unusual proportions, and no distinction between the royal and private sphere.

The pyramid had the modest—compared to those of the following kings of the Twelfth Dynasty—dimensions of 84 x 84 m and was probably 59 m high. Large-scale quarrying seems to have been a problem and many building blocks used were therefore taken from older buildings. A great number of decorated blocks of Old Kingdom temples with the names of Khufu, Khafre, Userkaf, Unas, and Pepy II were discovered in the masonry of the pyramid and surrounding buildings. The extensive reuse of relief blocks with the names of so many rulers may indicate a preceding wave of temple destruction.

Maspero opened the pyramid chamber in 1882 and found a vertical shaft in the chamber floor that disappeared into the ground water after seven meters. In 1994, our expedition from the Metropolitan Museum of Art lowered an underwater camera into the water that showed that the continuation of the shaft is filled with clean sand and that a shallow niche extends to the south. The pyramid, then, still holds some secrets, including the well shaft and the certainly existent, but inaccessible, reused Old Kingdom blocks that would permit us to reconstruct several Old Kingdom pyramid temples.

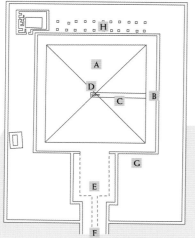

THE PYRAMID OF AMENEMHAT I AT LISHT
A   PYRAMID
B   ENTRANCE
C   ENTRANCE PASSAGE
D   BURIAL CHAMBER
E   PYRAMID TEMPLE
F   CAUSEWAY
G   INNER ENCLOSURE WALL
H   TOMB SHAFTS OF ROYAL FAMILY

345 top
The right half of a lintel from the pyramid temple of Amenemhet I at Lisht representing the enthroned king at his sed-festival receiving the symbol of countless years from the standard of the god Seth. Made of painted limestone, it was found by the Metropolitan Museum of Art, New York Excavation in 1907, close to the pyramid of Amenemhet I and dates to the Twelfth Dynasty, reign of Amenemhet I. Now in the Egyptian Museum, Cairo.

346 left and top right
This limestone statue of Senusret I is 200 cm in height. It was excavated by Gautier at the pyramid of Senusret I at Lisht in 1894–95, and dates to the Twelfth Dynasty. On the right is a detail of the base of the statue. Egyptian Museum, Cairo.

346 center right
The pyramid of Senusret I at Lisht, seen from west, was erected during the Twelfth Dynasty.

346 bottom right
Behind the pyramid of Senusret I at Lisht, looking down the northwest corner, can be seen the remains of the secondary pyramid no.5 dating to the Twelfth Dynasty.

Pyramids of the  Middle Kingdom

The Pyramid Complex of Senusret I

Senusret I, the son and successor of Amenemhet I, was able to stabilize the country's condition, strengthen the power of the royal family, and rebuild many major temples throughout Egypt. The king's builders designed a pyramid complex that followed to some extent the prototype of a pyramid complex of the Fifth and Sixth Dynasties but enriched them by innovative architectural features.

The pyramid base measured 105 x 105 m and the height was probably 61.25 m. The method by which the core was constructed shows technical experimentation. A grid of skeleton walls retained the core masonry of small fieldstone blocks. The steeply sloping entrance passage led from the north into the burial apartments of the king. In 1882, Maspero's workmen smashed several huge, obelisk-shaped granite beams that were blocking the entrance passage. At a distance of 48 meters from the entrance, the blockage ended, but ground water prevented further progress. Remains of the royal burial equipment found higher up in a robber's tunnel made it clear that ancient thieves had reached the king's chamber before the rise of the ground water by digging a parallel tunnel. Efforts to pump out the water in the passage have failed, challenging another generation of Egyptologists and engineers.

The pyramid temple was a huge limestone structure built against the east side of the pyramid. The plan followed the main features of the pyramid temples of the late Fifth and Sixth Dynasties. Several hundred fragments of the relief decoration of the interior walls of the pyramid temple were preserved; a few are now in the Metropolitan Museum of Art, and the rest reburied. The offering hall was decorated with figures of offering bearers, some still showing remains of the original painting. Processions of gods moved through the square antechamber and battle scenes were shown outside the temple, either in the court or causeway.

The inner pyramid court was surrounded on all sides by a five-meter-high limestone wall that was decorated with spectacular panels crowned with the Horus falcon. The panels were inscribed with the king's names on top of a so-called 'palace façade' supported by life-size fecundity figures. This ingenious decoration of the pyramid enclosure wall identifies the royal pyramid complex as a 'palace of eternity.'

Another amazing discovery was the detection by Gautier in 1894 of a group of ten completely preserved, seated limestone figures of Senusret I. The statues were ceremonially buried in pharaonic times, probably when a change in the building program rendered them superfluous.

The Private Tombs

The pyramids of Amenemhet I and Senusret I are surrounded not only by thousands of surface burials and tomb shafts, but also by a number of Twelfth Dynasty tombs that are distinguished by monumental *mastaba* superstructures or small mortuary temples. The tomb of Senusretankh was especially elaborate, with a *mastaba* decorated with the archaic paneling motif (now destroyed) and a completely preserved burial chamber inscribed with Pyramid Texts.

North of the causeway are the remains of the tomb enclosure of the priest Imhotep, with a sarcophagus pit inscribed with Coffin Texts. The vast tomb enclosure of vizier Mentuhotep was discovered 1987 southeast of the pyramid of Senusret I, containing not only remains of statuary and relief decoration, but also a granite sarcophagus with unusually well-preserved inscriptions and paintings.

THE PYRAMID OF SENUSRET I AT LISHT
A   UNEXPLORED PYRAMID CHAMBER
B   INNER PYRAMID TEMPLE
C   INNER ENCLOSURE WALL
D   'KA-PYRAMID'
E   PYRAMID OF QUEEN NEFERU
F   OUTER PYRAMID TEMPLE
G   OUTER ENCLOSURE WALL
H   CAUSEWAY

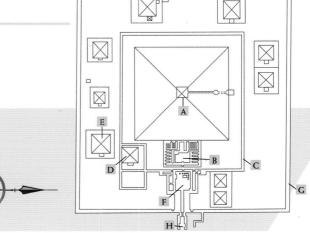

348-349
Aerial picture of the pyramid of Senusret II
at Illahun, dating to the Twelfth Dynasty,
seen from southwest.

349 bottom left
The uraeus of Senusret II, belonging to the
Twelfth Dynasty, has been realized in gold,
lapis lazuli, carnelian, and feldspar; it is 6.7
cm high and was found by the excavation of
Guy Brunton (British School) in 1920.
Now in the Egyptian Museum, Cairo.

PLAN OF THE PYRAMID AREA
OF ILLAHUN AND KAHUN

A *PYRAMID OF SENUSRET II*
B *VALLEY TEMPLE*
C *PYRAMID CITY OF KAHUN*

The Pyramid Complex of Senusret II at Illahun

Senusret II selected for his pyramid site an unexpected locality near the entrance into the Fayum oasis. The king's short reign of only nine years was apparently insufficient to complete the pyramid in a proper way, and several aspects of the complex indicate an early discontinuation of the works. The 107 x 107 m pyramid uses a limestone rock outcrop as a core or foundation. The rock carries a system of radial skeleton walls of huge limestone blocks as a support for the brick core. The limestone casing blocks seem to have had an angle of 42° 35′, suggesting a pyramid of modest inclination and height.

Petrie's engineer George Fraser opened the pyramid's interior in 1889–90. The crypt is a masterwork of granite building and houses an unusually shaped granite sarcophagus. Guy Brunton dug through the interior of the pyramid again in 1920. During this operation a magnificent royal uraeus was discovered in the debris, apparently part of the royal burial outfit and hidden by a thief.

A major achievement of Flinders Petrie was the discovery and excavation in 1888–90 of the pyramid city of Senusret II, now called Kahun. This settlement was—together with Tell al-Amarna, Elephantine, and Tell al-Dab'a—one of the most important domestic sites of pharaonic Egypt. The small city was enclosed by a 350 x 400 m wide enclosure wall and organized by a rectangular road system into blocks of buildings that included houses of different sizes and classes, ranging from four-room accommodations for workers to seventy-room estates for the upper class. The site also became known for its papyri, which give us important insights into the religious life of the small town. The population may have counted five to seven thousand persons.

PLAN OF THE PYRAMID OF SENUSRET II OF ILLAHUN

A PYRAMID
B PYRAMID ENTRANCE
C ENTRANCE PASSAGE
D FIND SPOT OF URAEUS

E CULT CHAPEL
F 'KA-PYRAMID'
G MASTABA TOMBS OF ROYAL FAMILY

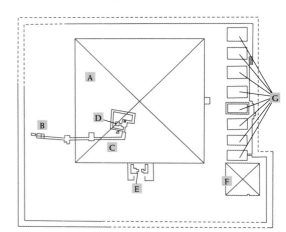

In this photo of the pyramid of Amenemhet III at Hawara, which dates to the Twelfth Dynasty, a fragment of a large limestone statue can be seen in the foreground.

Roman ruins on top of the 'Labyrinth' lie close to the pyramid of Amenemhet III of Hawara.

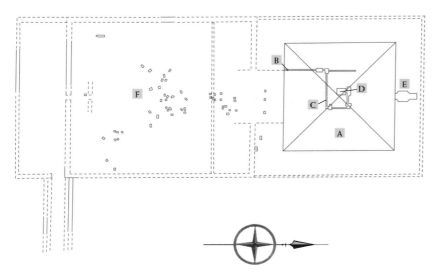

PLAN OF THE PYRAMID OF AMENEMHET III OF HAWARA

A PYRAMID
B ENTRANCE
C ENTRANCE PASSAGE
D BURIAL CHAMBER
E CULT CHAPEL
F 'LABYRINTH'

350-351
The pyramid of Amenemhet III at Hawara seen from the south, with the entrance to the pyramid in the center.

351 top
This statue of Amenemhet III, Twelfth Dynasty, in yellow limestone, is 160 cm high and was discovered in 1895 at Hawara during the excavation of a canal. Egyptian Museum, Cairo.

351 bottom
This isometric view shows the roof construction protecting the crypt of the burial chamber in the pyramid of Amenemhet III at Hawara. Reconstruction by Dieter Arnold.

Pyramids of the Middle Kingdom

The Pyramid Complex of Amenemhet III at Hawara

Amenemhet III built, as a replacement for his older pyramid at Dahshur (see below), a second pyramid at the entrance to the Fayum oasis, known by the modern name Hawara. This location, far from Memphis, is again unexpected. The move may be explained by the preexistence of a huge temple of Amenemhet III in the neighborhood, which was known in Greco-Roman times as 'The Labyrinth.' The temple compound was much admired by ancient visitors and writers such as Herodotus, Strabo, and Diodorus. Thereafter, the magnificent building was so much destroyed by stone robbers that neither excavation work at the site nor the analysis of ancient sources have been able to produce a clear picture of that unique structure. We may assume that the complex was a conglomerate of numerous small temples or chapels that seem to have housed an enormous collection of statues of the gods of Egypt.

The pyramid was added to the north side of the temple complex. In this pyramid, the royal builders took utmost care to guarantee the safety of the royal burial chamber. Flinders Petrie opened the burial chamber of the pyramid in 1890 under adventurous circumstances. Since the entrance to the pyramid was not found in the center of the north side, Petrie cut a narrow tunnel through the brick core. After one month, he reached the chamber roof. The conditions in the tunnel must have been incredible: "Occasionally falls of the side took place, and the false roof above broke away in parts, and hung in other places as if a touch would bring it down . . . . One of these falls would bring down tons of brick from the sides and roof, along perhaps twenty feet length." After such difficulties, Petrie's masons finally succeeded in breaking a hole into the quartzite chamber roof: "Into this I squeezed, sloping head downwards, on the mud that partially filled it, and managed to see that there was a chamber beneath with something in it, and a deal of water . . . and found it not more than chest deep . . . ." The underwater exploration of the chamber was no less unusual: 'The lads gradually picked up the stuff from the chamber, by shuffling it on the broad blade of a native hoe with the foot, and so lifting up a little at a time. One on the sarcophagus then examined all that came up, and threw what was not wanted into the sarcophagi, so as to keep the sorted stuff from the unsorted."

As questionable these methods may appear, Petrie probably found the basic archaeological information he wanted, and although the remains of the burial of Amenemhet III, nothing spectacular, they contained enough evidence to show that the king was actually buried here.

The crypt was carved from a single block of the hardest available stone, quartzite. A clever mechanism permitted the lowering of the roofing block of the chamber after the burial, thus sealing its access forever. Above, 55-ton limestone blocks shaped a second roof and were again relieved by an enormous brick vault. This ingenious construction protected the tomb very well against the pressure of the pyramid, but could not resist the efforts of the tomb robbers and could not prevent the flooding of the chamber by the groundwater that has since then reached the pyramid entrance.

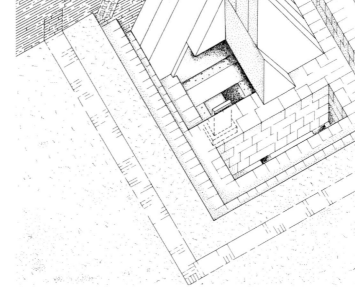

352
This black granite statue of Amenemhet III, 73 cm high and dating to the Twelfth Dynasty, was found in the cachette at Karnak in 1904 and is now conserved in the Egyptian Museum, Cairo.

353 top
The necklace of Neferuptah, made of gold, carnelian, feldspar, and vitreous paste, is 36.5 cm long and 10 cm wide. It dates to the Twelfth Dynasty reign of Amenemhet III, and was found at Hawara, close to the pyramid of Neferuptah, by the Antiquities Service Excavations in 1956. Now in the Egyptian Museum, Cairo.

353 bottom left
The flail of Neferuptah, made of faience, carnelian, gold-leaf, and wood (modern), is currently 36.5 cm long. It was found by the Antiquities Service Excavations at Hawara, close to the pyramid of Neferuptah, in 1956. It dates to the Twelfth Dynasty reign of Amenemhet III. Now in the Egyptian Museum, Cairo.

THE PYRAMIDS OF DAHSHUR

The Pyramid Complex of Amenemhet II

The monumental pyramid complex of the long-ruling Amenemhet II at Dahshur seems to have followed the prototypes of the Old Kingdom rather accurately, including a huge pyramid temple. However, the buildings suffered so much destruction at the hands of stone robbers that De Morgan, who excavated the site in 1894, could explore the pyramid chambers from above, in the open air. He found the royal sarcophagus empty, of course. De Morgan's

expedition gained unprecedented publicity when in 1895, he came upon the undisturbed burials of the two princesses, Ita and Khnumit, and the two disturbed tombs of the Princesses Itaweret and Sithathormeret along the west side of the pyramid. The reason for the excitement was the jewelry that still adorned the bodies of Ita and Khnumit: bracelets, anklets, collars, diadems, a dagger and other weapons, and many more objects; real treasures indeed, whose fame was only overshadowed much later by the discovery of the treasures of Tutankhamun and the treasures of the royal tombs of Tanis. De Morgan naturally thought that the princesses were royal women of the time of Amenemhet II; only recently have Egyptologists shown that the royal women were buried at the end of the Twelfth Dynasty.

354 left
The scarabs of Amenembet II, 2.57 and 2.51 cm long, and 1.46 and 1.64 cm wide, are made of amethyst and were found by the Metropolitan Museum of Art, New York Excavation in 1994–95, at the Dahshur funerary complex of Senusret III, in the tomb shaft of Queen Weret II, wife of Senusret III. Egyptian Museum, Cairo.

354-355
The necklace of Princess Khnumit, made of gold, carnelian, lapis lazuli, and amazonite, has a diameter of 21 cm. It was found in 1894 at Dashur in the funerary complex of Amenemhet II, in the tomb of Khnumit, by Jacques de Morgan. Twelfth Dynasty, reign of Amenembet III or later. Egyptian Museum, Cairo.

355 top left
This bracelet in gold, cornelian, lapis lazuli and amazonite was discovered in 1894 by Jacques De Morgan, in the tomb of Princess Khnumit, at Dahshur. The item has a 1.9 cm fastener. It is the Egyptian Museum, Cairo.

355 top right
This bracelet of Princess Khnumit, which dates to the Twelfth Dynasty reign of Amenembet III, is made of gold, carnelian, lapis lazuli, and amazonite. The clasp is 1.9 cm high. It was found in 1894 at Dashur in the funerary complex of Amenembet II, in the tomb of Khnumit, by Jacques de Morgan. Egyptian Museum, Cairo.

355 bottom
The diadem of Princess Khnumit, in gold, carnelian, lapis lazuli, and amazonite, has a diameter of 21 cm. It was found at Dashur in 1894 in the funerary complex of Amenemhet II, in the tomb of Khnumit, by Jacques de Morgan. It dates to the twelfth dynasty reign of Amenembet III or later. Egyptian Museum, Cairo.

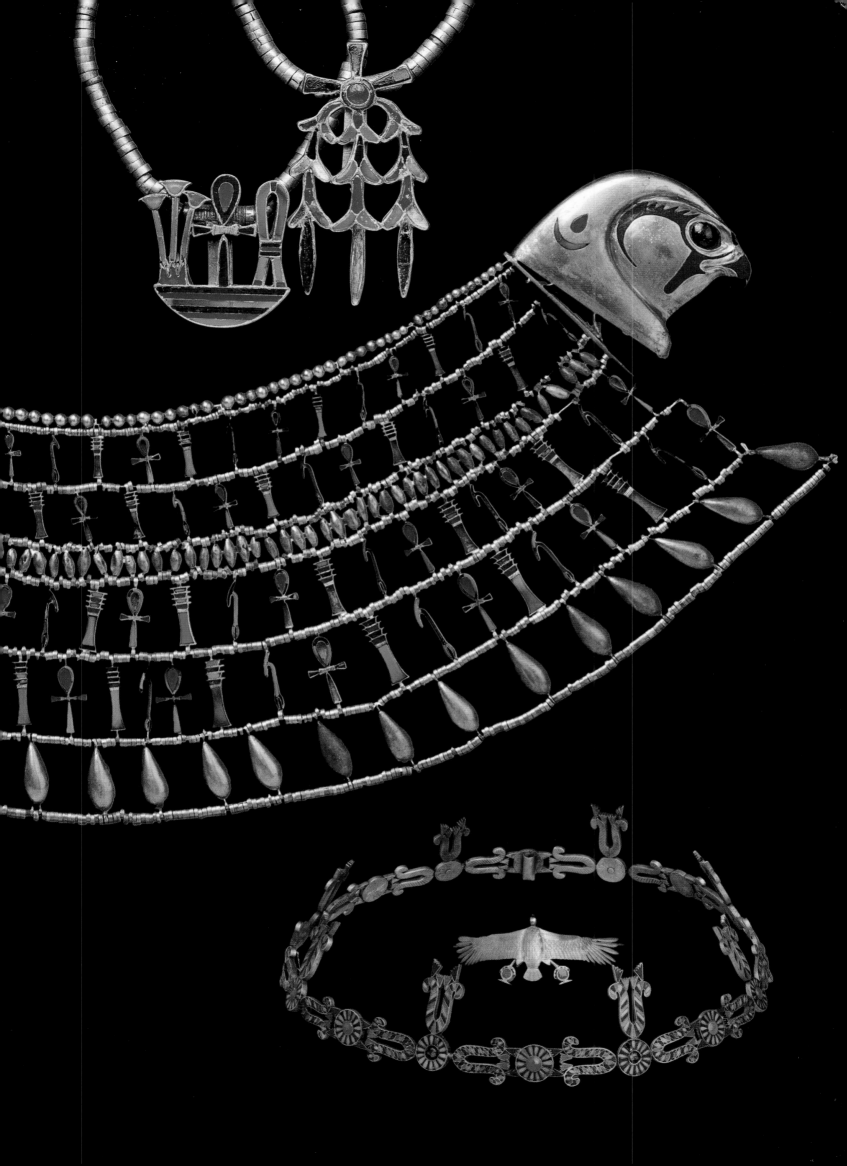

Pyramids of the ▲ Middle Kingdom

356-357

The pyramid complex of Senusret III at Dahshur, belonging to the Twelfth Dynasty, seen from the south. In foreground is the restored outer brick enclosure wall.

356 bottom

This reconstruction depicts the pyramid temple of Senusret III and the inner stone enclosure wall dating to the Twelfth Dynasty. Reconstruction by David Johnson.

357 top

This title, 'member of the elite and high official,' found in the mastaba of Nebit, north of the pyramid of Senusret III, by the Metropolitan Museum of Art in 1995, dates to the Twelfth Dynasty, reign of Senusret III.

357 bottom

This black granite statue of Senusret III, 150 cm high and dating to the Twelfth Dynasty, was found in front of the temple of Mentuhotep Nebhepetre at Thebes by Edouard Naville of the Egypt Exploration Fund in 1905. Egyptian Museum, Cairo.

The Pyramid Complex of Senusret III

The successor of Senusret II, Senusret III, chose the desert plateau northeast of the pyramid of Sneferu for his huge pyramid complex. Again, De Morgan worked here in 1894–95, and the expedition of the Metropolitan Museum of Art, New York, has resumed the exploration of the site since 1990.

The building style shows archaistic imitation of prototypes of the Old Kingdom on the one hand, and innovative development that lead to the royal mortuary installations of the New Kingdom on the other.

The pyramid had an inclination of 50 degrees and a base of 108 x 108 m. The underground apartments are lined with limestone and duplicate a royal tomb of the Old Kingdom. The proportions of the rooms and the quality of the stone treatment display the work of master builders of the highest rank, and the perfection of the royal granite sarcophagus is astounding.

Royal ladies were buried under smaller pyramids along the north and south sides of the king's pyramid. Only the main queen, Weret, received a chamber under the king's pyramid. In a hidden side-niche of her entrance shaft, a treasure was discovered in 1994. All burials in the queens' tombs had been thoroughly plundered, except for two boxes of jewelry discovered by De Morgan in 1895 in the burial gallery beneath the northern queens' pyramids. These treasures belonged to the princesses Merit and Sithathor, and

again contributed to the fame of Middle Kingdom jewelry.

The expedition of the New York's Metropolitan Museum of Art excavated thousands of fragments of the wall decoration of the pyramid temple and a so-called 'south temple' that was later added to a smaller pyramid complex on the south side. At present, a team from the expedition is working on the reconstruction of the decoration program.

The pyramid complex of Senusret III is surrounded by numerous Old and Middle Kingdom *mastabas*. Some were previously explored by De Morgan, and a few more are being excavated and studied by the expedition of the Metropolitan Museum. In 2001, part of the *mastaba* of the mayor of the pyramid city, Nebit, was rebuilt from ancient blocks that had been thrown down by an earthquake in antiquity. A shaft in the court of this tomb led to a much older tomb chamber. That tomb had been built in the early part of the Fourth Dynasty and closely followed the prototype of Sneferu's pyramid chambers, with corbelled ceilings, made of ten overhanging courses of limestone blocks. The *mastaba* of another Middle Kingdom official, Khnumhotep, was excavated in 2001. The remains of this *mastaba* are a jewel for architectural historians because the remaining casing blocks permit, for the first time, the reconstruction of a *mastaba* with the old paneling system of projections and recesses with a complicated false door.

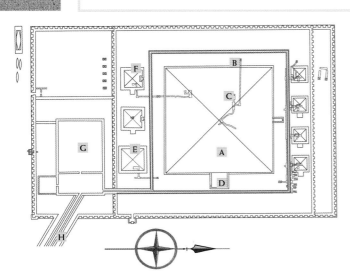

PLAN OF THE PYRAMID COMPLEX OF SENUSRET III AT DAHSHUR

A	PYRAMID
B	ENTRANCE
C	BURIAL CHAMBER
D	PYRAMID TEMPLE
E	'KA-PYRAMID'
F	PYRAMID OF QUEEN WERET II
G	SOUTH TEMPLE
H	CAUSEWAY

Pyramids of the Middle Kingdom

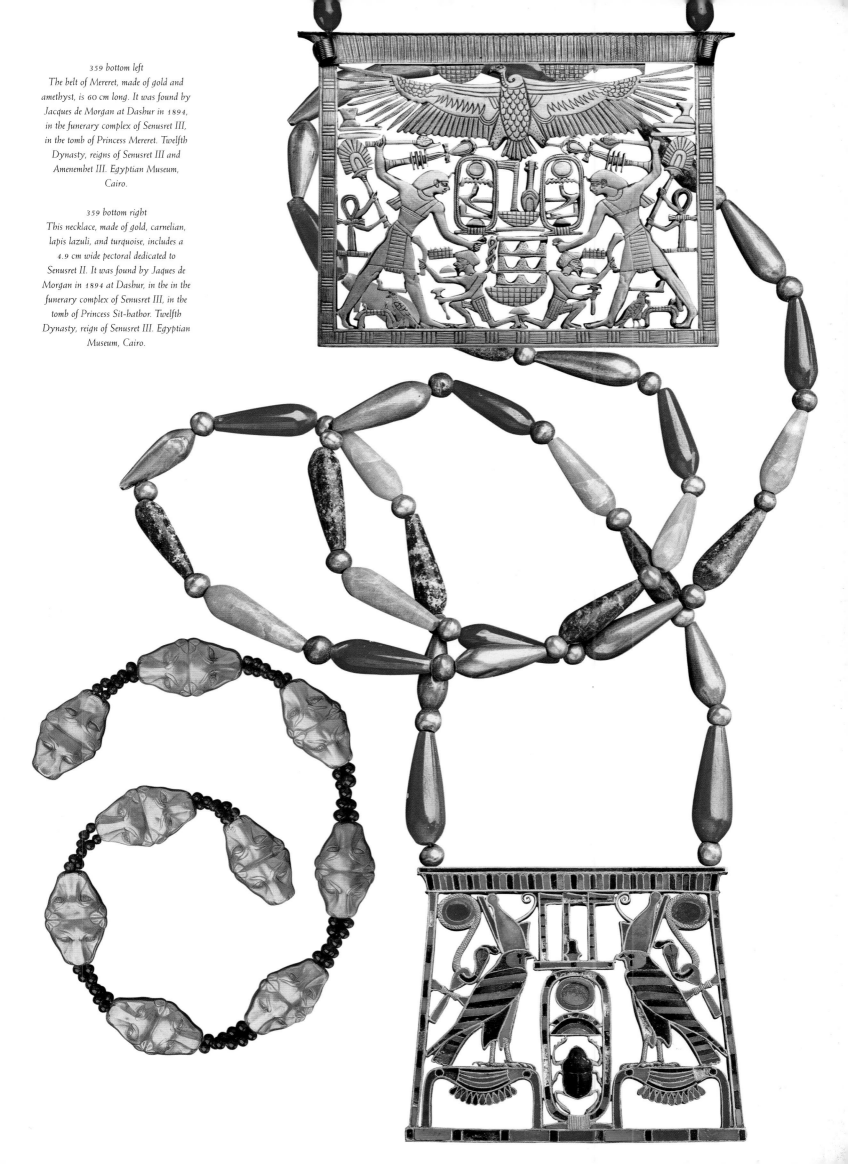

The Pyramid Complex of Amenemhet III

The son of Senusret III, King Amenemhet III, began his first pyramid early in his reign, apparently during his co-regency with Senusret III, when the construction work of his father's pyramid was not yet concluded. The 105 x 105 m pyramid reached a height of 75 meters and was again built of brick with a limestone casing. The interior shows a complex arrangement of corridors and chambers on two levels, comprising fifteen antechambers and a secondary 'ka-tomb' for the king. A magnificent granite sarcophagus decorated with projections and recesses was meant to house the king's body. However, the pyramid developed serious problems during construction: the chamber and corridor roofs were pushed into the ground by the weight of the

pyramid and cracked so much that they had to be propped up with timber and masonry. The king could not be buried in a damaged pyramid and therefore he had to build a new pyramid at Hawara. The consequences for the builders may have been unpleasant, to say the least.

King Auibre-Hor was a shadowy ruler of the Thirteenth Dynasty. His name was revived, however, when De Morgan discovered his simple, scarcely disturbed tomb within the enclosure of Amenemhet III at Dahshur. In addition to the sarcophagus, the small chamber contained a wooden shrine with a life-size wood statue of the king, a so-called 'ka-statue.' No visitor to the Egyptian Museum in Cairo can avoid the fascination of the magic eyes of the king standing in his chapel.

360 left
This statue depicts the ka of Auibre-Hor within his shrine. Made of wood, gold leaf, and semi-precious stones, the statue is 170 cm high, while the shrine is 207 cm. It was found by Jacques De Morgan in 1894. Thirteenth Dynasty, reign of Auibre-Hor. Egyptian Museum, Cairo.

360 right
The Twelfth-Dynasty pyramid of Amenemhet III at Dahshur, seen from the west.

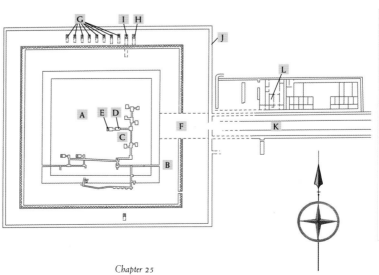

PLAN OF THE PYRAMID COMPLEX OF AMENEMHET III AT DAHSHUR

A PYRAMID
B ENTRANCE
C PASSAGE SYSTEM
D ANTECHAMBER
E BURIAL CHAMBER
F PYRAMID TEMPLE
G TOMBS OF THE ROYAL FAMILY
H TOMB OF KING AUIBRE-HOR
I TOMB OF PRINCESS NUBHETEPKHERED
J OUTER ENCLOSURE WALL
K CAUSEWAY
L PRIESTS' HOUSES

RECENT DISCOVERIES AT THE PYRAMIDS OF THE MIDDLE KINGDOM

The daily life of an excavator has changed much since the times of Petrie and De Morgan. Working conditions have improved tremendously. The crowds of local hoe men and basket boys have been replaced by a new generation of experienced excavation workers, and adventurous exploration has been transformed into methodic recording and conservation. One aspect has remained the same, however—the expectation and excitement about a discovery. Since most archaeologists are working now in sites which have been thoroughly 'explored' by generations of robbers and excavators, situations triggering such feelings have become rare.

In 1988, after long weeks of cleaning the shaft of the tomb of the Twelfth-Dynasty vizier Mentuhotep at Lisht-South, expedition members reached the devastated burial chamber which contained a totally smashed quartzite sarcophagus. What a surprise it was when they came upon a second granite

sarcophagus: the thieves had left it undamaged because it had never contained a burial. It was beautifully decorated with incised ornaments outside and perfectly preserved paintings and inscriptions inside.

In the 1994 season, the same expedition concluded the cleaning of the burial shaft of Queen Weret, the wife of Senusret III, at Dahshur. Standing at the bottom of the shaft, the excavation inspector, Ahmed Abdel Hamid, casually pointed out a barely noticeable irregularity of the side wall of the shaft: patches of mud smeared over the rock surface. Closer inspection revealed a cavity leading to a treasure belonging to the queen: a pair of bracelets and a pair of anklets made of gold spacers and clasps and carnelian, turquoise and lapis lazuli beads; a pair of amethyst scarabs of Amenemhet II; a girdle of golden cowrie shells; and a clasp with tiny, inlaid hieroglyphs. TThe team members will never forget the excitement of clearing the deposit shaft and sifting through the debris.

361 bottom left
The belt of Queen Weret II, wife of Senusret III, in gold, carnelian, lapis lazuli, and turquoise. It was found at Dahshur, in the funerary complex of Senusret III, in the tomb shaft of Weret II by the Metropolitan Museum of Art New York in 1994–95. It has been dated to the Twelfth Dynasty, between the reigns of Amenemhet II and Senusret III. Egyptian Museum, Cairo.

361 bottom right
The necklace of Queen Weret II, wife of Senusret III. This necklace, which dates to the Twelfth Dynasty between the reigns of Amenemhet II and Senusret III, is made of gold, carnelian, lapis lazuli, and turquoise. It is 62.9 cm long, with a pendant 1.7 cm high and 1.7 cm wide. It was found by the Metropolitan Museum of Art, New York in 1994-1995 at Dashur, in the funerary complex of Senusret III, in the tomb shaft of Weret II. Egyptian Museum, Cairo.

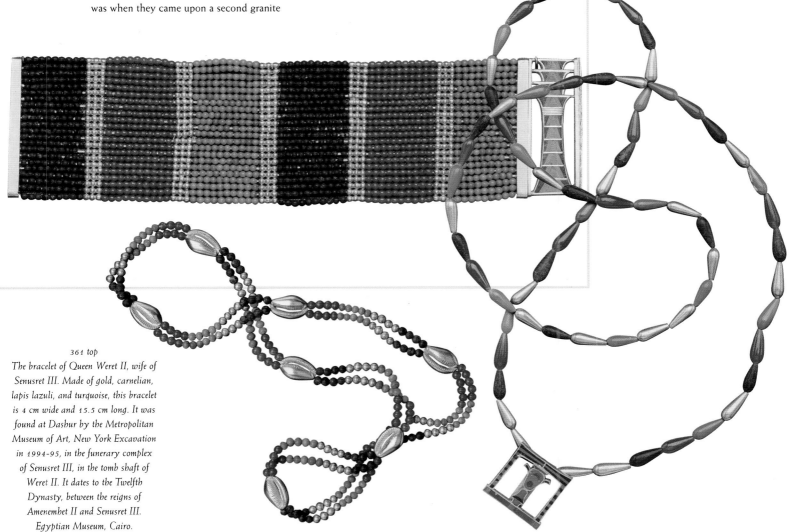

361 top
The bracelet of Queen Weret II, wife of Senusret III. Made of gold, carnelian, lapis lazuli, and turquoise, this bracelet is 4 cm wide and 15.5 cm long. It was found at Dashur by the Metropolitan Museum of Art, New York Excavation in 1994-95, in the funerary complex of Senusret III, in the tomb shaft of Weret II. It dates to the Twelfth Dynasty, between the reigns of Amenemhet II and Senusret III. Egyptian Museum, Cairo.

BUILDING A MIDDLE KINGDOM PYRAMID

The pinnacle of pyramid building was certainly reached under Sneferu and Khufu in the Fourth Dynasty, and it is difficult to imagine that this art could have been improved. The feat of producing, moving, lifting, and setting millions of blocks was probably never repeated again, but Middle Kingdom architecture shows an advancement in stone and brick building.

The remaining blocks of pyramid casing confirm that the stonework met the highest standards. The blocks have perfectly smoothed surfaces, sharply cut edges, and a precisely measured inclination. Numerous preserved cramps and cramp sockets suggest that a great number, if not all, of the casing blocks were connected with wood cramps. Meticulous stonework is also confirmed by the precisely cut and smoothed pyramidia of diorite and other hard stones, and of course by the granite and limestone wall blocks of the funerary apartments. Inevitable repairs to casing and wall blocks were expertly carried out with inserted patch stones.

The foundations of brick and stone buildings, which were rather poor or nonexistent in the Old Kingdom, were tremendously improved in the Twelfth Dynasty. In the pyramid complex of Senusret III, all stone masonry was not only laid on two courses of limestone foundation blocks, but these were supported by three to four courses of a brick subfoundation. Brick walls were built on massive foundation platforms that consisted of several courses of bricks and protruded from the foot of the wall on

both sides. The enclosure walls were battered on both sides and protected from the elements by layers of whitewashed mud mortar.

Another interesting technical detail was developed during the Twelfth Dynasty. The fillet stones that seal the roof slabs of the pyramid temple of Senusret III against rainwater have plain, mushroom-shaped sections. In the slightly later south temple, the fillet stones gained a much more sophisticated arrangement of tenons, which could have made the roof absolutely waterproof.

During the Middle Kingdom, the ancient traditions of brick building continued with visible technical advancement. In the royal pyramid complexes, the most prominent hallmark was the stepwise substitution of stone masonry with brickwork. One tends to interpret the creation of a pyramid with a brick core, as a sign of economic recession but there are no indications that the Egyptian economy of the Twelfth Dynasty was so weak that no stone pyramids could be built. I would interpret this phenomenon rather as an experiment by the builders to develop easier and faster construction methods than the archaic piling up of huge stone blocks.

The enormous mass of brickwork in the core of pyramids and enclosure walls was laid in sand, thus avoiding the cracking and sagging that could have occurred with wet mortar. The bricklayers also knew that they could increase the stability of the brickwork by laying the bricks as headers on all four faces of the pyramid.

The pyramid complexes of Senusret III and Amenemhet III at Hawara also demonstrate that the

bricklayers of the Middle Kingdom were able to build complicated brick arches and vaults. A discharging arch above the entrance of the causeway passage of Senusret III consisted of seven, 1.65 meter-thick rings of brick, which had to harmonize not only with the batter of the wall, but also with the bedding joints of the causeway. Another example, unfortunately now destroyed, was the 18.75 meter-long brick vault covering the large boat pit south of the pyramid complex, which consisted of five, 1.30 meter-thick rings that had a span of four meters. An enormous brick relieving vault also protected the stone roof of the royal burial chambers of the two last pyramids. The size of the rings cannot be measured, but they may well be 4.5 meters thick. These enormous vaults suggest development and a wide diffusion of brick construction during the Twelfth Dynasty.

Widespread remains of construction roads and ramps were found in the area around the pyramid of Senusret I. These 'slideways' consisted of five-meter-wide tracks of limestone chip and mortar into which rows of beams (reused boat timber) were inserted. The core and surface of the roads had a cement-like hardness. Another brick ramp climbing the eight degree angle of the plateau was made of builders' debris held in place by two retaining walls. Halfway up, two vertical wooden beams on both sides of the ramp were sunk into deep brick foundations and used to attach the ropes of a pulling device. The retaining walls of two brick ramps were found built at an angle against the pyramid and were certainly used for the construction of the pyramid.

362 top
The entrance of the pyramid of Senusret I (Twelfth Dynasty) at Lisht, seen from the north.

362 bottom
This photograph shows the transport roads east of the pyramid of Senusret I at Lisht (Twelfth Dynasty). Boat timber is reused to reinforce the mortar and chip fill of the road. The Metropolitan Museum of Art, New York expedition, 1988.

363 top
Perspective section showing the roof construction of the burial chamber of Senusret III in his pyramid at Dahshur.

363 center right
Cedar wood transport sledge, found by the Metropolitan Museum of Art, New York expedition in 1918 in the funerary complex of Senusret I at Lisht, in a deposit in the southern pyramid court of Senusret I. Length 173 cm, width 78.5 cm. Metropolitan Museum of Art, New York.

363 bottom
Reconstruction drawing of the two major construction ramps of the pyramid of Senusret I at Lisht, seen from the southwest. Twelfth Dynasty.

The Tombs of the Nobles of the Middle Kingdom

by David P. Silverman

364

Troop of Egyptian soldiers, in painted wood, from the tomb of Mesekhti, Asyut, Eleventh Dynasty, now in the Egyptian Museum, Cairo. Mesekhti included models as part of his burial equipment. His choice of military groups may be an indication of social and political situations at the time.

365

Statue of Mentuhotep II Nebhepetre, in painted sandstone, from Deir al-Bahri, Eleventh Dynasty, now in the Egyptian Museum, Cairo. This statue of Mentuhotep has an obvious monumentality. The pharaoh wears a cloak connected with the jubilee, and his beard, gesture, and skin color have Osiride associations.

The nobles of the Middle Kingdom continued the trend established early in Egyptian history of constructing large funerary monuments as part of the preparations that would help ensure the acquisition and maintenance of their eternal afterlife. Even though they maintained the custom overall, they did make some modifications. During much of the Old Kingdom, the nobles had built their tombs in cemeteries near the burial place of the pharaohs under whom they had served. These tombs were situated in the vicinity of the Memphite capital in Lower Egypt, near and/or around the pyramid of the pharaoh. As the Old Kingdom ended and the First Intermediate Period began, the central authority of the ruler lessened, and the powers of the nobility increased. The king no longer controlled the resources to construct large complexes with pyramids dominating the landscape. He was also he unable to maintain the same sphere of influence and power to draw the nobility near to him and have their cemeteries built close by his own monument.

Along with these shifts in control within the administration came a corresponding change in burial practices. Some of the high officials, especially those from the areas between Memphis and Thebes, preferred to build their mortuary structures in the localities in which their power was centralized. The high officials and administrators of the provinces, therefore, did not follow the reigning pharaoh in terms of his choice of burial location. Many of the nomarchs or 'governors' of the nomes (the administrative districts into which Egypt was divided), whose families had come to power in the late Old Kingdom and especially in the First Intermediate Period, built rather prepossessing monuments, not in the environs of the northern Memphite capital, but in their local areas of influence, especially in, but not limited to, Middle and Upper Egypt. This practice also continued during much of the succeeding Middle Kingdom, but it was by no means followed exclusively. Some high officials did in fact choose to be buried in a cemetery situated near the ruler under whom they had served. As the pharaoh consolidated his central authority during the Middle Kingdom, the nobles began to shift the locations of their tombs again. Later in the Twelfth Dynasty they clearly began to favor proximity to the sites that the king chose. This situation became much more common during the reign of Senusret III and may be related to the expansion of Egypt's boundaries during his reign. In any case, during the latter part of the Twelfth through the Thirteenth Dynasties, monarchs and high officials chose burial sites near the Memphite capital. Many middle and lower class burials, however, continued to cluster in provincial areas.

The architects of the large funerary monuments seem to have used elements from the earlier royal structures as models for the eternal dwelling places they designed for these non-royal high officials. Many of the tombs were located in the cliffs on the west bank, high above the Nile. Some had elaborate halls, porticoes, and courts cut out of the rock. Their plans could include a long causeway fronted by a covered entrance through which the funerary cortège would begin its ritual journey toward the burial chamber located in the upper terrace, deep in the rock cliffs. Some of the funerary complexes of high officials, especially those in the flat desert regions, followed other configurations and utilized a rectangular superstructure, as in previous periods. Constructed of stone or mud brick, they are called *mastabas*, an Arabic term meaning 'bench,' referring to their unique shape. The burial chamber was reached either directly through a sloping shaft or indirectly through a vertical shaft connected to an accompanying horizontal corridor. On other occasions, more simple burials with shallow pits were used.

The tombs of the Middle Kingdom incorporated many decorative elements that had appeared in burial complexes of the past, but they also employed innovative iconography, in both the reliefs and painting, that appears on the walls of the funerary structures. The officials expanded the standard formulae in the textual compositions to include a variety of additions, and they introduced several new compositions for use in tombs as well as cenotaphs. Unlike the situation in the private tombs of the Old Kingdom, the walls of the tomb (as well as those of the coffins and sarcophagi) now often had inscribed on them religious literature (Coffin Texts), whose purpose was similar to that of the texts (Pyramid Texts) which earlier royalty had inscribed inside their funerary monuments. Sometimes this material essentially duplicated what was originally on the walls of the pyramid chambers. Some are, however, clearly edited versions of such material. Still others appear to have been composed uniquely for this purpose and are not represented in earlier royal versions. During the Middle Kingdom, the repertoire of the sculptor broadened to include new and original forms of statuary fashioned specifically for use in the tomb complex. For example, the block statue appears first at the advent of the Twelfth Dynasty and becomes fairly common in funerary chapels above ground and later in commemorative settings or temples. Some of these innovations became quite popular and eventually saw uses in a variety of genres. Funerary equipment also showed signs of development and evolution, with mummy masks, anthropoid coffins, *shabtis* (an ancient Egyptian term, referring to statuettes used by the deceased in the afterlife to perform required labor), and canopic jars (a set of four receptacles for mummified internal organs) with stoppers in the form of human heads, appearing more regularly. These canopic jars were now often set in a chest and placed in a niche, most often on the east wall of the burial chamber.

366
Interior panel from the coffin of General Sepy in painted wood, found in Deir al-Barsha, Twelfth Dynasty, now in the Egyptian Museum, Cairo. Coffin Texts became popular in the Middle Kingdom. They consisted of funerary spells painted and/or carved on the interior walls of coffins (and sometimes of the burial chambers) and were intended to ensure an afterlife for citizens of the upper classes. A group of the spells, called The Book of Two Ways, was the first of the illustrated books of the afterlife, and is limited to this site.

367 top
Set of canopic jars belonging to Inepuhotep in painted wood and limestone, found in Saqqara, Twelfth Dynasty, now in the Egyptian Museum, Cairo. The mummification and separate storage of the lungs, liver, intestines, and stomach of the deceased continued throughout most of Egyptian history. Inscriptions associate each jar with one of the four sons of Horus who would protect the contents. The lid without the beard, on the far right, likely represents Imseti.

367 bottom
Elevation of the burial of Ihy, Saqqara, reign of Amenemhet I, Twelfth Dynasty. A vertical shaft in the courtyard of Ihy's offering chapel descends to a corridor that cuts across earlier burials until it opens onto his burial chamber, a room below the temenos wall surrounding the mortuary complex of Teti, Old Kingdom.

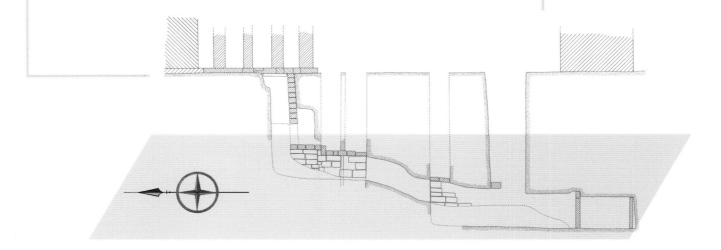

THE TOMBS OF THE SOUTH

The Middle Kingdom began with the successful reconsolidation of the country under the Eleventh Dynasty pharaoh Mentuhotep II Nebhepetre. Based in Thebes, he chose to rule from that area and established the city as his capital. Like his ancestors, he preferred the west bank for the location of his funerary monuments. Many of his predecessors from the end of the Old Kingdom onward had continued to build pyramidal monuments, although on a modest scale. Occasionally, they had them constructed out of mud brick. Mentuhotep II, however, built a stone complex on a grand scale in the cliffs at Deir al-Bahari, but it is unclear whether

or not it included a pyramidal component. He located it below the imposing conically shaped mountain, referred to in Arabic as *al-Qurn* ('the horn'), and he made his final resting place within the bedrock. Some Egyptologists now believe that the ancient Egyptians perceived this prominent feature of the landscape as a symbolic pyramid. Most of the high officials of his court seem to have followed his example in their choice of burial location, but those nobles from other provincial areas preferred to make their interment in the area of their local power base.

Theban tombs of the period were focused in or near the vicinity of the cliffs at Deir al-Bahari on the west bank at Thebes. This location today

recognized most by the remains of the mortuary complexes of Mentuhotep II and Queen Hatshepsut of the New Kingdom who had herself proclaimed pharaoh. Prior to the reunification, the rulers of the Eleventh Dynasty had selected a site for their burials about a mile to the east, near the plain of al-Tarif in the 'Intef Cemetery' (the name refers to the succession of kings of that name), and many contemporary as well as later private tombs were located here.

The custom of clustering private funerary monuments near burials of the rulers, albeit provincial (in this case of the Theban nome as well as a certain portion of Upper Egypt), reflects the tradition followed earlier in the Memphite royal

368 top
Royal temples built into the cliffs of Deir al-Bahri, on the west bank of Thebes. The temples of Mentuhotep II Nebhepetre of the Eleventh Dynasty and Thutmose III and Hatshepsut of the Eighteenth Dynasty were built below the prominent peak, called al-Qurn ('The Horn') in Arabic. This location may have been chosen in part because the pyramidal shape of the mountain above was to represent the same things as did the man-made pyramids of earlier times.

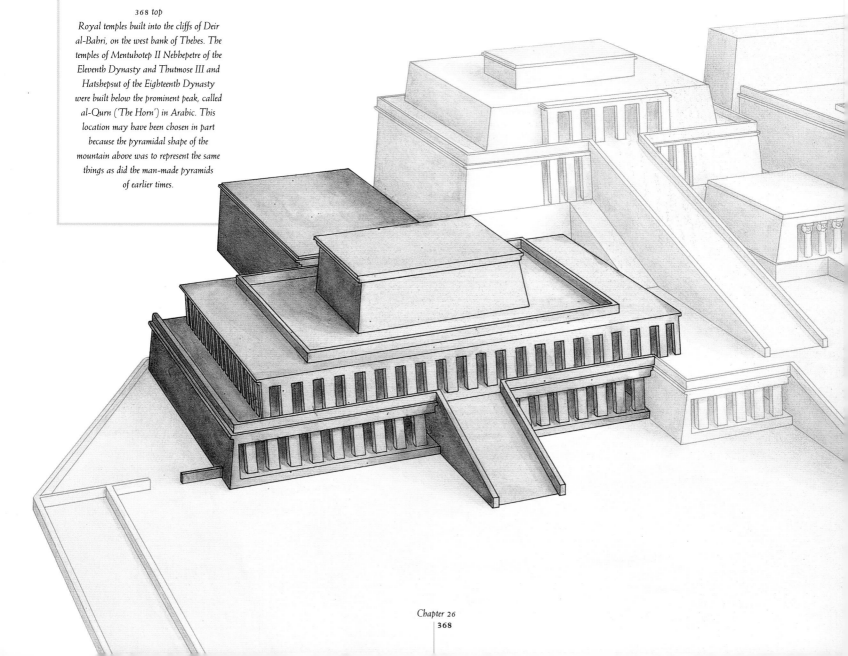

Tombs of ▲ the Nobles

cemeteries. Not all officials, however, followed this pattern, and some chose other areas for their burial. The orientation of some of these Eleventh Dynasty Theban tombs appears to have been influenced perhaps by another structure—the Temple of Montu at Karnak on the east bank—since their position is directly opposite that site. Located fairly low in the desert, near the modest mud-brick pyramids of their rulers, many of these private tombs had a courtyard whose rear wall consisted of a series of doorways next to each other and opening onto a transverse hall, occasionally with subsidiary rooms. Sometimes referred to as *saff* (an Arabic term meaning 'row,' used now in reference to their configuration) tombs, these structures often include a pillared portico.

368-369
The temples of Mentuhotep II Nebhepetre, Thutmose III, and Hatshepsut at Deir al-Bahri (West Bank of Thebes). The earliest structure, the mortuary temple of Mentuhotep of the Eleventh Dynasty (on the left), clearly served as a model for the other two temples, both of which date to the New Kingdom. Only Mentuhotep's incorporated a burial chamber within the complex.

369 right
Often fronted with large courts, the saff tombs of the Eleventh Dynasty derive from models introduced earlier and center in the area between Thebes and Dendera. Usually, two rows of pillars (A) in the rear wall form a façade that opens on to a central long hall (B) that extends back to a pillared chamber (C). A corridor (D) from that room leads to the burial chamber.

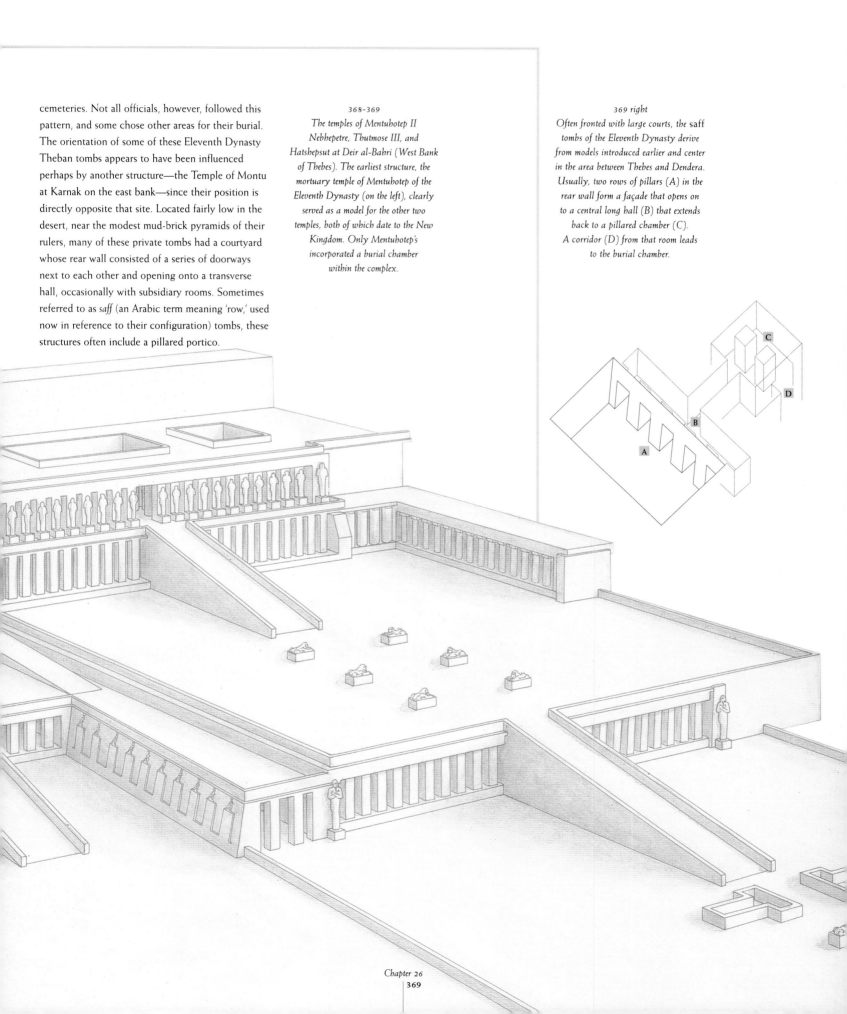

370 left

Female offering figure in painted wood, from the tomb of Meketre, Deir al-Bahari, end of Eleventh–beginning of Twelfth Dynasty, now in Cairo. Meketre, an official from the Theban area whose career spanned two dynasties, included this statue along with many tomb models as part of his burial equipment. Her larger scale and the details suggest that she may have been intended to play an important role in the funerary ritual and afterlife and may represent a domain in Meketre's funerary estate.

370 right

House model in painted wood, from the tomb of Meketre, Deir al-Bahari, end of Eleventh–beginning of Twelfth Dynasty, now in the Egyptian Museum, Cairo. Among the many models found in the tomb of Meketre was this miniature house façade and garden. The brightly painted columns support the roof of the portico, which opens on to a reflecting pool on three sides of which are sycamore trees bearing fruit.

Tombs of ▲ the Nobles

Recent re-analysis of many of the non-royal tombs in and adjacent to the area of Deir al-Bahari suggests that several of those previously dated to the Eleventh Dynasty belong to officials who survived into the early part of the Twelfth Dynasty. An example is the tomb of Meketre. As was the case with several of the other tombs belonging to owners of similar rank, it had a long pathway leading to a court, the back wall of which was cut into the face of the cliff. A portico was formed with a series of piers creating doorways to an interior transverse hall that led to a rock cut chapel and other rooms, and eventually to a subterranean sarcophagus chamber. The portico had scenes painted on plastered walls, and the corridor leading to the chapel had finely carved reliefs. Analogues to the scenes of daily life generally found on the walls of private burials of the past occur here in three-dimensional form as painted wooden models. In a side room, excavations revealed these groupings, and many of the figures were arranged in tableaux illustrating many different types of activities of daily life that Meketre wished to have preserved in his afterlife. Many other rock cut tombs were built in the area near the temple of Mentuhotep II, including that of his courtier Harhotep, the walls of whose coffin and burial chamber display primarily religious texts for the benefit of the deceased. The vizier Dagi possessed a large tomb in Sheikh Abd al-Gurna with an elaborate battered façade, formed from several large piers, and over the entrance was the architecturally interesting detail of embedded mud cones. The walls of the main entranceway had subtly carved and painted reliefs of the official and his family. Modest burials were also prepared for individuals of lower class, including multiple graves dug for soldiers.

371 left
Model of a carpenter's workshop in painted wood, from the tomb of Meketre, now in Cairo. Meketre's tomb contained three-dimensional models of many of the same scenes of daily life found carved and painted on the walls of tombs since the Old Kingdom. In this tableau, carpenters work busily on several woodworking projects.

371 right
Model of a workroom for weavers in painted wood, from the tomb of Meketre, Deir al-Bahari, end of Eleventh–beginning of Twelfth Dynasty, Egyptian Museum, Cairo. The action in this model reproduces in miniature a setting that was part of the daily life in the household of the deceased. Women are engaged in several different activities associated with weaving, including spinning and working looms.

Architects of the Middle Kingdom were aware of the need to protect all of the tombs from robbery, and they often employed the same devices, or variations of them, in both private and royal tombs. Such appears to be the case with the tomb of Khety, a noble in the court of Mentuhotep II, whose tomb was in the cliffs of Deir al-Bahari. Its designer employed a typical tomb plan, where the back wall of the forecourt formed the façade, but behind this he constructed several chambers that represented an attempt to lead would-be robbers away from the actual burial.

Shabti figurines, statuettes used by the deceased in the afterlife to perform forced labor, introduced earlier for other purposes as part of the funerary equipment, begin to appear more frequently in private tombs from Thebes, but their appearance here is later than it was in the north and other areas. The use of anthropoid coffins and mummy masks also takes root here. As in earlier times, scenes of daily life appear in registers on the walls of many tombs, especially in the areas visited by the public.

372-373
Model of the scene of counting the cattle, in painted wood, from the tomb of Meketre, Deir al-Bahari, end of Eleventh–beginning of Twelfth Dynasty, Egyptian Museum, Cairo. This tableau recreates in miniature a portico where Meketre sits higher than anyone else and reviews the counting and inspection taking place before him. Scribes seated nearby record the activity, a supervisor with an upraised staff maintains decorum, and herdsmen with sticks keep the herds from going astray.

373 bottom
In this model with fishermen in boats, again from the tomb of Meketre, oarsmen in the front and back of the two papyrus skiffs navigate carefully to maintain the parallel positions of the boats. This arrangement allowed the fishermen who held the ends of the ropes to manipulate the dragnet that is between the two vessels.

372 center and bottom
Meketre's tomb contained a variety of boats representing the many different riverine activities in Middle Kingdom Egypt. The top model, a transport vessel, conveyed the tomb owner and members of his family. Several of the crew on the bottom vessel manipulate the sail to take advantage of the prevailing wind.

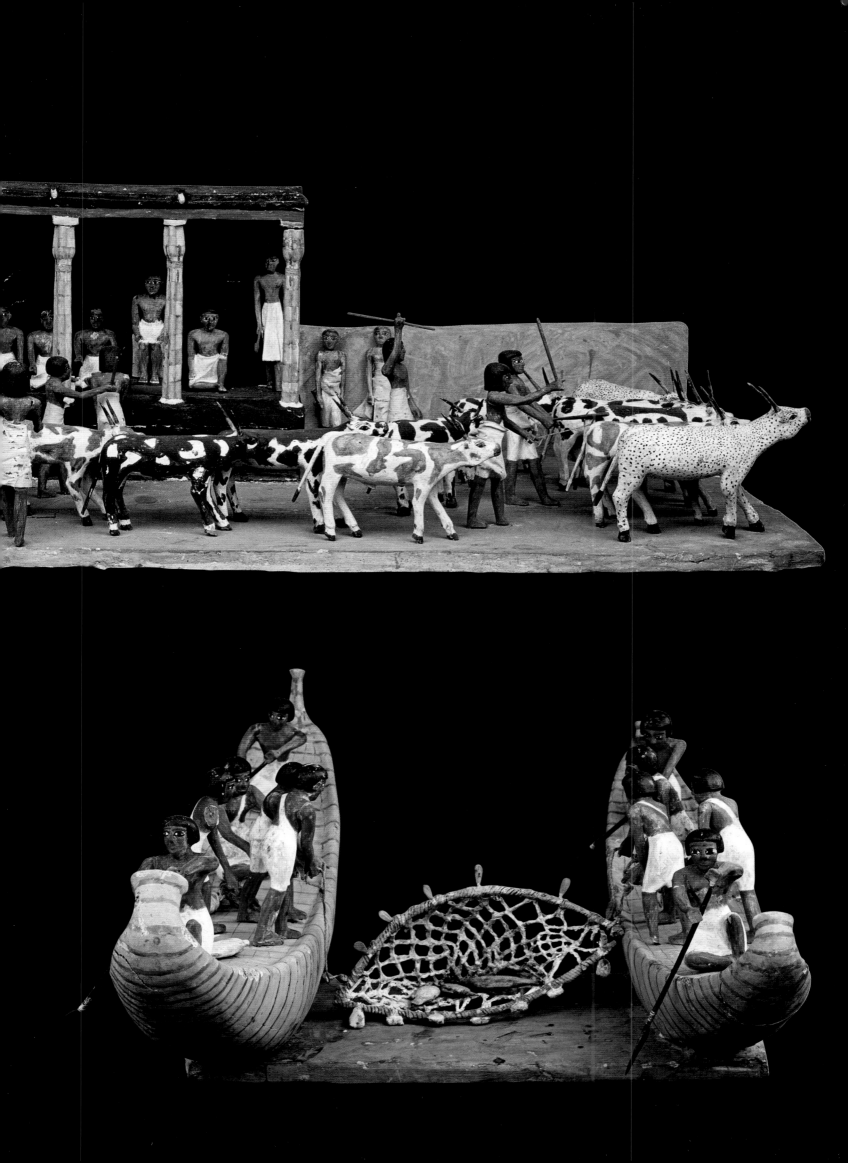

374-375
Stela of Amenemhet and his wife Iy in painted limestone, found in Thebes and probably dating to the early Twelfth Dynasty, now in the Egyptian Museum, Cairo. This stela is inscribed on behalf of Amenemhet and his wife Iy to ensure that they would receive appropriate funerary offerings. The couple is seated to the left and embrace their son, Intef, who sits between them. To the right stands a smaller-scale figure, identified as Hapy, perhaps Intef's wife.

374 bottom
Tomb of Sarenput I at Aswan, Qubbet al-Hawa, Twelfth Dynasty. Situated on the west bank at Aswan were the rock-cut tombs of officials, many of whom had been stationed at this important site at the first cataract of the Nile. Originally, an imposing court fronted a portico supported by six pillars. Carved representations of the deceased appear on the façade, on opposite sides of the entrance.

Occasionally, new iconography was introduced. For example, a scene of the reigning pharaoh in a private tomb first occurs in Thebes in the tombs of Khety and Intefoker. Frequently, however, the walls of the subterranean sarcophagus chamber were devoted to depictions of funerary equipment and copies of religious inscriptions for the benefit of the deceased in the afterlife. The texts can be in the form of Coffin and/or Pyramid Texts, and a similar program can also be found on the interior walls of the coffin and/or sarcophagus. This situation is not unique to Thebes; parallels exist at a number of sites throughout Egypt during the Middle Kingdom.

Many nobles from a variety of areas chose to build funerary memorials a bit farther north at Abydos, near the 'Terrace of the Great God,' i.e., Osiris, the deity sacred to that site. Then, at the time of the year when the festival of the god was commemorated, the memory of the departed would be revivified in part because of the presence of this monument. Built of mud brick, these structures were referred to in texts as a ***miḥꜥt*** . Often translated 'cenotaph,' and such a chapel could have dedicatory inscriptions on a single stela or on stelae for many members of the family for several generations. A courtyard might front the memorial, often with a separate section for a tree. Usually a vaulted brick chamber stood behind. Stelae identifying the individual and any other relative to be so honored would be placed in a niche in one of its walls. Occasionally, modest mud-brick tombs were also constructed on the desert plain, and the owners of some of them may have been associated with the owners of these chapels. They generally took the form of a *mastaba* with a substructure, usually containing more than one shaft. Some, however, have no indication of a superstructure. Recent excavations have also unearthed a cemetery of the same period devoted to the middle classes, and these are quite simple burials. The popularity of the site, as well as the restrictions applied to certain areas, are

indicated by the royal decree of Neferhotep I of the Thirteenth Dynasty, demarcating only particular quarters that could be used for burial.

Further south was Aswan, a strategic site from the earliest periods, located at the natural barrier of the First Cataract. On the cliffs of the west bank, many of the Middle Kingdom nomarchs of this area followed the tradition of the officials of the Old Kingdom and carved their final resting places on the high terrace, overlooking the Nile. A staircase ascends the cliff and opens onto a courtyard, the back wall of which becomes the façade, as in the tombs at Thebes. A portico can front the entrance, as is the case with the tomb of Sarenput I, and both this tomb and that of Sarenput II continue along an east-west axis with a rock-cut chamber with piers connected with another chamber by a fairly long corridor. The burials were reached through shafts or staircases. The corridor in the latter tomb has three niches on its north and south sides, and each contains a figure executed in such high relief that it approaches three-dimensional sculpture. These engaged statues are painted and are reminiscent of the anthropoid coffins that begin to appear during this period. While this tomb still has interior painted wall decoration (with the typical pale blue background color that is generally used here from the Sixth Dynasty on), such decoration appears to cease after the reign of Amenemhet II.

Additional sites in Upper Egypt, such as Dendera, Naga al-Deir, Gebelein, Moalla, and Akhmim also host Middle Kingdom tombs after the reunification, the private tombs at these locations were often constructed on a more modest level. These places had been in areas of importance during the First Intermediate Period. Many had large cemeteries of private individuals situated around the substantial funerary monument of the local administrator. This arrangement was not uncommon elsewhere in Egypt, and in a way, similar to the plan of the earlier royal pyramid complexes with their adjacent necropoli.

THE TOMBS OF MIDDLE EGYPT

Middle Kingdom tomb sites can be found throughout the country, although they tend to concentrate around the central areas that were the nuclei of provincial power in the preceding period. As noted above, the nomes around the Theban area in Upper Egypt represented one such focal point. The nomarchs of Thebes of the Eleventh Dynasty and their allies vied for supremacy with the Herakleopolitans of Middle Egypt of the Ninth and Tenth Dynasties and their supporters. The focus of Herakleopolitan influence was Middle Egypt, an area that had considerable provincial importance and where local nobles had begun to amass significant power toward the end of the Old Kingdom, and they may have increased that control during the early part of the First Intermediate Period to extend over much of the country. Nomarchs even dated inscriptions in their tombs according to their own reign, and not that of a king. The local officials who directly served these nomarchs refer in turn in their own inscriptions (for example, the Hatnub graffiti) to this district governor's tenure in office, not to that of the pharaoh. By the Middle Kingdom, the burials of the nobles tended to be large rock-cut complexes with porticoes that had pillars, and inside were chapels with false doors. Their plans had many architectural innovations as well as some affinities with earlier models. This style of burial had already appeared during the Old Kingdom at sites such as Giza, Meir, Deir al-Gebrawi, and Aswan, but now it evolved into a variety of forms. Iconography also has one foot in the past and one in the future, and the texts continue earlier traditions as well as introducing new material. Coffin Texts now become a staple in many high-ranking burials. Sites of importance in the Twelfth Dynasty include among others Beni Hassan, Deir al-Barsha,

Asiut, Meir, Deir Rifa, and Qaw al-Kebir.

The necropolis at Beni Hassan occupies two horizontal rows along the upper part of the cliffs that rise at the desert's edge. These final resting places of nomarchs and dignitaries of the sixteenth nome of the Eleventh and Twelfth Dynasty can be grouped into three different types based on their complexity. Many were constructed without porticoes and have only a few rooms, none with columns. Another group consists of those that have columns in a central hall and also a vault in the rear wall, similar to a plan of some tombs of the Old Kingdom. They also have no portico. The third group comprises the larger, more complex tombs with columned porticoes, and the columned main hall contains a shrine cut into the center of the rear wall. Some of the tombs have causeways ascending from the base of the hill.

The tomb of the nomarch Khety (no. 17) of the Eleventh Dynasty falls into the second category. There is a rectangular main chamber, the eastern half of which has two rows of columns, and near the southern wall are two burial shafts. The decoration painted on the wall depicts many typical scenes, but it also contains the representation of a battle, with some of the troops as well as some of the dead and wounded shown with details extending beyond the borders of the registers. The most elaborate type is well represented by the tomb of Amenemhet, a nomarch during the reign of Senusret I. Two columns adorn the portico in the center of whose rear wall is an entrance to the main chamber with four fluted columns. In its rear wall is a rock-cut shrine into which is carved a seated figure of the deceased with his mother and wife. Scenes of daily life are painted on the walls, and, as in other tombs, these include depictions of wrestlers and military activities. The tomb of Khnumhotep II, a nomarch during the reign of Amenemhet II also belongs to the third category.

On the walls of its porticoed main chamber is a unique representation of Asiatic Bedouin in a caravan, whose figures are portrayed with ethnic distinction in their physical features and the style and fabric of their garments. In the main hall, there is also a long inscription providing many details of provincial history. Coffins from the tombs in this area were inscribed with religious texts for the benefit of the deceased in the afterlife. Some of the tomb decoration from Beni Hassan includes interesting iconographic details, such as a griffin (also at al-Barsha), a caravan of Libyans, and dwarves.

Deir al-Barsha was the necropolis for the capital of the fifteenth nome during the First Intermediate Period and the Middle Kingdom, and the nomarchs as well as some of their retainers were buried in rock-cut tombs. Many of the names here can be associated with or identified as individuals specified in the graffiti carved in the rock quarry of Hatnub. It appears that the upper terrace of al-Barsha was reserved primarily for the higher officials, while the retainers were interred slightly below them on a lower level. Mud-brick *mastabas* were also used, but they were constructed earlier and were built along the desert plain at the base of the hill. As at Beni Hassan, the tombs range from the simple to the more elaborate to the complex. In the first, there is only one chamber entered through an entrance in the façade, and a shaft in the floor leads to the burial chamber. A statue niche was carved in the rear wall. A second group differs in that the rectangular chamber is fronted with a columned portico. The burial chamber in these can also be reached through a shaft near the portico. The third category increases the number of main chambers to two, and in the first of these are the shafts to the burials. The most prominent of the tombs, that of the nomarch Djehutihotep, belongs to the second group. Its

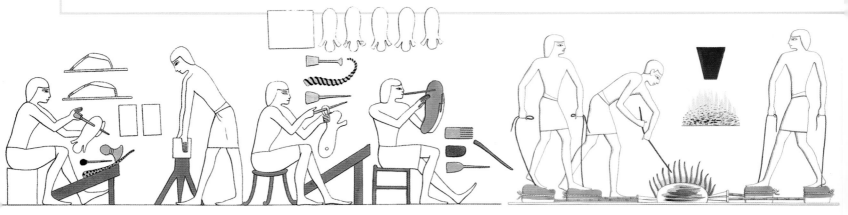

portico has two columns, and in its rear wall is an entrance to a large rectangular room. At the back of that is a raised shrine that originally had doors enclosing it. The most notable of the decoration on the walls depicts, in painted low relief, the transport of a colossal statue on a sledge from the quarry of Hatnub. The grand scale of the tomb, as well as that of the statue illustrated, attest to the power and importance of this nomarch and many of his equals, well into the Middle Kingdom (spanning the reigns of Amenemhet II and Senusret II and III). One tomb displays iconography symbolic of unification, unusual in a non-royal tomb (Djehutinakhte). One has both pre- and post-unification styles in its decoration (Ahanakhte). Another (Nehri II) uses the ceiling of the main chamber of the tomb as a surface on which to record particular Coffin Texts. A collection of spells, called *The Book of Two Ways*, appears almost exclusively at this locality. With the exception of one case where it occurs on the ceiling of a tomb (Nehri II), this composition is almost always limited to the floorboards of wooden coffins. Al-Barsha is one of the most significant sites in terms of coffins (and chambers) with Coffin Texts.

Meir, a necropolis for the officials of the fourteenth nome, has a series of funerary monuments whose continuous genealogy of the owners appears to indicate the hereditary nature of the office of nomarch from the end of the Old Kingdom through the Middle Kingdom. These are also rock-cut tombs, but they are not built on as impressive a scale as those discussed above, and none appear to have a portico. Some consist of one plain room with a statue niche in the rear wall, but the size and location of this shrine may vary; another group differs in that its single room is pillared; and a third category has a pillared chamber fronting a doorway to an inner room with a statue niche. Most, but not all, of the tombs have

decoration in low painted relief. The latest of the tombs, that of Ukhhotep III, who served under Senusret III, has only painted scenes in the large chamber with an offering niche at the back, but the workmanship is on a par with the best found at al-Barsha. The tomb of an ancestor with the same name contains a remarkable representation in relief of a Bedja tribesman, and in the main chamber of Senbi is a naturalistic desert scene where the animals are not linked to registers.

Rock-cut tombs are also the rule in the cemetery where the nomarchs of Asiut, the thirteenth nome, constructed their burials. While the earlier monuments, which date to the Herakleopolitan Period, are fairly simple, those of the officials of the Middle Kingdom generally utilize a more elaborate plan. Both of the major types of plans have several rooms that are set on a central axis. The first, typified by the tomb of Djefhapy, who served under Senusret I, has no pillars and contains two large halls, with the shrine centrally located in the rear wall of the last room. Along with two subsidiary chambers, it forms a tripartite arrangement. A similar configuration occurs in the first room, which has a subsidiary room opening onto it on either side of the entrance to the rear chamber. A successor with the same name who served under Amenemhet II built his monument, and it represents another type, but it is essentially a more elaborate version of the first. It has an outer court with a pillared hall (or portico) at its rear, which has a centrally located entrance to a rectangular chamber, which in turn is followed by a vaulted corridor that leads to a transverse hall. This last room has on its rear wall a tripartite shrine arrangement. This axial plan, with an emphasis on a rear tripartite offering area, is similar to that used in royal models of the Old Kingdom. It occurs also in a somewhat different

version in private Middle Kingdom chapels at Saqqara.

Similar in size and scope were the rock-cut tombs that the Middle Kingdom officials from the eleventh nome built at Deir Rifa. Although they used an axial plan, columns occur only in exterior areas, and there is no tripartite arrangement for the shrine. One tomb (Nekhetankhu) has stone beams carved on the architrave of the portico; this decorative motif is an interpretation of functional wooden ones in a prototype building. Similar details are known elsewhere (the tombs of Amenemhet and Khnumhotep at Beni Hassan and a model from the Theban tomb of Meketre). Monumental tombs were built during the reigns of Amenemhet II and Senusret III at Qaw al-Kebir, the necropolis constructed for three nomarchs of the tenth nome. Built on a longitudinal axis with chambers and corridors leading to a tripartite arrangement in the rear, the complex also included a riverine covered portico leading to a covered causeway ascending to the main parts of the tomb. The largest tomb is that of Wahka II, whose causeway extends more than 225 meters and opens onto a courtyard with a columned portico. Tomb shafts from the main chamber led to burial chambers of his relatives. A shaft from the innermost chamber led to his burial chamber. Elements of the architecture used here represent in part interpretations of and evolutions from models from the Old Kingdom (such as the causeway, lower landing area, and tripartite rear plan), but the use of open ramps, staircases, and terraced construction plans indicates the influence of Upper Egyptian models that are more contemporaneous. Interestingly, Wahka II does not seem to have held the title of nomarch, and his tomb, impressive as it was, appears to mark, more or less, the end of the line for this type of elaborate elite rock-cut tomb in the Middle Kingdom.

THE TOMBS OF NORTHERN EGYPT

The major distinction in the tombs of the north is that their locations tended to be mainly on the desert or Delta plains, and their plan, therefore, generally followed that of a *mastaba* type, similar to those common in the Memphite cemeteries of the Old Kingdom. While the Middle Kingdom versions clearly relied on models of the past for inspiration, they often were quite distinct from them, since they frequently employed different technological advances (such as devices to fool would-be robbers), architectural innovations (such as chapels separate from the *mastaba*), a distinguishing style and iconography, and certain textual variations (Coffin Texts). A superstructure in this particular rectangular form, however, was not always present. Burials without such structures above ground were also employed, although this situation may in fact be a result, in many cases, of destruction, reuse, or deterioration. Variations on some of the less complex arrangements found in the rock-cut tombs discussed above seem also to have been used on the tombs on the plains.

Northwest of Cairo, at the site of al-Qatta, most burials do not appear to have had superstructures, although excavators found a few traces of *mastabas* above ground in some areas. The former typically have significant burial chambers, and many have large barrel vaults. The canopic niche, ordinarily on the eastern wall in burial chambers at other sites, is located occasionally on the southern wall here. Further north and well to the east, is the site of Kom al-Hisn in the eastern Delta. In its vicinity is a cemetery in which a Middle Kingdom tomb belonging to the late Twelfth Dynasty official Khesu the Elder appears to be the most significant and 'upscale' of the burials in the cemetery. All that survives now is the single stone-lined burial chamber with finely carved representations of the deceased on the southern half of the west wall. The northern half of that wall, as well as most of the south and east, are incised primarily with hundreds of vertical lines of Coffin and Pyramid Texts, arranged in registers.

During the Twelfth Dynasty, the royal custom of burial in the south changed when Amenemhet I established his capital at Ity-tawi in the north, in an

378 top
The pyramid of King Senusret II at Lahun, Twelfth Dynasty. Senusret II chose not to follow his ancestors who built funerary monuments at Lisht and Dahshur; he constructed his pyramid

farther south, in the Fayum. On the northern side of his pyramid a series of mastabas for the royal family were constructed, as well as a small pyramid for the queen.

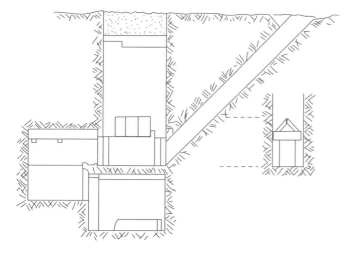

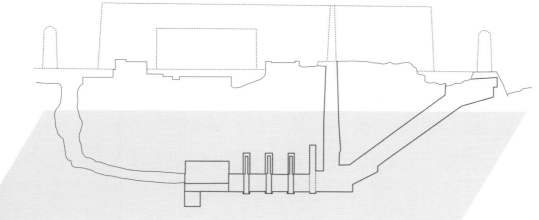

378 center and bottom
Plan and elevation of the tomb of Senusretankh at Lisht, Twelfth Dynasty. The architect of this official's tomb incorporated several methods to ensure the safety of the burial. He used a series of slabs of stone that slid into place to prevent entrance to the chamber, and he constructed a shaft full of rubble that would collapse on would-be tomb robbers. Neither device ultimately was successful.

area between Dahshur and Meidum, in the vicinity of the Fayum. This shift in the center of royal administration northward coincided with Amenemhet's establishment of a royal necropolis at the nearby site of Lisht. He may have begun construction on a funerary monument in Upper Egypt earlier in his reign, since there is at Thebes a platform of an unfinished funerary temple in the valley, northwest of the Ramesseum that some scholars have attributed to him (others, however feel it belonged to Mentuhotep III). Amenemhet may have abandoned it as his concentration was directed northward. In any case, at some point (suggestions range from as early as year three to five or as late as year twenty of his reign, with the earlier years seeming more likely), he made the decision to initiate construction of his new capital city and his nearby pyramid complex. Choosing a new capital city was not iconoclastic, as many predecessors who also had begun dynasties had chosen to do likewise. His successor Senusret I opted for interment at the same site. While most of the nomarchs of the provinces continued to build their pyramid complexes in the area of their power base, many officials who were close to these pharaohs decided to follow the model of their ruler and build tombs at Lisht. Undoubtedly, these individuals who headed the new departments of this transplanted capital were quite close to the pharaoh. Not all pharaohs of the Twelfth Dynasty chose this location as their final resting place. Some preferred other places, such as Dahshur, Lahun, Hawara, and perhaps Abydos (some scholars still question whether Senusret III was buried at Abydos or at Dahshur) for the locations of their pyramid complexes. Many of the high-ranking courtiers of these pharaohs followed their kings to the new sites. By the end of the reign of Senusret III, as a rule, officials abandoned their local associations in favor of establishing their tombs near the royal pyramid of their pharaoh.

Since the royal complexes of this dynasty were in the plains of the desert, the associated private tombs generally took the form of *mastabas*. Many had courtyards and mud-brick enclosure walls, and some of the superstructures had internal chambers. Burial chambers could be reached through vertical shafts or corridors, and in some cases, there were several additional subterranean rooms. In general, the *mastabas* were located outside the temenos wall that enclosed

the pyramid complex, presumably since it demarcated the royal sacred space. Royal exclusivity for this area, however, was not always maintained in the Middle Kingdom. For example, the *mastaba* of Intefoker at Lisht, although of a modest size with a shaft to the burial chamber, was erected within the enclosure of Amenemhet I, but well after the death of the king. Perhaps the proximity of this tomb to that of the king was an indication of the close personal relationship that this noble had with the pharaoh. Indeed, he too had come from Thebes and had constructed a tomb there, ostensibly for his mother, Senet.

In some cases, the architects used or modified protective devices similar to those found in royal burials (either Old or Middle Kingdom) for private tombs, such as portcullis stones that 'lock' in place, as well as plugging stones. The architect of the *mastaba* of Senusretankh, an official of Senusret I, used such mechanisms to protect the burial chamber and its contents. In addition, he also constructed a tapering shaft at the end of the sloping corridor leading from the superstructure, filled with rubble, which was set to collapse on any intruders just before the first of the four portcullis stones. This large monument had an enclosed chapel at the east end of its longitudinal axis. It had several other rooms as well, and it also included more than thirty subsidiary burials. The outer walls have some remnants of recessed panel decoration, similar to that found in the Old Kingdom. Many of the tombs of the most important officials in this area have a fairly complex subterranean burial plan that resembles the type that the reigning pharaoh had used. Some burials were less complicated, such as those with tripartite arrangements in shallow pits: an entrance, an offering chamber, and the burial chamber. A series of such tombs was situated near the pyramid of Amenemhet, and one of them (now dated at the earliest to Amenemhet III) belonged to Senebtisy, an apparently well-to-do individual, who, although not royal, possessed an extremely rich array of burial equipment and jewelry, close in quality and amount to that found in royal tombs at Dahshur. It appears that Lisht may have been the first site where *shabti* funerary figurines utilize a particular text, requesting the figure to perform required labor.

The pyramid of Senusret II was built at Lahun, and many of the high officials of the court were

interred in the necropolis there. Often these tombs had separate chapels, and some had pillared porticoes fronting a transverse hall with three shrines, a configuration known at other contemporaneous sites as well as in earlier times. For example, city temples built by kings of the Eleventh Dynasty sometimes have a rear broad hall with three niches. And such an arrangement is known also in royal pyramid temples. The tomb of Inpy also had such a plan with a forecourt, but it was partly cut into the rock cliff. It was adjacent to the tomb owner's massive mud-brick *mastaba*. The subterranean arrangement of the rooms is rather elaborate, and the architect positioned a false burial chamber in the upper part, while he 'hid' a functioning one below it. Many *mastabas* were constructed of mud brick, and occasionally these had recessed paneling, reflecting perhaps earlier architectural detailing. Some, however, were encased in stone. In some cases a shaft led to a horizontal or descending corridor. In others a sloping passageway would open on to the main subterranean chambers directly. They consisted of either a single room for burial or several rooms. Nearby, at the site of Hawara, Amenemhet III built one of his pyramids, and not far from it nobles constructed subterranean burial chambers with sloping corridors that led down from a stone chapel.

Dahshur, not far north of Lisht, was the location of the pyramid complex of Amenemhet II. The later Twelfth Dynasty king, Amenemhet III, also located his funerary complex at the same site. Senusret III chose to construct here as well. Whether the monument of the latter was a ceremonial or commemorative structure or one that actually served a funerary purpose for this monarch is still under deliberation. Some nobles of the court constructed their funerary monuments nearby. For example, a series of mud-brick *mastabas* are to the north of the complex of Senusret III. Recent excavations uncovered also three stone *mastabas*, one of which belonged to a vizier. The largest had a sloping corridor leading to a substantial burial chamber. An associated corridor led to the more modest burial of a woman, perhaps his wife. South of the enclosure wall of Amenemhet II is the burial chamber of the noble, Saiset, and on its walls were Pyramid Texts. Other sites such as Mazghuna, close by, also had tombs of the nobles. These were constructed not far from later pyramids, perhaps of the next dynasty.

380 left

The Middle Kingdom, Twelfth-Dynasty officials Ihy and Hetep built their tombs at Saqqara in the cemetery near the pyramid complex of the Old Kingdom pharaoh Teti. The plan and decoration of their tombs relied in part on royal models: the configuration of the court and chapel, the descending corridor, and the use of Pyramid Texts on the walls of their burial chambers.

380-381

Lector priests, identified by the band across their chest and the inscription before them, carry offerings before the seated image of Ihy depicted to the left. The horizontal register of hieroglyphs above the scene records that the fowl and haunches of meat pictured are among the products of Ihy's estates throughout the country.

Tombs of the Nobles

Saqqara, while not a site with a royal necropolis of the Twelfth Dynasty, still had a number of tombs of officials of the Middle Kingdom. Several were located in the vicinity of the Teti Pyramid complex, since most of these officials had associations with the mortuary cult of this Sixth Dynasty king. Perhaps the earliest of the Middle Kingdom tombs were those of Ihy and Hetep, now dated to the reign of Amenemhet I. While these individuals did not build a *mastaba*, they each had constructed for themselves an above-ground stone chapel with a mud-brick enclosure wall. The interior consisted of a courtyard with pillars, and at the south end of the rear wall was an opening to a narrow transverse room. Its rear wall had a tripartite arrangement consisting of two statue shrines and an offering chapel with a false door, resulting in a plan that suggests some archaizing elements as well as parallels to other more contemporaneous models mentioned above. The block statues that were set in these chapels represent an innovation and introduce a style of statuary that was to become extremely popular throughout this dynasty and later. In the courtyard of each chapel was a shaft to a slightly descending horizontal corridor, the length of which was just shy of about 10 meters, and each opened onto a burial chamber. That of Ihy actually consisted of two adjacent rooms, only one of which was

completed. Hetep had a single chamber, and the sarcophagus was set in a recessed floor with a slight projection into the south wall. Canopic equipment in both tombs was in a niche on the east wall. The subterranean section with a long corridor, leading to a burial chamber decorated entirely with Pyramid Texts, is reminiscent of earlier royal models. While not as dramatic a situation as that of Intefoker at Lisht, these two tombs were also situated within the boundaries of the royal sacred space. However, their encroachment would not have been visible to any passerby (unlike the situation with that of Intefoker, whose tombs was built later). Since the chapels were located on the north side of the pyramid, outside the enclosure wall, and the burial chambers were well below ground, they were under the wall and extended into royal sacred space.

Later in the Twelfth Dynasty, two other officials, Sekweskhet and Sahathoripy, built their burial chambers wholly within the enclosure walls of Teti's complex, perhaps indicating a lessening of restrictions or a change in decorum. There are indications that they, like their predecessors, had a superstructure outside the boundaries of the wall, but the structure may have been quite different, perhaps even a *mastaba*, judging from reliefs recently discovered that may originate from just such a structure. A very long horizontal corridor with a modest descent extended

underground almost 25 meters before it opened near the north wall of Sekweskhet's burial chamber. Thus far, two portcullis stones have been located, and there may be a third before the shaft is reached (perhaps a parallel to the pattern in Senusretankh's tomb).

Since this area of Saqqara was riddled with tombs dating from the Sixth Dynasty in a fairly unbroken sequence well into the Middle Kingdom, it is possible that the officials buried here during the Twelfth Dynasty may have had political or family connections with this area. Indeed, Ihy and Hetep held titles in the mortuary cult of Teti, and Sahathoripy and Sekweskhet appear also to have possessed similar positions. There is also the possibility that the latter two may have been associated with a family memorial chapel built on the opposite (south) side of the pyramid of Teti, which, some scholars believe may have functioned similarly to the memorial structures at Abydos. On the basis of the analysis of the iconography, paleography, and phraseology, it appears that it may span several generations, with its earliest use dating perhaps to the period about or just prior to reunification, and the latest usage into the Thirteenth Dynasty. It is possible that strong familial associations, as well as links to the earlier royal mortuary cults, here were primary in influencing these officials to choose interment at Saqqara rather than at a site near the ruling pharaoh.

*As the cutaway shows, the subterranean corridor in the
complex of both Ihy and Hetep descends at an angle quite
a distance toward the sarcophagus chamber, thereby
allowing the deceased to be buried in the sacred ground
of the royal pyramid complex of Teti to the south.*

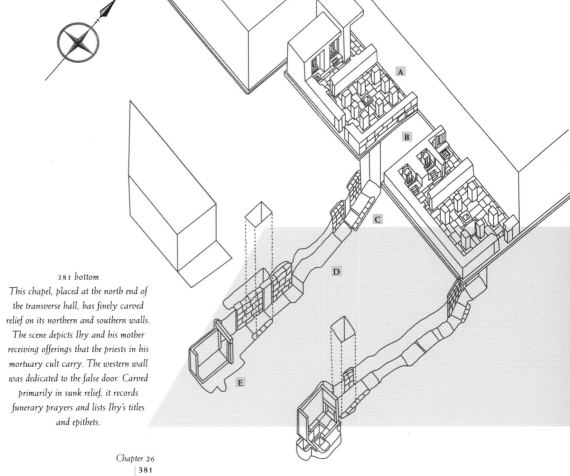

*381 bottom
This chapel, placed at the north end of
the transverse hall, has finely carved
relief on its northern and southern walls.
The scene depicts Ihy and his mother
receiving offerings that the priests in his
mortuary cult carry. The western wall
was dedicated to the false door. Carved
primarily in sunk relief, it records
funerary prayers and lists Ihy's titles
and epithets.*

Chapter 27

Royal and Private Statues of the Old and Middle Kingdoms

by Hourig Sourouzian

The statuary of the Old and Middle Kingdoms in Egypt is mainly dedicated to the king and his elite. Royal statuary appears in early royal funerary complexes at Abydos and Saqqara, as well as in the archaic divine temples of Hierakonpolis or Abydos. At that time, private statuary was rare, and was produced only as part of the king's surroundings. In the Old Kingdom, sculpture in the round flourished. The majority of the statues derive from royal funerary temples of the Memphite region and their auxiliary cemeteries comprising the tombs of the great officials. Fewer statues are found in divine temples, but that is essentially because those temples have seldom survived. Later kings strived to 'surpass all that had been done before,' rebuilding or replacing temples constructed under their predecessors. Any divine statues those temples might have sheltered have thus likewise rarely survived. As no trace remains of the palaces of the Old Kingdom, it is impossible to know what kind of statues would have represented the monarch in his residence. It is in the transformation of the royal residence into funerary complexes, built in durable materials for eternity and equipped with depictions of the deceased king and his elite, that we see a glimpse into the official appearances, duties, and performances of the king in his daily life and a glance at the courtiers who surrounded him, because that is what the statues were intended to illustrate and perpetuate. In the funerary complexes that surrounded the pyramid, royal and divine statues were part of the temple apparatus, together with stelae, barques, tables of offerings, stands, and other temple furniture. Both in the valley temple where the king was venerated and in the funerary temple through which the king gradually passed to the celestial world after being introduced and admitted into the sphere of the gods, certain types of statues were reserved for each temple division. They were translations into three dimensions of the funerary and ritual scenes that were represented in bas-relief on the walls of the temples. Thus, statues were an integral part of Egyptian architecture.

The repertoire of official statuary includes royal effigies of certain types showing the king in special attitudes, each corresponding to a certain ritual. These depictions extend from the gates of the temple, where the king was expected to repel chaos by smiting his enemies, and the first court where he was purified to present offerings to the gods, to the interior where, after his rebirth, he was welcomed, nursed, and raised by the lioness goddess or a mother goddess to be finally crowned as king of Upper and Lower Egypt and introduced to the great god who gave him the ruler's insignia for eternity. This itinerary, which we know in more detail from the better-preserved temples of the Middle and New Kingdoms, is not only described by scenes carved in relief on the temple walls, but also documented by statues, both monumental and of smaller size, that illustrate every moment of the divine kingship within the temple precinct, from his day of birth to the coronation, and finally, his admittance to the sphere of the gods. Major ceremonies, like the coronation or the jubilee festival that served to repeat the coronation rites after thirty years of reign, occupy an important place in the temple. Thus, each type of statue has a specific place within the funerary complex, with its corresponding costume and related attributes a special costume and related attributes.

382

Black granite sphinx of Amenemhet III, dated to the Twelfth Dynasty, 150 cm high, 236 cm long, and 75 cm wide. This monumental sphinx is one of an ensemble of Middle Kingdom royal effigies found reused in Tanis. Unlike classical sphinxes, it represents the king more realistically as a lion with a royal face bearing the uraeus and beard, and surrounded by real leonine ears and mane. The expressive face is rendered with heavily modeled features characteristic of Amenemhet III. Now in the Egyptian Museum, Cairo.

The material chosen for these statues varied from reign to reign and depended on the quality of the quarry in use during the reign. For royal statuary conserved or known from records, the materials were the hardest stones, the most precious metals, and the most durable woods. Due to the hazards of conservation, it is not possible to suggest any convention in the choice of the material, but from the preserved examples we may only observe that the reigns of Djoser and Sneferu favored limestone for statuary as well as for the architecture of their funerary complexes, and we know from the records of the Palermo Stone that Sneferu, like Khasekhemwy before him in the Second Dynasty, had produced copper statues. In Seila, west of Meidum, a chapel near the step pyramid of Sneferu has revealed alabaster fragments of a statue of the king. The same material was found in the valley temple of Khufu, who probably also used diorite, as his name was found in the corresponding quarries. Khafre mainly chose diorite and graywacke, as did Menkaure, who also used alabaster. In the Fifth Dynasty, the royal statuary in the pyramid temple of Neferefre used limestone, granite, and alabaster. In the divine temple of Hierakonpolis, Pepy I dedicated copper statues; smaller statues of the Sixth Dynasty kings attest to alabaster and graywacke, but their provenance is unknown. At this stage in the documentation, it is difficult to say if the material was merely the choice of the king or a compulsory requirement due to as yet unknown conventions, and if so, whether the selection of the material was dependent on the temple category, its place in the temple, or the symbolism of colors and material relative to the surrounding architecture.

The earliest types of statue are those of the king striding, standing, or seated. The king striding perpetuates the image of the monarch coming out of his palace to perform ceremonies. In the royal residence in the afterlife, what we call the funerary complex, these statues enable the monarch to come out from his eternal dwelling (the tomb) and participate in all rituals. This type is already attested in the archaic period, and the convention with the left foot forward will remain until the end of ancient Egyptian statuary. One

variant, mainly used for stone statuary, shows the king with both arms hanging down beside his torso. This type is best illustrated in the Old Kingdom by the formidable statue of King Sneferu that was inserted in the niche of one of the back chapels of his valley temple in Dahshur. Sneferu wears the white crown of Upper Egypt, and the pleated royal short kilt, which is held around the waist with a belt bearing a rhomboid decoration and a buckle in the form of a cartouche containing the name of the king. A large collar and a bracelet with floral decoration complete his attire. A second variant of this type shows the king striding, with one hand hanging down by his side and the other thrust forward, holding a staff. Known from the earliest two-dimensional royal representations, this variant with the raised forearm is difficult to execute in stone and was thus easier to render with statues in wood or metal where the arms were articulated, that is, fashioned separately and joined afterward to the body. The best representative of this type is the larger of the two copper statues of Pepy I, found in the deposit of the temple of Hierakonpolis and recently cleaned and conserved in the Egyptian Museum, in Cairo.

The king standing, wrapped in a festival cloak with his feet joined and hands crossed over his chest, holding the royal scepter and staff, is a type that appeared in the porticoes of the festival court of Djoser at Saqqara and was later transformed in the Middle Kingdom into a mummiform figure through a similarity of attitude with that of Osiris. At this stage, far before the first depictions of the mummified Osiris, this statue type represented an image of the king performing ceremonies at festivals, which were numerous, including the thirtieth-year jubilee festival. A variant of this type represents the king enthroned and wrapped in the jubilee cloak. This type is also known since the archaic period and is best illustrated in the Old Kingdom by the famous seated statue of Djoser, which depicts the king wearing a massive tripartite wig covered by an early form of the *nemes* headdress. A very long ceremonial false-beard is tied under his chin. From the cloak emerge his hands, the left one laid flat on the knee, the right fist clenched against his chest. On other similar but fragmentary statues of Djoser, the king holds a flail carved in bold relief on his torso and, in later examples from the Old Kingdom, the king was represented holding the two royal insignia, the crook and the flail, as he is shown on the alabaster enthroned statuette of Pepy I.

Another variant of the pose, holding only the flail, shows the ruler seated and wearing the short pleated kilt instead of the cloak, as is illustrated by the ivory statuette of Khufu that depicts him with the red crown of Lower Egypt.

Quite different is the more common statue type of the king seated, wearing the royal kilt with his hands resting on his lap, either one palm open and the other hand clenched, or both palms open and laid flat on the knees. This represents the classical type of the enthroned king and is frequently eancountered throughout the history of Egyptian art. Seated statues of this kind were placed in columned halls of the funerary complex as shown by the great statue of Khafre from his valley temple at Giza. This statue type depicts the king in his divine aspect, seated at the offering table. His left hand lies flat on his lap; his right hand is clenched and placed vertically on his thigh, holging a kerchief. The head of the king is covered by the *nemes* headdress behind which stands a falcon with opened wings, personifying the dynastic god Horus. The seat is supported by lions and the sides are decorated with the heraldic plants of Upper and Lower Egypt, symbolizing the unification of the Two Lands. This statue personifies the close relationship between the sovereign and the god. The king is the representative of Horus on earth and the god manifests himself through the appearance of the king, the living Horus. Several seated statues, smaller in size and sculpted in diorite and graywacke, were placed all around the court and the pillared hall of the valley temple of Khafre. From the examples found, now on display in the Egyptian Museum in Cairo, and the traces of their foundation in the temple, there are estimated to have been a total of twenty-seven statues.

385

This seated limestone statue of King Djoser, found in his funerary complex at Saqqara, dates to the Third Dynasty, is made of painted limestone, and is 142 cm high, 45.3 cm wide, and 95.5 cm in depth. Egyptian Museum, Cairo.

Royal and Private Statuary

386
The Great Sphinx of Giza, 20 m high and
73.50 m long, is a monumental rock-cut
sculpture at the southernmost limit of the pyramid
complex of Khufu. It combines for the first time
the head of a king wearing the royal headdress
with the powerful body of a lion.

387 left
Seated statuette of Khufu, now in the Egyptian
Museum in Cairo, found in the temple of
Khentamentui-Osiris at Abydos. Dating to the
Fourth Dynasty, reign of Khufu, it is ivory and
measures 7.5 cm in height, 2.5 in width, and 2.9
in depth. Egyptian Museum, Cairo.

387 right
This seated diorite statue of Khafre with the
falcon god Horus behind his head is from his
valley temple in Giza. Dated to the Fourth
Dynasty, the statue is 168 cm high and is in the
Egyptian Museum, Cairo.

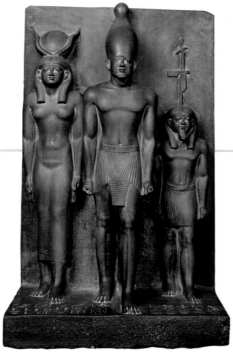

Four seated statues in alabaster were found in the court of the valley temple of Menkaure. All facing east, they flanked the entrance leading to the sanctuary in pairs.

Group statues representing the king with deities or with members of the royal family developed during the Old Kingdom. A group of four pairs of feet resting on a common base is conserved in the festival court of Djoser's pyramid complex, but the best preserved examples of this statue type are, of course, the famous statue groups of Menkaure: five triads and a dyad, masterfully executed in graywacke. Each of the triads represents the king standing between the goddess Hathor and the personification of a nome, except one, today at the Museum of Fine Arts, Boston, where Hathor is sitting in the middle, flanked by the king and the nome goddess. In each triad the king either holds the hand of Hathor or is embraced by her and the nome personification. On the triad where he appears standing near the enthroned goddess Hathor, the king holds a mace. He wears the crown of Upper Egypt, and the pleated short royal kilt is held at the waist by a belt. A striated beard adorns his chin. The attire of the goddesses is a striated tripartite coiffure and a long tight-fitting robe. The facial features and the anatomy of the figures are masterfully rendered. The sculpture was completed by painted elements, such as the facial cosmetics, the necklace, and the details of the king's belt.

The dyad represents the striding figure of Menkaure embraced by a queen. Here the king wears the *nemes* headdress, and the queen a tripartite wig under which part of the original hair is visible in front. Here again the details of the attire were probably gilded or completed with paint. Other statues of Menkaure populated the valley temple. Among them, the most remarkable are the seated statues in alabaster mentioned above. These

sculptures bear witness to the excellent skill of the Egyptian artists who harmoniously combined aesthetic quality with technical achievement. Fragmentary statue groups from the reigns of Sneferu and Djedefre attest to effigies of the enthroned king with the queen seated near his feet on the statue base. There is as yet no evidence of princes or male members of the royal family represented with the king. The first known instance of a king's son engraved on the side of a royal statue occurs only in the Thirteenth Dynasty.

An exceptional dyad from the reign of Niuserre, now in the Egyptian Collection, Munich, represents two almost identical figures of the king striding side by side. The essence of this double representation is not yet clear, but the type was abundantly imitated in private statuary with the production of 'pseudo-groups' displaying the same individual two, three, or more times, side by side.

Statues of the king kneeling and holding two pots of wine or milk in his hands were placed in front of a divine statue, which has rarely survived, and thus were parts of groups. A hand of a statue holding a wine pot was discovered in the funerary temple of Khafre, and the first known complete example of such a statue dates to the reign of Pepy I. The provenance of this statuette is not known and it is

impossible to determine if it derives from a funerary complex or a divine temple.

In the Fourth Dynasty, a sculptural innovation as extraordinary as the invention of the pyramids made its appearance. Merging the royal head with a lion's body, the Great Sphinx of Giza was sculpted from the rock at the southern edge of the funerary complex of Khufu. This extraordinary innovation in Egyptian art may be considered the first monumental sculpture of its kind. The Great Sphinx represents King Khufu, whose facial features repeat those of the seated ivory statuette of the king from Abydos and not those of his successor Khafre as was generally believed due to an incorrect interpretation of a lacunar text on the 'Dream Stela' of Thutmose IV, written some one thousand years later. Recent research and critical analysis in art history provides archaeologic, stylistic, and iconographic evidence for the attribution of the Great Sphinx to Khufu.

A smaller-sized sphinx in limestone comes from the pyramid temple of Djedefre in Abusir. In Giza, a pair of oblong pedestals with rounded back parts flank the entrance to the valley temple of Khafre and bear witness to the existence of a pair of royal sphinxes or lions. Recently, during excavations conducted by Egypt's Supreme Council of Antiquities at Saqqara, parts of four limestone sphinxes were discovered at the entrance of the valley temple of Unas. The Sixth Dynasty has left a few examples of monumental and small sphinxes, among them the first known example of a sphinx with human hands presenting offerings of wine pots.

Current excavations conducted by Waseda University, Japan, at Abusir have uncovered votive sphinxes in terracotta with a royal figure standing between the paws and bearing the name of Khufu. These votive offerings were deposited in a sanctuary during the reign of Pepy I and confirm the association of the Great Sphinx with Khufu.

388 and 389
These two triads of Menkaure, found in the valley temple of the king at Giza, are made of greywacke and represent the king standing between Hathor and a personification of a nome. In each dyad the king is depicted in the middle and is flanked by the goddess Hathor on his right side and the nome deity on his left. The excellent workmanship in the technique goes hand in hand with the high artistic quality of the sculptures. At left is the triad with the goddess of the seventh Upper Egyptian nome, which measures 96 cm in height, 61 cm in width, and 37cm in depth. On the right is the triad with the Theban nome. It is 89 cm high, 53 cm wide, and 40 cm deep. These two statues are now in the Egyptian Museum, Cairo.

Royal and divine statues received invocations and offerings. Thus, through them, the king was able to receive all offerings that were brought to the altars of his temple. The members of the court, buried in the official necropolis, also participated in these offerings. Beginning in the archaic period, tombs of courtiers and officials surrounded the tomb of the monarch. In the Old Kingdom, members of the royal family, architects and pyramid builders, leaders of expeditions, priests and scribes, surrounded the king in his eternal residence, just as they had done during their lifetime in the court around the royal palace. Their tombs, or *mastabas*, developed rapidly into important dwellings for the afterlife. Instead of a funerary temple, the private tombs have a niche or an offering chapel with a table of offerings, and instead of a sanctuary, a hidden chamber, the *serdab*. We know from well-preserved examples that both the niche and the *serdab* were occupied by statues of the deceased, like the funerary apartments of the king. For an official, it was a high honor to be the owner of a tomb granted by royal decree; likewise, it was a privilege to have a statue in his own image. It is thanks to the royal quarrymen, architects, and masons that a tomb was built, and it is by the royal workshops of sculptors, artists, and craftsmen that it was decorated and furnished. By royal order, these tomb owners could also participate in the official offerings. Their statues were constrained by certain rules, to special types and prescribed materials. Not just any individual had the right to possess a tomb in the vicinity of the pyramid of his king, and once he had obtained that favor in return for his extraordinary skill and achievements, he had a choice within a restricted range of statue types. From the recent excavations of Zahi Hawass in the southern part of the Giza plateau, we now know that the workmen and builders of the pyramids also had their own quarter of tombs, though modest, and a choice of statues.

At an early stage private statue types were reduced to two main attitudes, the seated and the standing, which evidently imitated those of the king. They differed from the latter by their limited number, their smaller size, differerences in costume and especially, different attributes.

The striding and seated attitudes are the most usual, as they imitate the corresponding attitudes of the king. The pose of the hands, whether palm open or clenched on the chest or on the thigh, largely depends on that of the effigies of the ruling king. With time, the statues become more numerous and the number of types increases to include scribal and group statues. Following the conventions of group statues of the king with deities, queens, or princesses, the officials put on display members of their family, such as their wife and children, and even pseudo-groups of themselves. These groups display a rich combination of both attitudes (seated and striding) with a great variety of poses: standing side by side; seated or striding, one embracing the other; one seated and the other(s) standing; or accompanied by naked children with their thumb in the mouth, as illustrated by the group statue of Seneb and Senetites. These group statues are numerous and extremely interesting, not only for the study of rank and titles, but for their great part in the history of Egyptian art in the Old Kingdom.

Although the kneeling pose is seldom preserved in royal statuary, the statue of the funerary priest Hetepdief dating from the early Old Kingdom attests to an early practice of that type in Egyptian sculpture.

The material used for private statuary is mainly limestone, which was painted with vivid colors to convey life, or sometimes painted red or black to imitate granite, as this stone was rarely or only occasionally granted to individuals in the Old Kingdom. The few known exceptions using red or black granite date to the end of the Third Dynasty: Ankh at the Museum of Leiden and at the Louvre, Ankhwa at the British Museum, Metjen in Berlin, and the princess Redjef in Turin, to cite the better known pieces. Examples from the Fourth Dynasty are the red granite statue of Setka in the Louvre, and the basalt effigy of Perniankhw in Cairo. By the end of the Fourth Dynasty, Babaf, chief of all works of the king, had a great number of statues cut in different materials such as graywacke, red granite, diorite, basalt, limestone, and alabaster. In the Fifth Dynasty, the vizier Ptahshepses not only had a very large *mastaba* near the pyramid of his king at Abusir, but also a large variety of life-sized and over-life-sized statues in various materials including quartzite. Finally, in the Sixth Dynasty, some officials like prince Tjaw from Saqqara owned a statue in graywacke, today in the Egyptian Museum in Cairo. All were princes or officials of very high rank, viziers, royal sons, and so on; a few others of lower rank may have been favorites of the king due to special services or achievements, such as the shipbuilder Ankhwa or the dwarf Perniankhw.

Wood is another standard material for private statuary. As with limestone, wood was also covered with a thin coat of plaster and painted. A great number of statues from the Old Kingdom had inlaid eyes that gave them such a vivid expression that statues like those of Rahotep and Nofret from Meidum, or Ka-aper ('Sheikh al-Beled') from Saqqara, are striking even now in their extraordinary liveliness.

At the beginning of the Old Kingdom, in the Third and part of the Fourth Dynasty, individuals were depicted with their attributes carved in bold relief on the statue itself, like the standing statues of Sepa, holding staff and scepter, the seated statues of Ankhwa holding the adze of the shipbuilder, and of Perniankhw with a scepter and a long staff in his hands. Under the reign of Sneferu at Dahshur, there is even a statue of the musician Ipi depicted as a flautist with a long reed flute in his hands.

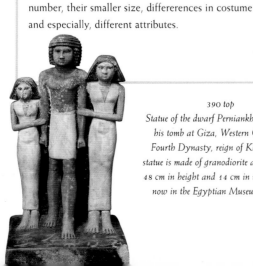

390 top
Statue of the dwarf Perniankhw, found in his tomb at Giza, Western Cemetery, Fourth Dynasty, reign of Khafre. The statue is made of granodiorite and measures 48 cm in height and 14 cm in width and is now in the Egyptian Museum, Cairo.

390 bottom
This group statue depicts Mersuankh and his daughters in painted limestone. Found in the mastaba of Mersuankh at Giza, the statue dates to the Fourth Dynasty and is 28 cm high, 21 cm wide, and 20.5 cm deep. Egyptian Museum, Cairo.

391
This group statue represents Seneb and his family and was found at Giza, in his tomb. The statue, now in the Egyptian Museum in Cairo, is in painted limestone and dates to the Fourth Dynasty. Height 34 cm, width 22.5 cm, and depth 25 cm. Egyptian Museum, Cairo.

Nevertheless, the attributes tend to disappear during the Fourth Dynasty, or to be replaced by short sticks used either as substitutes for longer staves or in imitation of the rolled kerchief and container of documents that the king holds in his hands.

The strong tendency to individualize the model, now depicted life-sized, dominates the private statuary of the Fourth Dynasty, producing a rich series of masterpieces that depict the master builders of the Great Pyramids. For example, we might mention the statues of prince Rahotep and Nofret, which were found in the funerary chapel of their *mastaba* in Meidum. Rahotep was a son of Sneferu, a high priest of Ra at Heliopolis, and chief of all construction projects for the king. He is sitting on a seat with a high backrest, his right arm bent over his chest and his left placed on his thigh, and his hands are clenched to suggest the attributes he would be holding. He wears a short kilt tied under his belly by a bold knot. He has short hair and a thin moustache. A heart-shaped amulet hangs around his neck. His wife Nofret, designated as 'one known to the king,' is likewise seated, and places both hands over her chest. She wears a heavy shoulder-length wig, encircled by a diadem that is ornamented with rosettes. Part of her natural hair is visible at the front. She is enveloped in a long mantle under which appear the straps of her tight-fitting dress. A broad collar composed of concentric rings of colored beads adorns her breast. In accordance with artistic conventions, the man's skin is painted ochre-brown, and that of the woman a pale cream color. Their eyes are inlaid in a copper frame: the white part of the eye is made of opaque quartz, the iris and pupil of rock crystal. On the high backrest, the name and the titles of the statue owners are written in black hieroglyphs. This pair of statues marks the beginning of a long range of portraits representing the illustrious personages of the court who witnessed not only the construction of the most extraordinary buildings of Egypt but also the development of a most glorious society.

392-393

The statues of Prince Rahotep and his wife Nofret, now in the Egyptian Museum in Cairo, were found in their mastaba at Meidum. They are made of painted limestone and date to the early Fourth Dynasty, beginning of the reign of Sneferu. Rahotep: height 121 cm, width 51 cm, depth 69 cm; Nofret: height 122 cm, width 48.5 cm, depth 70 cm.

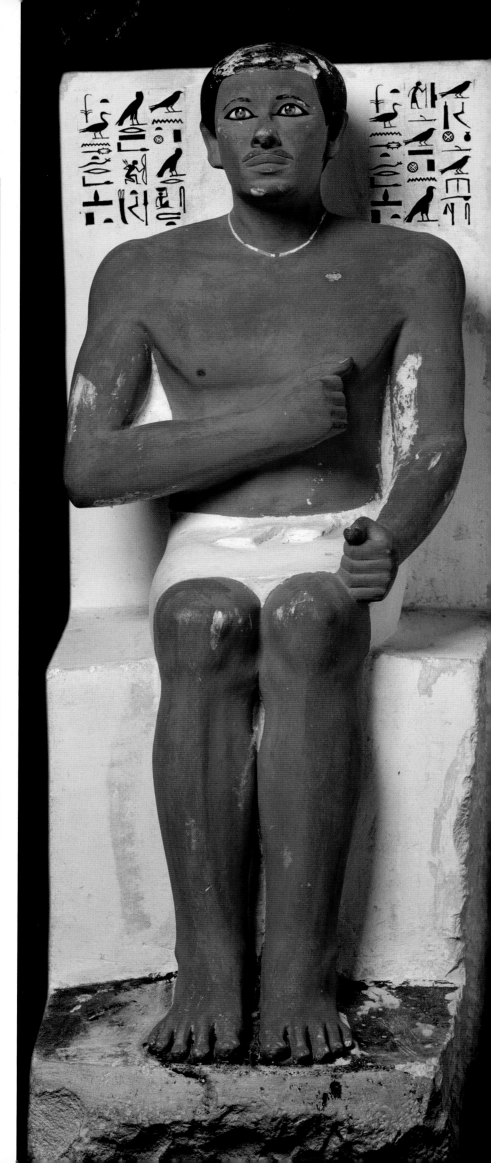

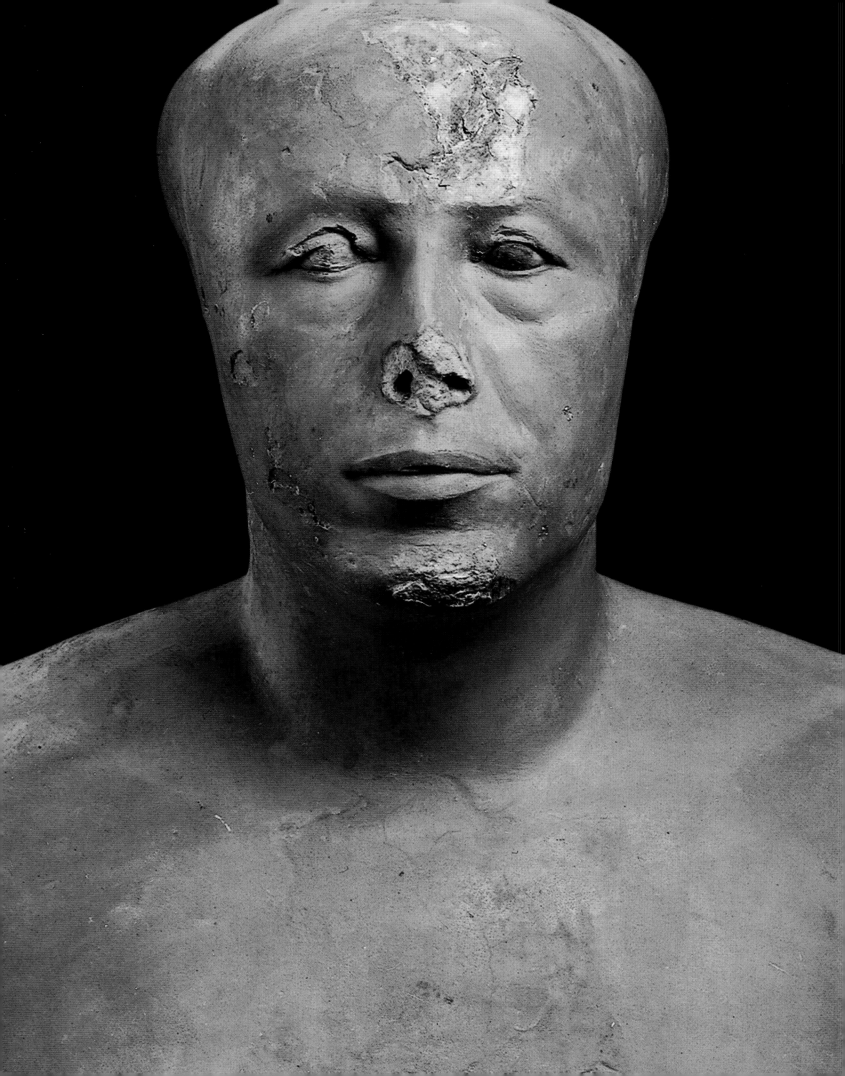

For a certain period during the reign of Khufu, most probably in relation to the Great Pyramid and the Great Sphinx, monumental statuary also appeared for members of the royal family, such as the extraordinary statue of Prince Hemiunu, a pyramid builder and vizier who had the title of 'king's son' by virtue of being Sneferu's grandson. He is the one who directed the building of the Great Pyramid of Khufu, whose nephew he was. His father Nefermaat, owner of a large *mastaba* at Meidum, was the eldest son of King Sneferu and older brother of Khufu. Hemiunu, as chief of all works of His Majesty, owned a tomb in the western cemetery of the pyramid of Khufu, with his statue placed in the *serdab*. The head was destroyed by tomb robbers, but it was possible to reconstruct it based on fragments recovered by Junker when he discovered the statue in 1912. It is a most remarkable statue, for its monumental dimensions as well as its imposing presence. Seated on a cubic stool, his left hand laid flat on his knee and his right fist clenched over his thigh, Hemiunu wears a short kilt tied at the waist by a knot. The physiognomy of the prince is impressive. The impressive head is accentuated by a double chin. His corpulence is executed with great realism: a heavy chest doubled by a ridge of fat. His massive arms frame a very thick abdomen where the navel is rendered by way of a furrow within the fat of the belly; his substantial legs and parallel feet with very clearly carved toenails enhance the monumentality of the sculpture. In all, this is clearly a portrait of a very high official of the elite, an evident declaration of royal power; as the portrait of an individual, it is the living image of a pyramid builder, majestic like the image of the king, eternal like the mass of the pyramid. The hieroglyphic text, inlaid with colored paste, a technique invented by Nefermaat at Meidum, gives his name and titles.

Hemiunu is exceptional. Perhaps already at the end of the reign of Sneferu and surely under the strict reign of Khufu, instead of statues, the tombs were equipped with rectangular slabs on which the deceased was represented seated at the offering table. At the bottom of their shafts, these tombs contained limestone heads of the owner, sculpted skillfully as heads only, generally called 'reserve heads.' They bear the features of the deceased and may therefore be considered as ideal portraits of the tomb owners. The most elaborate of this type is the bust of the prince Ankh-khaf, who was the brother of Khafre and his vizier.

394
The painted limestone bust of Ankh-khaf comes from his mastaba in the Eastern Cemetery of Giza. Height 50.6 cm; Fourth Dynasty. Conserved in the Museum of Fine Arts, Boston.

395
The statue of Prince Hemiunu, Fourth Dynasty, was found in his mastaba in the Western Cemetery of Khufu, in Giza (G 4000). Made of limestone, it measures 155.5 cm in height, 61.5 cm in width, and 104.7 cm in depth, and is conserved in the Pelizaeus Museum, Hildesheim.

396 left
*The wooden statue of the priest Ka-aper,
called the 'Sheikh al-Beled,' was found in
his mastaba at Saqqara, and now is
conserved in the Egyptian Museum,
Cairo. Sculpted of sycamore wood, the
statue dates to the Fourth Dynasty and
is 112 cm high.*

396 right
*This wooden statue of a female, found in
the mastaba of Ka-aper in Saqqara,
probably represents his wife. The lady
wears a short wig and a tight fitting dress.
Dated to the Fourth Dynasty, the statue
is 61 cm high, and can now be admired in
the Egyptian Museum, Cairo.*

Under Menkaure and by the end of the Fourth
Dynasty, private statuary again appears in the tombs
in large numbers. Another colossal statue of 2.40 m,
from Giza, unfortunately very damaged, represents
the queen Khamerernebty II, consort of Menkaure. It
is in the Egyptian Museum, Cairo. Several tombs of
the Memphite necropolis display rock-cut statues of
the tomb owner and members of the family, best
illustrated by the tomb of Meresankh III at Giza.

One of the most striking and celebrated likenesses
of the Fourth Dynasty is the life-size wooden statue
of the lector-priest Ka-aper, depicted in all his
corpulence and with his lively round face animated by
inlaid eyes, so lively that the workmen of Mariette
identified him as the 'Sheikh al-Beled,' the headman of
their village. In the Fifth Dynasty, officials like Ty and
Ptahshepses, owners of very large tombs, also
commissioned over-life-sized statues, whereas the
statuary of the common officials tends toward a
certain conformity in style and standardization of
scale and proportions. In the tomb of Mereruka at
Saqqara, the statue of the deceased is exceptionally
large and is cut into the back wall of the niche. In the
Sixth Dynasty, private statuary decreases in scale but
proliferates in number, diversifies in attitudes, and
changes in proportions. Individuals, like the kings,
appear now with smaller heads on long bodies with
high and narrow waists.

397
*This bust of a male statue in wood was
found in a tomb in Saqqara. The
extraordinary vividness of the face is
enhanced by the lively expression of the
inlaid eyes. The statue is 69 cm high
and dates from the Fourth to Fifth
Dynasty. Now in the Egyptian
Museum, Cairo.*

The statue type of the scribe figure appears in the early Fourth Dynasty and remains until the Late Period. Probably influenced by the attitude of the king kneeling and presenting offerings to the gods, the official was authorized to be represented squatting, with a papyrus containing divine writing unrolled on his lap. In this position, the individual can be depicted writing, reading, listening, or simply meditating or praying. Admittedly, not all persons portrayed as a scribe held that function in the royal court, but all were high-ranking officials eager to be depicted as possessing the faculty of writing, the highest distinction ever aspired to. Of all the numerous scribe statues, the most impressive are those of the scribe Kai in the Louvre and of his colleague in the Egyptian Museum, from Saqqara. In spite of their conventional and unnatural seated attitude, these statues show very realistic facial features, enlivened by the vividness of the paint and the inlaid eyes.

As the officials of the king surrounded their sovereign in the afterlife, the officials in turn gradually included in the repertoire of the tomb statuary servants and people of the household who were supposed to execute the domestic work and especially all activities related to the cultivation of land and the harvest, baking and brewing, fishing and hunting, navigation and transport—all professions that have a close relationship to the offerings that the deceased expected on his offering table in front of the false door. This is also how statues of servants gradually became part of the official statuary, as shown by a great number of figures of brewers, bakers, potters, and so on.

The prisoners held by the king were also part of his world, bound or trampled under his feet, especially when the king appears as a hybrid creature such as a griffin (a lion with a falcon head) or as a sphinx. In the Fifth Dynasty, such creatures trampling their enemies appear in two-dimensional representations on the walls of the causeways leading to the funerary temples at Abusir. The recumbent sphinx at the gates of the temples can be regarded as their translation to sculpture in the round. Heads of captives are known from the reign of Djoser onward, and statues of bound prisoners were discovered at the entrance of Sixth Dynasty temples at Saqqara.

In the Middle Kingdom, the royal residence, first at Thebes, moves back to the Memphite region and the construction of pyramids starts again. Besides the royal pyramid complexes and their funerary temples, a few divine temples dedicated by the kings to the major deities of their residence or capital are preserved from this period. They have revealed royal statues of old and new types, in hard stones, wood, and metal, now increased to colossal size. Moreover, the temples now also enclose a variety of private statues. Since the end of the Old Kingdom, the former administrators of the nomes had developed into practically independent governors, and accordingly had acquired prerogatives which had been previously reserved for the king alone. They dedicated statues in the temples of their residence. Their tombs in Middle Egypt grew to become large complexes preceded by pylons and courts, filled with the choicest equipment and naturally, with monumental statues. Some are preserved, like the very impressive ones from Qaw al-Kebir, today at the museum of Turin; others are lost, but one of them is known through an exceptional record: a colossal seated statue of Djehutyhotep, governor of the fifteenth nome, is represented on the wall of his tomb at al-Barsha. Mounted on a sledge, the statue is dragged by four rows of forty-three men each. By now the high ranking officials had also gradually obtained the privilege to deposit statues not only in their tombs but also in the divine temple precincts, within the processional ways and the first courts. These statues, which are numerous, include new variants of old attitudes as well as newly invented types. More hard stone than ever before was used for private statuary, which includes exceptional pieces of art as well as works of hasty craftsmanship.

398 left
The seated scribe writing on a papyrus roll, found in a tomb in Saqqara, is made of painted limestone and dates to the Fifth Dynasty. It is 53.7 cm high, 44 cm wide, and 35 cm deep. Musée du Louvre.

398 right
This statuette of a butcher cutting and cleaning a goose, in painted limestone, was found in a tomb in the Western Cemetery at Giza. Fifth Dynasty, now in the Cairo University Museum.

399
This seated scribe in the attitude of writing, dated to the Fifth Dynasty, was found in the Western Cemetery at Giza, and is 46.5 cm high and 23.5 cm wide. Now in the Cairo University Museum.

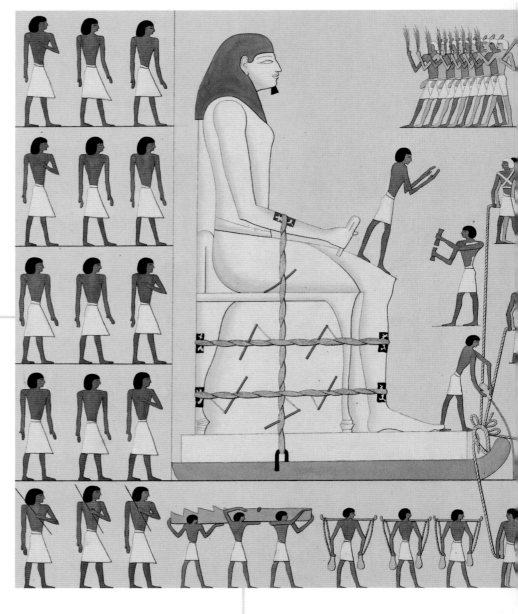

The classical statue types representing the king striding or seated, as well as the sphinx, continued in the Middle Kingdom with evident changes in style and additions in iconography. The kneeling king, holding in his hands two pots of wine or milk, is now definitely attested in divine temples and placed in front of a statue of a deity that has rarely survived.

Two examples of colossal statues of the classical type from the Twelfth Dynasty illustrate the new tendency in royal sculpture: the colossal striding statues of Senusret I in red granite and a seated statue of Amenemhet II in black granite. Like several other examples of Middle Kingdom colossal royal statuary, these were found in the temple of Tanis, which was the residence of the Third Intermediary Period kings

in the East Delta. These colossi originally derive from Memphis or the Ramesside residences in the Delta, where they had been re-inscribed and re-erected by Ramesses II, and eventually were reused in Tanis. Compared with the peaceful and majestic features of the Old Kingdom monarchs, the new portraits of the Middle Kingdom kings follow another aesthetic and hand down a new message: is it a question, a worry, a sadness that shows through these faces, or can it be understood as aggression or eagerness to rule? The anatomy of these kings is powerfully well rendered, with their athletic proportions suggesting force, smoothed surfaces transmitting youth, and tense, menacing musculature. This was a period when Egypt expanded into new territories and the monarchs now assumed the rule of a great empire.

400 left
This statue of King Senusret I, later reinscribed and reused by Ramesses II, was found in Memphis, in the southern processional way of the temple of Ptah. Sculpted from red granite and painted, it is 9.10 m high and is dated to the early Twelfth Dynasty with inscriptions and retouching from the Nineteenth Dynasty. Mit Rahina Museum Compound.

400-401
This drawing, after a scene painted on a wall of the tomb of Djehutyhotep at al-Bersha, depicts the transport of a colossal statue of a province administrator, the governor of the fifteenth Upper Egyptian nome, who depicted a colossal statue of himself mounted on a sledge being dragged along by four rows of 43 men each. Early Twelfth Dynasty.

Royal and Private Statuary

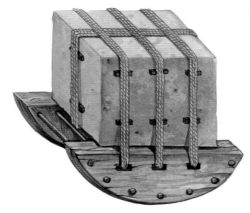

401 bottom left
This drawing suggests the possible use of a rocker for the transport of heavy blocks. Rockers are only known from models in the foundation deposits of temples.

401 right
This seated colossus of a Twelfth Dynasty ruler, restored and re-inscribed by Ramesses II, was found reused in Tanis during the Third Intermediate Period. Made of black granite, it is 320 cm high, and dates to the mid-Twelfth Dynasty, reigns of Amenemhet II or Senusret II. Egyptian Museum, Berlin.

A wooden statue of King Auibre-Hor striding, with the left hand hanging and holding a scepter, the right hand holding a long staff in front of the body, shows the continuity of the very archaic striding type, but its iconography adds an important element to our understanding of the statuary: the king is depicted with a divine beard and two raised hands (symbol of the *ka*) surmounting his tripartite wig. Therefore, this is a representation of the *ka* of the king, his alter ego who continues his life hereafter. Through the *ka*, the king is able to receive the offerings.

Among the new statue types that appear in both divine and royal funerary temples, one represents the striding king with hands placed flat on the triangular front panel of a pleated kilt, generally wearing the *nemes* headdress. Commonly called 'the king praying', this type corresponds, in representations on temple walls, to a standing royal figure adoring the gods or being purified by them before being introduced to the supreme deity. This attitude was naturally copied by the high officials, who imitate the gesture of the hands on their long skirts.

In royal funerary complexes, the archaic figure of the king wrapped in his jubilee cloak recurs in the Eleventh Dynasty at Thebes, with the renowned statues of Mentuhotep wrapped in a short cloak, both seated (in the Egyptian Museum, Cairo) and standing (in the Metropolitan Museum of Art, New York), and was still in use in major divine temples. Shortly after the middle of the Eleventh Dynasty, a mummiform effigy of the king made its appearance in the attitude of the festive king, the hands crossed on the chest and holding the royal insignia, but with the body completely wrapped in a shroud like that of Osiris, the god of death and rebirth: thus the appellation 'Osiride' statue. This type may be the result of a confusion with the form of Osiris, or more probably a deliberate assimilation with this god, whose popularity had increased since the end of the Old Kingdom. At any rate, the temples of the Twelfth Dynasty, be they royal funerary as under Senusret I at Lisht or divine as at Karnak, now display mummiform figures of the king in their courts, a type that will remain until late in the New Kingdom.

402

The statue of the ka of King Auibre-Hor, found at funerary complex of Amenemhet III in Dahshur, dates to the Thirteenth Dynasty. Made of wood, coated with a thin plaster of gypsum and painted, with inlaid eyes, it is 170 cm high, 27 cm wide, and 77 cm deep. Egyptian Museum, Cairo.

403

This statue of King Nebhepetre II Mentuhotep, found in a rock-cut chamber under the first court of the funerary temple of Mentuhotep II at Deir al-Bahari, is painted sandstone. Height 138 cm, width 47 cm, depth 101 cm,, Eleventh Dynasty. Now in the Egyptian Museum, Cairo.

Royal and Private Statuary

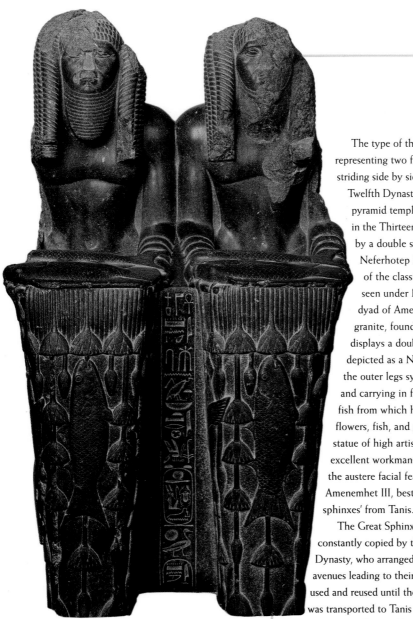

The type of the royal dyad representing two figures of the king striding side by side reappears in the Twelfth Dynasty in Amenemhet III's pyramid temple at Hawara, followed in the Thirteenth Dynasty at Karnak by a double statue of King Neferhotep I. Whereas these dyads of the classic type were already seen under Niuserre, a very original dyad of Amenemhet III in black granite, found reused in Tanis, displays a double effigy of the king depicted as a Nile deity, striding with the outer legs symmetrically advanced and carrying in front of them trays of fish from which hang strands of lotus flowers, fish, and geese. This double statue of high artistic quality and excellent workmanship exquisitely renders the austere facial features of King Amenemhet III, best seen on the 'mane sphinxes' from Tanis.

The Great Sphinx was a prototype constantly copied by the kings of the Twelfth Dynasty, who arranged them in pairs on the avenues leading to their temples. One pair, used and reused until the later periods when it was transported to Tanis where it was found, is so strongly influenced by the Great Sphinx that for a certain time, scholars tended to attribute it

to the Old Kingdom. A type of 'mane sphinx' already known in the Old Kingdom reappears on a larger scale in the Middle Kingdom, under the reign of Amenemhet III. A series of sphinxes with the face of the king surrounded by a realistic leonine mane and combined with the body of a lion also made their way to Tanis, after several re-inscriptions by rulers from the Hyksos to the Ramessides and to the Third Intermediate Period kings.

In the Twelfth Dynasty, a new type of private statuary appears and remains as a favorite type until the Late Period. This is the block statue, which represents the owner squatting with his body enveloped in a garment from which his hands emerge crossed over the knees, sometimes also leaving the legs or feet free. In later times, individual may hold a sprig of lettuce, a lotus, or other emblem. This extremely schematized sculptural type may have been inspired by representations of people carried in a sedan chair. Did these compact statues come into fashion to economize workmanship, to save material, to assure durability, to present a solid surface to receive offerings, or to offer smooth plane surfaces for the self-praising autobiographical inscriptions and offering formulae that covered their massive body? There may have been simply a practical reason, as the inscriptions on the statue usually contain an appeal to the living ones who pass by to say a prayer and offer some water and bread—the block-shaped statue could have indeed been the ideal form to receive the offerings. All these assumptions may be true, without

404 top left
The dyad of Amenemhet III as offering bearer was found reused in Tanis. Made of granite, its dimensions are: height 160 cm, width 100 cm, depth 80 cm. Now conserved in the Egyptian Museum, Cairo.

404 bottom
Quartzite statue of the vizir Gau, Thirteenth Dynasty, 99 cm high. Now in the Ny Carlsberg Glyptotheque, Copenhagen.

405 top
The block-statue of Hetep from his tomb at Saqqara, early Twelfth Dynasty, is made of grey granite, is 74 cm high, and is now in the Egyptian Museum, Cairo.

any one being the complete answer. In any case, Egyptian art attains an exceptional level of abstraction with these statues which will not be outdone thereafter.

Probably influenced by the representations of the king in the jubilee cloak, we now find more and more private statues in the seated, striding, or squatting attitude, showing the owner wrapped in a mantle. Likewise fashionable is the long skirt that is knotted just under the breast and most favored by viziers. Two examples brilliantly illustrate the extraordinary presence, splendor, and authority that radiates from these private effigies. The black granite statue of the vizier Sebekemsaf in the Kunsthistorisches Museum, Vienna, shows a corpulent man, slightly smaller than life size, striding, arms hanging on the side of his torso, which is enveloped in the viziers' long skirt, bordered by festoons. His head is bald, his face round with deeply carved eyes, plastic eyebrows, and modeled facial musculature; his expression is very stern. Another example, in red quartzite, on display in the Ny Carlsberg Glyptothek, Copenhagen, shows the vizier Gau seated in the attitude of the scribe with naturalistic eyebrows, bulging upper eyelids, and horizontal thin lips, features which foreshadow the Second Intermediate Period which will follow.

One word remains to be said about portraiture. The question is always asked: were these statues portraits, or were they idealized 'hieroglyphs' to represent the model? Without magic or criminological techniques to tell us exactly how these persons, kings, queens, priests, and officials looked, there is no way to answer that question. But in art history, that query is needless because, be they called conventions or stylistic differences, stylized or naturalistic character, idealized or realistic quality, it is through these official features that we recognize immediately Djoser, with his stern expression on his thick and bulging lips; Khufu, through his large square shaped face which we also detect on the Great Sphinx; Djedefre's harmonious smooth face; Khafre's distant majesty; Menkaure's small round head and athletic body; or the youthful features of Userkaf, so smooth that his portrait was thought to be that of the goddess Neith before we detected his moustache under certain lighting conditions. It is impossible to compare the serene visage of Pepy I with the menacing look of Mentuhotep II or the furrowed face of Senusret III. In private statuary, who could confuse Rahotep with Seneb, or Hemiunu with the 'Sheikh al-Beled', or the vizier Sebekemsaf, in spite of their common corpulence? The proper conclusion is that the Egyptian statues are likenesses of the models and may be considered as portraits. The artist will never have to justify whether the portrait resembles the subject or not; it is only important that the observer identify the model's characteristic features as they have been observed by the artist. The famous portraits of Dora Marr, by the brush of Picasso, are at once recognizable and cannot be confused with any of the other female heads painted by the artist.

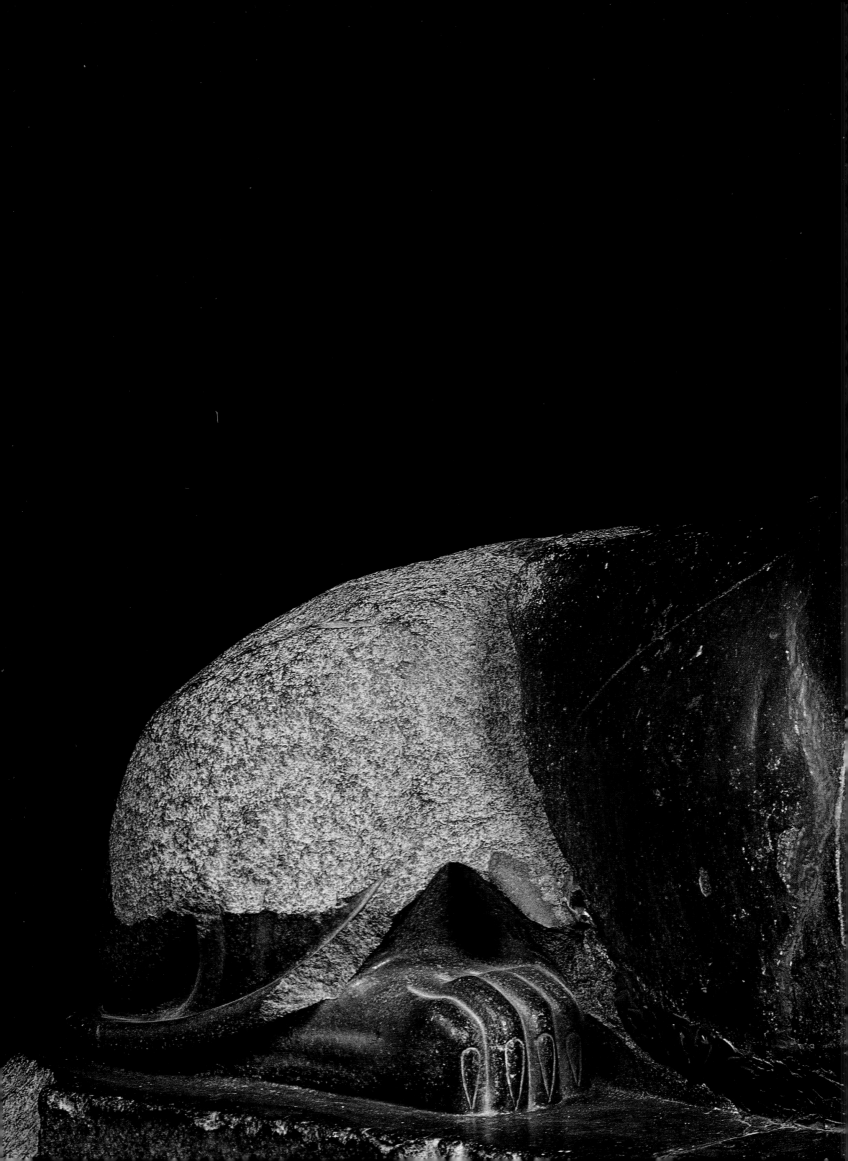

INDEX

BIBLIOGRAPHY

THE PYRAMIDS
Text by Zahi Hawass

World-renowned archaeologist **Zahi Hawass** has served in the field of Egyptian archaeology for over 40 years. He began as an inspector of antiquities and reached the top in 2011, when he was appointed Minister of Antiquities. Dr. Hawass received his doctorate from the University of Pennsylvania in 1987. He has written numerous books and made many major discoveries near the pyramids of Giza, such as the tombs of the pyramid builders. He plans to reveal the secrets behind the doors found inside the Great Pyramid soon. One of Dr. Hawass' most significant research efforts was the Egyptian Mummy Project (EMP), which used modern forensic techniques such as CT scanning and DNA analysis to answer questions about human remains from ancient Egypt. Through the EMP, Dr. Hawass was able to identify the mummy of Queen Hatshepsut, uncover the family of King Tutankhamun and solve the mystery of the murder of Ramesses III. He has received many prizes and awards, including five honorary doctorates from top universities around the world. Dr. Hawass has appeared in many documentary films shown all over the world, and has published articles in many international magazines. *Time Magazine* honored him as one of its Top 100 Most Influential People for 2005.

Photo credits:
1 Marcello Bertinetti/Archivio White Star
2-3 Giulio Veggi/Archivio White Star
4 Marcello Bertinetti/Archivio White Star
6-7 Araldo De Luca/Archivio White Star
8 Araldo De Luca/Archivio White Star
9 Araldo De Luca/Archivio White Star
10-11 Araldo De Luca/Archivio White Star
13 Kenneth Garrett
16-17 Kenneth Garrett
17 Mohamed Megahed
18 left Sharaf Mona/Reuters/Contrasto
18 right Mohamed Megahed
18-19 Kenneth Garrett
19 top Aladin Abdel Naby/Reuters/Contrasto
19 center Aladin Abdel Naby/Reuters/Contrasto
19 bottom Mohamed Megahed
20 top Kenneth Garrett
20 bottom Kenneth Garrett
20-21 Kenneth Garrett
21 top Kenneth Garrett
21 center Mohamed Megahed
21 bottom Angelo Colombo/Archivio White Star
22 top left and right Mohamed Megahed
22 bottom left and right Mohamed Megahed
22-23 Mohamed Megahed
23 Mohamed Megahed
24 top AP/LaPresse
24 center AP/LaPresse
24 bottom Mohamed Megahed
25 AP/LaPresse
26 Marc Deville/Getty Images
26-27 AP/LaPresse
27 top Mohamed Megahed
27 bottom left Patrick Chapuis/Gamma/Contrasto
27 bottom right Mohamed Megahed
28 Jean-Claude Aunos/Gamma/Contrasto
29 top Jean-Claude Aunos/Gamma/Contrasto
29 center right Mohamed Megahed
29 bottom left AP/LaPresse
29 bottom right Jean-Claude Aunos/Gamma/Contrasto
30 Mohamed Megahed
30-31 Jean-Claude Aunos/Gamma/Contrasto
31 left and right Jean-Claude Aunos/Gamma/Contrasto
33 Araldo De Luca/Archivio White Star
34-35 Araldo De Luca/Archivio White Star

WHY A PYRAMID? PYRAMID RELIGION
Text by James Allen

James Allen received his degree in Egyptology from the University of Chicago, with a dissertation on the grammar of the Pyramid Texts. He has served as epigrapher with the University's expedition in Luxor, Egypt, and as Cairo Director of the American Research Center in Egypt. Since 1986 he has held a research appointment at Yale University, and has taught there as well as at the University of Pennsylvania. He is currently Curator of Egyptian Art at the Metropolitan Museum of Art and Vice-President of the International Association of Egyptologists. Dr. Allen's specialties include ancient Egyptian language, texts, and religion, and he has written extensively on these subjects as well as the history of the Middle Kingdom and Amarna Period. He is the author of *Genesis in Egypt: the Philosophy of Ancient Egyptian Creation Accounts* and, most recently, *Middle Egyptian: an Introduction to the Language and Culture of Hieroglyphs*.

Bibliography:

Allen, J. "Reading a Pyramid," in *Hommages à Jean Leclant* (Bibliotheque d'Étude 106; Cairo: Institut Français d'Archéologie Orientale, 1994), vol. 1, pp. 5-28.
Barta, W. "Die Beudeutung der Pyramidentexte für den verstorbenen König," *Münchner Ägyptologische Studien* 39 (Munich, 1981).
d'Auria, S. H., et al., *Mummies & Magic: the Funerary Arts of Ancient Egypt*. Boston, 1988, pp. 27-59.
Quirke, S. *Ancient Egyptian Religion*, London, 1992.
Ritner, R. K. "The Cult of the Dead," in D. P. Silverman (ed.), *Ancient Egypt*, London, 1997, pp. 132-147.

Photo credits:
36 Araldo De Luca/Archivio White Star
36-37 Giulio Veggi/Archivio White Star
38, 39, 40, 41 Araldo De Luca/Archivio White Star

THE ADMINISTRATION OF THE PYRAMID
Text by Vassil Dobrev

Vassil Dobrev, a French archaeologist, was born in 1961 in Varna (Bulgaria). In 1992, he received is PhD in Egyptology from the University of Paris-Sorbonne for his dissertation "Researches on the Kings of the Fourth Egyptian Dynasty." From 1995 until 1998, he was Scientific Member of the French Archaeological Institute in Cairo (IFAO). Since 1987, he has worked on the excavations of the pyramids and temples of Pepy I and his Queens at South Saqqara. Since 2000, he has been responsible for the IFAO Mapping Project of South Saqqara and Director of the IFAO Mission at Tabbet al-Guesh (South Saqqara). The author of several scientific studies, and he is specialized in the inscriptions of the pyramid builders and pyramid history.

Bibliography:

Dobrev, V. "Les marques de la pyramide de Pépy Ier. Notes complémentaires," *BIFAO* 98 (1998), pp. 151-170.
Eyre, C. J. "Work and the Organisation of Work in the Old Kingdom," in M. A. Powell (ed.), *Labor in the Ancient Near East*, New Haven, 1987, pp. 5-47 (American Oriental Series, vol. 68).
Posener-Kriéger, P., *Les Archives du temple funéraire de Néferirkarê-Kakaï (Les papyrus d'Abousir). Traduction et Commentaire, 2 vol.* IFAO, Le Caire, 1976 (BdÉ 65).
Reisner, G. A. *Mycerinus: The Temples of the Third Pyramid*, Cambridge, Massachusetts, 1931, pp. 273-275, appendix E, pl. XI-XII.
Roth, A. M., "Egyptian Phyles in the Old Kingdom. The Evolution of a System of Social Organization," *SAOC* 48 (Chicago, 1991).

Photo credits:
42 Giulio Veggi/Archivio White Star
43 Vasko Dobrev
46 Marcello Bertinetti/Archivio White Star

BUILDING AN OLD KINGDOM PYRAMID
Text by Mark Lehner

Mark Lehner is one of the leading experts on Giza's Great Sphinx and Pyramids. He is president of the nonprofit research organization AERA, Inc., that sponsors the Giza Plateau Mapping Project. The project conducts excavations of Old Kingdom settlements near the Sphinx and Pyramids with a team of archaeologists, geochronologists, paleobotanists, and faunal specialists. Lehner has appeared on television in National Geographic's *Explorer* program, and on NOVA's *Secrets of Lost Empires* series on ancient technology including *This Old Pyramid and Obelisk*. He is author of *The Complete Pyramids* published in 1997. In addition to books and articles in print, Lehner's book on the Great Sphinx is in preparation with the University of Chicago Press. From 1990 until 1995 Lehner was Assistant Professor of Egyptian Archaeology at the University of Chicago. He is now a Research Associate at the Oriental Institute of the University of Chicago and at the Harvard Semitic Museum. Lehner was born, raised, and began his college education in North Dakota. He went to Cairo in 1973 as a Year Abroad Student at the American University in Cairo where he received his B.A. in Anthropology. He lived in Egypt in for thirteen years, working for American, Egyptian, British, French, and German archaeological projects. From 1979 until 1983 he was the Field Director and then Director of the Sphinx Project sponsored by the American Research Center in Egypt. In 1984 he began the Giza Plateau Mapping Project (GPMP), sponsored by ARCE and Yale University where Lehner received his Ph.D in Egyptology in 1990. In 1988 the GPMP began to excavate in search of the settlement and infrastructure that supported the pyramid work force. The team has discovered a workers' city that includes work shops, storage buildings, bakeries and a large royal administrative center from the time of the pyramids (ca 2,500 B.C.).

Bibliography:

GENERAL

Arnold, D., *Building in Egypt. Pharaonic Stone Masonry*, New York and Oxford, 1991.
Badawy, A., "The periodic system of building a pyramid," *JEA* 63 (1977), pp. 52-8
Dunham, D., "Building an Egyptian Pyramid," *Archaeology* 9, no. 3 (1956), pp. 159-65
Garde-Hansen, P., *On the Building of the Cheops Pyramid*, Cascais, 1974.
Hodges, P. and E. B. J. Keable, *How the Pyramids Were Built*, Shaftesbury, Dorset, England, 1989.
Isler, Martin, *Sticks, Stones, and Shadows: Building the Egyptian Pyramids*, Norman 2001.
Lauer, J.-P., "Comment furent construites les pyramides," *Historia* 86 (1954), pp. 57-66.
Mencken, A., *Designing and Building the Great Pyramid*, Baltimore, 1963.
Petrie, W. M. F., "The Building of a Pyramid," in *Ancient Egypt* (1930), pp. 33-9.
Smith, Craig, "Program Management B.C.," *Civil Engineering* (June 1999), pp. 34-41.

SUPPLY AND TRANSPORT

Bietak, M., "Zur Marine des Alten Reiches," in *Pyramid Studies and Other Essays Presented to I.E.S. Edwards* (London, 1988), pp. 35-40.
Bradbury, L., "Kpn-boats, Punt trade, and a lost emporium," *JARCE* 33 (1996), pp. 37-60.
Fischer, H. G., "Two tantalizing biographical fragments of historical interest, 1. a speedy return from Elephatine," *JEA* 61 (1975), pp. 33-5.
Goyon, G., "Les navires de transport de la chausée monumentale d'Ounas," *BIFAO* 69 (1971), pp. 11-41.
Goyon, G., "Les portes des pyramides et le grande canal de Memphis," *RdÉ* 23 (1971), pp. 137-53.
Haldane, C., "A new method of ancient Egyptian hull construction, preliminary report," *Mariner's Mirror* 74 (1988), pp. 141-52.
Haldane, C., "The Lisht timbers: a report on their significance," in D. Arnold (ed.), *The Pyyramid Complex of Senwosret I*, New York, 1992, pp. 102-12.
Landström, B., *Ships of the Pharaohs*, Garden City, 1970.
Schenkel, W., "Kanal," *LÄ* III, (1980), pp. 310-12.
Sølver, C. V., "Egyptian obelisk ships," *Mariner's Mirror* 33 (1947), pp. 39-43.

ORGANIZING THE LANDSCAPE

Aigner, T., "Facies and origin of nummulitic buildups: an example from the Giza Pyramids Plateau (Middle Eocene, Egypt)," *N. Jb. Geol. Paläont. Abh.* 166 (1983), pp. 347-68.
Aigner, T., "Zur Geologie und Geoarchäologie des Pyramidenplateaus von Giza, Ägypten," *Natur und Museum* 112 (1983), pp. 377-88.
Lehner, M., "The Development of the Giza Necropolis: The Khufu Project," *MDAIK* 41 (1985).

QUARRIES

Engelbach, R., *The Aswan Obelisk*, Cairo, 1922.
Engelbach, R., *The Problem of the Obelisks: From a Study of the Unfinished Obelisk at Aswan*, London, 1923.
Harrell, J. A., "An inventory ofancient Egyptian quarries," *NARCE* 146, (spring 1989), pp. 1-7.
Harrell, J. A. and T. M. Bown, "An Old Kingdom basalt quarry at Widan el-Faras and the quarry road to Lake Moeris," *JARCE* 32 (1995), pp. 71-92.
Harrell, J. A. and V. M. Brown, *Topographical and Petrological Survey of Ancient Egyptian Quarries*, Toledo, 1995.
Klemm, D. and R. Klemm, "Herkunftsbestimmung altägptischen Steinmaterials," *SAK* 7 (1979), pp. 103-40.
Klemm, D. and R. Klemm, *Steine der Pharaonen*, Munich, 1981.
Röder, J., "Steinbruchgeschichte des Rosengranits von Assuan," *Archäologischer Anzeiger* 3 (1965), pp. 461-551.

THE NOVA PYRAMID

Lehner, M., "The Pyramid," in *Secrets of Lost Empires*, New York, 1996, pp. 46-93.

TOOLS, TECHNIQUES, AND OPERATIONS

Hinkel, F. W., "Hölzernes Fördergerüst an der Cheopspyramide?" *Das Altertum* 2, no. 28 (1982), pp. 113-18.
Lane, M., "The pull-saw in Egypt," *Ancient Egypt and the East*, (June 1935) pp. 55-8.
Lucas, A. and J. R. Harris, *Ancient Egyptian Materials and Industries*, London, 1962.
Moores, R. G., "Evidence for the use of a stone-cutting drag saw by the Fourth Dynasty Egyptians," *JARCE* 28 (1991), pp. 139-48.
Petrie, W. M. F., *Tools and Weapons, Egyptian Research Account* 22, London, 1917.
Ryan, D. P., "Old rope," *KMT* 4, no. 2 (1993), pp. 72-9
Teeter, E., "Techniques and terminology of rope-making in ancient Egypt," *JEA* 73 (1987), pp. 71-7
Zuber, A., "Techniques du travail des pierres dures dans l'Ancienne Egypte," *Techniques et Civilizations* 29.5 , no. 5 (1956), pp. 161-78.
Zuber, A., "Techniques du travail des pierres dures dans l'Ancienne Egypte," *Techniques et Civilizations* 30. 5, no. 6 (1956), pp. 196-215.

SURVEY AND ALIGNMENT

Borchardt, L., 'Ein altägyptisches astronomisches Instrument,' ZÄS 37 (1899) pp. 10-7
Borchardt, L., *Längen und Richtungen der vier Grundkanten der grossen Pyramide bie Gise* (Berlin, 1926)
Cole, J. H., *The Determination of the Exact Size and Orientation of the Great Pyramid of Giza* (Survey of Eygypt Paper No. 39) (Cairo, 1925)
Dorner, J., 'Die Absteckung und astronomische Orientierung ägyptischer Pyramiden' (Innsbruck, 1981).
Dorner, J., 'Studien über die Bauvermessung und astronomische Orientierung,' AfO 32 (1985) pp. 165-66
Goyon, G., 'Quelques observations effectuée autour de la pyramide de Khéops,' BIFAO 47 (1969) pp. 71-86
Isler, M., 'An ancient method of finding and extending direction,' JARCE 26 (1989) pp. 191-206
Isler, M., 'The merkhet,' VA 7 (1991) pp. 53-67
Isler, M., 'The gnomen in Egyptian antiquity,' JARCE 28 (1991) pp. 155-86
Lauer, J.-P., 'À propos de l'orientation des grandes pyramides,' Bulletin de l'Institut d'Égypte (1960) pp. 7-15
Lehner, M., 'Some observations on the layout of thepyramids of Khufu and Khafre,' JARCE 20 (1983) pp. 7-25
Lehner, M., 'The Giza Plateau Mapping Project season 1984-85,' NARCE 131, no. (Fall 1985) pp. 23-56
Lehner, M., 'The Giza Plateau Mapping Project,' NARCE 135 (Fall 1986) pp. 29-54
Lepsius, R., *Die alt-ägyptische Elle* (Berlin, 1865)
Neugebauer, O., 'On the orientation of pyramids,' Centaurus 24 (1980) pp. 1-3
Petrie, W. M. F., *Ancient Weights and Measures* (London, 1926)
Pochan, A., 'Observations relatives au revetement des deux grandes pyramides de Giza,' Bulletin de l'Institut d'Égypte 16 (1934) pp. 214-20
Zába, Z., *L'orientation Astronomique dans l'ancienne Égypte, et la précession de l'axe du monde* (Prague, 1933)

RAMPS, LEVERS, LIFTING THEORIES

Arnold, D., "Überlegungenzum Problem des Pyramidenbaues," *MDAIK* 37 (1981), pp. 15-28.
Cunningham, J., "Techniques of pyramid building in Egypt," Nature 332, no. 3 (1988).
Dunham, D., "Building an Egyptian pyramid," Archaeology 9, no. 3 (1956), pp. 159-65.
Fitchen, J., "Building Cheops' pyramid," *Journal of the Society of Architectural Historians* 37 (1978), pp. 3-12.
Isler, M., "Ancient Egyptian methods of raising weights," *JARCE* 13 (1976), pp. 31-41.
Isler, M., "On pyramid building," *JARCE* 22 (1985), pp. 129-42.
Isler, M., "On pyramid building II," *JARCE* 24 (1987), pp. 95-112.
Lowdermilk, R., "Re-inventing the machine Herodotus said built the Great Pyramid," *KMT* 2, no. 4 (1991), pp. 45-53.

RISE AND RUN - CASING

Arnold, D., "Maneuvering casing blocks of pyramids," in John Baines, et al. (eds.), *Pyramid Studies and Other Essays presented to I. E. S. Edwards*, London, 1988, pp. 12-24.
Isler, M., "Concerning the concave faces on the Great Pyramid," *JARCE* 20, no. 27-32 (1983).
Lally, M., "Engineering a pyramid," *JARCE* 26, no. 207-218 (1989).
Lauer, J.-P., "Sur le choix de l'angle de pente dans les pyramides d'Égypte," *Bulletin de l'Institut d'Égypte* 37 (1956), pp. 57-66.
Lauer, J.P., "Observations sur les pyramides," *BdÉ* 30 (Cairo, 1960).

Robins, G. and C. C. D. Shute, "Determining the slope of pyramids," *GM* 57 (1982), pp. 49-54.

Photo credits:
47 top Archivio White Star
47 bottom Araldo De Luca/Archivio White Star
48, 49 Giulio Veggi/Archivio White Star
50, 51 Alberto Siliotti/Archivio Geodia
52 Mark Lehner
53 Alfio Garozzo/Archivio White Star
57, 59 Marcello Bertinetti/Archivio White Star

THE ARCHITECTURAL DEVELOPMENT OF THE EGYPTIAN ROYAL TOMB
Text by Zahi Hawass

Bibliography:
Edwards, I.E.S., *The Pyramids of Egypt. rev. ed.*, New York, 1985.
Hassan, S., *The Sphinx: Its History in the Light of Recent Excavations*, Cairo: Cairo University, 1949.
Hawass, Z., "The Khufu Statuette: Is It an Old Kingdom Sculpture?" *Melanges Gamal Eddin Mokhtar. Bibliotheque d'Etude, Institut Francais d'Archeologie Orientale* no. 971, (1985).
---, *The Funerary Establishments of Khufu, Khafra, and Menkaura During the Old Kingdom*, Ph. D. Dissertation University of Pennsylvanaia microfilm, Ann Arbor, MI, 1987.
---, "Histories, Mysteries of Man" in W.M.F. Petrie, *The Pyramid and Temples of Gizah*, London, 1990.
--- "Pyramid Construction: New Evidence Discovered in Giza," in H. Guksch and D. Polz (eds), *Stationen Beiträge zur Kultur-geschichte Ägyptens Gewidmet R. Stadelmann*, Mainz, 1998.
---,*The Pyramid of Ancient Egypt*, Carnegie Institute, Pittsburgh, 1990.
Lehner, M., "The Development of the Giza Necropolis: The Khufu Project." *MDAIK* 41, 1985.
Maragioglio, V., and C. Rinaldi., *L'Architettura della piramidi menfite*. Vols. 2-8. Turin and Rapello, 1963-77.
Reisner, G. A., *The Development of The Egyptian Tomb Down to the Accession of Chéops*, Cambridge, Mass., 1935.
Smith, W. S., *The Art and Architecture Of Ancient Egypt*. 2nd ed., revised by W. K. Simpson, Harmondsworth, 1981.

Photo credits:
60 Giulio Veggi/Archivio White Star
61 Marcello Bertinetti/Archivio White Star
62 Alfio Garozzo/Archivio White Star

THE ARCHITECTURAL COMPONENTS OF THE PYRAMID COMPLEX
Text by Zahi Hawass

Bibliography:
Badawy A., *A History of Architecture I*, Berkeley, University of California, 1966.
Brinks, J., *Die Entwicklung der Königlichen Grabanlagen des Alten Reiches*, Hildesheim, 1979.
Edwards, I.E.S., *The Pyramids of Egypt*, rev. ed., New York, 1985.
Fakhry, A., *The Pyramids. 2nd ed.*, Chicago: University of Chicago Press, 1974.
Hawass, Z., "The Pyramid," in D. P. Silverman and D. Baird (eds), *Ancient Egypt*, London and New York: Oxford University Press, 1998.
---, *The Funerary Establishments of Khufu, Khafra, and Menkaura During the Old Kingdom*, Ph. D. Dissertation University of Pennsylvanaia microfilm, Ann Arbor, MI, 1987.
---, "Pyramid Construction: New Evidence Discovered in Giza," in H. Guksch and D. Polz (eds.) *Stationen Beiträge zur Kultur-geschichte Ägyptens Gewidmet R. Stadelmann*, Mainz, 1998.
Maragioglio, V., and C. Rinaldi, *L'Architettura della piramidi menfite*, vols. 2-8. Turin and Rapello, 1963-77.
Petrie, W. M. F., *The Pyramids and Temples of Gizeh*, London, 1883.
Smith, W. S. *The Art and Architecture Of Ancient Egypt*, 2nd ed, revised by W. K. Simpson, Harmondsworth, 1981.
Stadelmann, R., *Die ägyptischen Pyramiden*, Mainz, 1985.

Photo credits:
66, 67 Araldo De Luca/Archivio White Star

THE PREDYNASTIC PERIOD
Text by Renee Friedman

Renee Friedman is the Heagy Research Curator in the Egyptian Department of the British Museum and Director of the Hierakonpolis Expedition, specializing in Egypt's Predynastic Period. Educated at the University of California, Berkeley, she has excavated at a number of sites in Egypt, including Giza, Mendes, Tell el-Muqdam, and Hierakonpolis, where she has worked since 1983. She has co-authored and edited several books including *Egypt Uncovered* (1998), *The Followers of Horus* (1992), and *Egypt and Nubia: Gifts of the Desert* (2002).

Bibliography:
Adams, B., *Predynastic Egypt* (Shire Egyptology 7), Aylesbury, 1988.
--- , *Ancient Nekhen: Garstang in the City of Nekhen* (ESA no.3), SIA Publishing, 1995.
Adams, B and K. Cialowicz, *Protodynastic Egypt* (Shire Egyptology 25), Great Britain, 1997.
Darnell, J.C., *Theban Desert Road Survey in the Egyptian Western Desert, Volume 1: Gebel Tjauti Rock Inscriptions 1-45 and Wadi el-Hôl Rock Inscriptions 1-45*, Oriental Institute Publications 119, Chicago, 2002.
Friedman, R. et al., "Preliminary Report on Field Work at Hierakonpolis 1996-1998," *JARCE* 36 (1999), pp. 1–35.
Friedman, R. and B. Adams (eds.), *The Followers of Horus: Studies dedicated to Michael Allen Hoffman*, Oxford, 1992.
Friedman R., *Egypt and Nubia: Gifts of the Desert*, London, 2002.
Hoffman, M. A., *Egypt Before the Pharaohs*, New York, Texas, 1979/1991.
Midant-Reynes, B., *The Prehistory of Egypt: From the First Egyptians to the First Pharaohs*, Oxford, 2000.
Spencer, A. J., *Early Egypt: The Rise of Civilization in the Nile Valley*, London, 1993.
--- (ed.), *Aspects of Early Egypt*, London: British Museum Press, 1996.
Shaw, I. (ed.), *The Oxford History of Ancient Egypt*, Oxford, 2000.
Wendorf, F. and R Schild, *Holocene Settlement of the Egyptian Sahara, vol. 1: The Archaeology of Nabta Playa*, New York, 2002.

Photo credits:
68, 69 Araldo De Luca/Archivio White Star
70, 71 left Renee Friedman
71 right Araldo De Luca/Archivio White Star
72, 73 Renee Friedman
74 The British Museum
75 Kenneth Garrett

THE TOMBS OF THE FIRST AND SECOND DYNASTIES AT ABYDOS AND SAQQARA
Text by Günter Dreyer

Günter Dreyer studied Egyptology, Assyriology and Ancient Near Eastern archaeology in Hamburg and Berlin, where he completed his Ph.D. in 1978 about temple donations in the early periods of Egypt. He excavated with the German Institute of Archaeology at Luxor, Elephantine, Wadi Garawi, Abydos and Giza. He became assistant director of the German Institute in 1989, and director in 1998. He completed his Habilitation at Berlin University in 1997 on Early Writing from Egypt and is now mainly conducting the excavations of the earliest Royal Tombs at Abydos.

Bibliography:
Spencer A. J., *Early Egypt*, London: British Museum Press, 1993.

ABYDOS
Amélineau, E., *Les Nouvelles Fouilles d'Abydos I-III*, Paris, 1895-1904.
---, *Le Tombeau d'Osiris*, Paris, 1899.
Petrie, W. M. F., *The Royal Tombs of the First Dynasty I-II* (Mem. Egypt Expl. Fund 18, 21), London, 1900-1901.
Dreyer, G., *Umm el-Qaab I, Das prädynastische Königsgrab U-j in Abydos und seine frühen Schriftzeugnisse* (Archäologische Veröffentlichungen 86), Mainz, 1998.
Dreyer G., et al., "Umm el-Qaab, Nachuntersuchungen im frühzeitlichen Königsfriedhof. Vorberichte (preliminary reports)," *Mitteilungen DAI Kairo (MDAIK)* 38, 46, 49, 52, 54, 56 (Mainz, 1982-2000).

SAQQARA
Emery, W. B., *Great Tombs of the 1st Dynasty I-III, Excavations at Saqqara*, Cairo, 1949; London, 1955-58.
--- *The Tomb of Hemaka, Excavations at Saqqara*, Cairo, 1938.
---, *Hor Aha, Excavations at Saqqara*, Cairo, 1939.
Lauer, J. Ph., "Histoire monumentale des pyramides d'Égypte," *Bibliothèque d'Étude* 39, Cairo, 1962.

Photo credits:
76 Araldo De Luca/Archivio White Star
77 Günter Dreyer
78 top RMN
78 center and bottom Günter Dreyer
80 Araldo De Luca/Archivio White Star
81 top Günter Dreyer
81 center Araldo De Luca/Archivio White Star
82-83 and 82 bottom Günter Dreyer
83 bottom left Araldo De Luca/Archivio White Star
84 and 85 private collection
86-87 private collection
87 top, center and bottom Araldo De Luca/Archivio White Star
88 Günter Dreyer
88 left and right Mohamed Megahed
88-89 Angelo Colombo/Archivio White Star
90 Mohamed Megahed
90-91 Angelo Colombo/Archivio White Star
91 left Loic Hamon/Photo RMN
91 right Araldo De Luca/Archivio White Star
92 top and bottom Araldo De Luca/Archivio White Star
92-93 Günter Dreyer

THE ROYAL MORTUARY ENCLOSURES OF ABYDOS AND HIERAKONPOLIS
Text by David O'Connor and Matthew Adams

David O'Connor is Lila Acheson Wallace Professor of Egyptian Art and Archaeology at the Institute of Fine Arts, New York University. He is also a Professor Emeritus of the University of Pennsylvania and Curator Emeritus of the Egyptian Section, University of Pennsylvania Museum of Anthropology and Archaeology. David O'Connor has excavated extensively in Egypt and the Sudan, and his publications include *Ancient Nubia: Egypt's Rival in Africa*, *Ancient Egypt: a Social History* (co-author), and several others. He is currently completing a book entitled *Abydos: The Evolution of a Sacred Landscape*.

Matthew Douglas Adams holds a dual Ph.D. in Anthropology and Egyptology from the University of Pennsylvania. He is Research Scholar at the Institute of Fine Arts, New York University, and a Research Associate of the University of Pennsylvania Museum. He has worked at Abydos since 1981 and has been a project director there since 1991. He is Director of the Abydos Settlement Site Project, and has undertaken excavations in the ancient town of Abydos. He is Associate Director of the Abydos Early Dynastic Project and has excavated many of north Abydos' Early Dynastic royal monuments. In addition to Egypt, Dr. Adams has also done archaeological fieldwork in Turkey, Syria, and North America. The author of several articles and reviews, his research interests include Egypt as a complex society, kingship and the nature of the early state in Egypt, Egyptian socio-economic organization, and the archaeology of settlement in Egypt.

Bibliography:
Kemp, B., "Abydos: The Royal Tombs of the First Dynasty," JEA 52 (1966), pp. 14-22.
O'Connor, D., "New Funerary Enclosures (Talbezirke) of the Early Dynastic Period," *Journal of the American Research Center in Egypt* 26 (1989), pp. 51-86.
---, "Boat Graves and Pyramid Origins: New Discoveries at Abydos, Egypt," *Expedition* 33/3 (1991), pp. 5-17.
O'Connor, D. and M. Adams, "Moored in the Desert: Digging an Ancient Armada," *Archaeology* (May/June 2001), pp. 44-45.

Photo credits:
94, 95, 96 top, 96-97 Giulio Veggi/Archivio White Star
97 top, 98-99, 99 David O'Connor
100, 101 Giulio Veggi/Archivio White Star

THE STEP PYRAMIDS
Text by Ali Radwan

Ali Radwan is a Professor at Cairo University where he teaches Egyptian Art and Archaeology. He was the former dean of Cairo Uninersity and excavated at Abusir.

Bibliography:
Allen, J. P., "Funerary Texts and Their Meaning," in S. D'Auria, P. Lacovara and C. H. Roehrig (eds.), *Mummies and Magic: The Funerary Arts of Ancient Egypt*, Boston, 1988, pp. 38-49.
Altenmüller. H., "Bemerkungen zur frühen and späten Bauphase des Djoserbezirkes in Saqqara," *MDAIK* 28 (1972), pp. 8-12.
Barsanti, A., "Ouverture de la pyramide de Zaouiét el-Aryan," *ASAE* II (1901), pp. 92-4.
Cwiek, A., "Date and Function of the So-called Minor Step Pyramids," *GM* 162 (1998), pp. 39-52.
Dreyer G. and W. Kaiser, "Zu den kleinen Stufenpyramiden Ober-und Mitteläegyptens," *MDAIK* 36 (1980), pp. 43-59, Taf. 68-77.
Dreyer G. and N. Swelim, "Die kleine Stufenpyramide von Abydos-Süd (Sinki)," in *MDAIK* 38 (1982), pp. 83-93, Taf. 11-14.
Dreyer, G., "Der erste König der 3. Dynastie," in H. Guksch and D. Polz (eds.), *Stationen, Fs. R. Stadelmann*, Mainz, 1998, pp. 31-34.
Dodson, A., "On the Date of the Unfinished Pyramid of Zawyet el-Aryan," *Discussions in Egyptology* 3 (1985), p. 21.
Edwards, I. E. S., *The Pyramids of Egypt*, Harmondsworth, 1961.
Fakhry, A., *The Pyramids*, Chicago, 1969.
Faulkner, R. O., *The Ancient Egyptian Pyramid Texts*, Oxford, 1969.
Firth, C. M., J. E. Quibell and J-Ph. Lauer, *The Step Pyramid, I, II*, Cairo, 1935, 1936.
Fischer, H. G., "Some Emblematic Uses of Hieroglyphs with Particular Reference to an Archaic Ritual Vessel," in *Ancient Egypt* in *The Metropolitan Museum Journal* (1977), pp. 31ff, 181 (palette from Helwan).
Friedman, F. D., "The Underground Relief Panels of King Djoser at the Step Pyramid Complex," *JARCE* 32 (1995), pp. 1-42.
Goneim, M. Z., *The Buried Pyramid*, London, 1956.
---, *Horus Sekhem-Khetm the Unfinished Step Pyramid at Saqqara, I* Cairo, 1957.
Greven, L., "Der Ka in Theologie und Königkult der Ägypten des Alten Reiches," *ÄF* 17 (Glückstadt, 1952).
Hawass, Z., "A Fragmentary Monument of Djoser from Saqqara," *JEA* 80 (1994), pp. 45-56.
Helck, W., "Der Name des letzten Königs der 3. Dynastie un die Stadt Ehnas," *SAK* 4 (1976), pp. 123-130.
---, "Gane," *LÄ* II (1977), pp. 391, n. 95.
---, "Die Datierung der Gefäßaufschriften aus der Djoserpyramide," *ZÄS* 106 (1979), pp. 120-132.
---, "Sanacht" *LÄ* V (1984), pp. 375f.
---, "Zum Statuensockel des Djoser," in I. Gamer-Wallert and W.Helck (eds.), *Gegengabe, Fs Emma Brunner-Traut*, Tübingen, 1992, 143-150.
Hornung, E., "Exploring the Beyond," in E. Hornung and B. M. Bryan (eds.), *The Quest for Immortality: Treasures of Ancient Egypt*, Munich, London and New York, 2002, pp. 33.
Kaiser, W., "Zu den Königlichen Talbezirken in Abydos und zur Baugeschichte des Djoser-Grabmals der 1. und 2. Dynastie," *MDAIK* 25 (1969), pp. 1-21.
---, "Ein Kultbezirk des Königs Den in Sakkara," *MDAIK* 41 (1984), pp. 47-60.
---, "Zur unterirdischen Anlage der Djoserpyramide und ihrer entwicklungsgeschichtlichten Einordnung," in I. Gamer-Wallert and W. Helck (eds.), *Gegengabe, Fs Emma Brunner-Traut*, Tübingen (1992), pp. 167-190.
Kees, H., *Der Götterglaube im Alten Agypten*, Leipzig, 1941, pp. 214ff.
Krejcí, J., "The Origins and Development of the Royal Necropolis at Abusir during the Old Kingdom," in M. Bárta and J. Krejcí (eds.), *Abusir and Saqqara in the Year 2000*, Praha, 2000, pp. 477, figs. 2 and 4.
Lauer, J-Ph., *La Pyramide à Degrés, I-III*, Cairo, 1936-1939.
---, "Histoire Monumentale des Pyramides d'Égypte I: Les Pyramides à Degrés (IIIe Dynastie)," *BdÉ* 39 (1962).
---, "Les petites pyramides à degrés de la IIIe dynastie," *Rev. archeologique* (1962), pp. 5-15.
---, "Recherche et découverte de tombeau sud de L'Horus Sekhem-Khet san son complexe funéraire à Saqqarah," *BIE* 48/49 (1969), pp. 121-131.
---, *Saqqara: The Royal Cemetery of Memphis*, London, 1976.
Leclant, J. and G. Clerc, "Fouilles et travaux en Égypte et au Soudan," *Orentialia* 57, no. 3 (1988), pp. 336, figs. 40, 41.
Lehner, M., "Z 500 and the Layer Pyramid of Zawiyet el-Aryan," in P. der Manuelian (ed.), *Studies in Honor of W.K. Simpson II*, Boston, 1996, pp. 507-522.
---, *The Complete Pyramids*, London, Cairo, 1997.
Lesko, L. H., "Seila 1981," *JARCE* 25 (1988), pp. 215-235.
Muller, H.W., "Lowenskulpturern," *MJbK* XVI (München 1965), pp. 20.
---, "Gedanken zur Entstehung, Interpretation und Rekonstruktion ältester ägyptischer Monumentalarchitektur," in Ägypten-Dauer und Wandel, in DAIK, Sonderschrift 18, Mainz 1985, pp. 7-33.
O'Connor, D., "New Funerary Enclosures (Talbezirke) of the Early Dynastic Period at Abydos," *JARCE* 26 (1989), pp. 51-86.
Otto, E., "Die Religion der Alten Ägypter," in *Handbuch der Orientalistik*, Abt 1, Bd VIII, 1, Leiden 1964, p. 55.
Parra Ortiz, J. M., "Houni et Snéfrou: Les Pyramides de Meïdoum et Dahschour," *GM* 154 (1996), pp. 77-91.
Radwan, A., "Recent Excavations of the Cairo University at Abusir: A Cemetery of the 1st Dynasty," in D. Kessler and R. Schultz (eds.), *Gedenkschrift für Winfried Barta*, in *MÄU* 4 (1995), pp. 312, n.11.
---, "Mastaba XVII at Abusir (First Dynasty): Preliminary Results and General Remarks," in M. Bárta and J. Krejcí (eds.), *Abusir and Saqqara in the Year 2000*, Praha, 2000, pp. 509-514, fig. 2.

---, "Some Remarks Concerning the Superstructure of Some Mastabas at Abusir," in Z. Hawass (ed.), *Egyptology at the Dawn of the Twenty-First Century. Proceedings of the Eighth International Congress of Egyptologists, Cairo 2000*, Cairo, 2002.
Ricke, H., "Bemerkungen zur ägyptischen Baukunst des Alten Reiches I," *Beiträge*, Bf 4 (1944).
Ritner, R. K., O. "Gardiner 363: A Spell Against Night Terrors," *JARCE* 27 (1990), pp. 37f., fig. 5.
Schraff, A., "Die Ausbreitung des Osiriskultes in der Frühzeit und wärend des Alten Reiches," *SBAW* Heft 4, (1948).
Seidel, M., and D. Wildung, in C. Vandersleyen (ed.), *Das alte Ägypten* (Propyläen Kunstgeschichte 15), Berlin, 1975, pp. 218-220.
Seidel, M., "Die koniglichen Statuengruppen I," *HAB* 42, 1996, pp. 5-9.
Sourouzian, H., "Inventaire iconographique des Statues en Manteau Jubilaire," in *Hommages à J. Leclant, BdÉ* 106, vol.1 (1994), pp. 50ff.
---, "L'iconographie du roi dans la statuaire des trois premières dynasties," in *Kunst des Alten Reiches, DAIK*, Sonderschrift 28 (1995), pp. 133ff.
---, "Concordances et Écarts entre Statuaire et Représentations à deux dimensions des Particuliers de L'Époque Archaïque," in N. Grimal (ed.), *Les Critères de Datation Stylistiques, BdÉ* 120 (1998), pp. 305ff.
Stadelmann, R., "Pyramiden," *LÄ* IV (1982), pp. 1205ff.
---, "Das vermeintliche Sonnenheiligtum im Norden des Djoserbezirkes," *ASAE* 69 (1983), pp. 373-378.
---, "Die Oberbauten der Königsgräber der 2. Dynastie in Sakkara," Mélanges G. E. Mokhtar II, *BdÉ* 97/2 (1985), pp. 295-307.
---, *Die ägyptischen Pyramiden - vom Ziegelbau zum Weltwunder*, Mainz, 1985.
---, *Die großen Pyramiden von Giza*, Graz, 1990.
--- "Zur Baugeschichte des Djoserbezirks, Grabschacht und Grabkammer der Stufenmastaba," *MDAIK* 52 (1996), pp. 295-305.
---, "Origins and Development of the Funerary Complex of Djoser," in P. der Manuelian (ed.), *Studies in Honor of W. K. Simpson*, Boston, 1996, pp. 787-800.
---, "Représentations de la famille royale à l'Ancien Empire," in Chr. Ziegler (ed.), *L'Art de l'Ancien Empire*, Paris: Musée du Louvre, 1999, p. 174, fig. 5.
Stiénon, J., "El-Kolah," *Chronicle d'Égypte* 59 (1950), pp. 43-45.
Swelim, N., "Additional Views Concerning the Monument Called Sinki," *MDAIK* 38 (1982), pp. 94f.
---, *Some Problems on the History of the Third Dynasty*, Alexandria, 1983.
---, *The Brick Pyramid at Abu Roash, Numbered I by Lepsius*, Alexandria, 1983.
---, "Some Remarks on the Great Rectangular Monuments of Middle Saqqara," *MDAIK* 47 (1991), pp. 389-402.
Tray, L., *Patterns of Queenship in Ancient Egyptian Myth and History*, Uppsala, 1986, pp. 56ff.
Verner, M., *The Pyramids: The Mystery, Culture and Science of Egypt's Great Monuments*, Cairo, New York, 2002.
Westendorf, W., *Das Alte Ägypten*, Baden-Baden, 1968, p. 30.
Wildung, D., "Die Rolle ägyptischer Konige im Bewustsein ihrer Nachwelt," *MÄS* 17 (1969).
---, "Imhotep" *LA* III (1980), pp. 145-148.
---, "Two Representations of Gods from the Early Old Kingdom," *Miscellanea Wilbouriana* I (1972), pp. 145ff.
Wilson, J. A., "Buto and Hierakonpolis in the Geography of Egpyt," *JNES* 14 (1955), pp. 209-236.
Ziegler (ed.), Chr., *L'art égyptien au temps des Pyramides, Cat.* Paris, 1999, pp. 34-51; 148-165.

Photo credits:
102 Oriental Institute of The University of Chicago
103, 104, 105, 106, 107, 108, 109 Araldo De Luca/Archivio White Star
110-111 Marcello Bertinetti/Archivio White Star
111 top Giulio Veggi/Archivio White Star
112 Marcello Bertinetti/Archivio White Star
114, 115 Araldo De Luca/Archivio White Star
116, 117 Giulio Veggi/Archivio White Star
118, 118-119, 119 bottom left Marcello Bertinetti/Archivio White Star
119 bottom right Giulio Veggi/Archivio White Star
120 top Marcello Bertinetti/Archivio White Star
120-121, 122-123, 123 bottom Marcello Bertinetti/Archivio White Star
123 top, 124 top, 125 bottom right Giulio Veggi/ Archivio White Star
124-125, 125 bottom left Marcello Bertinetti/ Archivio White Star
126 top Araldo De Luca/Archivio White Star
126 center and bottom Giulio Veggi/Archivio White Star
127 Miroslav Verner

THE PYRAMIDS OF THE FOURTH DYNASTY
Text by Rainer Stadelmann

Born October 24, 1933 in Oettingen/Bavaria as son of a professor of classical languages, he studied Egyptology at the Universities of Munich and Heidelberg. He first visited Egypt between December 1955 and April 1956 and participate in excavations at the Sun Temple of Userkaf at Abusir. Completed his PhD in spring 1960 with a thesis on "Syrisch-Palästinensische Gottheiten in Ägypten" and became Assistant Lecturer of Egyptology at the University of Heidelberg. In 1967 he completed a second Ph.D., Habilitation, in Heidelberg with a thesis on: "Altägyptische Bauinschriften und Namen von Bauteilen" and became Assistant Professor. In April 1968 he became Scientific Director of the German Institute of Archaeology in Cairo and Honorary Professor at the University of Heidelberg. In 1989 he became First Director of the German Institute of Archaeology in Cairo. He has at Elephantine Island and the Mortuary temple of Sety I at Gurna and the Pyramids of Sneferu at Dahshur. Newest excavation and conservation work at the Temple of Amenhotep III and the Colossi of Memnon. He has published several books about the pyramids and ca. 100 scholarly articles in German, English, and French in international periodicals.

Bibliography:
Edwards, I. E. S., *The Pyramids of Egypt*, London, 1985.
Fakhry, A., *The Monuments of Sneferu at Dahshur, vol. I-II*, Cairo, 1959.
Hawass, Z., *The funerary establishment of Khufu, Khaefra and Menkaura*
Lauer, J. Ph., *Le Mystère des Pyramides*, 1988.
during the Old Kingdom, Pennsylvania, 1987.
Lehner, M., *The Complete Pyramids*, 1997.
Stadelmann, R., *Die Großen Pyramiden von Giza*, ADEVA, 1990.
---, *Die Ägyptischen Pyramiden*, Mainz, 1997.
Vercoutter, J., *L'Egypte et la vallée du Nil, NOUVELLE CLIO Tome I, Des Origines à la Fin de l'Ancien Empire*, Paris, 1992.

Photo credits:
128 Araldo De Luca/Archivio White Star
129 Private collection
130-131 Marcello Bertinetti/Archivio White Star
130 bottom Araldo De Luca/Archivio White Star
131 Giulio Veggi/Archivio White Star
132-133, 133 top Marcello Bertinetti/Archivio White Star
133 bottom Giulio Veggi/Archivio White Star
134, 135, 136-137 Marcello Bertinetti/Archivio White Star
137 Marcello Bertinetti/Archivio White Star
138-139 Marcello Bertinetti/Archivio White Star
138 bottom Giulio Veggi/Archivio White Star
139 top Araldo De Luca/Archivio White Star
140 top Giulio Veggi/Archivio White Star
140 bottom Araldo De Luca/Archivio White Star
142-143 Giulio Veggi/Archivio White Star
144-145, 145 bottom Marcello Bertinetti/Archivio White Star
145 top Giulio Veggi/Archivio White Star
146 Araldo De Luca/Archivio White Star
147, 148-149, 149 Marcello Bertinetti/Archivio White Star
148 bottom left Giulio Veggi/Archivio White Star
148 bottom right, 150, 151, 152 bottom left and right Araldo De Luca/Archivio White Star
152-153, 153 Marcello Bertinetti/Archivio White Star

THE QUEENS' PYRAMIDS OF THE FOURTH DYNASTY AT GIZA
Text by Zahi Hawass

Bibliography:
Badawy A., *History of Egyptian Architecture I*, Giza, 1954.
Borchardt, L., *Das Grabdenkmal des Königs Sabu-Re II*, Leipzig, 1913.
Edwards, I. E. S., *The Pyramids of Egypt, rev. ed.*, New York, 1985.
Fakhry, A., *The Pyramids*, Chicago and London, 1969.
Hawass, Z., *The Funerary Establishments of Khufu, Khafra, and Menkaura During the Old Kingdom*, Ph.D. Dissertation, University of Pennsylvania microfilm, Ann Arbor, MI, 1987.
---, update in W. M. F. Petrie, *The Pyramid and Temples of Gizah*, London: Histories & Mysteries of Man, 1990.
Lehner, M., *The Pyramid Tomb of Hetep-heres and the Satellite Pyramid of Khufu*, Mainz am Rhein, 1985.
Maragioglio, V. and C. Rinaldi, *L'Architettura della piramidi menfite. Vols. 2-8*, Turin and Rapello: Tip. Artale, 1963-77.
Reisner, G. A., *A History of the Giza Necropolis, vol. II: The Tomb of Hetepheres, Mother of Cheops*, Cambridge, MA, 1955.
Riser, E., *Der Königliche Harim im alten Ägypten und seine Verwaltung*, Vienna, 1972.
Simpson, W. K., *The Mastabas of Kawab, Khafkhufu I, II, and III*. Boston, 1978.
Stadelmann, R., *Die ägyptischen Pyramiden*, Mainz, 1985.
Vyse, H., *Operation carried on at the Pyramids of Giza 2*, London, 1841.

Photo credits:
148 bottom left Giulio Veggi/Archivio White Star
148 bottom right, 150, 151, 152 bottom left and right Araldo De Luca/Archivio White Star
152-153, 153 Marcello Bertinetti/Archivio White Star
154, 155 Giulio Veggi/Archivio White Star
156, 157 Marcello Bertinetti/Archivio White Star
158, 159, 160, 161 right Giulio Veggi/Archivio White Star
161 left Marcello Bertinetti/Archivio White Star
162, 164-165, 165 bottom Giulio Veggi/Archivio White Star
165 top Marcello Bertinetti/Archivio White Star

THE SATELLITE PYRAMID OF KHUFU
Text by Zahi Hawass

Bibliography:
Hassan, S., *Excavations at Giza 10. The Great Pyramid of Khufu and its Mortuary Chapel*, Cairo, 1960.
Hawass, Z., "The discovery of the Satellite Pyramid of Khufu, GID" in P. Der Manuelian (ed.), *Studies in Honor of William Kelly Simpson*, Boston: Museum of Fine Arts, 1996.
---, *The Funerary Establishments of Khufu, Khafra, and Menkaura During the Old Kingdom*, Ph.D. Dissertation, University of Pennsylvania microfilm, Ann Arbor, MI, 1987.
---, update in W. M. F. Petrie, *The Pyramid and Temples of Gizah*, London: Histories & Mysteries of Man, 1990.
---, "The Discovery of the Pyramidion of the Satellite Pyramid of Khufu (GID)," *Iubilate Conlegae: Studies Memory of Abd Aziz Sadek, Part I, Varia Aegyptiaca, Vol. 10*, (1997).
Lauer, J. P., *Pyramide à degrés I*, Cairo 1935.
Lehner, M., *The Pyramid Tomb of Hetep-heres and the Satellite Pyramid of Khufu*, Mainz am Rhein, 1985.
Maragioglio, V. and C. Rinaldi, *L'Architettura della piramidi menfite, vols. 2-8*, Turin and Rapello: Tip. Artale, 1963-77.
Reisner, G. A. A., *History of the Giza Necropolis, vol II: The Tomb of Hetepheres, Mother of Cheops*, Cambridge, MA, 1955.
Reisner, G. A., *Mycerinus: The Temples of the Third Pyramid at Giza*, Cambridge, MA, 1931.
Smith, W. S., *The Art and Architecture of Ancient Egypt*, Harmondsworth, 1981.
Stadelmann, R., "Die Pyramiden des Sneferu in Dahschur: Erster Bericht über die Grabungen an den nördliehen Steinpyramide," *MDAIK* 38, 1982.
---, *Die ägyptischen Pyramiden*, Mainz, 1985.
Vyse, H., *Operation carried on at the Pyramids of Giza 2*, London, 1841.

Photo credits:
167 Giulio Veggi/Archivio White Star

THE MYSTERY OF HETEPHERES
Text by Zahi Hawass

Bibliography:
Lehner, M., "The Development of the Giza Necropolis: the Khufu project," *MDAIK* 41 (1985).
Hawass, Z., *The Funerary Establishments of Khufu, Khafra, and Menkaura During the Old Kingdom*, Ph.D. Dissertation, University of Pennsylvania microfilm, Ann Arbor, MI, 1987.

Photo credits:
169, 170, 171 Araldo De Luca/Archivio White Star

THE SECRET DOORS INSIDE THE GREAT PYRAMID
Text by Zahi Hawass

Bibliography:
Hawass, Z., M. Waters, and C. Sandreal, "The Recent Investigation of the so-called doors inside the great pyramid"
Stadelmann, R. with the contribution of R. Cantenbrink, "Die Sogenanntem Luftkanle der kheopspyramide. Modellkorridore für den Aufstiey des Kings Zum Himmel," *MDAIK* 50 (1994), pp. 285-294.

Photo credits:
173, 174 Kenneth Garrett

THE PYRAMIDION
Text by Zahi Hawass

Bibliography:
Arnold, D., "Rituale und Pyramidentempel," *MDAIK* 33 (1977).
Badawy A., *A History of Architecture*, I Berkeley: University of California, 1966.
Edwards, I .E. S., *The Pyramids of Egypt, rev. ed.*, New York, 1985.
Fakhry, A., *The Pyramids, 2nd ed.*, Chicago: University of Chicago Press, 1974.
Hawass, Z., "The discovery of the Satellite Pyramid of Khufu, GID" in Peter Der Manuelian (ed.) *Studies in Honor of William Kelly Simpson*, Boston: Museum of Fine Arts, 1996.
---, *The Funerary Establishments of Khufu, Khafra, and Menkaura During the Old Kingdom*, Ph.D. Dissertation, University of Pennsylvania microfilm, Ann Arbor, MI, 1987.
---, "Pyramid Construction: New Evidence Discovered in Giza," in H. Guksch and D. Polz (eds.), *Stationen Beiträge zur Kultur-geschichte Ägyptens Gewidmet R. Stadelmann*, Mainz, 1998.
---, "The Discovery of the Pyramidion of the Satellite Pyramid of Khufu (GID)," *Iubilate Conlegae: Studies Memory of Abd Aziz Sadek, Part I, Varia Aegyptiaca*, Vol. 10, 1997.
---, "The Old Kingdom Pyramidion: Is It Cased with Gold?" *Fayza Heikel Festschrift, BIFAO*, 2000.
Hölscher, U., *Das Grabdenkmal das Königs Chephren*, Leipzig, 1912.
Maragioglio, V. and C. Rinaldi, *L'Architettura della piramidi menfite, vols. V and VI*, Rapallo, 1966.
Petrie, W. M. F., *The Pyramids and Temples of Gizeh*, with an update by Z. Hawass, London: Histories & Mysteries of Man, 1990.
Reisner, G. A., *A History of the Giza Necropolis, vol. I: The Tomb of Hetepheres, Mother of Cheops*, Cambridge, MA, 1942.
Stadelmann, R., "Die Pyramiden des Snofru in Dahschur: Erster Bericht über die Grabungen an den nördliehen Steinpyramide," *MDAIK* 38 (1982).

Photo credits:
176 Araldo De Luca/Archivio White Star
178 Giulio Veggi/Archivio White Star
179 Giulio Veggi/Archivio White Star

THE ROYAL BOATS AT GIZA
Text by Zahi Hawass

Bibliography:
Abubakr, A. M., "Divine Boats of Ancient Egypt," *Archaeology* 8 (1955).
Abubakr, A. M. and A. Y. Mustafa, "The Funerary Boat of Khufu," *Festschrift Ricke, BÄBA* 12 (1971).
Borchardt, L., *Das Grabdenkmal des Königs Ne-user-Re*, Leipzig, 1907.
Černy, J., "A Note on the Recently Discovered Boat of Cheops," *JEA* 41 (1955).
Edwards, I. E. S., *The Pyramids of Egypt, rev. ed.*, New York, 1985.
Fakhry, A., *The Pyramids*, Chicago and London, 1969.
Faulkner, R. O., *The Ancient Egyptian Pyramid Texts*, Oxford, 1969.
Grinsell, L., *Egyptian Pyramids*, Gloucester, 1947.
Hassan, S., *Excavation at Giza*, vol. I, Oxford, 1932; vols. II-X, Cairo, 1936-60.
Hawass, Z., "The Pyramids," in D. P. Silverman, Duncan Baird (eds.), *Ancient Egypt*, London, New York: Oxford University Press, 1998.
---, *The Funerary Establishments of Khufu, Khafra, and Menkaura During the Old Kingdom*, Ph.D. Dissertation, University of Pennsylvania microfilm, Ann Arbor, MI, 1987.
Jenkins, N., *The Boat Beneath the Pyramid*, New York, 1980.
Jéquier, G., *Le Monument funéraire de Pepi* II, vol. I, Cairo, 1938.
Landstrom, B., *Ship of the pharaohs: 4000 Years of Egyptian Shipbuilding*, London, 1970.
Lauer, J. P., "Les barques de Chéops," *RC* 33 (1955).
Lehner, M., *The Pyramid Tomb of Hetep-heres and the Satellite Pyramid of Khufu*, Mainz, 1985.
Lipke, P., *The Royal Ship of Cheops* (Greenwich Archaeological Series, no. 9), Greenwich, 1984.
Lucas, A., J. R. Harris (eds.), *Ancient Egyptian Materials and Industries*, London, 1962.
Maragioglio, V. and C. Rinaldi, *L'Architettura della piramidi menfite, vols. 2-8*, Turin and Rapello, 1963-77.
Nour, M. Z. et al., *The Cheops Boat, vol. I*, Cairo, 1960.
Petrie, W. M. F., *The Pyramids and Temples of Gizeh*, London, 1883.

Saleh, A., "Excavation around Mycerinus Pyramid Complex," *MDAIK* 30 (1974).
Stadelmann, R., "Pyramiden," *LX* 32, IV8 (1982).
Thomas, E., "A Further Notes on Rock-cut Boats," *JEA* 42 (1956).
Thomas, E., "Solar Barks prow to prow," *JEA* 42 (1956).

Photo credits:
180, 181, 182-183, 183 Araldo De Luca/Archivio White Star
182 top and center Marcello Bertinetti/Archivio White Star
184, 185 Araldo De Luca/Archivio White Star/Service of Antiquities
186-187 Araldo De Luca/Archivio White Star

THE SPHINX
Text by Mark Lehner

Bibliography:

Anthes, R., "Was veranlasste Chefren zum bau des Tempels vor der Sphinx?" *Festschrift Ricke, BÄBA* 12 (1971)
Baikie, J., "The Sphinx," in J. Hastings (ed.), *Encyclopeida of Religion and Ethics, Vol 11*, Edinburgh, 1920, pp. 767-68
Bergmann, E. V., "Die Sphinx," *ZÄS* 18 (1880), pp. 50-1
Birch, S., "On excavations by Capt. Caviglia, in 1816, behind, and in the neighborhood of the Great Sphinx," *The Museum of Classical Antiquities* 2 (1852), pp. 26-34
Borchardt, L., "Uber das Alter des Sphinx bei Giseh," *Sitzungsberichte der Preussischen Akademie der Wissenschaften, Berlin* 35 (1897), pp. 752-60
Brock, L. P., "Problems of the Great Sphinx," *KMT* 1, no. 3 (1990), pp. 24-8
Esmael, F. A. (ed.), *Book of Proceedings: The First International Symposium on the Great Sphinx*, Cairo, 1992.
*Gauri, K. L., "Deterioation of stone on the Great Sphinx," *NARCE* 114, (Spring 1981), pp. 35-47.
---"Geologic Study of the Sphinx," *NARCE* 127 (Fall 1984), pp. 24-43.
*Hassan, S., *The Sphinx: Its History in Light of Recent Excavations*, Cairo, 1949.
Hawass, Z., *The Secrets of the Sphinx: Restoration Past and Present*, Cairo, 1998.
*Hawass, Z. and M. Lehner, "The Passage Under the Sphinx," *Hommages à Jean Leclant, BdÉ* 106/1 (1994,) pp. 201-16.
---, "The Sphinx: Who built it, and why?" *Archaeology* 47, no. 5 (Sept./Oct. 1994), pp. 30-47.
Jordan, P., *Riddles of the Sphinx*, Phoenix Mill, 1998.
*Lehner, M., J. P. Allen, K. L. Gauri, "The ARCE Sphinx Project: A Preliminary Report," *NARCE* 112 (Fall 1980), pp. 3-33.
*Lehner, M., *Archaeology of an Image: The Great Sphinx of Giza*, Ph.D. dissertation, Yale University, 1991.
Lehner, M., "Computer rebuilds the ancient Sphinx," *National Geographic* 179, no. 4 (April 1991), pp. 32-9.
Lehner, M., "Reconstructing the Sphinx," *Cambridge Archaeological Journal* 2, no. 1 (1992), pp. 3-26.
*Mariette, A. and M. D. Rougé, "Note sur le fouille executées par Mariette autour du grand Sphinx de Gizeh. Lettre de Mariette citées par M. de Rouge," *l'Athenaeum française* 3, no. 28 (1854).
*Ricke, H., "Der Harmachistempel des Chefren in Giseh," *BÄBA* 10 (1970), pp. 1-43.
Schott, S., "Le temple du Sphinx á Giza et les deux axes du monde," *BSFE* 53-54 (1969), pp. 31-41.
Schott, S., "Ägyptishce quellen zum plan des Sphinxtempels," *BÄBA* 10 (1970), pp. 49-79.
Stadelmann, R., "Le grand Sphinx de Giza, chef-d'oeuvre de régne de Chéops," *Académie des Inscriptions & Belles-Lettres* (July-October 1999), pp. 863-879.
Zivie-Coche, C., *Sphinx, History of a Monument* (D. Lorton, trans.), Ithaca and London, 2002.

Photo credits:
188 Giulio Veggi/Archivio White Star
189 Archivio White Star
191, 192-193, 194 Marcello Bertinetti/Archivio White Star
195 Marcello Bertinetti/Archivio White Star
197 bottom left and right Giulio Veggi/Archivio White Star
196-197 Marcello Bertinetti/Archivio White Star
198 Giulio Veggi/Archivio White Star
199 The British Museum
200, 201, 204-205 Giulio Veggi/Archivio White Star

THE TOMBS OF THE HIGH OFFICIALS AT GIZA
Text by Peter Der Manuelian

Peter Der Manuelian (B.A., Harvard University; Ph.D. in Egyptology, University of Chicago) is Mellon Research Fellow in Egyptian Art at the Museum of Fine Arts, Boston, and Lecturer in Egyptology at Harvard University and Tufts University. He is co-editor of the *Giza Mastabas Series* along with William Kelly Simpson, and is currently working on the "Giza Archives Project," intended to create a scholarly Web site of excavation images and archival materials from the Giza Necropolis.

Bibliography:

Abu-Bakr, A-M., *Excavations at Giza 1949-1950*, Cairo, 1953.
Allen, J. P., "Rce-wer's Accident," in *Studies in Pharaonic Religion and Society in Honour of J. G. Griffiths* (EES Occassional Publication 8), London: Egypt Exploration Society, 1992, pp. 14-20.
Altenmüller, H., "Daily Life in Eternity–The Mastabas and Rock-cut Tombs of Officials," in R. Schulz and M. Seidel (eds.), *Egypt: The World of the Pharaohs*, Cologne, 1998, pp. 78-93.
Arnold, D., *When the Pyramids Were Built: Egyptian Art of the Old Kingdom*, New York, 1999.
Baud, M., *Famille royale et pouvoir sous l'Ancien Empire égyptien. 2 vols.* Cairo: Institut français d'archéologie orientale, 1999.
Bolshakov, A. O., *Man and His Double in Egyptian Ideology of the Old Kingdom* (Ägypten und Altes Testament 37), Wiesbaden, 1997.
Brovarski, E., *The Senedjemib Complex Part I: The Mastabas of Senedjemib Inti (G 2370) Khnumenti (G 2374), and Senedjemib Mehi (G 2378). Giza Mastabas 7*, Boston: Museum of Fine Arts, 2001.
Brunner-Traut, E., *Die altägyptische Grabkammer Seschemnofers III. aus Gîsa, 2nd edition*, Mainz am Rhein, 1982
Brunner, H. and E. Brunner-Traut, *Die Ägyptische Sammlung der Universität Tübingen*, Mainz am Rhein, 1981, pp. 13–26.
Callender, V. G., and P. Jánosi, "The Tomb of Queen Khamerernebty II at Giza. A Reassessment." *MDAIK* 53, (1997), pp. 1–22.
Cherpion, N., *Mastabas et hypogées d'Ancien Empire. Le Problème de la Datation*, Brussels: Conaissance de l'Egypte ancienne, 1989.
Covington, L. "Mastaba Mount Excavations." *Annales du Service des Antiquités de l'Egypte 6* (1905), pp. 193-218.
Curto, S., *Gli Scavi Italiani a el-Ghiza (1903)*, Rome, 1963.
Dunham, D., *The Egyptian Department and its Excavations*, Boston: Museum of Fine Arts, 1958.
Dunham, D. and W. K. Simpson, *The Mastaba of Queen Mersyankh III (G 7530-7540). Giza Mastabas 1.* Boston: Museum of Fine Arts, 1974.
Eyre, C. J., "Work and Organisation of Work in the Old Kingdom," in M. A. Powell (ed.), *Labor in the Ancient Near East* (American Oriental Series, vol. 68), New Haven, CT: American Oriental Society, 1987, pp. 5–47.
Fisher, C. S., *The Minor Cemetery at Giza* (The Eckley B. Coxe Jr. Foundation, New Series Vol. I.) Philadelphia: University Museum, 1924.
Fischer, H. G., *Egyptian Women of the Old Kingdom and of the Heracleopolitan Period, second edition*, New York: The Metropolitan Museum of Art, 2000.
Gamer-Wallert, I., *Von Gîza bis Tübingen. Die bewegte Geschichte der Mastaba G 5170*, Tübingen, 1998.
Harpur, Y., *Decoration in Egyptian Tombs of the Old Kingdom: Studies in Orientation and Scene Content*, London and New York, 1987.
Hassan, S. *Excavations at Giza. 10 vols.*, Oxford: Oxford University Press, and Cairo, 1932–1960.
Hawass, Z., "The Workmen's Community at Giza," in *Haus und Palast im alten Ägypten. Internationales Symposium 8. bis 11. April 1992 in Kairo*, Vienna, 1996, pp. 54-67.
---, "The Pyramids," in D. P. Silverman, *Ancient Egypt*, London, 1997, pp. 168-191.
Jánosi, P., "Die Grabanlagen der Königin Hetepheres II," *Zeitschrift für Ägyptische Sprache und Altertumskun* 123 (1996), pp. 46–62.
Junker, H., *Gîza 1–12. Akademie der Wissenschaften in Wien, Phil.-Hist. Klasse. Denkschriften, 12 vols.*, Vienna, 1929–1955.
---, *The Offering Room of Prince Kaninisut*, Vienna: Kunsthistorisches Museum, 1931.
Lehner, M., *The Pyramid Tomb of Hetep-heres and the Satellite Pyramid of Khufu* (Sonderschriften Mitteilungen des Deutschen Archäologischen Instituts Abteilung Kairo 19), Mainz am Rhein, 1985.
---, *The Complete Pyramids: Solving the Ancient Mysteries*, London and New York, 1997.
---, "The 1988/1989 Excavation of Petrie's "Workmen's Barrack at Giza." *Journal of American Research Center in Egypt* 38 (2001), pp. 21–60.
Lichtheim, M., *Ancient Egyptian Literature: A Book of Readings. Vol. 1, The Old and Middle Kingdoms*, Berkeley: University of California Press, 1973.
Málek, J., "The Old Kingdom," in I. Shaw (ed.), *The Oxford History of Ancient Egypt*, Oxford: Oxford University Press, 2000, pp. 89-117.
Málek, J., *In the Shadow of the Pyramids: Egypt during the Old Kingdom*, Norman, OK: University of Oklahoma Press, 1986.
Der Manuelian, P., "Excavating the Memphite Cemeteries: The Giza Necropolis," in *L'Art égyptien au temps des pyramides and Egyptian Art in the Time of the Pyramids* (exhibition catalogues chapter), Paris: Musée du Louvre, pp. 124–33; New York: Metropolitan Museum of Art, 1999, pp. 139–53.
---, "The Problem of the Giza Slab Stelae," in H. Guksch and D. Polz (eds.)*Stationen: Beiträge zur Kulturgeschichte Ägyptens: Festschrift für Rainer Stadelmann*, Mainz, 1998, pp. 115–34.
--- "March 1912: A Month in the Life of American Egyptologist George A. Reisner." *KMT* 7, no. 2 (Summer 1996), pp. 60–75.
---, "George Andrew Reisner on Archaeological Photography." *Journal of the American Research Center in Egypt* 29 (1992), pp. 1–34.
--- "Digital Epigraphy. An Approach to Streamlining Egyptological Epigraphic Method." *Journal of the American Research Center in Egypt* 35 (1998), pp. 97–113.
---. "A Race against Time in the Shadow of the Pyramids. The Museum of Fine Arts, Boston and the Giza Necropolis, 1902–1990." *KMT* 1, no. 4 (1990–91), pp. 10–21.
Mariette, A.,*Les mastabas de l'ancien empire. Fragment du dernier ouvrage de A. Mariette, publié d'après le manuscrit de l'auteur par G. Maspero*,Paris, 1889. Reprint New York, 1976.
The Metropolitan Museum of Art, *Egyptian Art in the Age of the Pyramids*, New York: The Metropolitan Museum of Art, 1999.
Petrie, W. M. F., *The Pyramids and Temples of Gizeh*, London, 1883, 1885; new edition, with update by Zahi Hawass, London: Histories & Mysteries of Man, 1990.
Priese, K-H., *Die Opferkammer des Merib*, Berlin: Staatliche Museen zu Berlin, 1984.
Reisner, G. A., *Mycerinus: The Temples of the Third Pyramid at Giza*, Cambridge, MA, 1931.
---, *A History of the Giza Necropolis, vol. 1*, Cambridge, MA: Harvard University Press, 1942.
Reisner, G. A. and W. Stevenson Smith. *A History of the Giza Necropolis. Vol. 2, The Tomb of Hetep-Heres the Mother of Cheops: A Study of Egyptian Civilization in the Old Kingdom*, Cambridge, MA, 1955.
Roehrig, C. H., "Reserve Heads: An Enigma of Old Kingdom Sculpture," in *Egyptian Art in the Age of the Pyramids, Exb. cat.* New York: The Metropolitan Museum of Art, 1999, pp. 72–81.
Roth, A. M., "The Practical Economics of Tomb-Building in the Old Kingdom: A Visit to the Necropolis in a Carrying Chair," in D. P. Silverman (ed.), *For His Ka. Essays Offered in Memory of Klaus Baer* (SAOC 55). Chicago: Oriental Insitute, 1994, pp. 227–40.
---, *A Cemetery of Palace Attendants. Giza Mastabas 6*, Boston: Museum of Fine Arts, 1995.
Saleh, A-A., "Excavations Around Mycerinus Pyramid Complex," *Mitteilungen des Deutschen Archäologischen Instituts, Abteilung Kairo* MIDAIK 30 (1974), pp. 137–154.
Schmitz, B, et al., *Untersuchungen zu Idu II, Giza. Ein interdisciplinäres Projekt* (Hildesheimer Ägyptologische Beiträge 38), Hildesheim, 1996.
Simpson, W. K., *The Mastabas of Qar and Idu (G 7101 and 7102). Giza Mastabas 2.* Boston: Museum of Fine Arts, 1976.
---, *The Mastabas of Kawab, Khafkhufu I and II (G 7110–20, 7130–40, and 7150 and subsidiary mastabas of Street G 7100). Giza Mastabas 3*, Boston: Museum of Fine Arts, 1978.
---, *Mastabas of the Western Cemetery: Part I Sekhemka (G 1029), Tjetu I (G 2001), Iasen (G 2196), Penmeru (G 2197), Hagy, Nefertjentet, and Herunefer (G 2352/33), Djaty, Tjetu II, and Nimesti (G 2337X, 2343, 2366). Giza Mastabas 4*, Boston: Museum of Fine Arts, 1980.
---, "Topographical Notes on Giza Mastabas," in M. Görg and E. Pusch (eds.), *Festschrift Elmar Edel 12 März 1979* (Ägypten und Altes Testament 1), Bamberg, 1979, pp. 489–499.
Seidel (eds.) *Egypt: The World of the Pharaohs*, Cologne, 1998, pp. 46–77.
Siliotti, A., *Guide to the Pyramids of Egypt*, New York: Vercelli, 1997.
Smith, W. S., "The Stela of Prince Wepemnofret," *Archaeology 16* (1963), pp. 2–13.
---, *The Art and Architecture of Ancient Egypt. Rev. and enlarged by William Kelly Simpson*, New Haven: Yale University Press, 1998.
Stadelmann, R., "Giza," in D. B. Redford (ed.), *The Oxford Encyclopedia of Ancient Egypt*, Oxford: Oxford University Press, 2001, pp. 25-30.
---, "Der Strenge Stil der frühen Vierten Dynastie" in R.
---, "Royal Tombs from the Age of the Pyramids," in R. Schulz and M.
---. "Builders of the Pyramids," in J. Sasson (ed.), *Civilizations of the Ancient Near East II*, New York, 1995, pp. 719-734.
Stadelmann, R. and H. Sourouzian (eds.), *Kunst des Alten Reiches* (DAI Sonderschrift 28), Mainz am Rhein: Philipp von Zabern, 1995, pp. 155–166.
Strudwick, N., *The Administration of Egypt in the Old Kingdom: The Highest Titles and Their Holders*, London and Boston, 1985.
Tefnin, R., *Art et Magie au Temps des Pyramides. L'énigme des tetes dites 'de remplacement,'* (Monumenta Aegyptiaca 5), Brussels: Fondation Egyptologique Reine Elisabeth, 1991.
Weeks, K., *Mastabas of Cemetery G 6000. Giza Mastabas 5*, Boston: Museum of Fine Arts, Boston, 1994.

Photo credits:
206, 207 Araldo De Luca/Archivio White Star
208, 209 Marcello Bertinetti/Archivio White Star
210 Courtesy Museum of Fine Arts, Boston
211 left Peter Der Manuelian
211 right Courtesy Museum of Fine Arts, Boston
212-213 Hearst Museum of Anthropology, University of California at Berkeley
215 bottom Courtesy Museum of Fine Arts, Boston
From 216 to 225 Araldo De Luca/Archivio White Star
226-227, 227 left Giulio Veggi/Archivio White Star
From 227 right to 239 Araldo De Luca/Archivio White Star
240-241 Giulio Veggi/Archivio White Star

THE 'UNFINISHED' PYRAMIDS OF THE FOURTH DYNASTY
Text by Michel Valloggia

Michel Valloggia, Professor of Egyptology at the University of Geneva, Switzerland and field Director of the Archaeological Mission at Abu Rawash, Egypt, is former "Membre scientifique à titre étranger" of the French Institute of Oriental Archaeology in Cairo. He was in charge of the archaeological excavations between 1976 and 1993 in the Kharga Oasis (Douch) and the Dakhla Oasis (Balat). He is also Corresponding Member of the German Institute in Cairo and Consultant on behalf of UNESCO.

Bibliography:

Hassan, S., *Excavations at Giza IV*, Cairo, 1943.
Jequier, G., *Le Mastabat Faraoun*, Le Caire, 1928.
Lehner, M., *The Complete Pyramids*, Cairo, 1997.
Maragioglio, V. and C. Rinaldi, *L'architettura delle Piramidi Memfite, 7 vols.*, Rapallo, 1963-77.
Valloggia, M., *Fouilles archéologiques à Abu Rawash, Rapports préliminaires des campagnes 1995-2002 in Genava, n.s. 43-50*, Genève, 1995-2002.
---, *Au cœur d'une pyramide. Une mission archéologique en Egypte*, Gollion, 2001.

Photo credits:
242 top, 242-243 RMN
242 bottom Michel Valloggia
243, 244 Giulio Veggi/Archivio White Star
246, 247 Michel Valloggia
248 Courtesy Museum of Fine Arts, Boston
248-249, 250-251 Marcello Bertinetti/Archivio White Star
250 top Giulio Veggi/Archivio White Star

THE PYRAMIDS OF THE FIFTH DINASTY
Text by Miroslav Verner

Born in 1941, he graduated in Egyptology and prehistory at Charles University in Prague. He directed the Czech Institute of Egyptology for twenty five years and since 1976 has been leading the excavations by

Czech archaeologists in Abusir, Egypt. He is professor at Charles University in Prague and also serves as guest professor at the universities of Vienna and Hamburg and at the American University in Cairo.

Bibliography:

Borchardt, L., *Das Re-Heiligtum des Königs Ne-woser-re, vol. I., Der Bau.* Berlin, 1905.

---, *Das Grabdenkmal des Königs Ne-user-re*, Leipzig, 1907.

---, *Das Grabdenkmal des Königs Nefer-ír-ke-re*, Leipzig 1909.

---, *Das Grabdenkmal des Königs Sa-hu-re*, Leipzig, 1910-13.

Edwards, I. E. S., *The pyramids of Egypt*, rev. ed., Harmondsworth, 1993.

Fakhry, A., *The Pyramids*, Chicago, 1961.

Jánosi, P., *Die Pyramidenanlagen der Königinnen*, Wien, 1995.

Lehner, M., *The Complete Pyramids*, London-Cairo, 1997.

Maragioglio, V. and C. Rinaldi, *L'architettura delle piramidi menfite. VII*, Rapallo-Torino, 1977.

Stadelmann, R., *Die ägyptischen Pyramiden. Vom Ziegelbau zum Weltwunder, 2nd ed.*, Mainz, 1985.

Verner, M., *The Pyramid Complex of Khentkaus*, Prague, 1995.

---, *The Pyramids: Their Archaeology and History*, London 2002.

---, *Abusir: The Realm of Osiris*, Cairo, 2002.

---, "The Mysterious Sun Temples," *KMT* 14/1 (2003), pp. 44-57.

Photo credits:

252, 253 Araldo De Luca/Archivio White Star
254-255 Marcello Bertinetti/Archivio White Star
254 bottom, 255 top Giulio Veggi/Archivio White Star
256 top, 256-257 Marcello Bertinetti/Archivio White Star
256 bottom, 258 Araldo De Luca/Archivio White Star
259, 260-261 Marcello Bertinetti/Archivio White Star
260 bottom, 261 top Giulio Veggi/Archivio White Star
261 bottom Araldo De Luca/Archivio White Star
262-263 Marcello Bertinetti/Archivio White Star
263 Miroslav Verner
265 Marcello Bertinetti/Archivio White Star
265, 266, 267 bottom Araldo De Luca/Archivio White Star
267 top Giulio Veggi/Archivio White Star
268, 269, 270 top left, 270 right, 271 Marcello Bertinetti/Archivio White Star
270 center left, 270 bottom left Giulio Veggi/ Archivio White Star
272 top Miroslav Verner
272-273 Giulio Veggi/Archivio White Star
273 Araldo De Luca/Archivio White Star
274 Marcello Bertinetti/Archivio White Star
275 Araldo De Luca/Archivio White Star

THE SURPRISING ABUSIR BLOCKS
Text by Zahi Hawass and Miroslav Verner

Bibliography:

Borchardt, L., *Das Grabdenkmal des Königs Ne-user-re'*, Leipzig, 1907.

Fakhry, A., *The Monuments of Snefru I: The Bent Pyramid*, Cairo, 1959.

Firth, C.M., J.E. Quibell, *The Step Pyramid I*, Le Caire, 1935.

Ghoneim, Z., Hours Sekhem-Khet I, Le Caire, 1957.

Grinsell, L., *Egyptian Pyramids*, Gloucester, 1947.

Hawass. Z, "Newly Blocks from the Causeway of Sahure," MDAIK 32, (1996).

Hölscher, U., *Das Grabdenkmal das Königs Chephren*, Leipzig, 1912.

Jéquier, G., *Le Mastabat Faraoun*, Le Caire, 1928.

---, G. *La Pyramide d'Oudjebten*, Le Caire, 1928.

---, G. *Le monument Funéraire de Pepi II*, Le Caire, 1940.

Lauer, J. P., *La Pyramide à degrees I*, Le Caire, 1936.

Maragioglio, V. and C. Rinaldi, *L'architettura delle piramidi menfite II and VI*, Rapallo, 1963-70.

---, *Notizie sulle piramidi di Zedefra, Zedkara Isesi, Teti*, Turin, 1962.

Petrie, W. M. F., *Meidum*, London, 1892.

Posener-Kriéger, P. and J. L. Cenival, *The Abusir Papyri: Hieratic Papyri in the British Museum. 5th Series*, London, 1968.

Reisner, G.A. W., S.T. Smith, *A History of the Giza Necropolis, vol. II.*, Cambridge, 1955.

Stadelmann, R., *Die ägyptischen Pyramiden*, Mainz, 1985.

Verner, M., *Forgotten Pharaohs, Lost Pyramids, Abusir*, Praha, 1994.

Photo credits:

276, 277 Giulio Veggi/Archivio White Star
278 Miroslav Verner Star

THE PYRAMIDS OF THE SIXTH DYNASTY
Text by Audran Labrousse

Architect and Doctor of, Literature and Human Sciences, he earned his Ph.D. at the University of Sorbonne in 1988 and is researcher at the CNRS. He carried out excavations in Iran between 1969 and 1973 and at Sedeinga, in the Sudan, from 1976 to 1994. He has worked in Egypt since 1973, where he is the Director of the French Archaeological Mission of Saqqara.

Bibliography:

Berger-El Naggar, C., J. Leclant, B. Mathieu, and I. Pierre-Croisiau, *Les Textes de la pyramide de Pépy Ier, 1. Description et analyse, sous la direction de J. Leclant*, Le Caire: Ifao, 2001.

Jéquier, G., *La pyramide d'Oudjebten*, Le Caire, 1928.

---, *Les pyramides des reines Neit et Apouit*, Le Caire, 1933.

---, *Le monument funéraire de Pepi II, t. I : Le tombeau royal, t. II : Le temple, t. III : Les approches du temple*, Le Caire, 1936, 1938, 1940.

Labrousse, A., *L'architecture des pyramides à textes, 3 vol., Saqqara Nord, 1 et 2*, 1996, *Saqqara Sud*, 2000, Le Caire, Ifao.

---, *Les pyramides des reines, une nouvelle nécropole à Saqqâra*, Paris, 1999.

Piacntini, P., *L'autobiografia di Uni, principe e governatore dell'Alto Egitto, Monographia di SEAP I, Series Minor*, Pisa,1990.

Photo credits:

280 Araldo De Luca/Archivio White Star
281 Audran Labrousse
282, 283 bottom left and right Araldo De Luca/ Archivio White Star
282-283 Giulio Veggi/Archivio White Star
284 Araldo De Luca/Archivio White Star
284-285 Marcello Bertinetti/Archivio White Star
285 top, 286 top, 286-287 Audran Labrousse
286 bottom National Museum of Warszawa, Poland
287 bottom National Museum of Scotland
288 top, 289 top, 289 center Araldo De Luca/Archivio White Star
288-289 Marcello Bertinetti/Archivio White Star
290, 291 top left and top right Giulio Veggi/ Archivio White Star
291 center and bottom RMN
292 Audran Labrousse
294-295 Marcello Bertinetti/Archivio White Star
294 bottom Giulio Veggi/Archivio White Star
295 right Audran Labrousse
296 left Brooklyn Museum of Art
296 right Audran Labrousse

THE DECORATIVE PROGRAM OF THE OLD KINGDOM PYRAMID COMPLEXES
Text by Zahi Hawass

Bibliography:

Arnold, D., "Rituale und Pyramidentempel," *MDAIK 33* (1977).

Bleeker, C.J., *Egyptian Festivals: Enactments of Religious Renewal*, Leiden, 1967.

Bonnet, H. *Reallexikon der Ägyptischen Religionsgeschichte*. Berlin, 1952.

Borchardt, L., *Das Grabdenkmal des Königs Sahure II*, Leipzig, 1913.

Brinks, J., *Die Entwicklung der Königlichen Grabanlagen des Alten Reiches*, Hildesheim, 1979.

Edwards, I.E.S., *The Pyramids of Egypt*, Harmondsworth, 1961.

Fakhry, A., *The Monuments of Sneferu at Dahshur II: The Valley Temple*, 2 pts., Cairo, 1961.

Goedicke, H., *Re-used Blocks from the Pyramid of Amenemhet I at Lisht*, New York, 1971.

Hawass, Z., *The Funerary Establishments of Khufu, Khafra, and Menkaura During the Old Kingdom*, Ph. D. Dissertation, University of Pennsylvanaia microfilm, Ann Arbor, MI, 1987.

Hornung, E. and E. Staehelin, Studien zum sedfest, Genf-Basel, 1974.

Jéquier, G., *Le Monument funéraire de Pepi II, vol. I: Le Temple funéraire*, Cairo, 1936.

Maragioglio, V. and C. A. Rinaldi, *L'Architettura della Piramidi menfite*. Vols. 2-8, Turin and Rapello, 1963-1977.

Posener-Kriéger, P., *Les Archives du temple funéraire de Neferirkare-Kakai: Les Papyrus d'Abousir, vol. I, II*, Cairo, 1976.

Reisner, G. A. and W. S. Smith, *A History of Giza Necropolis, vol. II*, 1955.

Reisner, G. A., *Mycerinus: The Temples of the Third Pyramid at Giza*, Cambridge, MA, 1931.

Smith, W. S., *A History of Egyptian Sculpture and Painting in the Old Kingdom*. Boston and London, 1946.

Smith, W. S., *The Art and Architecture of Ancient Egypt*, Harmondsworth, 1981.

Wilson, J., "The Artist of Egyptian Old Kingdom," JNES 6 (1947).

Photo credits:

298 Araldo De Luca/Archivio White Star
299, 300-301 Giulio Veggi/Archivio White Star

THE TOMBS OF THE FIFTH AND SIXTH DYNASTIES AT SAQQARA
Text by Karl Myśliwiec

Karol Myśliwiec is the director of the Research Center for Mediterranean Archaeology at the Polish Academy of Sciences and professor of Ancient Egyptian Archaeology at the Warsaw University. He is also director of Polish-Egyptian excavations at Saqqara. Excavating in Egypt on various sites since 1969. K. Myśliwiec also directed the Polish-Egyptian rescue excavations at Tell Atrib (Nile Delta) in 1985-1995. He is the author of many books and articles on Egyptian archaeology, art, and religion.

Bibliography:

Altenmüller, H., *Die Wanddarstellungen im Grab des Mehu in Saqqara* (Archäologische Veröffentlichungen DAIK 42), Mainz, 1998.

Donovan L. and K. McCorquodale (eds.), *Egyptian Art: Principles and Themes in Wall Scenes* (Prism Archaeological Series 6), Cairo, 2000.

Harpur, Y., *Decoration in Egyptian Tombs of the Old Kingdom*, Oxford, 1987.

Jánosi, P., "The Tombs of Officials: Houses of Eternity," in *Egyptian Art in the Age of the Pyramids* (exhibition catalogue), New York, 1999, pp. 27-39.

Kanawati N. and A. Hassan, *The Teti Cemetery at Saqqara, vol. II: The Tomb of Ankhmahor* (The Australian Centre for Egyptology Reports 9), Warminster, 1997.

Kanawati N.and M. Abder-Raziq, *The Teti Cemetery at Saqqara, vol. VI: The Tomb of Nikauisesi* (The Australian Centre for Egyptology Report 14), Warminster, 2000.

Moussa A. M. and H. Altenmüller, *Das Grab des Nianchchnum und Chnumhotep* (Archäologische Veröffentlichungen DAIK 21), Mainz, 1977.

Myśliwiec, K., Kuraszkiewicz, K., Czerwik, D., Rzeuska, T., Kaczmarek, M., Kowalska, A., Radomska, M., Godziejewski, Z., *The tomb of Merefnebef (Saqqara I)*, Varsavia 2004.

Rzeuska, T., *Pottery of the Late Old Kingdom. Funerary Pottery and Burial Customs (Saqqara II)*, Varsavia 2006.

Photo credits:

302, 303, 304 left and right Araldo De Luca/ Archivio White Star
304-305 Marcello Bertinetti/Archivio White Star
305 bottom Giulio Veggi/Archivio White Star
From 306 to 321 Araldo De Luca/Archivio White Star
322 top left, right, 323 Araldo De Luca/Archivio White Star
322 bottom left Giulio Veggi/Archivio White Star
From 324 to 333 top Araldo De Luca/Archivio White Star
333 bottom, 334, 335, 336, 337, 338 center and bottom Karol Myśliwiec
338 top, 339, 340, 341 Araldo De Luca/Archivio White Star

THE PYRAMIDS OF THE MIDDLE KINGDOM
Text by Dieter Arnold

Dieter Arnold is Curator at the Metropolitan Museum of Art, New York, and has for forty years been conducting excavations in Egypt, at Thebes, El-Lisht, and Dahshur, among other sites. He is the author of numerous books on Egyptian architecture, including *Building in Egypt: Pharaonic Stone Masonry* (1991), *Temples of the Last Pharaohs* (1999), and *The Pyramid Complex of Senwosret III at Dahshur* (2000).

Bibliography:

AMENEMHAT I

Gautier, J.-E. and G. Jèquier, *Mèmoire sur les fouilles de Licht*, Cairo, 1902, pp. 87-107.

Excavation reports in the *Bullettin of the Metropolitan Museum of Art*, New York from July 1907 to December 1922.

SENWOSRET I

Arnold, Dieter, with contributions by Dorothea Arnold and an appendix by Peter Dorman, *The Pyramid of Senwosret I*, New York, 1988.

Gautier, J.-E. and G. Jéquier, *Mémoire sur les fouilles de Licht*, Cairo,1902, pp. 1-85.

Excavation reports in the *Bullettin of the Metropolitan Museum of Art*, New York from September 1908 to November 1934.

AMENEMHAT II

Morgan, Jacques de, *Fouilles à Dahchour en 1894-1895*, vol. 2, Vienna,1903, pp. 28-37.

SENWOSRET II

Petrie, W. M. F., *Illahun, Kahun and Gurob 1889-90*, London, 1891

---, *Kahun, Gurob and Hawara*, London, 1890.

Petrie, William Flinders, G. Brunton, and M.A. Murray, *Lahun II*, London, 1923.

SENWOSRET III

Arnold, D., with contributions and an appendix by Adela Oppenheim and contributions by James Allen, *The Pyramid Complex of Senwosret III, Architectural Studies*, New York,2003.

Morgan, J. de, *Fouilles à Dahchour Mars-Juin 1894*, vol.1, Vienna, 1895, pp. 47-85

AMENEMHAT III AT DAHSHUR

Morgan, J. de, *Fouilles à Dahchour Mars-Juin 1894*, vol. 1, Vienna, 1895, pp. 87-117.

Arnold D., *Der Pyramidenbezirk des Konigs Amenemhet III in Dahschur.* Mainz, 1897.

AMENEMHAT III AT HAWARA

Petrie, W. F., *Hawara, Biahmu and Arsinoe*, London, 1889.

Petrie, W. F., G.A. Wainwrights and E. Mackay, *The Labyrinth, Gerzeh and Mazghuneh*, London, 1912.

Photo credits:

342, 343 Araldo De Luca/Archivio White Star
344-345 Alfio Garozzo/Archivio White Star
345, 346 left, 346 top right Araldo De Luca/Archivio White Star
346 center and bottom right Giulio Veggi/Archivio White Star
348-349 Marcello Bertinetti/Archivio White Star
349 Araldo De Luca/Archivio White Star
350 Giulio Veggi/Archivio White Star
351 top Araldo De Luca/Archivio White Star
351 bottom Dieter Arnold
352, 353, 354, 355 Araldo De Luca/Archivio White Star
356 top Giulio Veggi/Archivio White Star
356 bottom, 357 top Dieter Arnold
357 bottom, 358 left, 358 top right, 359 Araldo De Luca/Archivio White Star
358 bottom right Dieter Arnold
360 left, 361 Araldo De Luca/Archivio White Star
360 right Marcello Bertinetti/Archivio White Star
362 top Alfio Garozzo/Archivio White Star
362 bottom Dieter Arnold
363 right Dieter Arnold

THE TOMBS OF THE NOBLES IN THE MIDDLE KINGDOM
Text by David P. Silvermann

David P. Silverman is the Eckley B. Coxe, Jr., Professor of Egyptology and the Curator-in-Charge of the Egyptian Section of the University of Pennsylvania Museum of Archaeology and Anthropology in Philadelphia. Having received his PhD from the University of Chicago, he has curated several major exhibitions, including the *Treasures of Tutankhamen*. He has conducted fieldwork at a number of sites in Egypt, including Abydos, Bersheh, the Delta, and Giza, and, since 1990, Dr. Silverman has led an ongoing expedition to Saqqara. He has written numerous articles on language, religion, and art and has authored, co-authored, and edited several books including *Ancient Egypt, Kingship in Ancient Egypt, Religion in Ancient Egypt, Interrogative Constructions*, and *Masterpieces of Tutankhmaun*.

Bibliography:

Akoris, *Report of the Excavations at Akoris in Middle Egypt 1981-1992*, The Paleological Association of Japan, Inc. Egyptian Committee, Kyoto, Koyo Shobo, 1995.

Allen, J. P., "Some Theban Officials of the Early Middle Kingdom," in *P. Der Manuelian (ed.), Studies in Honor of William Kelly Simpson. Volumes I-II*, Boston: Department of Ancient Egyptian, Nubian, and Near Eastern Art. Museum of Fine Arts, 1996, pp. 1-26.

Arnold, Dieter, *Das Grab des Jnj-jtj.f. Die Architektur*, Mainz am Rhein: Philipp von Zabern, 1971.

---, "Sechster Vorbericht über die vom Deutschen Archäologischen Institut Kairo in Qurna unternommenen Arbeiten (8. Kampagne)," *MDAIK* 27 (1971), pp. 125-130.

---, "Gräber des Alten und Mittleren Reiches in El-Tarif," *Archäologische Veröffentlichungen* 17, (Mainz, 1976).

---, *Building in Egypt: Pharaonic Stone Masonry*, New York, Oxford: Oxford University Press, 1991.

---, "Royal Cult Complexes of the Old and Middle Kingdoms," in B. E. Shafer, *Temples of Ancient Egypt*, London, New York: I.B., 1997, pp. 31-85.

---, *The Encyclopedia of Ancient Egyptian Architecture*, Princeton: Princeton University Press, 2003.

Arnold, Dieter, with contributions by Dorothea Arnold and an appendix by P.F. Dorman, *The Pyramid of Senwosret I*, New York: The Metropolitan Museum of Art, The South Cemeteries of Lisht, vol. 1. Publications of the Metropolitan Museum of Art Egyptian Expedition, 22, 1991.

Arnold, Dieter, with contributions by Dorothea Arnold and F. Arnold and an appendix by C. Haldane, *The Pyramid Complex of Senwosret I*, New York: The Metropolitan Museum of Art. The South Cemeteries of Lisht, vol. 3. Publications of The Metropolitan Museum of Art Egyptian Expedition, 25, 1992.

Arnold, Dieter and J. Settgast. "Bericht über die Arbeiten des Deutschen Archäologischen Instituts Kairo in Qurna von 1963 bis 1970," *ASAE 61* (1973), pp. 177-190.

Arnold, Dorothea, "Amenemhat I and the Early Twelfth Dynasty at Thebes," *Metropolitan Museum Journal 26* (1991), pp. 5-48.

---, "The Metropolitan Museum of Art's Work at the Middle Kingdom Sites of Thebes and Lisht," in N. Thomas (ed.), *The American Discovery of Ancient Egypt. Essays*. Los Angeles: Los Angeles County Museum of Art / American Research Center in Egypt, 1996, pp. 56-77,

Badawy, A., *A History of Egyptian Architecture: The First Intermediate Period, the Middle Kingdom, and the Second Intermediate Period*, Berkeley and Los Angeles: University of California Press, 1966.

---, "Ancient constructional diagrams in Egyptian architecture," *Gazette des Beaux Arts, Paris 128* (1986), pp. 51-56.

Bourriau, J., "Patterns of Change in Burial Customs During the Middle Kingdom," in S. Quirke (ed.), *Middle Kingdom Studies*, New Malden, Surrey: SIA, 1991, pp. 3-20.

---, *Pharaohs and Mortals: Egyptian art in the Middle Kingdom. Catalogue by Janine Bourriau, with a contribution by Stephen Quirke*. Cambridge University Press, Cambridge and Fitzwilliam Museum, 1988.

Brovarski, E., "Ahanakht of Bersheh and the Hare Nome in the First Intermediate Period and Middle Kingdom," in W. K. Simpson and W. M. Davis (eds.), *Studies in Ancient Egypt, the Aegean, and the Sudan: Essays in honor of Dows Dunham on the occasion of his 90th birthday, June 1, 1980*, Boston: Department of Egyptian and Ancient Near Eastern Art, Museum of Fine Arts, 1981, pp. 14-30.

---, "Akhmim in the Old Kingdom and First Intermediate Period," in *Mélanges Gamal Eddin Mokhtar. Publié sous la direction de Paule Posener-Kriéger. 117-153. Volume I et II*, Le Caire: Institut français d'archéologie orientale, 1985.

Brovarski, E. et al., *Report of the 1990 Field Season of the Joint Expedition of the Museum of Fine Arts, Boston, University Museum, University of Pennsylvania, Leiden University* (Bersheh Reports 1), Boston: Museum of Fine Arts, , 1992.

Calendar, G., "The Middle Kingdom Renaissance (c.2055-1650 BC)" in I. Shaw (ed.), *The Oxford History of Ancient Egypt*, Oxford: Oxford University Press, 2000, pp. 148-183.

D'Auria, S., P. Lacovara, and C. H. Roehrig, *Mummies and Magic: The Funerary Arts of Ancient Egypt*, Boston: Museum of Fine Arts, 1988.

Firth, C. M. and B. Gunn, *Teti Pyramid Cemeteries*, Cairo: Impr. de l'IFAO, 1926.

Fischer, H. G., *Dendera in the Old Kingdom and its Aftermath*, Dissertation Abstracts, Ann Arbor, Michigan, Vol. XV, No. 11, 1955.

---, *Inscriptions from the Coptite nome: Dynasties VI-XI*, (Analecta Orientalia 40), Roma: Pontificium Institutum Biblicum, 1964

---, *Dendera in the Third Millennium B.C., down to the Theban Domination of Upper Egypt*, Locust Valley, New York: J. J. Augustin Publisher, 1968.

Franke, D., "The Career of Khnumhotep III of Beni Hasan and the So-Called Decline of the Nomarchs," in S. Quirke (ed.), *Middle Kingdom Studies*, New Malden, Surrey: SIA, 1991, pp. 51-68.

Freed, R. E., *The Development of Middle Kingdom Egyptian Relief Sculptural Schools of Late Dynasty XI with an Appendix on the Trends of Early Dynasty XII (2040-1878 B.C.)*, New York University Dissertation, 1984.

Lustig, J., "Kinship, Gender and Age in Middle Kingdom Tomb Scenes and Texts," in J. Lustig (ed.), *Anthropology and Egyptology. A Developing Dialogue*, Sheffield: Sheffield Academic Press, 1997, pp. 43-65.

Marochetti, E. F., "Variations of the mastaba tomb during the Middle Kingdom," in *Atti del VI Congresso Internazionale di Egittologia. Volume I-II*, Torino: Comitato Organizzativo del Congresso, 1993, pp. 121-127.

---, "On the Design, Symbolism, and Dating of some XIIth Dynasty Tomb Superstructures," *GM 144* (1995), pp. 43-52.

Newberry, P. E., *Beni Hasan*, London: Egypt Exploration Fund, 1893-1900, Parts 1-4.

Quirke, S. (ed.), *Middle Kingdom Studies*, New Malden, Surrey: SIA, 1991.

Richards, J. E., "Understanding the Mortuary Remains at Abydos. Northern Cemetery Project: Preliminary Research Report," *Newsletter ARCE 142* (Summer 1988), pp. 5-8.

---, *Mortuary variability and social differentiation in Middle Kingdom Egypt*, dissertation, University of Pennsylvania, Philadelphia, 1992.

---, "Ancient Egyptian Mortuary Practice and the Study of Socioeconomic Differentiation," in J. Lustig (ed.), *Anthropology and Egyptology: A Developing Dialogue*, Sheffield: Sheffield Academic Press, 1997, pp. 33-42.

Roehrig, C. H., "The Early Middle Kingdom Cemeteries at Thebes and the Tomb of Djari," in J. Assmann, E. Dziobek, H. Guksch, F. Kampp (eds.), *Thebanische Beamtennekropolen. Neue Perspektiven archäologischer Forschung, Internationales Symposion Heidelberg, 1993*, Heidelberg: Heidelberger

Orientverlag, 1995, pp. 255-269.

Seidlmayer, S. J., *Gräbfelder aus dem Übergang vom Alen zum Mittleren Reich: Studien zur Archäologie der Ersten Zwischenzeit*, Heidelberg: Heidelberger Orientverlag, 1990.

Silverman, D. P., "Middle Kingdom Tombs in the Teti Pyramid Cemetery," in *Abusir and Saqqara in the Year 2000* (Archiv orientální Supplementa IX), Prague: Academy of Sciences of the Czech Republic Oriental Institute, 2000, pp. 259-282.

Silverman, D. P., Jennifer Wegner, and Josef Wegner (eds.), *Middle Kingdom Egypt*. Philadelphia: University of Pennsylvania Museum of Archaeology and Anthropology Press, 2004.

Simpson, W. K., "Lepsius Pyramid LV at Dahshur: the Mastaba of Si-Ese, Vizier of Amenemhet II," in J. Baines, T. G. H. James, A. Leahy, A. F. Shore (eds.), *Pyramid Studies and Other Essays Presented to I.E.S. Edwards*, London: The Egypt Exploration Society, 1991, pp. 57-60.

Spanel, D. B., *Beni Hasan in the Herakleopolitan Period*, University of Toronto, Dissertation, 1985.

---, "The Herakleopolitan Tombs of Kheti I, Jt(.j)jb(.j),and Kheti II at Asyut," *Orientalia 58* (1989), pp. 301-314.

Willems, H., *The Coffin of Heqata (Cairo JdE 36418): A Case Study of Egyptian Funerary Culture of the Early Middle Kingdom*, Leuven: Uitgeverij Peeters en Departement Oriëntalistiek, 1996.

---, "The Nomarchs of the Hare Nome and Early Middle Kingdom History," *JEOL 28* (1983-1984), pp. 80-102.

---, *Chests of Life: A Study of the Typology and Conceptual Development of Middle Kingdom Standard Class Coffins*, Leiden: Ex Oriente Lux, 1988.

---, "Deir el-Bersheh. Preliminary Report," *GM 110* (1989), pp. 75-95.

---, "A Note on the Date of the Early Middle Kingdom Cemetery at Ihnâsiya al-Madîna," *GM 150* (1996), pp. 99-109.

Winlock, H. E. "The Theban Necropolis in the Middle Kingdom." *AJSL 32* (1915-1916), pp. 1-37.

---, "Graffiti of the Priesthood of the Eleventh Dynasty Temples at Thebes." *AJSL 58* (1941), pp. 146-168

---, "The Eleventh Egyptian Dynasty." *JNES 2* (1943), pp. 249-283.

---, *The Rise and Fall of the Middle Kingdom in Thebes*, New York: The Macmillan Company, 1947.

Photo credits:

364, 365, 366, 367 Araldo De Luca/Archivio White Star

368 top Marcello Bertinetti/Archivio White Star

370, 371, 372, 373, 374-375 Araldo De Luca/Archivio White Star

374 bottom, 375 top, 376 top David Silverman

376 bottom, 377 Archivio White Star

378, 380 top, 380-381 Giulio Veggi/Archivio White Star

380 bottom, 381 bottom Araldo De Luca/Archivio White Star

ROYAL AND PRIVATE STATUES OF THE OLD AND MIDDLE KINGDOMS
Text by Hourig Sourouzian

Egyptologist and Art Historian. Corresponding member of the German Archaeological Institute of Berlin in Cairo. She has studied Egyptology, Art History and Ancient Languages in Paris. Graduated from the Ecole des Langues Orientales in Classical Arabic and Ancient Armenian. Diplomed from the Ecole du Louvre with a dissertation on the Monuments of King Merenptah, published in 1989. PhD in Egyptology (Doctorat d'Etat ès Lettres) at the University of Paris IV-Sorbonne, with Research on the Royal Statuary of the Nineteenth Dynasty, in print. Work in Egypt with participation in several archaeological missions at Karnak, Thebes-West, Dahshur and Tanis. Joined the excavations of the Swiss Institute at the temple of Merenptah in Thebes where she was entrusted with the study and the publication of the temple statuary. Has made thorough research at the Cairo Museum and published with co-author Mohamed Saleh a catalogue of the most important works of the Egyptian Museum Cairo. Teaching of Egyptian Art and Archaeology in the American University in Cairo and the University of Munich. Has published several articles and reports on her work, and participated in numerous exhibition catalogues and books. She has also worked in Armenia with a Survey on the monuments endangered by the earthquake of 1989. Since 1988 she directs the archaeological mission at the Temple of Amenophis III at Thebes, after having introduced the site in the list of the '100 most endangered monuments' of the World Monuments Watch.

Photo credits:

382, 384, 385 Araldo De Luca/Archivio White Star

386 Giulio Veggi/Archivio White Star

387, 388, 389, 390, 391, 392, 393 Araldo De Luca/Archivio White Star

394 Courtesy Museum of Fine Arts, Boston

395 Roemer- und Pelizaeus- Museum

396, 397, 398, 399 Araldo De Luca/Archivio White Star

400 left Reiner Stadelmann

400-401 Archivio White Star

401 right Reiner Stadelmann

402, 403, 404 left Araldo De Luca/Archivio White Star

404 bottom Reiner Stadelmann

405 top Araldo De Luca/Archivio White Star

405 right Kunsthistorisches Museum

406-407 Araldo De Luca/Archivio White Star

WS White Star Publishers® is a registered trademark property of Edizioni White Star s.r.l.

© 2003, 2011 Edizioni White Star s.r.l.
Via M. Germano, 10
13100 Vercelli, Italy
www.whitestar.it

New extended and up-dated edition in 2007

ISBN 978-88-544-0607-0
1 2 3 4 5 6   15 14 13 12 11

Printed in China